大商业2

SUPER COMMERCILA COMPLEXES II

—多元复合商业地产

Multiple Complex Commercial Real Estate

金盘地产传媒有限公司 策划
香港建筑科学出版社 编著

中国林业出版社
China Forestry Publishing House

EXCLUSIVE INTERVIEW

专访

Hong Kong Architecture Science Press
Katrina Question:

what are the highlights and features of the project?

香港建筑科学出版社
张燕清问：

该项目具有哪些亮点与特点?

Architect:James Goettsch
建筑师：James Goettsch

Architect:Travis Soberg
建筑师：Travis Soberg

James Goettsch (GP): Sowwah Square is a major new commercial development on Abu Dhabi's Al Maryah Island (formerly Sowwah Island). The city's new urban framework plan, entitled Plan Abu Dhabi 2030, has designated the previously undeveloped island and the adjacent edges of Mina Zayed and Reem Island as the city's new Central Business District. The project totals over 290,000 square meters of office space and features the iconic new headquarters building for the Abu Dhabi Securities Exchange surrounded by four office towers, all overlooking the water. In addition, the project integrates two levels of retail and two parking structures.

The centerpiece of the development's first phase is the business center, which includes a 21,650 m stock exchange building, four Class A office towers totaling 271,750 m, parking for approximately 5,000 cars, and 23,220 m of retail. The complex emphasizes a sustainable design approach throughout and looks beyond the LEED certification process to integrate both active and passive sustainable design strategies.

As the distinctive new headquarters of the Abu Dhabi Securities Exchange, the stock exchange building is an iconic, four-level facility. Glass-enclosed with a roof the size of a football field, the building rises 27 m above a 49-meter-diameter water feature on massive stone piers. The four granite piers house the stairs, mechanical risers and service elements for the exchange. The building projects an image of strength and solidity as it overlooks the water facing back toward the city's existing downtown.

Four office towers frame the stock exchange building: two at 31 stories and the other two at 37 stories. The first full office floor of each building starts 34 m above the ground level, providing a highly transparent, open lobby and elevating the views on all tenant floors. A landscaped plaza connects the four buildings and the exchange.

Beneath the plaza, a two-story retail podium weaves through the development, providing upscale shopping along the waterfront. At the north and south boundaries of the site, two parking structures, partially submerged, serve the complex with more than 2,400 parking spaces each.

Distinctions/Innovations

•Sustainable Design: First mixed-use project in Abu Dhabi to be pre-certified LEED-CS Gold based on sustainable initiatives.

•Anchor Development: Complex establishes the heart of Abu Dhabi's new master planned CBD on Al Maryah Island.

•International Business Hub: Complex offers new standards for Grade A+ office space to attract international companies.

•Timeless Design: Clear massing and organization defines a lasting urban gesture and pedestrian-friendly environment.

•Lighting/Energy Use: Active and passive lighting controls conserve energy while providing optimal conditions for workers.

James Goettsch(GP): 沙瓦哈广场是阿布达比阿尔玛雅岛（以前的索沃岛）的一个重量级新商业型地产开发项目。根据城市新框架方案（即阿布达比 2030 计划），将把未开发的阿尔玛雅岛、扎伊德港及里姆岛与该岛相邻区域建设成为城市未来的中央商务区。项目总办公面积超过 290 000 平方米。项目的一大亮点就是一栋地标性的阿布达比证券交易所新总部大楼，大楼四周围绕着另外 4 栋写字楼。无论是哪栋大楼，你都可以将水景尽收眼底。此外，项目还将建设两层楼的商场与两个停车场。

项目一期的重点建设内容就是商务中心，其中包括建筑面积达 21 650 平方米的证券交易所大楼、4 栋 A 级写字楼（建筑面积共计 271 750 平方米）、能容纳 5 000 辆车的车库、建筑面积达 23 220 平方米的商场。整个综合体表达出可持续发展的设计方法，力求超越绿色建筑认证水准，实现主动与被动可持续设计战略的完美结合。

阿布达比证券交易所新总部大楼造型别具一格。这是一栋具有标志性的四层证券交易所大楼。四根巨型砖柱将建筑高高托起，矗立在直径为 49 米水景上方的 27 米空中。四根巨型柱砖柱之间安置了多个扶梯与电梯以及多家服务于交易所的商店。建筑俯瞰水景，以现有的城市中心为背景，俨然向众人传达出一幅力量与坚实的图画。

4 栋写字楼围绕证券交易所大楼四周：其中两栋高 31 层，另外两栋高 37 层。每栋楼首层楼面高 34 米，第二层才是办公楼层。这样的设计旨在打造出高透明、开放式的大厅，让租户能享受更广阔的美景。一个景观广场将四栋写字楼与证券交易所大楼形成串联。

广场下方便是 2 层高的商场裙楼。商场贯穿整个场地，给海滨路带来高端购物体验。在场地的南北侧修建了 2 个半路半露半掩的车库，给综合体提供了共计 4 800 个停车位。

• 可持续性设计：倡导可持续性发展概念，作为阿布达比首个提前获得 LEED-CS 黄金认证的综合型项目。

• 超大型地产开发项目：根据阿布达比新总体规划方案，该综合体将成为拟建于阿尔玛雅岛上的 CBD 的核心内容。

• 国际商务中心：综合体提供新标准的 A+ 级办公空间，以吸引跨国公司。

• 永恒的设计：建筑体轮廓分明与布局清晰合理，传达永恒的城市气质，散发温馨体贴的步行气息。

• 照明 / 能源使用：同时采用主动与被动式照明控制，力求在提供最佳办公条件的同时也达到节约能源的效果。

Exclusive interview with

Travis Soberg AIA,LEED AP Principad, Director, Sustainable Design

James Goettsch, FAIA, The Architect

独家专访：
Travis Soberg AIA LEED AP Principad, Directou, Sustainable Design
James Goettsch, FAIA, The Architect

Hong Kong Architecture Science Press
Katrina Question:

From the architecture point of view, how do you help the developer to realize their ivestment plans?

香港建筑科学出版社
张燕清问：

你如何从建筑本身帮助开发商实现他们的投资计划？

James Goettsch (GP): Development occurs in a competitive environment. Developers are usually competing with other developers to attempt to convince tenants to lease space in their building. Tenants make their leasing decisions based on their cost of occupancy which is affected by the cost per sq meter of their proposed lease, the efficiency of the building in terms of how many square meters are required to satisfy the tenants space needs, and the quality of the building in terms of architecture and building systems.

1 - We try to design buildings that are very efficient, which means the tenant may be able to reduce the amount of space that he must lease and thus reduce the tenant's cost of occupancy.

2 - We try to design buildings that give the developer the best use of his money (the highest quality of building in terms of architecture and engineering systems for a given budget) which allows the developer to offer the most attractive lease terms to the tenant, thus reducing the tenant's cost of occupancy.

Simply stated, we design buildings that make the best use of the developer's money, that are as efficient as possible at the same time providing high quality design in terms of architecture and building systems. It sounds simple, and everyone says the same thing, yet the results of various developments are dramatically different.

James Goettsch（GP）：地产行业竞争激烈。为了吸引租户，地产开发商之间通常会互相竞争。租户根据租金来做决定，然而除了每平方米的单价以外，影响租金的因素还包括建筑的空间使用效率，建筑自身质量以及所采用的系统的质量。

1. 我们努力设计出高效率的空间。也就是说，租户对空间使用效率的最大化，从而降低租金。

2. 我们努力设计出给开发商带来最大投资效益的建筑。（在既定的预算下，从建筑自身以及建筑所采用的工程系统都能实现最高品质）在这样的前提下，开发商可以对租户提出最具吸引力的租约条件，从而降低租金。

简而言之，我们设计出给开发商带来最大投资效益的建筑。不仅保证高的空间使用效率，而且实现建筑自身与建筑所采用的工程系统的高品质。听起来很简单，而且大家都是如是说。但每个地产项目最终取得的成果却相差甚远。

Hong Kong Architecture Science Press
Katrina Question:

Green building very mature in western country, but in China basic didn't develop. how do you think to use western's successful experience to implement in China? And what do you think the trend of commercial building?

香港建筑科学出版社
张燕清问：

在欧洲，环保概念的建筑已经进入成熟的发展期，然而中国的环保概念的建筑几乎还没有起步。以你高见，如何可以将西方的成功经验应用到中国呢？你如何看待商业型建筑的发展趋势？

Travis Soberg (GP): Western urbanization is at a very mature level when considered globally. Modern cities have been developed over hundreds of years and the migration of people to the cities is increasing at a fairly steady percentage. For this reason, the necessity for new developments is not as expansive as what is happening in China. If a new development is to be undertaken in a mature city, there needs to be significant advantages over the existing building stock in order for tenants to find it desirable. Some of the advantages could be location, infrastructure, amenities, space planning efficiency, operational efficiency or improved indoor environment. In this way, green building development has been integrated as a way to differentiate developments as more healthy or more efficient than other properties, ultimately making the properties more valuable in the marketplace.

In comparison, urbanization in China is happening at an unprecedented level. Thirty years ago, the urban population of China was 20%. Today it is 54% and continuing to rise. The very nature of the rapidly rising urban population demands that new developments be undertaken, and as quickly as possible. It's not to say that green building is not a consideration; with all the new building stock coming on line, the ability to provide sufficient power to the buildings has severely taxed the capability of the power industry in China, which is highly dependent on high-emission coal burning facilities. Yet, when demand for new development remains at such a high level, the need to differentiate properties with elements such as green building technology remains low. Instead, the speed with which a property can be brought to market becomes the key driver in a developments undertaking.

In time, the urbanization of China's cities will level out and the demand for building developments will follow. Once developments begin to need to compete for tenants, the necessity of green technology will take on a more meaningful role within China's building industry.

Travis Soberg（GP）：纵观全世界，西方国家的城市化进展已进入非常成熟的阶段。西方国家的现代化城市是经历了上百年的发展而来。而且，城市移民增长率也相当稳定。鉴于此，西方国家城市对新地产项目的需求就不如中国那么多。若要在一座发展成熟的城市开启一个新地产项目，那么为了让租户对项目感到满意，该项目相对其他已有建筑而言就应具备显著的优势。这些显著的优势可以体现为地理位置、基建、便利设施、空间规划效率、经营效率或经改善的室内环境。因此，环保概念的建筑已被标榜为更健康或效率更高的建筑，从而不同于其他普通建筑，最终创造出更高的市场价值。

与西方相比，中国正经历前所未有的城市化进程。30 年前，中国城市人口只占总人口的 20%。而如今这个数字已变成 54%，而且还在不断攀升。在城市人口快速增长的推动下，需要尽快完成新的地产项目。随着众多新建筑如雨后春笋般的走入市场，中国电力行业为了供应足够的电力已不堪重负（中国的电力高度依赖高排放的煤热力发电厂）。在这样的背景下，环保建筑也将成为一张选择。但是，虽然中国仍保持对新建项目的高需求，但对那些能让建筑与众不同的技术仍需求较低（比如，环保建筑技术），建设速度反而成为了推动地产项目发展的主要动力。

到时候，中国城市的城镇化将会呈现平稳状态，自然而然也将影响建设项目的需求。一旦中国建筑行业到了以租户为核心的发展阶段，环保技术将显得更加必要。

EXCLUSIVE INTERVIEW

专访

Hong Kong Architecture Science Press
Katrina Question:

The architectural form represents a new classicism. What is the idea to organize these classic elements?

香港建筑科学出版社
张燕清问:

建筑的形式是一种新古典主义的形式，请问是怎么在设计上组织这些古典元素的？

Hua Lei: There are numerous classic elements to be found from Shanghai Global Harbour. We made a selection of elements applicable to commercial architectural style at the beginning of design. A variety of spatial detailings are used to meet commercial demands based on architectural functions and scale. For overall design, the development features traditional symmetry, repeated rhythm, large colonnade and shadow in contrast. For example, the use of stone and copperplate mixes with detailed decoration. Thus, we created a decent architecture of classicism as it is true of classicism. Working as a ground rule, classicism has been robustly executed throughout the detailing, including the division of stone. It is these rigorous detailings that created a majestic, exquisite and well-proportioned building. The interior design features Italian Renaissance style. In combination with a perfect control of scale, the use of gold and red and other colors not only sheds glory and nobility on the building but also gives prominence to details. Excessively gorgeous decoration is not necessary when all is combined with a perfect control of scale. All these happens to create a warm, cosy and vibrant commercial building space.

华镭：上海环球港采用的古典元素很多，在设计之初我们对适用于商业建筑风格的元素进行了选择，再根据建筑功能和尺度选用不同的空间处理手段以满足商业的需求。建筑在整体设计上采用的是传统对称，韵律重复，大型柱廊和阴影对比，包括石材和铜板的使用配合细部装饰，原汁原味地打造了一个正宗的古典主义建筑。细节上也丝毫不放过古典主义的原则，包括石材分割上都严格执行古典主义的原则，正是这些严谨的细节使建筑不但端庄宏伟，而且细腻匀称。室内设计采用的是意大利文艺复兴的风格，金色、红色等色彩辉煌而不落俗套，同时也十分强调细节，把握尺度，不至使建筑过度装饰，恰如其分地把一个商业建筑空间打造得热烈、温馨、明快。

Hong Kong Architecture Science Press
Katrina Question:

What is your idea to design and organize consumers' shopping experience?

香港建筑科学出版社
张燕清问:

你们是怎样设计和组织消费者的购物体验的？

Hua Lei: Sense of "experience" is an indispensable element of commercial building. Global harbour tries to enhance a sense of experience with its retail outlets. A variety of business forms are used to enrich the experience. We make effort to diversify visitors' experience in sense of sight with designed decoration style and creation of varied space. As a result, the architectural design incorporates large scale, classic rhythm and melody, strong decoration, aiming at shaping up a variety of "themes". Visitors are attracted as they make their first step into the space. They feel the things they never felt anywhere else with their eyes. Meanwhile, they also feel spatial variation, repeated rhythm and detailed decoration. All is about consumers' experience of environment.

华镭："体验"感目前是商业建筑中必不可少的元素，环球港以商业内容来强调体验感，以不同的业态带来不同的体验经历。在设计上我们则是以设计的装饰风格，以建筑上打造不同的空间感给人在视觉感官上带来丰富的"体验"。所以建筑设计上采用大尺度、古典韵律和节奏、强烈的装饰以刻画出不同的"主题"，让人进到空间就被建筑本身所吸引，用眼睛去体验这种在其他地方所见不到的内容，同时体验空间的变化、韵律的重复和细节的装饰。这一切全都是消费者的环境体验。

Architect: Hualei
建筑师：华镭

Exclusive interview with Hua Lei

独家专访：
华镭

Hong Kong Architecture Science Press
Katrina Question:

Was there anything you pay more attention to when designing? Like material and form?

香港建筑科学出版社
张燕清问：

在设计过程中有什么是你们特别注重的吗？比如材料和形式的方面？

Hua Lei: We paid more attention to how to cope with the contradiction between classic style, modern architectural functions and technology. As required by the client, a ramp with access to a 32-meter-high roof shall be designed. How to integrate such a slash into the exterior facade with a rigorous classic style poses as a great challenge for architectural design. The design team ended up with hiding the 200 m-long ramp behind a row of colonnades, keeping it as perfect as it should be. A rare experience comes alive with such a ramp going all the way up through colonnades. For interior design, we did not use too much of natural materials. Instead, we present a decent European classic interior style with the help of fine and clever design. Techniques were used to create a pretty, elegant and pleasant commercial environment, such as colors, patterns, textures, frescos and others. As a result, we have an impressive commercial environment that deserves your everlasting appreciation. Compared to some other commercial buildings of classic style in China, it gets rid of columns and walls monotonously made of marble and cuts back on costs of construction. The root cause is the blind use of western concept and religious architectural style in commercial and "folk" buildings. This is a dead wrong.

华镭： 我们在设计过程中特别注重古典风格与现代建筑功能和技术的矛盾的处理。根据甲方的需求，要设计一坡道直通 32 米高的屋顶，如何将这条斜线与严谨的古典风格的外立面相结合，给建筑设计带来极大的挑战。设计团队最终把这条 200 米长的坡道隐藏在一排柱廊后，丝毫没有破坏建筑的效果，同时这条坡道通过柱廊一直向上，成为另一种难得的体验。

室内设计上，我们并没有采用过多的华贵的天然材料，而是通过精细而巧妙的设计来体现真正欧洲古典的室内风格，用色彩、图案、纹样、壁画等一系列的手法打造了一个美丽、典雅同时又让人赏心悦目的商业环境，使人流连忘返，久看不厌。相比国内其它一些商业建筑，同样采用古典风格但只是一味地在柱子和墙面上使用大理石，看上去单调至极，而且提高了造价，殊不知其根本问题在于盲目地把西方观念和宗教建筑风格应用到一个商业和"民俗"建筑中，这样是大错特错的。

LANDMARK COMPLEX REAL ESTATE
地标型复合地产

014

SHENZHEN OCEAN WORLD PLAZA COMPLEX
深圳海上世界广场综合体

Ocean World Plaza is designed to be an European sunken plaza which envelops an extensive space of human scale where socializing, recreational activities and exchange occur.

"海上世界广场"采用欧洲下沉式的广场设计，形成的围合空间可为人们提供宽松的社交场合、休闲娱乐及交流的人性化空间。

ABU dhabi SOWWAH SQUARE

The layout of building follows the classical proportionally balanced principle.

建筑的布局遵循古典式的对称比例原则。

038

阿布扎比沙瓦哈广场

The different arrangement of skin textures on a individual building gives identity to all of them.

通过在建筑单体上对于表皮肌理的不同搭配，使每一栋单体建筑都呈现出独特的个性。

KUALA LUMPUR EMPIRE DAMANSARA
吉隆坡白沙罗帝国大楼

062

050

BEIJING CHAOYANG PARK PLAZA
北京朝阳公园广场

With an overall black look, the project has employed some techniques, such as water and rocks in the landscape painting.

建筑呈现黑色调的整体形象，运用山水画中山石形象直译过来的建筑形式等手法。

The building conveys the solemn atmosphere of regional financial center while the cold and straight building mass represents the emotional modern capital sanctuary in a very good way.

整体的建筑气氛一方面传达了一种区域金融中心的庄重大气，另一方面其冰冷挺拔的整体形式有意无意地暗示着一种金融组织去情感化的现代资本圣殿。

072

CHINA-TAIWAN CROSS STRAIT FORUM AND CBD DEVELOPMENT
平潭海峡论坛及中央商务区发展

To reflect the aspiration of transparency and dialogue the buildings are formed by converging elements that combine with the landscape and waterfront to create a fluid and open series of public spaces that meld into the buildings themselves.

建筑设计结合了景观及滨海的自然元素，创造了一个流动的、空间开放的、与建筑融为一体的公共场所，充分体现了建筑的透明度和与周围环境互动的特征。

078

SINGAPORE ASIA SQUARE TOWER
新加坡亚洲广场

Expressed as a singular, unifying element, it is conceived as an "ice block" floating above the ground. It encapsulates the whole site to provide a large city room known as "The Cube".

这座裙楼可堪称悬浮在地面的"冰块"，单一中却也透露出一种和谐感。它仿佛将整座建筑的精华浓缩在此，才创造出"The Cube"这样大型的都市空间。

088

NANJING ZENDAI HIMALAYAS CENTER
南京证大喜玛拉雅中心

The overall white architectural style may be closer to traditional Chinese landscape painting featuring lightness and transparency.

整体建筑白色系的风格可能更加接近传统中国山水艺术轻盈通透的气质。

096

WUXI COMPLEX
无锡综合体

In the project of Wuxi city many design products address the presence of the lake. The water becomes a tool to design landscape and buildings; the waterscape is brought in the inner part the project and also until the top of buildings designing the main facade of the Hotel with a waterfall.

在无锡的项目中，众多设计产品围绕湖的存在而展开，水成为了设计景观与建筑的工具。水景表达了项目的内涵，比如通过房顶设计的瀑布来烘托酒店主立面的内涵。

THE TWO PILLARS OF EASTLAKE
杭州东湖双子大楼

102

The towers' volume delivers two integral geometrical forms in the design plan for Hangzhou twin towers delivers two integral geometry. Such detailing features a strong style-based orientation by relinquishing different views of aesthetics. However, this processing has a strong sense of the style orientation.

在这个杭州双塔的方案中，塔楼的体量取了两个完整的几何体形式。抛开美学上的见仁见智，这样的处理有一种强烈的风格化取向。

108

NINGBO YINZHOU SOUTHERN CBD PORTAL
宁波鄞州南部商务区门户区

The surface shape of individual building and fusion of walls and floors of the project is an expression of rising of a new aesthetic genre achieved by new technology.

本方案中建筑单体曲面的塑造，墙体楼板的融合等等，体现了一种新技术带来新的审美流派的兴起。

COMMERCIAL COMPLEX REAL ESTATE

商业型复合地产

120 FUZHOU WUSIBEI THAIHOT PLAZA 福州五四北泰禾广场

The stylish and cool-looking pleated skin working with gigantic volume looks striking in the city. Interior space and interior design present a clear style. The purple automatic escalator catches eyeballs.

外观上时髦酷炫的折叠表皮配合其大体量在城市中格外显眼。内部环境中空间和内饰设计风格明快，紫色调自动扶梯非常抢眼。

130 SHIJIAZHUANG WONDER MALL 石家庄万象天成

The architects create a commercial complex with a brand new look different from others with constrained construction technology in China and via a unique design. What is more, the project delivers another highlight, a clever use of lighting design which complements the expression of architectural curve skin and forms a speech that speaks to building's commercial property. A powerful sense of landmark is shown.

设计师们运用在国内可行的技术建构手段通过设计的方式得出一种不同于一般商业综合体建筑的全新风貌。同时本项目的另一个亮点在于灯光设计的运用，其很好地烘托了建筑曲线型表皮的表现力，与建筑的商业属性相得益彰，地标感强

142 QUANZHOU WANDA PLAZA 泉州万达广场

The new Quanzhou Wanda Plaza is located at one of the cities' most extraordinary locations, directly at the Jinjiang River, noble at day and shiny at night time. The scheme is respecting and defining the natural and urban space. The entire design is made by highlighting the most present element of the surrounding nature element "water".

由于泉州万达广场坐落在锦江河边，一个非凡的城市地理位置，白天显得高贵而晚上霓虹闪烁，为了使环境与自然更加和谐，设计强调了周边最有代表性的自然元素"水"。

Behind this concept is the idea to promote the interaction of this natural element and the human made systematic, valuate the attracting wildness by combining it with a background of dignity, capture a fragile moment of beauty into a frame of eternity.

方案的概念是促进自然元素和人造体系间的相互作用，以结合纯粹的设计理念来应对极具吸引力的繁杂，将美丽的瞬间凝固在永恒的画框之中。

152 ZIBO LIVING MALL 淄博华润五彩城

There are several differences designing retail projects in the west versus in Asia, particularly in China. The retail mix and tenant types are obviously different to suit the local markets.

亚洲与西方在设计商业型项目方面存在几处差别，尤其以中国的商业型项目更加突出。为了迎合当地市场需求，亚洲与西方的商业型项目在功能匹配与租户类型方面存在明显差别。

160 SHENZHEN VANKE ONE CITY 深圳万科壹海城

The abstract narrative defined each of the facades, creating a unifying layer that was able to transition between each of the parcels.

抽象的立面展现创造出统一、协调的韵律，从而使各地块前呼后应，过渡自然。

168 HUIZHOU HUAMAO CENTER 惠州华贸中心

Residential areas are arranged around the square in a pinwheel fashion, which creates a dynamic flow to the scheme. Townhouse apartments feature retail lots at the lower levels, forming the podiums for the fifty-story residential towers that pierce the sky above the city skyline and create an iconic landmark within the city.

住宅区以旋转风车的时尚结构排列在广场四周，为整个设计方案形成了一种动感的流线结构。联排别墅式公寓的底层设有零售商店，形成 50 层住宅楼的裙楼，在城市天际线三方直直插入云霄，为这个城市打造一个极具标志性的地标建筑。

176 CHENGDU BACK GARDEN PHASE 4 成都后花园 4 期

Inspired from "Urban landscape", designers expect to create a unique commercial project by imitating enjoyable scenery found in Chinese traditional painting, with architectural fengshui theory serving as the tutor for architectural layout and function.

"城市山水"，设计师们希望能借鉴国画写意山水的意境，让建筑的布局和功能在建筑风水学的指导下成为一个不同的商业项目。

180 SANYA CHINA RAILWAY SUNSHINE PLACE 三亚中铁子悦薹

A series of public facilities are arranged under the roof, showing the respect for roof space design in marseille apartments that made by Le Corbusier. The neighboring office building adopts the exaggerated setback structure, showing the unique features fully.

屋顶下是一系列公共活动设施，仿佛一种对柯布时期马赛公寓开发屋顶空间的一个致敬。紧邻地块的办公塔楼采取了一种夸张的退台形式。向所处环境努力展现出一种与众不同的存在感。

190 BEIJING GREENLAND COLORFUL TOWN 北京绿地缤纷城

As a community commercial complex, it not only offers neighboring residents an easy life and a prime quality of development but also delivers a good supporting environment for business, office, serviced apartment at the later stage of development.

缤纷城不仅保证了周边居住区的生活便利、楼盘品质，更为后期开发的商务办公、酒店式公寓提供了良好的配套环境。

SHOPPING COMPLEX REAL ESTATE

购物型复合地产

Reflection, light and pattern are used throughout the Hanjie Wanda Square to create an fantastical world.

整个汉街万达广场都运用了光线的反射、照明、图案，旨在营造出一种奇幻的世界。

This modern commercial building collects and conveys many classical architectural languages. It has the biggest area in Shanghai commercial complex building. It is the epitome for Art Deco building style in Shanghai.

古典建筑语汇在现代商业建筑的大合体。冠绝上海的商业综合体面积体量。上海地区泛滥的 Art Deco 建筑风格的集大成者。

The Jockey Plaza has achieved this with costumers, through the creation of semi-urban areas with architectural elements that serve as references and encourage the visitors to explore a worth remembering experience.

服装商，城乡结合区的打造，建筑元素的借鉴都促就了赛马广场的成功。建筑元素无时无刻不吸引游客们去探索一种值得回忆的体验。

Both the materials and forms of the massing are organic or natural with gentle curves and arcs overlapping to make the building reflect the topography. The result is a harmonious facade, both in color and form, symbolic and unique within its context.

通过对柔和曲线与弧线的堆叠，采用天然材料，塑造自然形体，让建筑与周遭地貌融为一体。从而，无论是颜色还是形体，都打造出与环境相交融的立面，不仅别具一格，而且相映成趣。

Filtered daylight, timber colonnades , and natural stone paving create an approachable and inviting experience; a new landmark for a historic city.

柔和的日光，木质柱廊，自然石材铺装，这一切都营造出一种温馨，亲民的体验。已然一座历史名城的新地标。

Poly Water City takes full account of its own advantage to use the "water" element in a scientific and reasonable way.

"水"元素是保利水城项目对于自身的优势最为科学合理的应用。

The project emphasizes the integration of urban function and form, the building rich more porosity and gives space back to citizens.The project implements in Chengdu architecture and regional emotion, architecture and human interaction and integration, and achieves the concept of modern environmental protection technology to build a super green building. The project hopes to give residents here an exciting experience.

项目强调整体化都市功能与形式，建筑体富多孔隙性，还空间于市民。该项目实现了成都建筑与地域情感、建筑与人的互动与融合，实现了现代环保技术打造超级绿色建筑的概念，项目希望带给成都市民一种兴奋的体验。

The design and programmatic focus are based primarily on the location in Solingen, known as the German City of Blades. The mall has been designed with the themes of nature, industry and fashion. The first two subjects strongly relate to the City of Solingen and its surrounding regions.

商场以自然、工业、时尚作为设计主题。前两个主题与索林根市及其周边区域息息相关。整个主题围绕着商场的室内室外，并通过强调不同区域的设计来对顾客起引导作用。

OFFICE COMPLEX REAL ESTATE
办公型复合地产

312

TURKEY ZORLU CENTER

土耳其佐鲁中心

The excellent project should be designed according to the terrain. Row houses under the building shell are configured with a large garden on its first floor,while the residents could enjoy the view of the Bosphorus Bay from the large terrace of second floor. Both the garden and the terrace can be entranced through the open atrium. This atrium is a space that is rich, bright and pleasant.

根据地形来设计的优秀项目。建筑外壳下的联排住宅在一层配置了大型的花园，二层的大露台使住户可以在此欣赏博斯普鲁斯湾的景色。花园和露台都可以经由露天的中庭进入。这座中庭是一处内容丰富、色调明亮、令人愉悦的空间。

The Zorlu Center Site is just at the junction of the Bosphorus Bridge European connection and the glamorous Büyükdere axis that connects the city center with the great business district Maslak. It is reached from various important centers of Istanbul and moreover,topographically is one of the few plain sites that face south, with the old city view. With all these significant qualities, it has been a "subject of desire" and was owned by the Zorlu Property through a tender, being watched by all levels of the public. In this sense, the mixed use project being developed on this area deals with contradictions such as grandeur and modesty, public and private, international and domestic, social and distinguished, together with structural and topographical considerations.

佐鲁中心位于土耳其伊斯坦布尔博斯普鲁斯大桥和迷人的布伊克德尔轴线的交汇处，布伊克德尔轴线连接了市中心和马斯拉克商业区。佐鲁中心不仅连接了城市几个重要的中心地带，同时它也处在城市少有的几处平坦地形之上，靠近南部的旧城区。因其综合这些重要的品质，它被称为"欲望的主体"，佐鲁中心归佐鲁地产所有，是在公众的目光下投标所得。这个多功能项目将多个对立的元素融合在一起 ：宏伟和谦逊、公开和私密、国际性和本土化、社会化和独特性等都在结构和地形的设计上有所体现。

344

ABU DHABI GUARDIAN TOWER

阿布扎比 GUARDIAN 大厦

The commercial building is of neighborhood.

Module design comes along with energy saving. The Middle East economic crisis happened during the creation. But the final design brought value to the investment.

The key to the commercial project lies in the success of sustainability. It will last forever instead of an one-off opening ceremony.

商业属于街区社区类型、小而美；

模块化设计结合节能。营造过程经历了中东经济危机，但最终设计为投资带来了价值；

业项目最关键的是可持续的成功、而非昙花一现的开幕式、要永不落幕。

332

GERMANY KÖ-BOGEN DÜSSELDORF

德国杜塞尔多夫库伯根项目

Kö-Bogen is a six-storey 40,162□office and retail complex in downtown Düsseldorf and marking an important transition between urban space and landscape.

建筑高 6 层，建筑面积为 40 162 平方米，兼有办公和零售功能。它位于杜塞尔多夫的市中心，在城市空间和景观空间之间发挥承前启下的作用。

Permeated cuts into the facades towards Königsallee and Hofgarten allow for the landscape to naturally blend and flow into the building.

人们的视线可穿过立面上的切口，直达国王大道与宫廷公园，让建筑与远处的景观形成自然的交融，成为建筑物一幅美丽的背景画。

Kö-Bogen completes the Königsallee boulevard at Hofgarten park and shapes the new Hofgarten promenade and terraces, places that have already become popular with the people of Düsseldorf. The building also gives shape to Schadowplatz square and forms a passage towards Hofgarten, busy with boutiques, restaurants and cafes with outdoor seating.

Kö-Bogen 的存在填补了宫廷公园国王大道的空缺，形成了已受杜塞尔多夫人民热捧的宫廷新散步道、露台与聚集地。此外，建筑的存在不仅塑造了沙多广场，而且还是通往宫廷公园的通道。建筑内设有众多精品店，餐馆，咖啡，并在室外安置了座椅。

On the sides towards Schadowplatz and Gustaf-Gründgens Platz, using components of various heights within the same sized facade elements a horizontal pattern is created. The staggered horizontal bands amplify the dynamic character of the building along the newly shaped pedestrian spaces.

在朝沙多广场与格林德根斯 • 古斯塔法广场一侧的立面上采用水平格局，在同样宽度的立面元素内采用不同高度的构件。以新形成的步行空间为背景，纵横交错的横条纹更加凸显建筑的动态感。

ACCESSIBLE COMPLEX REAL ESTATE
交通型复合地产

352

HARBIN TWIN TOWERS
哈尔滨双子大楼

The main concept of the Harbin towers was Sharing the same DNA - but positioned differently - the Twin Towers form a new icon for the Haxi Business Development Zone. The Towers creates a balanced relationship between empty and full, mass and void, private and public. Each tower creates a program specific dialogue with the site, with the north SOHO and Service Apartment tower atrium opening toward the Plaza, and the south Office Tower atrium oriented toward the Business District.

哈尔滨大厦的主要设计理念：同样的血统，不同的定位。作为哈西商务开发区的新地标，双子塔在虚与实、私密与公共之间找到了一种平衡关系。大厦的功能定位与场地布局紧密相连。北侧是SOHO与酒店式公寓大厦，其大厅入口正对广场。南侧则是写字楼，其入门大厅正对商务区。

374

AEROVILLE
爱萝维莉购物娱乐中心

Uses are changing with new ways of life, and technology affecting our relationship to space and time. New uses will be the most interesting sources of innovations in the future. Form has to follow and serve new uses.

建筑用途正随着新的生活方式发生变化。技术影响着我们跟空间与时间的关系。在未来，首当其冲的是建筑用途的创新，随后才是形式创新，这是因为形式创新是随用途创新而来。

We truly believed that a the right working environment is generating money! Today we are obligate to create a comfortable working space even though the cost is more expensive in construction but when its get to rent the rent is higher.

我们从骨子里认为，只要能营造出舒适的工作环境，大家就能开心工作、赚钱！尽管建设成本高昂，但从当今社会角度考虑，我们有义务营造出舒适的工作场所，而且还可抬高楼面租金。

Promoting human interaction is an important guideline for spatial practice, we truly believe that its the essence of design today.

促进人际互动是如何布局空间的主要纲领。我们的确认为促进人际互动就是当今设计的核心内容。

MALL FORUM MITTELRHEIN, KOBLENZ
科布伦茨中部莱恩的 Mall Forum Mittelrhein

366

The task was to make a design for a facade which gave the building a "shell" with a unique character, to hide the parked cars on the top floors, while offering enough openings for ventilation. We approached that challenge with the "Wine Leave Facade".

我们的一个目标就是设计出一种具有特色，类似于"壳"的立面，遮住停在顶层的汽车。与此同时，立面还具备保证充分通风的孔洞。最后，我们的解决方法就是"葡萄叶立面"。

By creating spaces that are amiable to be in and offer the user a pleasant ambience. In addition, it needs the great spaciousness, clear orientation and sightlines, and can lead people's sightline, providing a lot of daylight and pleasant lighting.

创造出和蔼可亲的空间，让人们能感到愉悦。此外，还需要广阔的空间、明确的朝向，能引导人们的视线，充足的自然采光，让人心情舒畅的照明设计。

The essential qualities were the strong incorporating in the urban microstructure of the routes and ways and the easy accessibility of the projects. We wanted an introverted mall but also a building that could function independently and invites the user to stroll through.

本项目内涵就是从微观层面上看，如何将城市空间中的人流、物流、交通便利性有效地整合在一起。我们既希望打造一个含蓄的商场，也希望打造一个具有独立功能的建筑，可以吸引人们到此畅游。

By using production techniques from car body manufacturing in the architectural process we could stay within the scope of technical requirements, design issues and building costs. By designing one "Wine Leave" element and using it 2,900 times in the facade it was possible to achieve the benchmark of the budget while getting a high end quality of the product. The chosen material aluminium had great advantages and made it feasible to make a lightweight element which saved a lot of primary construction while introduce the deep draw technique in the building sector.

在建筑设计过程中，我们借助了取自于汽车车身的生产工艺，从而帮助我们解决在技术要求，设计以及建造成本方面的困难。我们设计了以"葡萄叶"为单位的立面构件，安装了2 900个"Wine Leave"，最终可以在不超出预算的情况下打造出如此高品质的产品。我们选用铝作为材料，铝具有很大的优势，可以制造出轻量的立面构件。这样不仅可以大幅度节约建设成本，而且还可借用汽车制造行业采用的深冲成形工艺。

358

SINGAPORE CLEMENTI MIXED DEVELOPMENT
新加坡金文泰综合体

Clementi Mall stands out because it is part of the first mixed-use development in Singapore that has seamlessly integrated a retail mall with public housing units, an air-conditioned bus interchange as well as a Mass Rapid Transit (MRT) station. The project is a true reflection of what it means to build spaces that are socially-conscious and yet, commercially viable.

由于克莱门蒂商场是新加坡首个综合型商业项目，所以她的存在自然就与众不同。该项目在商场，公共住房单位，空调巴士换乘站以及新加坡地铁站之间形成了无缝连接。项目真实地反应了什么才是既服务大众又适合经商的空间打造。

A mall should not be just another high density development standing in isolation. It should be designed for the community in mind, with features such as interactivity and connectivity incorporated into not only the mall but every aspect of the entire development living, commuting and retail experience.

商场不应是一个独立的且高密集型建筑。设计应该以人为本，考虑到与人的互动，与周边环境的互通。不仅是商场本身，还是整个建筑的各方面，包括住户生活体验、路人感受、购物体验等等，都应体现出一种互动与连通。

386

SINGAPORE CHANGI AIRPORT TERMINAL 4
新加坡樟宜机场 4 号航站楼

The large areas of vertical greening and interior green garden, are exactly consist with the title of "garden city" of Singapore, creating the comfortable interior green life. In addition, two layers of glaze appearance, colorful light lanterns hanging in the entrance hall and unique old Nyonya-style buildings, show people the brand-new feelings.

项目大面积的垂直绿化、室内的绿色花园，与新加坡的"花园城市"的称号非常相符，营造非常舒适的室内林荫生活。另外，两层内釉面外观、色彩斑斓的天窗灯笼挂在入口大厅，以及设计独特的娘惹风格建筑，给人耳目一新的感觉。

TOURISM COMPLEX REAL ESTATE

旅游型复合地产

392

BEIJING TONGZHOU RESORT CITY

北京通州度假城

The main concept for the project was to create a unique year-round mixed-use resort destination in the heart of Tongzhou while providing a dramatic silhouette along the Wenyu River.

该项目的主要设计理念就是在通州的核心地段打造一个四季开放的综合型度假胜地，给人们带来另一番风味的体验。建筑在文字河边画出美丽的轮廓，生机快然。

The design intent was to energize the commercial street frontage, activate the adjacent waterfront while also engaging the nearby Yuan Toudao island.

设计旨在点燃正街的商业氛围，让毗邻的滨河地区充满生机，同时还唤醒附近的源头岛。

这个问题对建筑师是挑战，很多建筑师持排斥态度，我想在建筑设计进程中因项目的特点，产生了更多影响设计的因素，对建筑师而言，其设计的过程会更显设计的价值。对商业建筑，建筑师充分研究商业运营与投资回报也是从不可少的课题，只有了解了问题的实质，才能在设计中合理的解决。

The first job is to integrate and plan commercial functions to cater to business practice and deliver an excellent organization of flows when a commercial project is not influenced by any specific external factor.

对于商业项目，在无特定的外部条件影响下，首要的是将商业功能整合规划成符合商业运营的模式，组织好各种流线。

420

CHENGDU'S NEW CENTURY GLOBAL CENTER

成都新世纪环球中心

The project was small in scale in the early phase. The design proposal is quite based on concept. With change of external factors, we saw an increasingly improved core of this project which became a signature project in Chengdu. And the project saw an enhancement both in scale and functions.

项目的前期规模不大，设计方案也是在设计理念基础上进行，但是随着外部因素的变化，项目主体不断提升，成为成都市的名片项目，其规模和功能也不断的放大。

While the curving nature of the design concept references the historical narrative of a traditional Sampan boat sailing along the river it also serves the functional purpose of providing a larger footprint area to be designated for public plaza and gathering spaces.

中国自古以来就有小船荡漾在河上的美景。以此为灵感，我们在设计理念中引入了曲线的元素。从功能上说，度假胜地给游客带来更宽阔的散步空间，引领游客通往公共广场与聚集空间。

Careful consideration is paid to zoning and building arrangement within the site to maximize views and ventilation to all buildings, while at the same time maintaining the existing important sight lines and breeze corridors. Leisure facilities are designed on podium rooftops raised from the undulating landscape, while spaces are carved into the high-rise towers to form sky gardens for residents.

设计师细心考虑了基地分区和基地内建筑物的布局，以获得最佳的景观效果及自然通风，但同时也保留了现有的景观和通风回廊。在高低起伏的景观的烘托下，裙楼屋顶设计了休闲设施，同时高层塔楼上挖出空间，为住户打造空中花园。

INTERNATIONAL BUSINESS CENTER AND INTERCONTINENTAL HOTEL

412

国际商务中心与洲际酒店

A certain dualism has been sought in the project- a reference and connection between Mount Ararat and the twin peaks together with the dynamic equilibrium of the two parts as a whole. The hotel building has been designed as an accent both in the architectural composition of the complex and in the general layout of the city.

该项目力图寻找某种两重性，寻找阿勒山双子峰之间的关联；同时当两者作为一个整体时，两者之间形成的一种动态平衡。无论在综合体建筑布局方面，还是在城市总体布局方面，酒店大楼都是焦点。

Combining three functions- hotel, office and residential building in one complex is always challenging. Following the design concept of the two integral elements, considering them not as separate units, but as a part of the whole, point our idea. The volumes appear as a united complex of ovals by plan, but each expresses its individual purpose.

功能上，该综合体集酒店、办公以及家居为一体。如何实现功能的集合，总是颇具挑战。遵循合二为一的设计理念，我们既要将各建筑视为一个整体，同时又传递出他们的不同之处。从平面图上看，各建筑好似整合在一起的综合体，但同时也表达出各自不同的用途。

400

GALAXY MOONBAY RENAISSANCE HOTEL AND MIXED USE DEVELOPMENT

星河澜月湾万丽酒店及综合发展

The masterplan design was inspired by the local craft of bamboo carving and the aerodynamic shapes of naval design. The landscape design forms the foundation of the overall planning and design of the masterplan. A mixture of public spaces including parks, plazas, an amphitheatre and playgrounds are designed to support a variety of uses. The nature of public usage of landscape areas allows the site to integrate seamlessly with the existing lake-side promenade to the east of the site.

此总体规划设计的灵感来自当地竹雕工艺以及具有流线外形的现代船舶设计。景观设计构建了总平面规划和设计的基础。一系列的公共空间如公园、广场、圆形剧场和操场为多种用途提供支持。景观区域的公共用途性质使基地与东面现有的湖滨人行道无缝对接。

The buildings are curved to reflect the fluidity of the lake. A section of each tower is carved to house a large floating garden to give the masterplan a softer, resort like feel.

建筑物呈弧形设计，以呼应湖泊的流动性。每座塔楼的一部分都被挖开，镶嵌大型的漂浮花园，使总体规划看起来更柔软、更具度假地的美感。

The energy of the space is very important. We really focused on the spatial flow of the spaces as this is important to connect back to the streets of Kuta so the people can flow and walk in naturally at the surrounding areas,beachwalk became an extension of the street in a natural way. It is the first semi open lifestyle commercial hub in Indonesia with a great focus on nature and landscape design.

赋予空间以活力是非常重要的要素。保持与库塔街风格的连贯至关重要，于是我们的确把重心放在了如何营造出一种过渡自然的空间。这样，人们很自然地穿行于周边各个区域，而且海滩步道也自然地成为库塔街的延伸。这是有史以来在印度尼西亚第一次采用半开放式生活体验购物中心，如此关注自然，如此关注景观设计。

432

SAHID KUTA LIFESTYLE RESORT

萨希迪库塔生活方式度假村

LANDMARK COMPLEX REAL ESTATE

地标型复合地产

GOETTSCH PARTNERS (GP)

GP 建筑设计有限公司

SHENZHEN OCEAN WORLD PLAZA COMPLEX
深圳海上世界广场综合体

014

Ocean World Plaza is designed to be an European sunken plaza which envelops an extensive space of human scale where socializing, recreational activities and exchange occur.

"海上世界广场"采用欧洲下沉式的广场设计，形成的围合空间可为人们提供宽松的社交场合、休闲娱乐及交流的人性化空间。

GOETTSCH PARTNERS (GP)

GP 建筑设计有限公司

038

ABU DHABI SOWWAH SQUARE
阿布扎比沙瓦哈广场

The layout of building follows the classical proportionally balanced principle.
建筑的布局遵循古典式的对称比例原则。

ONGGONG Pte Ltd

王及王有限公司

KUALA LUMPUR EMPIRE DAMANSARA
吉隆坡白沙罗帝国大楼

062

The different arrangement of skin textures on a individual building gives identity to all of them.
通过在建筑单体上对于表皮肌理的不同搭配，使每一栋单体建筑都呈现出独特的个性。

MAD Architects

MAD 建筑事务所

052

BEIJING CHAOYANG PARK PLAZA
北京朝阳公园广场

With an overall black look, the project has employed some techniques, such as water and rocks in the landscape painting.
建筑呈现黑色调的整体形象，运用山水画中山石形象直译过来的建筑形式等手法。

10 DESIGN

10 DESIGN（拾稼设计）

CHINA-TAIWAN CROSS STRAIT FORUM AND CBD DEVELOPMENT
平潭海峡论坛及中央商务区发展

072

The building conveys the solemn atmosphere of regional financial center while the cold and straight building mass represents the emotional modern capital sanctuary in a very good way.

整体的建筑气氛一方面传达了一种区域金融中心的庄重大气，另一方面其冰冷挺拔的整体形式有意无意地暗示着一种金融组织去情感化的现代资本圣殿。

Architects 61, Denton Corker & Marshall

Architects 61, Denton Corker & Marshall

SINGAPORE ASIA SQUARE TOWER
新加坡亚洲广场

078

Expressed as a singular, unifying element, it is conceived as an "ice block" floating above the ground. It encapsulates the whole site to provide large city room known as "The Cube".

这座裙楼可堪称悬浮在地面的"冰块"，单一中却也透露出一种和谐感。它仿佛将整座建筑的精华浓缩在此，才创造出"The Cube"这样大型的都市空间。

MAD Architects

MAD 建筑事务所

NANJING ZENDAI HIMALAYAS CENTER
南京证大喜玛拉雅中心

088

The overall white architectural style may be closer to traditional Chinese landscape painting featuring lightness and transparency.
整体建筑白色系的风格可能更加接近传统中国山水艺术轻盈通透的气质。

To reflect the aspiration of transparency and dialogue the buildings are formed by converging elements that combine with the landscape and waterfront to create a fluid and open series of public spaces that meld into the buildings themselves.
建筑设计结合了景观及滨海的自然元素，创造了一个流动的、空间开放的、与建筑融为一体的公共场所，充分体现了建筑的透明度和与周围环境互动的特征。

COOP HIMMELB(L)AU Prix, Dreibholz & Partner ZT GmbH

COOP HIMMELB(L)AU Prix, Dreibholz & Partner ZT GmbH

NINGBO YINZHOU SOUTHERN CBD PORTAL
宁波鄞州南部商务区门户区

108

The surface shape of individual building and fusion of walls and floors of the project is an expression of rising of a new aesthetic genre achieved by new technology.
本方案中建筑单体曲面的塑造，墙体楼板的融合等等，体现了一种新技术带来新的审美流派的兴起。

ATENASTUDIO

阿特拉斯建筑事务所

WUXI COMPLEX
无锡综合体

096

In the project of Wuxi city many design products address the presence of the lake. The water becomes a tool to design landscape and buildings; the waterscape is brought in the inner part the project and also until the top of buildings designing the main facade of the Hotel with a waterfall.

在无锡的项目中，众多设计产品围绕湖的存在而展开，水成为了设计景观与建筑的工具。水景表达了项目的内涵，比如通过房顶设计的瀑布来烘托酒店主立面的内涵。

amphibianArc

amphibianArc

102

THE TWO PILLARS OF EASTLAKE
中国杭州东湖双子大楼

The towers' volume delivers two integral geometrical forms in the design plan for Hangzhou twin towers delivers two integral geometry. Such detailing features a strong style-based orientation by relinquishing different views of aesthetics. However, this processing has a strong sense of the style orientation.

在这个杭州双塔的方案中，塔楼的体量取了两个完整的几何体形式。抛开美学上的见仁见智，这样的处理有一种强烈的风格化取向。

PROJECT NAME 项目名称

SHENZHEN OCEAN WORLD PLAZA COMPLEX

深圳海上世界广场综合体

Architect: Architectural Design & Research Institute of Guangdong Province Shenzhen Branch/ Callison Architect/SOM/AECOM

设计公司：广东省建筑设计研究院深圳分院 / 美国凯里森设计事务所 / SOM / AECOM

PROJECT INFORMATION 项目信息

Client	China Merchants Property Development Co. Ltd.	**客户**	深圳招商房地产有限公司
Location	Shenzhen, Guangdong Province, China	**地点**	中国广东省深圳市
Gross Floor Area	107,275m^2	**总建筑面积**	107，275 平方米
Building Height	211m	**建筑高度**	211 米
Floor Area Ratio	1.02	**容积率**	1.02
Photograhy	Shenzhen Pioneer Culture Media	**摄影**	深圳先锋文化传媒

OVERVIEW 项目概况

Ocean World is located in Nanshan District, Shenzhen City and is designed to be a new international waterfront town with all rolled into one. It is a generous redevelopment project incorporating business office, recreation and entertainment, dinning, shopping, hotel, vocation, residence, culture, art and others. The new project covers China Merchants Plaza, a landmark as high as 211m, Finance Center phase II, Prince Plaza phase II and others.

海上世界位于深圳市南山区，是一座应有尽有的国际滨海新城，集商务办公、休闲娱乐、餐饮购物、酒店、度假、居住、文化艺术等于一体。新建项目包括：高 211 米的地标建筑招商局广场、金融中心二期、太子广场二期等。

FEATURE ANALYSIS 特色分析

Ocean World Plaza is designed to be an European sunken plaza which envelops an extensive space of human scale where socializing, recreational activities and exchange occur. The plaza is comprised of western bars with exotic flavors and specialty catering areas with cultural delicacies across the world. Delivering music, dance, delicacies, humanity custom and artworks that can be representative globally, the plaza gives an emphasis on harmony between human and natural environment by embracing a global community, disseminating international culture and building up global brands as well.

“海上世界广场”采用欧洲下沉式的广场设计，形成的围合空间可为人们提供宽松的社交场合、休闲娱乐及交流的人性化空间；整个广场由独具异域风情的西餐酒吧区、荟萃各国美食文化的特色餐饮区域构筑而成，以世界各地代表性的音乐、舞蹈、美食、人文风俗和工艺品为经营载体，营造国际风情，传播国际文化，打造国际名牌，强调人与自然环境的和谐共处。

Terrace 露台

In the spirit of "twin fish" flag displayed by China Merchants, Back Plaza presents a vista toward the project's promising future as part of conceptual design of Ocean World and presents a rich and unique design concept in Ocean world.

As the commercial core, "Ocean World" ANCEEVILLA at the southeastern corner of the site is the centerpiece of the whole design. Taking into account ANCEEVILLA's unique historic culture, elements in relation to the ocean are shown. The design gives a full thought to the climate characteristics at Shekou while combining the project's recreational climate and focusing on sustainable building and both interior and exterior healthy ecology as well as offering natural ventilation, daylight and others through architectural means or technic means, with a purpose to create a comfortable small climate.

秉承中国招商局历史上"双鱼"旗帜的精神，船后广场之设计作为海上世界整体概念设计的一部分，表现了对项目对未来的畅想和展望，赋予了海上世界丰富独特的设计理念。

本项目设计围绕场地东南侧"海上世界"明华轮这一商业核心展开，考虑明华轮独特的历史文化，展示与海洋有关的元素。设计充分考虑蛇口的气候特征，结合项目的休闲氛围，注重建筑节能和室内外生态环境设计，利用建筑或技术手段解决自然通风、日照控制等问题，营造宜人舒适的小气候。

LÖWENBERG

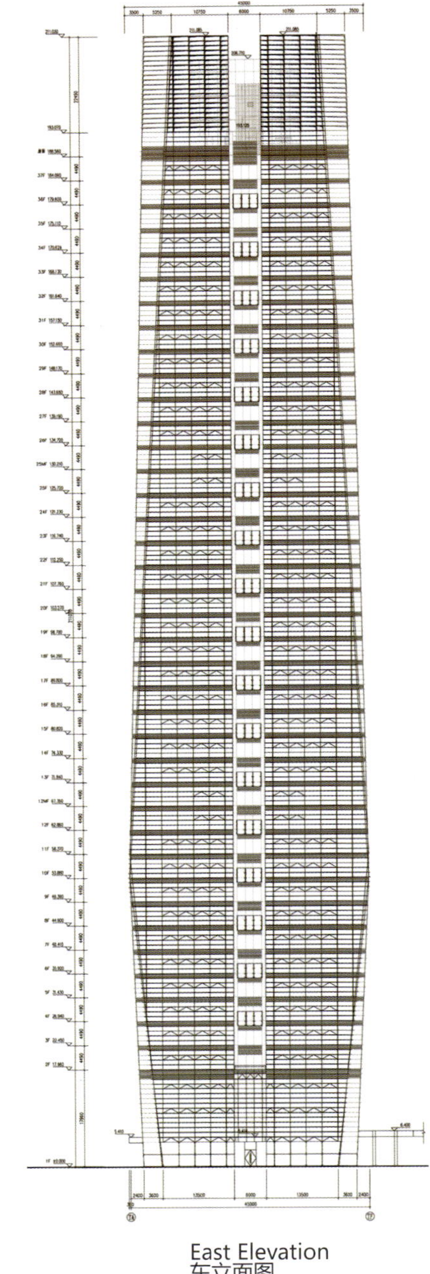

East Elevation
东立面图

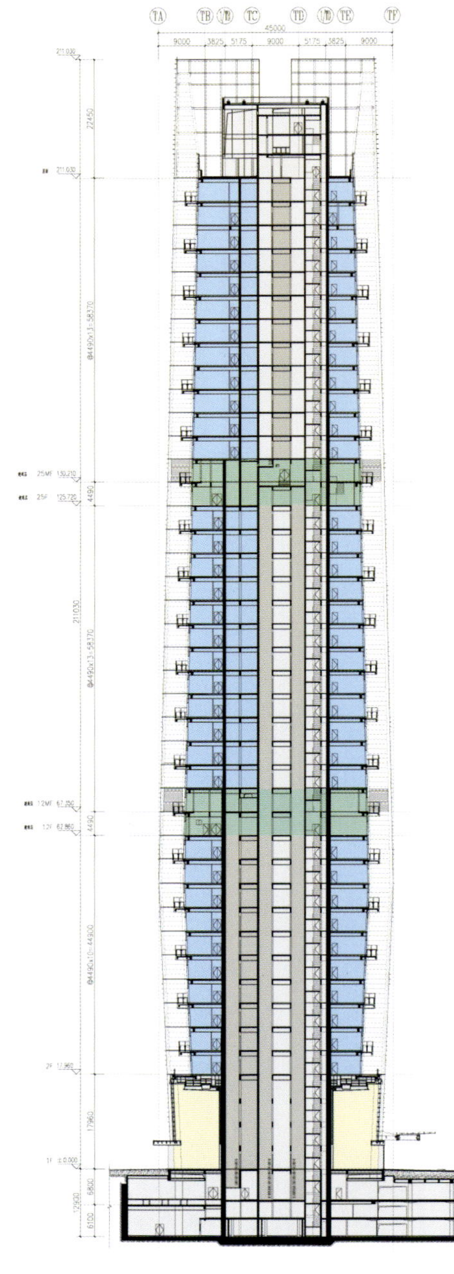

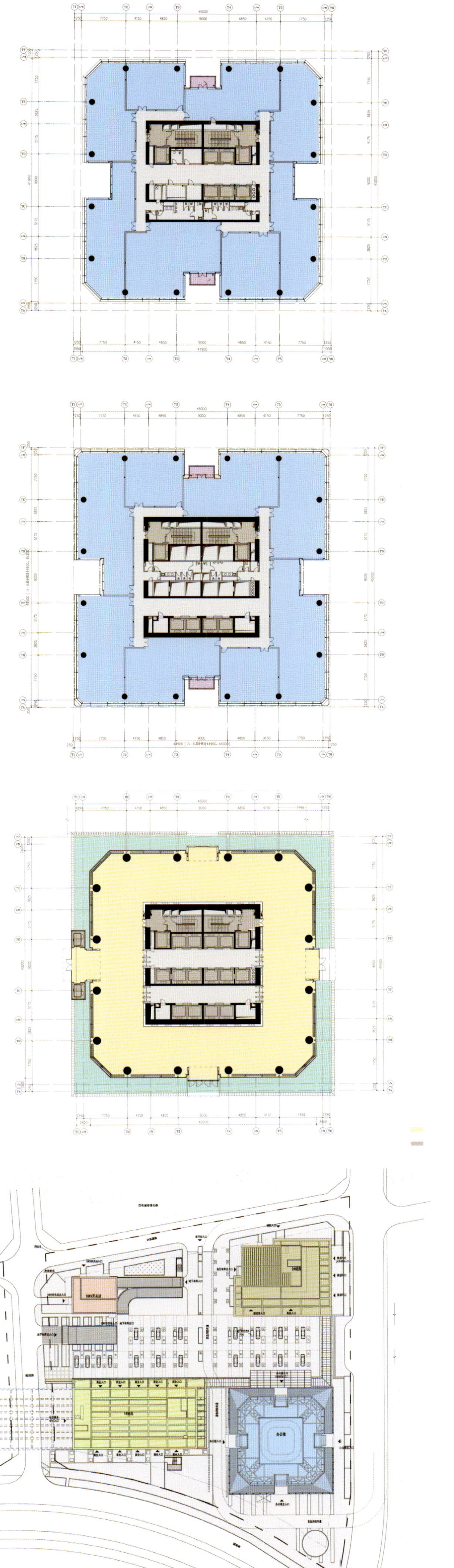

Floor Plan
楼层平面图

The ground floor falls into separate interior spaces organically linked by communal open corridor. The adjacent two floors above ground floor offer areas organically linked by exterior corridors which form an integrated building. The volume stretches along Wanghai road in the south and planned road No. 3 in the east, centering around ANCEEVILLA and embracing elegantly it like two fishes connecting from end to end.

The entrance lobby at ground floor has a ceiling height of 17.96m. The generous and open space helps enhance the quality of office building. The shelter levels at floor 12 and 25 respectively divide the building into lower area, medium area and upper area. The floor area varies with change of architectural form. All floors are designed to be office area with broad space and can be separated into isolated areas for a variety of occupants' demands.

首层分为多个室内空间，内部设有公共使用的开敞连廊，使各室内空间相对独立，又有机联系。地上 2、3 层各区域通过室外连廊有机联系，形成一个整体建筑。体量上以南侧望海路及东侧规划三路沿街伸展，以明华轮为中心，呈双鱼环抱姿态，形式优美。

首层为办公楼的入口大堂，高 17.96 米，宽敞高大的空间提升了办公楼的品质。结合 12 层、25 层的避难层将办公分成低、中、高 3 个区，各个楼层的面积随造型的收分而变化；各楼层均设计为大空间的办公区域，可根据不同用户的要求进行灵活间隔。

The exterior space is designed to offer employees and visitors a variety of open spaces with sun shade. The main public plaza in the east of office building serves as a gate for the site. With a proper set-back from the street, the building provides privacy. A large area of green land behind the tower creates an oasis for occupants to take a breath from busy and suffocating urban life. The pools around the tower provide the pedestrians a natural setting. At night, a colorful world emerges with visual effect of special lighting.

The project has employed the latest system and skin material which gives a more modern statement of forms of facade and wall surfaces with continuous transformation and delivers a dramatic and fluid form. The solid part of skin uses white acrylic as exterior wall material with addition of LED back light. The semi-transparent and reflective skin looks mysterious with application of LED throughout the building. The semi-transparent facade consists of ceramic fritted glass attached to elegant-looking spatial frame. It provides unique medium of light for terrace catering while covering the plaza.

室外空间设计秉承了为员工和来访者提供各种开敞的，有遮阳空间的设计理念。办公楼东面的主要公共广场作为地块的门户，建筑退离街道一定的距离从而提供一定的私密性，塔楼后面的大片绿地为使用者在繁忙紧张的城市中创建了一片绿洲，塔楼四周的水池也为行人提供了一种自然的环境，夜晚在特殊灯光的照射下，异彩纷呈。

项目设计采用了最新的系统和表皮材料，以一种更加现代的方式表述连续转变的屋面墙面形态，生动表现自然流畅的特性。表皮的实体部分采用高品质的白色亚克力外墙材料，可加入 LED 背光，白色半透明及反光度加上 LED 的应用在整个建筑上，使之富于神秘感。建筑的半透明部分采用异形彩釉玻璃附着在优雅的空间框架结构上，覆盖广场的同时为露台餐饮提供独特的采光介质。

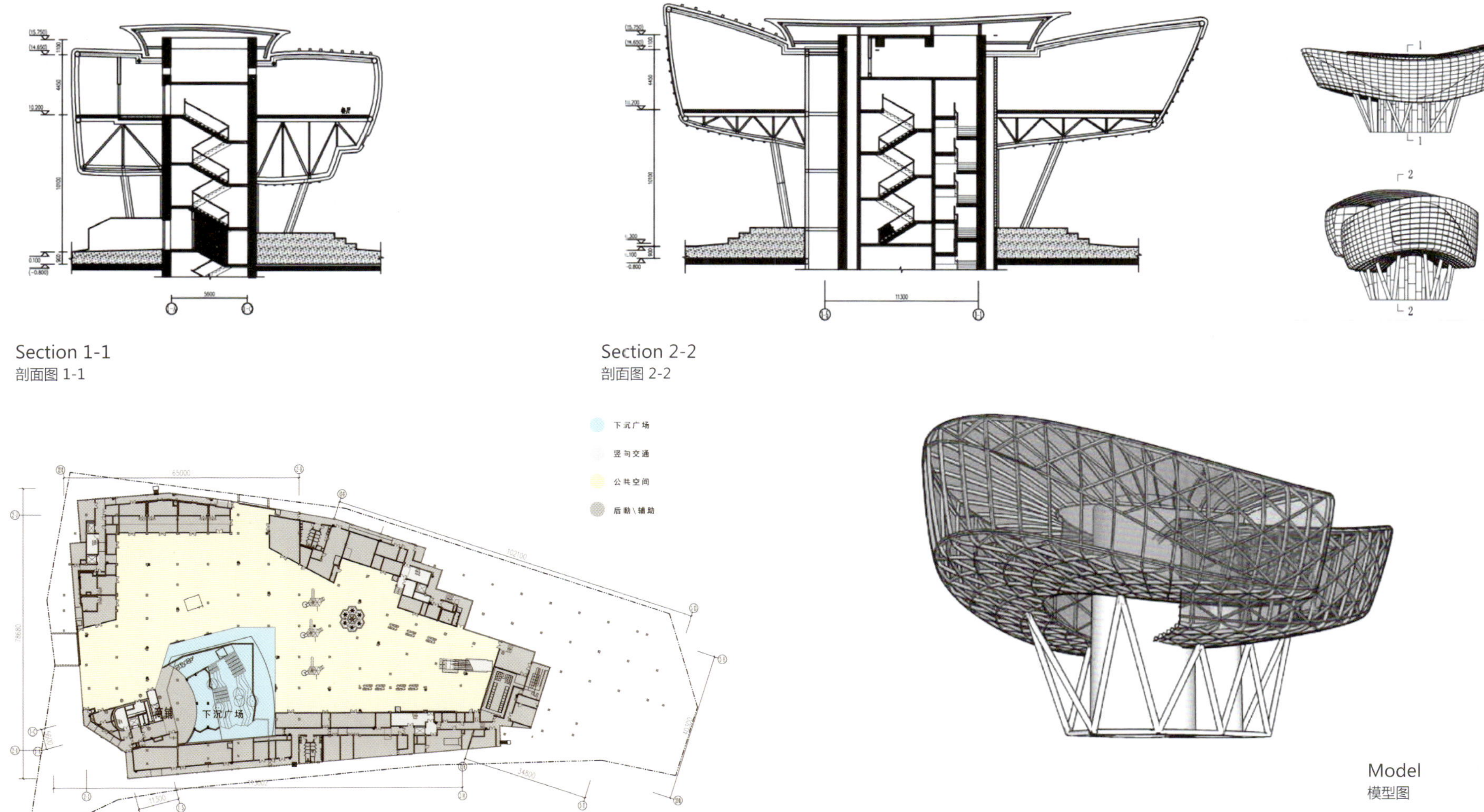

Section 1-1
剖面图 1-1

Section 2-2
剖面图 2-2

B1 Floor Plan
负一层平面图

Model
模型图

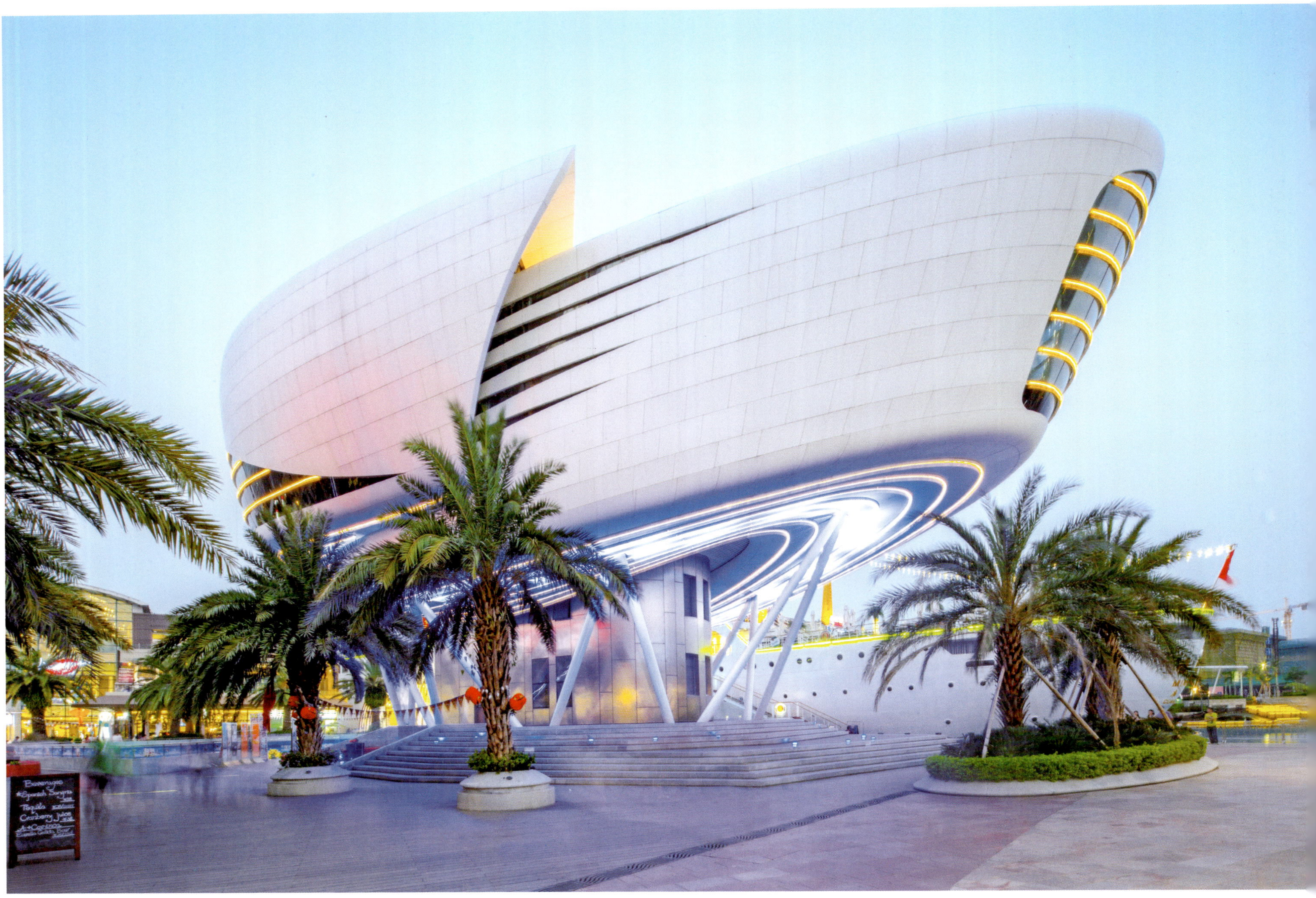

双玺花园
美食广场
MINGHUA

With a careful planning, the building provides cozy and isolated public spaces and private terrace setting for having dinner by maximizing availability of space in a proper manner. Meanwhile, there is a balance achieved among business, catering and entertainment. The looping circulation running through all circular retail programs of Ocean World serves as a major demarcation line between solid structure and semi-transparent structure. The eastern building and western building are connected with wide and flat steel which also supports the upper floors, forming a major monumental space at the entrance of the building.

Vertical mullion of four facades delivers a stronger vertical quality. Based on efficient plane organization and proper structure, facade represents an inspiring spirit by rolling all elements into one like sea, sail, beacon and others, giving a perfect expression of "incorporating maturity, restraining and pioneering" of Merchant enterprises and allowing Merchant Plaza to become a new generation of icon and landmark of Shekou.

该建筑经过精心策划，充分合理利用空间，提供舒适无干扰的公共空间、私人露台用餐环境，同时在商业、餐饮和娱乐功能之间达到平衡。实体与半透明体间的主要界线是连接整体海上世界环船商业的环形通廊。通过宽扁钢将建筑东西两部分连接并支撑起上部分的楼层结构，形成建筑主要的入口大空间。

建筑的四个立面设计上采用竖向线条来强化建筑垂直品质。外立面设计在平面高效、结构合理的前提下，综合了海、帆、灯塔等元素的外部造型表达了一股向上的精神，完美地表现了"集成熟、内敛和敢为天下先为一身"的招商局企业特质，使招商局广场成为蛇口新一代的标志和象征。

整体鸟瞰图（效果图）

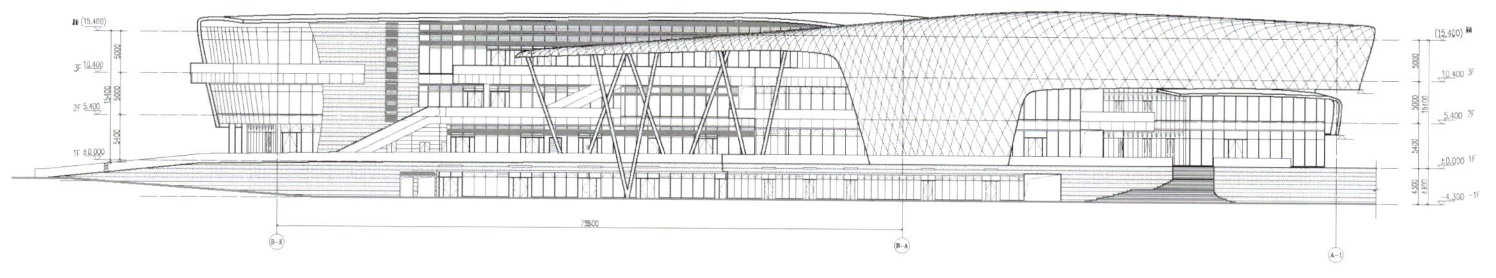

Elevation 1
立面图 1

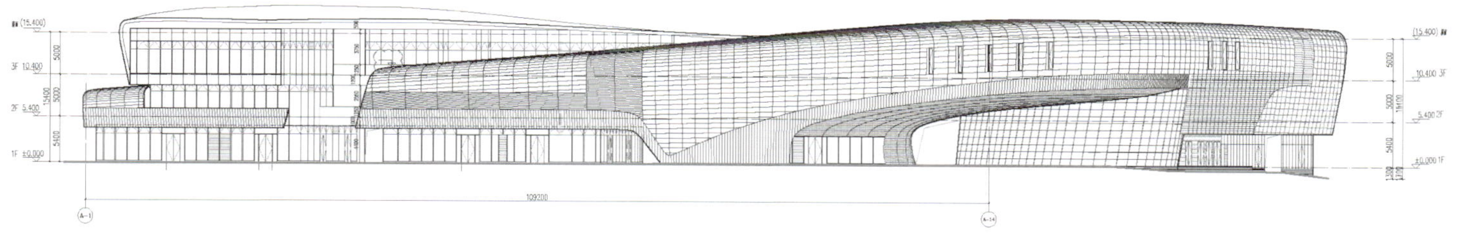

Elevation 2
立面图 2

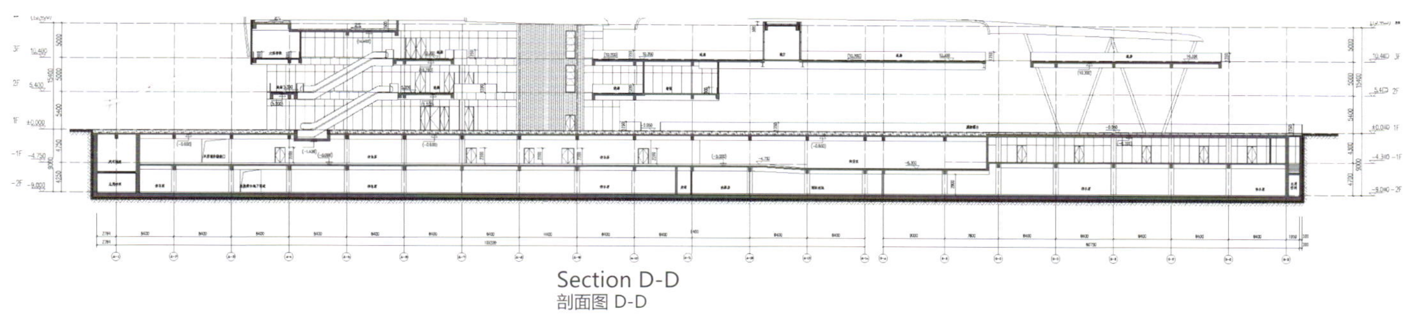

Section D-D
剖面图 D-D

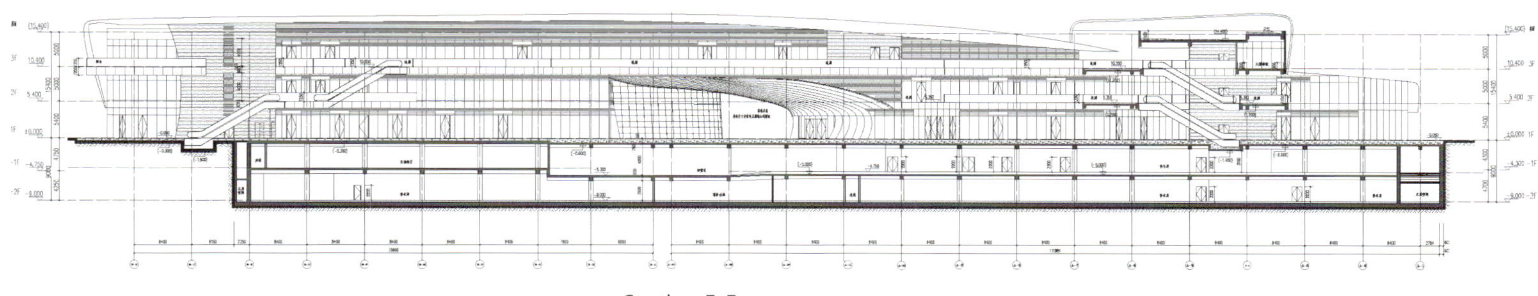

Section E-E
剖面图 E-E

2nd Floor Plan
二层平面图

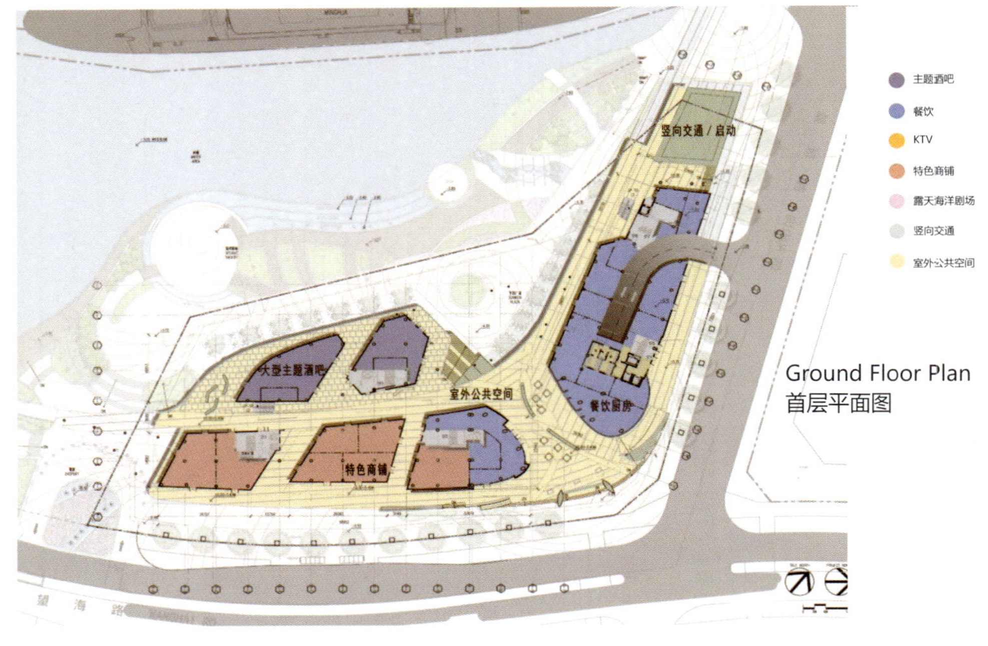

Ground Floor Plan
首层平面图

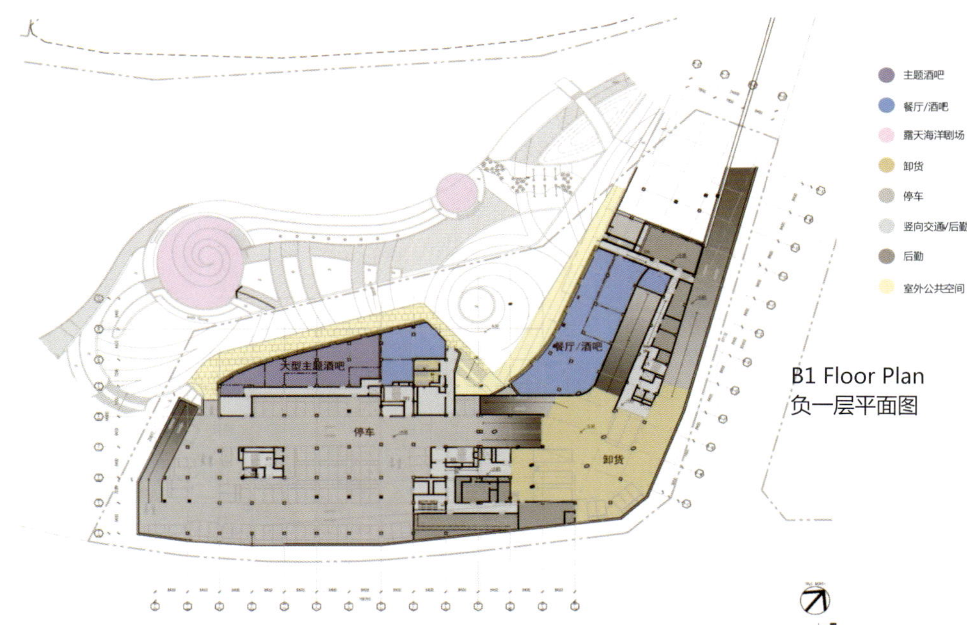

B1 Floor Plan
负一层平面图

总平面图

The exterior envelop consists of customized extruded aluminium unitized glass facade. The outer glass is of high-performance low-E hollow glass which can be heated and strengthened. Unitized glass facade is used in combination with rock wool insulated layer and transparent sheet glass with high-performance painted aluminium-alloy thermal veneer at walls between opaque windows. 0.35m-wide horizontal sun shades made of white opaque laminated glass louver are set about every 0.9m in vertical direction over the glass facade, which not only complements facade in form but also bring more benefits in energy saving.

Merchant plaza office building has 37 levels above ground, with a height of 211.03m and a floor area of 61, 025m^2. Floor 12 and its interlayer, floor 25 and its interlayer serve as refuge floor which is also used as equipment floor. The lobby at ground floor has a ceiling height up to 17.96m. The refuge floor has a ceiling height up to 8.98m. Office building's standard level averages at 4.49m in height. Two podiums have 3 levels above ground and are 16.5m high, with a gross floor area of 6,650 m^2. The ground floor of two podiums has a ceiling height of 6.5m, with ceiling height of floor 2 and 3 averaging at 5m. Switch station with a power of 10KV enjoys an area of 300 m^2 and is 6m high. Merchant Plaza sets 3 levels below ground which work mainly as garage and equipment room and partly serve as civil defense area during war.

建筑的外围护是由定制挤压成型铝制单元式玻璃幕墙构成。外层玻璃是高性能的 low-E 中空玻璃，根据需要进行热强化。在不透明的楼层窗间墙位置处结合单元式玻璃幕墙设置岩棉热层，并包括带有高性能喷涂铝合金保温衬板的透明平板玻璃。在建筑玻璃幕墙的垂直方向每隔约 0.9 米设 0.35 米宽白色不透明夹胶玻璃百叶的水平遮阳，既丰富了建筑外立面的造型又对建筑的节能有利。

招商局广场办公塔楼地上 37 层，高度 211.03 米，办公建筑面积为 61，025 平方米；其中 12 层及夹层、25 层及夹层为避难层，避难层兼作为设备层；首层大堂层高 17.96 米，避难层高 8.98 米，办公楼标准层高均为 4.49 米。2 栋裙房为地上 3 层，高度 16.5 米，总面积为 6,650 平方米；其中首层高 6.5 米，2、3 层高均为 5 米。10kv 开关站面积 300 平方米，高度 6 米。招商局广场设 3 层地下室，主要是车库和设备用房，地下三层局部为战时人防区。

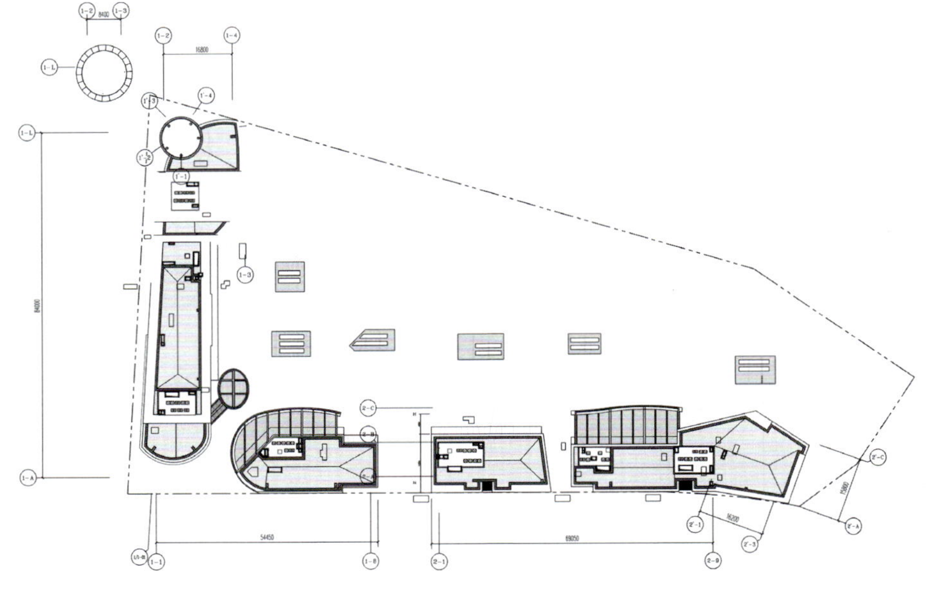

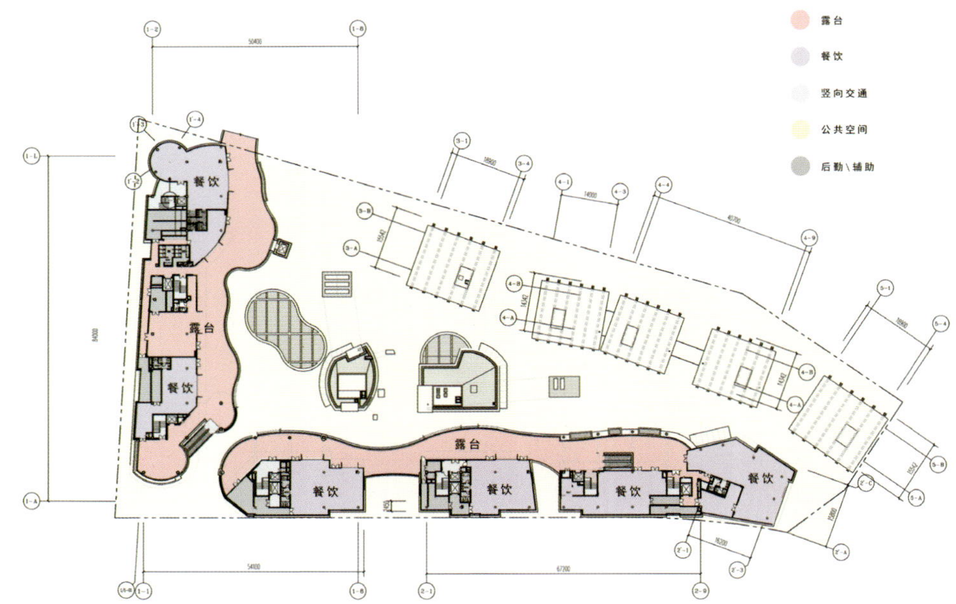

Floor Plan
楼层平面图

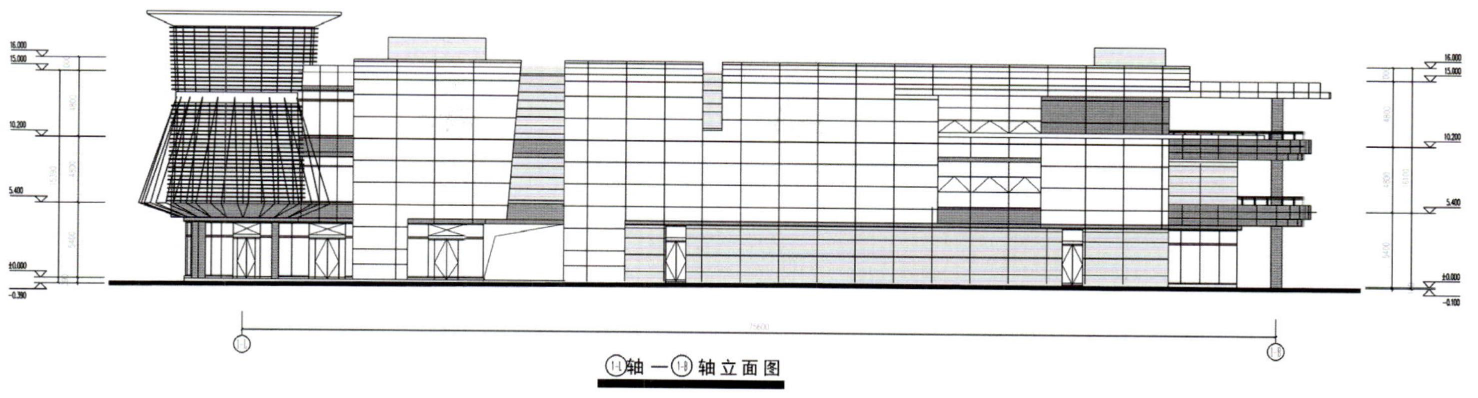

(1-L)轴—(1-B)轴立面图

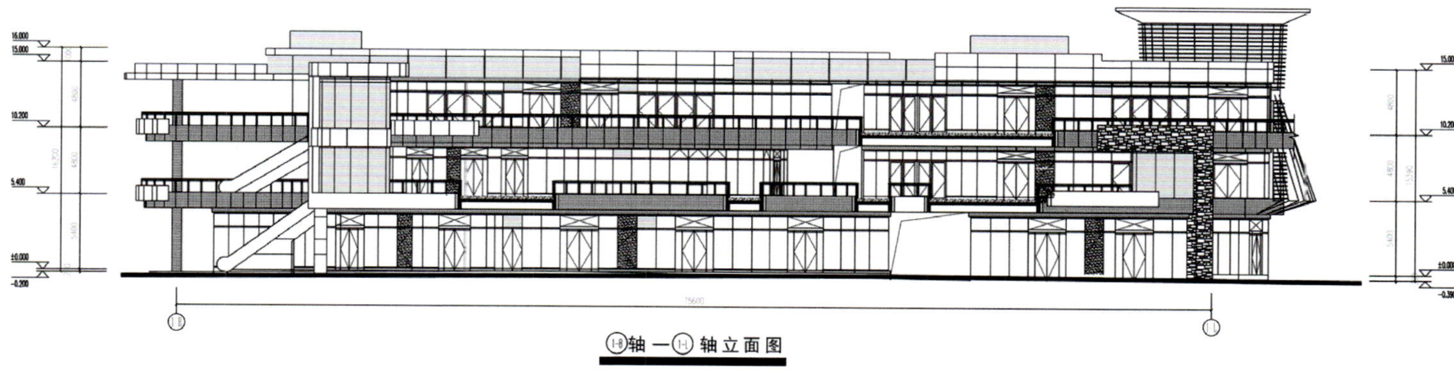

(1-B)轴—(1-L)轴立面图

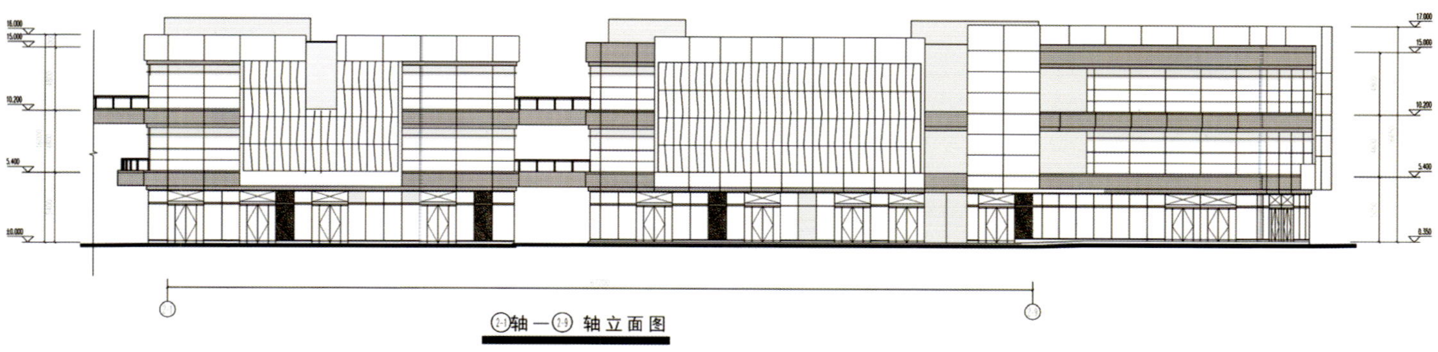

(2-1)轴—(2-9)轴立面图

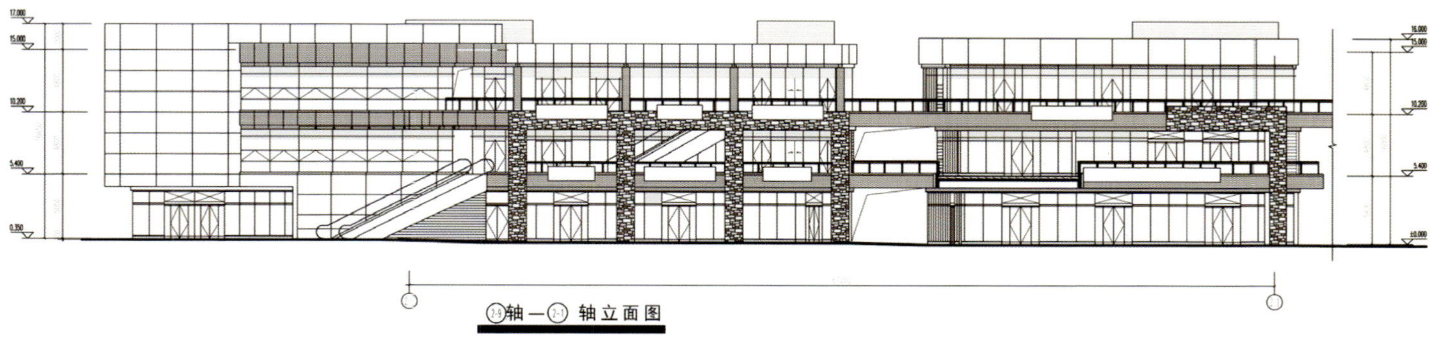

(2-9)轴—(2-1)轴立面图

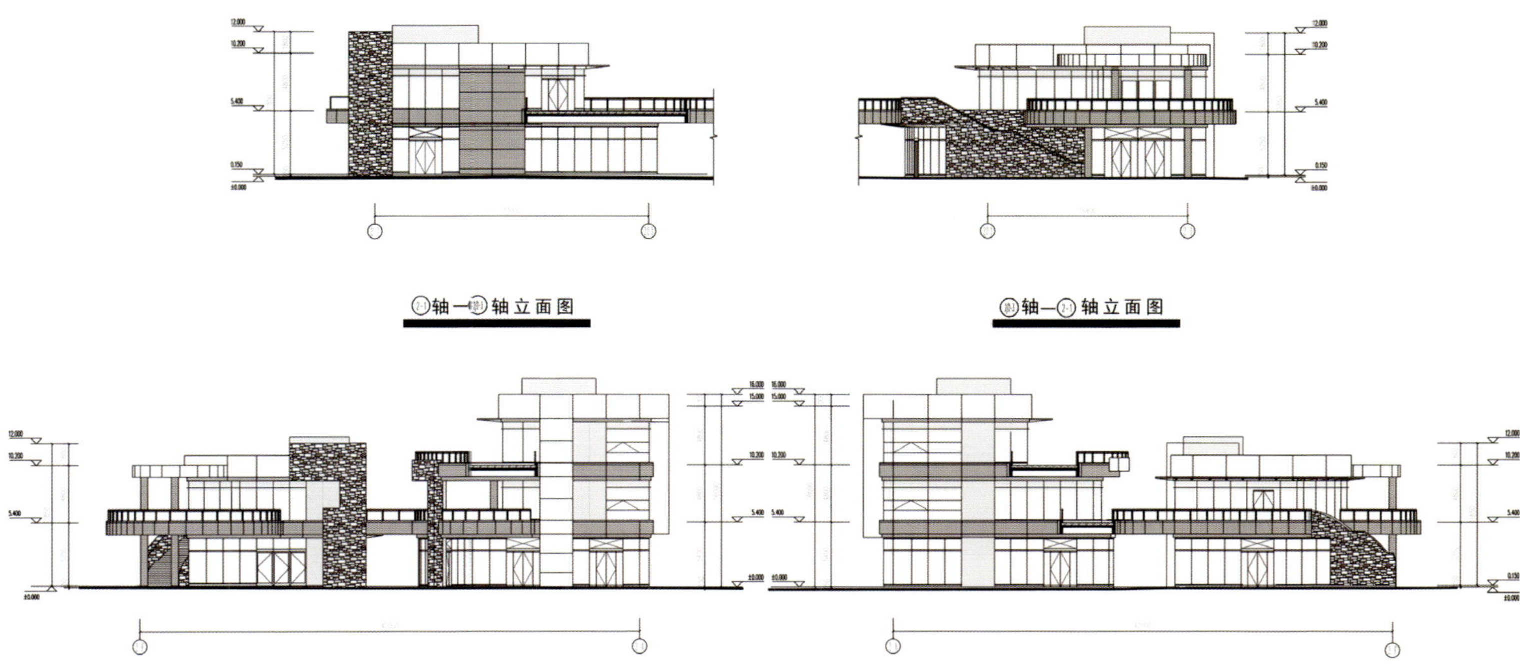

(2-1)轴—(静-1)轴立面图　　(静-1)轴—(2-1)轴立面图

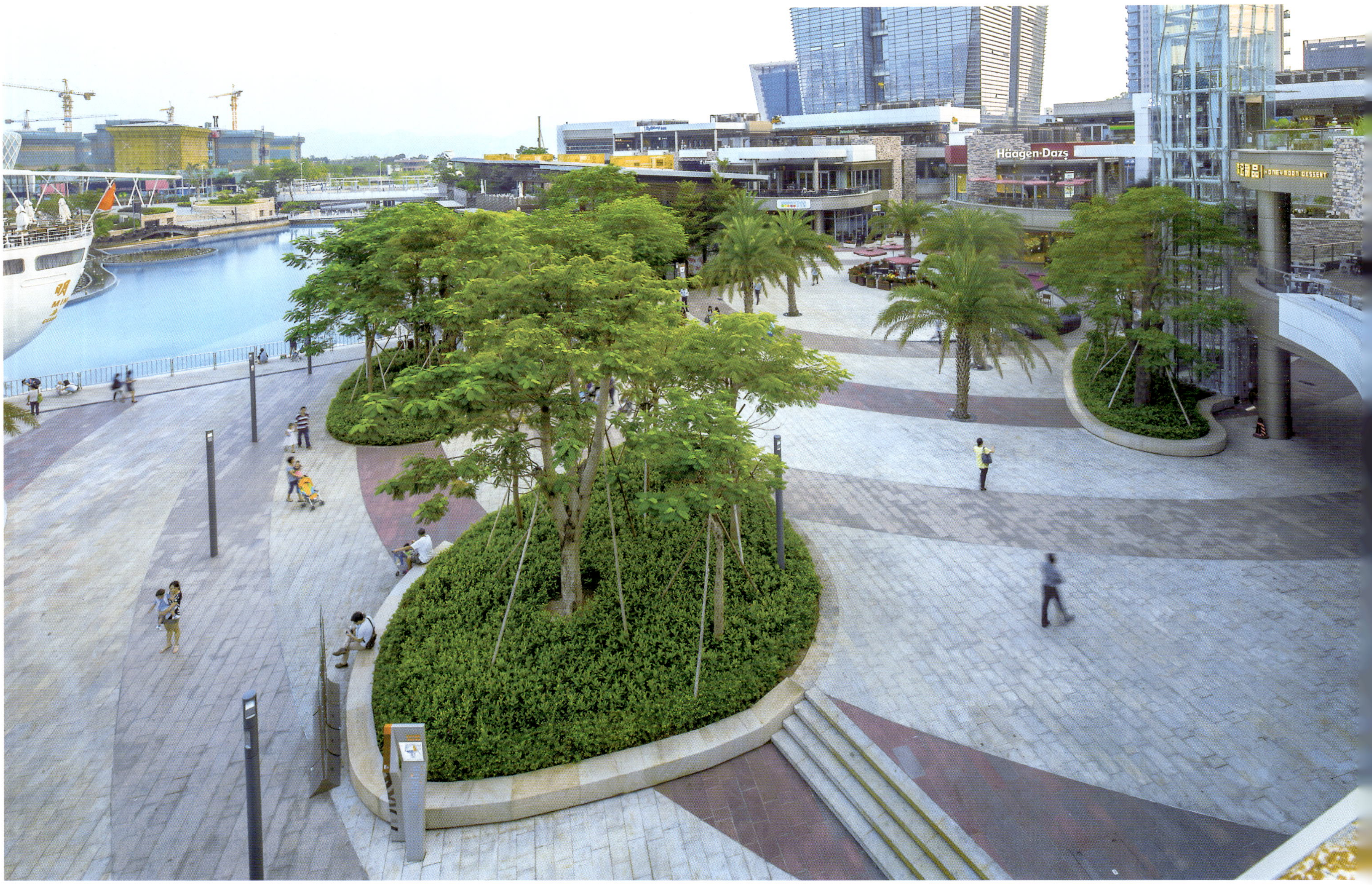

COSTA CO

Häagen-Dazs

element fresh
新元素

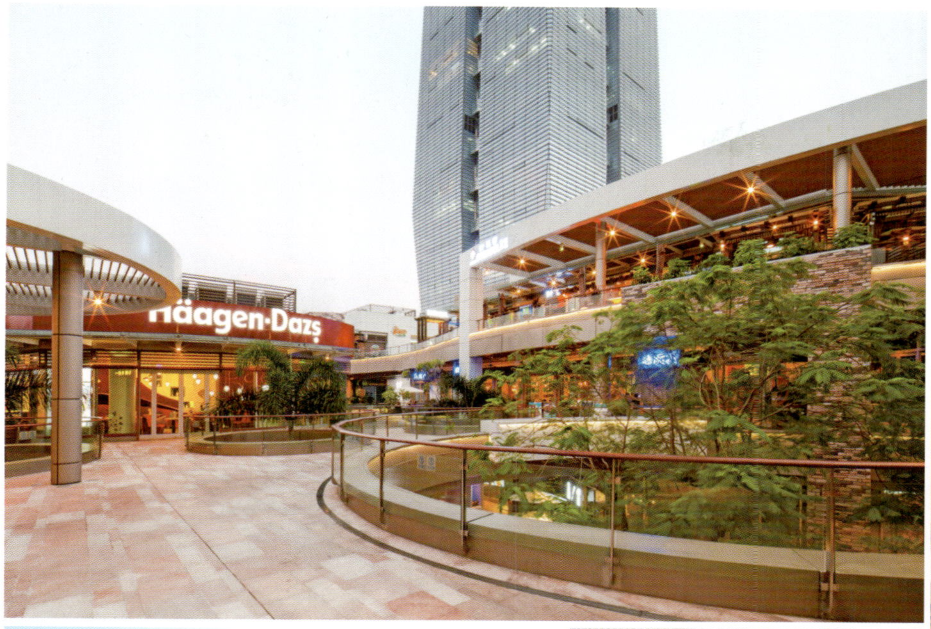
Häagen-Dazs

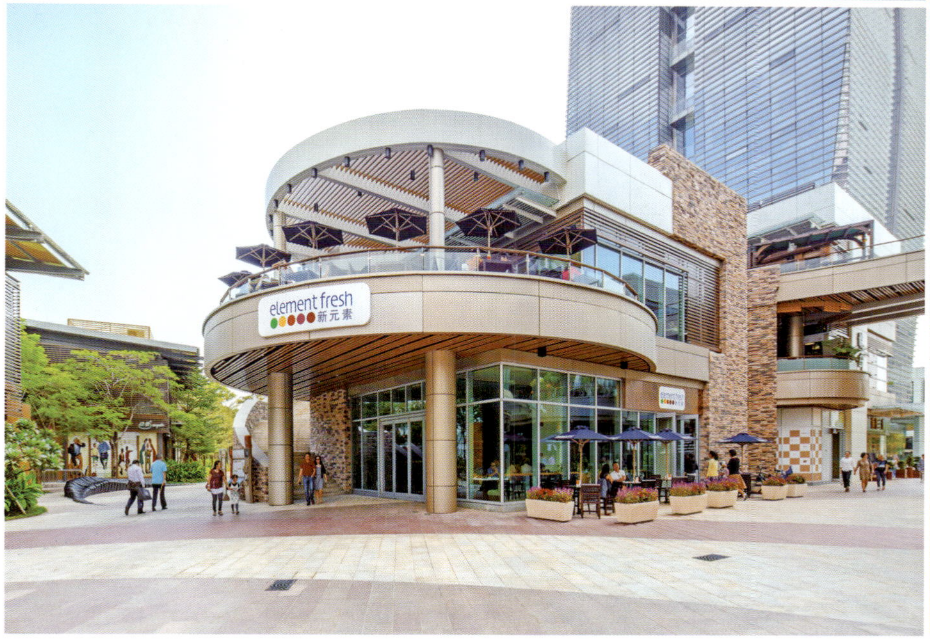
element fresh
新元素

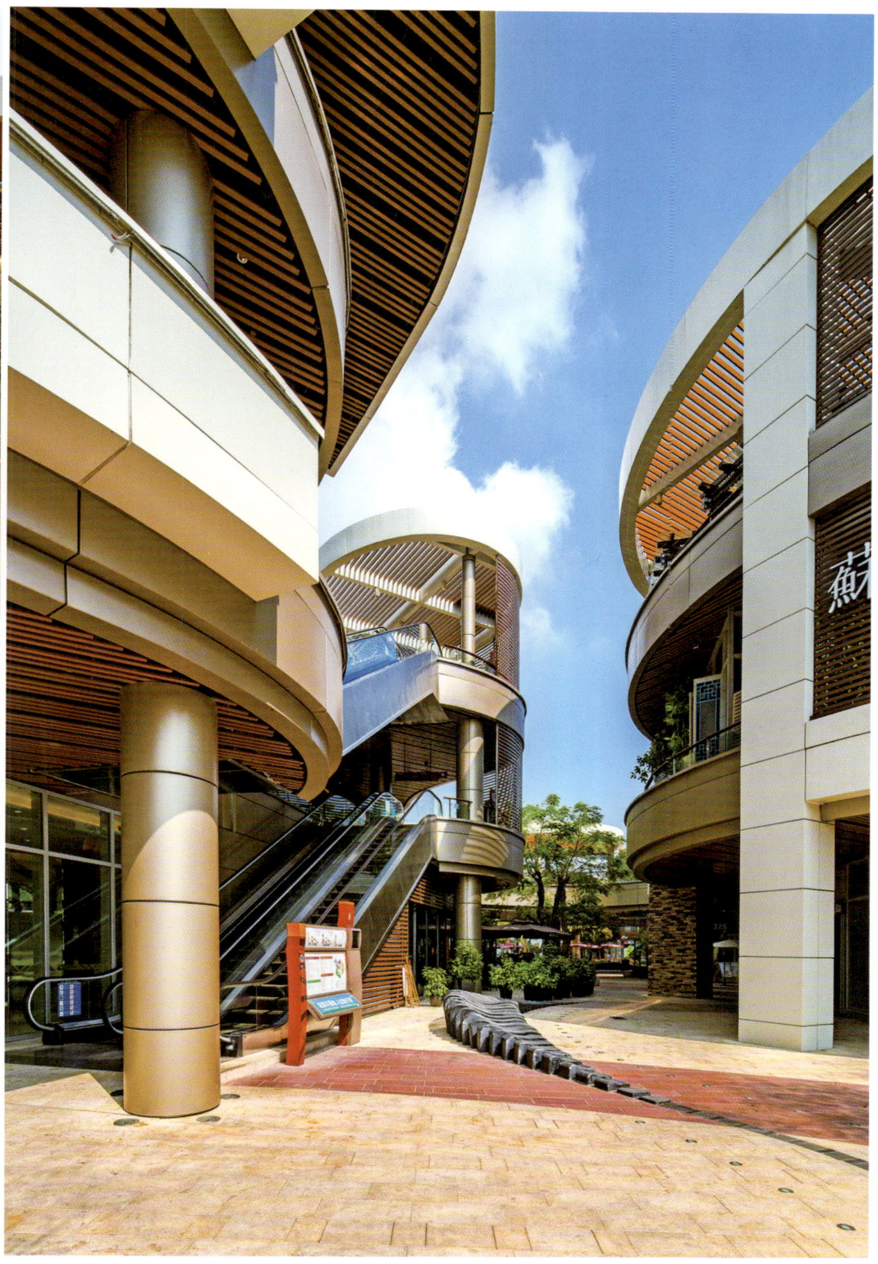

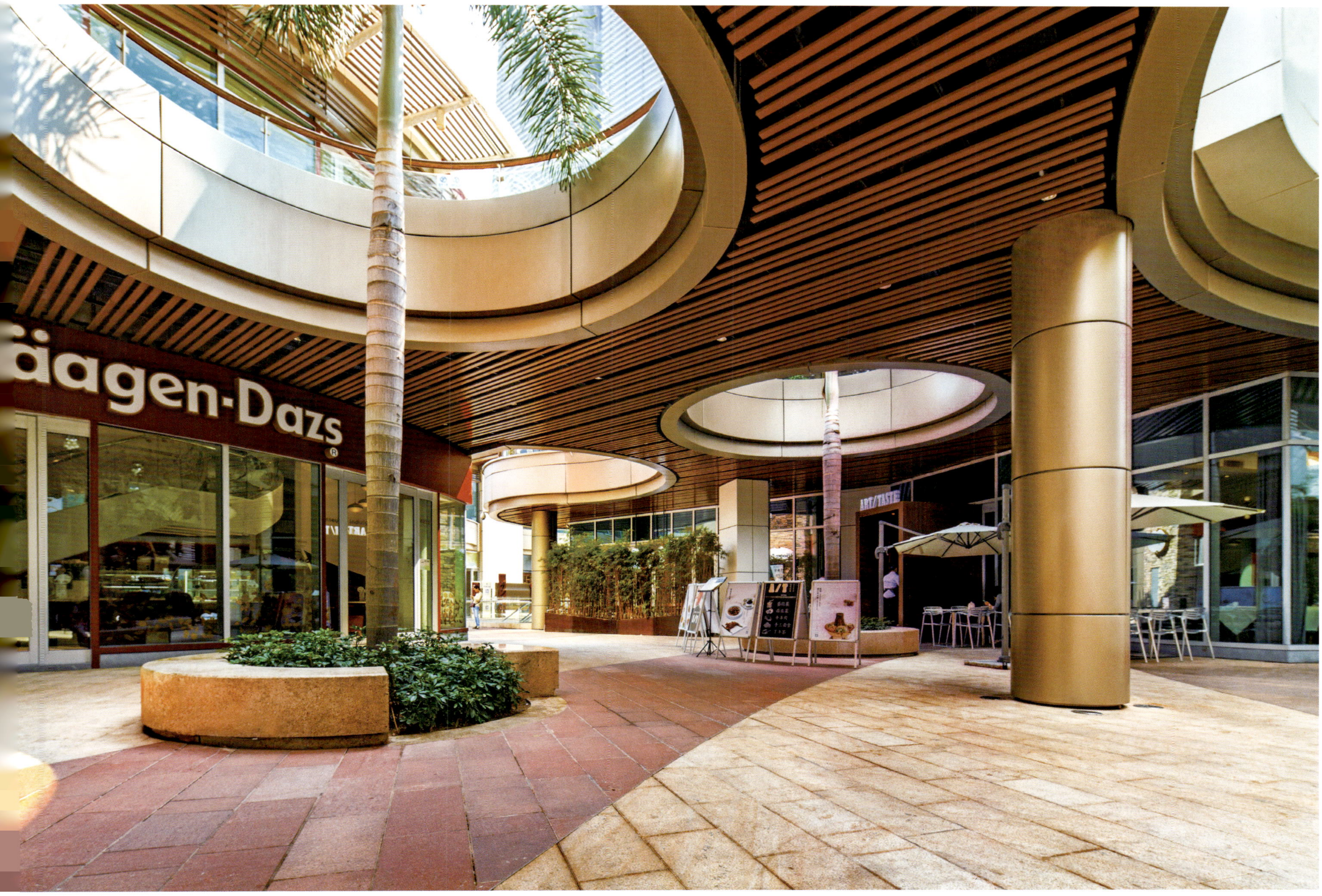
äagen-Dazs

PROJECT NAME 项目名称

ABU DHABI SOWWAH SQUARE

阿布扎比沙瓦哈广场

Architect: Goettsch Partners (GP)

设计公司：GP 建筑设计有限公司

PROJECT INFORMATION 项目信息

Client	Mubadala Real Estate & Infrastructure	**客户**	Mubadala Real Estate & Infrastructure
Location	United Arab Emirates	**地点**	United Arab Emirates
Area	5,698,000 sf / 529,360 m²	**面积**	5,698,000 平方英尺 / 529,360 平方米

OVERVIEW 项目概况

Goettsch Partners (GP) has been commissioned by Mubadala Development Company to design Sowwah Square, their flagship commercial development on Abu Dhabi's Sowwah Island in the United Arab Emirates. The project totals 3,125,500 square feet of office space and features the iconic new headquarters building for the Abu Dhabi Securities Exchange surrounded by four office towers, all overlooking the water. In addition, the project integrates two levels of retail and two underground parking structures. Abu Dhabi's recently published urban framework plan, entitled Plan Abu Dhabi 2030, has designated Sowwah Island and the adjacent edges of Mina Zayed and Reem Island as the city's new Central Business District.

美国 GP 建筑设计有限公司 （GP） 由 Mubadala Development Company 委任为沙瓦哈广场提供建筑设计，这是他们在阿拉伯联合酋长国阿布扎比沙瓦哈海岛的旗舰商业项目。项目共计 3,125,500 平方英尺办公面积，有着四座办公塔搂，标志性的阿布扎比证券交易所总部围绕于其中，并俯视底下的水景，还有着二层零售和二层地下停车。阿布扎比最近推出了命名为“阿布扎比 2030”的都市规划计划，选定了沙瓦哈岛和毗邻的 Mina Zayed 和 Reem 岛作为城市的新中央商业区。

FEATURE ANALYSIS 特色分析

ARCHITECT
James Goettsch
设计师
James Goettsch

ARCHITECT
Travis Soberg
设计师
Travis Soberg

The building layout follows the classical proportionally balanced principle. The iconic stock exchange is located in the center of cite, expressing the dignity and ritual of capitalism symbolic venue. The office and commercial towers are arranged around with a retreated construction base. 4 totems just like grow from the ground, showing the strong sense of potency in the desert environment. The building facade adopts the glass body that modern office building always used and horizontal grates that featured in tropical zone. The building conveys the solemn atmosphere of regional financial center while cold and straight building mass represents the emotionless modern capital sanctuary in a very good way.

建筑的布局遵循古典式的对称比例原则。标志性的证券交易大厅位于布局正中，烘托出一个资本主义标志性场所的仪式感与庄严感。办公和商务塔楼布局四周，其结构在建筑的底部收缩。仿佛地面生长出来的四座图腾在沙漠热带苍凉的环境中显得格外具有力量感。立面的处理是现代办公建筑惯用的玻璃体配合热带地区的水平格栅。整体的建筑气氛一方面传达了一种区域金融中心的庄重大气，另一方面其冰冷挺拔的整体形式有意无意地暗示着一种金融组织去情感化的现代资本圣殿。

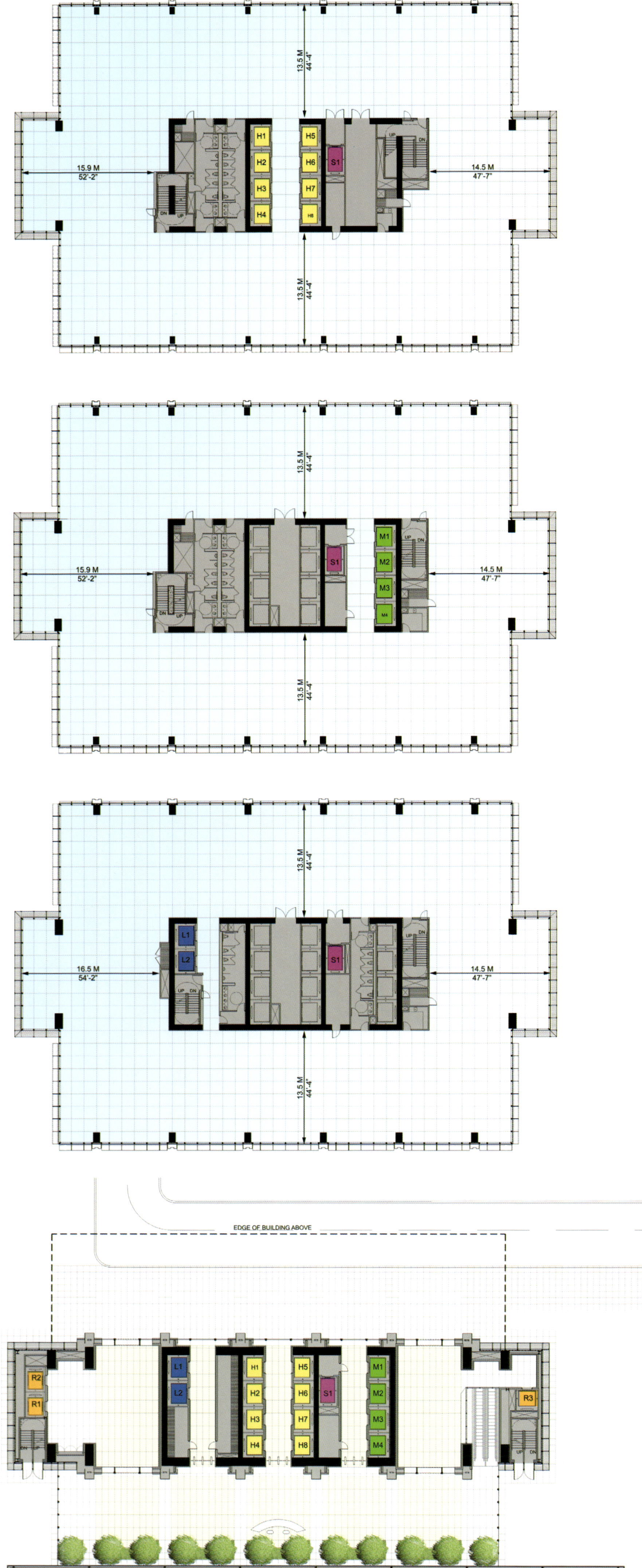
13.5 M
44'-4"
15.9 M
52'-2"
14.5 M
47'-7"
16.5 M
54'-2"
H1
H2
H3
H4
H5
H6
H7
H8
S1
M1
M2
M3
M4
L1
L2
R1
R2
R3
UP
DN
EDGE OF BUILDING ABOVE

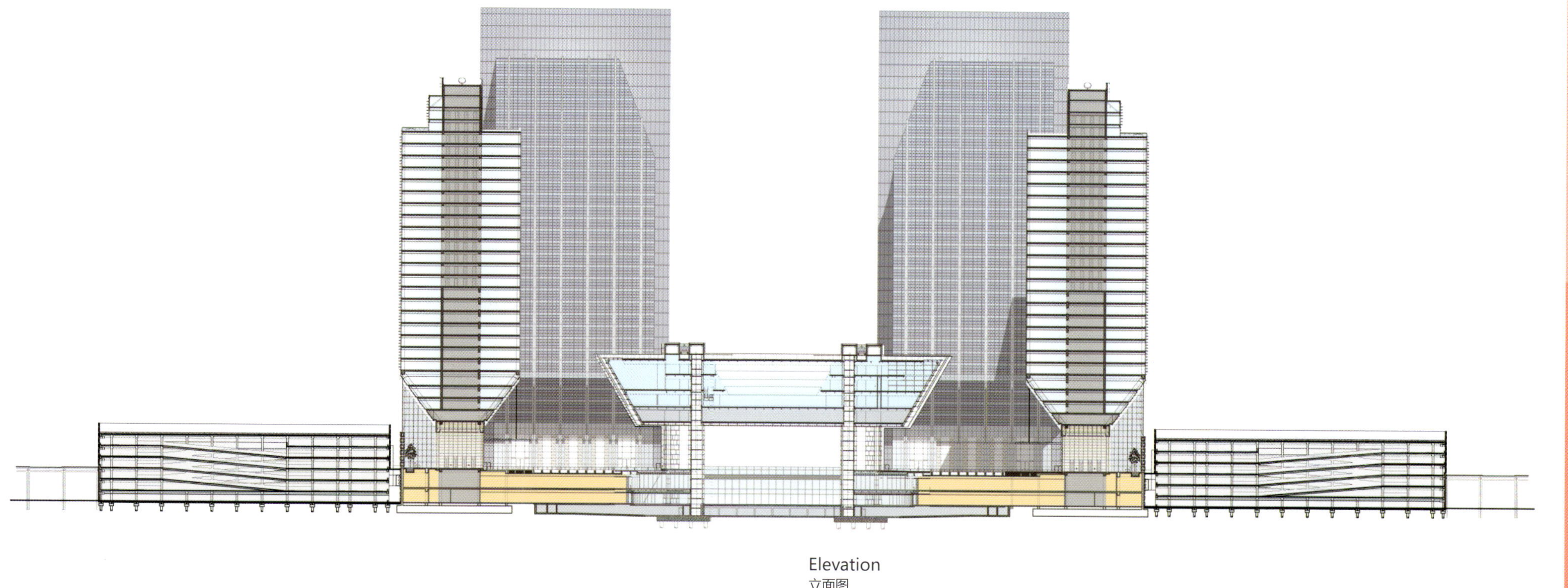

Elevation
立面图

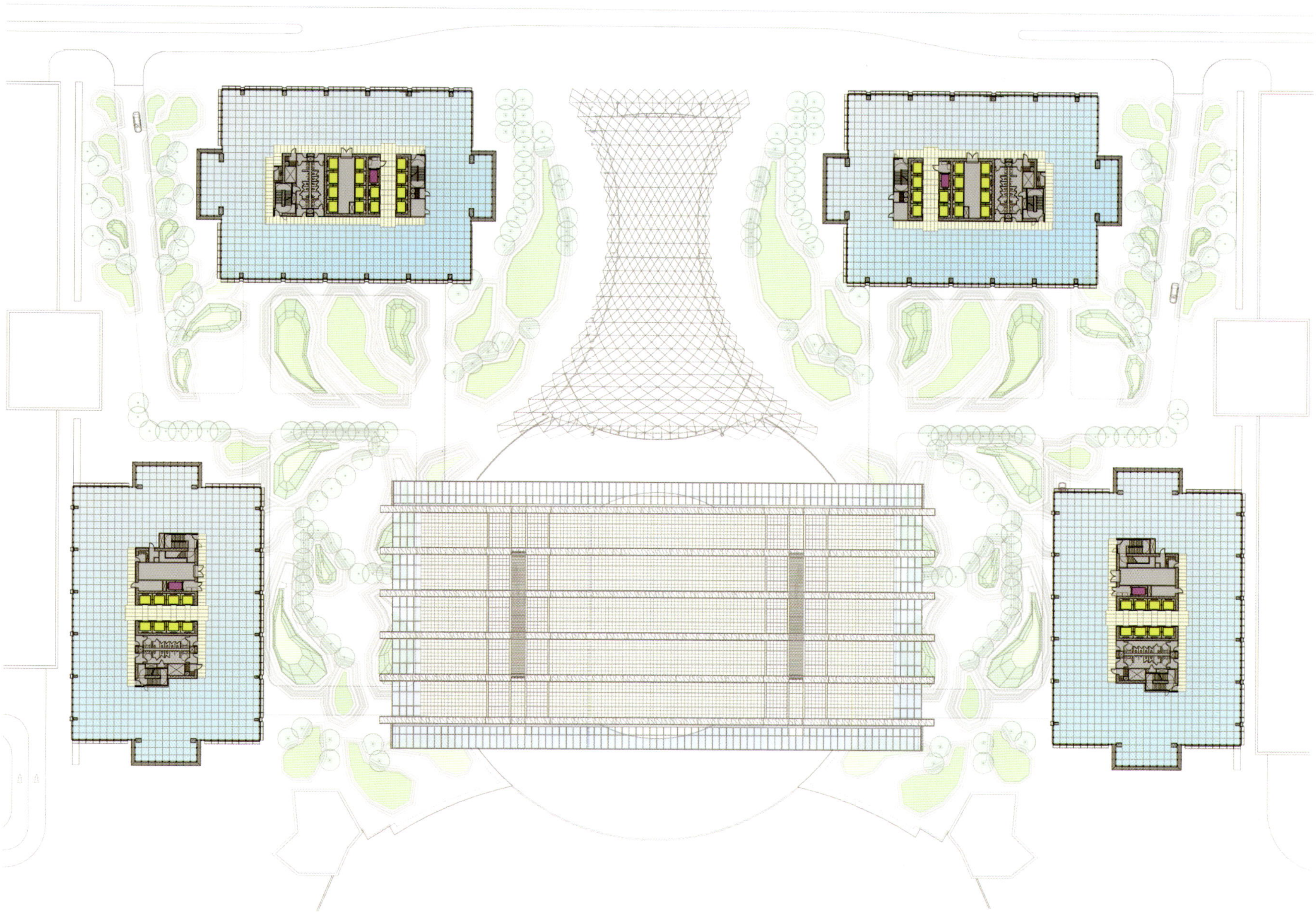

Sowwah Square

The centerpiece of the development's first phase will be the business center, which will include: a 21,646m2 stock exchange building, four Class A office towers totaling 268,722m^2, parking for 5,200 cars and 23,225m^2 of retail. Construction commenced on the site of Sowwah Square in summer 2007, with the full development scheduled for completion in 2010.The complex emphasizes a sustainable design approach throughout and looks beyond the LEED certification process to integrcte both active and passive sustainable design strategies.

沙瓦哈广场

沙瓦哈广场项目第一阶段的重点是商业中心，这包括一个21,646平方米的证券交易所大夏，共计268、722平方米的四座甲级办公塔楼，以及5,200停车位的地下停车场和23,225平方米零售。施工于2007年夏天开始，预定于2010年完成。项目由始至终强调可持续性设计，以及使用静态和动态的设计策略，使之不但达到并超过了LEED标准。

Abu Dhabi Securities Exchange Building

As the distinctive new headquarters of the Abu Dhabi Securities Exchange, the stock exchange building is an iconic, four-level facility. Glass-enclosed with a roof the size of a football field, the building rises 90 feet above a 160-foot-diameter water feature on massive stone piers. The four granite piers house the stairs, mechanical risers and service elements for the exchange. The building projects an image of strength and solidity as it overlooks the water facing back toward the city's existing downtown.

阿布扎比证券交易所总部

因为本项目将成为阿布扎比证券交易所的新总部大厦，证券交易所大厦被设计的极有标志性、四层、玻璃包覆以及一个橄榄球球场大小的屋面。建筑在一个160英尺直径水景上，由四个巨大的花岗岩石柱支撑上升90英尺，楼梯、电梯和建筑配套设施位于四个花岗岩石柱内。在体现了力量和稳健的同时，建筑背靠现在的城市中心俯视水面。

Retail and Parking

Beneath the plaza, a two-story retail podium weaves through the development, providing upscale shopping along the waterfront. At the north and south boundaries of the site, two parking structures, partially submerged, serve the complex with more than 2,600 parking spaces each.

High-Performance Enclosure

The environmentally responsive enclosure system uses a mechanically ventilated cavity and a double-skin facade system over large portions of the office buildings. These elements mitigate the 40 °F interior/exterior temperature differential and protect building occupants from the intense sand storms and constant corrosive mist of the neighboring Gulf coast.

零售和停车

广场下为两层的零售裙房，提供了滨水高级购物场所。在项目场地的南北两侧有着两个连通的停车场，各提供超过2,600个的停车位使之服务于本项目。

高性能帷幕墙系统

大面积的办公塔楼外墙使用了机械通风的双层幕墙来准确地对外界环境做出反应，这些措施缓和了40 °F的室内外温差，保护了使用者免受强烈的沙尘暴袭击和来自邻近海湾腐蚀性湿气的侵蚀。

Office Buildings

Four office towers frame the stock exchange building: two at 31 stories and the other two at 37 stories. The first full office floor of each building starts 110 feet above the ground level, providing a highly transparent, open lobby and elevating the views on all tenant floors. A landscaped plaza connects the four buildings and the exchange at grade.

Sustainable Design

Sustainability is a main focus of the development, and the design of the complex integrates many sustainable initiatives, including: ventilated, double-skin facades in order to insulate the buildings against extreme temperatures; active and passive solar shading to further control light and heat gain; 27,500 square feet of photovoltaic panels on the roof of the exchange; condensation collection from cooling coils to supply the water feature and provide irrigation; and active lighting controls to balance natural and artificial light.

办公楼

四座办公塔楼围绕着证券交易所：两座31层，另外两座37层。第一层办公楼层在110英尺处开始，有着高透明度、开放大堂和挑高的视角。还有景观花园在地面连接四座塔楼和证券交易所。

可持续性设计

可持续性设计是项目的设计重点，集成了多种可持续性措施，包括可通风的双层幕墙，使建筑在极端气温下得到隔热保温，还有动态和静态的遮阳设计，进一步控制了光线和热量吸收，以及屋面上27,500平方英尺的光电太阳能板，并且回收制冷系统的冷凝水作水景用水和灌溉用水，还使用智能灯光控制来平衡自然光和人造光。

The double-skin cavities run uninterrupted along the entire height of the four office towers, starting from the fourth floor and extending to the penthouse mechanical floors. Within these cavities, active solar shades continuously track and adjust for the sun angle in order to provide optimal shading to the building's interior. The cavity is sealed to protect the gears from airborne particulates.

Active solar shading and glass selection keep the cavity from heating up and increasing the internal radiant temperature. To minimize the amount of solar energy penetrating the outer layer of the double-skin system, an outboard lite with a very high shading coefficient (76%) was selected. The remaining energy was then blocked from reaching the inner facade by the active shading; however, its presence contributed to an elevated air temperature within the double-skin cavity.

To alleviate the accelerated temperature and achieve the moderating air buffer, the warm cavity air needed to be flushed out using an air source cooler than the natural air temperature. The solution GP developed was to collect the exhaust air from the tower offices and, instead of allowing it to escape into the atmosphere, redirect it back down the double-skin cavities where it is exhausted at the fourth floor mechanical level. Sensors within the cavities will modulate dampers at the top of the building, directing the air to the optimal zones of the cavity depending on the time of day and outdoor temperature. Additional dampers will allow filtered exterior air to enter directly into the cavity during economizing periods such as night and winter, when the outdoor air is cooler than the collected exhaust air.

Through these efforts, the design team expects the double-skin cavity to be an average temperature of 89 °F when the exterior temperature reaches 115 °F. This condition will allow the high U-value of the insulated inner glazing to more easily block the air cavity's radiating energy. Most importantly, calculations estimate that the double-skin system designed for Sowwah Square will generate a savings of 7200 kwh of electricity per day across all four towers and provide a more comfortable thermal environment near the perimeter wall, all while protecting itself from the harsh external elements.

四座办公塔楼有着全高的双层幕墙，双层幕墙的空腔从四层起延伸至建筑上部的机电层。在这些空腔内，动态遮阳设施连续地跟踪太阳的角度来调整及提供理想的遮阳。同时这些空腔被密封来保护遮阳设施免受空气中悬浮粒子的侵害。

动态遮阳设施和玻璃的选择使幕墙中的空腔以及室内免于过热。为了将穿透双层幕墙外层的太阳热量减到最小，外层选择了遮阳系数（76%）非常高的玻璃，剩余的热量由内部的动态遮阳阻挡在外，然而，这使得双层幕墙内的温度升高。

为了减缓温度的上升并形成一个空气缓冲带，空腔内的热空气通过空气降温器排出而不是自然降温。GP 的解决办法是收集建筑室内的排气，而不是直接排至室外，将其引至双层幕墙内部带走热空气，然后在建筑四层机电层排出。通过空腔内的感应器来控制建筑上部的风阀，并根据时段和室外温度来将空气引至指定部位的空腔。还有更多的风阀可以将过滤后有着合适温度的室外空气，如夜晚或冬季比所收集的室内排气温度低的空气引入空腔内。

通过这些措施，当外部温度达到 115 °F 时，双层幕墙空腔的平均温度保持在 89 °F。这会允许高隔热性能内部玻璃可以更加容易地遮挡空腔的热辐射。最重要的，节能计算显示双层幕墙为沙瓦哈广场的四座办公塔楼节省了 7200 KWh/ 日的能耗，以及在接近外墙的内部空间处提供更舒适的温度，最后，保护建筑免受恶劣外部环境的破坏。

PROJECT NAME 项目名称

BEIJING CHAOYANG PARK PLAZA

北京朝阳公园广场

Architect: MAD Architects

设计公司：MAD 建筑事务所

PROJECT INFORMATION 项目信息

Directors in Charge	Ma Yansong, Dang Qun, Yosuke Hayano	**主持建筑师**	马岩松，党群，早野洋介
Client	Junhao Real Estate Beijing Jingfa Properties Co., Limited.	**客户**	骏豪地产北京京发置业有限公司
Location	Chaoyang ,Beijing, China	**地点**	中国北京朝阳区
Site Area	30,763 m²	**占地面积**	30，763 平方米
Gross Floor Area	Above ground 128,177 m² ,Belowground 94,832 m²	**总建筑面积**	地上 128，177 平方米，地下 94，832 平方米
Height	120 m	**高度**	120 米

OVERVIEW 项目概况

Chaoyang Park Plaza is located in the central business district (CBD) of Beijing, and is composed of over 120,000㎡ of commercial, office, and residential buildings. The site is on the Southern edge of Chaoyang Park, one of the largest public parks in Beijing. Its proximity to the park will not only create breathtaking views of the city, but will also highly impact the skyline of Beijing. By transforming features of Chinese classical landscape painting, such as lakes, springs, forests, creeks, valleys, and stones, into modern "city landscapes", the urban space creates a balance between high urban density and natural landscape.

项目总建筑面积约为 120，000 平方米，以办公、商业和住宅为主。位于北京 CBD，毗邻朝阳公园，建筑与公园借景，建筑形态与公园内的自然景观相呼应、相观望。自然存在的湖、泉、林、溪、谷、石、峰这些中国山水的传统意境被转换为建筑中的意象运用在现代的“城市景观”建造中，创造出一个高密度城市与自然景观和谐过渡的空间。

FEATURE ANALYSIS 特色分析

ARCHITECT
Ma Yansong – Founder & Principal Partner, MAD Architects

设计师
马岩松
-MAD 建筑事务所创始人、合伙人

Amazing form. Mayansong who goes increasingly deeper into landscape architecture has gone to the extreme in form with Chaoyang project in Beijing. With an overall black look, the project has employed some techniques, such as architectural forms with image of mountain and stones literally translated from landscape painting. MAD definitely has found a new approach to explore Chines style buildings with a combination of tradition and modernity. Recently, MAD presented the public with visual feast of landscaped architecture. But the final evaluation will not shape up until the landmark is completed.

瞠目结舌的形式。在山水建筑这一概念上越走越远的马岩松在北京朝阳这一项目中走到了一个形式上的极端。黑色调的整体形象，山水画中山石形象直译过来的建筑形式等手法。如果把美学上和合理性上的讨论先搁置一边，MAD 确实在所谓的传统结合现代的穿衣戴帽式的中式建筑中探索了一条新的路子。近几年 MAD 山水建筑的探索给公众呈现了许多视觉饕餮。但是具体的评价如何还需要等标志性的项目建成后再作评判。

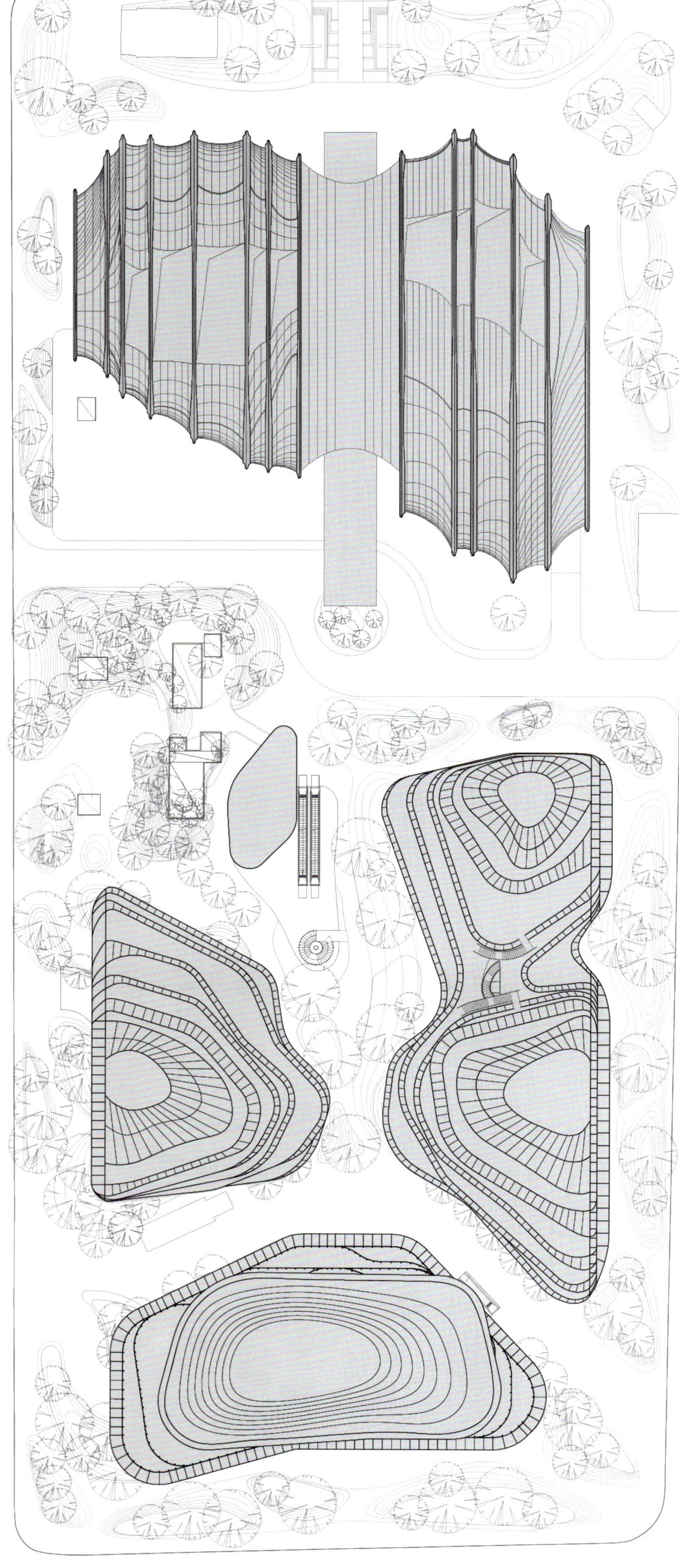

Site Plan
总平面图

As a recent realization of the concept "Shanshui City" ,"Chaoyang Park Plaza"has begun construction. It marks another milestone in one of the practices of MAD's design theory. This project pushes the boundary of the urbanization process in modern cosmopolitan life by creating a dialogue between artificial scenery and natural landscapes.

Like the tall mountain cliffs and river landscapes of China, a pair of asymmetrical towers creates a dramatic skyline in front of the park. Ridges and valleys define the shape of the exterior glass facade, as if the natural forces of erosion wore down the tower into a few thin lines. Flowing down the facade, the lines emphasize the smoothness of the towers and its verticality. The internal ventilation and filtration system of the ridges draw a natural breeze indoors, which not only improves the interior space but also creates an energy efficient system.

作为 MAD“山水城市”建筑理念的重要实践，“朝阳公园广场项目”目前全面破土动工。建筑通过人工与自然景致的和谐营造，探索现代都市的人居理想。

位于基地最北侧的主体高层建筑由不对称的双塔组成，如光滑挺拔的山岩立于水景之中。外立面纵向突出的脊线如自然风化的力量把塔楼融为成数个片状体，流畅的竖向线条与公园水面相映成趣；脊线内部贯穿的通风过滤系统，将自然风引入空间，实现节能环保。

Sketch
草图

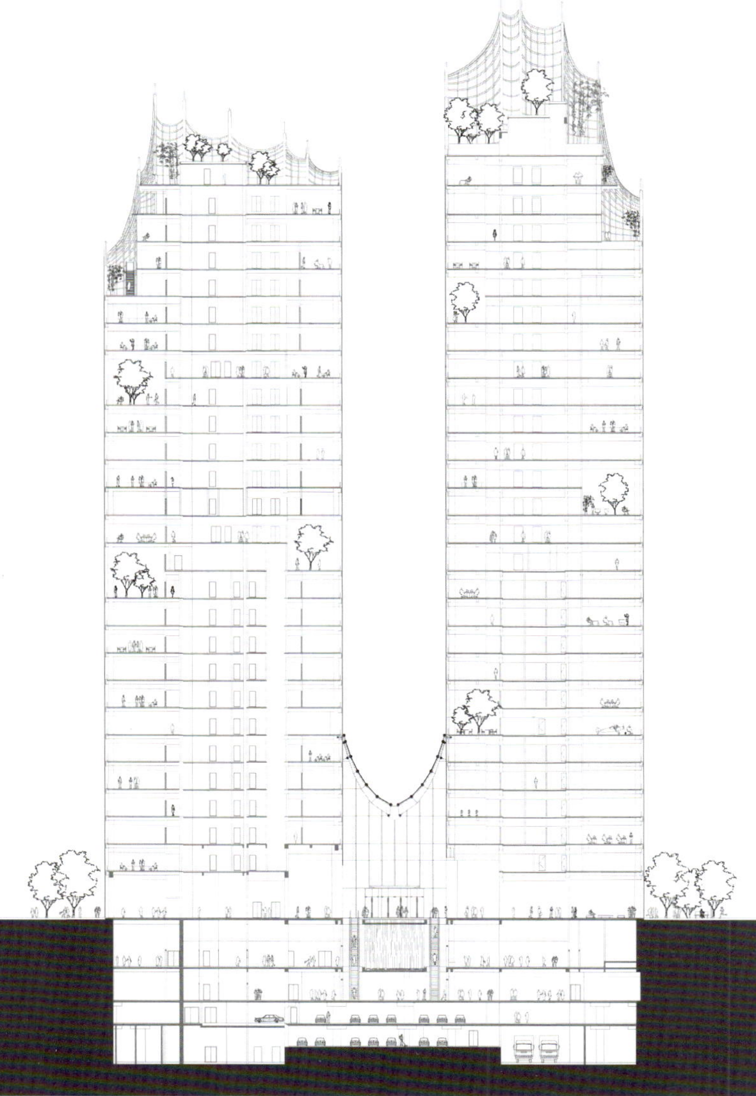

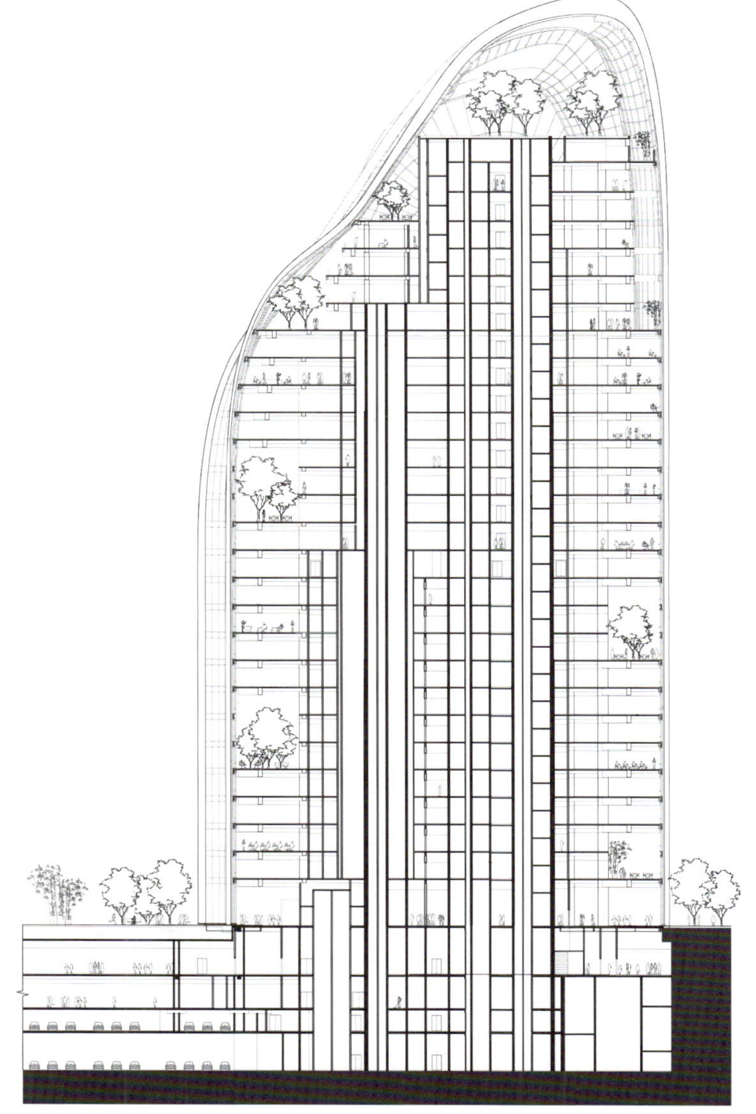

Section
剖面图

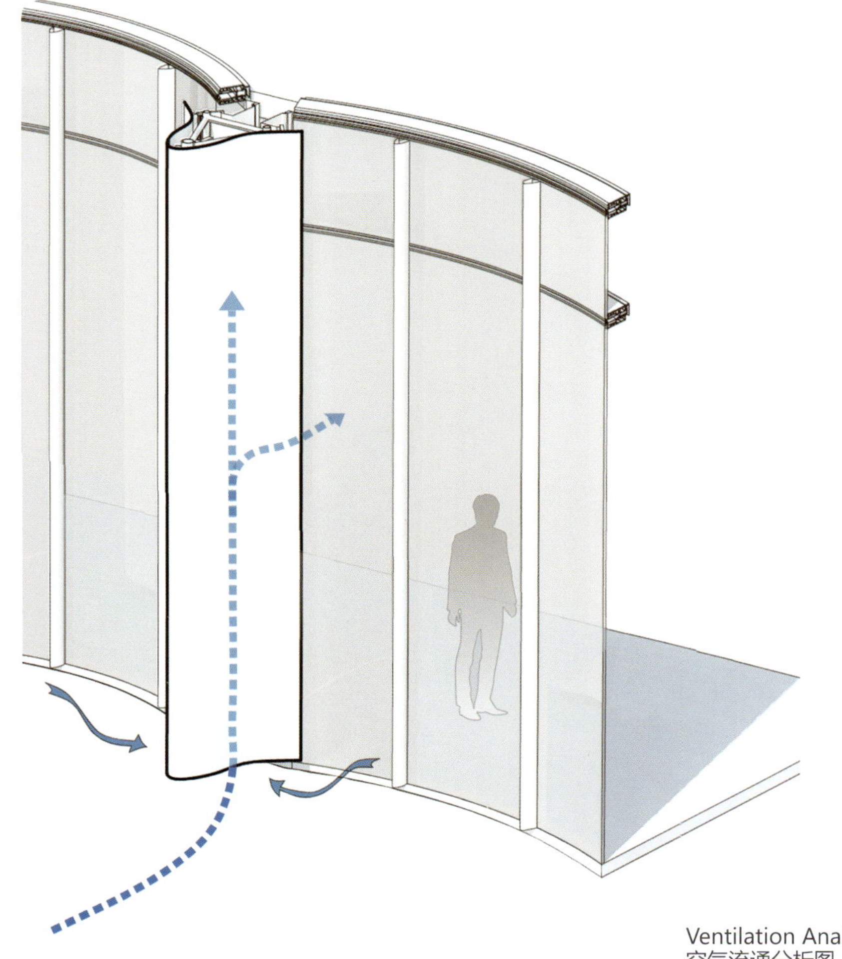

Ventilation Analysis
空气流通分析图

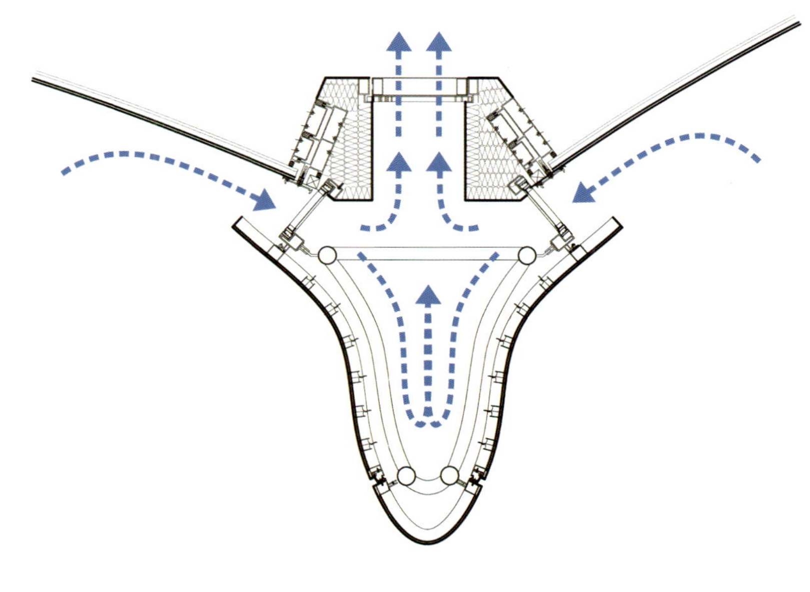

Facade Detail
幕墙节点图

Landscape elements are injected into the interiors of the towers to augment the feeling of nature within an urban framework. The two towers are connected by a tall courtyard lobby with a ceiling height of up to 17 m. The site and sounds of flowing water make the entire lobby feel like a natural scene from a mountain valley. At the top of the towers, multi-level terraces shaped by the curving forms of the towers are public gardens where people can gaze out over the entire city and look down at the valley scene created by the lower buildings on the site.

同时，自然元素作为景观始终贯穿在建筑之中：两座塔楼通过通高 17 米的中庭空间连接，室内瀑布流动的水声让整个大堂如同山间谷地；在建筑顶部、结合建筑曲线的交错平台伸入多层通高的公共空间，让人们如同置身空中花园，既可以远眺整个公园与 CBD，又可俯瞰多层建筑群的山谷景致。

Ermenegildo Zegna

Located to the South of the towers, four office buildings are shaped like river stones that have been eroded over a long period. Smooth, round, and each with its own features, they are delicately arranged to allow each other space while also forming an organic whole. Adjacent to the office buildings are two multi-level residential buildings in the Southwest area of the compound. These buildings continue the "mid-air courtyard" concept, and provide all who live here with the freedom of wandering through a mountain forest.

位于建筑群南端的多层办公楼形如被流水长期冲刷的山石，圆润而各有特征，·疏密有致的布局，相互退让而又形成有机的整体。基地西南段的两栋多层住宅延续了"空中庭院"的概念，错层的设计让每户都拥有更多的日照和与自然亲近的机会。

The project was awarded the "Leadership in Energy and Environmental Design (LEED)"Gold certificate by U.S. Green Building Council. Its use of natural lighting, intelligent building, and air purification system make this project stand out from others being built today. The ideal of " Shanshui "is not only embodied in the innovation of green technology, but also in the planning concept. This project transforms the traditional model of buildings in a modern city's central business district（CBD）. By exploring the symbiotic relationship between modern urban architecture and natural environment, it revives the harmonious co-existence between urban life and nature. It creates a Shanshui city where people can share their individual emotions and a sense of belonging.

整个建筑充分利用自然光，实现空气净化和楼宇智能控制，获得美国绿色建筑协会LEED金奖认证。“山水”的理念不仅体现在技术革新上，更体现在整体规划观念上——朝阳公园广场项目尝试改变传统CBD模式，将传统诗意带入城市，在高密度快节奏的区域重构建筑和环境的共生关系，创造一种给人以情感寄托和有归属感的未来山水意境。

PROJECT NAME 项目名称

KUALA LUMPUR EMPIRE DAMANSARA

吉隆坡白沙罗帝国大楼

Architect: ONG&ONG Pte Ltd

设计公司：王及王有限公司

PROJECT INFORMATION 项目信息

Architect	Ong&Ong Architects	**设计公司**	新加坡王及王建筑事务所
Studio Directors	Studio Directors:Lau JakShen, Tan KeeKeat, YeohThiam Yew	**项目负责人**	Lau JakShen, Tan KeeKeat, YeohThiam Yew
Location	Kuala Lumpur, Malaysia	**地点**	马来西亚吉隆坡
Photographer	RupajiwaStudio	**摄影师**	RupajiwaStudio

OVERVIEW 项目概况

Located in Damansara Perdana, Empire Damansara strives to differentiate itself from its competitors through its mix of programmes, which capitalises on its strategic island site's street frontage as well as individual drop-off points.

白沙罗帝国大楼位于白沙罗柏兰岭，其努力将自己打造成为与众不同的项目，充分利用其战略岛、临街以及独特的下客点的优势。

FEATURE ANALYSIS 特色分析

ARCHITECT
Lau Jak Shen

设计师
Lau Jak Shen

ARCHITECT
Tan Kee Keat

设计师
Tan Kee Keat

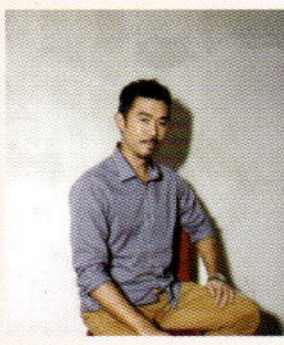

ARCHITECT
Yeoh Thiam Yew

设计师
Yeoh Thiam Yew

A vibrant case generated from expression of skin. The mix of skin textures on a stand-alone gives identity to all of them. Such individuality is exposed with different techniques used in color, material and facade units. There is no sense of mess when all stone-alones come into a regional system. However, they remain complete landmark in urban context. The design strategy achieving integration with differentiation is extremely rare among current urban complexes of common nature in China.

表皮表现力发掘的一个生动案例。通过在建筑单体上对于表皮肌理的不同搭配，使每一栋单体建筑都呈现出独特的个性。这种个性或因色彩，材质，立面单元的不同手法而显现出来。而这些单体组成一个区域系统的时候却并不令人感觉到杂乱无章。而仍然能够感觉到它是城市环境中的一个整体地标区域。这种通过差异化达到整体化的设计策略在国内目前大一统的城市综合体设计中还极为鲜见。

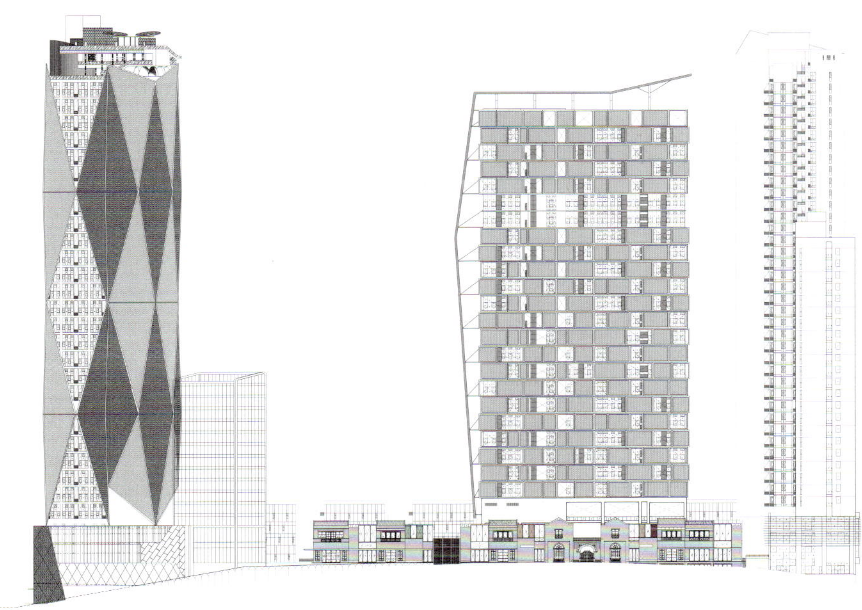

Section 1
剖面图 1

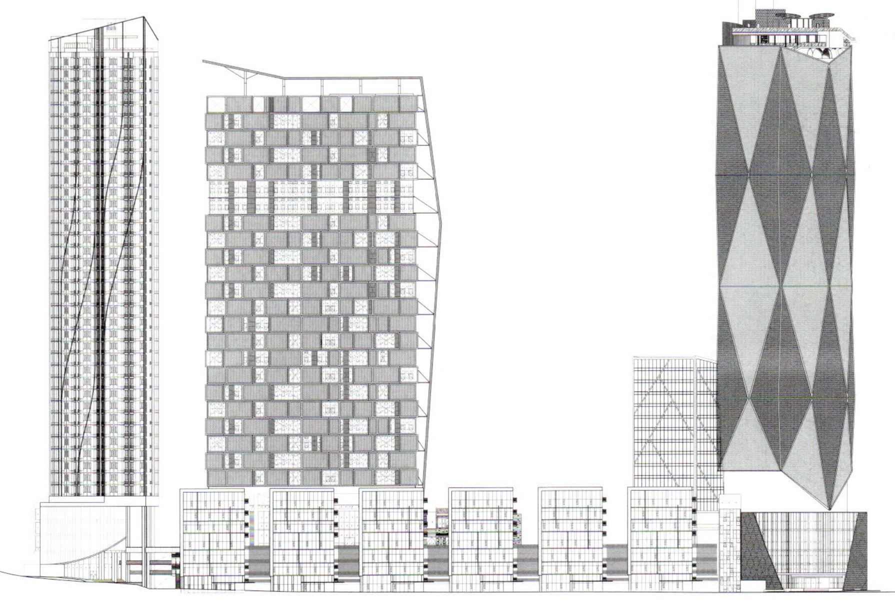

Section 2
剖面图 2

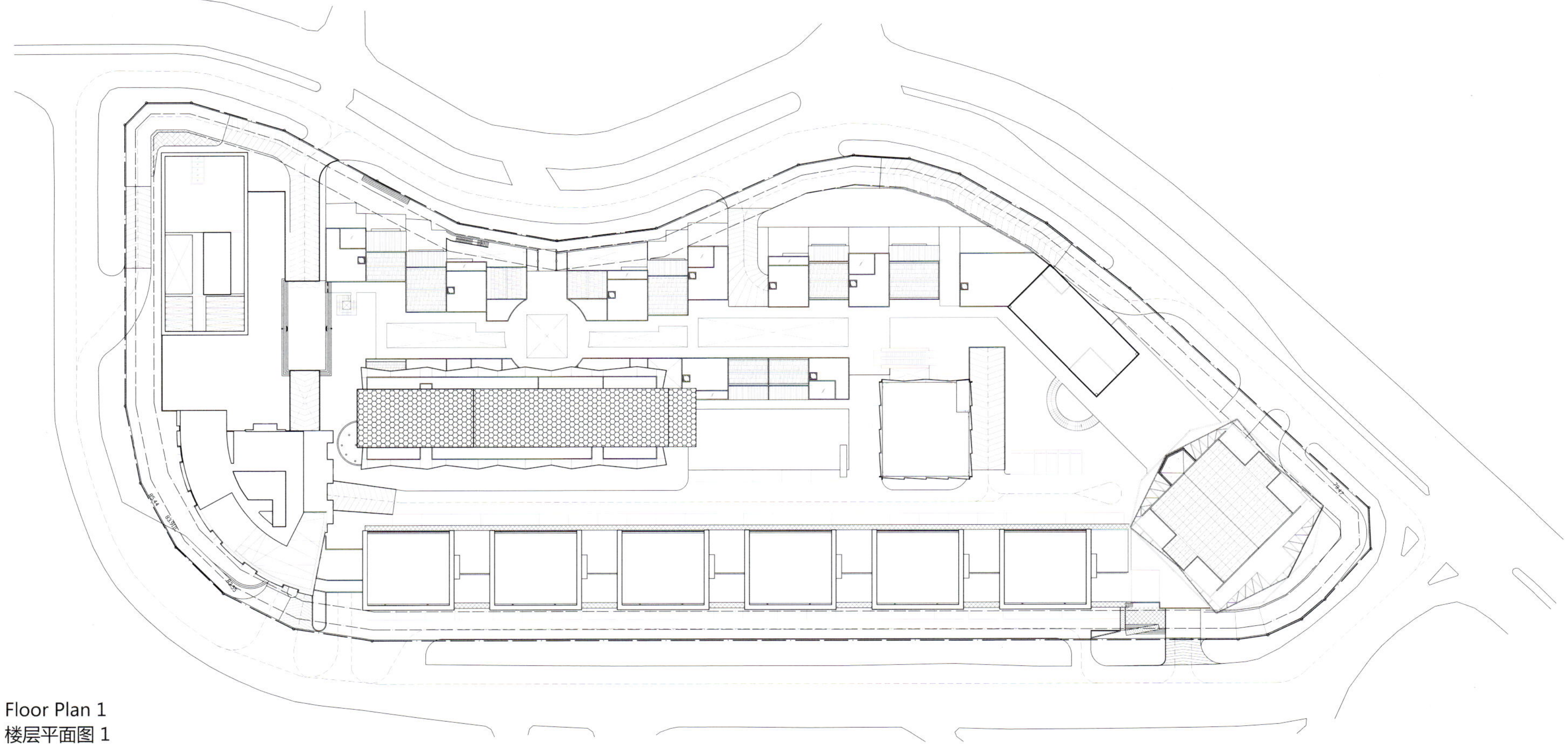

Floor Plan 1
楼层平面图 1

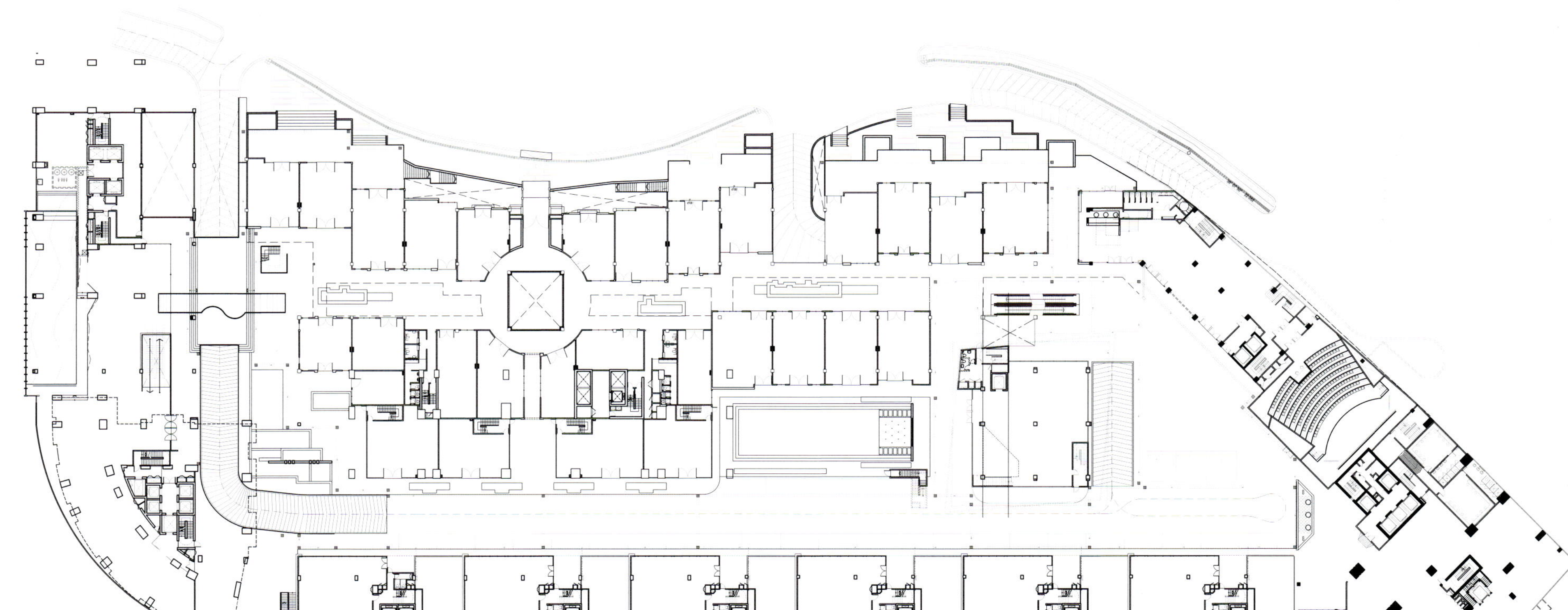

Floor Plan 2
楼层平面图 2

PJ Trade Centre
Bata

REINVENT WORK
REINVENT TASTE
EMPIRE

MUSIC
DANCE

A theatre, as well as the club facilities and sky deck located on each tower, complete the leisure and entertainment element of the programme mix. The podium car park, which is recessed from the street, ensures pedestrian connectivity from all directions of the site.Empire Damansara's dynamic mix of programmes allows it to establish its uniqueness in the new and thriving neighbourhood of Kuala Lumpur.

白沙罗帝国大楼有五栋塔楼组成，包括酒店、SOHO公寓和办公场所，这三个是签名办公室以及文物主题的群落，餐饮和零售等，设计灵感来自于旧的世界新仓库。群落部分采用特别从中国进口的可回收砖，连接着中央庭院的五栋塔楼。每栋塔楼都布置了剧院、俱乐部及空中平台，提供休闲和娱乐元素。停车场的设置保证了在场地各个方向都与人行道有所连接。白沙罗帝国大楼项目的动力组合使其能在吉隆坡繁荣的新地区建立起这座独一无二的建筑。

PROJECT NAME 项目名称

CHINA-TAIWAN CROSS STRAIT FORUM AND CBD DEVELOPMENT

平潭海峡论坛及中央商务区发展

Architect: 10 DESIGN

设计公司：10 DESIGN（拾稼设计）

PROJECT INFORMATION 项目信息

Client	Pingtan Comprehensive Planning Bureau of Experimental zone	**客户**	平潭综合实验区规划局
Location	Pingtan, Fujian, China	**地点**	中国福建
Site Area	93,000m²	**占地面积**	930，000 平方米
GFA	518,000m²	**建筑面积**	518，000 平方米

OVERVIEW 项目概况

"Following a design competition 10 DESIGN (often referred to as "10") has recently been awarded both the master plan of a 930,000m² waterfront CBD development and a new Cross Straits Forum in the island of Pingtan in China.", says Gordon Affleck,Design Partner.

"自赢得了平潭海峡论坛的总体规划竞赛后，近来 10 DESIGN（拾稼设计）又被委任了位于平潭的两个新项目的总体规划设计——一个是93 平方米的海滨商务中心项目，另一个则是平潭海峡论坛中心项目。"，艾高登 ——设计合伙人说。

BRIEF INTERVIEW 访谈录

ARCHITECT
Gordon Affleck,
Design Partner

设计师
Gordon Affleck,
Design Partner

HKASP: What is the main concept behind the whole project?

10 DESIGN: To reflect the aspiration of transparency and dialogue the buildings are formed by converging elements that combine with the landscape and waterfront to create a fluid and open series of public spaces that meld into the buildings themselves.

香港建筑科学出版社：设计背后主要的概念是什么？

10 DESIGN（拾稼设计）：建筑设计结合了景观及滨海的自然元素，创造了一个流动的、空间开放的、与建筑融为一体的公共场所，充分体现了建筑的透明度和与周围环境互动的特征。

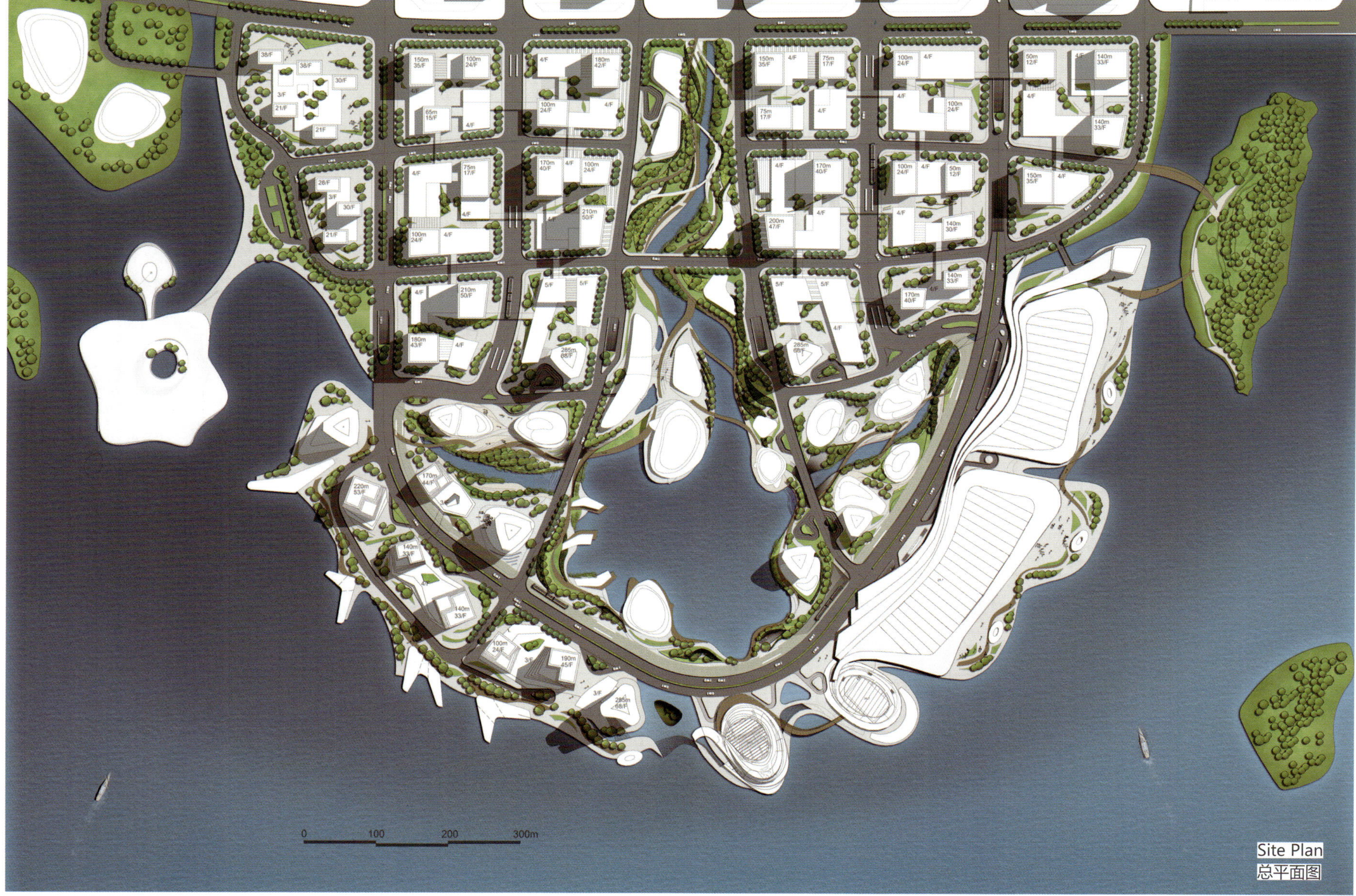

Site Plan
总平面图

Pingtan is planned as a new commercial hub to drive communication and commercial trade between China and Taiwan. Part of the competition included the design of a new Cross Straits Forum including theatre, convention, exhibition and auxiliary commercial and cultural facilities.

At the centre of the CBD and Forum district has a newly created fresh water lake that conserves fresh water from run off through the urban grain.The masterplan cater for some 3.3 million ㎡ of urban development, while the Cross Straits Forum would be in the first phase of development.

Service traffic, roads and trams are integrated into a series of terraced landscape levels to minimize impact of car traffic on pedestrian circulation routes and to createfree access from the central axial park canal through the lake towards the waterfront through a series of leisure and retail lined canals.

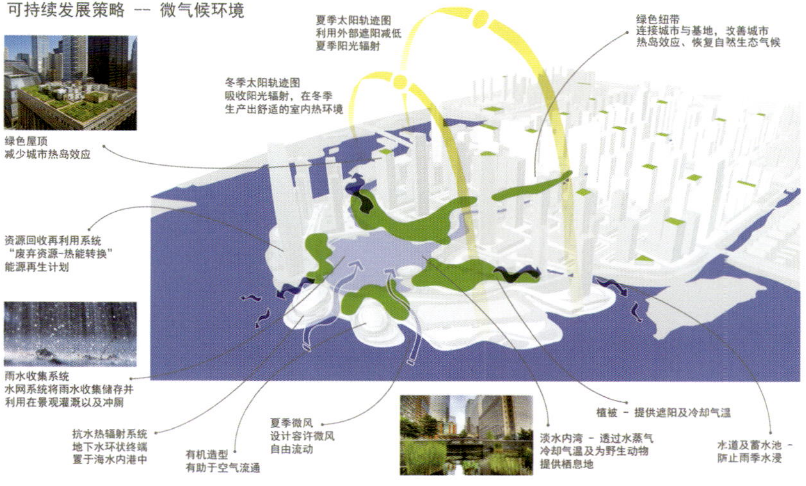

Sustainability Strategies ciagram
可持续策略图示

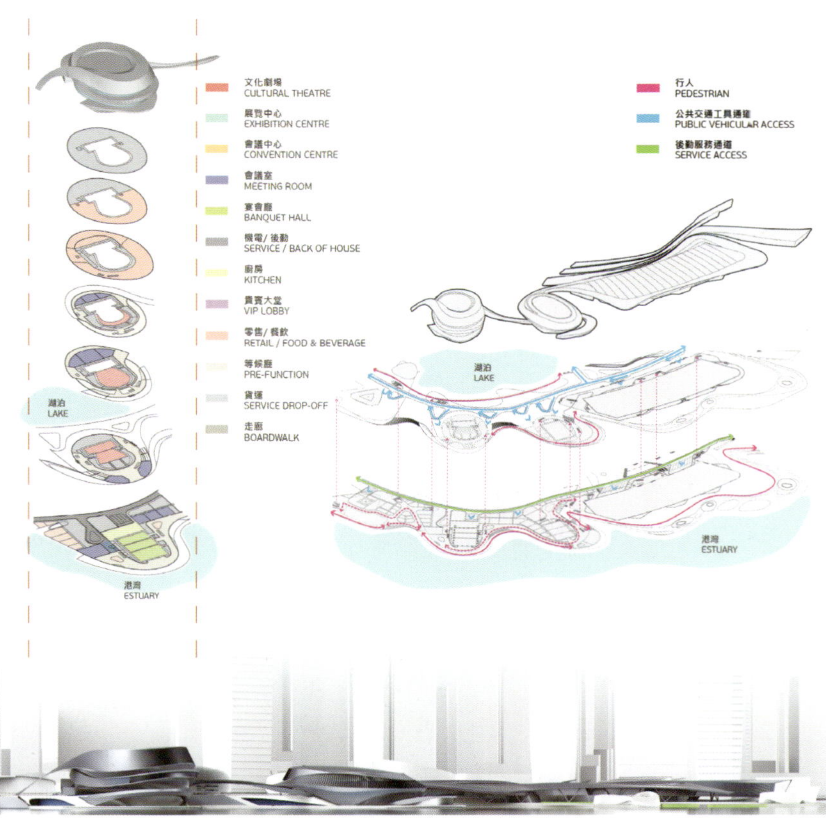

Function Circulat on Plan
功能循环图

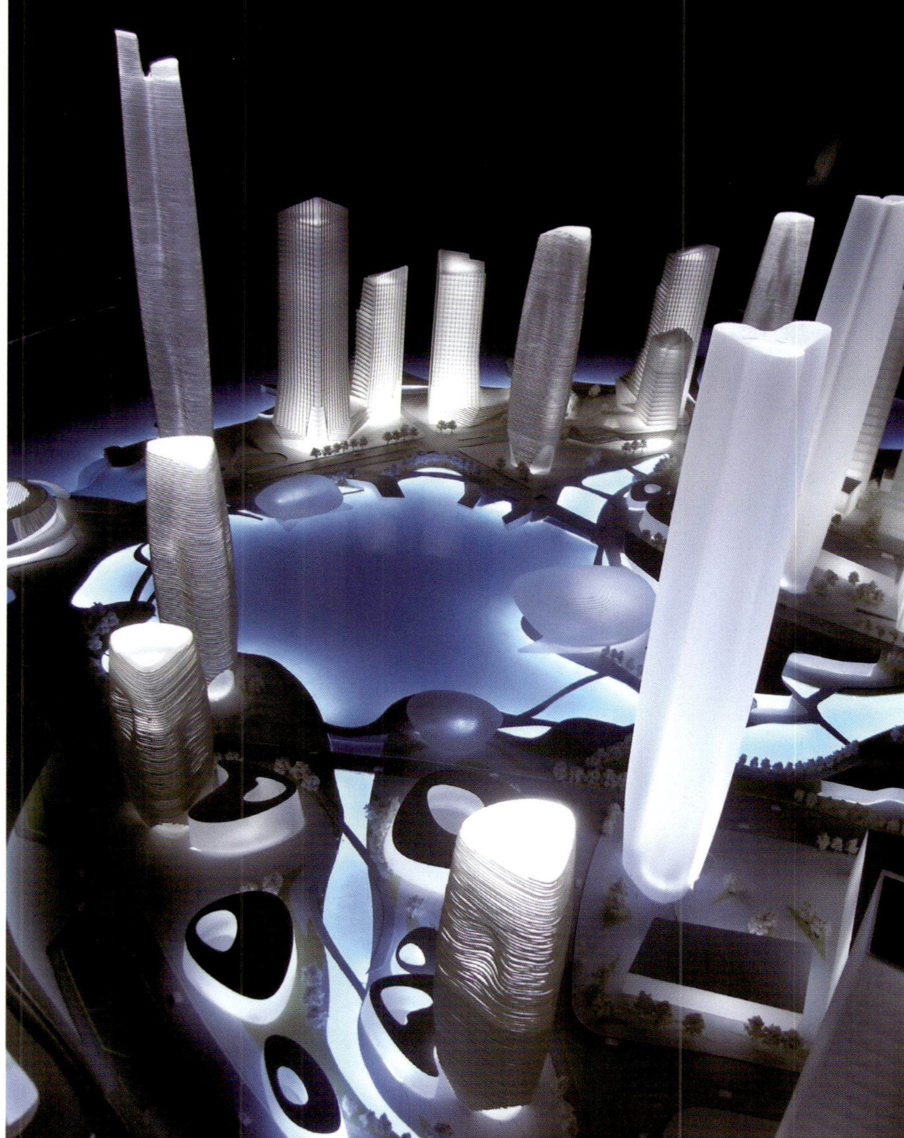

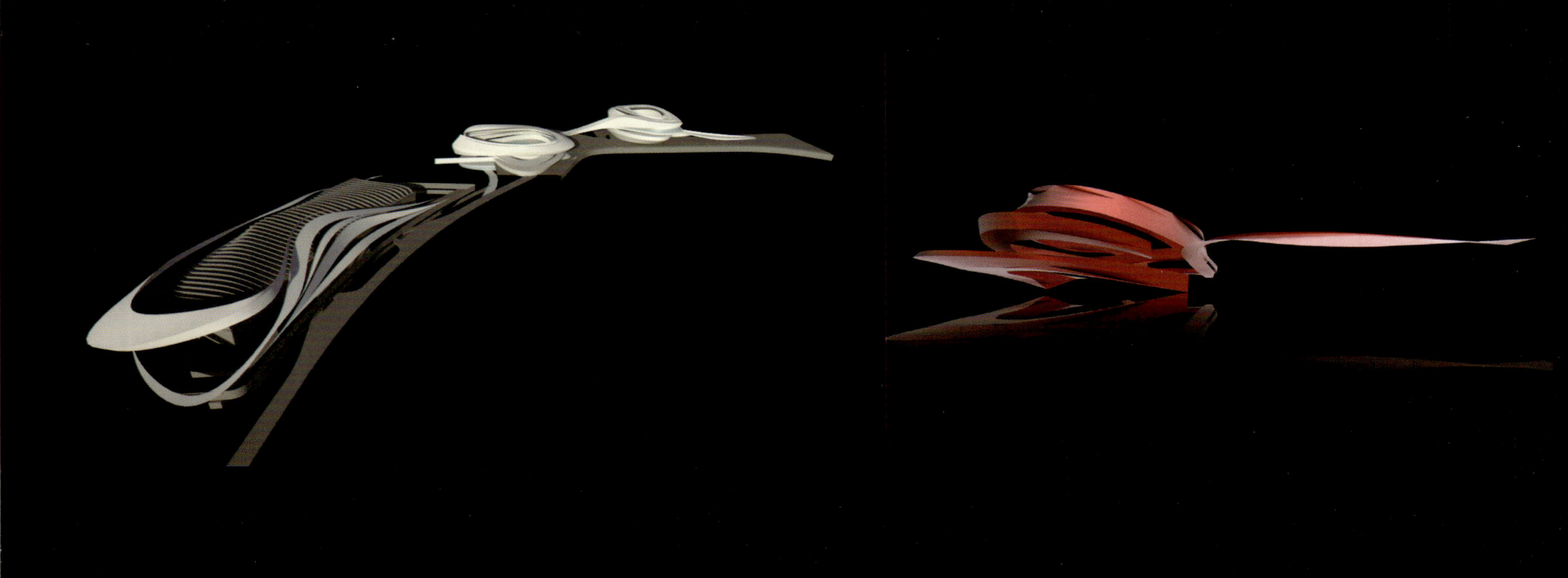

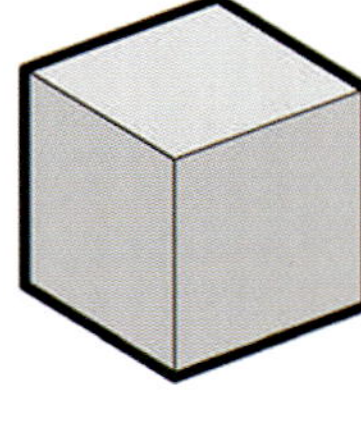

传统模式
封闭盒子
CONVENTIONAL MODEL
AN ENCLOSED BOX

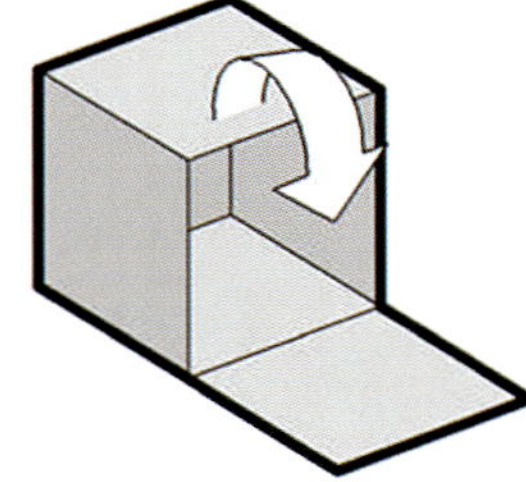

传统模式
限制进入
CONVENTIONAL MODEL
LIMITED ACCESS

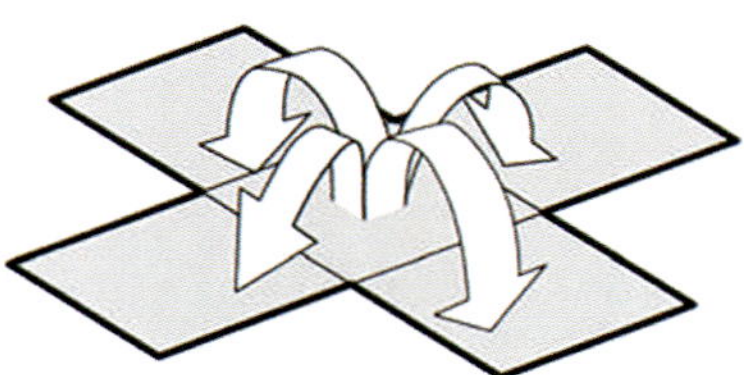

打开盒子
OPENING UP 'THE BOX'

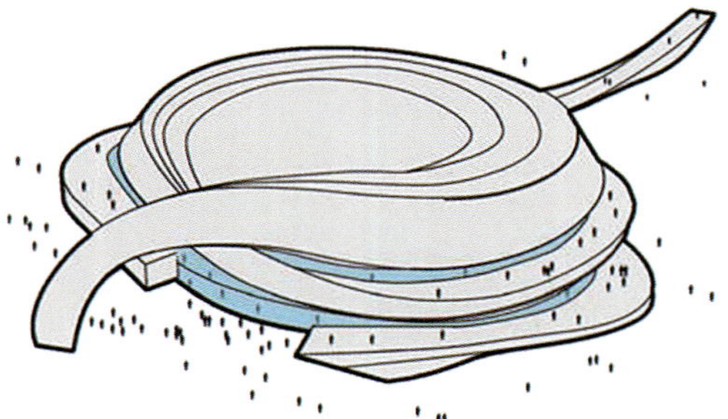

新模式
从全方位进入
NEW MODEL
ACCESS FROM ALL DIRECTIONS

平潭是一个新兴的，推动中国大陆和台湾之间沟通和商贸往来的商业中心。10 DESIGN 被委任的平潭项目的竞赛任务包括了平潭海峡论坛中心项目的设计，该项目包含了剧院、会展中心、展览中心及配套商业和文化设施的设计。

在商务和论坛区中心坐落了一个新创建的淡水湖泊，它能为整座城市节约淡水用量。整个项目的总体规划将包括 330 万平米的城市规划，而平潭海峡论坛中心将作为整个项目第一阶段的设计发展目标。

为使车辆对行人道路的影响降至最低，为创造一条经由中央公园、穿过湖泊和一系列的休闲零售服务设施场所，直至滨海的自由畅通的线路，道路等要素被设计安排成景观梯田的组合。

PROJECT NAME 项目名称

SINGAPORE ASIA SQUARE TOWER

新加坡亚洲广场

Architect: Architects 61 Pte Ltd

设计公司：Architects 61 Pte Ltdall

Foreign design consultant: Denton Corker & Marshall

国外设计顾问：Denton Corker & Marshall

PROJECT INFORMATION 项目信息

Location	Marina Bay,Singapore	**地点**	新加坡滨海湾区
Site Area	191,941.90 m^2	**占地面积**	191, 941.90 平方米

CONCEPT 设计理念

Located at the heart of Singapore's business and financial precinct of Marina Bay is Asia Square – a premium integrated commercial development. This new district at Marina Bay, known as the New Downtown, houses the largest organizations in Singapore's financial sector and provides a seamless extension from the existing Central Business District at Raffles Place. Planned for prime office, residential, and mixed-use developments, the New Downtown ushers in a new concept of a live-work-play garden city.

Asia Square sits at the heart of the well planned district where tenants can enjoy great accessibility due to its close proximity to the existing Raffles Place and Marina Bay MRT stations. It is also connected to the upcoming Landmark MRT station by direct underground pedestrian links, making it one of the most accessible landmarks in the vicinity.

亚洲广场位于新加坡的商业和金融中心的滨海湾区，是由MGPA开发的高端综合商业区。这片滨海湾新区被称为新市区，覆盖了新加坡金融区最大的组织机构，与莱佛士坊现有的中央商务区完美融合。为了打造高档办公室、住宅和多功能综合体，新市区引进了生活、工作、娱乐一体化的花园城市的新理念。

亚洲广场坐落在规划区的核心位置，由于其临近现有的莱佛士坊和滨海湾地铁站，租户可以很好地来此享受。通过连接地下人行通道，它还与即将完成的地标性的地铁站相连，使其成为附近最便利的地标之一。

BRIEF INTERVIEW 访谈录

HKASP: What are the highlights and features of the project?

Architects 61 Denton Corker & Marshall: Asia Square is a 246,500m^2 twin tower development of premium office space, a 5 star hotel and prime food, beverage and entertainment / public space. Each tower emerges from a simple, orthogonal glass podium and is composed of a cluster of eight slender shafts, rising to varying heights, to create a distinctive signature on the Singaporean skyline. In contrast to the towers, the white fritted glass podium is expressed as a singular, unifying element and is conceived as an 'ice block' floating above the ground plane.

Within this 9,000m^2 glass podium is a 6,000m^2, 17 metre high city room known as The Cube. A centrepiece of the project, The Cube is designed to accommodate both local office workers as well as, major public gatherings and events. It shelters, shades and defines the public realm, creating a memorable place in the city. It is characterised by:

–a random pattern of square skylights providing both natural light and natural ventilation;
–activating cafes, restaurants and bars around the edges;
–entry and address to the tower lobbies;
–covered vehicular drop off and arrival;
–a video wall;
–trees and fountains;
–a food court on the upper level.

香港建筑科学出版社：该项目具有哪些亮点及特色？

Architects 61 Denton Corker & Marshall: 亚洲广场是座双塔式建筑，占地 246，500 平方米，集高档办公区、休闲空间和公共空间为一体，集五星级酒店及餐饮娱乐于一身。每栋大厦都矗立在一座简约的矩形玻璃裙楼之上，分别由 8 根修长、高耸的轴柱复合体构成，彼此高度不一，它们为新加坡的天际画上了美丽独特的一笔。相比于两幢大厦，这座白色多孔玻璃裙楼虽然只是个单体，却也能将大厦合二为一。它可堪称悬浮在地面的“冰块”。

这块玻璃平台占地 9，000 平方米，在其内部赫然可以看见一片熟悉的城市空间，覆盖面达 6，000 平方米，高 17 米，这里就是 The Cube。它是该项目的重头戏，举足轻重。这儿不仅是办公人员及普通公共休憩或聚会的场所，也适合举办活动。这里没有风吹日晒，可以乘凉庇荫，可以说是这座城市里绝佳的公共场所。如果人们来到这里，定会看到如下特点，难以忘怀。

– 无规律分布的方形天窗，提供自然采光及自然通风；
– 咖啡店、餐馆及酒吧遍布周遭；
– 大厦大堂入口；
– 设有遮雨棚的车辆停放处；
– 电视墙；
– 树木及喷泉；
– 高层就餐区。

HKASP: What was the greatest challenge? And what was the final solution?

Architects 61 Denton Corker & Marshall: One of the key challenges associated with the project was the accommodation of large floor plates of approximately 3,300m². To reduce the visual mass of the plates, the two towers emerge from a simple, orthogonal, pedestrian scaled podium. The towers are each seemingly composed of a cluster of eight slender shafts that individually rise to differing heights, a 'mini Manhattan' concept.

The integration of two separate parcels of land was also a key challenge and was resolved by the inclusion of the podium. Expressed as a singular, unifying element, it is conceived as an 'ice block' floating above the ground plane. It encapsulates the whole site to provide a large city room known as The Cube. A centrepiece design feature of the project, The Cube is a 6,000m² roofed public space with a 17 metre high ceiling. Skylights provide both natural light and ventilation. Cafes and bars activate this major contribution to the public realm of the CBD.

香港建筑科学出版社：所面临的最大挑战是什么？解决之道是什么？

Architects 61 Denton Corker & Marshall: 该项目主要挑战之一为如何巧妙地安置巨型地板，它们覆盖面几乎达至 3，300 平方米。这些地板太巨大，为了创造更好的视觉效果，两幢大厦这才从一座简约且近人尺度的矩形裙楼平台上拔地而起。当然，这也使得这座庞然大物稍显小巧玲珑。大厦都分别由 8 根修长、高耸的轴柱复合体构成，彼此高度不一，好似一座“迷你型曼哈顿”。

两个独立的地块也可谓不可忽略的关键，然而该裙楼设计也对此给出完美的答复。这座裙楼可堪称悬浮在地面的“冰块”，单一中却也透露出一种和谐感。它仿佛将整座建筑的精华浓缩在此，才创造出“The Cube”这样大型的都市空间。它可以算是整个项目的点睛之笔，这片覆以屋顶的公共空间面积达 6，000 平方米，高至 17 米。其天窗可供自然采光及通风。咖啡馆及酒吧也促成了中心商务区公共场所内的人来人往，熙熙攘攘。

Designed by Australian-based architect, Denton Corker Marshall, and Singapore-based architect, Architects 61, the primary design challenge was in the integration of two separate land parcels, the accommodation of large regular floor plates, and the provision of a crown signature to articulate the towers.

At the heart of the development is the unique podium structure with its semi-transparent glass walls and ceiling punctuated with roof lights. Essentially, the development comprises twin commercial towers "floating" above the podium structure which accommodates "The Cube". The Cube provides an architectural address to the towers and a vibrant landscaped plaza which is an impressive, 9,290 m^2 all-weather covered space with a 17-metre ceiling height that blends the excitement of shopping, al fresco dining and public entertainment with the tranquillity of shade, shelter and natural landscaping.

项目由澳大利亚建筑师Denton Corker Marshall和新加坡建筑公司Architects 61设计，设计面临的主要挑战是如何将两块独立的地块结合在一起，如何巧妙地安置呈规则形状的巨型楼板；如何设计连接塔楼顶层的天桥，使其具有标志性。

开发区的中心是一个独特的平台结构，带有半透明的玻璃墙壁及吊灯点缀着的天花板。实际上，开发区包括双子商业塔楼，"漂浮"在平台结构上，调节这个"立方体"。从建设角度而言，立方体诠释了塔楼的内涵。立方体给人们提供了一个充满活力，绿意快然的广场。广场设有屋顶，高17米，全年开放，总面积达9,290平方米，令人叹为观止。广场呈现一片热闹的场景，有购物者的热情，有露天餐厅的惬意，也有大众的欢腾，一切跟树荫、栖息地以及自然景观的寂静融为一体，浑然天成。

Site Plan
总平面图

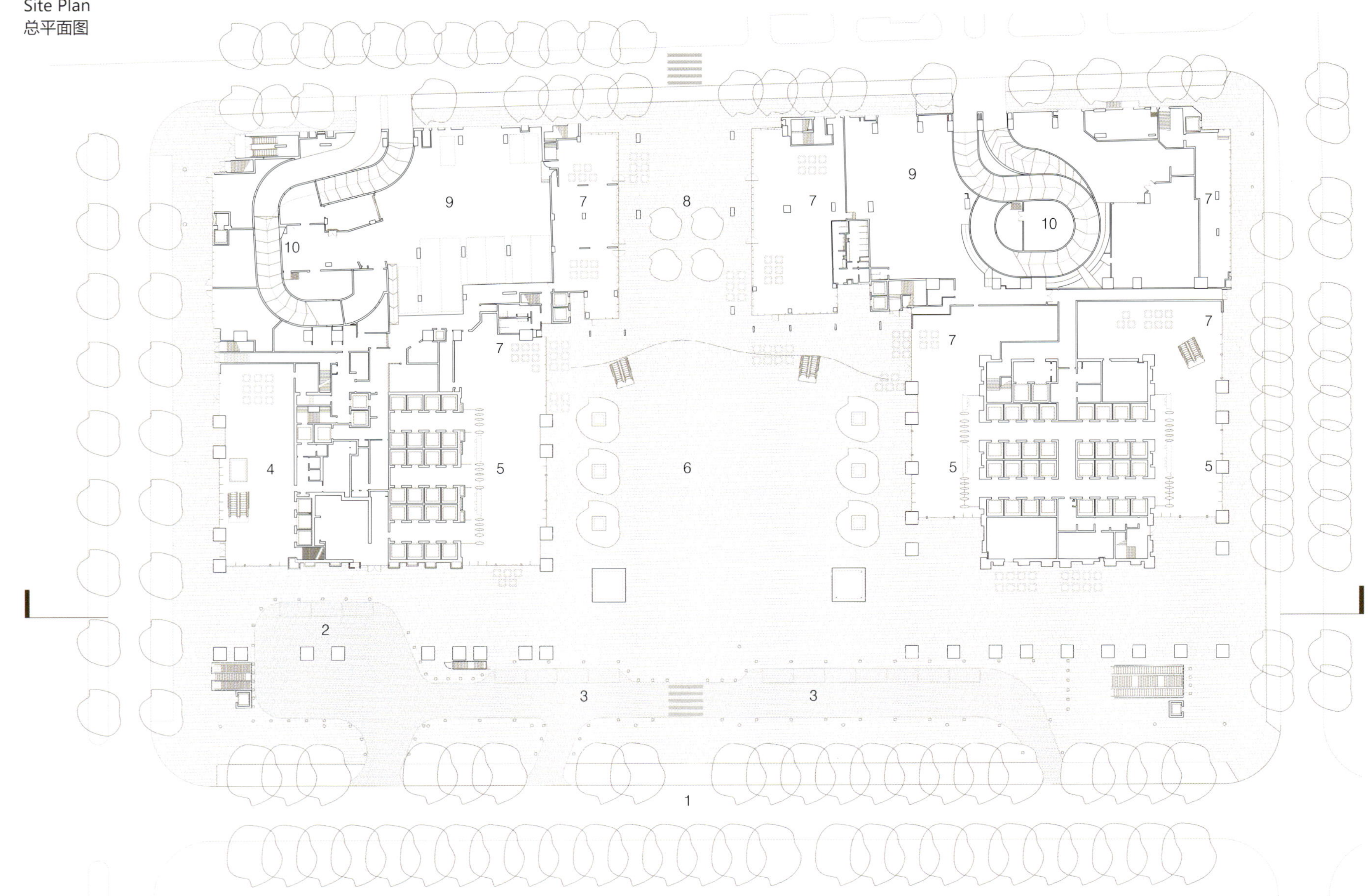

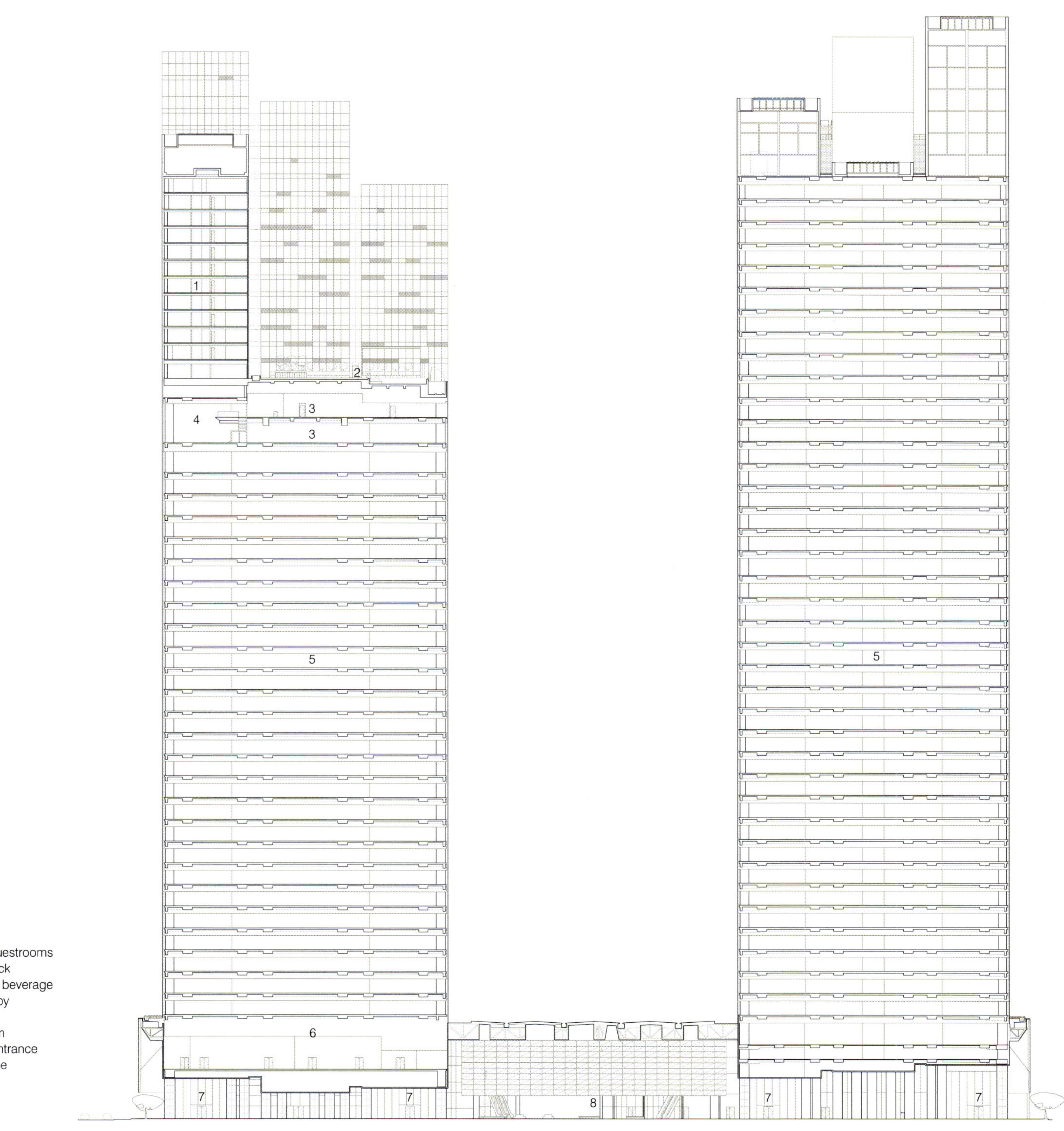

1 Hotel guestrooms
2 Pool deck
3 Food + beverage
4 Sky lobby
5 Office
6 Ballroom
7 Foyer entrance
8 The cube

Section 1:1000

Section
剖面图

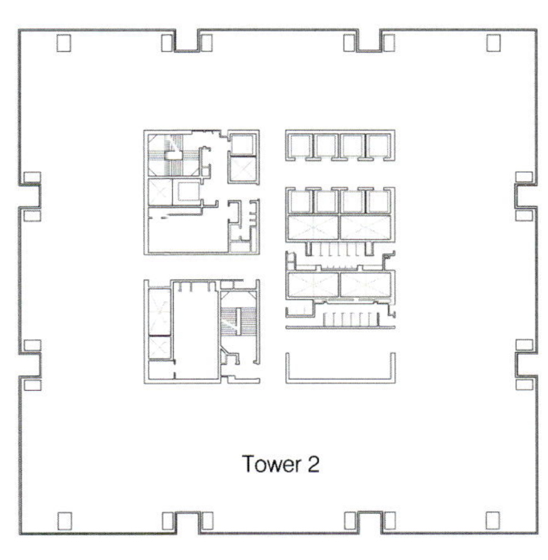

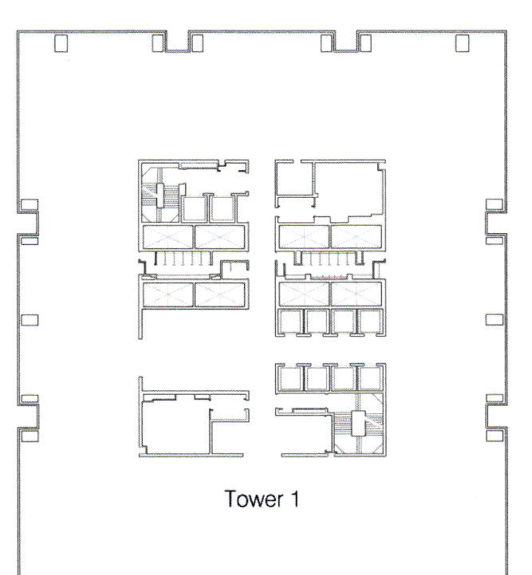

Typical Office Plan Mid Rise
中层典型办公平面图

Mid Rise Office Plan 1:1000

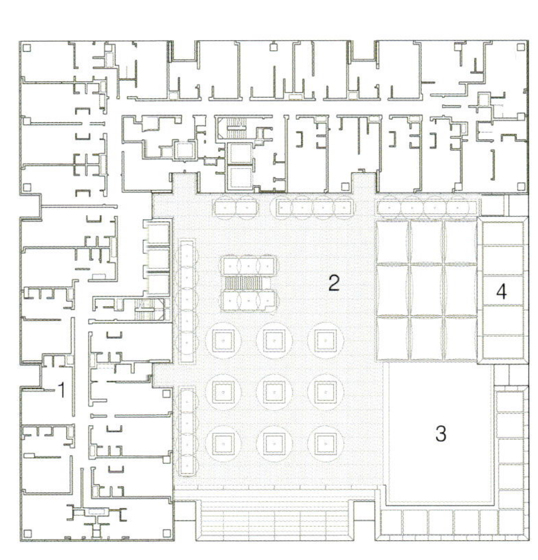

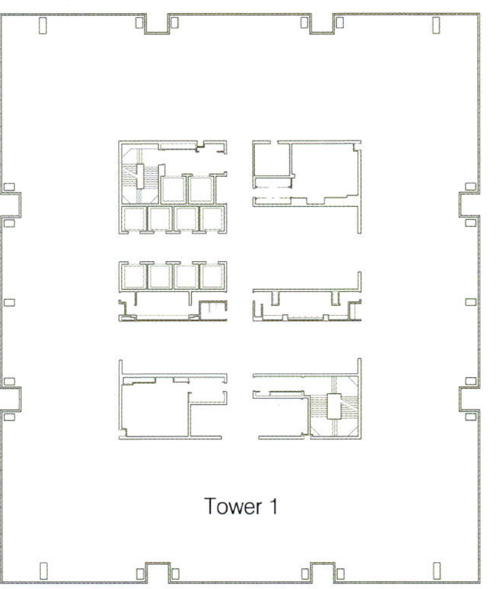

Typical Hotel Plan and Typical Office Plan High Rise
高层典型办公酒店平面图

1 Hotel Guestrooms
2 Pool deck
3 Infinity edge pool
4 Pool bar

High Rise Hotel + Office Plan 1:1000

Asia Square's innovative building design and features deliver unparalleled levels of space efficiency and cost effectiveness giving businesses that extra competitive edge.The large floor plates in Asia Square's twin towers extend up to 3,251m^2 and benefit from being column-free and regular in shape. This enables tenants to have easier direct access around the office, and maximises occupiable and productive space.

Asia Square's facade is an impressive statement of energy efficiency and high technology. The facade minimizes solar heat transmission. This conserves energy and reduces cooling costs while maximising natural daylight and further minimising heat transfer into the interior.

亚洲广场的创新设计和特点展示了空前的空间利用效率和成本效率的水平，带来很大的竞争优势。亚洲广场双子塔的楼板面加大到3 251平方米，得益于没有圆柱及既定的形状，这使租户在办公室更直接访问，并最大化占用并高效利用空间。

亚洲广场的外立面集能源高利用率和高科技为一体，给人印象深刻。外立面尽可能地降低热传导。最大化地利用阳光的同时，节约能源，降低制冷成本，进一步减小热量传递到室内。

citi
citi

North Lobby
Levels 25-43

PROJECT NAME 项目名称

NANJING ZENDAI HIMALAYAS CENTER

南京证大喜玛拉雅中心

Architect: MAD Architects

设计公司： MAD 建筑事务所

PROJECT INFORMATION 项目信息

Client	Jiangsu Zendai Commercial Culture Development Co., Ltd	**客户**	江苏证大商业文化发展有限公司
Location	Nanjing, China	**地点**	南京
Site Area	93,595 m²	**占地面积**	93 ,595 平方米
Gross Floor Area	Above Ground 383,307 m², Below Ground 181,562 m²	**总建筑面积**	地上：383 ,307 平方米；地下：181 ,562 平方米
Building Height	120 m	**建筑高度**	120 米
Floor Area Ratio	4.06	**容积率**	4.06

OVERVIEW 项目概况

The Nanjing Zendai Himalayas Center is a city-scale urban project, with an overall building area of approximately 560,000 m². Working at this scale, MAD strives to capture a fully realized "Shanshui City".

The Nanjing Zendai Himalayas Center project is currently under construction, and is estimated to be completed in 2017.

最近全面开工的"南京证大喜玛拉雅中心"总建筑面积约 56 万平方米。MAD 正在尝试通过这一城市尺度的作品，实践一座理想中的"山水城市"。

"南京证大喜玛拉雅中心"项目已经在有序施工中，预计将于 2017 年完工。

FEATURE ANALYSIS 特色分析

ARCHITECT
Ma Yansong
Founder & Principal Partner, MAD Architects

设计师
马岩松
MAD 建筑事务所创始人、合伙人

Continued from MAD's landscape city in last article. Nanjing Zhengda Himalayas Center is the latest work released from MAD landscape city plan. Compared to Chaoyang project in Beijing, we find numerous interesting differences, which show architect's initiative to seek more than one thinking for such concept. The white color as a whole may be closer to traditional Chinese landscape painting featuring lightness and transparency. The design lays more emphasis on the creation of landscape. In combination with number and volume of buildings, the project makes people feel like a "creation of urban park" of super urban scale. The rendering also makes great effort to present the visitors a picture of landscape, taking an implicative tension in urban elites to usher a new architectural aesthetic sentiment.

继上篇对 MAD 山水城市的介绍后，南京证大喜马拉雅中心项目是 MAD 山水城市计划发表的最新作品。通过和北京朝阳项目的比较我们可以发现许多有趣的不同点，也反映出设计师主动追求这一内涵的更多变种的思考。整体建筑白色系的风格可能更加接近传统中国山水艺术轻盈通透的气质。设计也将更多的精力放在景观的营造上。结合建筑的数目与体量，颇有在进行一个超级城市尺度的"都市造园"的感觉。建筑在效果图上也极力向观者呈现出一种山水生活的文化意境，隐约中蕴含着一种引导城市精英新的建筑审美情趣的目的。

Site Plan
总平面图

Sketch
草图

Built over 2600 years ago, Nanjing is an iconic city with equally rich traditional heritage and high modernization. With these two motifs in mind, MAD strives to achieve a balance of the city's historic past and its high-tech future. The design of the Zendai Himalayas Center maintains and develops the philosophy of cooperation between humanity and nature, albeit in a modern setting. The carefully planned project seeks to restore harmony between humans and the environment by creating integrated, contemplative spaces that still meet the material needs of modern life.

有着 2600 多年建城史的南京，极具人文传统，同时是中国现代化程度很高的城市之一。MAD 一直秉持的理念，就是在现代城市中人和自然共生的传统哲学，重建人与环境之间的和谐关系。在满足现代生活的各种需求的同时，营造融合而富有生机的空间，实现人与自然在精神上的契合。

The site is composed of six lots, two of which are linked by a vertical city plaza. Curving, ascending corridors and paths weave through the undulating commercial complexes, bringing people from the busy ground level to the vertical park for opportunities to wander among the buildings and gardens.

At the center of the site is a village-like community of low buildings, connected by footbridges and nestled into the landscape. This scene of footbridges, artificial hills and flowing water together creates a poetic moment at the heart of the project. The simplicity of the design concept is further captured through the use of clean construction materials, such as concrete.

项目基地由六个地块组成，其中两个街区被一座立体城市广场连接。不同尺度的连廊、走道穿插在几个连绵起伏的商业综合体中，引领人们从繁忙的地面街道漫步到立体公园，游走于建筑与景观之间。

基地的中心区域由一些散落在绿毯上的坡顶小屋构成，呈现出小村落式的环境，为大尺度的城市项目提供了宜人的城市空间。小桥连接着村落，从一个街区到另一个街区，串联了假山、流水，构成了一幅充满诗意的画作。建筑采用混凝土作为材料，表现出材质本身的朴素。

On the edge of the site, the mountain-like towers are characterized by vertical sun shading and pervious glass screens that "flow" like waterfalls. These features provide interior spaces with energizing light and wind to form a subtle, calming ambience. The project mimics the site's surrounding mountains and meandering rivers that are essential parts of Chinese aesthetic philosophy. Towers along the edge of the site act as a mountainous backdrop, while water features such as ponds, waterfalls, brooks, and pools connect buildings and landscapes to integrate all of the Center's elements. This integration goes beyond form, with the water features functioning as reservoirs to collect and recycle rainwater for irrigation.

位于基地外侧的塔楼宛如高山，竖条的遮阳玻璃百叶窗，遮阳又透光，为室内空间提供了怡人的光线和风，如瀑布般流动于山体上，让整座建筑充满意境。塔楼扮演了高山流水的远景，而基地内水池、瀑布、溪流、水潭等的水景承接了意象并把隐喻具现化，模糊了远景与近景的边缘。这些项目内的水景同时也是雨水收集池，让基地内的水再用于浇灌、循环利用。

PROJECT NAME 项目名称

WUXI COMPLEX

无锡综合体

Architect:ATENASTUDIO

设计公司：阿特拉斯建筑事务所

PROJECT INFORMATION 项目信息

Client	Wuxi Taihu Pearl Estates Development Co., LTD, ; Cheng Hsiung International Corporation,	**客户**	无锡太湖明珠房地产开发有限公司，程雄国际集团
Assignment	ATENASTUDIO + Archmaster studio	**特邀设计**	阿特拉斯建筑事务所与 Archmaster 工作室
Lot Area	336.340 m^2	**占地面积**	336，340 平方米
Built Area	561.411 m^2	**建筑面积**	651，411 平方米

OVERVIEW 项目概况

The Masterplan project called ""CONCEPT DESIGN FOR BUILDING'S PROJECT - LOT A.02.08 - LIHU AREA, WUXI, CHINA" takes a 200.000 sqm buildable zoning lot (inside the property lot with bigger dimensions) located in the South-East part of Wuxi City, China.The North border of this land is along the Taihu Lake Avenue, the East is along the Hongqiao Road, the South is along the natural river, Dingchang River and the West is along the Taihu Lake.

The area appears to be of exceptional paesistic value because of the condition of a waterfront both West towards Taihu Lake, and South towards Dingchang River and of the view of the mountain chains to the North.

中国无锡蠡湖区域第 A0208 号地块建筑工程概念，规划的可建筑地块面积 200,000 平方米（区内较大规模的地块），地块位于无锡市东南部。规划范围北沿太湖大道，东临鸿桥路，南接天然河道鼎昌河，西靠太湖。

规划区域因其西面紧靠太湖水岸、南面紧靠鼎昌河水岸和北接连绵山脉景观的自然条件，它的特别价值由此显现出来。

BRIEF INTERVIEW 访谈录

ARCHITECT
Rossana Atena, Marco Sardella

设计师
Rossana Atena，Marco Sardella

HKASP: Can you share with us the design process of this project? Like how do you develop the form?
ATENASTUDIO: Design process starts finding balance between landscape, waterscape and buildings demands. Those three issues are developed together and overlap each other in very organic and mutual respects. The building shapes come from the site where design, views and solar orientation are able to deform skyscrapers researching the highest quality of life space from insides to outsides. The fluid way to design waterscape and landscape together involves the buildings as well, that developed in five different typologies to provide more diverse offers and flexibility for the developers.

HKASP: Did the concept/design change much during that time?
ATENASTUDIO: The concept design has remained the same as the first initial idea while types, orientation and shape of buildings improved during the process to answer local demands and flexibility issues of developers.

HKASP: When designing, is there something in particular that you focus on? (Material, form, use etc)
ATENASTUDIO: Design is a process, an integrated net of input rather than a final shape that involves all issues together: ecology, local values, materials, technology, program, etc. Main characteristics come from the site where specificities of the place are values that are then valorized in the projects. In Wuxi project many inputs address the presence of the lake. The water becomes a tool to design landscape and buildings; the waterscape is brought in the inner part the project and also until the top of buildings designing the main facade of the Hotel with a waterfall.

香港建筑科学出版社：你能跟我们分享一下该项目的设计过程吗？例如，你们是如何设计造型的？
阿特拉斯建筑事务所：设计之初，我们力求在景观、水景、建筑需求之间寻找一种平衡。我们把这三者融合在一起，使他们成为一个整体，相互影响，相互作用。建筑的造型需迎合项目所在地的环境，通过设计、景观以及建筑朝向来确定高楼大厦的造型，开拓一条从里到外都体现至高品质生活的道路。在设计中，为了将水景与景观形成完美的融合，也必须考虑建筑物本身。我们对此采用了五种迥异的设计风格，给开发商营造更加丰富多彩的内容与空间自由。

香港建筑科学出版社：在设计过程中，你们对设计理念或设计的改动大吗？
阿特拉斯建筑事务所：设计理念一如既往的保持不变。然而，在设计过程中，我们对优化了建筑的外形，朝向与造型，目的是为了迎合当地的需要，给开发商更多空间使用的自由。

香港建筑科学出版社：设计过程中，你有什么特别关注的地方吗？（比如，材料、形体、用途等）
阿特拉斯建筑事务所：设计是一个过程，它属于整个产出过程中不可分割的一部分。但设计不代表所有问题已找到最终的答案，包括生态、本地价值创造、材料、工艺、服务设施等。项目所在地的环境因素决定了建筑的主要特点。项目所在地的特质已赋予项目既定的价值。在无锡的项目中，众多设计产品围绕湖的存在而展开，水成为了设计景观与建筑的工具。水景表达了项目的内涵，比如通过房顶设计的瀑布来烘托酒店主立面的内涵。

The Masterplan presents two main keywords which are the base of all design choices and that can be defined as generator elements of all the project: Landscape and Waterscape.

Landscape

The ground is not thought as a flat plate element on which the buildings are simply located, on the contrary it is used as if it would be a "3D solid material" and shaped both horizontally and vertically.In this way force lines are developed from East to West, always dynamic, which find their highest points on the 2 hills which enclose the villas, that all have a view to the Taihu Lake.The movement of these force lines produce in-between spaces, which create the squares system and the whole public spaces.

This movement partially generates the buildings themselves, mainly the 5 high rise buildings, the Hotel, the Facilities and the Shopping area, which in this way assume a plastic and dynamic shape.Other buildings appear to be "on" the landscape instead, particularly the villas, the courtyard building and the multy-storey buildings, these last two detached from the ground, and anyway always using green as a "design material": private gardens and roof gardens for the villas, green facades and roof gardens for the courtyard buildings and hanging gardens for the multy-storey buildings.Tight linear trees add up to this integrated Landscape system following and underlining the Landscape bands and represent an integrated project system of essences, most of all made of plum trees.

Waterscape

The intention is to emphasize to the maximum the presence of water making it become a diffuse system, introducing it inside the area and in every part of the project, and using it as if it was a "3D liquid material". Following as a model the idea of the city of Venice an estuary is created to the South with an artificial island for open air shows, a series of buildings which represent the Yacht Club thought as an archipelago, a small lake system, a timed waterfall (for example 10 minutes per hour, mainly in the evening and with scenographic artificial lighting) coming from the last floor of the Hotel. In this way a perfect fusion between Earth, Water and Architecture is gained in complete harmony of the parts according to a design and attention to landscape approach typically Italian and Mediterranean and pursuing the goal of always researching as a reference the human scale. The result is a "Landscape Resort Community Park" in respect to the law of humanity and nature.

总体规划突显两个关键词：陆地景色和水上景观。这是所有设计选择的基础，也被定为义为全部项目的生成元素。

陆地景观

地面并不是建筑可以简单坐落的平板，相反，它被看着是一种 3D 固体材料，可以同时进行水平和垂直两个方向的造型。这样，形成了自东向西的动态力线，两座山丘是力线的最高点，别墅隐于山丘之间却又都能观看到湖景。空间之间产生的力线运动，创造了广场系统和整个公共空间。

动线的一部分生成建筑本身，座高层塔楼、酒店、裙楼和购物区就这样呈现了可塑的动态造型，而与此不同是其它建筑则呈现“站”在景观上的景象，特别是别墅、庭院建筑和多层建筑，最后这两类建筑从地面分开。无论哪类都总是以绿色作为设计材料：别墅的私家花园和屋顶花园，庭院建筑的绿色立面和屋顶花园，多层建筑的悬垂花园。排列成行的树木，紧贴着景观带的边缘融入景观，体现着一种本质的综合工程系统，这些树中大部分是李树。

水上景观

水上景观力图着重最大化发挥水的效果，使其形成散开的系统，在区域内项目的每个部分都能出现并把它作为“立体的液态材质”加以运用。借鉴了水城威尼斯的表现手法，在南面创造了一个可供露天演出的人工小岛。游艇俱乐部的建筑群则变形为一系列海岛造型、小湖造型和一处从酒店顶层落下的时控瀑布（主要在晚上每小时 10 分钟的水幕艺术灯光），这样，陆地、水、建筑之间根据设计达到了完美的融合。设计吸取了典型的意大利和地中海景观方法，追求以人为本不断探索的目标，最终形成了这个崇尚人文与自然的“度假社区景观公园”。

Site Plan
总平面图

landscape Analysis
景观绿化分析图（请核对）

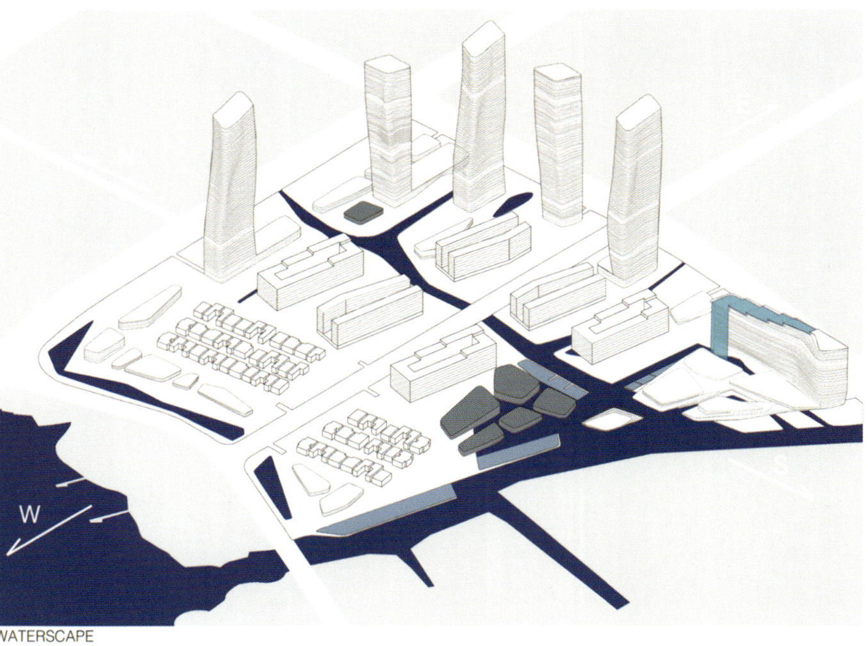

Waterscape Analysis
水景分析图

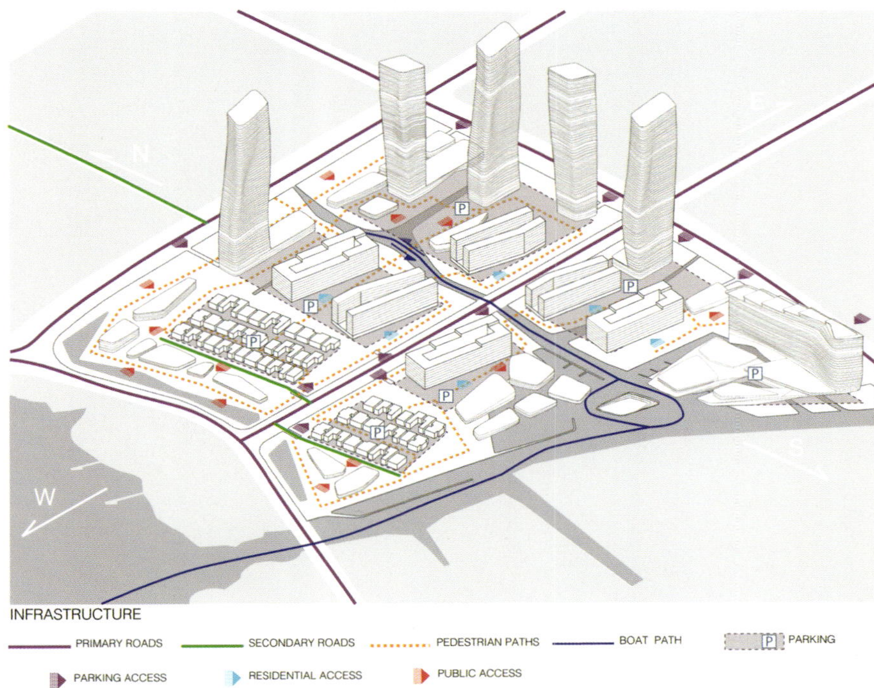

Infrastraucture Analysis
基础设施分析图

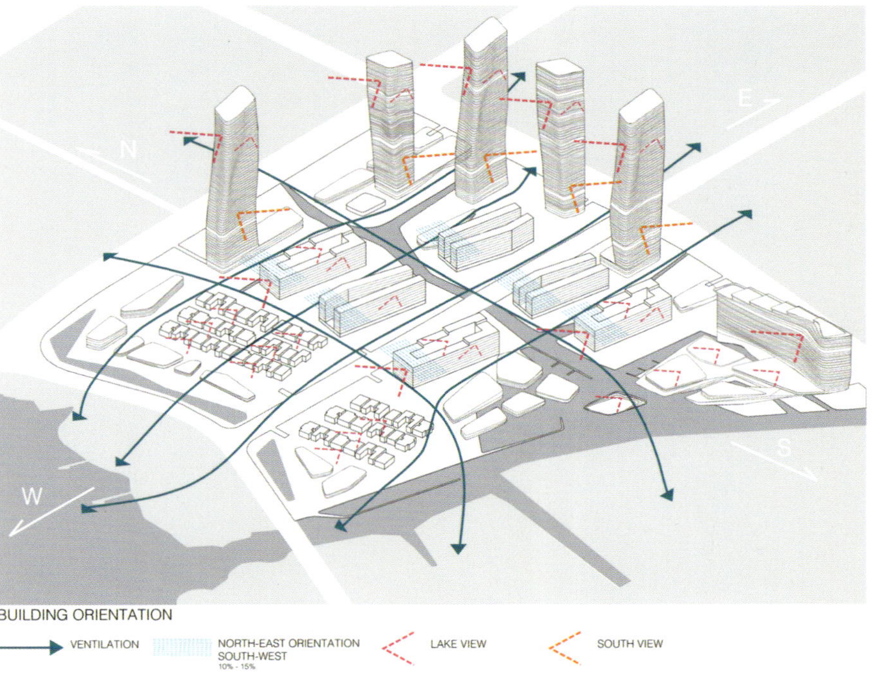

Building Orientation Analysis
建筑物方位分析图

PROJECT NAME 项目名称

THE TWO PILLARS OF EASTLAKE

杭州东湖双子大楼

Architect: COOP HIMMELB(L)AU Prix, Dreibholz & Partner ZT GmbH

设计公司：COOP HIMMELB(L)AU Prix, Dreibholz & Partner ZT GmbH

PROJECT INFORMATION 项目信息

Location	Hangzhou,China	**地点**	中国杭州
Site Area	77,600 m²	**占地面积**	77，600 平方米
Renderings and Plans	COOP HIMMELB(L)AU	**效果图和设计图纸**	蓝天组
Model Images	Markus Pillhofer	**模型图**	Markus Pillhofer

CONCEPT 设计理念

Our proposal for the new Twin Towers seeks to transform the Olympic Expo site into a new "Eastlake"district in Hangzhou inspired by the powerful relationships of architecture, water and landscape of world-renown Westlake, but reconsidered as a new kind of Urban Garden of the 21st Century. This new Garden contains variable architectural, landscape and functional elements in composed and dynamic relationships to each other, reflecting the vibrant nature of the future of Hangzhou. As the main symbolic and physical icons of this Garden, two 300 meter uniquely shaped towers balance next to each other in a sculpted ensemble, creating an unmistakable new skyline. The Two Pillars of Eastlake are subtly shaped in response to the each other's complementary but distinct forms creating a new and memorable image for the future of Hangzhou representing the values of dynamic interaction and cooperation.

本案将以两座崭新的双子大楼将奥林匹克博览会区域改造成杭州的新"东湖"。设计灵感来源于世界闻名的西湖，设计师希望本案能像西湖一样在紧密联系建筑、水系和景观的同时，又转型为一座 21 世纪的新型都市花园。花园里有不同的建筑、景观和功能设施，相辅相成又各自独立，展现出杭州充满生机与活力的未来。花园里的代表元素和象征就是这两座高 300 米的东湖双子大楼：造型各异，相互呼应，相互平衡，打造出一条清晰可见的新天际线。双子大楼的形状都有微妙的不同之处，巧妙地在互补的同时又展现出各自的独特，更为杭州打造出一个令人难忘的新形象及活力互动和紧密合作的价值观。

FEATURE ANALYSIS 特色分析

ARCHITECT
Mr. Wolf D. Prix

设计师
Mr. Wolf D. Prix

PHOTOGRAPHONS
Alfons Kowatsch

摄影师
Alfons Kowatsch

Coop Himmelblau is famous for a design style featuring expressionism. The towers' volume delivers two integral geometrical forms in the design plan for Hangzhou twin towers delivers two integral geometry. Such detailing features a strong style-based orientation by relinquishing different views of aesthetics. However, he design is focused on organization and shaping of internal space of towers.As an early concept of design, the architects give a discussion on the forms of internal space of a both stereotyped and cutting-edge super high-rise building, which deserves our reference.

蓝天组的设计风格以表现主义式的张扬闻名。在这个杭州双塔的方案中，塔楼的体量取了两个完整的几何体形式。抛开美学上的见仁见智，这样的处理有一种强烈的风格化取向。而其设计着力点则在于完成塔楼内部的空间组织塑造。作为一个比较前期的概念方案，设计师在塑造一个地标的同时，对于限于窠臼的先进的超高层建筑设计的内部空间形式进行了值得借鉴的探讨。

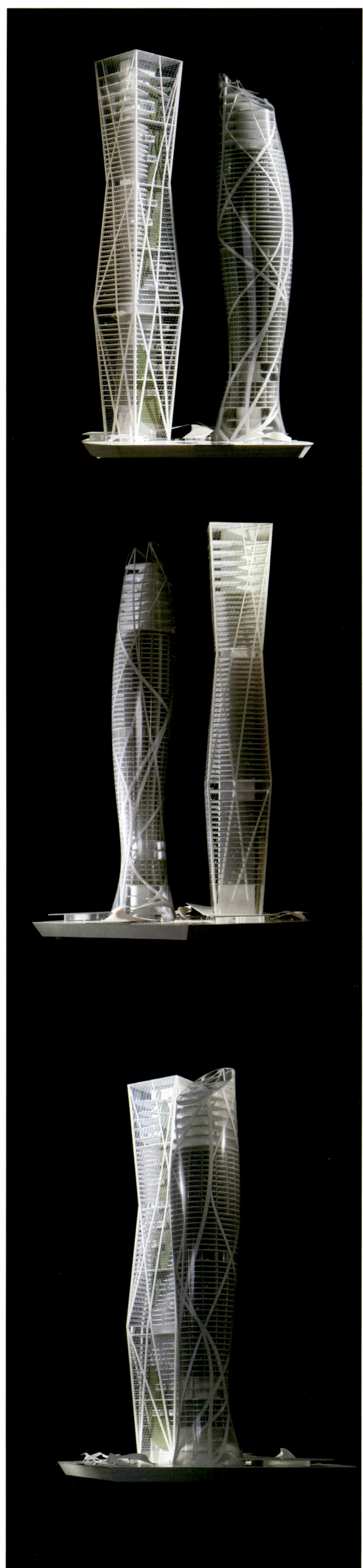

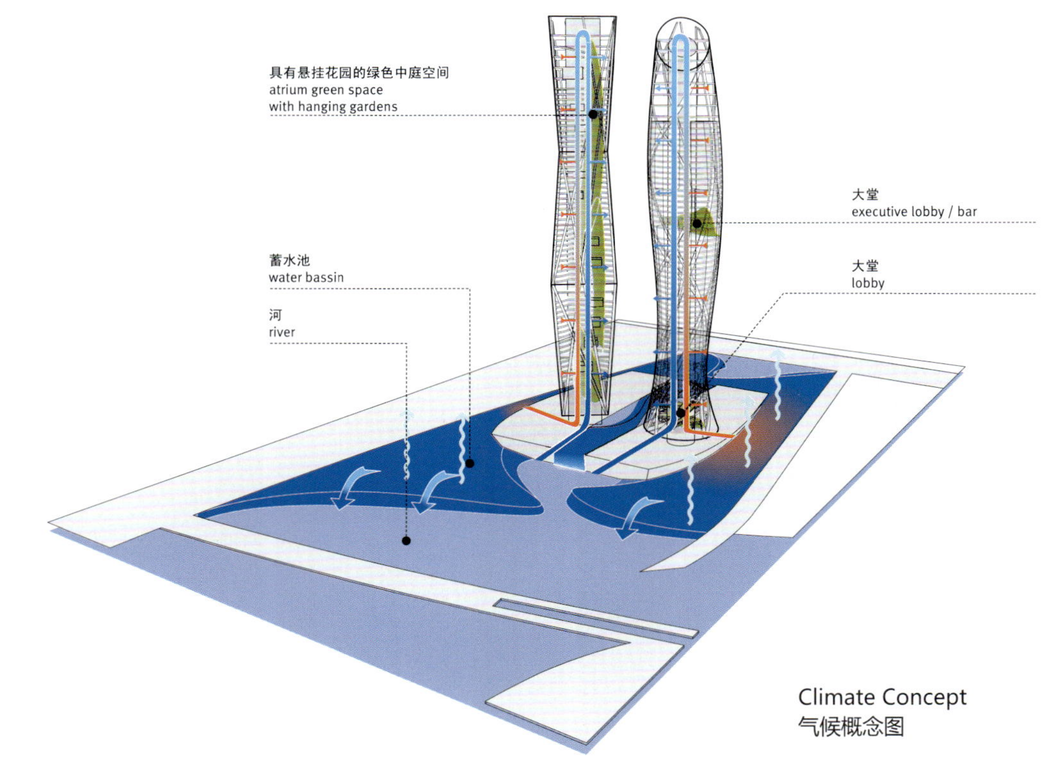

Climate Concept
气候概念图

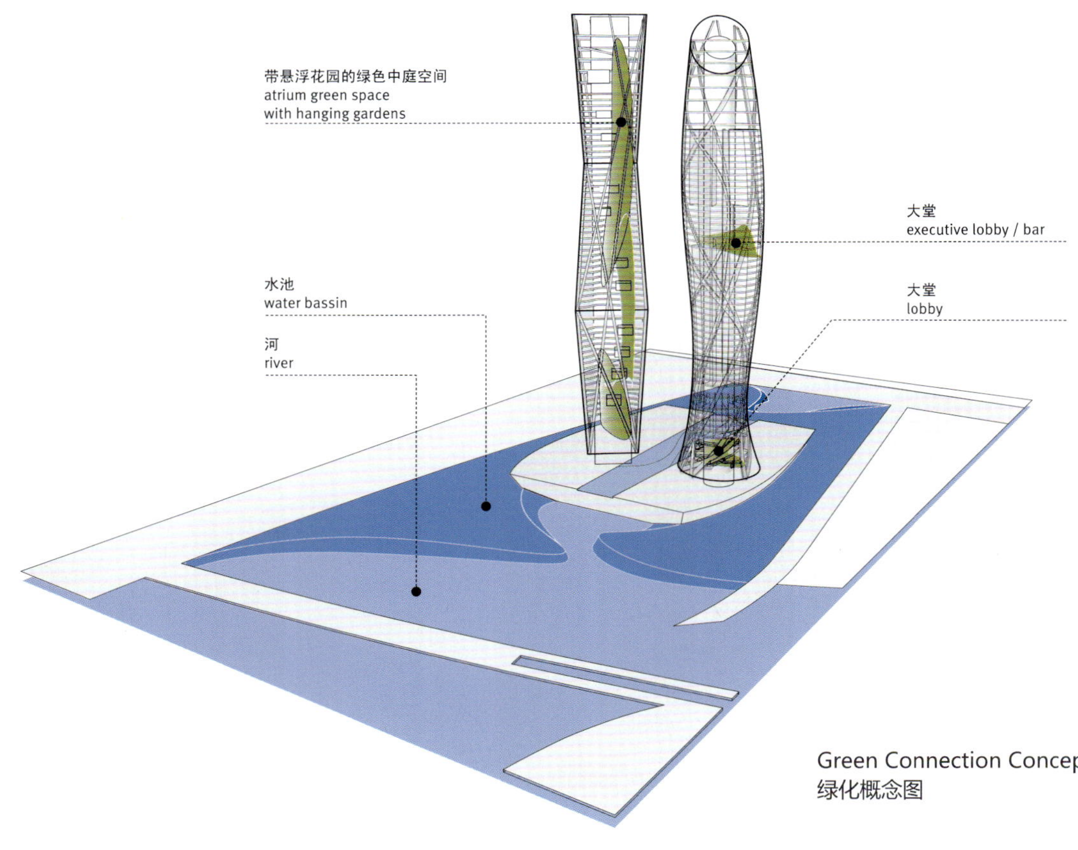

Green Connection Concept
绿化概念图

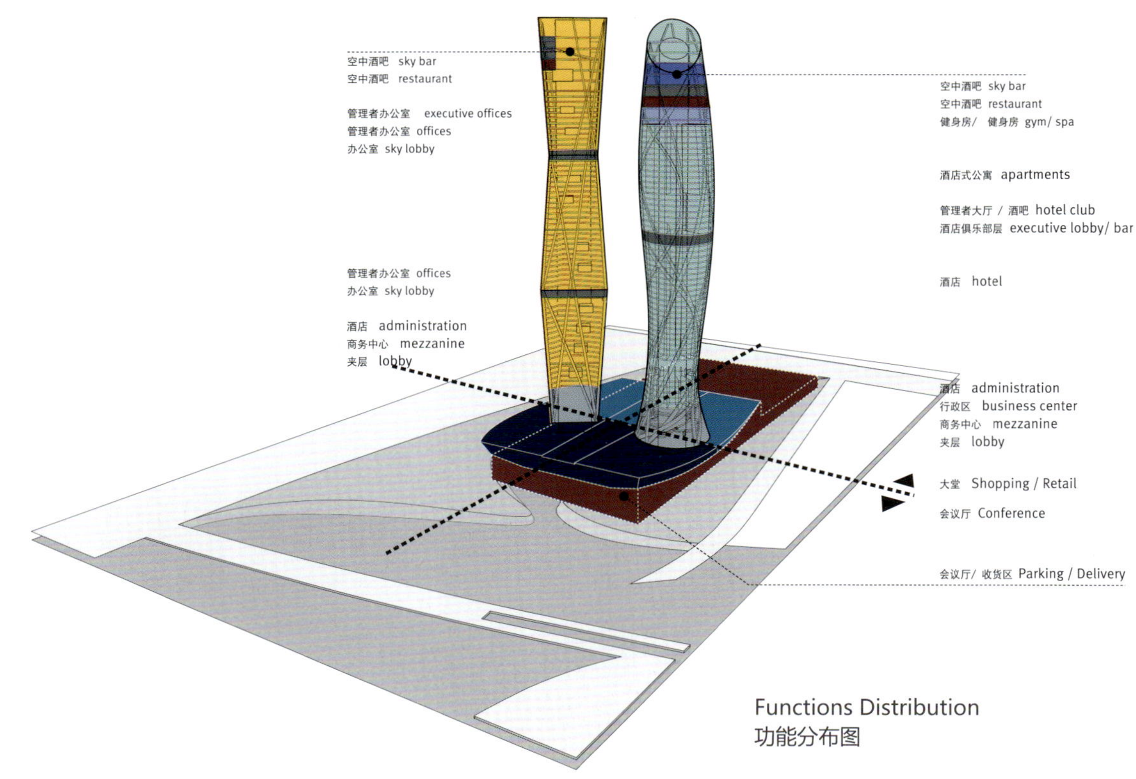

Functions Distribution
功能分布图

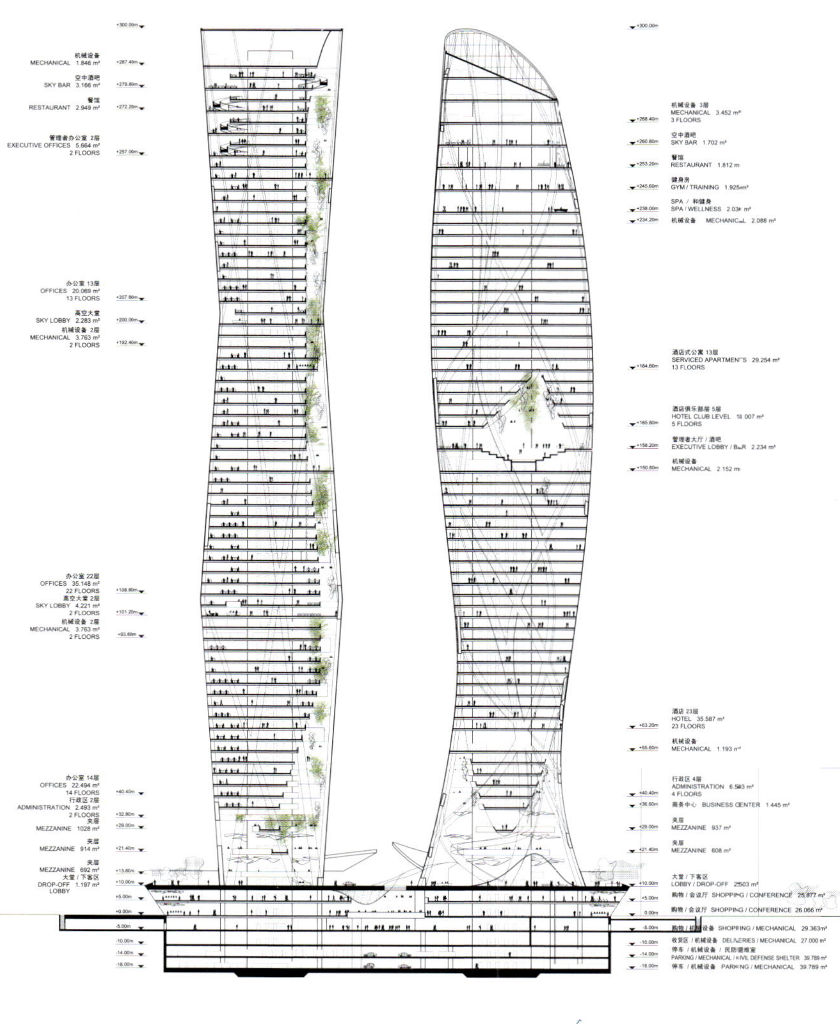

剖面图 Section A-A | 1:1000

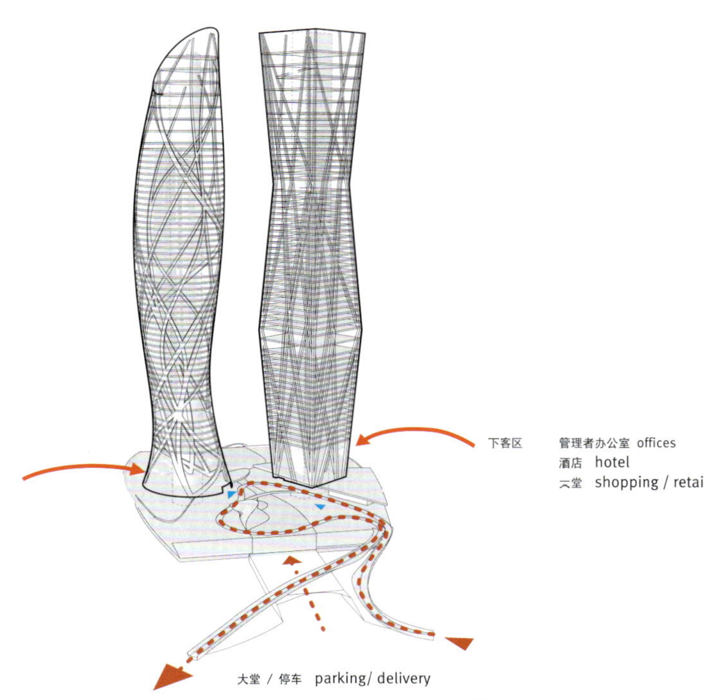

Traffic Circulation Diagram
交通流向图

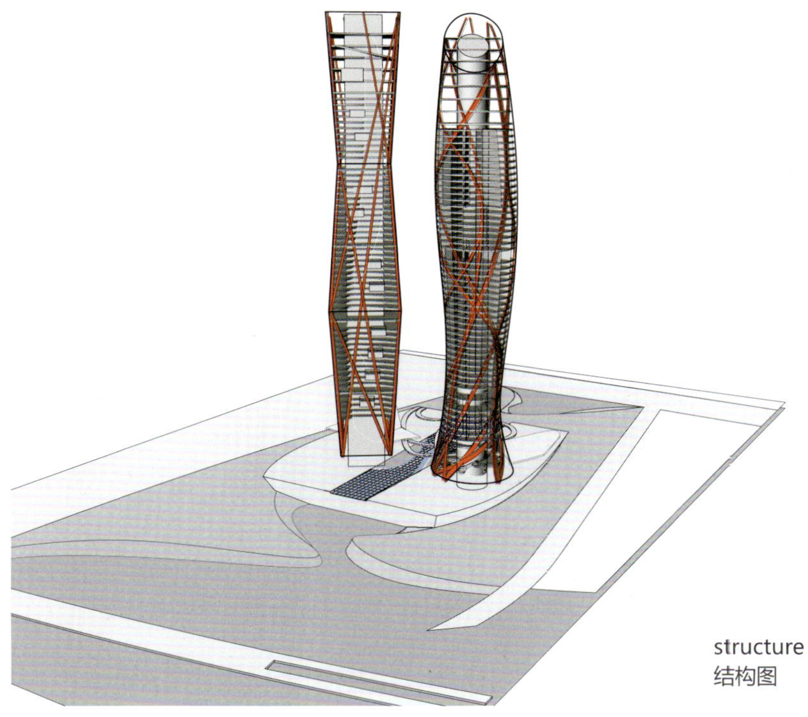

structure
结构图

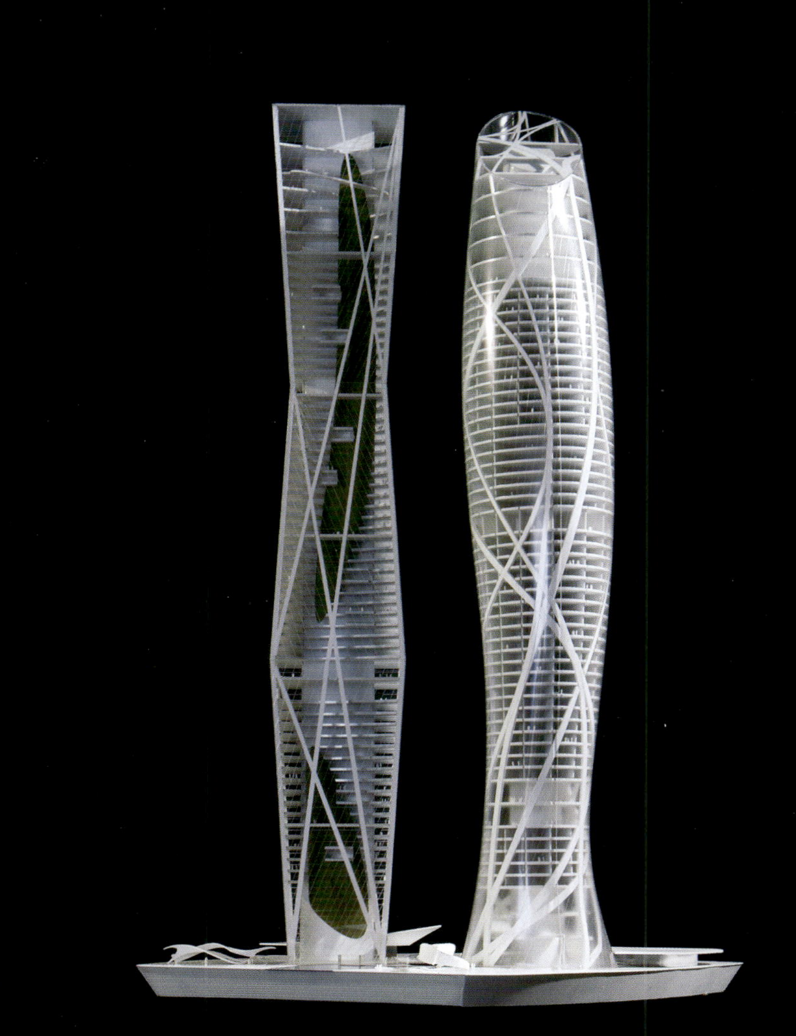

EastLake

Water—the source of Hangzhou's identity - is the source of orientation and serves to establish the identity for "Eastlake" as well as act as the main organizing feature for the mixed use medium and large scale buildings surrounding it. The confluence of the waterways of the QiJia River and LiMin River crossing on the site are expanded into a new central "lake" creating a pedestrian level experience focused on moving next to, around and over water in a lush landscape with distinct but changing perspectives to landmark building objects.

Verdant gardens and landscaping surround the lakeshore and line pathways used by pedestrians and automobiles connecting the various points of interest, plazas and entrances to buildings.The new "Eastlake", highlighted by the Two Pillars towers, is the symbolic main space of the district and becomes a distinct new urban venue in Hangzhou combining water, urban and leisure activities and a new representative architecture.

东湖

水——杭州的身份象征，是建筑物定向的依据，也是东湖的代表元素，还作为周围的大中型建筑的布局参照物。由Qijia河和Limin河交汇而成的河道穿过本案场地，并注入到新建的中央湖中，让湖边的行人能沿着、绕着湖边，或通过湖上的桥梁走进葱葱郁郁的风景中，周围的地标建筑也随着角度的变化而移步异景。

翠绿的花园和景观环绕着湖岸和各条小路，为行人和车辆连接各个景点、广场和各座建筑的入口。新东湖的最大亮点就是双子大楼，也是本案的象征性空间，更是杭州的新城市空间：一个水、城市、休闲活动和新地标建筑共存的地方。

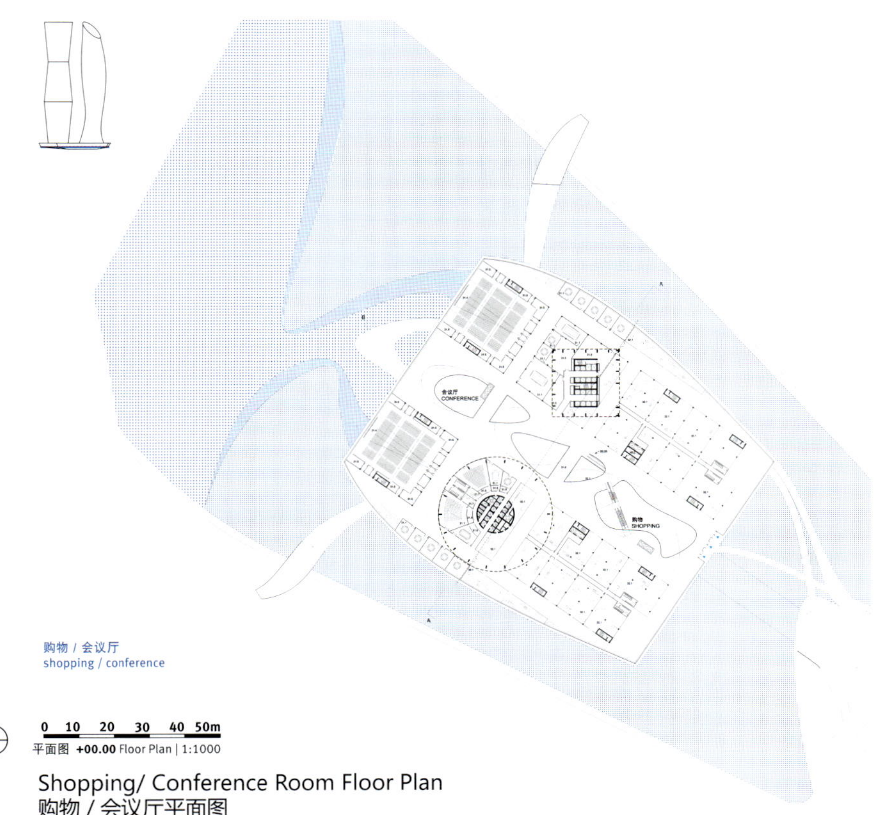

Shopping/ Conference Room Floor Plan
购物 / 会议厅平面图

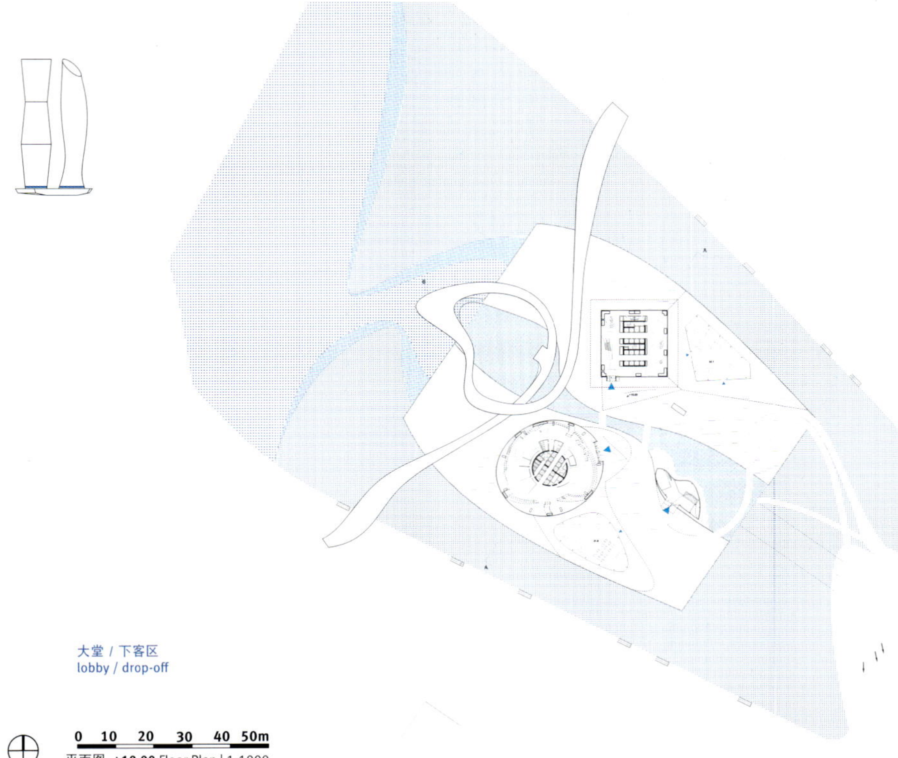

The Lobby/Area Under The Floor Plan
大堂 / 下客区平面图

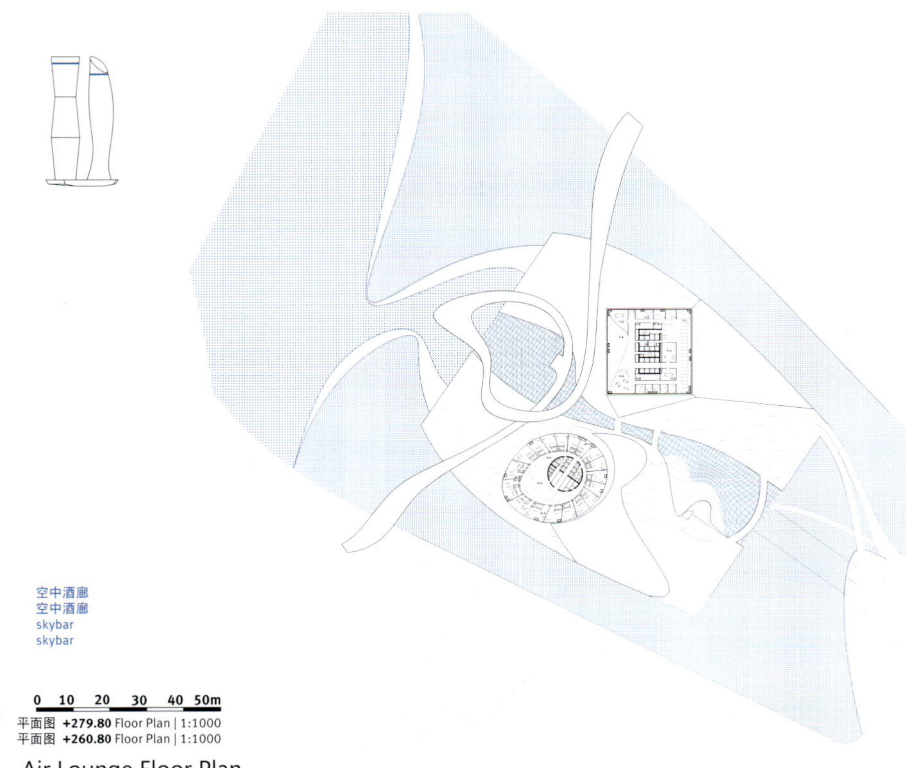

Air Lounge Floor Plan
空中酒廊平面图

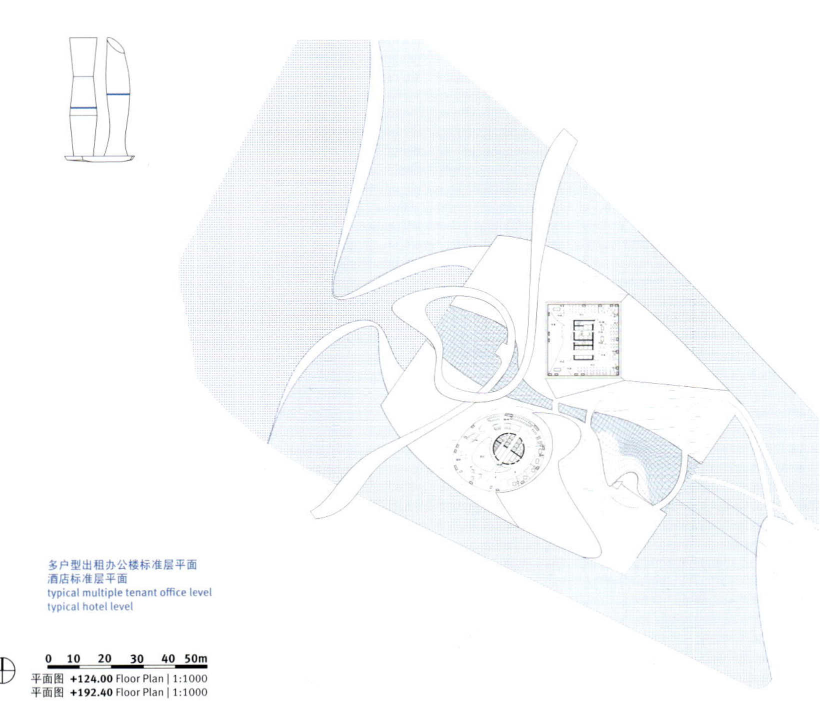

Multi-Family Rental For Gong Building/Hotel Standard Layer Of Floor Plan （请核对）
多户型出租帮贡楼 / 酒店标准层平面图

Towers - Balance and Dynamic Interaction

The Two Pillars towers are two sculpturally unique objects that work in tandem to form a single powerful image of the future Hangzhou. Inspired by the Pagodas and towers of Westlake, but reflective of the contemporary, dynamic era of Hangzhou, the paired objects use the concept of Composed Balance found in the perspectives of the Chinese Garden to create a positive tension between different elements. This unifying force created by a sculptural and dynamic relationship of solid and void and between the soft and hard shapes, creates visual balance in a manner more complex and nuanced than simple symmetry of two identical objects. The balanced poise of the two related bodies creates a situation of dynamic interaction and cooperation - a condition more reflective of the modern and dynamic future of Hangzhou

Boat-shaped Base

Functionally and formally the Two Pillars are placed on top of a boat-like podium floating in the center of Eastlake. Like the "Pagoda Boats" of Westlake, this "Boat" carries the new Twin Towers and serves as their functional podium. All access ways and support functions, such as shopping, conference, ballrooms and parking are located in the "Boat". Fluid bridges and pathways connect it to the shores of Eastlake and the multifunctional uses of the district.

双子大楼——平衡与动感的结合

双子大楼虽然是两座造型各异的个体，却又相互配合，创造出杭州强大的未来形象。项目灵感来源于杭州的传统塔楼，又希望表现出杭州现代、动感的新时代印象。中国园林中常用平衡对称的双数元素作为不同元素之间的缓冲。虚实空间之间的动态联系、软质与硬质景观之间能创造出视觉上的平衡，比两个完全相同的元素之间的简单对称更为复杂和微妙。这两座相互联系的大楼的平衡造型就模拟出了互动与合作——更能反应出杭州现代与动感的未来形象。

船型底座

东湖中心上漂浮着一座船型底座，双子大楼就是建造在此底座之上。如同西湖的“宝塔船”一样，这个船型底座承载着新建的双子大楼，并作为其附带的功能裙楼，承担着作为进出通道和购物、会议、宴会、停车等各种辅助功能。流动的小桥和小路将底座连接到东湖岸边和此多功能区域。

Towers -Function and Identity

Reflecting their different respective functions of Office and Hotel, and like "Brother and Sister", the two towers each have a different geometric principal but share a common architectural language. They are different corresponding to their function, but work together so that the overall effect is more than the sum of the parts.

The Office tower is a faceted form of three truncated pyramids alternating on top of each other, while the Hotel tower is a fluid, ellipse-based cylindrical tower whose profile changes in an elegant flow from top to bottom. The soft form and 3-dimensionality of the Hotel tower is reflected in the inner atrium void of the Office tower, and the negative space between the two towers is seen as a virtual "third tower" connecting the two objects into one. The sculpted void space of the "third tower"between the two pillars plays as important a role in the composition as the solid objects do themselves.

Structural Description

The Twin Tower Hang Zhou building project is a highrise structure with 2 towers with a height of 300m and around 70 storeys.The round tower houses mechanical floors, a sky bar and restaurant on the top, 13 floors of residences and a hotel in the middle and lower part, with an atrium over 5 floors and technical floors for mechanical services in the middle and the lower quarter. The elliptic footprint of the tower has a diameter of 50 to 60 m.The quadratic tower houses also mechanical floors, a sky bar and restaurant on the top and offices down to the basement with technical floors for mechanical services in the thirds. The quadratic footprint has a side-length of 37 meters. The basement contains three stories of shopping and conference centre, one story for delivery and mechanical and two stories of parking area, The dimensions of the base are 165 meter x 190 meter.

双子大楼——功能和特征

为表现出双子大楼的不同功能——办公大楼和酒店大楼，两座大楼就如“兄妹”般有自己独自的几何特征，又享有共同的建筑语言。它们各自对应自己的建筑功能，又相互配合工作，产生的协同效果自然比各自独立工作更为高效。

办公大楼的立面由三个楼锥三角形组成的面彼此向上叠加而成；酒店大楼则是椭圆底座、流线型的圆柱造型，从下到上表现出优雅的波浪曲线变化。酒店大楼的柔软形态和立体造型和办公大楼内部中庭的宽阔空间相互呼应。两座大楼之间的负空间在视觉上就如同“第三座大楼”。这座“第三座大楼”就如同有实体一般，在整体构成中起到了重要的作用。

结构概述

杭州东湖双子大楼为超高层建筑，高达 300 米，共 70 层。圆形大楼包括机电层、顶层的空中酒吧和餐厅、13 层公寓住宅、一家包揽中下层的酒店等，5 楼之上还有一座中庭，机械层位于建筑的中下部分。椭圆形的底座直径达 50~60 米。另一座大楼也设置了机电层和顶层空中酒吧及餐厅，从上层到地下层全为办公空间，其中第 3 层为机械层。该大楼的底座单边长达 37 米。地下层包括 3 层的购物和会议空间、一层运输和机械层及 2 层的停车场。底座的面积为 165 米 x 190 米。

PROJECT NAME 项目名称

NINGBO YINZHOU SOUTHERN CBD PORTAL

宁波鄞州南部商务区门户区

Architect: amphibianArc

设计公司：amphibianArc

PROJECT INFORMATION 项目信息

Chint	Ningbo, Yinzhou cuban construction investment and Development corporation	**客户**	宁波鄞州区城市建设发展公司
Location	Ningbo, Zhejiang Province, China	**地点**	中国浙江省宁波市
Area	710,000 m^2	**面积**	710，000 平方米

OVERVIEW 项目概况

The project is located in the southernmost tip of Yinzhou Southern CBD, north to Tai'an East Road, east to Tiantong South Road, west to Ningnan South Road, and south to of Huanqiu City plot. The plan emphasizes the strategic position of the portal area while facilitating its urban center feature. Based on transit-oriented development model, it also seeks to create a new regional center around the transportation hub, so as to maximize the urban public space and to achieve vertical sustainable development of the landscape levels. With Ningbo being one of the starting points of the Maritime Silk Road, the booming economy of Yinzhou plays a critical role in both the ancient and the modern trade routes. So the planning concept draws inspiration from the Silk Road, as a manifestation of Chinese cultural heritage.

本项目位于鄞州南部商务区最南端，北至泰安东路，东到天童南路，西靠宁南南路，南面为环球城地块。规划强调门户区的战略重点地位，深化塑造都市中心功能的城市意向。并围绕交通枢纽中心，创造一个T.O.D的新型发展模式的区域中心，实现城市公共空间最大化、景观层次纵向可持续发展的都市发展计划。宁波是海上丝绸之路的起点之一，而鄞州的蓬勃经济无论是在古代丝绸之路或现代商路都占居了重要地位。本规划故以“丝绸之路”作为设计概念，以促成历史文化的延续。

FEATURE ANALYSIS 特色分析

ARCHITECT
Nonchi Wang

设计师
王弄極

As an urban design for a new urban plot in the early stage, architects play a game of form with use of some cutting-edge urban form and organization as well as architectural concept in the design plan. Some architects having a good command of latest modelling technology tend to be handy with facility in their exploration into form of buildings when they are armed with increasingly updated design software. The shaping of curvy stand-alone comes along with integration of wall, floor plates and other components that speak to each other. The project is an expression of rising of a new aesthetic genre achieved by new technology.

作为一个城市新区区块的前期城市设计，建筑师在其中玩了一次形式游戏。他们将一些前卫的城市形态组织和建筑理念运用到本方案中，随着设计软件的更新换代，掌握着最新建模技术的公司往往在建筑形式的探索上能够更加得心应手。本方案中建筑单体曲面的塑造，联系性的墙体楼板的融合等等，体现了一种新技术带来的新的审美流派的兴起。

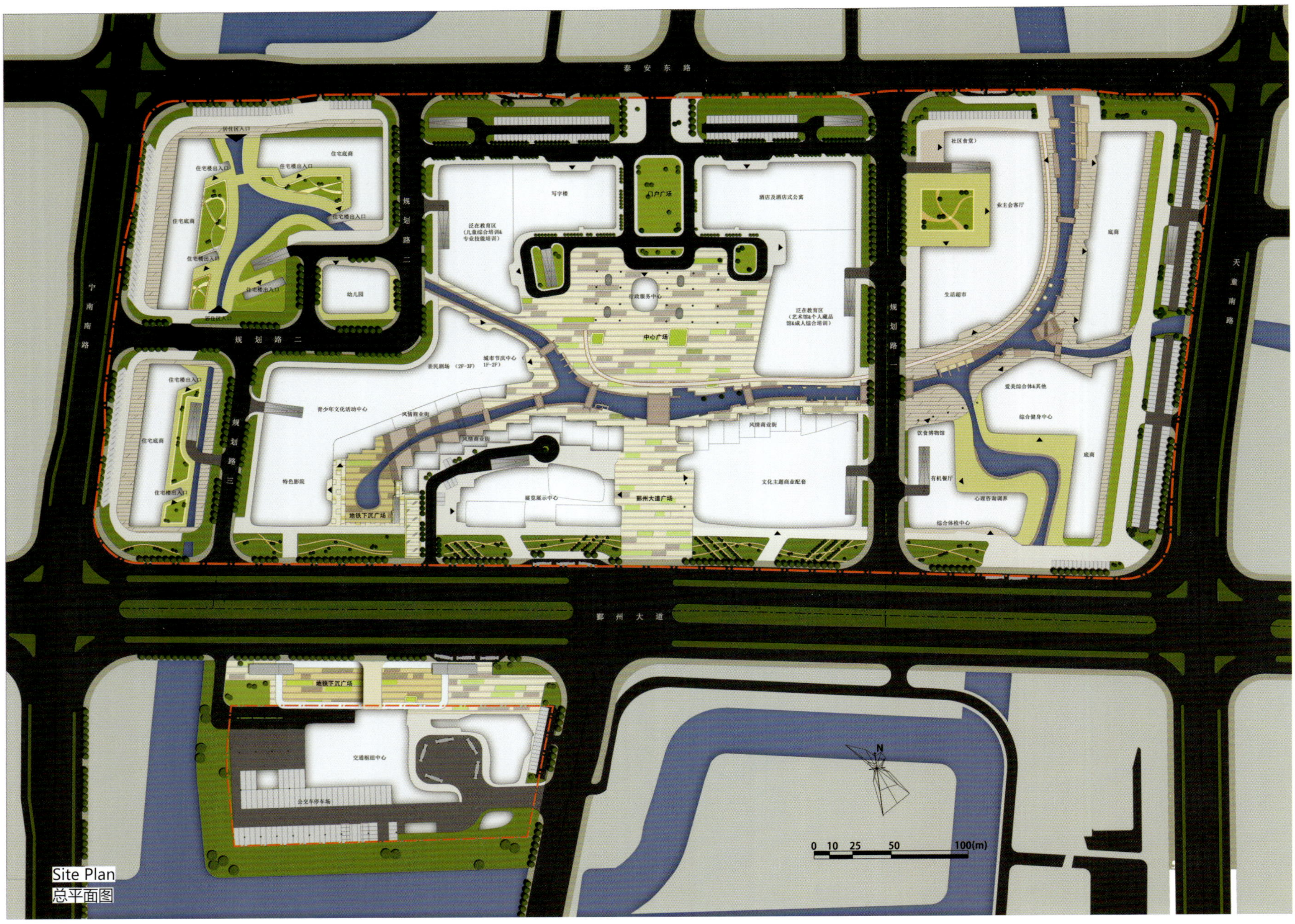

Site Plan
总平面图

In January 2014, amphibianArc won first prize in the Ningbo Yinzhou Southern CBD Portal Project Planning Design Competition. The competition was commissioned by Ningbo Yinzhou Urban Construction Investment and Development Corporation, who is responsible for successfully implementing the Ningbo Museum project designed by Wang Shu. The subject of the competition was the fourth phase of the Ningbo Yinzhou Southern CBD, the Portal Project. The winning plan is not only a successful summary of the first three developing phases of the CBD, but a driving force for the area's future dynamic urban life. Six international design firms from China, U.S. and France participated in the competition, including URBANUS.

The plan divides the buildings of the site into two categories. The first category is the main buildings, including the Twin Towers, the Public Service Center, the Museum, the Customs Street and the Transportation Hub. The five main buildings have the most highlighted features and body mass. With different styles and forms, they compose a diversified group, unfolding a variety of environments and cultural characters. The second category is the background buildings, including the shopping center at the Vibrant Culture Area, the education center at the Pan-asian Education Area, the health center at the Holographic Health Area and the residential apartments at the Commercial & Residential Area. Simple changes in the body mass and building facades are utilized in the design of these buildings to set off the distinctive and diverse manifestations of the main buildings.

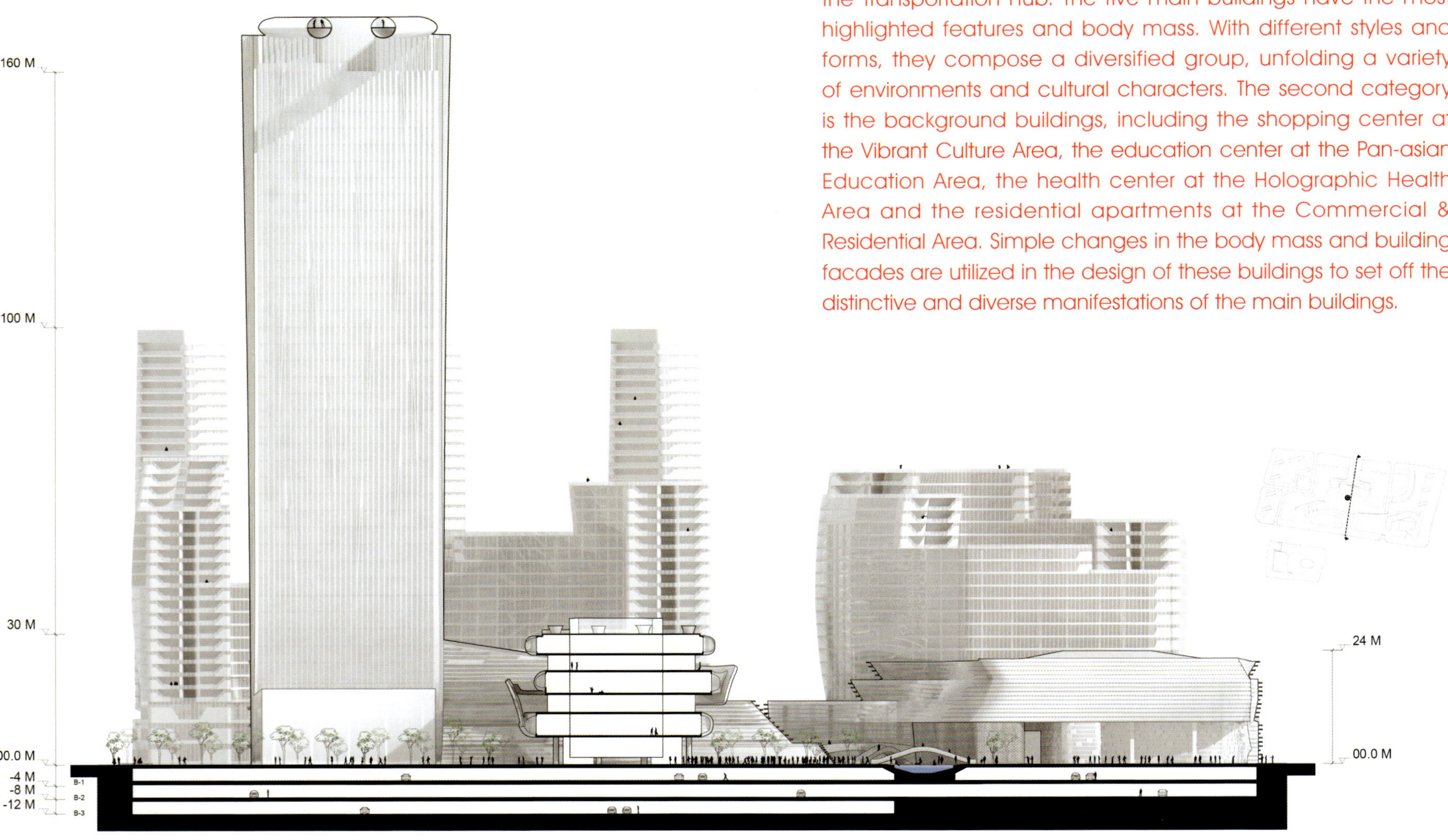

Section C
剖面图 C

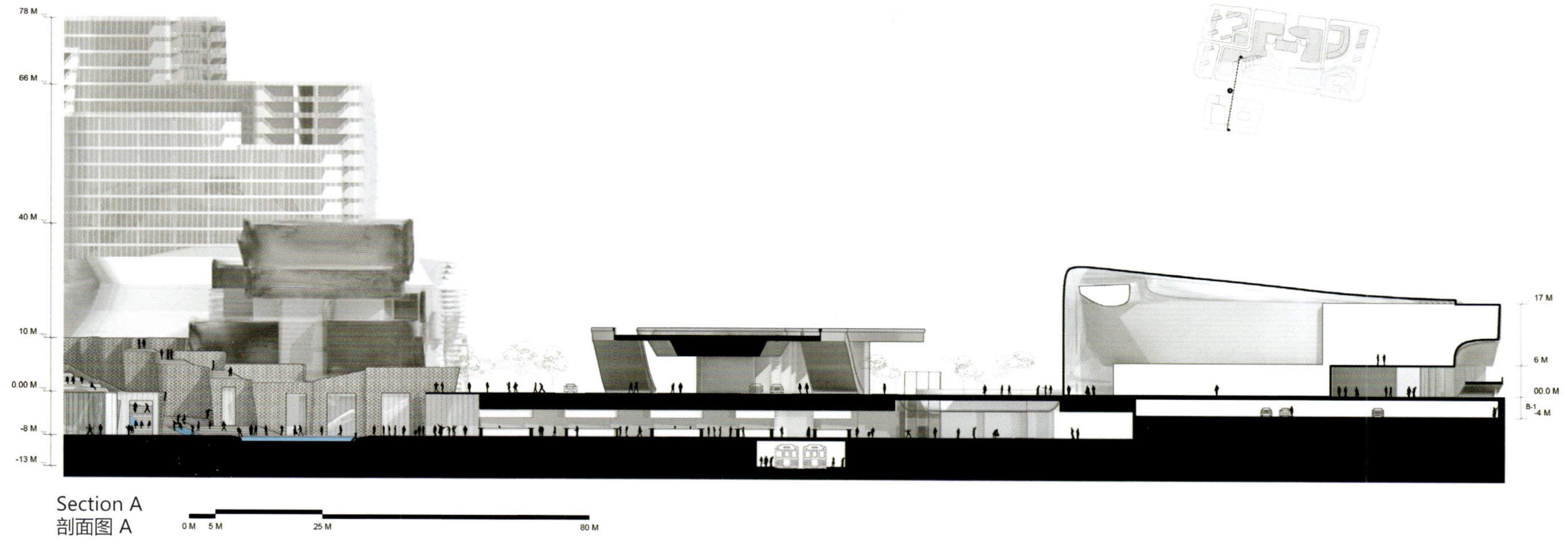

Section A
剖面图 A

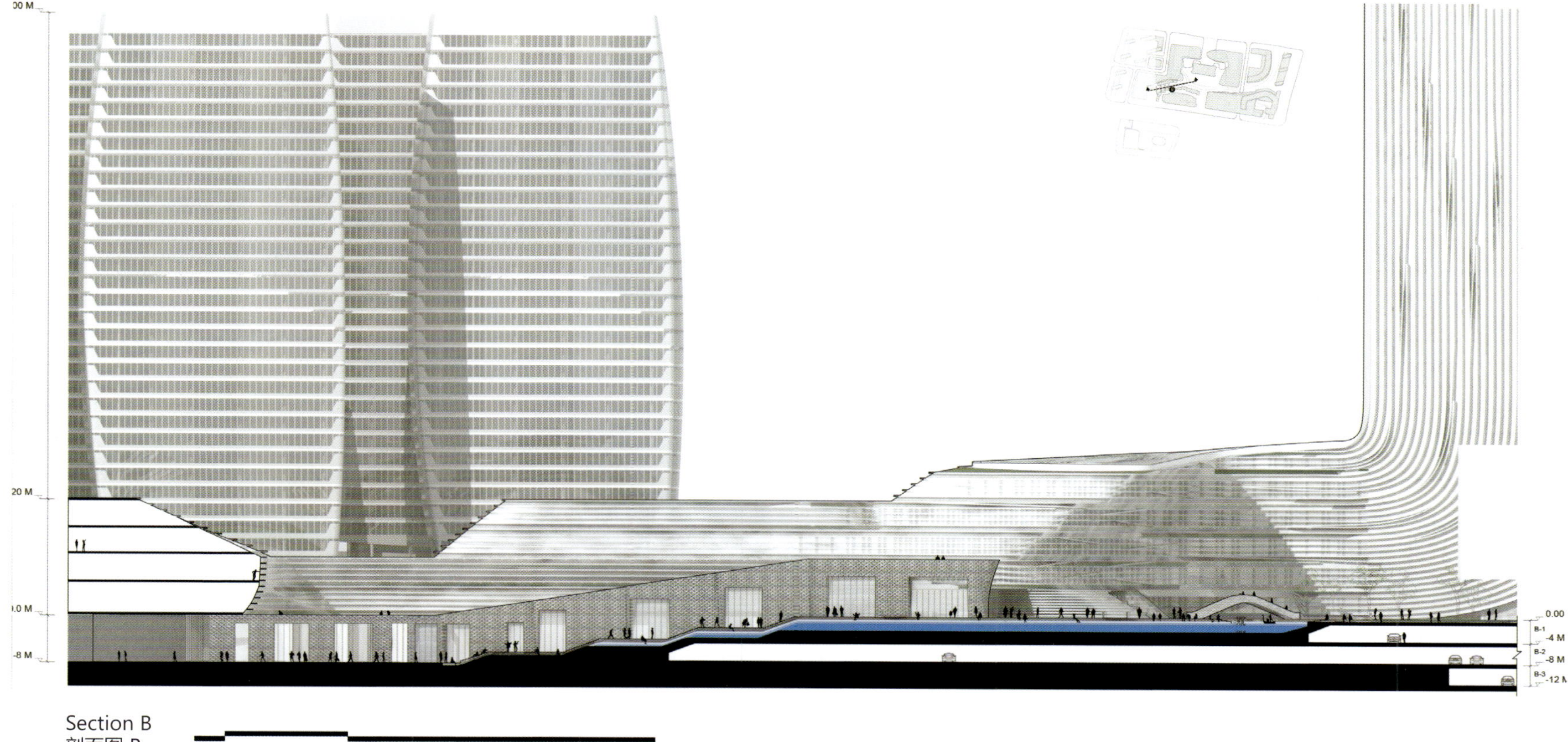

Section B
剖面图 B

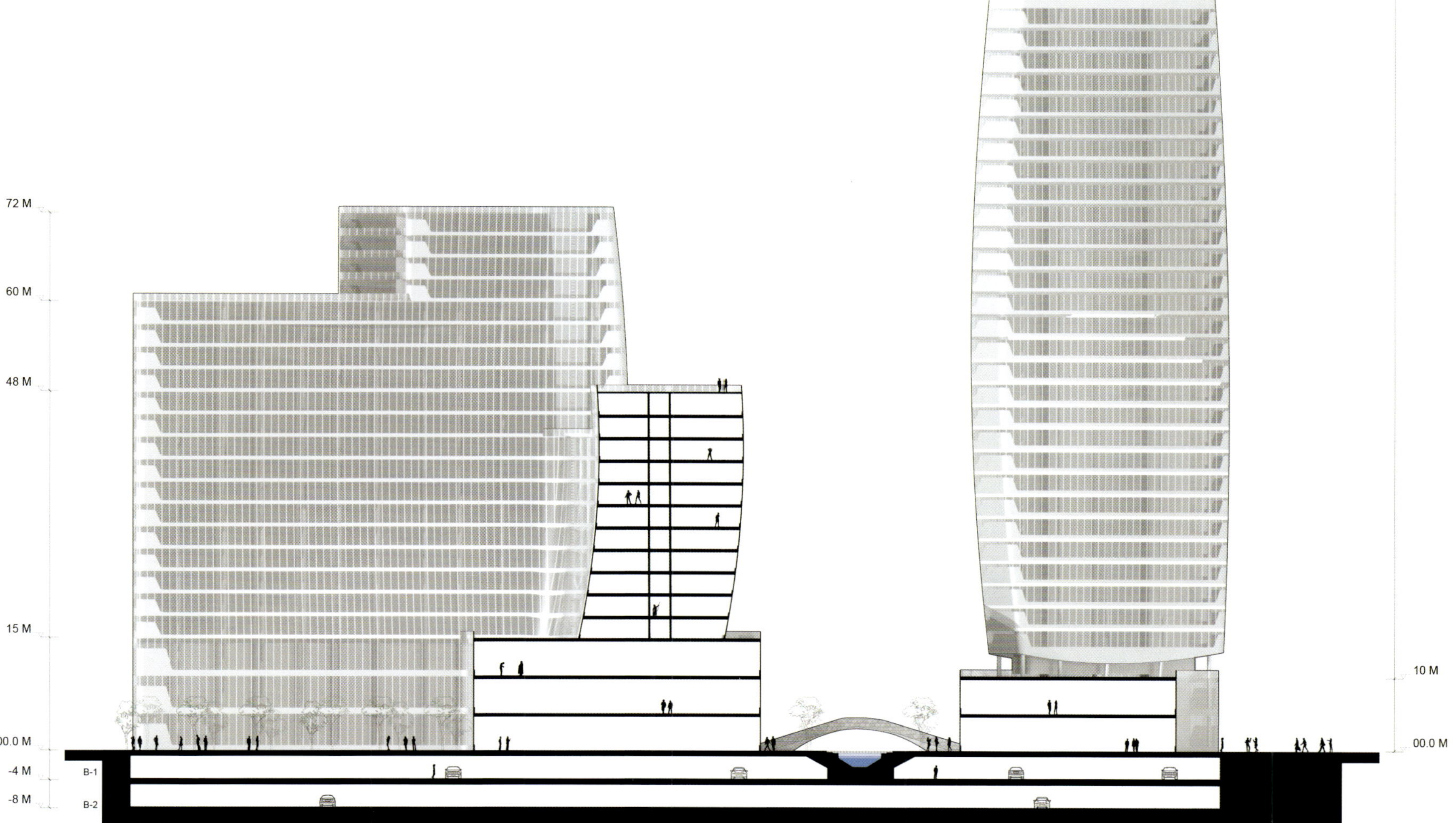

Section D
剖面图 D

Location Plan
区位图

2014年1月，amphibianArc的方案赢得了宁波鄞州南部商务区门户区项目概念规划设计竞赛一等奖。本城市竞赛甲方是宁波市鄞州区城市建设投资发展公司，他们曾经成功实施了王澍设计的宁波博物馆项目。竞赛设计对象是宁波鄞州南部商务区四期——门户区项目。此项目既是对商务区前三期开发的成功总结，也将成为未来都市生活新的活力引擎。竞赛邀请了包括都市实践在内的中美法六家国际设计团队参赛。

规划将建筑分为两类：第一类是主建筑，包括门户双塔、市民服务中心、展览馆、风情街和交通枢纽。这五个主要建筑功能或体量最突出，且各具风格，形式不一，是一个多元的组合，展现出不同的环境和人文气息。第二类是背景建筑，包括活力文化区中的购物中心、泛亚教育区中的教育中心、全息健康区中的健康中心及商务居住区的公寓或住宅。背景建筑以简单的体量变化和建筑立面处理，烘托主建筑，在主建筑多元的表现中达到协调陪衬的作用。

DENNIS

COMMERCIAL COMPLEX REAL ESTATE

商业型复合地产

Behind this concept is the idea to promote the interaction of this natural element and the human made systematic, valuate the attracting wildness by combining it with a background of dignity, capture a fragile moment of beauty into a frame of eternity.

方案的概念是促进自然元素和人造体系间的相互作用，以结合纯粹的设计理念来应对极具吸引力的繁杂，将美丽的瞬间凝固在永恒的画框之中。

SPARK

SPARK 思邦

The stylish and cool-looking pleated skin working with gigantic volume looks striking in the city. Interior space and interior design present a clear style. The purple automatic escalator catches eyeballs.

外观上时髦酷炫的折叠表皮配合其大体量在城市中格外显眼。内部环境中空间和内饰设计风格明快，紫色调自动扶梯非常抢眼。

130 SHIJIAZHUANG WONDER MALL 石家庄万象天成

amphibianArc

双栖弧建筑设计公司

The architects create a commercial complex with a brand new look different from others with constrained construction technology in China and via a unique design. What is more, the project delivers another highlight, a clever use of lighting design which complements the expression of architectural curve skin and forms a speech that speaks to building's commercial property. A powerful sense of landmark is shown.

设计师们运用在国内可行的技术建构手段通过设计的方式得出一种不同于一般商业综合体建筑的全新风貌。同时本项目的另一个亮点在于灯光设计的运用，其很好地烘托了建筑曲线型表皮的表现力，与建筑的商业属性相得益彰，地标感强烈。

FUZHOU WUSIBEI THAIHOT PLAZA 福州五四北泰禾广场 120

5+design, Inc

五杰建筑设计

ZIBO LIVING MALL 淄博华润五彩城 152

There are several differences designing retail projects in the west versus in Asia, particularly in China. The retail mix and tenant types are obviously different to suit the local markets.

亚洲与西方在设计商业型项目方面存在几处差别，尤其以中国的商业型项目更加突出。为了迎合当地市场需求，亚洲与西方的商业型项目在功能匹配与租户类型方面存在明显差别。

142

HPP

HPP

QUANZHOU WANDA PLAZA 泉州万达广场

The new Quanzhou Wanda Plaza is located at one of the cities' most extraordinary locations, directly at the Jinjiang River, noble at day and shiny at night time. The scheme is respecting and defining the natural and urban space. The entire design is made by highlighting the most present element of the surrounding nature element "water".

由于泉州万达广场坐落在锦江河边，一个非凡的城市地理位置，白天显得高贵而晚上霓虹闪烁，为了使环境与自然更加和谐，设计强调了周边最有代表性的自然元素"水"。

SHENZHEN VANKE ONE CITY 深圳万科壹海城 160

5+design, Inc

五杰建筑设计

The abstract narrative defined each of the facades, creating a unifying layer that was able to transition between each of the parcels.

抽象的立面展现创造出统一、协调的韵律，从而使各地块前呼后应，过渡自然。

Perkins Eastman

Perkins Eastman

建筑设计事务所

HUIZHOU HUAMAO CENTER 惠州华贸中心 168

SANYA CHINA RAILWAY SUNSHINE PLACE 三亚中铁子悦薹

TongJi Architects (TJA)

深圳市同济人建筑设计有限公司

Residential areas are arranged around the square in a pinwheel fashion, which creates a dynamic flow to the scheme. Townhouse apartments feature retail lots at the lower levels, forming the podiums for the fifty-story residential towers that pierce the sky above the city skyline and create an iconic landmark within the city.

住宅区以旋转风车的时尚结构排列在广场四周，为整个设计方案形成了一种动感的流线结构。联排别墅式公寓的底层设有零售商店，形成 50 层住宅楼的裙楼，在城市天际线三方直直插入云霄，为这个城市打造一个极具标志性的地标建筑。

CHENGDU BACK GARDEN PHASE 4 成都后花园 4 期

As a community commercial complex, it not only offers neighboring residents an easy life and a prime quality of development but also delivers a good supporting environment for business, office, serviced apartment at the later stage of development.

缤纷城不仅保证了周边居住区的生活便利、楼盘品质，更为后期开发的商务办公、酒店式公寓提供了良好的配套环境。

Australia PT Design Consultants Limited

澳大利亚柏涛建筑设计有限公司 180

Inspired from "Urban landscape", designers expect to create a unique commercial project by imitating enjoyable scenery found in Chinese traditional painting, with architectural fengshui theory serving as the tutor for architectural layout and function.

"城市山水"，设计师们希望能借鉴国画写意山水的意境，让建筑的布局和功能在建筑风水学的指导下成为一个不同的商业项目。

176

BEIJING GREENLAND COLORFUL TOWN 北京绿地缤纷城 190

UA International

UA 国际

A series of public facilities are arranged under the roof, showing the respect for roof space design in marseille apartments that made by Le Corbusier.The neighboring office building adopts the exaggerated setback structure, showing the unique features fully.

屋顶下是一系列公共活动设施，仿佛一种对柯布时期马赛公寓开发屋顶空间的一个致敬。紧邻地块的办公塔楼采取了一种夸张的退台形式。向所处环境努力展现出一种与众不同的存在感。

PROJECT NAME 项目名称

FUZHOU WUSIBEI THAIHOT PLAZA
福州五四北泰禾广场

Architect: SPARK 思邦
设计公司：SPARK 思邦

PROJECT INFORMATION 项目信息

Project Director	Jan Felix Clostermann	**项目总监**	Jan Felix Clostermann
Client	Thaihot Group	**客户**	泰禾集团
Location	FuZhou, China	**地点**	中国福州
Gross Floor Area	300,000 m^2 (Above ground: 212,600m^2, basement: 87,400m^2 Commercial: 100,890m^2 SOHO: 199,110m^2)	**总建筑面积**	300，000 平方米（其中地上建筑面积 212，600 平方米，地下建筑面积 87，400 平方米；商业：100，890 平方米，SOHO 199，110 平方米）
photography	ShuHe	**摄影**	ShuHe

OVERVIEW 项目概况

Fuzhou Wusibei Thaihot Plaza's central location at WuSi Bei Dajie, Jinan District makes it Fuzhou's most successful retail mall. Its design enhanced Thaihot's brand as a forward thinking innovative retail developer. SPARK's design entwines the plaza, the street and the mall interior into a continuous circulation route that transforms the building into a living entity full of movement and energy. 12-hour daytime retail activities are concentrated in a 7-level shopping mall from which routes to the rooftop are carved out. Here various activities such as full service dining and cinema effectively create 24-hour traffic-free streets and squares attracting visitors not only to shop but also enjoy as a new social and entertainment destination.

福州五四北泰禾广场位于福州核心区位五四北大街秀峰路，独特的区位优势使之成为福州最成功的购物中心。设计彰显并强调了泰禾作为具有前瞻性视野的零售商业开发商的独特品牌特征。SPARK 思邦的设计将广场、街道和商场内部等元素有机地糅合成了一个环形的延续路径，并于此将建筑转换成了一个充满动感和能量的有机个体。每天 12 小时的购物活动主要集中在一座 7 层的商场内，自下而上流线型的动线设计将引导着顾客通往商场的顶层，当这里全天候的餐饮娱乐和电影院等设施全部启动时，商场内便出现了一道 24 小时人流穿梭、熙熙攘攘于集市间的独特风景，这不仅吸引着游客们纷纷来此驻足休憩、购物休闲，更使得这里成为了人们社交娱乐的新地标。

FEATURE ANALYSIS 特色分析

ARCHITECT
Stephen Pimbley

设计师
史蒂芬 · 平博理

Among malls found in all today's cities and in a time of fierce competition, to set a mall apart from others and attract flows of people lie in distinguished form and richer spatial experience. Fuzhou Thaihot project realized both interior and exterior success. The stylish and cool-looking pleated skin working with gigantic volume looks striking in the city. Interior space and interior design present a clear style. The purple automatic escalator catches eyeballs. A wide range of new skin materials have been used, delivering a distinguished look. It is of a masterpiece of large-sized mall.

在商业 mall 在各大城市随处可见的今天，在竞争空前激烈的今天，一个 mall 要想脱颖而出吸引更多的客流一定要在形式上更加突出，在空间上、体验性上比对手更佳。福州泰禾的项目由内而外做到了这两点。外观上时髦酷炫的折叠表皮配合其大体量在城市中格外显眼。内部环境中空间和内饰设计风格明快，紫色调自动扶梯非常抢眼。多种新型表皮材料的使用也别具一格，属于大型 mall 中的佳作。

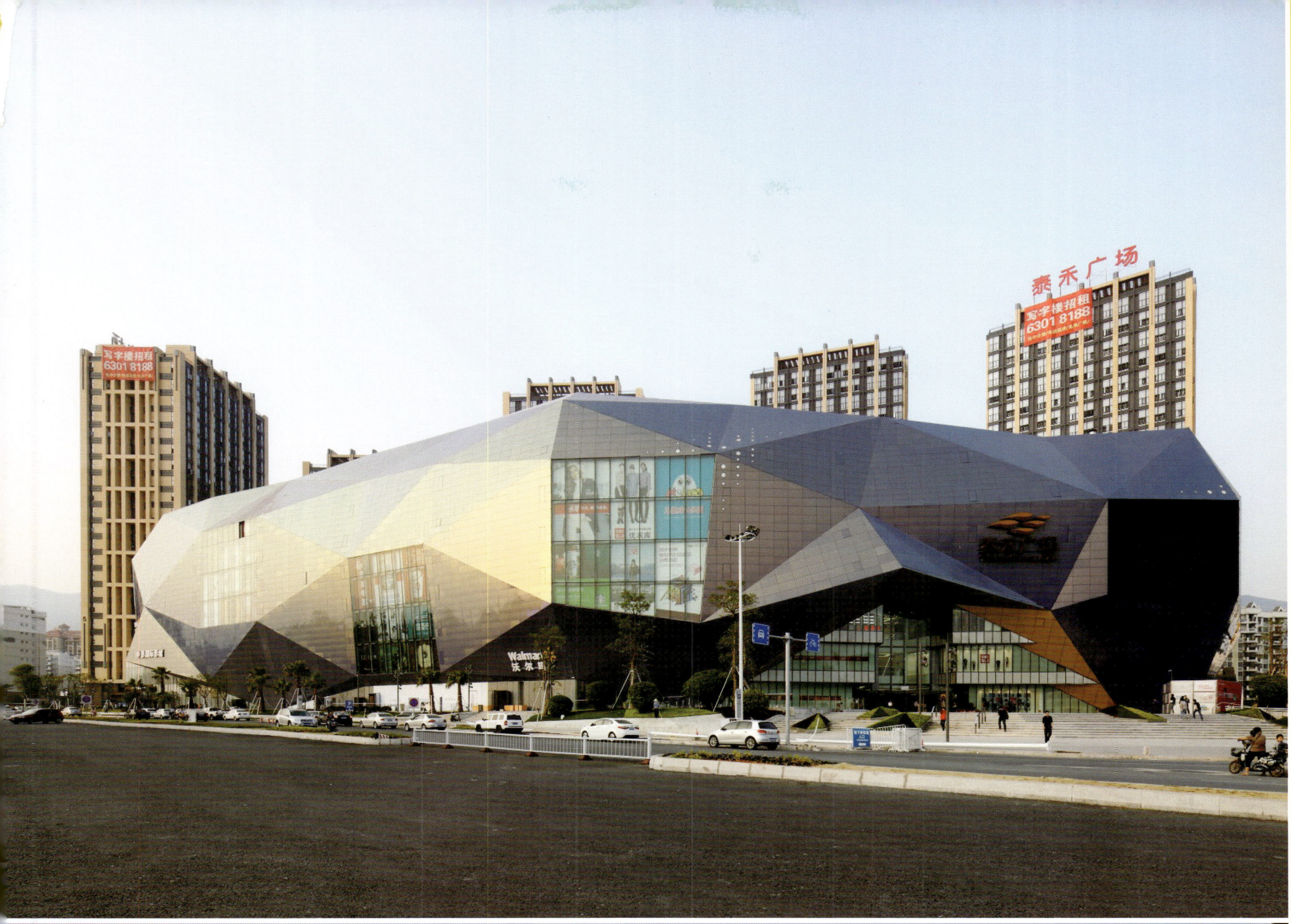

泰禾广场
写字楼招租
6301 8188
Walmart

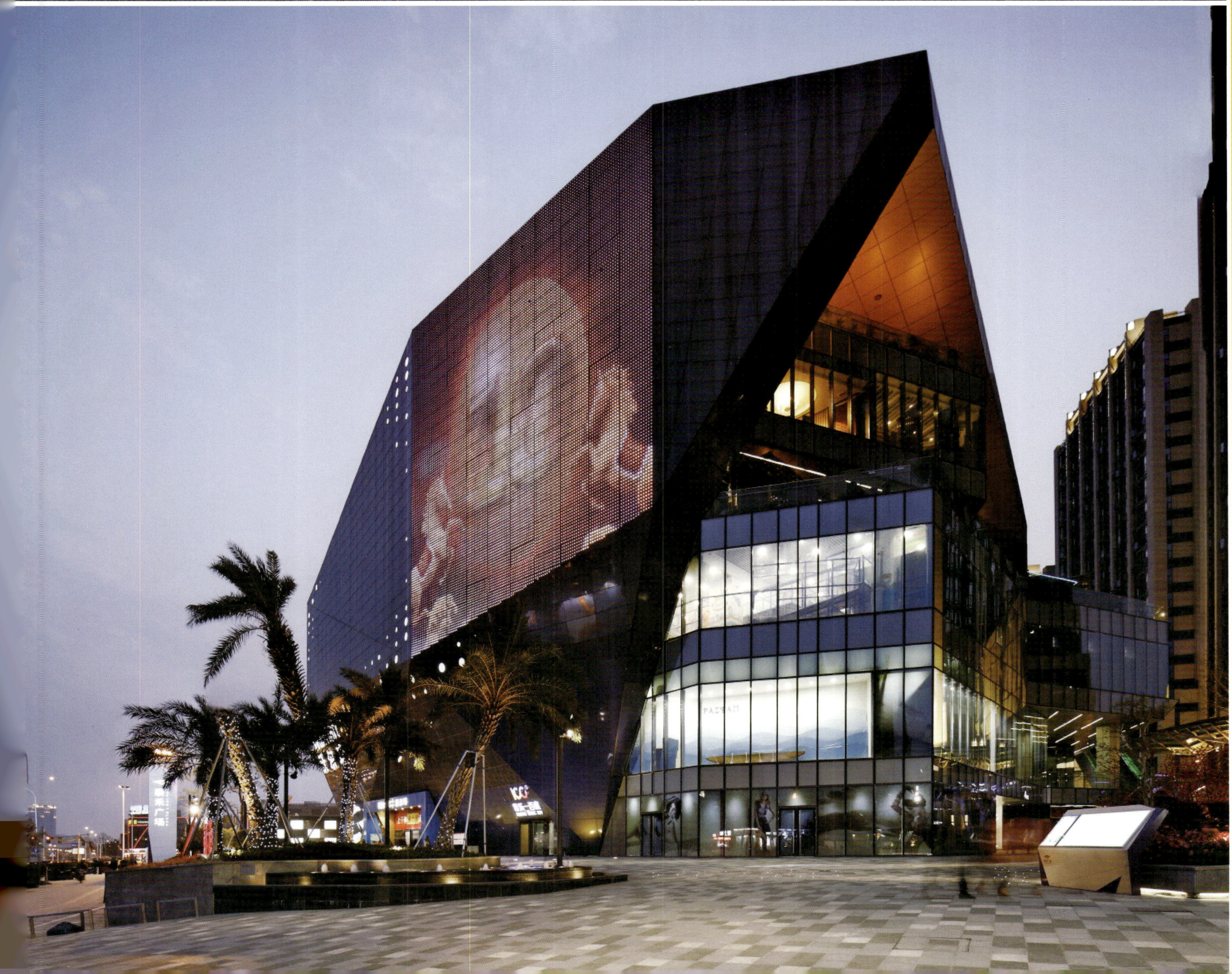

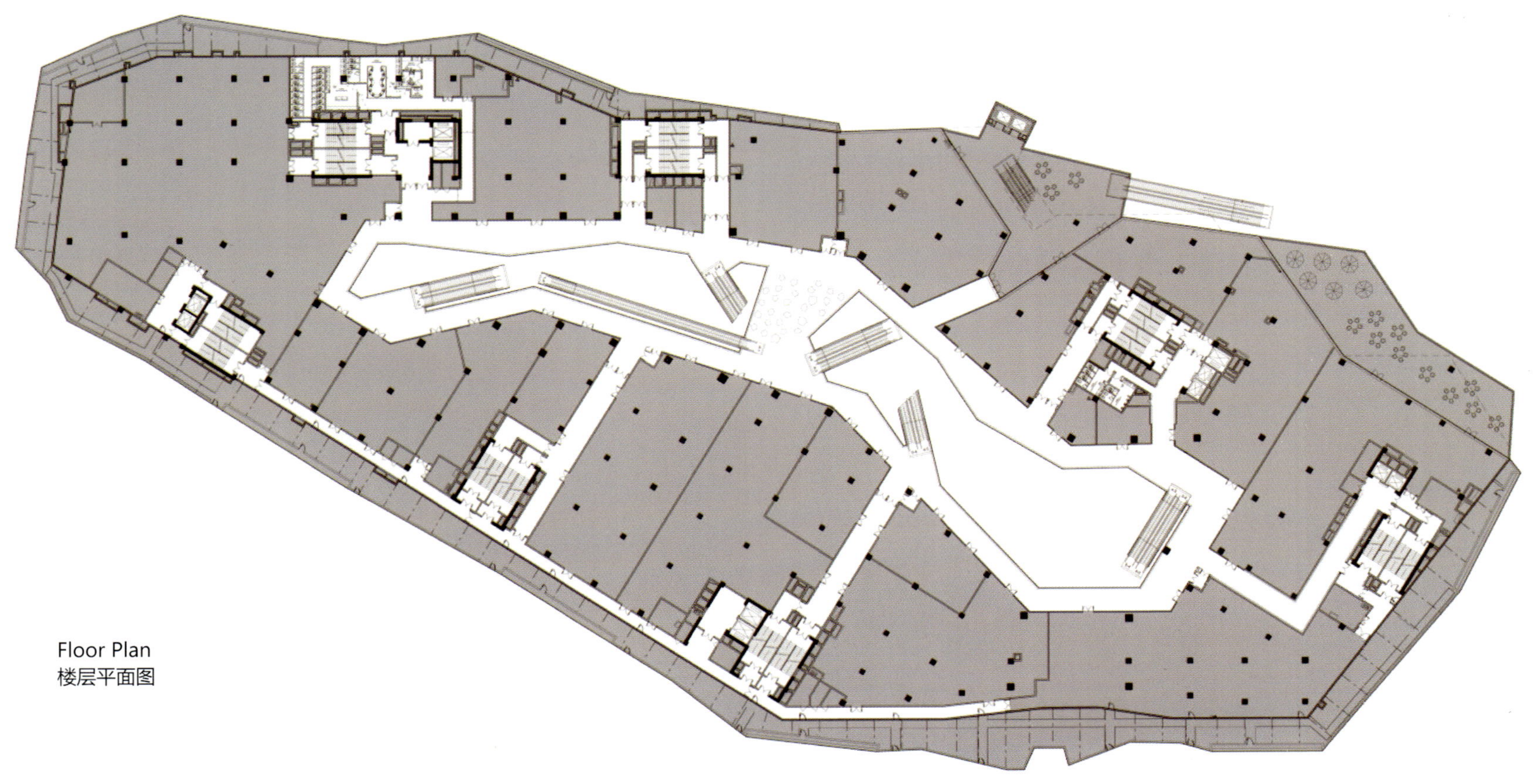
Floor Plan
楼层平面图

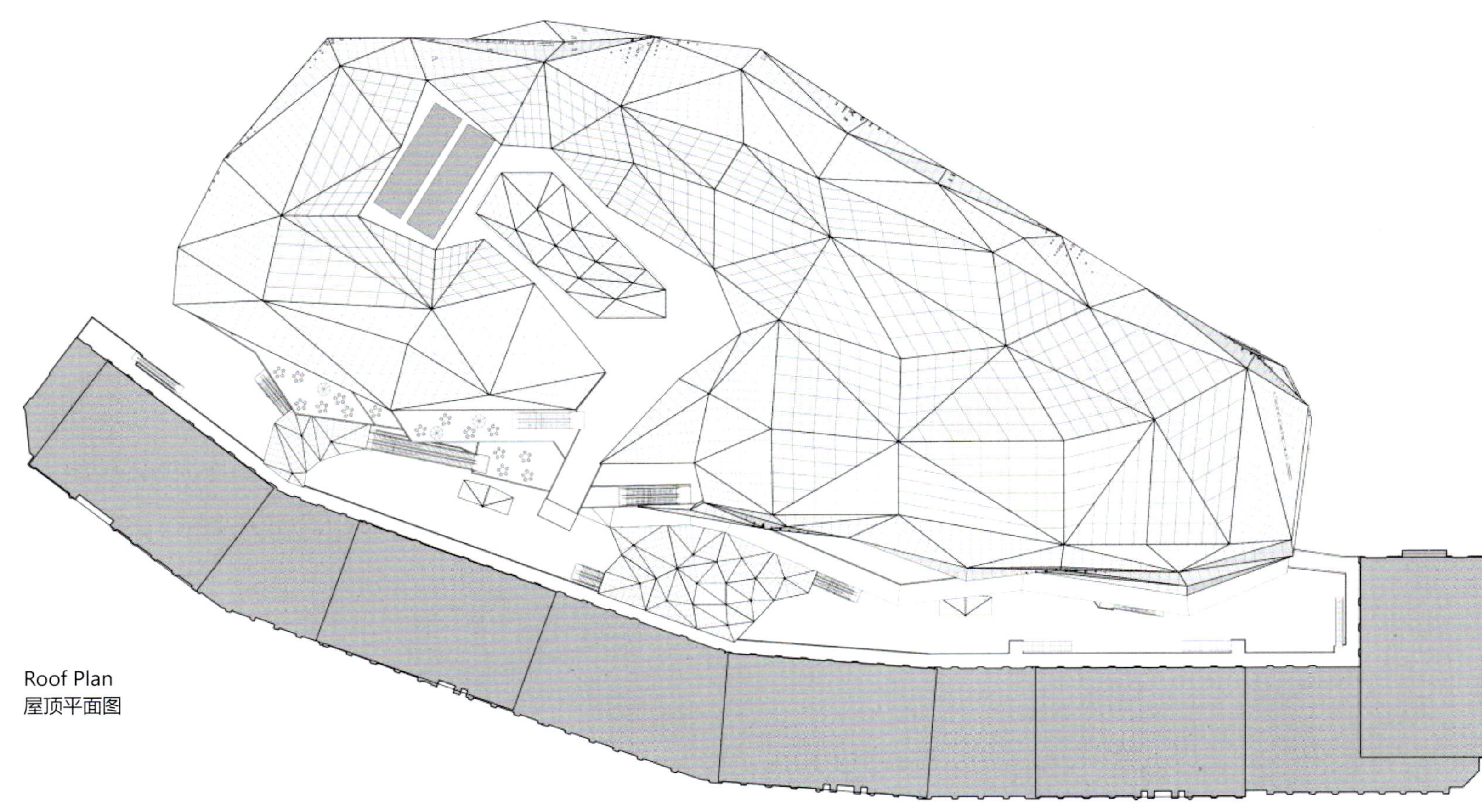
Roof Plan
屋顶平面图

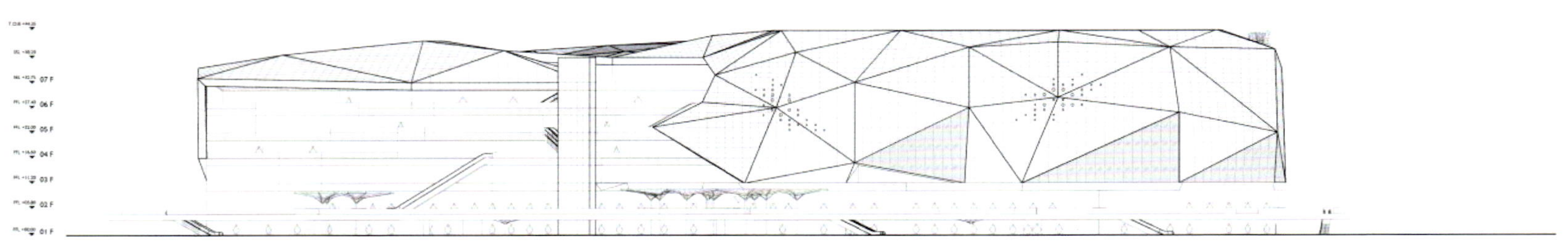
Elevation 1
立面图 1

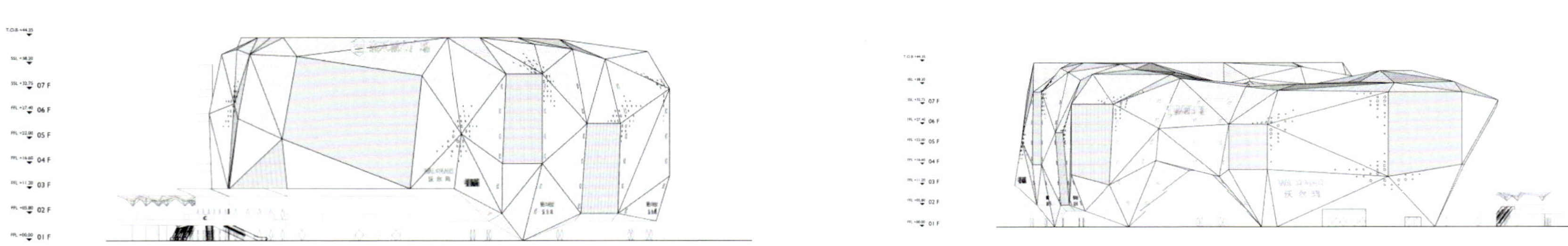
Elevation 2
立面图 2

Elevation 3
立面图 3

Design Description

It is recorded history that after visiting Fuzhou, Marco Polo described the city as "an important centre of commerce in precious stones."Fuzhou Wusibei Thaihot Plaza is the modern day "precious stone", a gem, located in the heart of Fuzhou soon to be discovered by many alike.

The Building

The many facets of the building exist to serve different functions in plan and the building facade. Easing the edges of the building in plan increases sightlines into the pedestrian street, which helps draws people in. Unlike some straight streets that shoot pedestrians quickly through, an undulating tenant facade facilitates the natural ebb and flow of pedestrian traffic, creating a dynamic shopping experience.

设计说明

根据历史记载，马可伯罗到访福州之后，将其描述为一个如宝石般珍贵的重要商业中心。福州五四北泰禾广场的造型就仿佛当代的珍贵宝石，镶嵌在福州市中心，作为一个崭新的城市地标建筑，让人们发出无尽的赞叹。

建筑

建筑造型由多组三角板块组成，板块间的排布定位结合了平面商业功能和不同的立面要求。通过板块组的功能定位自然的构筑成建筑曲折的线条。这种形式与功能相结合的设计理念，不仅实现了将人流引导进入到商业街的功能，同时更将各个店面的造型塑造成整体灵动的线条，曲折的线条化店面相互映衬，使得购物者无论身处哪一个角度，都会有一间面向他们的店面在恭候他们光临。此设计手法最大限度地提升了商业街内部的购物体验。

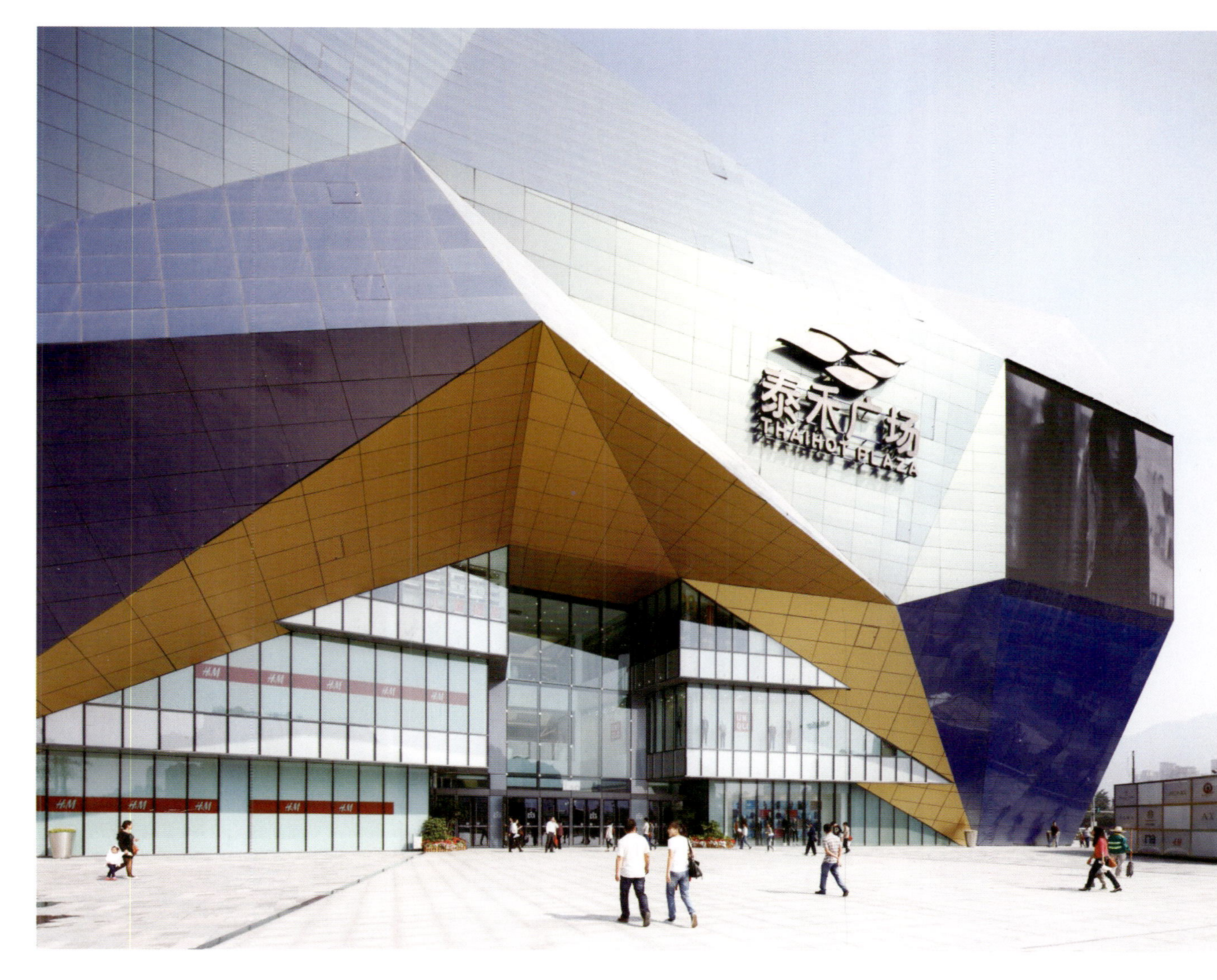

Colour shifting aluminium panels on the facade creates an exterior appearance that is constantly changing. While most panels are the building skin, select facets serve key visual functions such as illuminated signage boxes, advertisements, and three LED screens. At night, perforations in the aluminium panels allow light to pass through to create a starry night effect.

幕墙材料的选用是此次外立面设计的又一亮点，通过运用绚彩复合铝板，形成一个色彩缤纷的外幕墙效果。同时，出于渲染整体商业气氛的考虑，幕墙结合了一些必要的展示功能，如广告标识，灯箱和3个LED屏幕，位置面向人流活动的主要区域，加强了商业的综合气息。此外被设计在复合铝板上的洞口，通过其后面所带的暗藏灯箱，在晚间亮起时放射出柔和的点式灯光，形成了繁星点缀的效果。

The Circulation

The typical mall typology locates functions such as cinemas & KTV at upper levels of malls. These functions operate into the early hours of the morning long past the closing time of other retail facilities necessitating the public to navigate a difficult journey down out of darkened non air conditioned space.

To mitigate this dilemma, Fuzhou Wusibei Thaihot Plaza has two complementary circulation routes, a 12 hour day route and a 24 hour route. Retail programs that operate in the day are consolidated into a shopping mall podium typology (12hour). Circulation routes and terraces are carved out of the podium facilitating access to the roof top where there are a variety of activities such as miniature golf and full service dining can be found(24 hour).

商业流线

此次商业流线的设计思考，分析了多数的综合性购物商场会将一些功能性场所，如电影院和KTV设置在商场的顶层空间，作为目的性的商业。此类商业一般营业至深夜凌晨时分，有别于其他主题性店面商业的营业时间。一般情况下，在此类商场活动至深夜凌晨，或是在观赏完电影、结束唱歌后，人流量很多，如果是简单的疏散流线设计，就只能通过扶梯进入到已经关闭的商场室内再到达出口，结果造成公众不得不途经黑暗而又没有空调的空间，这样的商业流线非常不理想。

为了解决这个问题，五四北泰禾广场设计了两个互为辅助的商业流线：12 小时流线和 24 小时流线。普通正常营业时间的商店都组织在建筑的商场群楼以内，形成购物商场内的 12 小时日间流线。与此同时，我们也在室外增加了 24 小时的全天候流线。24 小时全天候流线通过在外幕墙部分设置垂直交通流线如电梯 / 扶梯，并在当中适当地增加商店延伸的室外集散平台，直达顶层 24 小时的商业功能空间如电影院、KTV 或餐饮区。

When the normal shopping functicns have closed, customers are provided with an alternate route lined with shops and terraces snaking along the podium facade (24 hour). This route is further animated by its adjacency to the pedestrian street. The entire north facade becomes a living entity full of movement and energy.

"The project is an important step for SPARK to bring our 24 hour vertical street concept to reality. The opening day has shown that it will make a big impact to this street culture city" says Jan Clostermann, Director of SPARK.

这样的流线设计，使得当购物商场关门以后，仍然在光顾 24 小时功能空间如电影院，KTV 或餐饮区的人们有另一个有趣的室外流线可以通达顶层空间与地面出口。在这种流线空间中，中小型的晚间商业如餐饮、咖啡厅等特色主体可以被设计在其中，并结合留给穿过热闹区域的人们设计的户外交谈观景平台，形成更加富有动感和活力的整体室外商业街。

“此项目是 SPARK 思邦实践 24 小时垂直流线商业街概念的重要一步。项目开业的盛况已经显示了此项目将给这个街市文化的城市带来的巨大影响。” SPARK 思邦董事 Jan Felix Clostermann 先生这样说到。

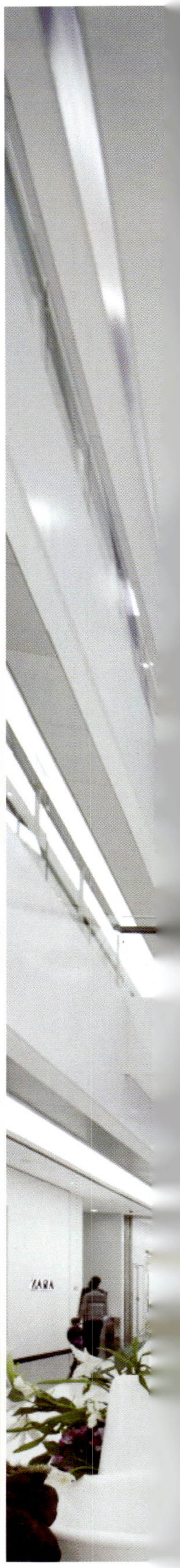

The Interior Space

On a rare occasion, chipping away at a stone will lead to the discovery of a cavernous core lined with mineral deposits exploding with radiant colour and light. The experience of entering Spark's proposed mall in Fuzhou is equally dazzling as a voluminous atrium filled with vibrant colour and light greets the visitor.

As an extension of the faceted facade a crystalline LED advertisement gem hovers over the atrium concierge as the visual focal point upon entering the mall. The pristine white interior atrium is accentuated by colour highlights on the escalators which are sculpturally composed in the middle of the atrium. Linear LED light chandeliers sit over the interior events plaza. Back lit floor peepholes strew across the atrium bridges like scattered jewels as a playful addition to the space, attracting curious onlookers.

室内空间

在非常稀有的情况下，雕凿天然石头至其核心将会发掘出散射着迷人光芒与色彩的宝石。进入思邦设计的福州商业空间的过程，就是一个由生动的色彩与光丰富起来的中庭空间，愉悦参观者的炫目旅程。

作为外立面钻石面延续入室内的晶体LED广告宝石悬吊于中庭，成为人们进入商场后的视觉中心。质朴的白色室内中庭由于具有雕塑感且位于中庭中部的彩色扶梯而变得异常生动起来。线型LED灯极具仪式感的悬吊于室内广场。散落在错落布置的连桥上的内置LED灯的窥视孔，如同散发着眩目光彩的宝石，吸引人驻足与探索。

mothercare

CITY CHAIN
太平洋咖啡

PROJECT NAME 项目名称

SHIJIAZHUANG WONDA MALL

石家庄万象天成

Architect: amphibianArc

设计公司：双栖弧建筑设计公司

PROJECT INFORMATION 项目信息

Designer	Nonchi Wang, Yu-I Chan, Tomoyuki Sudo, Yulis Wardjiman	**设计负责人**	王弄极 ，詹于仪 ，Tomoyuki Sudo ，Yulis Wardjiman
Client	Hebei Tiancheng Enterprise Group	**客户**	河北天成房地产开发集团有限公司
Location	Shijiazhuang, Hebei Province,China	**地点**	中国河北省石家庄市
Area	170,000 m^2	**面积**	170，000 平方米
Photographer	Nicholas May, Ruogu Zhou	摄影师	Nicholas May, 周若谷

OVERVIEW 项目概况

Wonder mall is a mix-use development located in Shijiazhuang, China. It includes a 60,000 m^2 of shopping mall, 30,000 m^2 of office space, 35,000 m^2 for hotel use and 45,000 m^2 of condominiums.

万象天成是一个位于石家庄的综合开发项目，包括 6 万平方米的商场，3 万平方米办公空间，3.5 万平方米的酒店以及 4.5 万平方米的住宅。

FEATURE ANALYSIS 特色分析

ARCHITECT
Nonchi Wang

设计师
王弄極

The architects deliver an extraordinary work with much care in a third-tier city. They seek to explore a brand new modern style and look for opportunities in limits. They create a commercial complex with a brand new look different from others with constrained construction technology in China and via a unique design. What is more, the project delivers another highlight, a clever use of lighting design which complements the expression of architectural curve skin and forms a speech that speaks to building's commercial property. A powerful sense of landmark is shown.

虽然作为一个中国三线城市的商业项目，建筑师并没有随意交出一个在普通城市随处可见的平庸设计，而是积极探索一种全新的现代风格，在限制之中寻找机会，运用在国内可行的技术建构手段，通过设计的方式得出一种不同于一般商业综合体建筑的全新风貌。本项目的另一个亮点在于灯光设计的运用，其很好地烘托了建筑曲线型表皮的表现力，与建筑的商业属性相得益彰，地标感强烈。

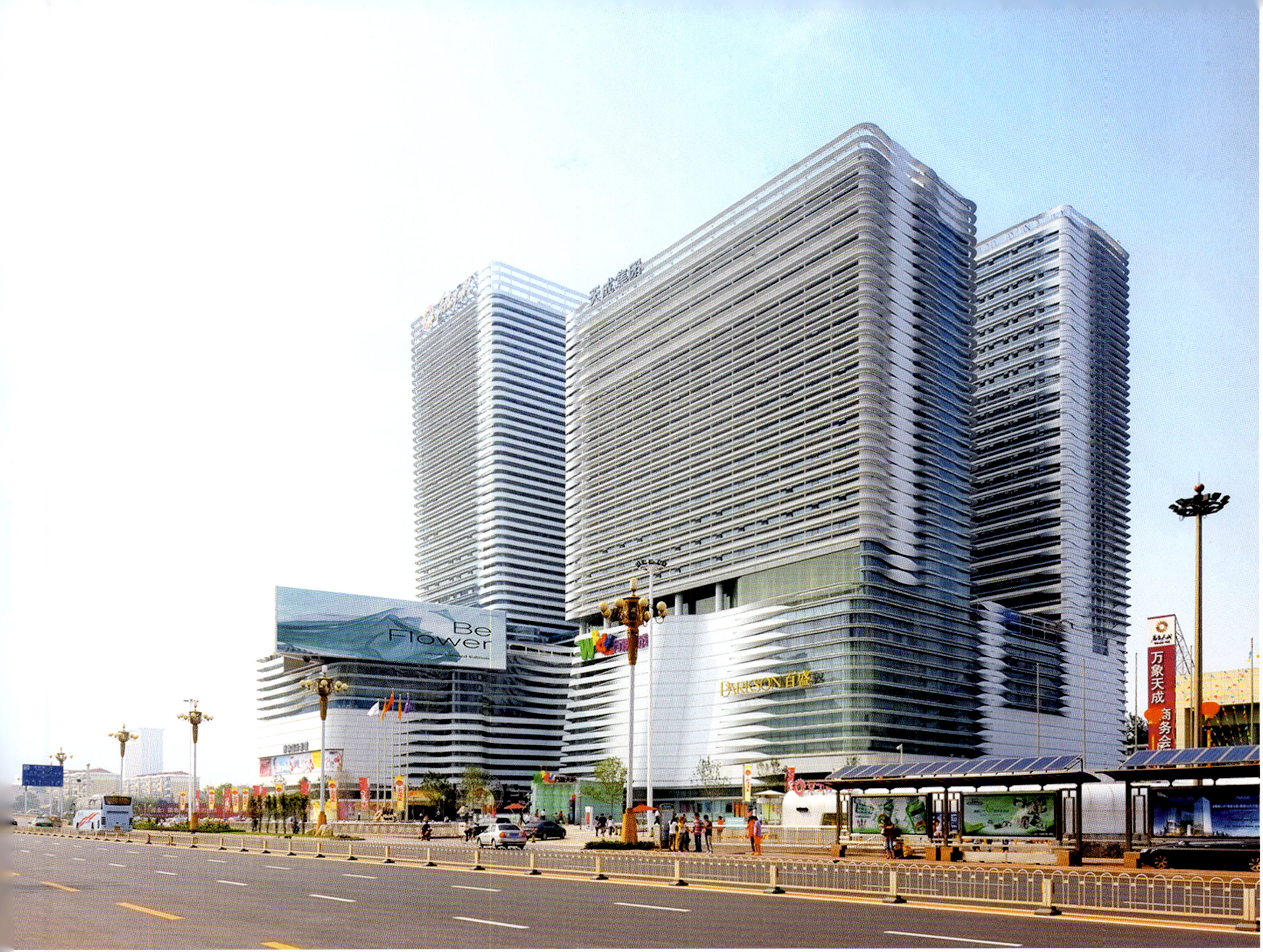
天成集团
Be
Flower
PARKSON 百盛
万象天成

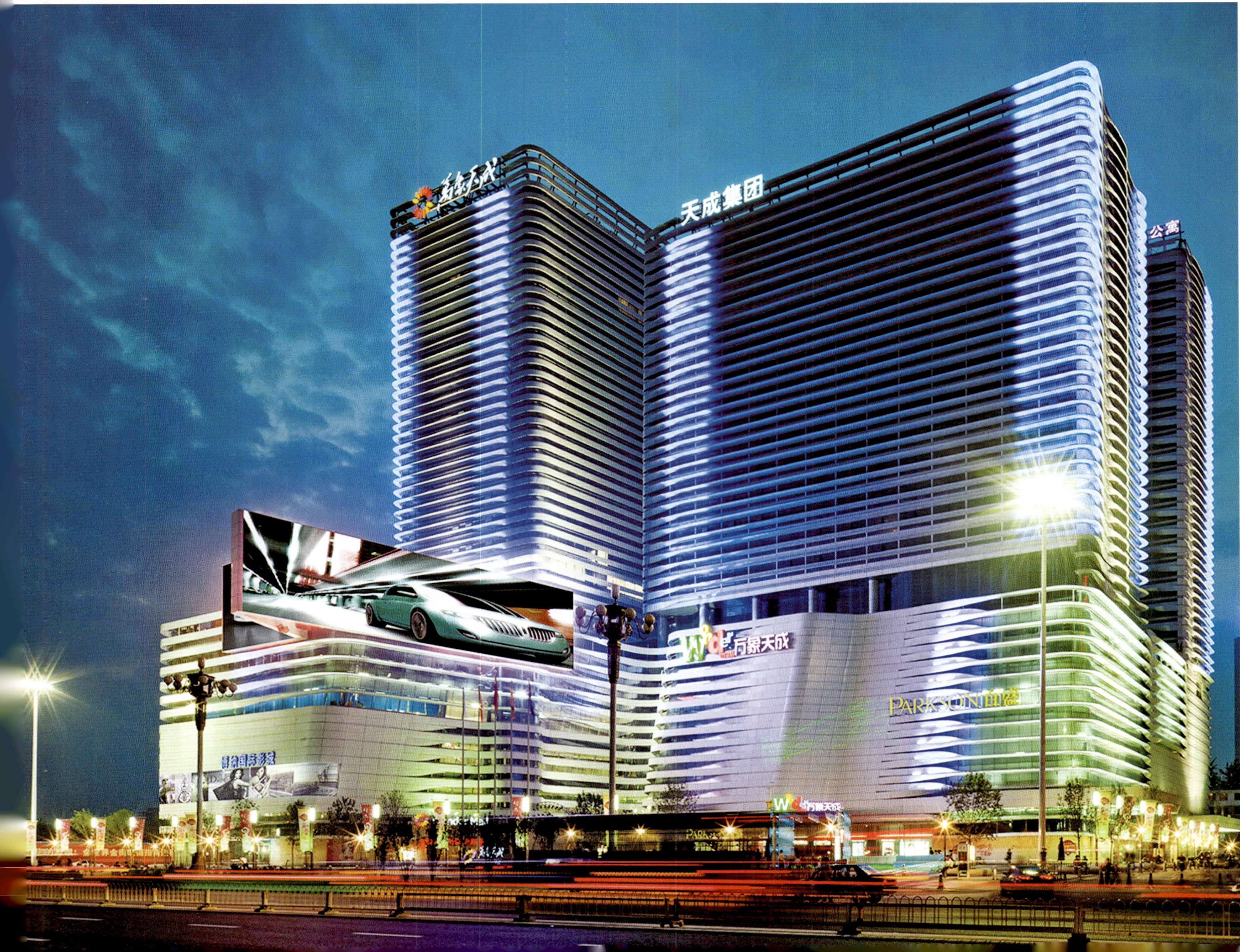
天成集团
万象天成
PARKSON 百盛

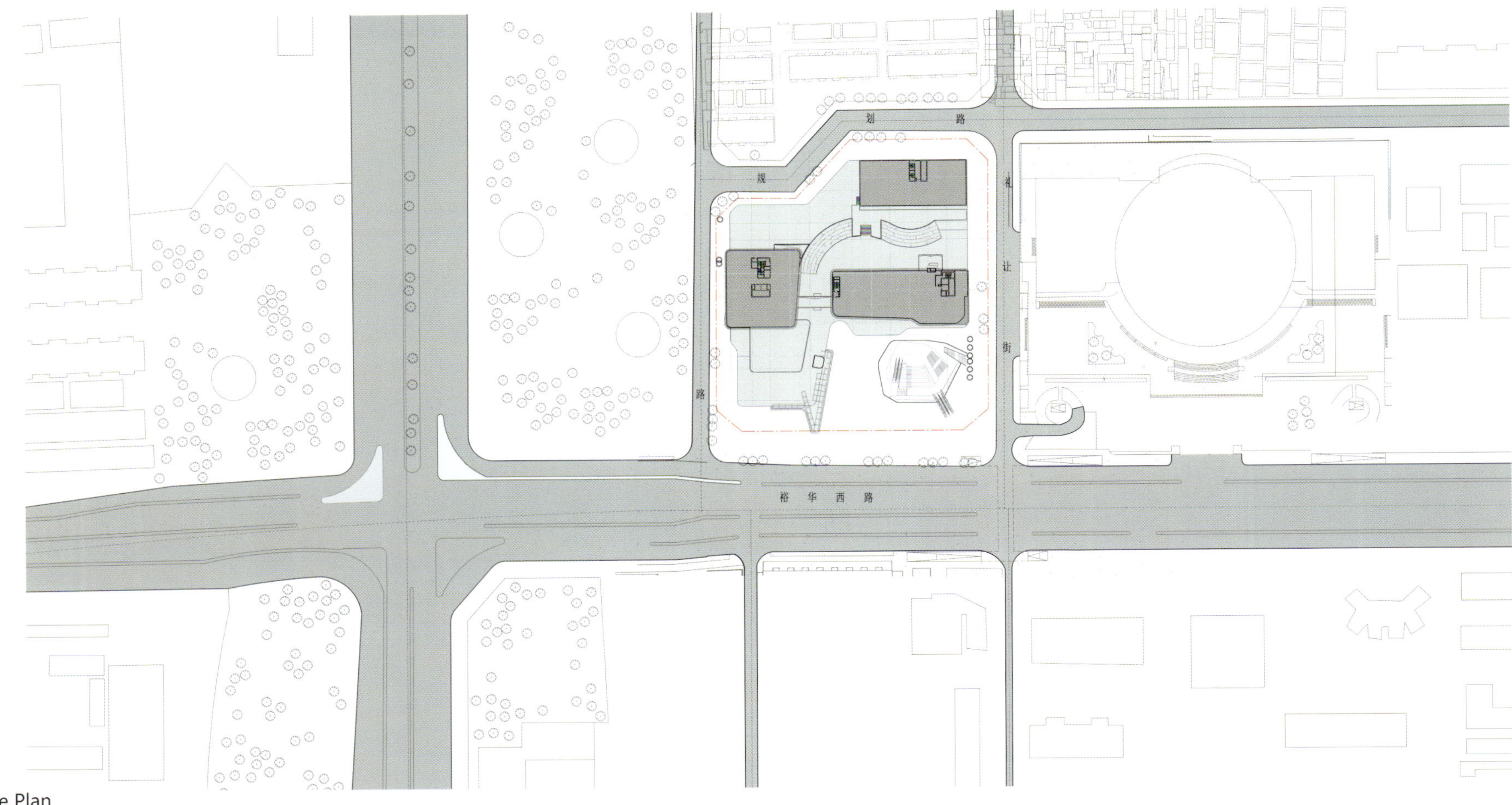

Site Plan
总平面图

Fashion is ubiquitous in this world's most populated country after 30 years of its opening-up since the late 1970s. It is defining the heart and soul of urbanites in both first tier cities, such as Beijing and Shanghai, and second tier cities, including Shijiazhuang. Wonder mall, a mix-use development with a shopping mall at the podium as its anchor, is a celebration of China's contemporary urban life that has been partly defined by its pursuit and consumption of fashion.

自从七十年代末改革开放的三十年来，在中国这个拥有世界上最多人口的国家，时尚无处不在。时尚不只为北京、上海等一线城市都市精神作定义，还深刻影响着包括石家庄在内的二线城市。拥有王层旗舰商业裙房的天成购物中心，是以追逐和消费时尚为代表的当代中国都市生活的解读。

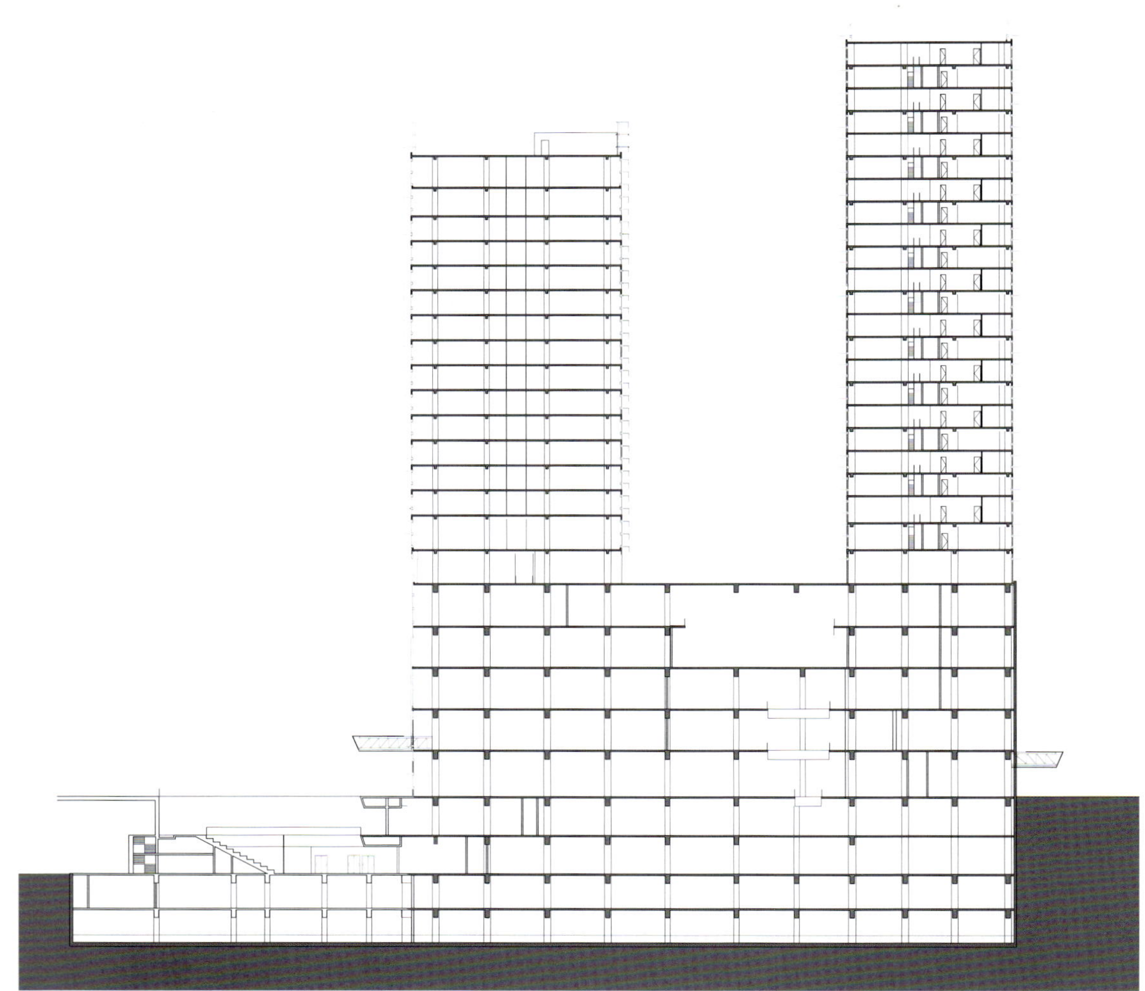

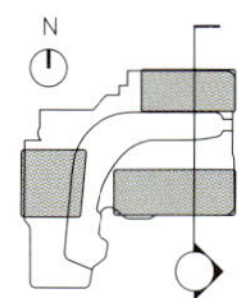

Section B-B
剖面图 B-B

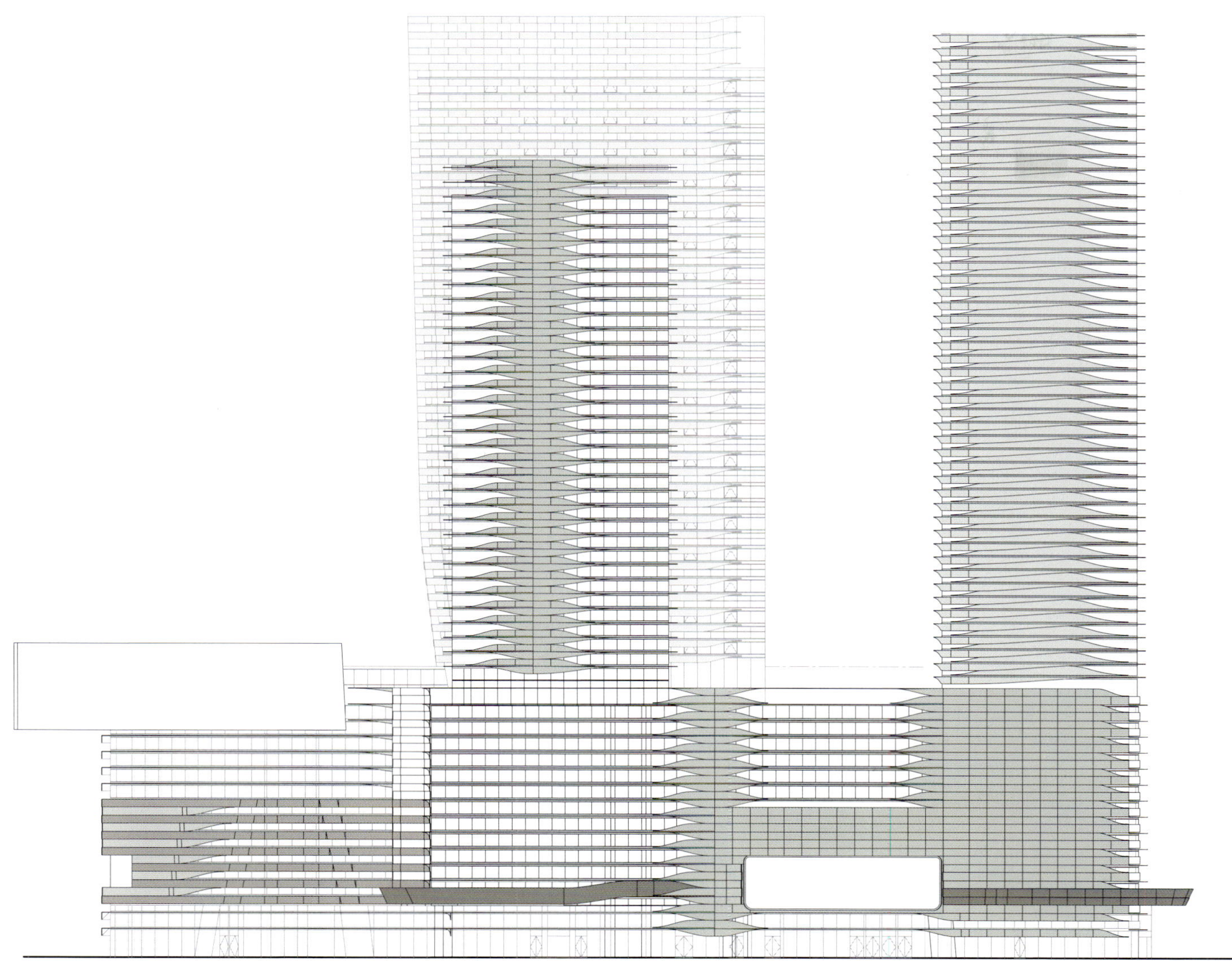

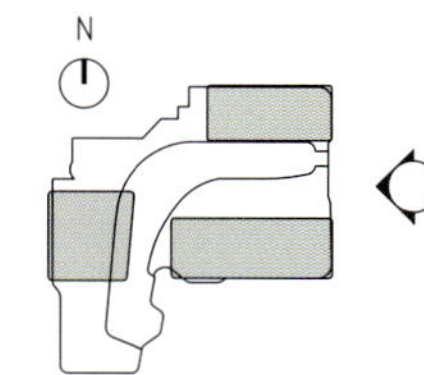

East Elevation
东立面图

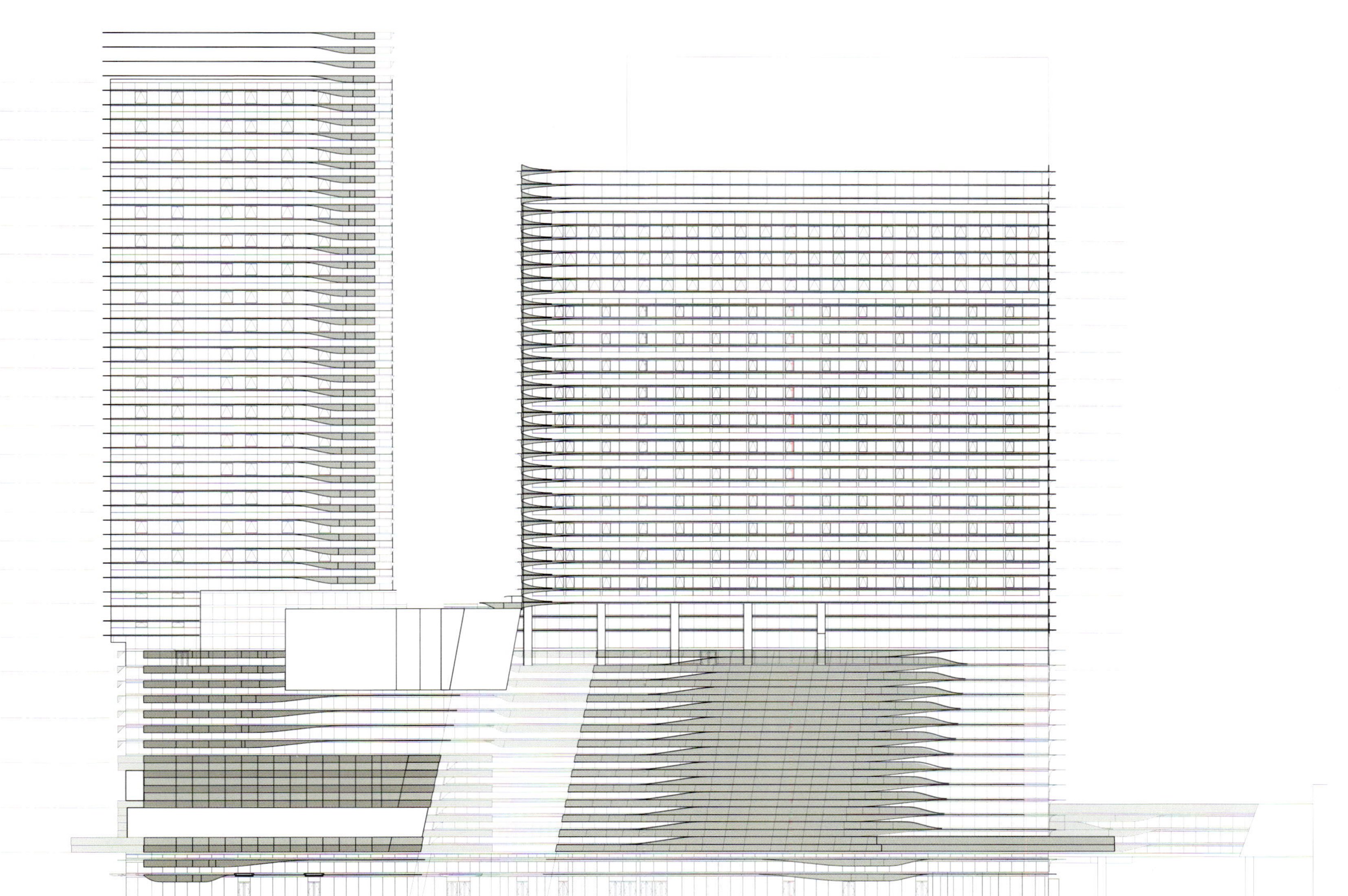

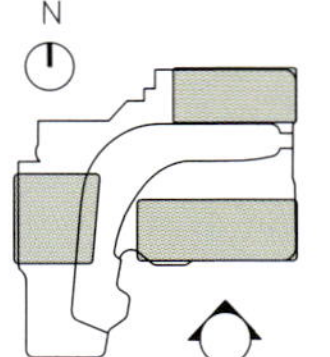

South Elevation
南立面图

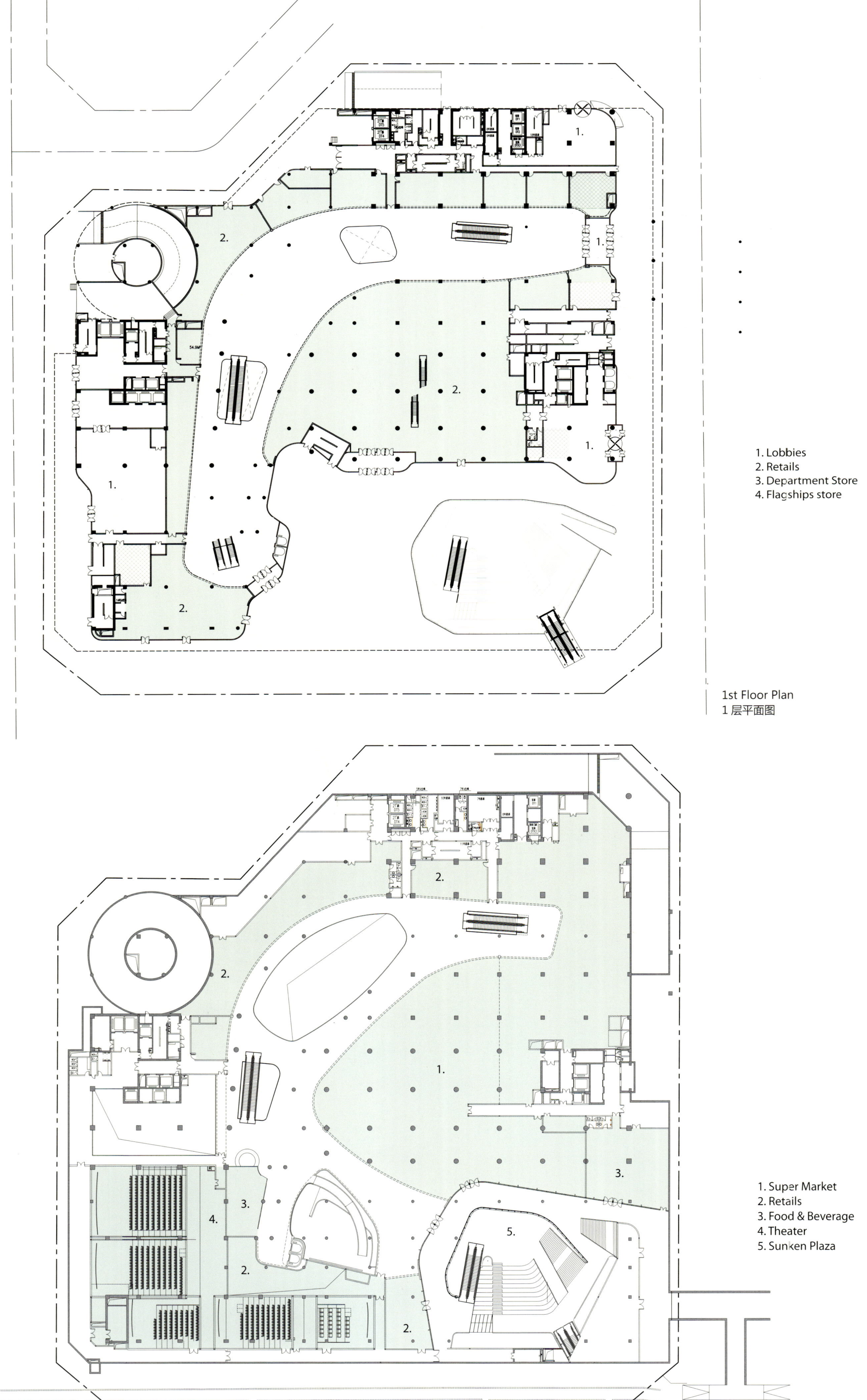

1st Floor Plan
1 层平面图

B1 Floor Plan
地下 1 层平面图

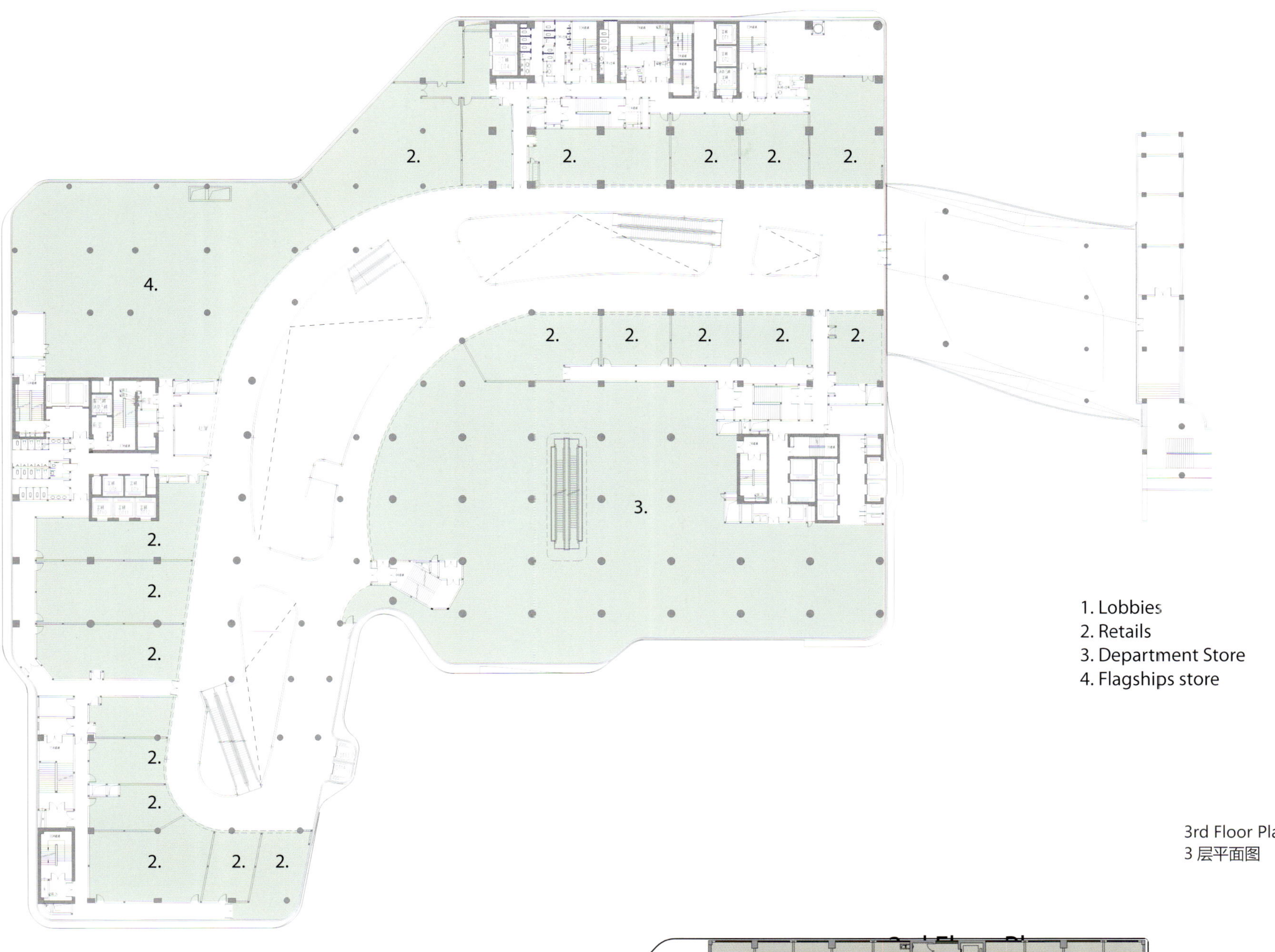

1. Lobbies
2. Retails
3. Department Store
4. Flagships store

3rd Floor Plan
3 层平面图

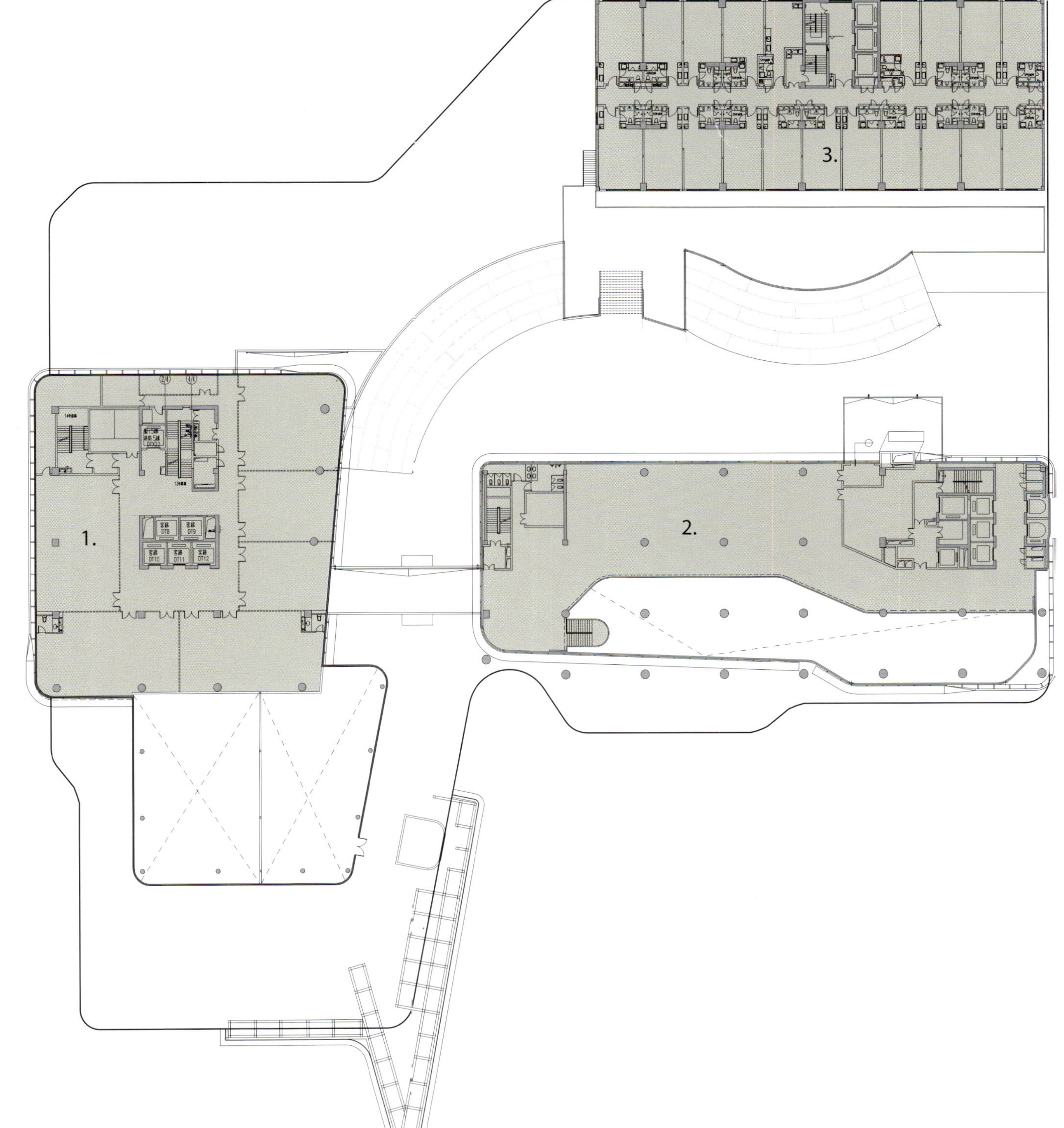

7th Floor Plan
7 层平面图

Architectural Solution

To fulfill the client's vision of creating a locus for fashion and urban amenities, the architect employed an intricate louver system as an agent of free expression that will capture contemporary Chinese enthusiasm toward fashion. The louver system at the same time functions as shading device to mediate sun light and heat gain, making the building more sustainable. The twisting geometry of the louver, from vertical to horizontal and vice versa, allows the louver panels on different elevations to respond to changing angle of the sunlight.

建筑设计解决方案

为了满足客户创造一个时尚与城市便利设施场所的愿景，设计师采用了精细的百叶窗来更加自由地表达当代中国人对时尚的热情。百叶窗的设计同时实现了遮阳功能——防止阳光的灼晒和减少热量的获得，使得整幢建筑更加环保。此外，金属窗蜿蜒的几何造型更使得不同立面的窗板随太阳照射角度的变化而发挥着自身的作用。

万象天成

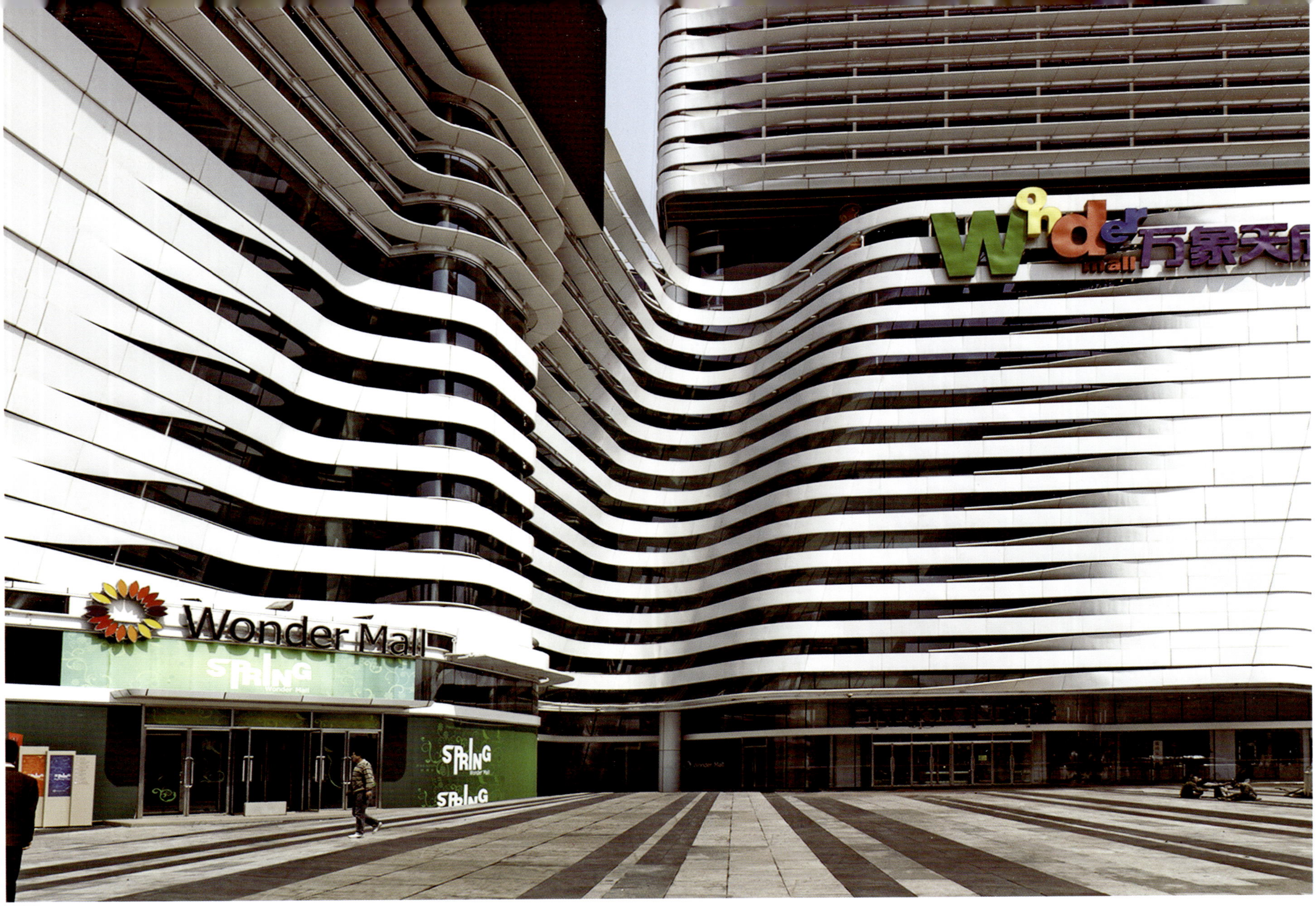
Wonder Mall
SPRING
SPRING

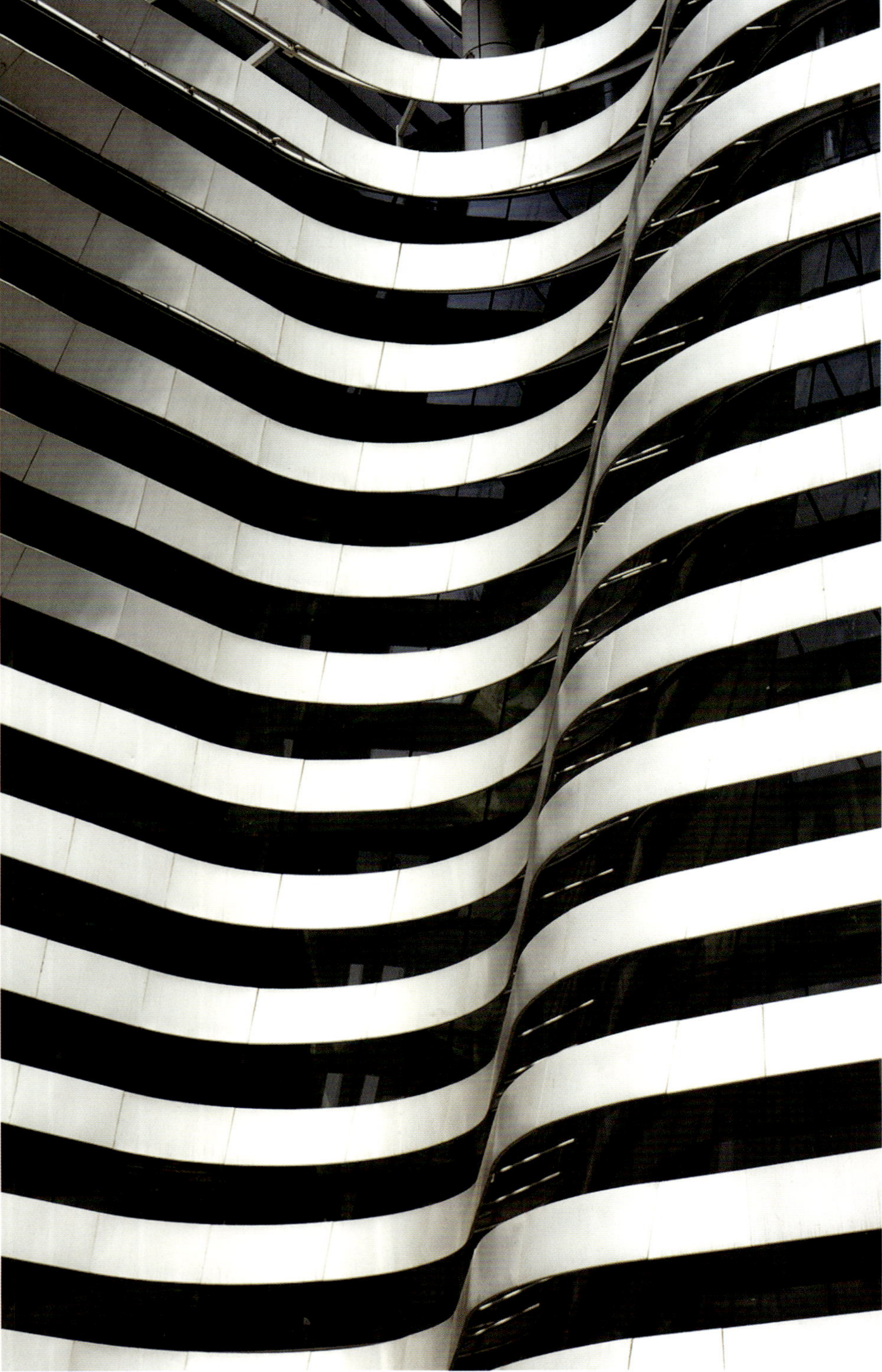

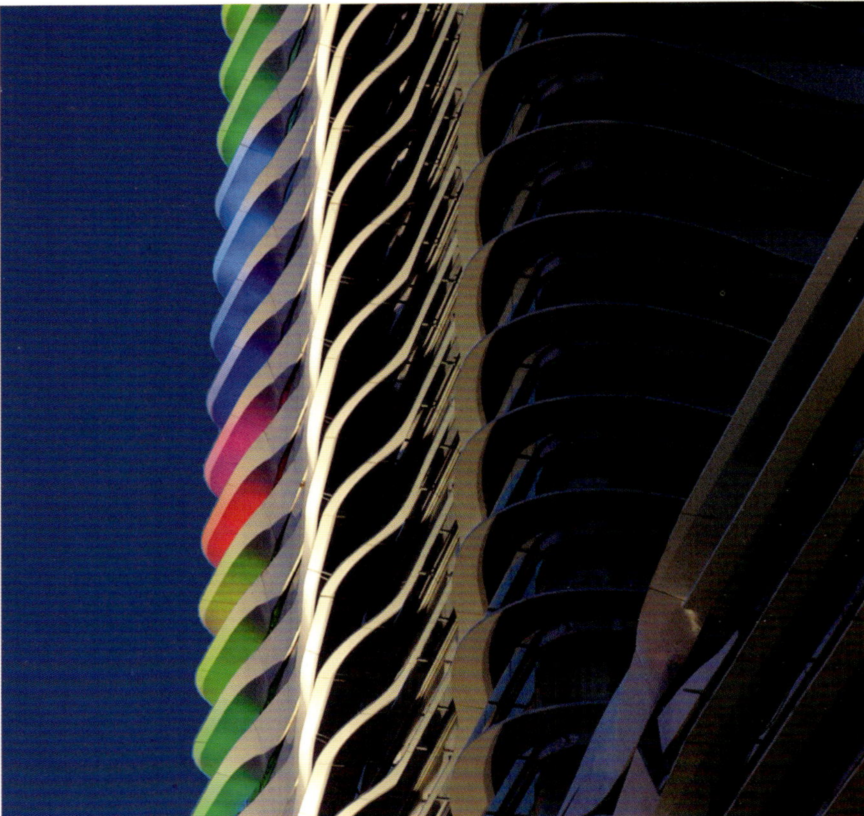

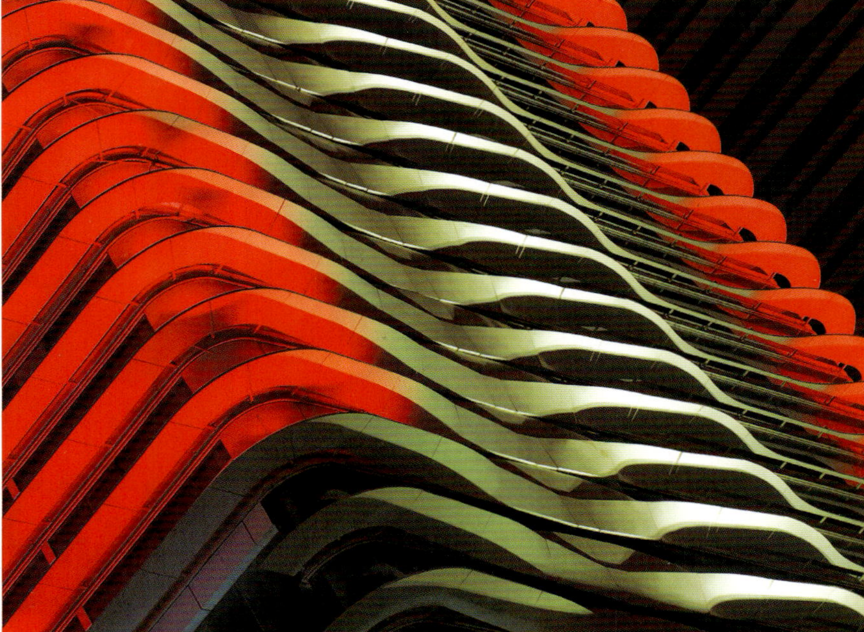

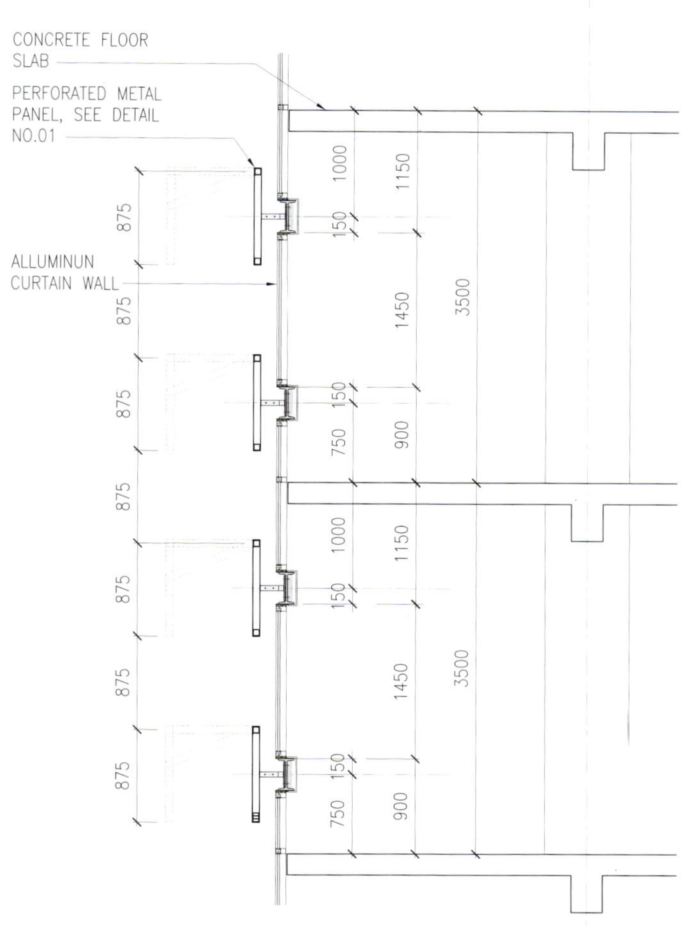

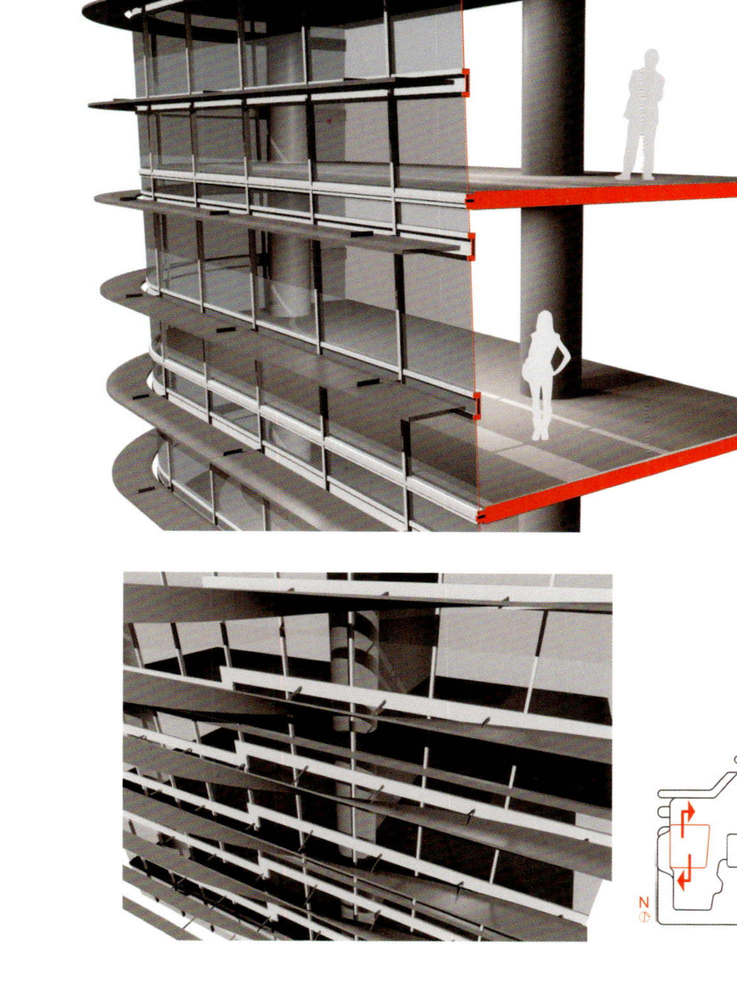

Wall Section
外墙剖面图

While fashion is ever changing and multiple in expressions, Wonder Mall strives to embody the essence of fashion by articulating fashion as an act of wearing and accessorizing oneself. It is a conscious act of covering the naked body with items, either utilitarian or frivolous, that create identity and self-expression. The architecture of Wonder Mall takes place at the building's surface where the naked curtain wall as body skin is covered with weaves of metal louvers, the ready-to-wear of architecture.

自从70年代末改革开放的三十年时尚的表达方式是不断变化的，同时又是多种多样的，万象天成试图用“穿衣”和“配饰”这两种行为来表达时尚这个核心概念。它有意识地用物品覆盖着裸体，功利或轻浮，创建身份特征或者自我表达方式。万象天成的设计将建筑体量作为“身体”，而编织状的金属百页则是遮盖身体的表皮，这就是“整装待发”的建筑。

Louvers details
百叶窗细节图

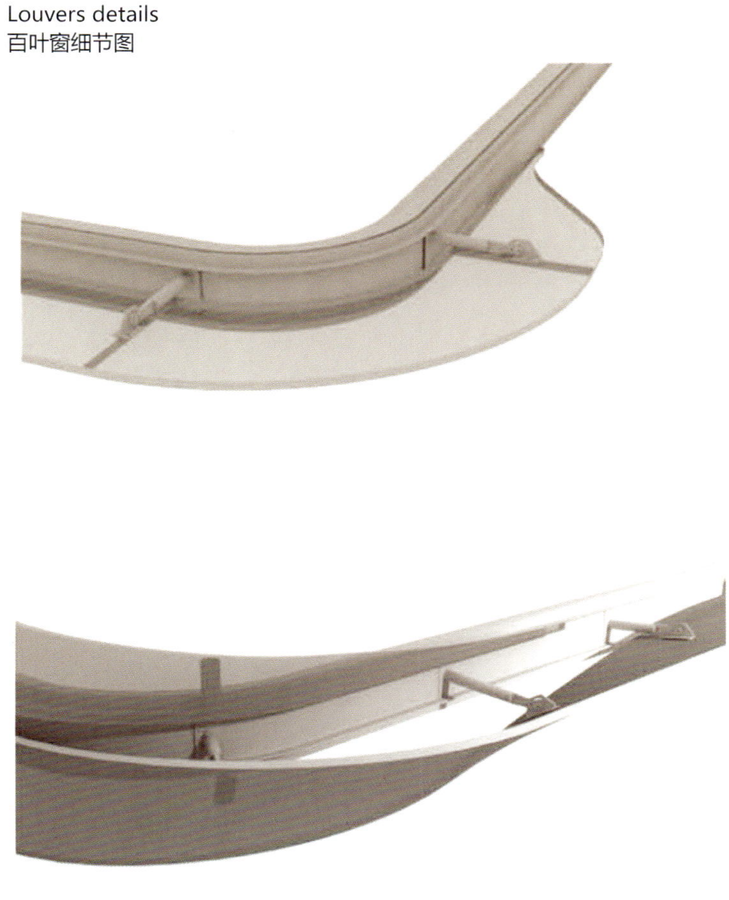

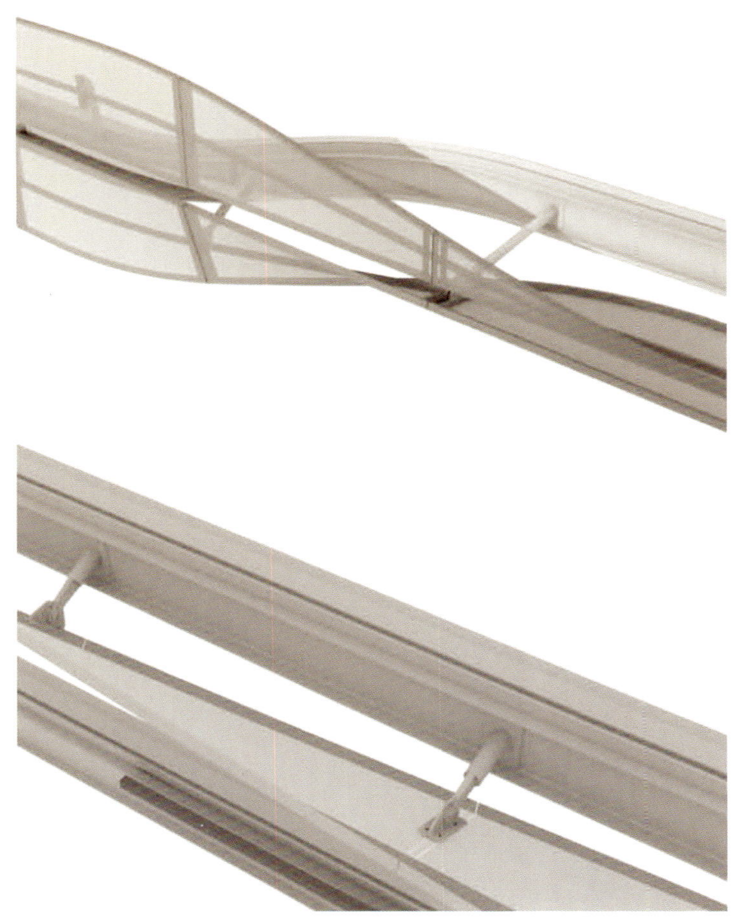

PROJECT NAME 项目名称

QUANZHOU WANDA PLAZA

泉州万达广场

Architect: HPP

设计公司：HPP

PROJECT INFORMATION 项目信息

Client	Wanda Group	**客户**	万达集团
Location	Quanzhou,China	**地点**	中国泉州
Gross Floor Area	342, 800 m^2	**建筑面积**	342，800 平方米（总计）

OVERVIEW 项目概况

Wanda Plaza owns 5 multi-functional towers consisting of shopping mall, a office building, a 5-star hotel and a SOHO office, which will be a new city centre in Quanzhou, a southern harbor city in China.Located closely to Jinjiang River as a new landmark in this city with a population of 8,000,000, Wanda Plaza includes 2 volumes of 180m office towers and 3 slightly lower residential and commercial buildings, which are connected by terraces in several floors to form rhythmic commercial paths and a favorable business atmosphere.

万达广场是拥有五个塔楼的多功能城市综合体，集购物中心、办公、五星级酒店、公寓和 SOHO 办公（小型办公室，家庭办公室）为一体，成为中国南方海港城市泉州新的城市中心。项目紧临晋江，项目的目标是在这个 800 万人口的城市中建设一个新地标。两座 180 米高的办公塔楼和三个高度略低的住宅和商业建筑，通过交互平台，连接部分楼层，形成有节奏感的商业步道和良好的商业氛围。

BRIEF INTERVIEW 访谈录

ARCHITECT
Jens Kump,
HPP Architects,
Project Partner

设计师
彦斯库，
HPP 项目合伙人

HKASP: Please describe the design process to develop the proposal for Quanzhou Wanda Plaza?

HPP : The design is the result of a long term cooperation over many years with the Wanda Group, one of the leading and most professional developers in China. HPP entered into the design of this multifunctional City Complex after being awarded 1st prize in the design competition in Summer 2010.The new Quanzhou Wanda Plaza is located at one of the cities most extraordinary locations, directly at the JinJiang River, noble at day and shiny at night time. The scheme is respecting and defining the natural and urban space. The entire design is made by highlighting the most present element of the surrounding nature, "water". Behind this concept is the idea to promote the interaction of this natural element and the human made systematic, valuate the attracting wildness by combining it with a background of dignity, capture a fragile moment of beauty into a frame of eternity. From design competition to the functional opening in September 2012, it took 2.5 Years. HPP was responsible for the design in all phases from concept over development design, lead detailing and site control.

HKASP: How would you compare the dynamic and its difference when doing retail projects between Asia and Europe ?

HPP : The dynamic of Chinese cities has its origin in the dynamic of its people. As a River-Metropolis, Quanzhou is a growing, young and energetic city, currently experiencing rapid development. The new Wanda Plaza has special chances as well as responsibilities to be a positive part towards the city's future, reflecting a whole region's individuality and pure spirit. The HPP design answer is to give the shopping center a calm and classic frame of dignity. Taming the wild and necessarily omnipresent commercial elements of the Shopping Complex by defining a pure and neutral background is the expertise of our design.

香港建筑科学出版社：请描述一下泉州万达广场的整个方案设计过程。

HPP: 这个设计是与中国最领先和最专业的开发商万达集团长期合作的结果，HPP 通过 2010 年夏季的竞赛获得该城市综合体的项目。由于泉州万达广场坐落在锦江河边，一个非凡的城市地理位置，白天显得高贵而晚上霓虹闪烁，为了使环境与自然更加和谐，设计强调了周边最有代表性的自然元素——" 水 "。方案的概念是促进自然元素和人造体系间的相互作用， 以结合纯粹的设计理念来应对极具吸引力的繁杂， 将美丽的瞬间凝固在永恒的画框之中。从设计竞赛到 2012 年 9 月项目开业，历时两年半，此间 HPP 负责了从方案、初设、到细节把控和现场控制等所有阶段。

香港建筑科学出版社：您觉得在亚洲和在欧洲做商业项目有什么区别？

HPP: 中国城市的不断发展起源于人的变化。作为一个河岸都市，泉州是一个成长中、年轻和充满能量的城市，正经历着快速的发展。新的万达广场拥有特殊的机会和责任为城市的未来带来积极的影响，并反映出地域特点和精神。把冗杂但不可或缺的各种商业元素通过一个纯粹和中性的理念来重新定义，是我们的设计专长。最后，以我的所见所闻而言，亚洲的客户通常对设计抱以很高的期望。他们喜欢令人咋舌的设计方案，他们喜欢你能提供多种方案。无论在哪里，这种想法是可以理解的，也是在意料之内的。只是觉得在亚洲，这些要求显得有点苛刻。这可能是因为当地房地产迅速发展，从而更需要每个项目能达到脱颖而出的效果。

Sketch of Elevation
立面草图

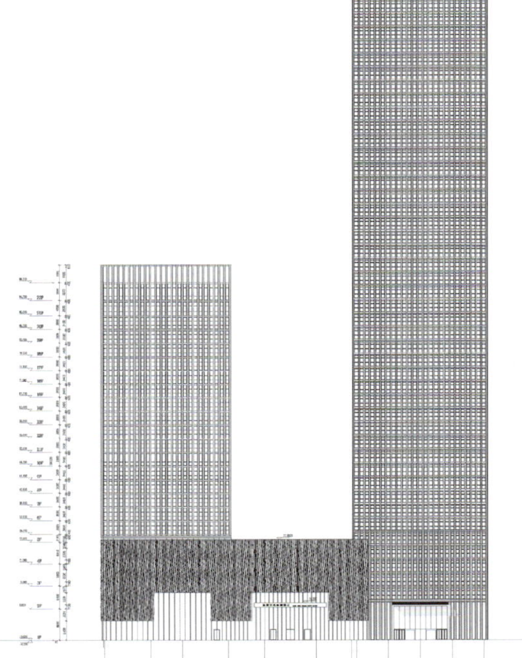

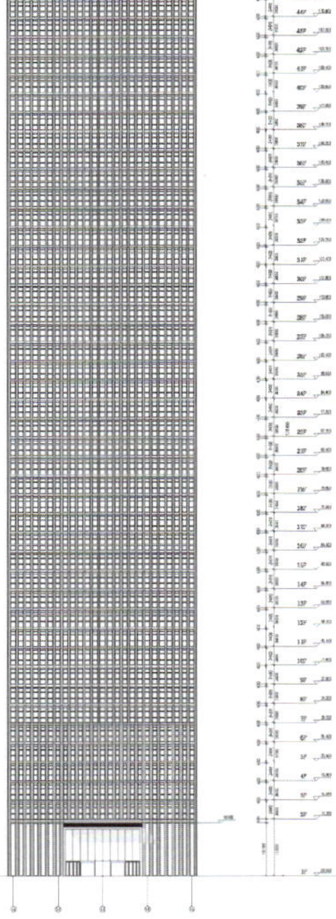

Elevation 1
立面图 1

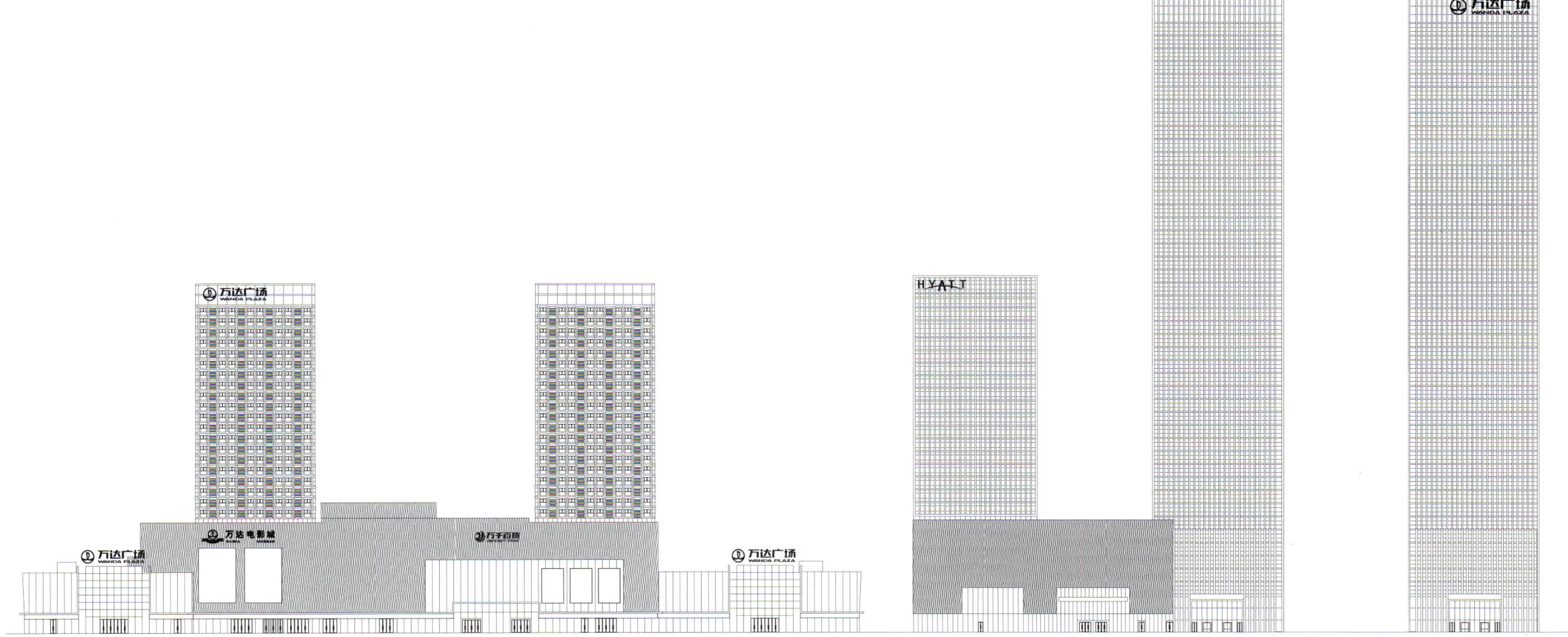

Elevation 2
立面图 2

The podium covered by LED lighting highlighting a vibrant commercial atmosphere. Additionally, double glazing and beige aluminum walls offer a harmonious architectural language and a sense of classcial doctrine. Double glazing will effectively reduces carbon emissions to be sustainable. Quanzhou Wanda Plaza builds itself a identity which helps the emmerging metropolis strengthes its city image.

裙房的外墙通过LED灯照明，凸显充满生机的商业氛围。除此之外，双层玻璃和米黄色铝制墙面营造和谐的建筑语言，闪耀着经典主义的光芒。双层玻璃的运用有效降低了建筑的碳排放，使建筑更加可持续。泉州万达广场帮助这座新兴的大都市，营建属于自己的新地标，在很大程度上加强了城市形象。

万达广场
WANDA PLAZA

万达百货
MUJI
無印良品
万达广场
WANDA PLAZA

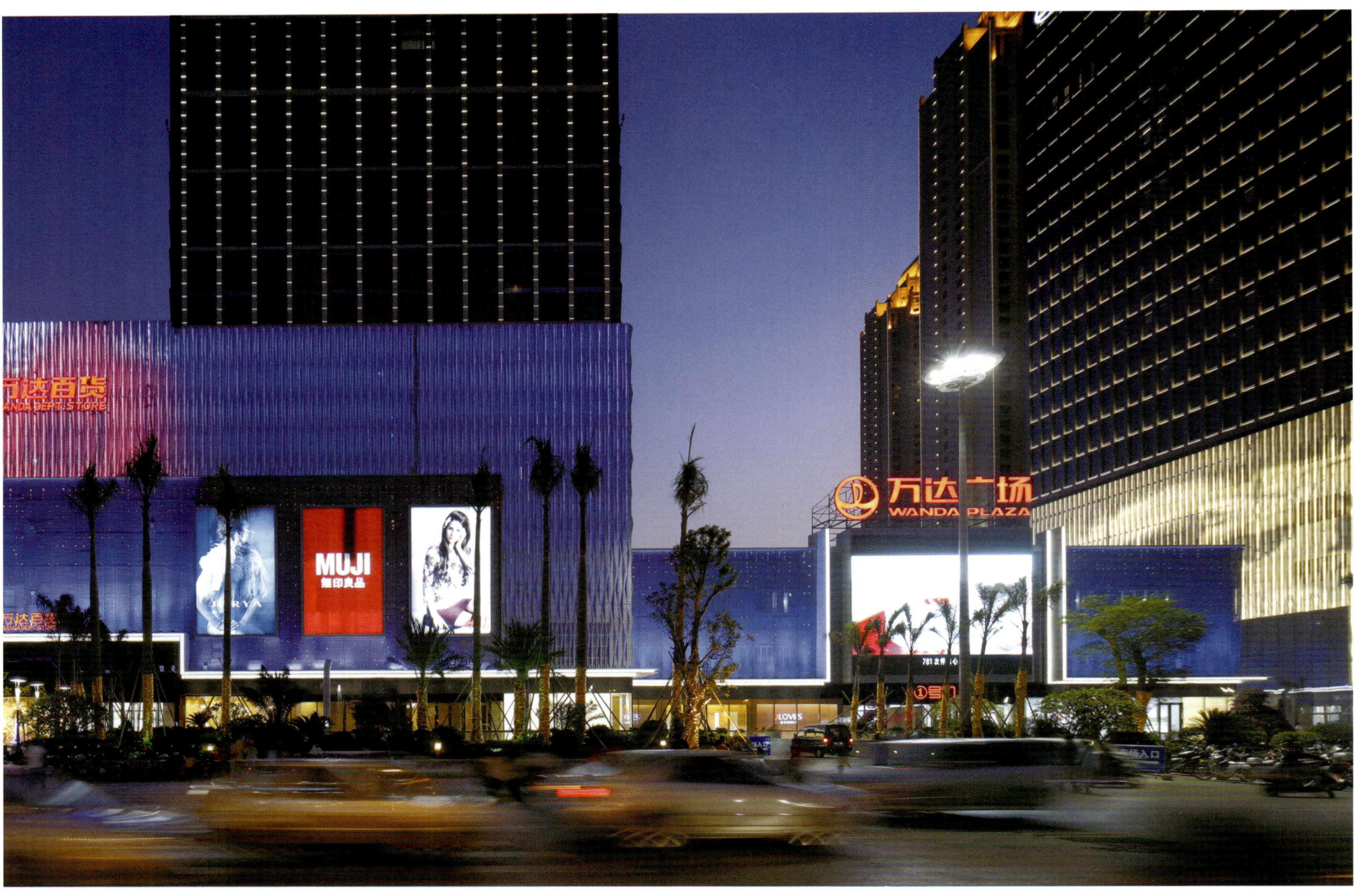

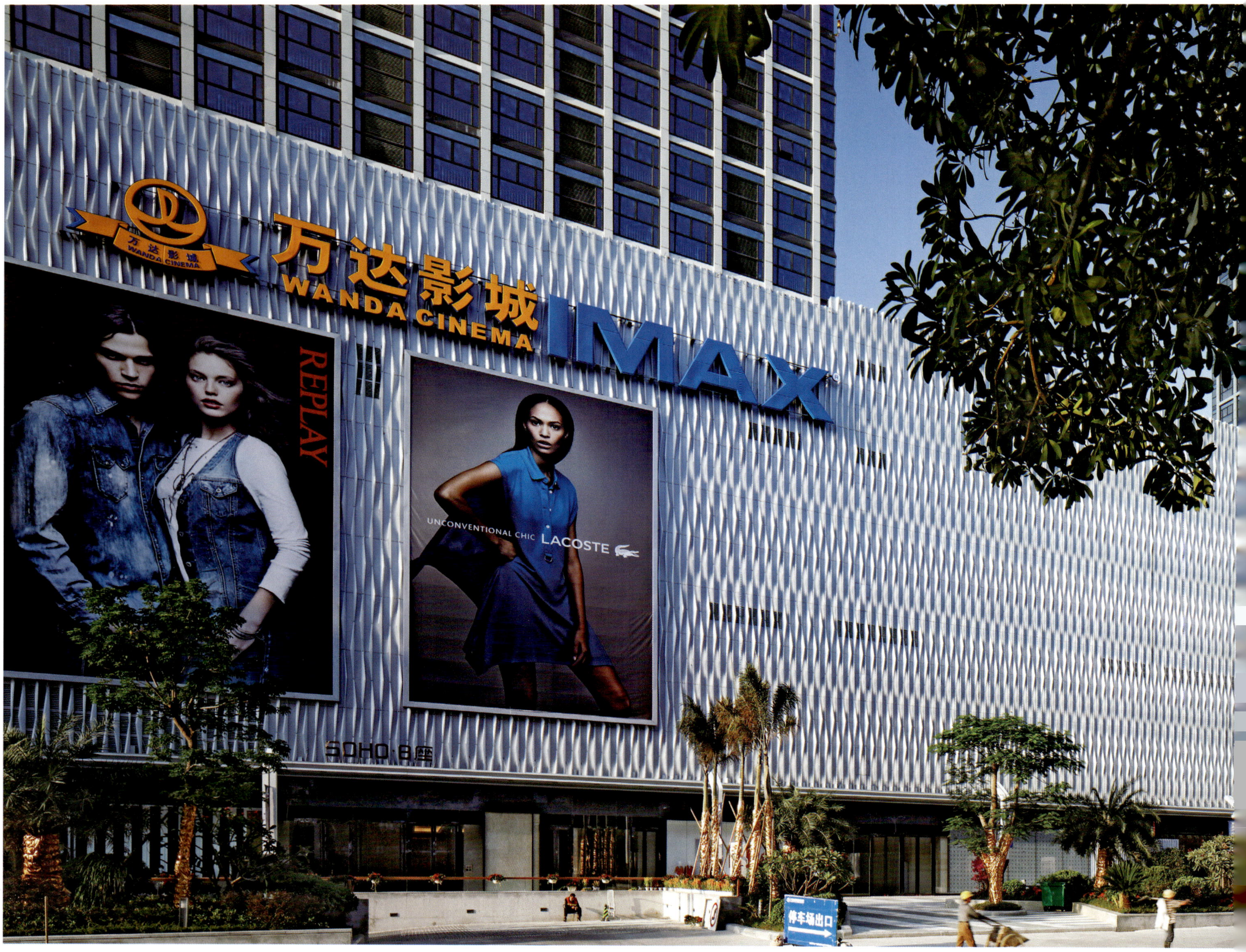
万达影城
WANDA CINEMA
万达影城
WANDA CINEMA
IMAX
REPLAY
UNCONVENTIONAL CHIC LACOSTE
SOHO B座
停车场出口

MUJI
JORYA

東海大酒店

PROJECT NAME 项目名称

ZIBO LIVING MALL

淄博华润五彩城

Architect:5+design, Inc
设计公司：五杰建筑设计

PROJECT INFORMATION 项目信息

Client	China Resources Land	**客户**	华润置地
Location	Zibo, Shandong Province, China	**地点**	中国山东省淄博市
Site Area	50,000 m²	**占地面积**	50，000 平方米
Building Area	250,000 m²	**建筑面积**	250，000 平方米

OVERVIEW 项目概况

China Resources Land, after developing mixed-use centers in many of China's larger cities, is now focused on emerging cities as well. The Living Mall represents their first third-tier city development, and will serve as a prototype and testing platform for other developments to come. Located at a major intersection in the city's historic commercial district,the 240,000 m² center promises to become the city's destination of choice residents and visitors alike. It will feature a six-story retail mall, showcasing stores, restaurants, nightclubs, bars, movie theaters and an ice rink. A 39-storey office and hotel tower will rise on one corner of the block-long site, while a 28-storey business apartment tower will anchor the other. Seven residential towers and an inner street lined with art galleries complete the project.

华润置地，继在中国很多大城市推出综合体项目后，现在又将目光转向新兴城市。华润五彩城就是他们在三线城市项目开发的首个代表。它将作为公司未来在新兴城市开发的雏形和探索平台。五彩城坐落于历史商业区的主要路口，占地240，000 平方米，必将成为城市居民和游人的首选。六层商场，集展馆、餐厅、夜总会、酒吧、电影院和溜冰场于一体，39 层写字楼和酒店大楼将从街区的一角拔地而起，而 28 层楼的商务公寓楼则位于街区的另一角。除此之外，该项目还有 7 幢住宅楼和与艺术画廊并行的内大街。

BRIEF INTERVIEW 访谈录

ARCHITECT
Paul Gasiorkiewicz

设计师
Paul Gasiorkiewicz

HKASP: How long did it take the project team to develop the proposal? Did the concept/design change much during that time?

5+design, Inc: The conceptual design process for the overall project took about six months to establish. The process took a little longer than usual because during the concept design the client increased the scope and added a 5-star hotel that required more space, which in turn added more retail space, resulting in the overall project becoming 50% larger.

HKASP: Is there any different when doing retail projects between Asia and Western? Or do you agree that the customer behaviors are globally the same?

5+design, Inc: There are several differences designing retail projects in the west versus in Asia and particularly in China. The retail mix and tenant types are obviously different to suit the local markets. In Asia, the quality of tenants varies tremendously from one project to the next. This is particularly true in China, however, the overall quality is improving at an accelerated pace. Generally, restaurants are more common, much larger in size, and more plentiful in Asia. On the other hand, department stores are not very common, and have smaller tenants which are preferred over larger tenants.

For better or worse, working in Asia is different in many ways from working on projects in the west. First, projects in China tend to be designed and built at a much greater speed than in the west. Secondly, the design process for projects in China tends to be more fluid. During the design phases (and sometimes in the construction phase as well), there can be many substantial changes along the way. In contrast, projects in the west tend to be more planned, engineered, coordinated and reviewed, before going through extensive municipal approvals, which naturally takes more time.

In my personal opinion,, clients in Aisa typically expect highly of design. They tend to appreciate novel and unique design solution and expect you to deliver multiple alternatives. These requirements are somewhat demanding, but it's also understandable. This may be a result of booming local real estate, which expects all projects to be outstanding.

香港建筑科学出版社：拟定设计方案花费了多长时间？ 期间，设计理念或设计方案发生过重大变动吗？

五杰建筑设计：耗时大约 6 个月才确定了整个项目的概念设计方案。这比往常要久一点，这是因为在确定概念设计过程中，客户扩大了设计范围，增加了一家 5 星级酒店的设计，从而需要更多空间。自然而然也就增加了商业空间，最终导致整个项目的规模扩大了一半。

香港建筑科学出版社：亚洲与西方国家的商业型项目有什么不同之处？换言之，你认为全世界客户的处事方式是如出一辙的吗？

五杰建筑设计：亚洲与西方在设计商业型项目方面存在几处差别，尤其以中国的商业型项目更加突出。为了迎合当地市场需求，亚洲与西方的商业型项目在功能匹配与租户类型方面存在明显差别。在亚洲，不同项目的租户在质量方面存在巨大差别。这种情况在中国尤为显著。然而，总体而言，中国的租户质量正在迅速攀升。一般而言，亚洲的餐馆更加普遍，规模更大，数量更多。另外一方面，亚洲的百货本就不那么普遍，往往更青睐于小型租户。

不管怎样，西方与亚洲之间的项目存在诸多方面的差别。首先，中国的项目在设计与建设进度方面通常比西方的更为紧张。其次，在中国项目的设计过程中通常会存在更多的不稳定因素。在设计阶段中，甚至有时在建设阶段中，一路上通常会发生很多次重大变动。相反的是，西方的项目在通过一系列繁琐的政府审批之前，通常会经过更加周密的计划，更加详尽的调配，通过工程验证并经过专业评审把关。自然而然，西方的项目在概念设计阶段会耗时更长。

在我看来，亚洲的客户对设计通常抱以很高的期望。他们喜欢新颖独特的设计方案并且希望你能够提供多种备选方案，这些要求显得有些苛刻，但也是可以理解的，这可能是因为当地房地产迅速发展，从而更需要每个项目能达到脱颖而出的效果。

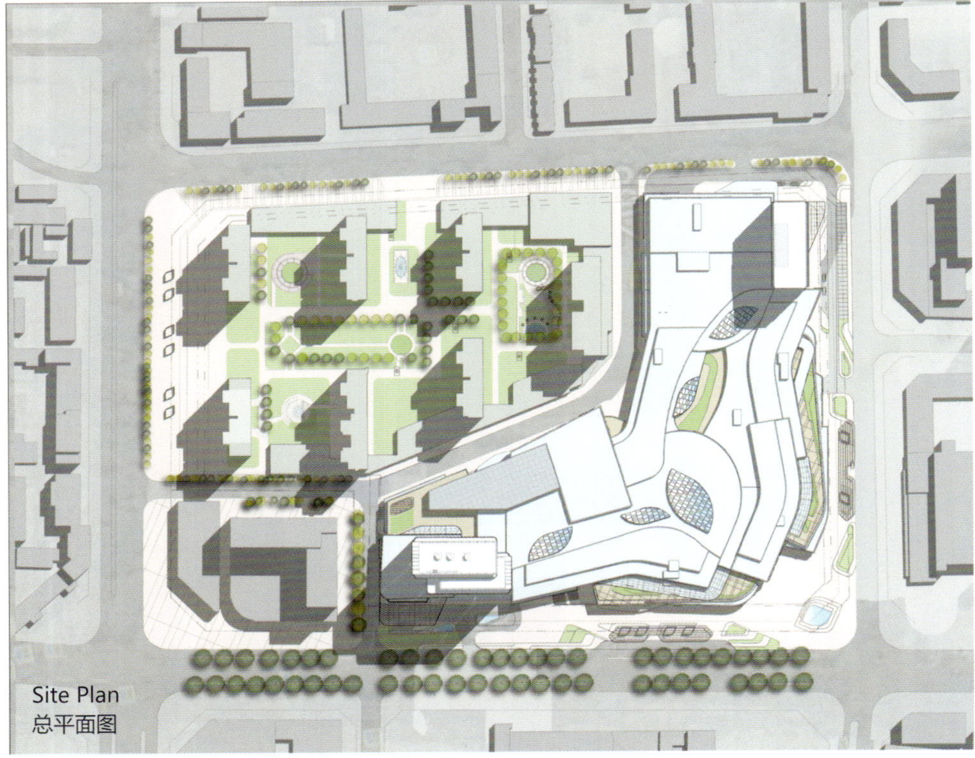
Site Plan
总平面图

5+design has respected the client's request for a simple and elegant interior retail configuration, while providing Vamenities wherever possible that link the project to the outdoors and connect it to the city. A large plaza with stepped landscaping and a fountain serves as an outdoor living room and event space, as well as the main entrance to the mall. While alfresco terraces draw visitors to upper-level shops, a sunken garden attracts them to the basement hypermarket. Ribbon-like exterior walls of glass, stone, terracotta tile and metal convey a fresh, fluid aesthetic that is echoed inside, where curvilinear atriums are accentuated by warm wood paneling and soft up lighting. Completing and complementing the retail center, the two towers provide unique faces to the city that are in keeping with their functions, integrating with the center to create a true mixed-use destination.

5+design设计团队顺应客户的要求，除了为项目提供连接自身与户外、以及整个城市的便利设施之外，还要保证内部商业布置简洁典雅。阶梯式景观工程和喷泉的大型广场为市民提供露天生活和活动空间，同时也是去往商场的主入口。通过露天看台可以到达高层零售店，穿过下沉式花园则可以进入地下大卖场。丝带般的玻璃外墙、石材、陶土砖和金属溢出一种鲜活的流线美，与在暖色木镶板及柔和屋顶灯光的映衬下脱颖而出的室内曲线式中庭风格相呼应。作为对商业中心的补充，两座塔楼造型独特，功能完善，与中心相融合，是一个真正的多功能场所。

Hand-drawn Sketches
手绘草图

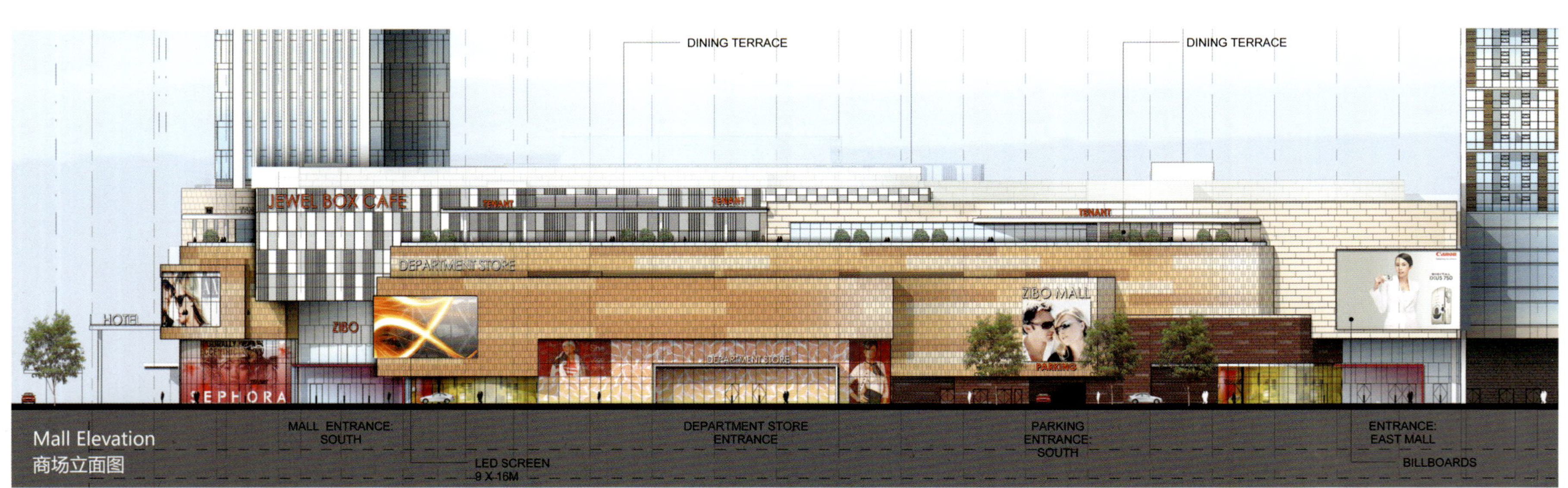

Mall Elevation
商场立面图

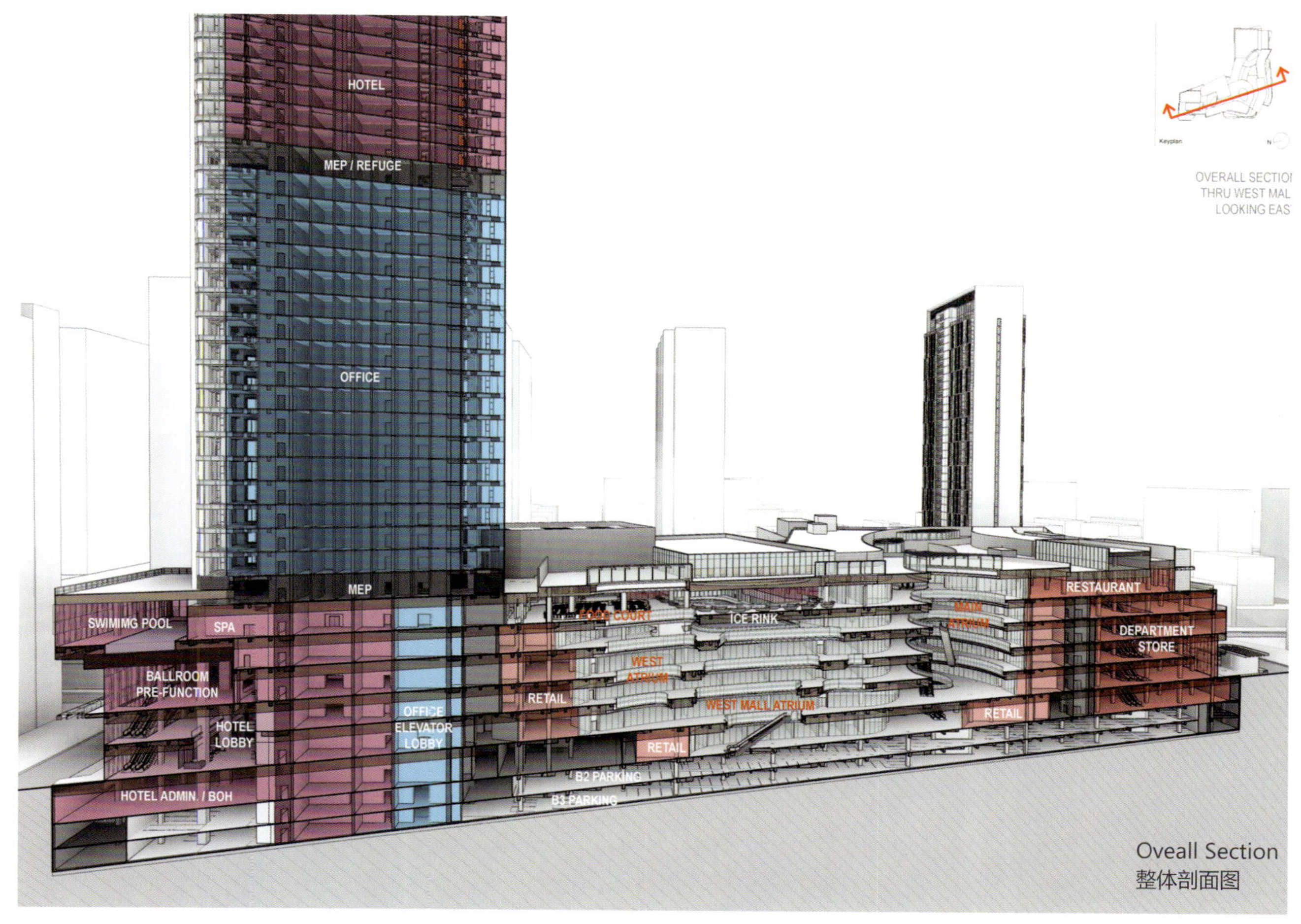

Oveall Section
整体剖面图

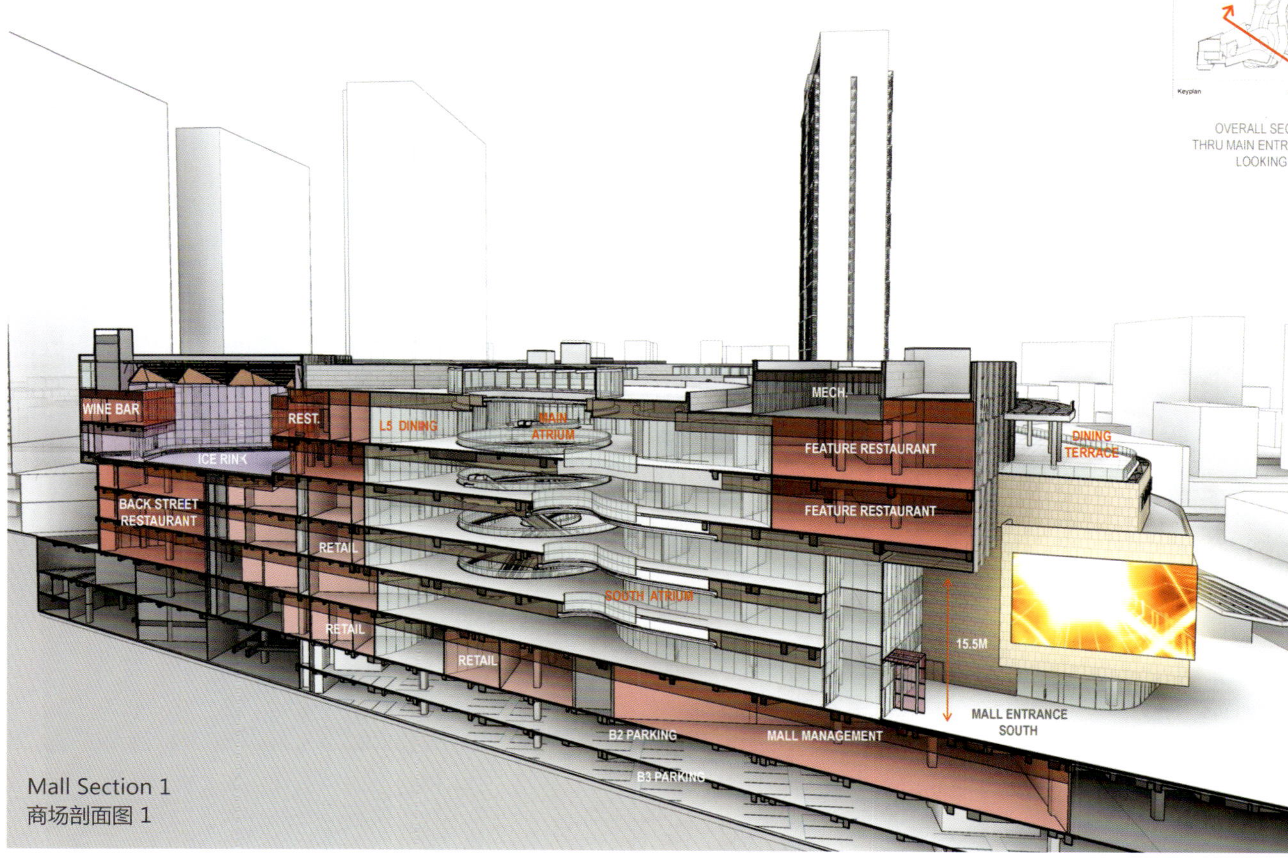

Mall Section 1
商场剖面图 1

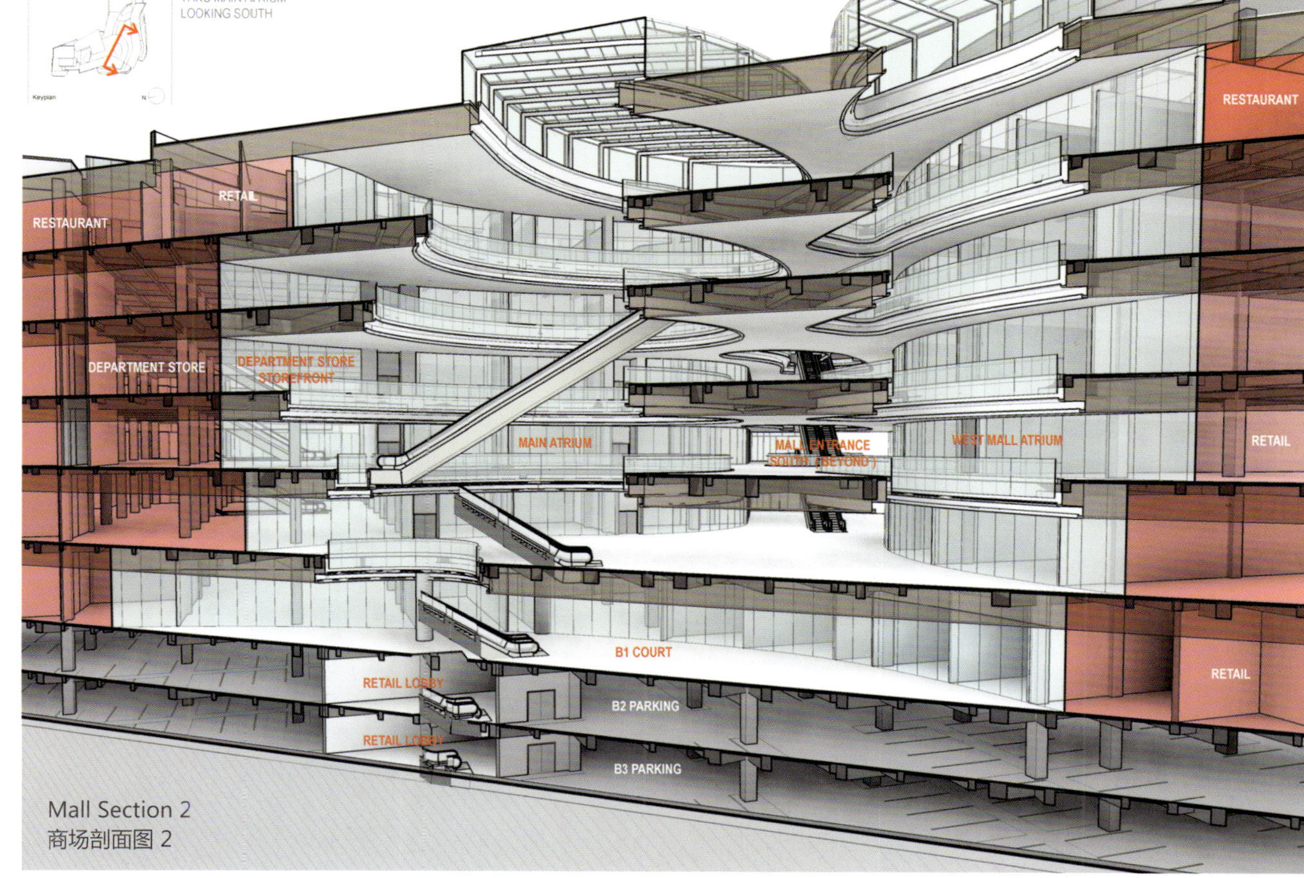

Mall Section 2
商场剖面图 2

Elevation 1
立面图 1

Elevation 2
立面图 2

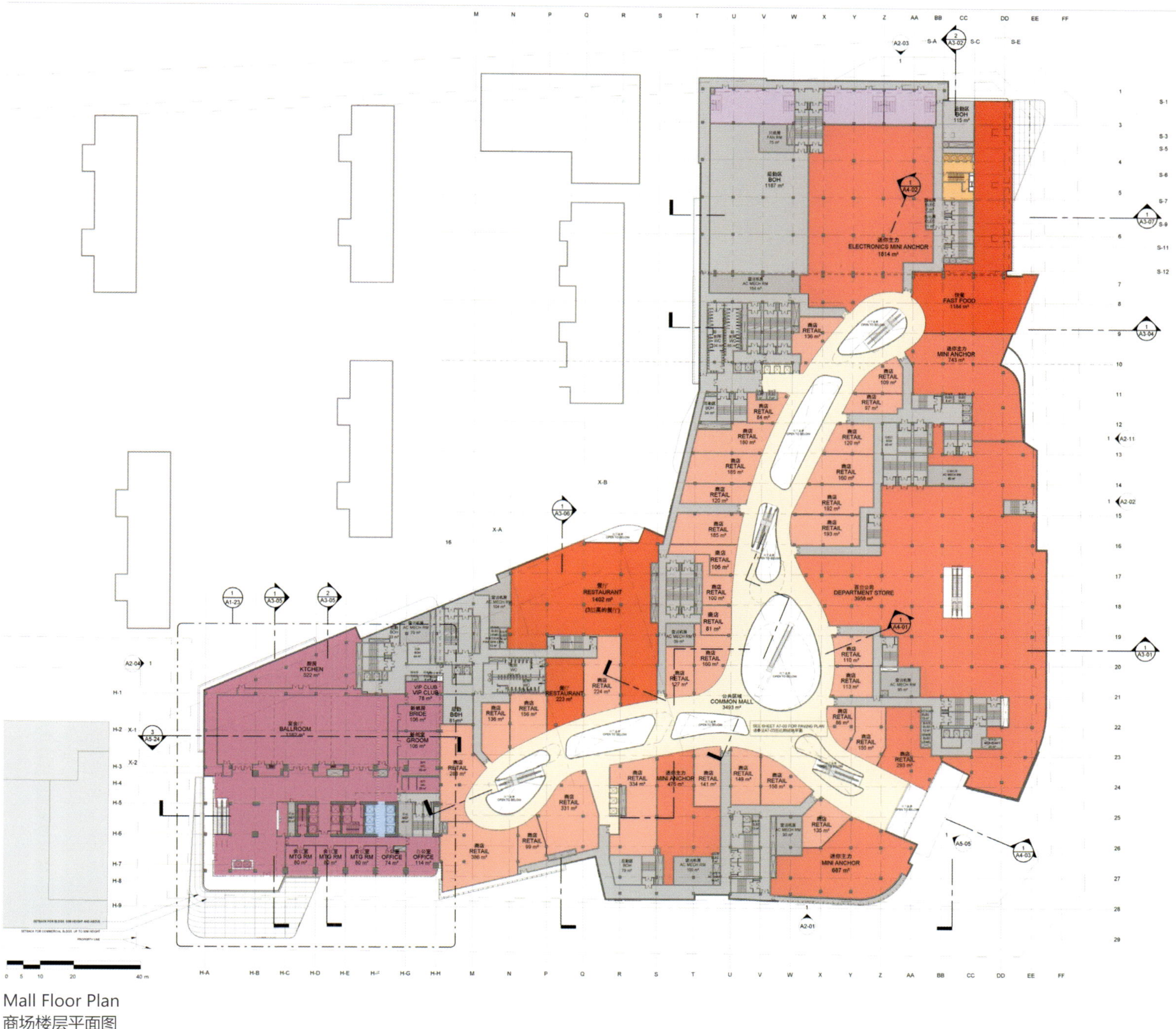

Mall Floor Plan
商场楼层平面图

Level 5 floor plan
商场 5 层平面图

Jewel Box
BISTRO
DEPARTMENT STORE
ZIBO
MALL
NARA
NARA
SHANGHAI
ZIBO
MALL

ICE BOX
ZIBO
MALL
SEAFOOD HARBOR
HOTEL DINING

PAUL & JOE
MIELE

PROJECT NAME 项目名称

SHENZHEN VANKE ONE CITY

深圳万科壹海城

Architect: 5+design, Inc

设计公司：五杰建筑设计

PROJECT INFORMATION 项目信息

Client	Shenzhen Vanke Real Estate	**客户**	深圳万科地产集团
Location	Shenzhen, China	**地点**	中国深圳
Site Area	137,250 m²	**占地面积**	137，250 平方米
Renderings	Vanke Public Relations Firm	**图片**	万科公关公司

OVERVIEW 项目概况

Vanke One City, a large-scale mixed-use development in the Yantian District of Shenzhen, promises to return the existing government center to local prominence while introducing many exciting new public amenities to the area. Located between Wutong Mountain, the city's tallest peak, and Mirs Bay, the project will feature a 200 m office tower, several residential buildings, a five-star hotel, four restaurant pavilions and a three-level shopping complex containing a movie theater, food court and department store.

万科壹海城为一个大型综合开发项目。该项目位于深圳市盐田区，旨在使现有的政治中心重新回到核心地位。与此同时，该开发项目将引入各种有趣的公众娱乐项目。地处深圳最高峰梧桐山与大鹏湾之间的又一城项目将以高达 200 米的办公大厦为中心，周边配有少量住宅楼，一座五星级酒店，四所餐馆以及一座三层楼高的综合购物中心；在购物中心内则配设有电影院、餐厅及百货商店。

BRIEF INTERVIEW 访谈录

ARCHITECT
Arthur Benedetti

设计师
Arthur Benedetti

HKASP: What has been the greatest design challenge ?

5+design, Inc:The project site consists of four separate development parcels bookending two open-greenspace parcels , each of which had varying development objectives. One of the biggest challenges was in creating a harmonious language to unify the parcels while respecting the individuality and the objectives of each of the parcels. The center two parcels were to be a public space, which we activated with children's' play areas, greenspace, promenades, and sunken plazas to create a 'family room' for the nearby residents and visitors.

HKASP: What was the final design solution?

5+design, Inc:Being adjacent to the Yantian Government Center, we made use of the primary organizational device – the perfect axial alignment from the top of Wutong Mountain passing through the Yantian Government Center and continuing axially through the park and Starling Inlet and terminating on the rolling hills of Hong Kong New Territories. By establishing a narrative between the mountain and the sea we created a 'fabric' of textures to be applied to the buildings which transformed the facades from the warm tones of vertical slats representing the forest along the mountain to white fritted glass facades representing the crashing waves over a rocky shore. Colorful glass facades behind the 'wood' screen responded to the colorful ripples of water along the shorefront. The abstract narrative defined each of the facades, creating a unifying layer that was able to transition between each of the parcels. Highrises along the western fronting parcels allowed for dramatic views of the Inlet while lower pavilions on the waterfront edge allowed for a permeability to the site from the public waterfront walk.

The solution created a harmonious environment between lots which would eventually have different ownerships, but which formed an enlivened backdrop of-retail, restaurants and entertainment in a comfortable, safe ocean-front enclave for local residents and visitors alike to enjoy a day near the sea.

香港建筑科学出版社：最大的挑战是什么？

五杰建筑设计：项目所在地由四片独立的地块组成。地块两端分别是露天绿地。每片地块都有自己特定的开发目标。最大的挑战在于如何在四片地块之间形成一种协调与统一，而同时又保留各自的特点并凸显各自的功能。中间的两片地块将作为公共空间，这里我们将设置儿童游乐区、绿地、散步走廊与沉降广场，旨在给周边的居民与游客提供一片具有浓郁家庭氛围的场所。

香港建筑科学出版社：最终的设计方案是什么？

五杰建筑设计：鉴于项目毗邻盐田政府大楼，我们利用了主要的布局方案（即一条完美的轴向排列，轴线始于梧桐山顶，穿过盐田政府大楼，然后在轴向上继续延伸、穿过公园与沙头角海，最后至于香港新界的连绵群山）。为了反映出山与海之间的自然过渡，我们在建筑立面上创造了一种自然过渡的肌理，从由暖色竖条板形成的立面逐渐过渡到由白色多孔玻璃形成的立面，因为前者代表大山中的森林，而后者则代表拍击在岸边岩石上的浪花。木质屏风后面采用缤纷多彩的玻璃幕墙，这恰巧呼应了岸边荡起的绚丽多彩的涟漪。抽象的立面展现创造出统一、协调的韵律，从而使各地块前呼后应，过渡自然。人们可在西侧临街边上的高层楼观赏海湾美景。同时，散步于海边走廊的人们可从位于海边的矮层生活馆进入场地。

设计方案不仅在各地块之间形成了和谐的环境，而且也保留了各自的功能特点。这里有商店、餐厅、休闲娱乐场所，功能齐全，环境舒适，真可谓安全的海边圣地，以供本地居民与游客到此尽享海边生活。

壹海街
ONE CITY AVENUE

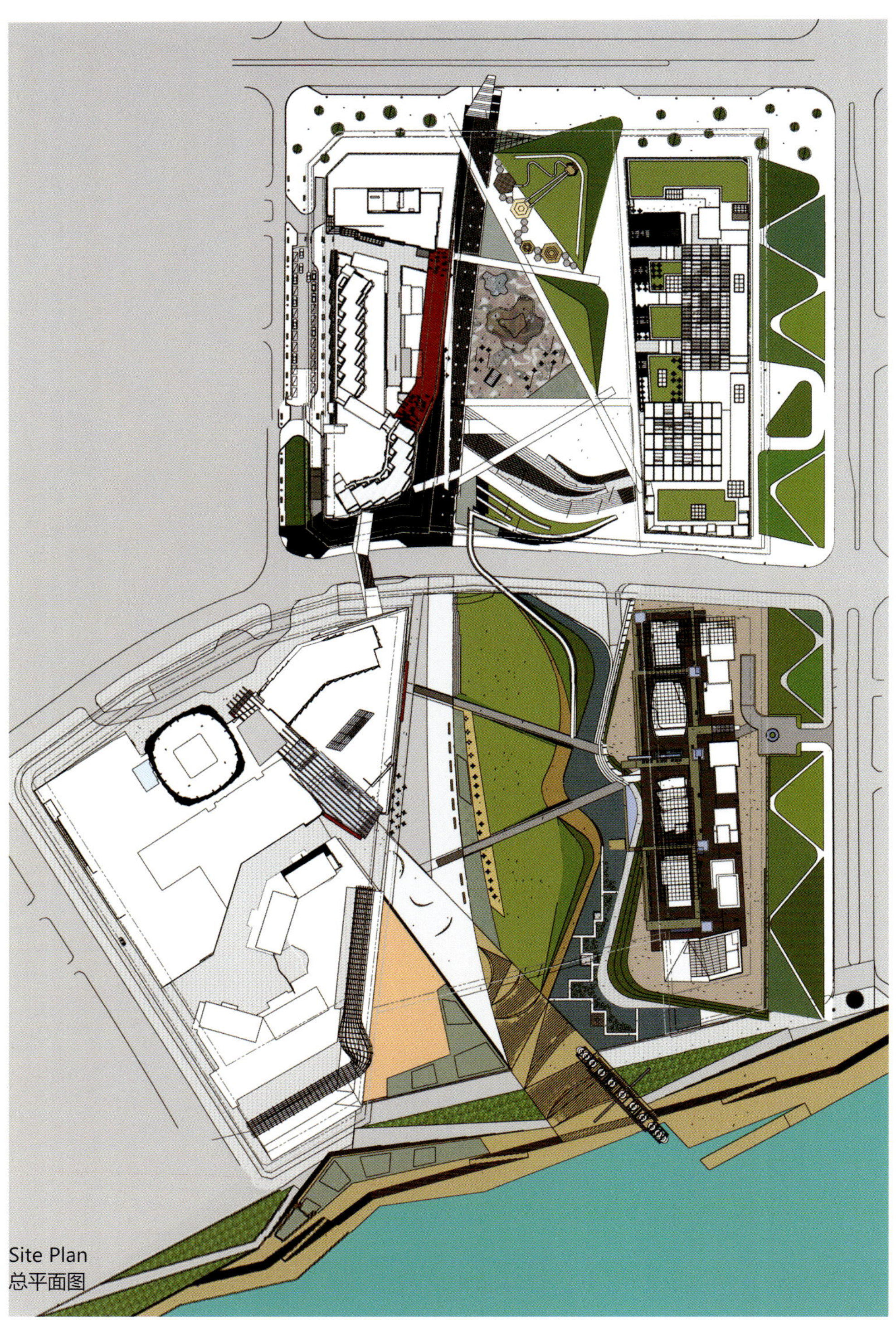
Site Plan
总平面图

In master-planning Vanke One City, 5+design re-established and celebrated the view corridor between the forested summit and the sea. The project's retail components were designed to reflect their connection to the site, with building forms and materials changing between the mountains and the bay. Exterior wood slats will provide dappled light like a tree canopy as well as evoke a boardwalk. The park at the project's center will serve as the district's principal green space. Accessible from nearby residences, tourist beaches and beyond, it will offer a man-made inlet, playgrounds and playing fields, refreshment kiosks and a large central green.

对项目做总体规划时，五杰建筑设计对绿色山峰与蓝色海湾之间的观景走廊进行了重新设计与架构。项目旗下所有商店的设计风格都传递着它们与所处环境的融合，而且山水之间建筑的形态以及建筑材料的变换也都完全与周边环境相契合。另外，建筑外墙采用木条，在阳光照耀下会形成斑驳光影，一如置身于森林之中，令人想起浪漫的木板小道。而位于项目中心位置的公园则会成为这一地区主要的绿色地带。在壹海城，邻近的住宅，近在咫尺的观景沙滩都唾手可得；再加上人工水湾、活动和娱乐场所、小食档以及一个超级大的绿色中心带，显然，壹海城为人们提供的还有更多。

华润万家

8283
8880
名校学位
赢在起点
STARBUCKS COFFEE
盛大开业

壹海城

床上用品
质优价廉

开业酬宾
全天

PROJECT NAME 项目名称

HUIZHOU HUAMAO CENTER

惠州华贸中心

Architect:Perkins Eastman

设计公司：Perkins Eastman 建筑设计事务所

PROJECT INFORMATION 项目信息

Client	Beijing Guohua Property Real Estate Company Ltd.	**客户**	北京国华房地产有限公司
Location	Huizhou, Guangdong Province, China	**地点**	中国广东省惠州市
Site Area	135,920 m²	**占地面积**	135，920 平方米
Gross Floor Area	771,450 m²	**用地面积**	771，450 平方米

OVERVIEW 项目概况

The Huizhou Huamao Center is envisioned as a vibrant retail commercial and residential destination on a 136,000m² site—redefining the city center while setting the stage for Huizhou City's future. It is the final piece of a comprehensive city master plan, presenting a momentous opportunity to reinforce the overall plan while adding a lively and distinctive block to the city center. The development consists of a group of buildings with a sleek and contemporary aesthetic, a complement to the bold and visually contemporary architectural language of other developments in the region. The site's three major components are retail, commercial, and a residential community totaling almost 771,500 m². More specifically, it comprises a large pedestrian plaza, a five-story shopping mall with 100,000 m² of central retail space, and six 30-to 50-storey residential towers clustered in three groupings. Additionally, the site is anchored by two office towers that provide more than 130,000 m² of commercial space. As a focal point in the city, the open space and buildings will allow for a variety of civic activities, while the development's proximity to major sports and cultural facilities will make it a desirable urban destination. The Huizhou Huamo Center will become the landmark within the City that is integrated into the surrounding urban fabric, has a sense of place, and creates value.

惠州华贸中心总占地面积 136，000 平方米，将以充满活力的零售商业据点和住宅区姿态为惠州市打造别具前景的未来。它是综合城市主体规划的收官项目，为市中心新增充满活力且别具特色的地标建筑的同时，更带来了巩固总体规划的重要机会。此项开发项目将囊括多个外观时尚、现代的建筑群，与该区域颇具粗犷视觉感的现代建筑风格形成完美互补。项目集商业、写字楼、住宅区三大组成部分于一体，总建筑面积约为 771，500 平方米。具体而言，项目包括一个大型步行广场、一座五层楼购物中心（设 100，000 平方米的中央零售区）以及 6 栋 30~50 层的住宅公寓，分别集聚于三大建筑体。此外，项目还包括两栋写字楼作为标志性建筑，提供逾 130，000 平方米的商业面积。作为惠州市的焦点，这里开放的空间和建筑将是市民活动的理想选择，而靠近主要体育、文化设施的便捷地理位置将让这里成为一流的城区娱乐场所。惠州华贸中心将一跃成为惠州市的地标性建筑，融于城市肌理，充满地域动感，势必为这座城市创造崭新的价值。

BRIEF INTERVIEW 访谈录

ARCHITECT
Nicholas Leahy

设计师
Nicholas Leahy

ARCHITECT
Perkins Bradford

设计师
Perkins Bradford

HKASP: What was the main concept behind the whole project?

Perkins Eastman: Nicholas Leahy AIA, LEED AP (Principal) ：The design concept was to create a new destination within the new larger city center plan, "a place to be and be seen" that is centered around a new urban square—a human scaled plaza that acts as the hub for several connections to the surrounding context—so that it is activated day and night with people.

The design is anchored by a large urban shopping mall, an important urban edge that draws visitors into the development, and two tall office towers that create an important portal. Residential areas are arranged around the square in a pinwheel fashion, which creates a dynamic flow to the scheme. Townhouse apartments feature retail lots at the lower levels, forming the podiums for the fifty-story residential towers that pierce the sky above the city skyline and create an iconic landmark within the city. – Nicholas Leahy

HKASP: How long did it take the project team to develop the proposal? Did the concept/design change much during that time?

Perkins Eastman: Nicholas Leahy AIA, LEED AP (Principal) :The team worked on the project for a little more than two years. The design concept package was developed in 3 months, and the design process continued until the project was built. The design concept did not change once throughout the process, although it was refined and developed through a collaborative process with the client, ranging from the overall concept to the smallest details. – Nicholas Leahy

HKASP: Is there any different when doing retail projects between Asia and Europe? Or do you agree that the customer behaviors are globally the same?

Brad Perkins FAIA (Chairman and CEO) : All major retail markets have significant differences. Many of these differences have major design implications. Project size, the number of levels, the internal circulation, the size and distribution of the stores, the amenities, pedestrian access, vehicular access, service access, and many other important issues.

香港建筑科学出版社：项目背后的主要概念是什么？

AIA, LEED AP 的 Nicholas Leahy（主建筑师）设计概念计划在新的大城市中心规划中打造一个新的目的地，这是一个“值得一去并令人欣赏的地方”，周围环绕着一个全新的都市广场，这个人性化的广场可作为联系周围环境的中心枢纽，日日夜夜人流川流不息。

设计中规划出一个大型城市购物中心，作为重要的城市边缘区可吸引消费者的光临，还有两栋高高的办公大楼，打造出一个重要的城市门户区域。住宅区以旋转风车的时尚结构排列在广场四周，为整个设计方案形成了一种动感的流线结构。联排别墅式公寓的底层设有零售商店，形成 50 层住宅楼的裙楼，在城市天际线三方直直插入云霄，为这个城市打造一个极具标志性的地标建筑。– Nicholas Leahy

香港建筑科学出版社：项目团队开发方案用了多长时间？设计期间，项目概念 / 设计是否经过多次修改？

Perkins Eastman 建筑设计事务所 :AIA, LEED AP 的 Nicholas Leahy（主建筑师）：团队在这个项目上花了两年多时间。提出设计概念大概用了 3 个月时间，并且在项目建设过程中也一直持续对设计做更改。在整个建造过程中，设计主要概念并没有做过更改，只是随着客户的意见对整体概念和细节都作了提炼和修改。

香港建筑科学出版社：在亚洲和欧洲建设零售项目有何区别？您是否全球的消费者都有相同的行为认知？

AIA, LEED AP 的 Nicholas Leahy（主建筑师）：所有主要的零售市场都有着明显的差别。这些差别都影响着主要设计概念：项目规模、层数、内部循环、商店规模和分布、设施、人行通道、车辆通道、服务通道以及其他方面。

Tower 2
7190000
STARBUCKS COFFEE
GUESS
DKNY JEANS
Calvin Klein Jeans
LACOSTE

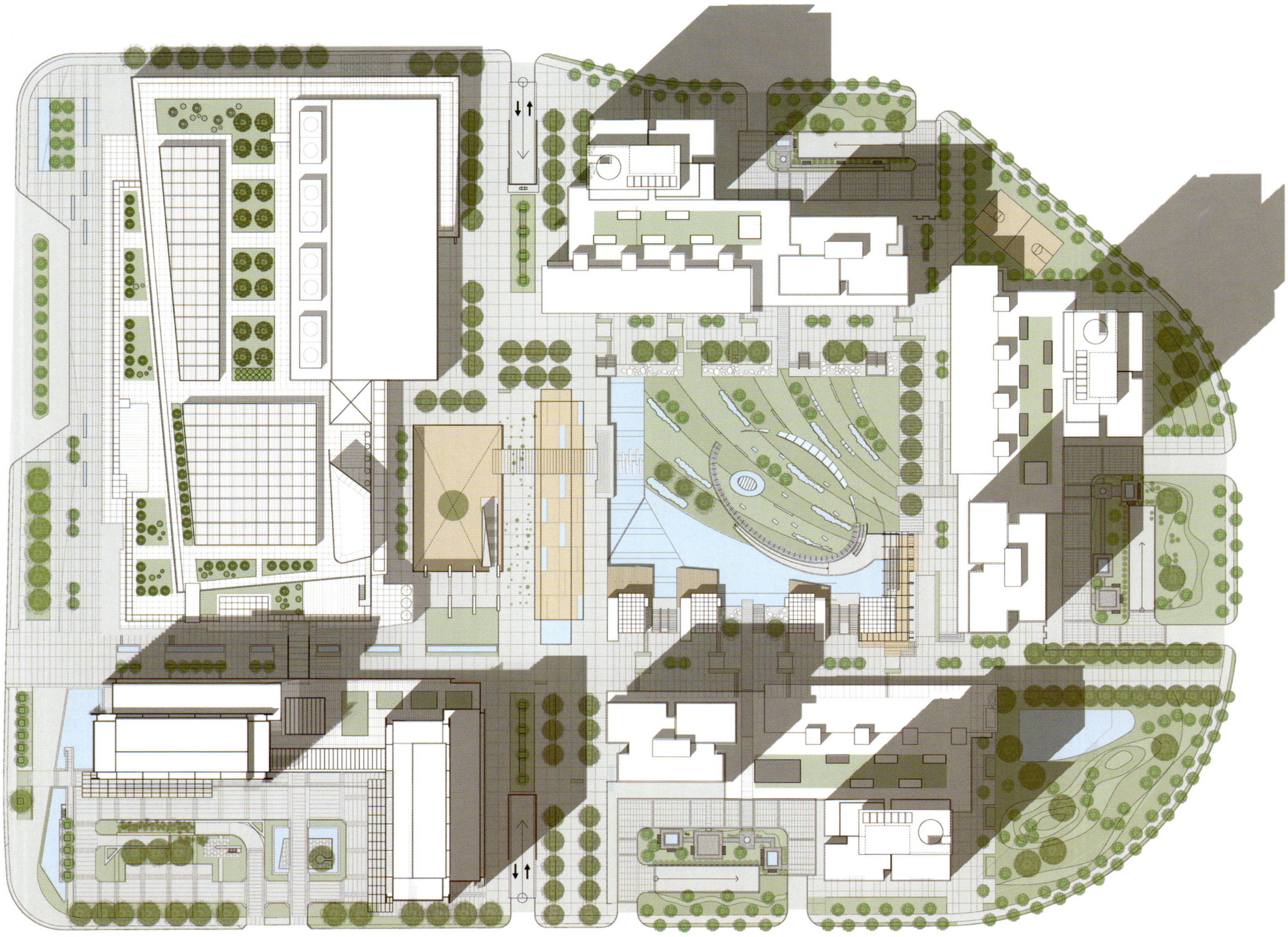

Site Plan
总平面图

Perkins Eastman's vision for a contemporary multi-use community was designed to complement the existing recreational, cultural, and residential projects in the area. It creates a user-friendly singular hub that is full of vitality and memorable, even in the larger context. The overall configuration of the major architectural elements strives to create synergies with surrounding land-uses while simultaneously maintaining distinct environments within the site. To accomplish this, the site has been arranged as a largely pedestrian zone. Vehicular access is confined to drop-off points around the periphery of the site while major service traffic is directed below-grade, allowing for a large public pedestrian open-space at the heart of the site. The result is a comfortably human-scaled space designed to support a variety of activities that will become a unique and vibrant destination, a place to "see and be seen".

Perkins Eastman 建筑设计事务所的设计愿景在于打造一座多用途社区，与该区域目前的娱乐、文化、住宅项目共同形成完整配套体系，营造出充满生命力的人性化独立城市综合体，甚至能从更广层面上体现其标新立异的特性。主建筑元素的总体布置力求与周边用地相辅相成，同时保有项目鲜明的环境特征。为实现这一设计愿景，项目整体设计以大型步行区为基准理念，仅在项目区域外围设有车辆上客、落客点，主要交通服务则位于地下层，以此在项目中心留出宽敞的公共行人区，最大化空间利用，实现舒适的人性化空间设计，让这里成为众多活动的开展园地，从而树立起独一无二、充满活力的新型城区地位，成为人们津津乐道、乐于前往的全新场所。

Tower 2

Tower 2
DKNY JEANS

Critical to the success of any urban scheme is how well it is woven and integrated into the existing urban fabric. Therefore, careful consideration was given to how this scheme ties into the surrounding city blocks while allowing for improved amenities. By promoting public pedestrian circulation through the site and creating en route destinations, the master plan establishes links into a wider context of inter- and extra-urban networks. The placement of such a core with relevant connections to the rest of the city is crucial to the success of a city with distinct, divided areas.

任何城市规划成功的关键都在于它能否与现有城市结构完美交融。因此，针对该项规划如何融入周边街区、同时保有设施提升空间进行了谨慎考量。通过刺激项目区域内的行人往来量并沿途设立引人驻足的目的地，主体规划在整个市区内外创建了更为广阔的城市网络链接。对于区域特征明显的城市而言，核心位置与其余部分实现有效融合是城市规划成功的关键。

Another predominant goal of the plan was to create a sense of place that would be vibrant and inviting while remaining pedestrian-friendly. Sited around the open activated pedestrian space that functions as a major organizing element, the buildings will also bolster this space as an identifiable urban focal point. Together, the open space and buildings will allow for a variety of civic activities, distinguished on both city planning and architectural levels. The development was carefully designed to incorporate proven "place-making" practices that underline the positive virtues of mixed-use planning. Mixed-use sites create efficiencies in the use of infrastructure, allowing for convenient access to public services while supporting pleasant environments for social interactions. To achieve an adequate level of accessibility that is always tied to a sense of place, the plan features multi-storey retail bases that frame the streets and animate the pedestrian's experience.

Another critical factor to the long-term success of any major urban development is its potential to create value. Through smart urban planning practices and boldly designed architecture, the development will generate special addresses for high-profile retail establishments and professional tenants. This will, in turn, promote a positive urban setting for residents seeking an exclusive environment. Such environments can be achieved through the careful placement of buildings on the site. By capitalizing on the views of the surrounding landscape, majestic vistas, and view corridors will be incorporated into the urbanscape. Intelligent planning of the site, such as optimizing the orientation of the buildings with regard to views, light, and the strategic distribution of open spaces will create remarkable transitions between the public and private domains. One very unique aspect of the project involves a water feature in the plaza that not only enlivens the pedestrian plaza, but also serves as a catalyst for revenue. Retail pavilions and a tea house were developed on one side of the feature, and an ice skating rink sculpted into a green lawn was developed on the other.

该规划另一个主要目标便是营造出场所感，在充满活力、别具吸引的同时还要有方便行人的特性。建筑群坐落于充满生气的开放式步行区，在该区域本身即为主要结构元素的条件下，为其更添光辉，成为特色鲜明的城市焦点。二者结合，打造出市民活动的理想去处，而在城市规划和建筑层次的基础上又别有不同。项目设计独具匠心，巧妙采用已经验证的“场所构建”实践，凸显出了综合规划的长处。项目多用设计让基础设施更具使用效率，在为公共服务提供便利的同时，让社交互动活动也能享有怡人的环境。为了让整个项目更具亲民性，同时营造出通常与之同在的场所感，规划提出了多层零售商业区理念，为街道构建出整体框架，打造更具活力的行人体验。

任何主要城市规划项目要想取得长远的成功都脱离不了另一个关键因素，即创造价值的潜能。有了巧妙的城市规划实践和大胆的建筑设计，此规划项目必将是高端零售店和专业承租人的理想选择，转而为寻求独有环境的居民构建出积极向上的城市环境。通过巧妙的楼宇布局即可轻松呈现这样的环境。项目设计中包括观景廊，充分利用周围设计风貌，呈现壮丽风光，为城市景观增添一抹新亮色。整个项目规划巧妙，充分考量楼宇朝向，获取最佳周边景观和入室光线，此外，通过对开放空间进行布局定位，让公共和私人领域实现完美过渡。项目一大亮点在于广场水景，其不仅让步行广场绽放蓬勃生气，更为创造营收增添助力。水景一侧设有零售亭和茶楼，另一侧则建有溜冰场，为青青绿草地增添不一样的视觉感受。

PROJECT NAME 项目名称

CHENGDU BACK GARDEN PHASE 4

成都后花园 4 期

Architect:TongJi Architects (TJA)

设计公司：深圳市同济人建筑设计有限公司

PROJECT INFORMATION 项目信息

Location	Chengdu, China	**地点**	中国成都
Occupied Area	52,971.51 m²	**用地面积**	52，971.51 平方米
Gross Floor Area	379,772.2 m²	**用地面积**	379，772.2 平方米
Plot Area	4.9	**容积率**	4.9

OVERVIEW 项目概况

The design principle of project takes consideration of consumer's feelings and business benefits to achieve the double win. Combined with the poetic landscape of Chengdu and commercial industry model, a familiar and poetic commercial space was created for consumers. The construction symbolizes the hills and valleys while the dynamic water represents the source of fortune and the ecological lawn serves as the resting platform, with all of these elements, this project combined with sunshine, mountain, water, greenery and business complex organically, creating an urban living model with leisure and fashion and resulting in the authentic "black garden" of Chengdu.

本项目的设计核心是将消费者的感受与商家的盈利实现双赢。其将诗意的成都山水与商业业态模式结合渗透，为消费者提供一个熟知而又诗意的消费空间，以建筑的实体象征山谷山丘，以灵动的立体水体为象征财运的源，以立体生态草坪作为休息平台，将阳光、山、水、绿化有机的组织渗透到商业综合体中，创造一个闲适与时尚兼有的都市生活范本，成就真正意义上的成都“后花园”。

BRIEF INTERVIEW 访谈录

ARCHITECT
Zhang Lingfei

设计师
张凌飞

ARCHITECT
Zhao Junwei

设计师
赵军维

HKASP: What was the main concept behind the whole project?
TongJi Architects (TJA) :Inspired from "Urban landscape", we expect to create a unique commercial project by imitating enjoyable scenery found in Chinese traditional painting, with architectural fengshui theory serving as the tutor for architectural layout and function.

HKASP: When designing, is there something in particular that you focus on?
TongJi Architects (TJA) :The integration of architectural fengshui theory into modern commerce is quite important for such project. The prominent difference between the project and other commercial projects lies in combining such two factors with the needs of architectural function.

HKASP: What are the important things that this project does for the city?
TongJi Architects (TJA) :Known as "land of abundance", Chengdu enjoys unique cultural heritage and climate, with an emphasis in carrying on traditional culture. As a result, we expect to combine architectural fengshui theory from traditional culture with modern architecture, forming a blending of the past and the present as well as a harmonious form of architecture. In addition, we also hope the buildings can be part of Chengdu and her culture.

香港建筑科学出版社：建筑背后的主要概念是什么？
深圳市同济人建筑设计有限公司："城市山水"，我们希望能借鉴国画写意山水的意境，让建筑的布局和功能在建筑风水学的指导下成为一个不同的商业项目。

香港建筑科学出版社：在设计的过程中有什么是你们特别注重的吗？
深圳市同济人建筑设计有限公司：建筑风水和现代商业的融合在这个项目里是比较重要的，把这两个因素和建筑功能的需求结合，是这个项目和其他商业综合体项目最大的不同点。

香港建筑科学出版社：你觉得这个项目给这座城市带来了什么重要的东西呢？
深圳市同济人建筑设计有限公司：成都有“天府之国”的称谓，有独特的文化底蕴和氛围，比较注重国学文化的承接，所以在设计上我们希望把国学文化里的建筑风水和现代建筑结合，形成一个古今交融并且和谐的建筑形式，也希望建筑能融入城市，融入成都的文化中。

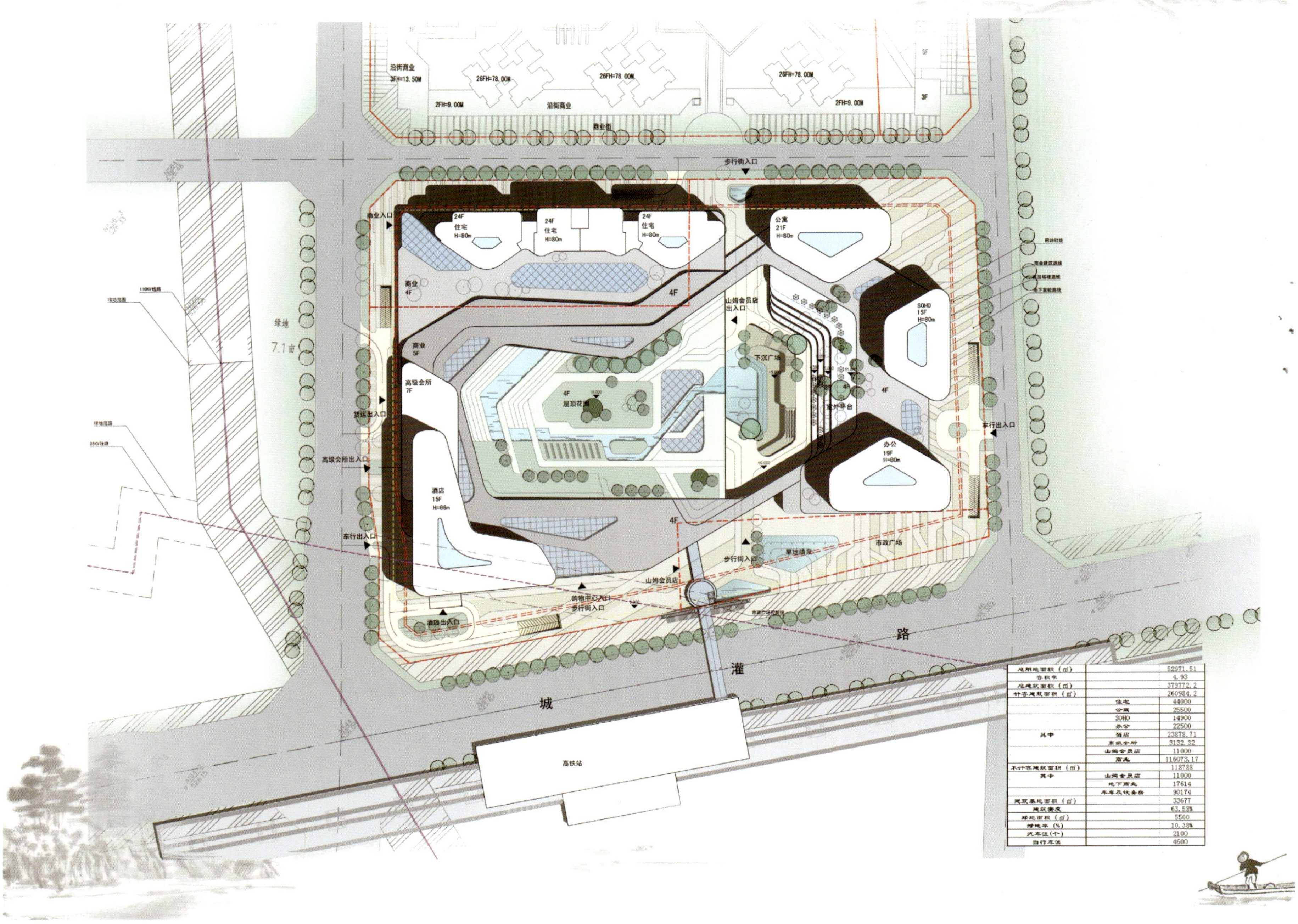

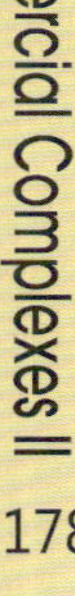

总用地面积（㎡）		52971.51
容积率		4.93
总建筑面积（㎡）		379772.2
计容建筑面积（㎡）		260984.2
其中	住宅	44000
	公寓	25500
	SOHO	14900
	办公	22500
	酒店	23878.71
	高级会所	3132.32
	山姆会员店	11000
	商业	116073.17
不计容建筑面积（㎡）		118788
其中	山姆会员店	11000
	地下商业	17614
	车库及设备房	90174
建筑基地面积（㎡）		33677
建筑密度		63.58%
绿地面积（㎡）		5500
绿地率（%）		10.38%
汽车位(个)		2100
自行车位		4600

Site Plan
总平面图

This project combines the poetic landscape of Chengdu and modern business models, providing a friendly and innovative experience space that brings actual benefit to businesses. The building mass symbolizes the hills and mountains while the dynamic three-dimensional waters represents the source of wealth, this modern urban complex takes the solid ecological grass slope as the platform to mix the sunshine, wind, water, greenery together. This urban life sample space features with highly leisure and comfort, creating the "Back Garden of Chengdu" in the real sense.

将诗意的成都山水与现代的商业业态模式结合渗透，为消费者提供一个熟知而又富有新意的体验空间，为商家带来有实际效益的经营。以建筑的实体为象征性的山谷山丘，以灵动的立体水体为象征财运的源，以立体生态草坡为平台，将阳台光、风、水、绿化糅和进现代城市综合体，创造一个闲适兼有的都市生活范本，成就真正意义上的“成都后花园”。

PROJECT NAME 项目名称

SANYA CHINA RAILWAY SUNSHINE PLACE

三亚中铁子悦薹

Architect: Australia PT Design Consultants Limited

设计公司：澳大利亚柏涛建筑设计有限公司

PROJECT INFORMATION 项目信息

Client	Sanya, China railway real estate co., LTD	**客户**	三亚中铁置业有限公司
Location	Sanya, Hainan	**地点**	海南三亚
Site Scale	3#Plots 13,977m², 4#Plots 18334m²	**用地规模**	3# 地块 13，977 平方米，4# 地块 18，334 平方米
Site Area	total construction area of 3#Plots,Planning Volume,42,142m²,total construction area of 4#plots,PlanningVolume,56,063m²	**图纸和规划图**	3# 地块总建筑面积（计容）：42，142 平方米，4# 地块总建筑面积（计容）：56，063 平方米；
Area Ratio	3#Plots 3.02, 4#Plots 3.0	**容积率**	3# 地块 3.02，4# 地块 3.0
Architecture Properties	Retail Complex	**物业类型**	商业综合体

OVERVIEW 项目概况

Built according to international grade-A criteria, China Railway Property Square is the very first high-end office tower, with a total covered area of 31,000 m². The concept of master planning is one centre with two axes, to create a comfortable and warm space in the city, presenting an abstract concept of entrance to Luna River. The base is located at the city's central area. The back of the base serves as the city's major landscaped gallery. The south side of the base serves as the urban political and cultural center. In concert with the landscape range behind the base, the height of two plots is limited at 100 levels to allow the continuity of the skyline. The overall design goes as follows:

三亚中铁置业广场作为三亚第一个按照国际甲级标准建设的高品质写字楼，总建筑面积 31，000 方米。该项目的总体规划理念为：一心两轴，城市客厅，月川之门。整个基地位于城市的中心区，背面为城市的主要景观长廊，其南面为城市的政治与文化中心。为了迎合背后的景观山脉，两地块的至高点均设置 100 高层建筑，使得城市的天际线得以延续。整体设计如下：

BRIEF INTERVIEW 访谈录

ARCHITECT
Shi Xudong

设计师
施旭东

HKASP: Is there anything unique in this project that different from other business retail projects?

Shi Xudong :The biggest difference between architectural design and other product designs is that every architectural project is unique as its design is to dig out and express the special values and features for itself. The first feature for this project is it is adjoins to Landscape avenue in the south and next to the Mountain Park in Yuechuang District in the back, the project layout adopts the echoing towers at a 45 degree angle to form the "Yuechuang Door", which emphasize the landscape gallery of 60 meters in the center of plot to build the opposite landscape relationship between project and Jin Ji Ling Park in the axis structure. The second feature lies in its special complex types of operation, we take fully consideration of local market's needs before we set up the functions of project, and the office adopts the layout of dual core wall structure, providing an open space with ocean view and broad sight in two sides. This space could be divided into several small units with different sizes by flexible division. Without the limitation of central core tube, the high and open lobby produces the refreshing image for the visitors. Point-type towers, plate-type hire-rise buildings and "Commercial HOUSE" were arranged around the inner garden. The third feature could be the concept of green and ecological environment. In addition to the sunshade component in the facade, we also specially emphasize on the relationship between buildings and nature, which expressing the local life style and urban leisure. Next to two core tubes in the office building, sky gardens were set up in alternating floors to create the comfortable office space. We brought the concept of "transmission patio", which not only introduces nature lighting in the vertical space, but also lead into the sky gardens to form the three-dimensional sky garden system, allowing the users that living in the high levels close to the nature.

HKASP: What is your special attention on this project in your design process, such as materials, patterns?

Shi Xudong: We thought the image of building should source from the plot feature and internal spatial function logic. The design of side core tubes create the thick and straight corner for main office building, and the terrace garden in the towers that face to Yingbin Avenue adopts the drop and ladder-type structure accordingly, forming the special geometry cutting effect to echo to the mountain shape of northern Jin Ji Ling, which is contrast to most water-friendly buildings in waterfront area of Sanya. We mainly use the warm colored travertine for the building facade.

The hotel and office space adopt the unified vertical aluminum sun shade to realize the consistent visual effect.There was an open swimming pool in the roof garden of plate-type hotel building, we configured the steel sunshade above the pool to avoid direct sunshine. The sunshade structure adopts the charming orange canvas to create a bright point for this building. As this is an urban complex project, we always focus on the shape of urban public space. We arranged a slanting commercial inner street in commercial space, which brought the street front commercial atmosphere into inner space of complex, forming the public space system with the combination of 60 meters of urban landscape belt. We tried to design a sunken urban plaza and landscape tower between the office building and hotel, but it is could not be true unfortunately.

香港建筑科学出版社：你觉得这个项目和其他的商业零售项目比起来有什么与众不同的地方？

施旭东：：建筑设计与其他的产品设计最大的一个不同就是每个项目都是独一无二的，设计的过程其实就是挖掘和表现项目本身的独特价值和气质。子悦台项目的特点一是项目南临景观大道，背靠月川区山体公园的位置，在布局上我们通过塔楼 45 度围合呼应的方式，形成”月川之门”，限定强调了地块中心 60 米宽城市绿化带的景廊，建立项目本身与金鸡岭公园的轴线对景联系。特点之二是复合型的特色业态，项目的每个功能我们都详细考虑了当地市场的需求，办公采用了双核心筒的布局，提供了可以双面看海望山，视线通畅的开敞办公空间，这个大空间通过灵活分割平面也可以形成不同模数的小单元办公，大堂由于没有中央核心筒的限制，两层挑高的通透大跨效果令人耳目一新。酒店设计则围绕一个内花园安排了点式塔楼，板式高层和位于商业区域的“商 HOUSE”多种房型。第三个特点是绿色和生态的概念。除了在立面上根据南方的炎热日晒上重点设计了遮阳构件，在空间上我们特别强调建筑与自然的联系，反映本地的生活习惯和城市的休闲特色。办公楼两个核心筒旁边都隔层安排了空中花园，营造舒适宜人的办公环境。酒店设计上我们大胆引入了“穿透式中庭”的概念，中庭空间不仅竖向上引入了天光，水平方向也间隔的引入贯穿的空中花园，形成镂空的立体空中花园体系，最大限度地让居于高层的使用者接触自然。

香港建筑科学出版社：有什么是你们特别关注的吗，比如材料或者形式？

施旭东：我们认为建筑的形象应来源于场地的特质和内部的空间功能逻辑，主体办公楼由于边核心筒的设计，转角显得厚实和挺拔，我们借势对沿迎宾大道的塔楼露台花园采用了跌落和退台的手法，形成富有特色的几何体切割效果，呼应北侧金鸡岭的山形，与三亚滨海区域的大部分建筑的亲水柔美形象形成反差，形成自身特色。建筑材料上使用了比较温暖的浅色洞石。

酒店和办公则利用统一的竖向铝合金遮阳板达成一致效果。在板式酒店的屋顶花园中，我们设计了露天泳池，考虑到炎热的日晒，泳池上方配置了钢构遮阳 . 构造采用出挑和橙色帆布编织肌理的效果，成为建筑的一个有特色的亮点。作为城市综合体，我们始终比较关注的是城市公共空间的塑造。在商业空间中我们布置了一条斜向的商业内街，把沿街商业氛围引入综合体纵深，与 60 米的城市景观带形成公共空间体系。在办公楼和酒店两个地块中间，重点设计了一处下沉式的城市广场和景观塔，比较遗憾的是这个概念最终没有实现。

HKASP: What is your special attention on this project in your design process, such as materials, patterns?

Shi Xudong :Guiding by the city principles, this planning strives to build a project that could improve the city functions of Sanya and lead the development of city center.

Sanya is the first-tier tourism city, the waterfront tourism estate projects develop quickly in recent years, and most of them are with highly market orientated principles. But the fact is that the related supporting facilities in this city could not match the development, the scale and level of design development is decreasec apparently from waterfront to inland area. This project is located in the middle section of Yingbin Road (the main image road in this city) and adjoins to Jin Ji Ling Park, it is about 2 km away from the coastline. The planning concept focuses on the base characteristics and existing resources tc create the regional center that combines office, hotel, retail and urban public space together. Our design tries to improve the city development of inner city based on planning layout, to enrich the diversity of city function from the aspect of function positioning and to create a new visiting card for Sanya from the aspect from architecture image.

香港建筑科学出版社：方案背后的主要概念是什么？

施旭东：方案最初的考虑是从城市的角度入手，希望能建设一个完善三亚城市功能，引导城市腹地发展的项目。三亚作为一线旅游城市，近年旅沿海岸线旅游项目发展迅速，定位也比较高，但城市相关配套的功能相对薄弱，发展很不均衡，设计开发的规模和水准从海边往内陆呈现明显递减现象．中铁子悦台位于城市主要形象道路迎宾路中段，离海岸线约 2 公里，毗邻金鸡岭公园。方案的构思立足于强调基地特色，依托自身资源打造融办公、酒店、商业和城市公共空间于一体的区域中心。从规划布局上提升内城区的城市发展，从功能业态上丰富城市功能的多样性，从建筑形象上打造三亚的一张新名片。

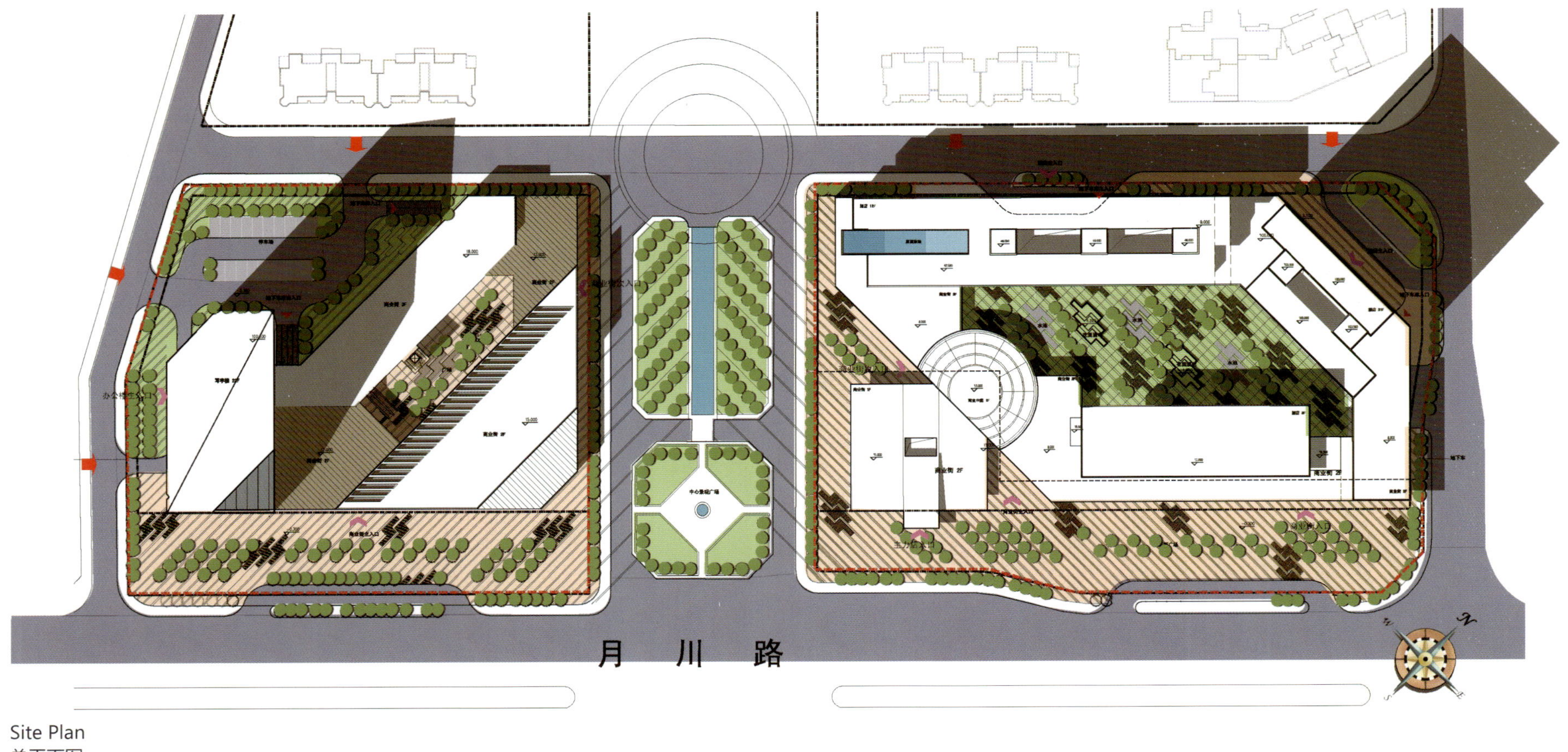

Site Plan
总平面图

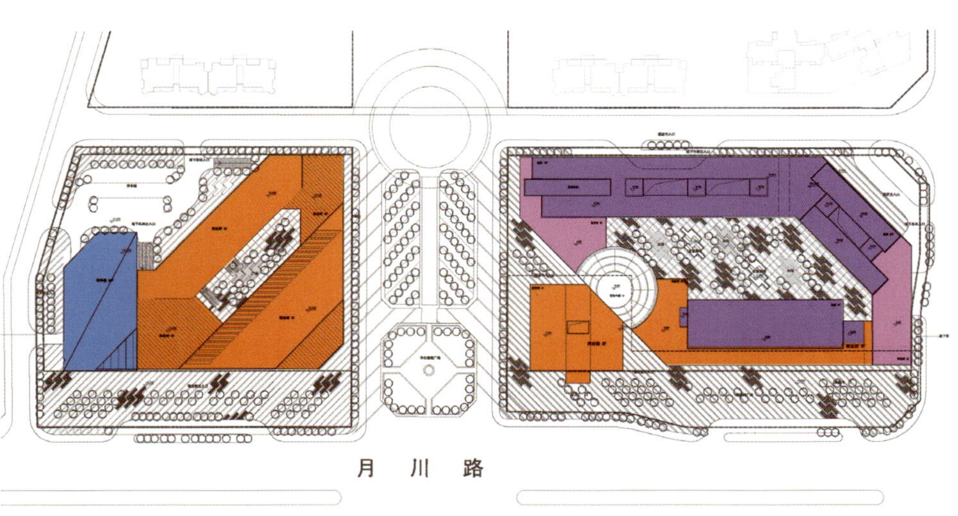

Functions Distribution
功能分析图

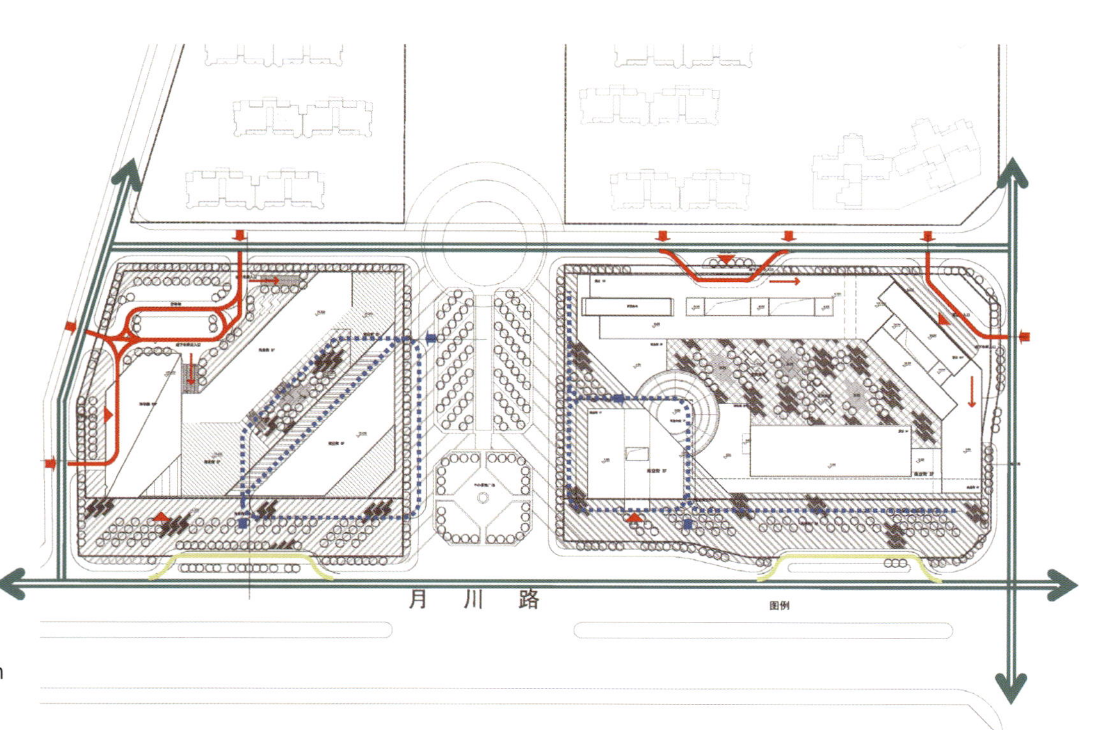

Traffic Circulation Diagram
交通流向图

19

20

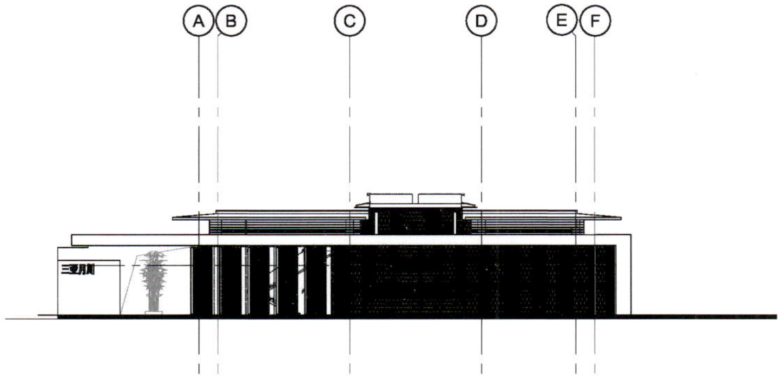

South Elevation
南立面图

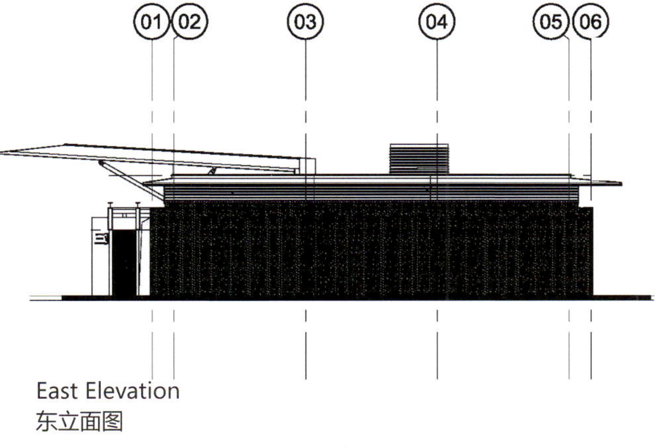

East Elevation
东立面图

1.Conceptual design :two block using integrated design on the layout, business line and the figure.
2.Design of Office Building: to create a flexible space features landscape view and ecological system. It is a symbolic architecture with prestigious quality lobby and office automation.
3.Design of High Street: to present a retail area with integrated design plan to maximize the commercial value.
4.Design of Apartment: the design is to integrate garden landscape view with corridor in interior space and hanging garden in exterior.
5.Transportation and Logistic Service: priority is given to pedestrians, to implement the separation of people and vehicles.
6.Architecture Configuration: it demonstrates a modern architecture style, an ecological landscape and high quality building.
7.Landscape Design and Open Space: key elements in landscape design are Space Consequence, Space Layer, Space Dimension, Sophisticated Technology and Lighting Design.

1. 概念设计：两片地块在布局、商业动线、造型上采用整体式设计。
2. 办公楼设计：灵活空间，景观办公，生态办公，标志造型，典雅大堂，智能办公。
3. 商业街区设计：整合设计，价值优化，沿街展示，商业氛围。
4. 酒店公寓设计：点板结合，景观庭院，内廊布局，空中花园。
5. 交通与后勤服务：步行优先，人车分流。
6. 建筑造型：有机现代，山水交融，生态景观，品质建造。
7. 景观设计与开放空间：空间序列，空间层次，空间尺度，精细设计，亮化设计。

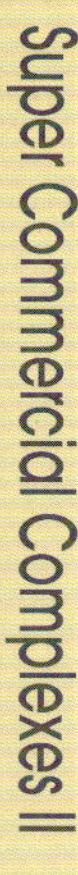

中铁置业广场

PROJECT NAME　项目名称

BEIJING GREENLAND COLORFUL TOWN

北京绿地缤纷城

Architect: UA International

设计公司：UA 国际

PROJECT INFORMATION　项目信息

Client	Greenland Group	**客户**	绿地集团
Location	Daxing district, Beijing	**地点**	北京大兴区
Floor area	224, 202 m^2, ground floor area: 140,263 m^2	**建筑面积**	224，202 平方米，其中地上建筑面积：140，263 平方米
Site Area	40,086 m^2	**占地面积**	40，086 平方米

OVERVIEW　项目概况

As an urban complex, Beijing Greenland Colorful Town and Beijing Greenland Central Square under construction have won the attention of people in the rising Daxing district. As a commercial project, it is the result of the design team's long-term endeavor, research and innovation. It shows architects' dialogues with time, base and reality.

Beijing Greenland Colorful Town (Plot B) and Beijing Greenland Central Square under construction (Plot A) are located the east of New area of Daxing district, Chongqing, south of Hougao road, west of Xingfeng avenue and north of Jinxing road. Xinghua avenue and Jinxing west road are primary road. Hougao road and Xingfeng avenue are sub-arterial road.

北京绿地缤纷城及在建中的北京绿地中央广场作为一个城市综合体，已经在逐渐崛起的大兴区赢得了众人的瞩目。作为一个商办项目，她的绚丽背后有着设计团队长时间的努力、研究和创新，有着建筑师与时间、与基地、与现实的一次次对话。

北京绿地缤纷城（B 地块）及在建中的北京绿地中央广场（A 地块）位于北京市大兴新区兴华大街以东、后高路以南，兴丰大街以西，金星西路以北；其中兴华大街与金星西路为城市主干路，后高路和兴丰大街为城市次干路。

BRIEF INTERVIEW　访谈录

HKASP: What are the highlights and features of the project?

UA International: The project features four major design highlights:

At first, the way to enter has been marked with distinct identity. With main entrance locating at commercial central plaza on southeastern most point of site, the project faces Sisley mansion in the east, a cluster of residential housings. The vertical mullion features distinction. A full use of 1.5m-thick earthing gives rise to a plaza space that gently sinks, reconnecting human activity to commercial entrance; to the west of commercial volume lies the subway station. An immediate and efficient gigantic step has been designed to direct human traffic to the level under grade; commercial volume that runs along the river interacts with office building. At noon and night, the white collars go to the riverside bars for a rest or a party through bridges over the river or they may go directly to the commercial dynamic line at level 2 via the gigantic step to have a nice dinner or go shopping with companies. The diversified entrances not only cater to demands of different customers but also inject the underground floor, ground floor and 2nd floor of commercial building with vigor, greatly enhancing its commercial value.

Second, central plaza is created to have highlights. The step and landscape deliver a sense of security and a sense of being enclosed at the slightly-sunk plaza. A 2000 ▯ activity space serves as a platform for the city, citizens nearby to hold events as well as a platform for commercial events. It has gained great popularity. That is to say, the plaza will be extremely popular among people. On the other hand, sinking by 1.5 m gives rise to near-7m-high retail stores at ground floor. It goes without saying that we see marked additional value of retail stores coming together with greater influence.

Third, there is designers' wholehearted care and though behind large projection along the river. On west of the site lies Xinfeng river. The control line requires a 16 m-long set-back to blue line at riverway, which exerts great impact on coverage rate at ground floor and creation of commercial value. Hence, the designers devised a projection by extending cinema at floor 4 and 5 toward "riverside" by 8 meters, which not only adequately expands area at a single floor, but also create a grey space along the river for rest or sightseeing. In addition, such volumetric change generates a stronger visual impact, impressive and unforgettable.

Fourth, overall form gives prominence to cinema as a functional block at the top. The gigantic box is clad in dynamic glazed skin in colors of tangerine, medium yellow and dark grey, forming a visual focal point and intensifying dramatic theory based on which "colorful town" is designed. The rest of walls features mainly grey and glass color, accenting architectural core and identity.

香港建筑科学出版社：项目的亮点和特色是什么？

UA 国际：北京绿地缤纷城项目有四个主要设计亮点：

首先，进入方式各具特点。主入口位于东南角的商业中心广场，面向东侧西斯莱公馆的住宅客群。竖向设计独具匠心，充分利用了 1.5 米的覆土厚度，形成一个缓缓下沉的广场空间，将人们的活动和商业入口进行紧密衔接；商业体西侧连接了地铁客群，设计了直接而高效的大台阶，将人流引导入地下一层；商业体沿河则与商务办公楼形成了互动，午间和傍晚，白领青年可以通过河上小桥来到河畔的酒吧街休憩聚会，或直接从大台阶汇入二层的商业动线，享受美食或结伴购物。通过多样化的入口设计，不仅迎合了不同客群的诉求，更同时激活了商业建筑的地下一层、首层和二层多个界面，大大提升了商业价值。

其次，中心广场的场所营造颇具亮点。微微下沉的广场通过台阶、景观的设计，形成了一个具有安全感和场所感的 40 米 x50 米的活动空间，给城市、周边居民、商业营销活动提供了开展的场所，也深受欢迎。可以说，这个广场成为了一个吸纳人气的漩涡。另一方面，1.5 米的下沉使得首层商铺层高近 7 米，铺位的附加值和影响力增长不言而喻。

第三，沿河大出挑背后，隐藏了设计师的良苦用心。本项目西侧为新凤河河道，按照相关规定，一层控制线需要退让河道蓝线 16 米，这对首层覆盖率和商业价值挖掘有很大影响。因此，设计师通过出挑的方式，将位于四层至五层的影院向“河边”延伸了 8 米，不仅充分扩大了商业单层面积，同时营造了一片可供休憩停留的沿河灰空间，更通过这个体块变化增加了视觉冲击力，令人印象深刻。

第四，整体建筑造型突出了顶部的影院功能体块，以富有动感的橘红、中黄、深灰三色玻璃包裹了这个大盒子，形成视觉焦点，强化了“缤纷城”的活力理念。其余墙体主要以灰色和玻璃本色为主，保证建筑的重点突出，标示性强。

HKASP: From point of view of consumer, how to set commercial experience? What is the theme about?

UA International: As for Beijing Greenland Colorful Town, atrium represents the most interesting space with a graphic sense. Being positioned as a community commercial complex, it is a family-oriented lifestyle commercial building, which sets itself apart from those shopping-oriented buildings with multiple atria. The project has only an atrium. We expect to provide recreational space and interactive commercial programs around the atrium. All targeted customers engage in their activities around it. The architects embedded carefully an irregular glass block shaped like "Mickey Mouse' s Head" between the atrium and the exterior. This is an architectural block composed of glass and metal vertical rods. All single-level dynamic lines go through the middle of it, with the main entrance just lying beneath it. That is to say, it connects the interior to the exterior, and serves as an interchange on a dynamic line and is more like an excitement in the atrium. The designers recommended that as to leasing, an extra focus is put on incorporating experiential commercial activities with graphic sense into the glass block, allowing them to be a scenery throughout the mall.

HKASP: From the prospective of architecture, how do you help the developer to realize the investment plan?

UA International :It is best to have a broader view when it comes to development of a commercial complex. In this case, Beijing Greenland Colorful Town is only a parcel at Jinxing road area. Functional areas including hotel and conference rooms lie on north of it. Large-sized residential housing cluster lies on east of it. "Green Central Square" functioning as business, office, apartment and others lies on west of it. Using comprehensive development as foundational model, the project starts from residence to business and office.

Therefore, Beijing Greenland Colorful Town not only sits on the heart of the area but also serves as a key point for operation. As a community commercial complex, it not only offers neighboring residents an easy life and a prime quality of development but also delivers a good supporting environment for business, office, serviced apartment at the later stage of development. Just like Wanda and Plaza MIXC that drive urban flourishing, a commercial complex is able to exert a forward influence like product premium, enhanced land price and others. This is exactly what developers desire. And, this is also what urban people expect to see in a city.

香港建筑科学出版社：从消费者角度， 如何设定商业体验？什么主题？

UA 国际：对于北京绿地缤纷城而言，最具有趣味和设计感的空间是建筑的中庭区域。缤纷城定位于社区商业综合体，是面向家庭的、生活为主题的商业建筑，因此有别于以购物为导向的多中庭商业，本项目仅有一个主中庭。我们希望围绕这个空间提供休闲的场所和商业互动活动的平台，所有目标客群的活动轨迹都围绕这个中庭发生，而在中庭和室外之间，设计师非常用心地植入了一个"米老鼠脑袋"形状的玻璃异形体。

这是一个以玻璃和金属竖向杆件组成的建筑体块，所有单层动线都需要从中间穿过，商业主入口也在其下部进入。可以说，这是一个室内外空间的接驳体，一个动线的中转站，更是中庭的兴奋点。设计师建议，商业招商也有所侧重，将一些具有设计感和体验性的业态补充到玻璃体中，成为整个 mall 的一道风景。

香港建筑科学出版社：从建筑角度出发，如何更好地协助开发商实现投资计划？

UA 国际：一个商业综合体的开发应着眼于更大区域，在这个案例中，北京绿地缤纷城仅是开发商在金星路片区的一块用地，她的北侧是酒店、会议功能片区，东侧为大型居住组团，西侧为商务办公、公寓等功能的"绿地中央广场"。在整体运营中，以综合开发为基本模式，以住 - 商 - 办为启动顺序。

因此，缤纷城不仅占据了片区的地理核心，更是运营的关键点。作为社区商业综合体，缤纷城不仅保证了周边居住区的生活便利、楼盘品质，更为后期开发的商务办公、酒店式公寓提供了良好的配套环境。正如万达广场、华润万象城带来的兴城效应，一个商业综合体所能起到的远期影响，往往包括产品溢价、地价的提升等等，这是开发商希望看到的，也是城市乐于看到的。

The base sits next to 5h loop, offering convenient transportation. Beijing subway line 4 extension or the former Daxing line which was put into operation by the end of 2011 establishes Jinxing station No.2 and 3 exits within the plot, which will carry a huge amount of subway circulation and also help the project gain great popularity.

Daxing people's court and people's procuratorate are adjacent to the southwestern end of the base. The base faces the south campus of high school affiliated with Central Conservatory of Music in the east, and faces residential neighborhoods in both north and west. Sisley mansion, a high-series residential area, locates in the east of the base.

The base falls into Beijing Greenland Colorful Town (Plot B) and Beijing Greenland Central Square (Plot A) between which Xinfeng river, a natural riverway, runs in. The bridge over the riverway integrates them into one.

基地紧邻五环，交通便捷；另有2011年年末已通车运营的的北京地铁4号线延伸段（原为大兴线），在地块内设有金星路站2号、3号口两个地铁出入口，将承载未来巨大的地铁客流，也为项目带来巨大的人气和商机。

基地西南角不远处为大兴区人民法院和大兴区人民检察院，东面为中央音乐学院附中南校区，北面及西面以住宅区为主，东侧为已建成的绿地西斯莱公馆高档住宅区。

基地分为A地块绿地中央广场以及B地块绿地缤纷城，中间被天然河道新凤河穿越，隔河相望，同时通过连桥形成整体。

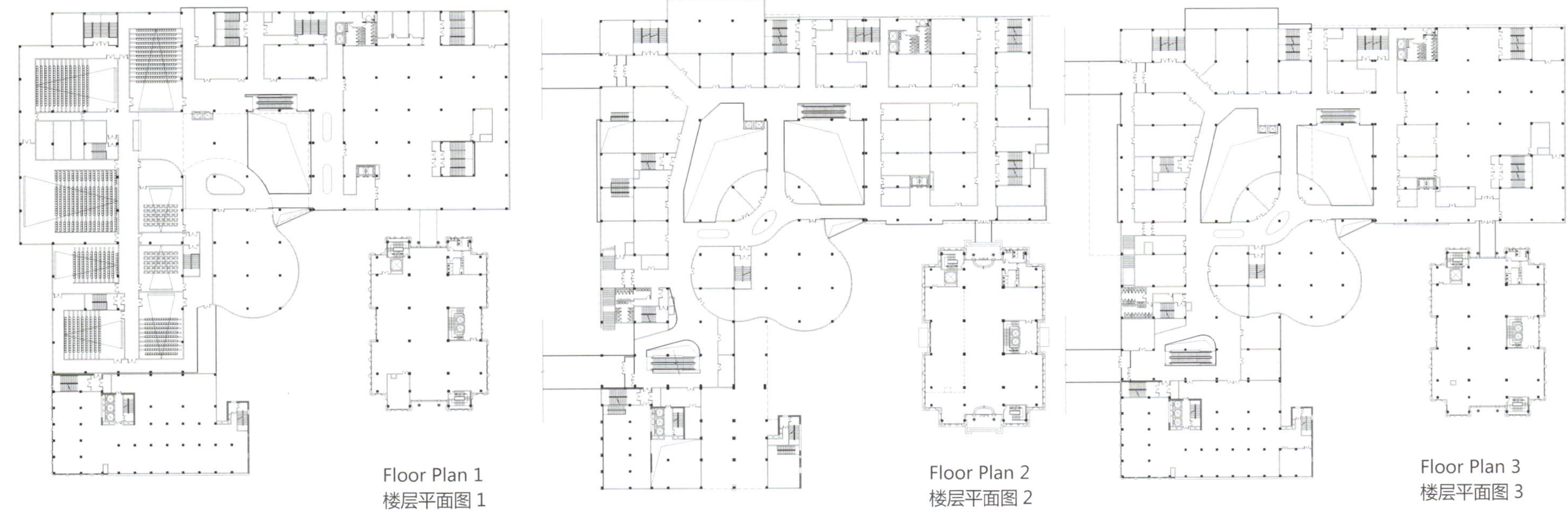

Floor Plan 1
楼层平面图 1

Floor Plan 2
楼层平面图 2

Floor Plan 3
楼层平面图 3

Overall layout

We base the overall plane layout on current situation. We take into a full consideration the original landform and surrounding geographic environment and bring it into a full play. Considering the fact that the wider south-north plane of flattening does no good in fire control, we set a 8 m-wide vehicular way in the central plot A, which happens to run all way down to the northern end of plot B and ends at Xingfeng avenue. The vehicular way can be a logistics corridor for the commercial complex. In addition, there is a 6 m-wide drive way along the west side of plot B and east side of plot A, which carries the vehicular circulation from egress/ingress of underground garage and office tower. We establish three ways on the principle of "go simple and straightforward", trying to minimize the size of road and realize the highest efficiency.

We first have identified the area at the intersection between Xinghua avenue and Jinxing west road as the ideal location for high-end office tower. High-series road and the location of subway egress/ingress make such a standard Grade-A office tower a local landmark. The south-north stretch of plot A can exactly show a full skyline of 4 high risings.

The integration with Beijing Daxing line is another traffic design feature borne by the base. Daxing line is the extension of line 4 and establishes egress/ingress No. 2 and 3 at Jinxing station located within the base. Egress/ingress No.3 is required to be under the planned design for the building, with a purpose to pursue an integrated style. Therefore, the design is focused on how to introduce a huge amount of human influx into the commercial space and on delivering a clear and rational circulation flow, with an u timate target to realize "smooth public traffic and activating potentiality of plot". We consider connecting the commercial space to the subway by the subway lobby level or 2nd underground floor of commercial building. Thus, human flow can be led to the commercial building immediately and to the boutiques at 1st underground floor and floors above via the escalator. The ground-level subway Egress/ingress just sits next to the main entrance of the commercial building, allowing subway Egress/ingress to share the grey space in front of the commercial building and keep their independence.

总体布局

总平面布局上，我们坚持从实际现状出发，充分考虑和发挥了原有地形和周边地理环境优势。鉴于基地南北向延展面较宽，不利于消防扑救，我们在 A 地块中央开设了 8 米宽的行车辅道，正好贯穿至 B 地块的北侧至兴丰大街，可作为商业综合体的后勤通道；另外，在 B 地块西侧和 A 地块的东侧开设了 6 米宽的车道，解决地库出入口和办公塔楼出入口的交通问题。我们本着“最精简、最直接”的原则开设了这三条道路，将地块内的道路面积降到最低，效率达到最高。

从适合度角度出发，我们首先确定了兴华大街和金星西路交叉口的区域为最适合建设高级办公楼的地点，高等级的道路和地铁出入口的位置都决定了这栋准甲办公楼将成为本区域的地标。而 A 地块南北延展的界面，正能完整地展示四栋高层的天际线。

基地的另一个交通设计特点是与北京大兴线的结合。北京大兴线为 4 号线的延伸段，在本基地设有金星路站的 2 号、3 号地面出入口。其中 3 号口要求与建筑统一规划设计，力求一体化。因此，本设计的重点在于如何将地铁的巨大人流吸引进入商业空间，并组织合理清晰的交通流线，达到“通畅公共交通，激活地块潜能”的目的。在设计上，我们考虑在地铁站厅层，即商业地下二层就与地铁对接，第一时间分流客群，将潜在的顾客吸引到商业建筑内，通过便捷的自动扶梯引导至地下一层精品商业内街和以上楼层。地铁地面出入口同样与建筑紧密结合，紧挨着商业主要出入口，既能与商业共享入口前的灰空间，又能单独使用互不干扰。

Plot B is organized based on a human-oriented principle. Human traffic, cargo traffic and human traffic all find their ways without mutual intervention, making sure that they all can be evacuated in an efficient manner. The main entrance of Greenland Colorful Town is located at the southeastern end of the square, linking Jinxing road with the sunken square. The main entrance of shopping mall is located at Xingfeng avenue on the east, which offers easy access to shopping for residents. The other main entrance is located at the sunken square on the south, aiming to attract human flow from the subway. There is another entrance located along the riverway, interacting with Greenland Central Square. The bars along the riverway become visitors' first choice in a cozy afternoon. The car parking is located on the south side of the town, serving the vehicles from the logistics corridor and the shuttle bus to the shopping mall. The traffic flow is completely separated from the commercial flow without mutual intervention, greatly enhancing the commercial quality.

B地块的布局本着以人为本的原则，有效地组织了各种流线，避免车流、货流、人流的交叉，并且使人流、车流、货流快速、高效的疏散。绿地缤纷城的商业主要入口位于东南角的广场内，通过下沉广场与金星路相连；大卖场的主入口位于东侧兴丰大街，便于居住区居民就近购物，另一个主入口位于南侧下沉广场，吸纳来自地铁的人流。绿地缤纷城的另一个商业入口位于沿河界面，与绿地中央广场遥相呼应，在宜人的午后，沿河风情酒吧街将成为休闲碰面的第一选择。缤纷城的北侧为后勤道路及卖场班车停靠点，交通流线与商业流线完全分离，互不影响，大大提升了商业品质。

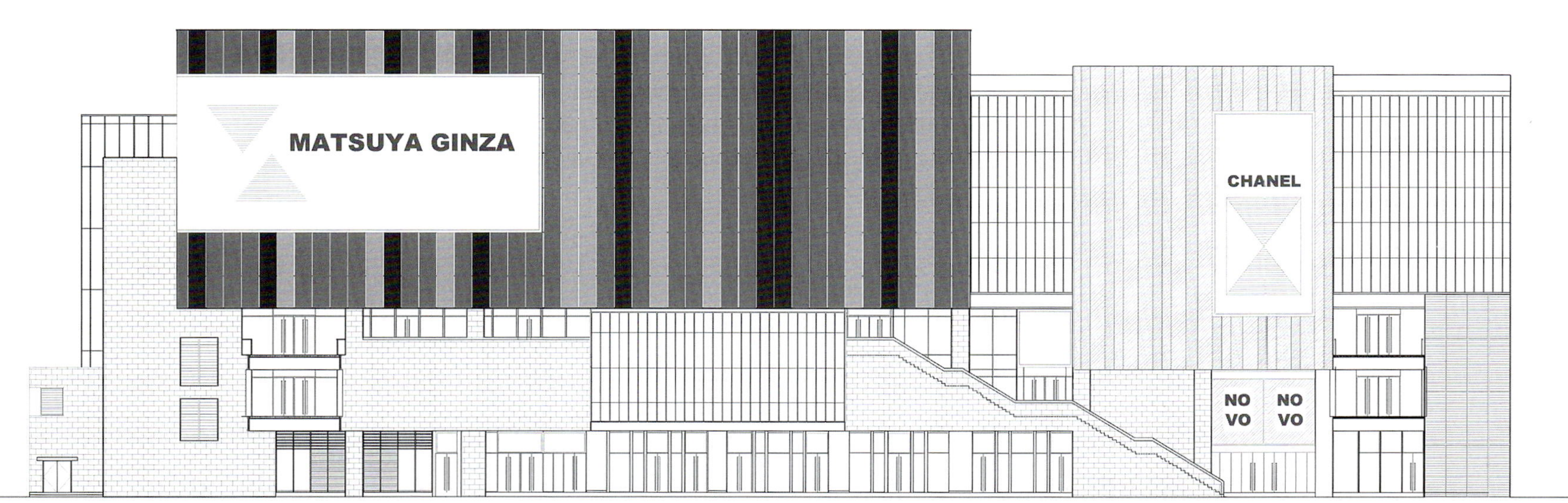

Details
节点图

Facade

The facade of plot A and plot B is oriented differently as two plots have separated positioning and their own functional complexity.

Greenland Central Square represents a mix of modern style and classic styling as a whole. As a grade-A landmark, the building has a modern and simple styling. The rising and sophisticated architectural form is taken into shape with glass curtain wall and vertical lines. The styling presents a picture of the tower wrapped in limbs. At the street corner rises a canopy as the main entrance, a clever design. Facing predominating direction, a strip of exquisite core is exposed in the air and shines brilliantly at night, becoming an impressive urban landmark. SOHO office and LOFT office tower are improved version of art deco style. The detail design that shows sense of value not only embodies a kind of low-profile aesthetics but also sets the main buildings off to advantage.

Greenland colorful town presents a modern style of vivid vogue as well as lays an emphasis on combination of virtual & essence and interweaving of blocks. The form of commercial building uses "gigantic roof cap" as the element for governing all. The stack of "boxes" of varied materials and textures breathe more life and transparence into the form of base of building. The conciseness and decorous feeling of the roof can be realized by clever use of stones and ads. position at higher levels. The collage of enamelled glass and aluminium plates with varied gray levels generates two kinds of eye-catching boxes which look colorful, exquisitely carved and fine.

Elevational
立面图

立面造型

由于两块基地定位的区别、功能的复杂，本设计的立面风格在A、B两块地也有不同倾向。

绿地中央广场整体为现代风格与古典造型的杂糅。准甲办公作为地标性建筑，其造型较为现代、简洁，以玻璃幕墙和竖向线条勾勒出挺拔、干练的建筑形体。其造型形似瓣片包裹着塔楼，在街角掀起一角巧妙地作为主入口的雨棚，面向主导方向露出一条精致的核心，在夜色下更透出熠熠光彩，成为令人难以忘怀的城市标记。SOHO办公和LOFT办公建筑为改良的art deco风格，通过价值感的细节设计，体现其低调的美感，同时衬托主楼。

绿地缤纷城为鲜明时尚的现代风格，强调虚实结合和体块穿插。商业建筑形体以“大顶盖”作为统摄全局的元素，将不同材质和肌理的“盒子”堆叠起来，使得底部建筑形体更为活跃和通透。上层则利用石材和广告位控制顶部的简洁性和厚重感，更通过彩釉玻璃和不同灰度铝板的拼贴，形成夺人眼球的两种盒子效果——剔透绚丽和精致耐看。

绿地缤纷城
GREENLAND BEING FUNNY
保利电影院线
Etam
COSTA COFFEE

COSTA COFFEE

MICHELLE BELAU
Cartier

SHOPPING COMPLEX REAL ESTATE
购物型复合地产

UNStudio
UNStudio

Reflection, light and pattern are used throughout the Hanjie Wanda Square to create an almost fantastical world.

整个汉街万达广场都运用了光线的反射，照明，图案，旨在营造出一种奇幻的世界。

Chapman Taylor
查普门泰勒建筑设计咨询（上海）有限公司

This modern commercial building collects and conveys many classical architectural languages. It has the biggest area in Shanghai commercial complex building. It is the epitome for art deco building style in Shanghai.

古典建筑语汇在现代商业建筑的大合体。冠绝上海的商业综合体面积体量。上海地区泛滥的 artdeco 建筑风格的集大成者。种

Metropolis
Metropolis

The Jockey Plaza has achieved this with costumers, through the creation of semi-urban areas with architectural elements that serve as references and encourage the visitors to explore a worth remembering experience.

服装商，城乡结合区的打造，建筑元素的借鉴都促就了赛马广场的成功。建筑元素无时无刻不吸引游客们去探索一种值得回忆的体验。

HMD
HMD

Both the materials and forms of the massing are organic or natural with gentle curves and arcs overlapping to make the building reflect the topography. The result is a harmonious facade, both in color and form, symbolic and unique within its context.

通过对柔和曲线与弧线的堆叠，采用天然材料，塑造自然形体，让建筑与周遭地貌融为一体。从而，无论是颜色还是形体，都打造出与环境相交融的立面，不仅别具一格，而且相映成趣。

5+ design
五杰建筑设计

DWP
DWP

Filtered daylight, timber colonnades , and natural stone paving create an approachable and inviting experience; a new landmark for a historic city.

柔和的日光，木质柱廊，自然石材铺装，这一切都营造出一种温馨，亲民的体验。已然一座历史名城的新地标。

5+ design
五杰建筑设计

Nanjing Yangtze River Urban Architectural Design Co.,
南京长江都市建筑设计股份有限公司

Poly Water City takes full account of its own advantage to use the "water" element in a scientific and reasonable way.

"水"元素是保利水城项目对于自身的优势最为科学合理的应用。

GLC
杰奥斯建筑设计

The project emphasizes the integration of urban function and form, the building rich more porosity and gives space back to citizens.The project implements in Chengdu architecture and regional emotion, architecture and human interaction and integration, and achieves the concept of modern environmental protection technology to build a super green building. The project hopes to give residents here an exciting experience.

项目强调整体化都市功能与形式，建筑体富多孔隙性，还空间于市民。该项目实现了成都建筑与地域情感、建筑与人的互动与融合，实现了现代环保技术打造超级绿色建筑的概念，项目希望带给成都市民一种兴奋的体验。

HPP
HPP

The design and programmatic focus are based primarily on the location in Solingen, known as the German City of Blades. The mall has been designed with the themes of nature, industry and fashion. The first two subjects strongly relate to the City of Solingen and its surrounding regions.

商场以自然、工业、时尚作为设计主题。前两个主题与索林根市及其周边区域息息相关。整个主题围绕着商场的室内室外，并通过强调不同区域的设计来对顾客起引导作用。

PROJECT NAME 项目名称

HANJIE WANDA SQUARE, WUHAN

武汉汉街万达广场

Architect: UNStudio

设计公司：UNStudio

PROJECT INFORMATION 项目信息

Client	Wuhan Wanda East Lake Real State Co., Ltd	**客户**	武汉万达东湖置业有限公司
Location	Wuhan, China	**地点**	武汉
Gross Floor Area	80,000 m²	**总面积**	80，000 平方米
Commercial Space	65,000 m²	**商业面积**	65，000 平方米
Local cooperative design company	CSADI, Central South Architectural Design Institute, INC.	**当地合作设计公司**	中南建筑设计院股份有限公司
Photography	Edmon Leong	**摄影师**	Edmon Leong

OVERVIEW 项目概况

Hanjie Wanda Square is a new luxury shopping plaza located in the Wuhan Central Culture Centre, one of the most important areas of Wuhan City. The multifunctional organisation of the master plan - which includes cultural and tourist facilities as well as commercial, office and residential components—acts as an attractor to the area for visitors, inhabitants and commuters alike.

武汉中央文化中心在这座城市享有重要的地位。而汉街万达广场作为一个全新的豪华购物商场就坐落于此。根据总体规划，整个广场采用多功能布局，集文化、旅游、商业、办公以及家居为一体，是游客，住户以及路人共聚的天堂。

BRIEF INTERVIEW 访谈录

ARCHITECT
Ben van Berkel

设计师
Ben van Berkel

PHOTOGRAPHY
Inga Powilleit

摄影师
Inga Powilleit

HKASP: The project looks quite impressive.what experience bring to the vistor ?

Ben van Berkel: "Reflection, light and pattern are used throughout the Hanjie Wanda Square to create an almost fantastical world. New microcosms and experiences are created for the shopper, similar perhaps to the world of theatre, whereby the retail complex becomes almost a stage or a place of performance and offers a variety of different impressions and experiences to the visitor."

HKASP: When designing, is there something in particular that you focus on?

Ben van Berkel: "In Hanjie Wanda Square a circular motif is repeated in many different ways, both in the facade and throughout the interior. The patterns used were influenced by numerous cultural references, both traditional and contemporary and are connected to fashion, products and everyday consumer items, but also to the use of pattern in art and in our cultural history. Patterns drive our aesthetic choices, whether they be personal or shared and in Hanjie Wanda Square act as a background to the world of desire encapsulated in the contemporary shopping plaza."

香港建筑科学出版社：这个项目令人印象深刻，那么它将给游客带来怎样的体验？

Ben van Berkel 说："整个汉街万达广场都运用了光线的反射，照明，图案，旨在营造出一种奇幻的世界。给购物者打造全新的微观世界与体验，如同电影世界一样，这里的商店都如同舞台或表演场所，总之这里将给游客带来缤纷多彩的体验，让人流连忘返。"

香港建筑科学出版社：设计过程中，你有什么特别注意的地方吗？

Ben van Berkel 说："汉街广场的设计以圆形为基调，通过五花八门的方式重复展现出来，这样的基调随处可见，包括外立面以及室内装饰。图案的设计与各种文化元素有着千丝万缕的关联，我们巧妙地将传统与当代文化元素结合起来，并且将这些文化元素融入到服装，各类产品以及各类日用消费单品当中。此外，文化元素也被融入到了图案的设计当中，这不仅是艺术的表达，也蕴含了历史传统。图案支配着我们对审美角度的选择。无论这种审美角度是个人行为，亦或是大众品味，图案在这里都成为了诉说欲望世界的背景故事。这是一个封装在当代购物广场里的欲望世界。

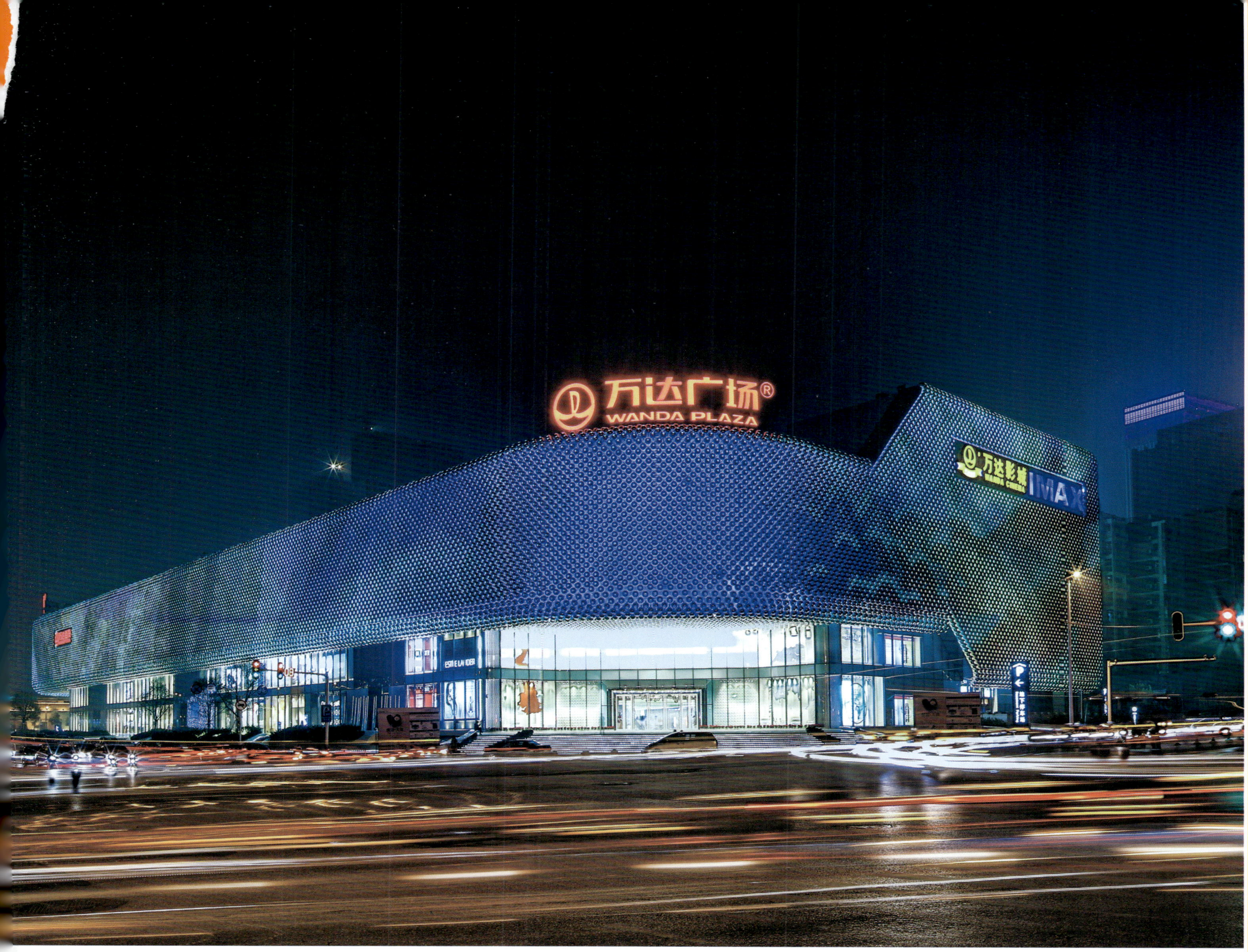
万达广场®
WANDA PLAZA
万达影城
IMAX

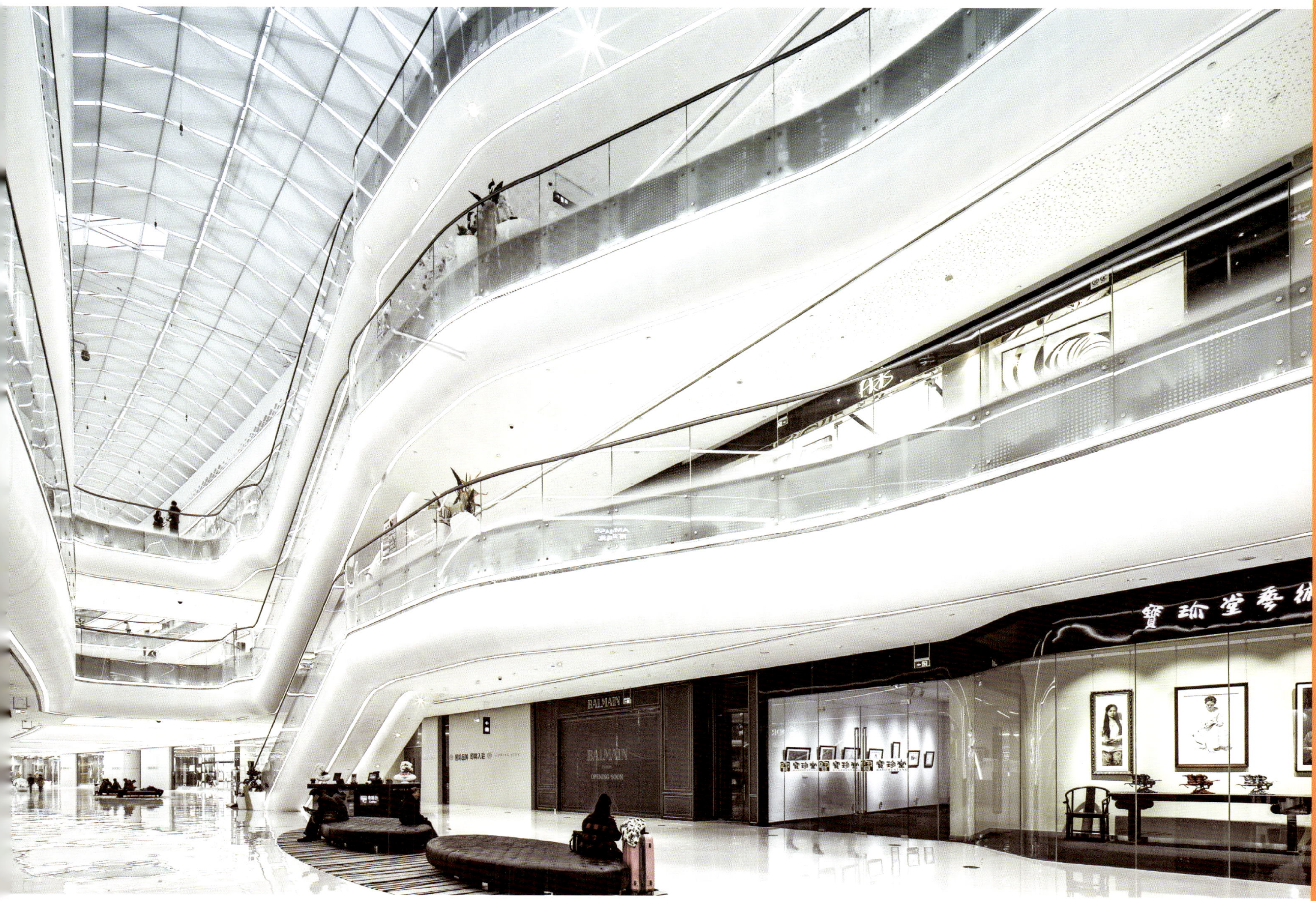
BALMAIN

不锈钢结合木材球体 * STAINLES STEEL WITH WOOD SPHERE

制作过程 * PRODUCTION PROCESS

应用汽车和产品设计的工业技术提高批量模块生产的效率
模块生产过程允许单独的灯光设计
最终产品抵抗不同气候
工厂预制能为每个预制件安装保护材料
减少工地安装时间

- USING SIMILAR PROCCESSES AS THE CAR AND/OR INDUSTRIAL DESIGN MANUFACTURES ALLOWS EFFICIENT MASS PRODUCTION OF ELEMENTS
- MOLDING ALLLOWS INDIVIDUAL DESIGN PROCESS FOR LIGHT FIXTURES ETC
- FINISHES ARE RESISTANT TO CLIMATE
- PRE ASSEMBLING IN FACTORY ALLOWS CLIMATE PROTECTED INSTALLATION OF ALL COMPONENTS
- CONSTRUCTION TIME ON SITE ARE MINIMIZED

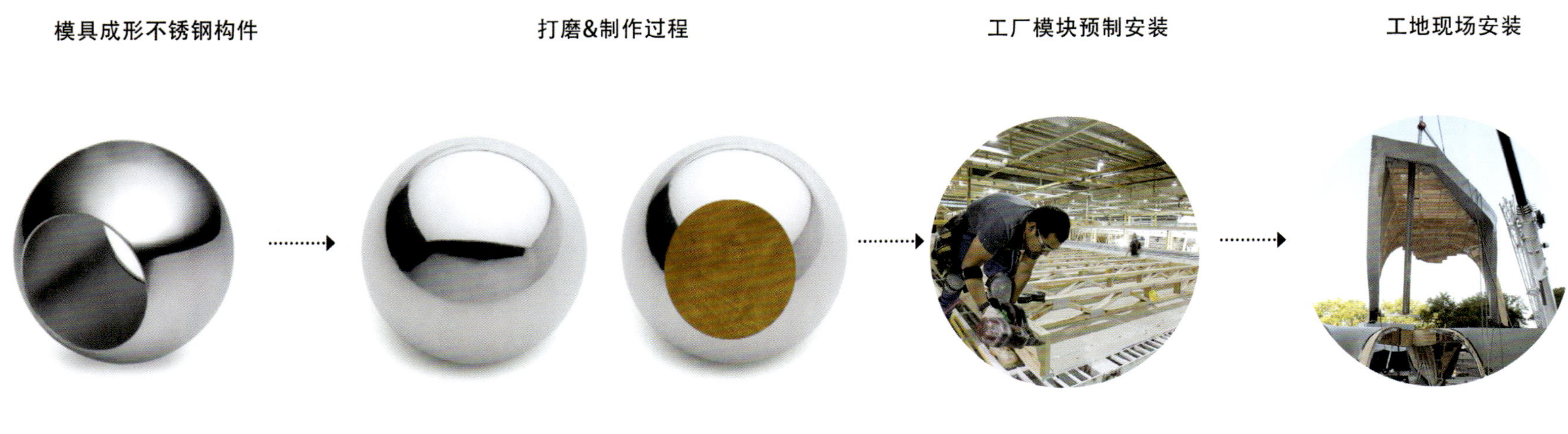

Following a competition with design entries from national and international architects, UNStudio's overall design was selected by Wanda as the winning entry for the facade and interior of the Hanjie Wanda Square. Hanjie Wanda Square was completed in September 2013. It houses international brand stores, world-class boutiques, catering outlets and cinemas.

UNStudio's design concept capitalises on the strategic location for the shopping plaza within the context of the master plan area. The concept of luxury is incorporated by means of ideas focussing on the craftsmanship of noble, yet simple materials. Unstudio's approach considers the Hanjie Wanda Square as a contemporary classic, combining both contemporary and traditional design elements in one concept.

在经过跟国内外建筑设计事务所的一番竞标之后，UNStudio的总体设计方案脱颖而出，最终成功入选为汉街万达广场立面与内部的设计方案。汉街万达广场已于2013年9月竣工。这个广场享有国际品牌店，世界级专卖店，餐饮店以及电影院。

UNStudio的设计理念利用了购物商场在总体规划中所具备的战略位置优势。根据设计思路，将强调对既显高贵而简单的材料的精雕细琢，以此来纳高端品质的设计理念。Unstudio的设计方法充分考虑了汉街万达广场作为当代经典作品的定位，将当代元素与传统元素融入到同一个设计理念当中。

Site Plan
总平面图

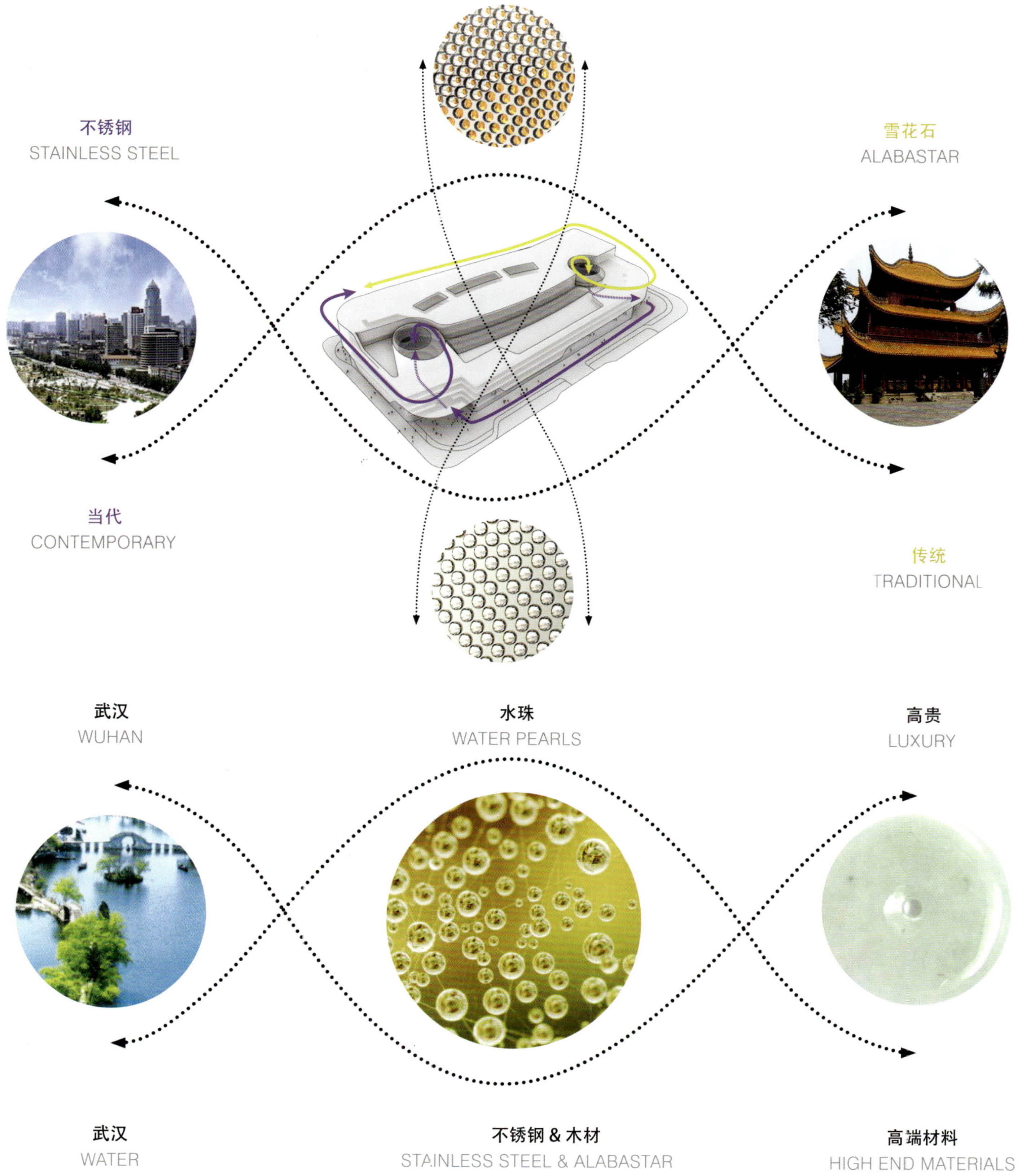

不锈钢
STAINLESS STEEL
雪花石
ALABASTAR
当代
CONTEMPORARY
传统
TRADITIONAL
武汉
WUHAN
水珠
WATER PEARLS
高贵
LUXURY
武汉
WATER
不锈钢 & 木材
STAINLESS STEEL & ALABASTAR
高端材料
HIGH END MATERIALS

Retail Shops
商店
North Atrium / Tradition
北中庭/传统
South Atrium /Contemporary
南中庭/当代
Cosmetic Area
化妆区
Shopping Street Connections
购物街连结
Elevator Lobby
电梯厅
Entrance Area
入口
Toilet / North Atrium
洗手间（北中庭）
Toilet / South Atrium
洗手间（南中庭）
10
25
50
100m

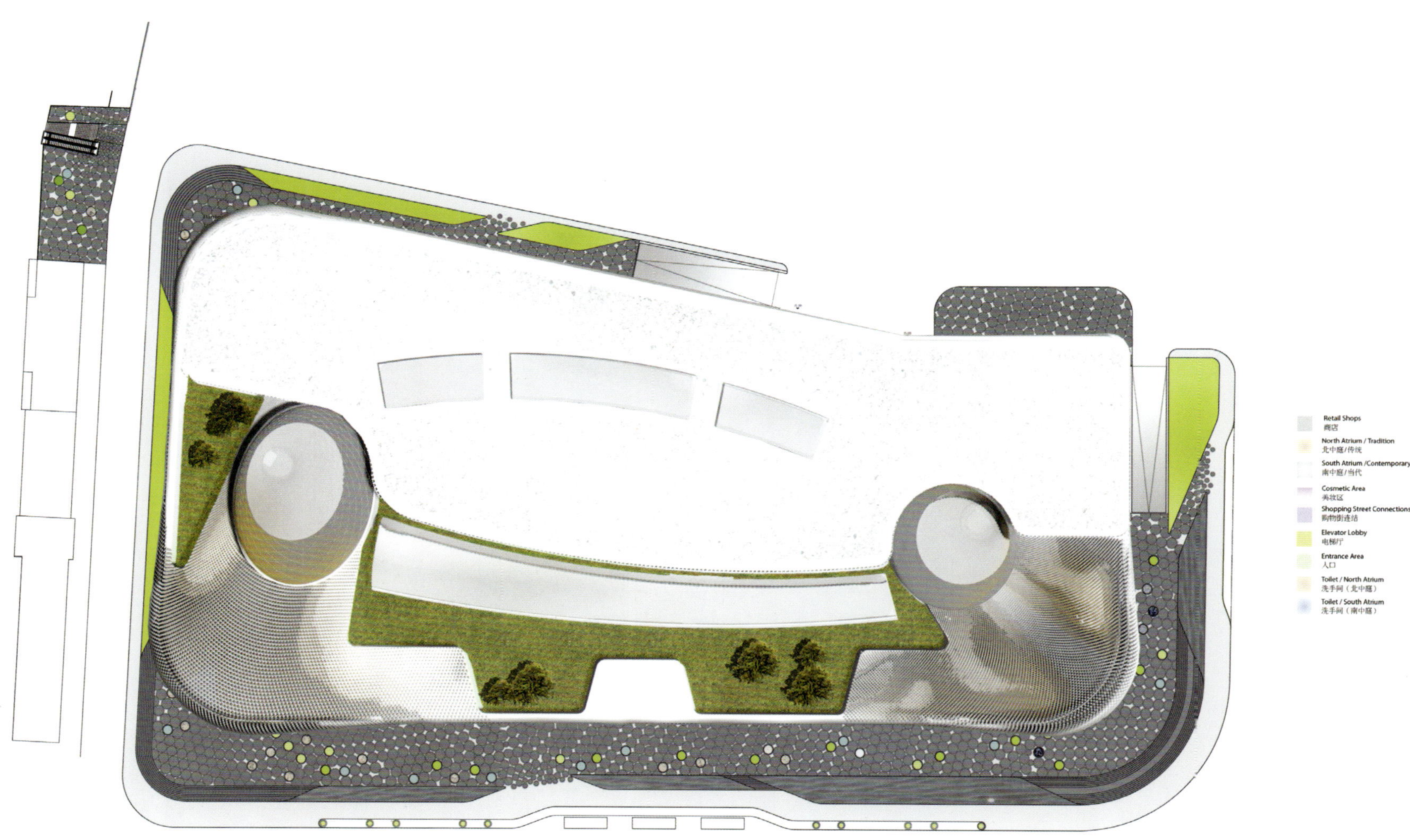

Functions Distribution
功能分布图

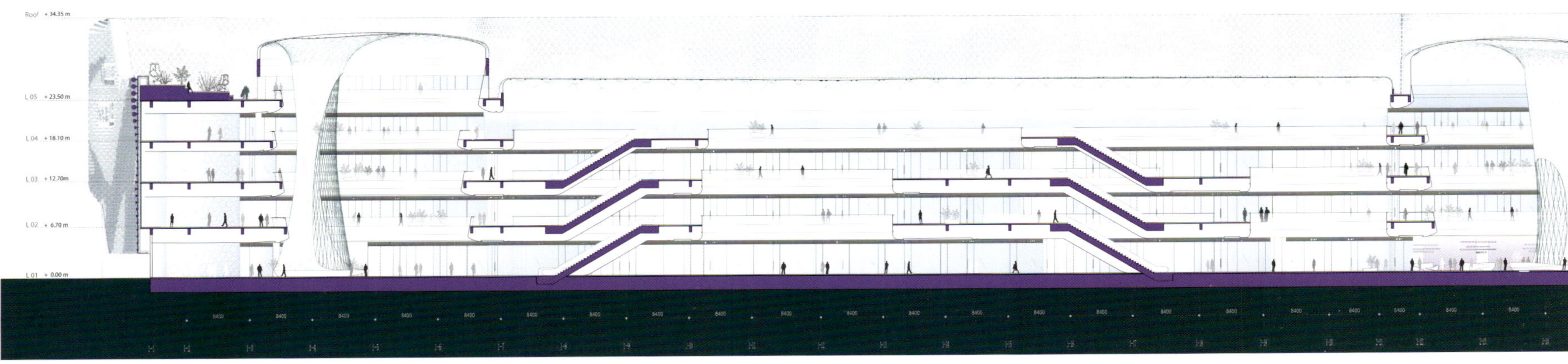

Long Section
整体剖面图

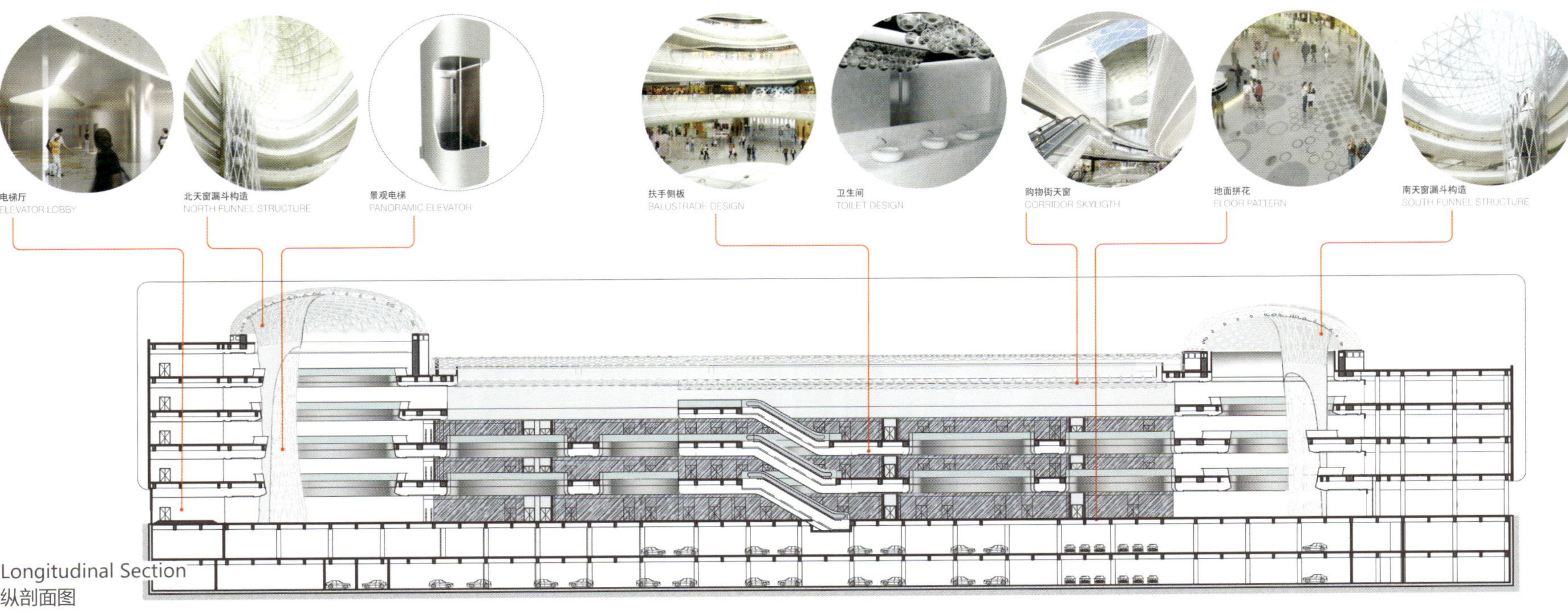

Longitudinal Section
纵剖面图

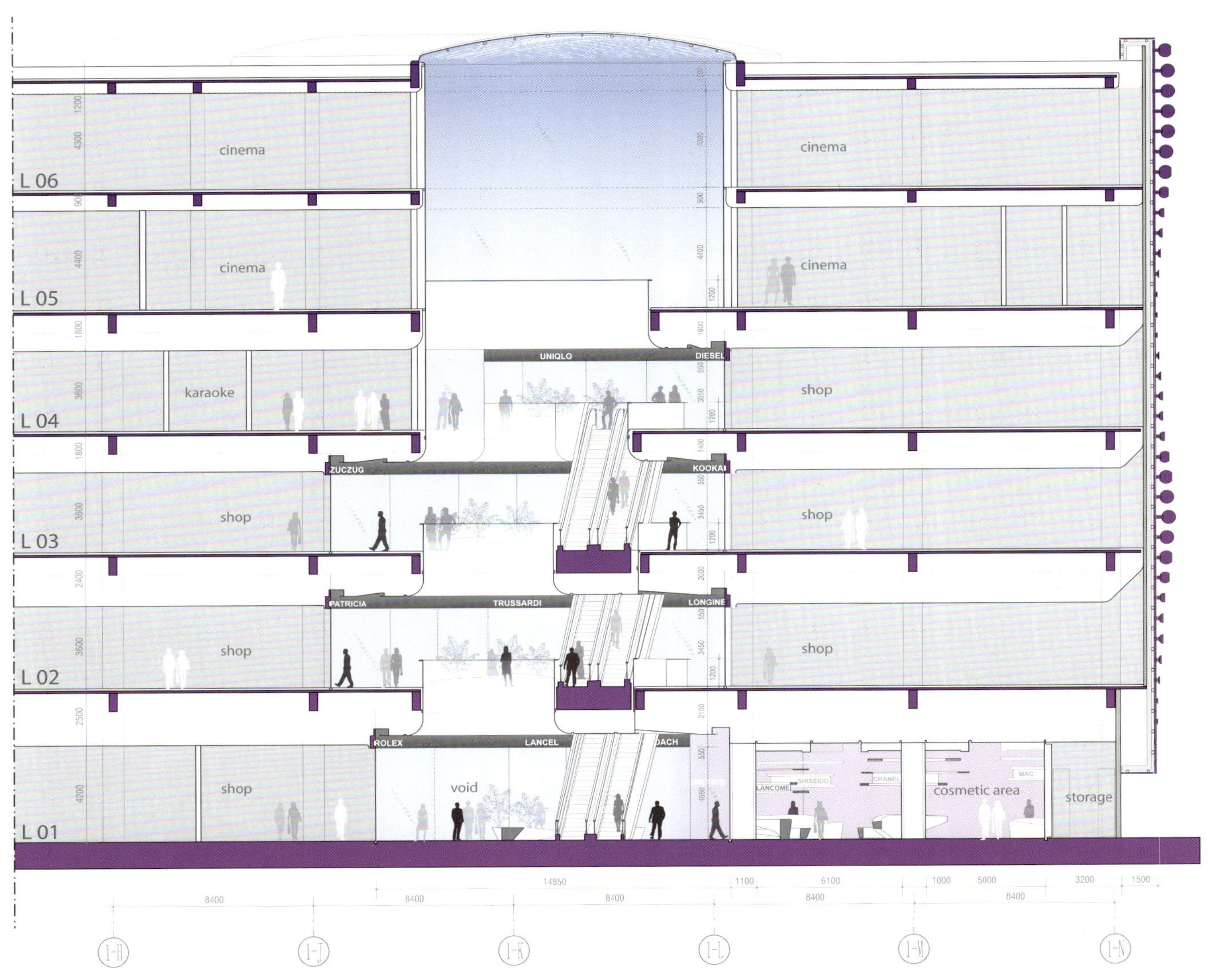

interior cross section
内部横截面图

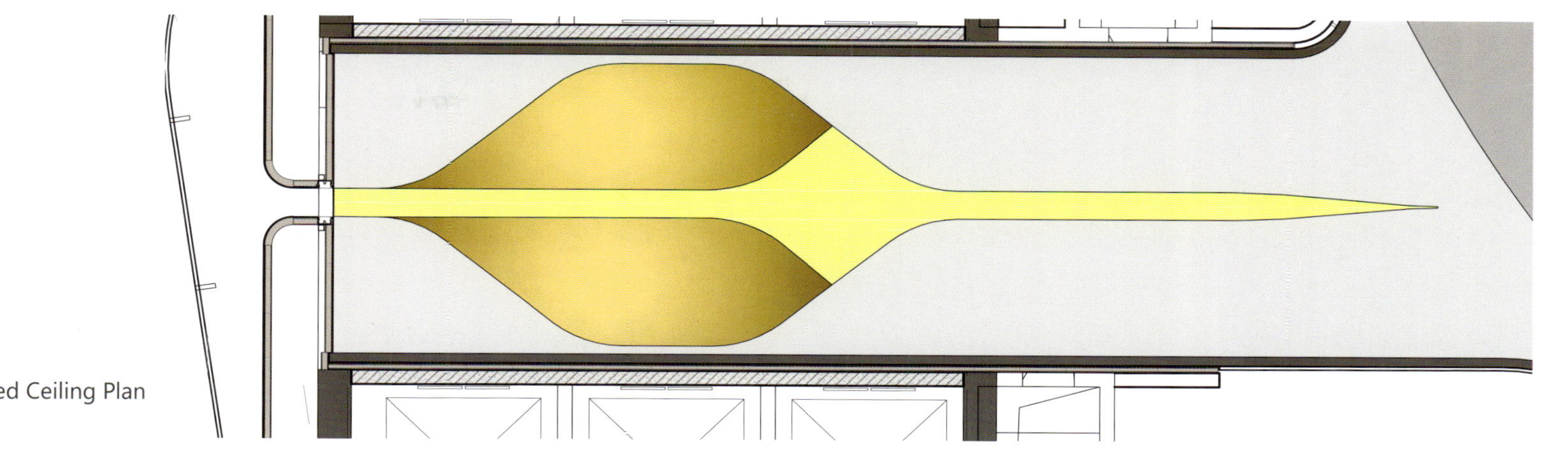

Elevator Lobby Reflected Ceiling Plan
电梯大厅天花板反向图

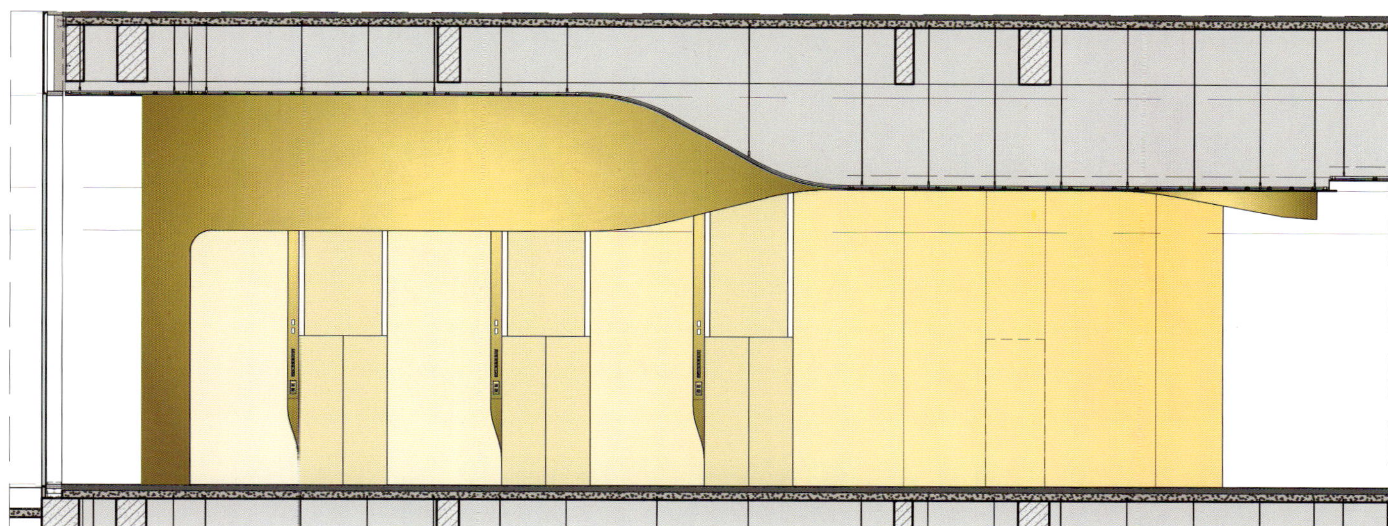

Elevation/ Section Elevator Lobby
电梯大厅立面图 / 剖面图

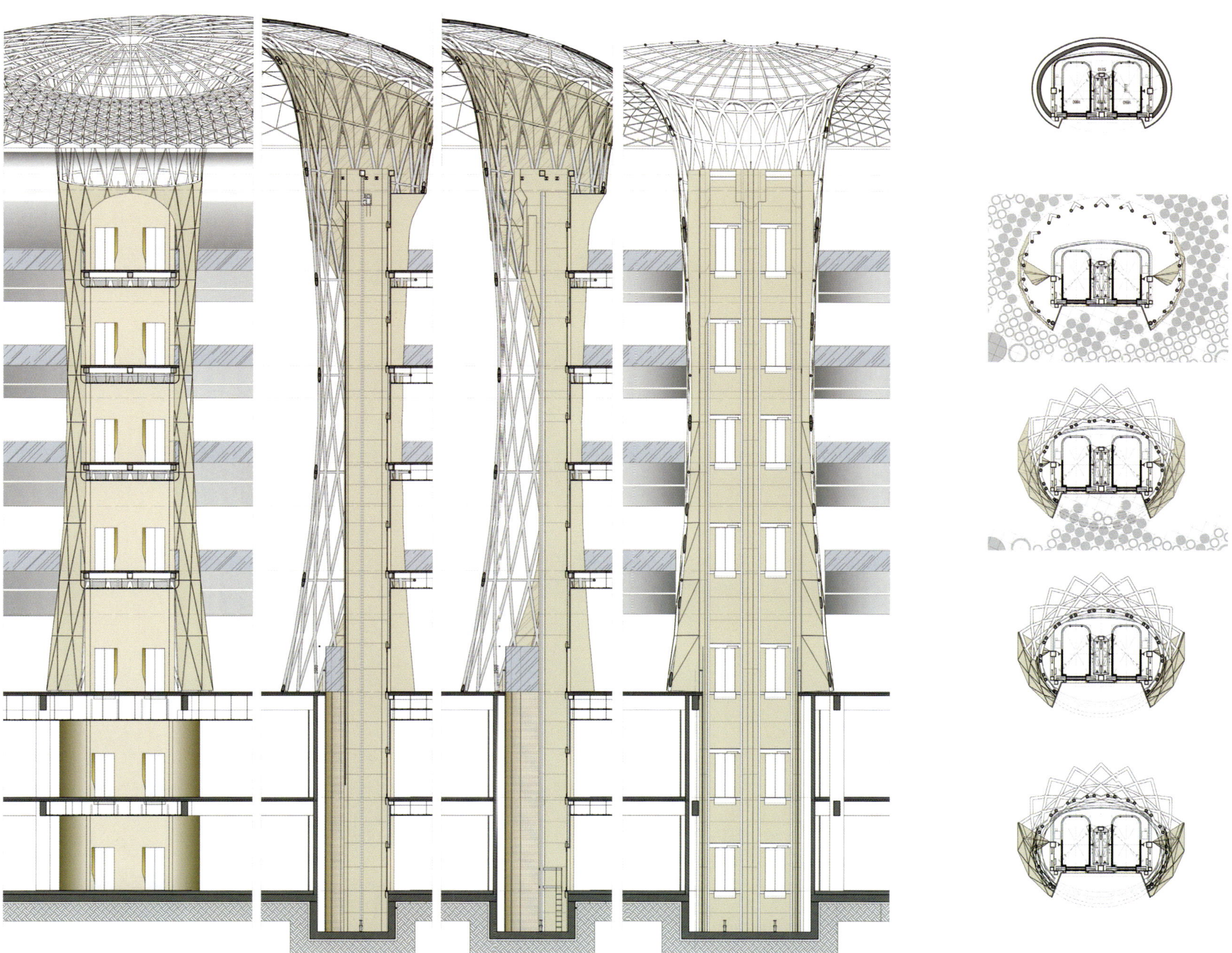

Funnel panoramic lift drawing
漏斗全景电梯图纸

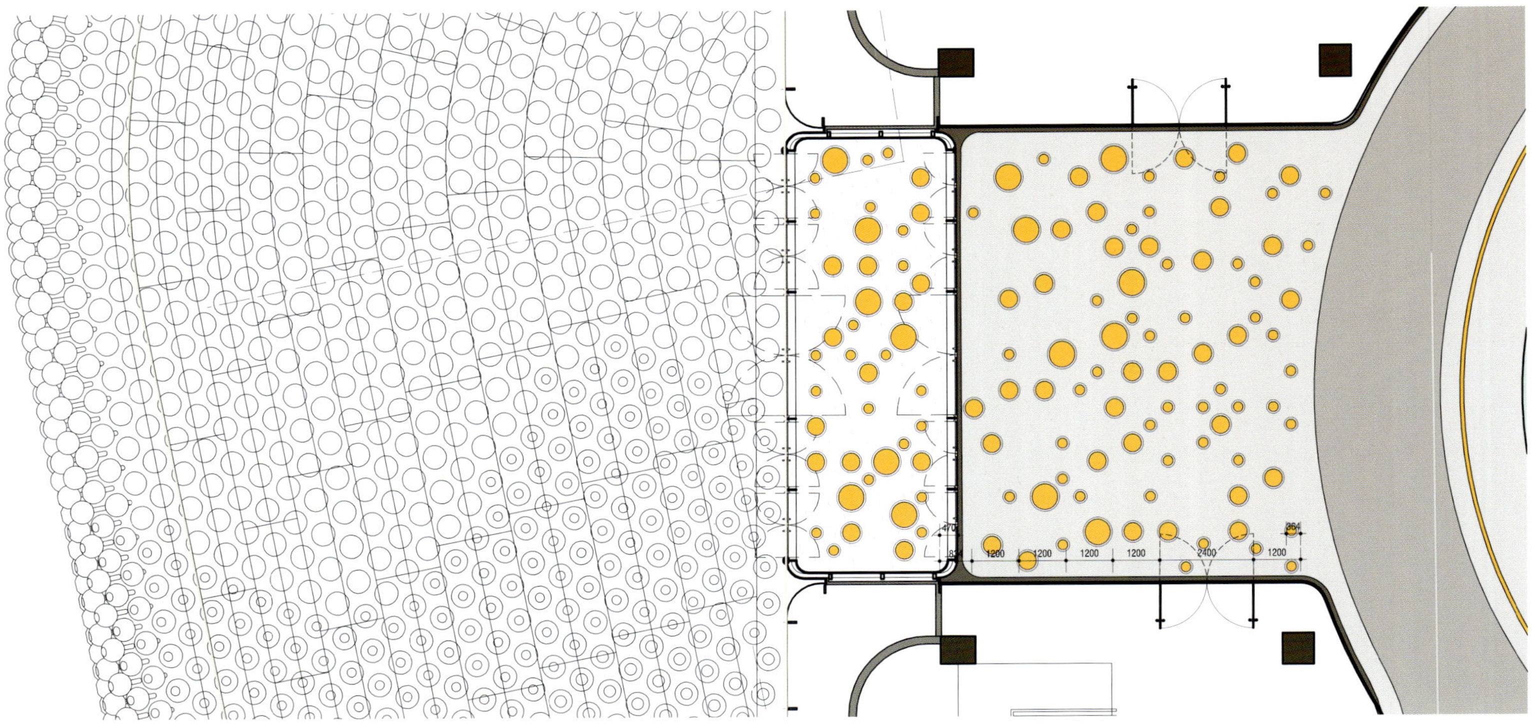

North West Entrance Reflected Ceiling Plan

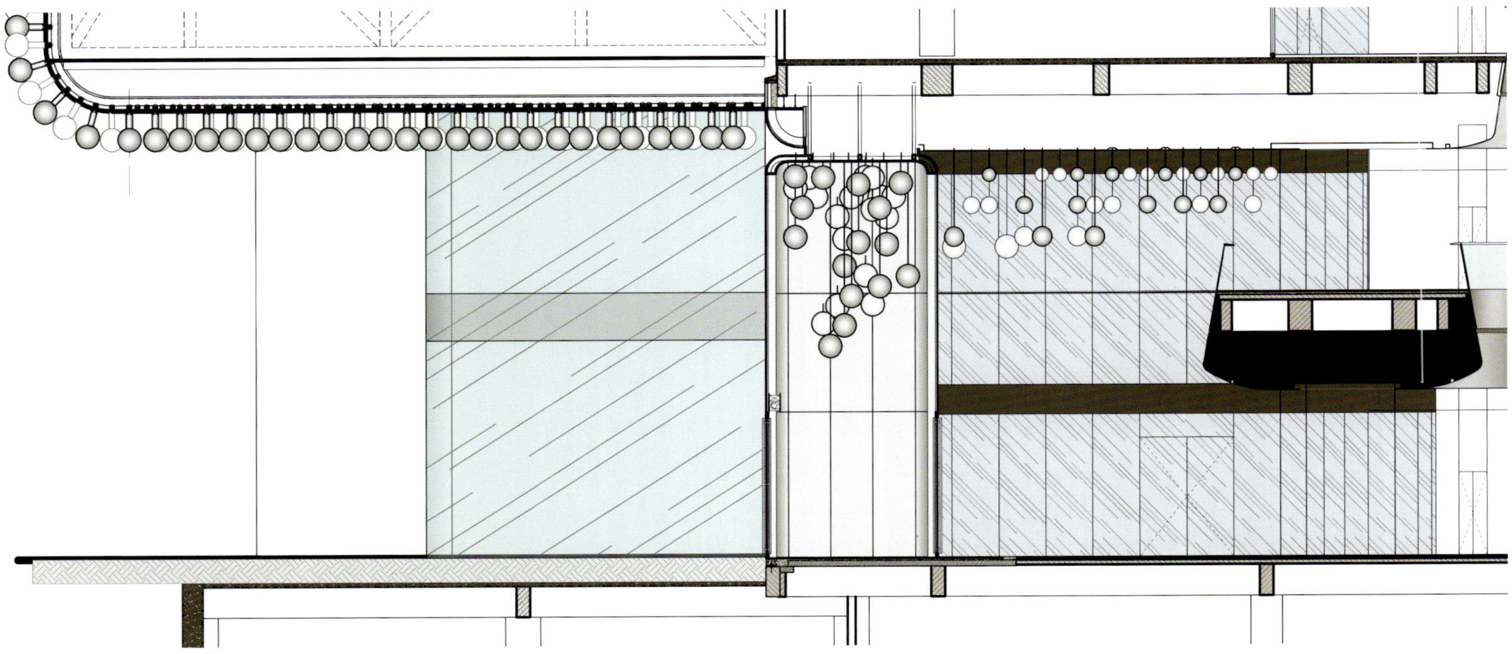

North West Entrance Cross-section Plan

North West entrance plan
西北入口平面图

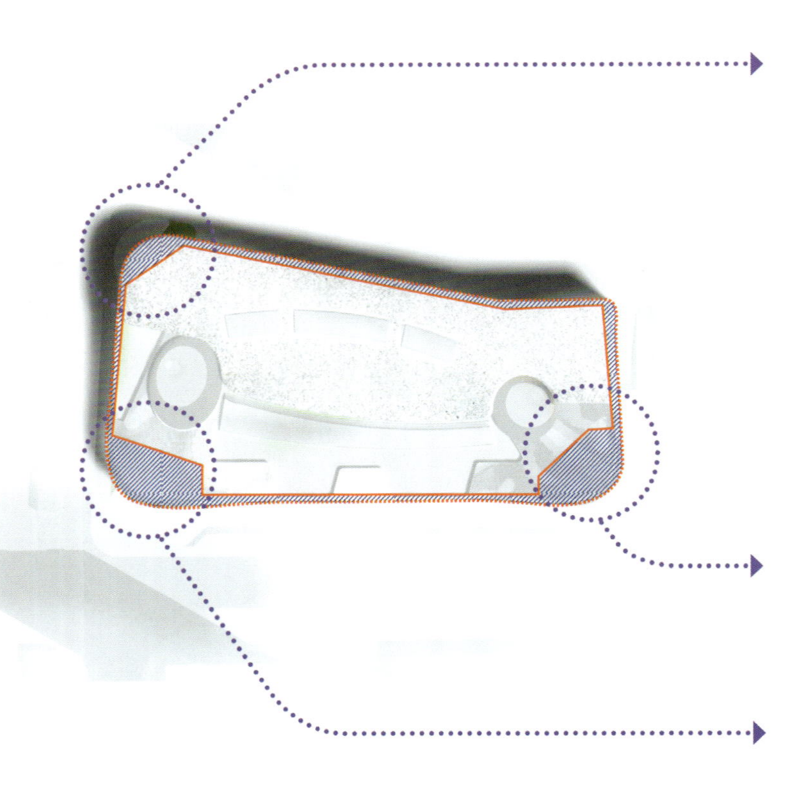

顶视图
TOP VIEW

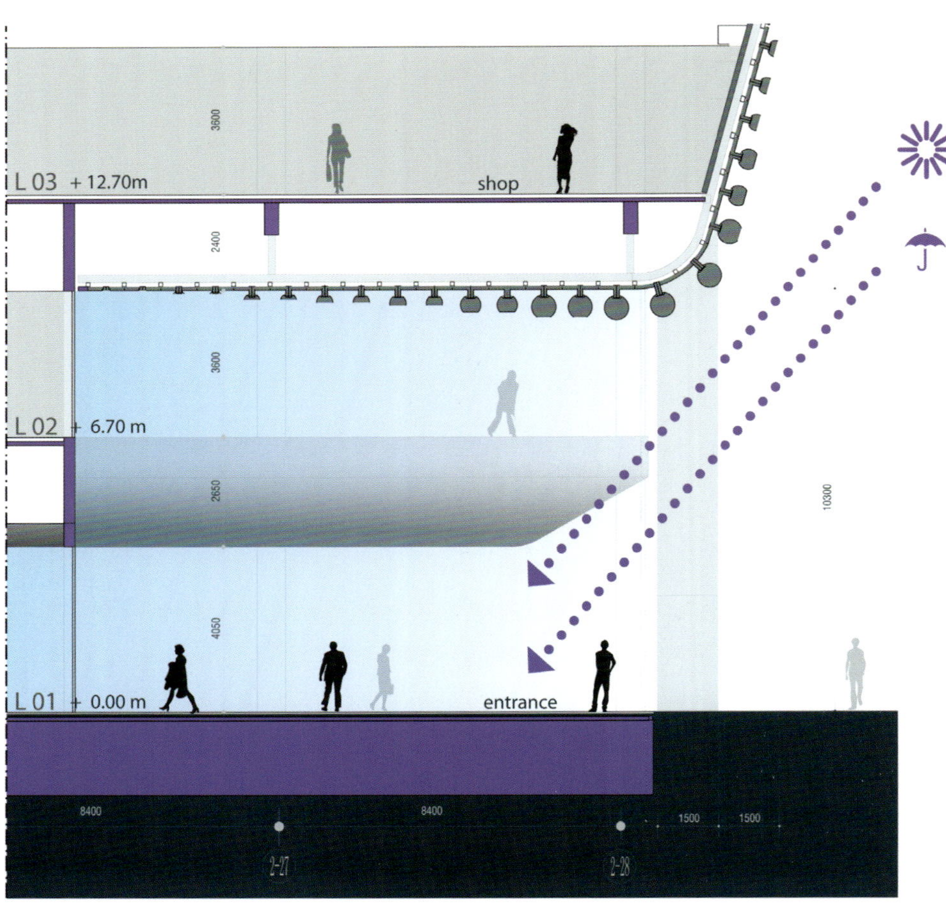

剖面
SECTION

Entrance section
入口剖面图

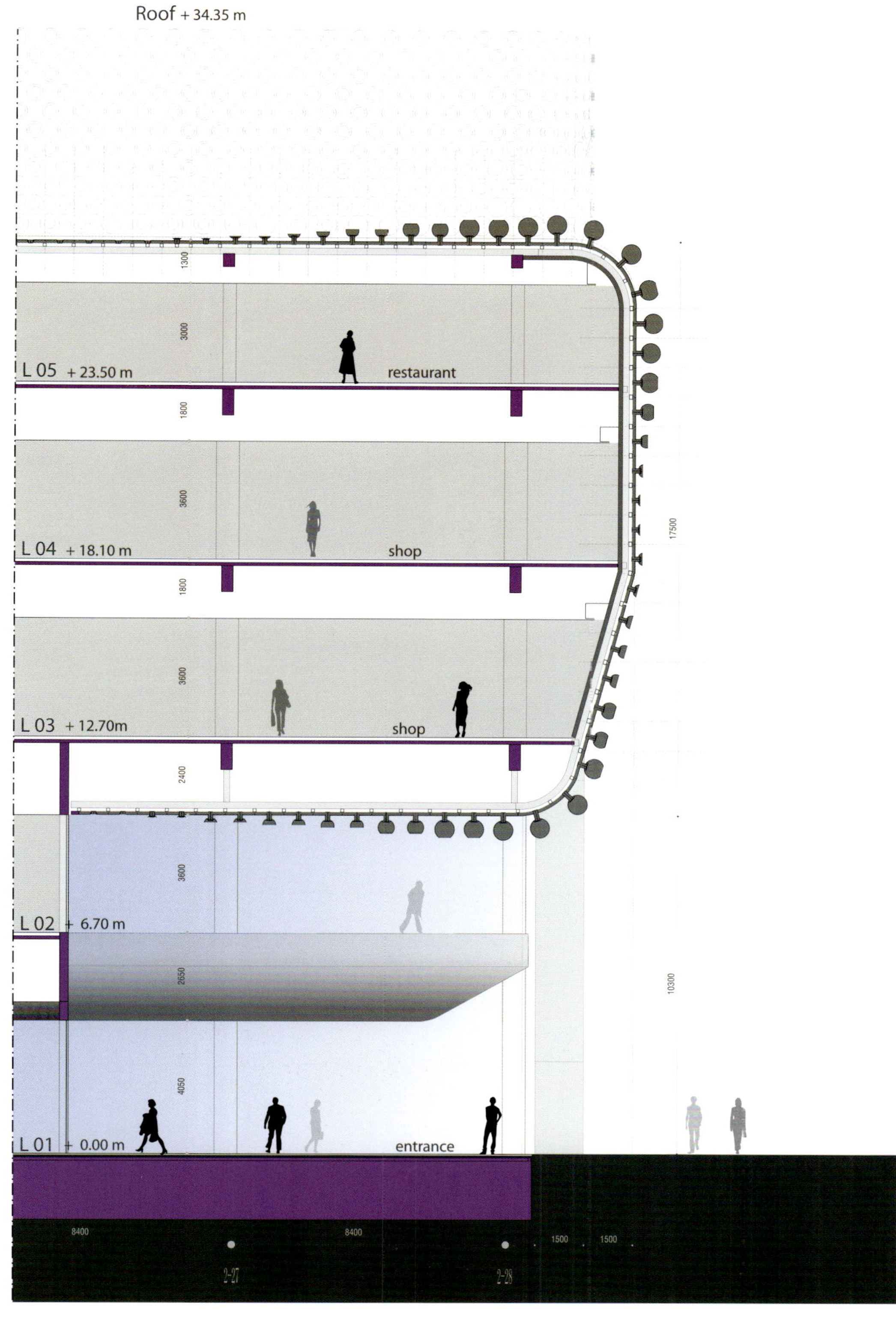

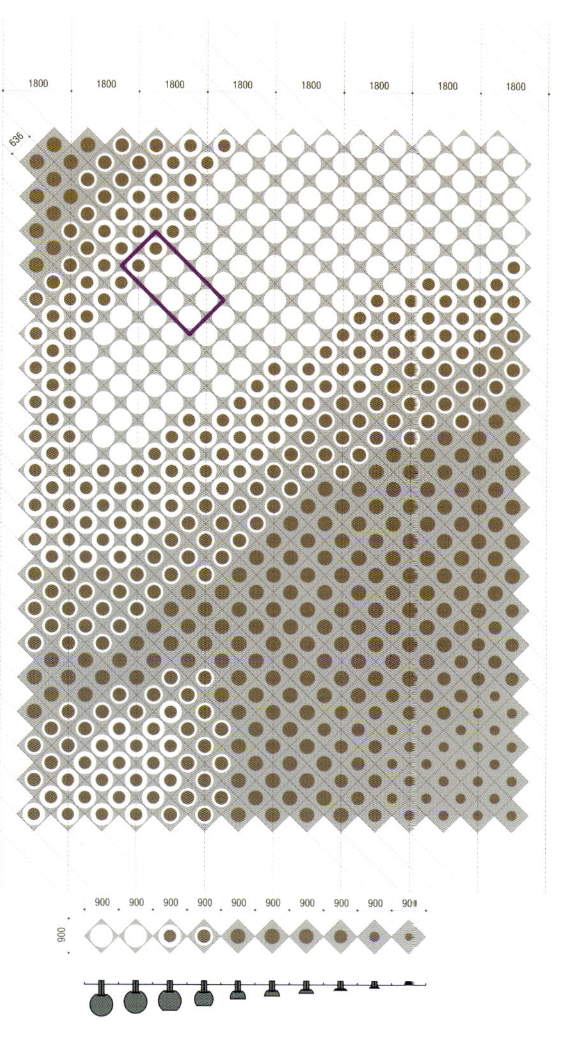

Facade Section
外立面剖面图

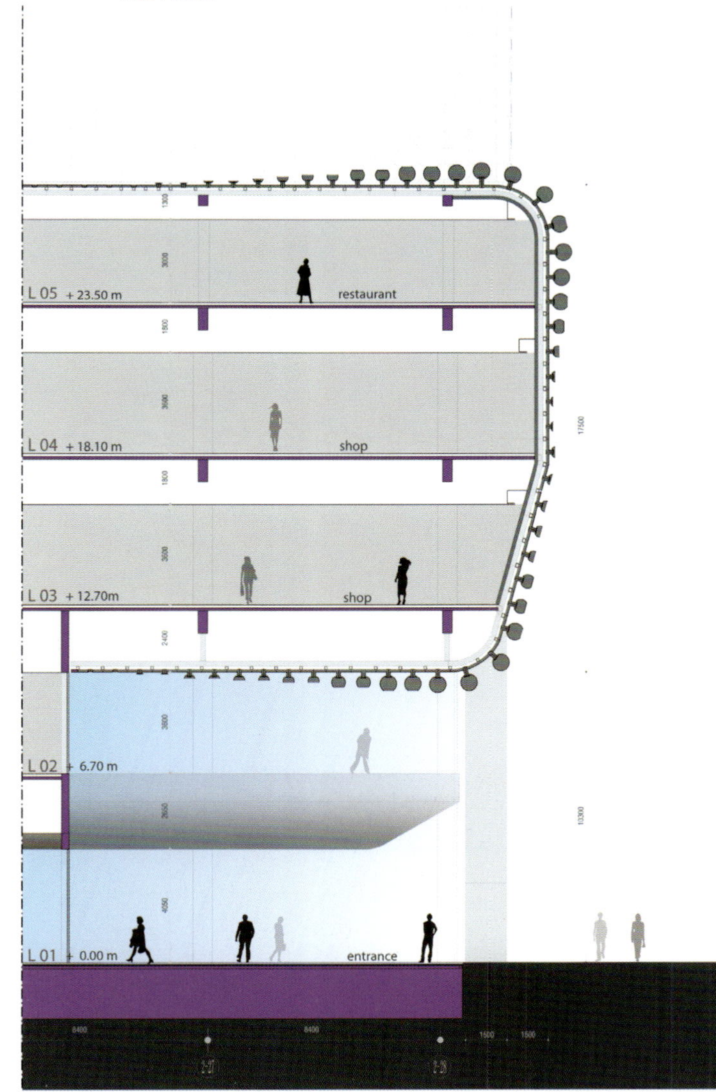

入口处表皮剖面 * FACADE SECTION @ SECTION

Entrance Facade section
入口处表皮剖面图

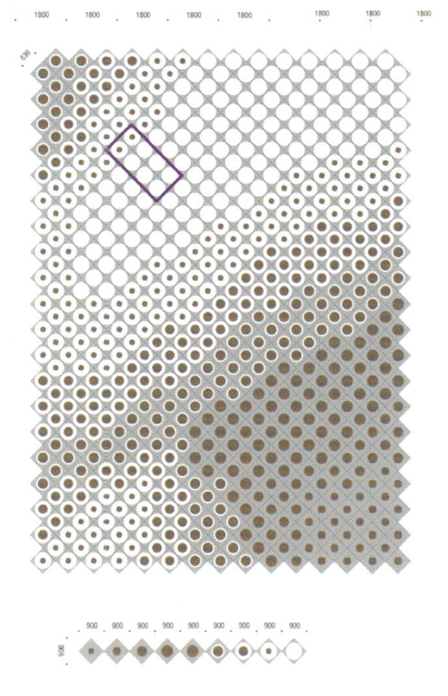

入口处立面 * ELEVATION @ ENTRANCE

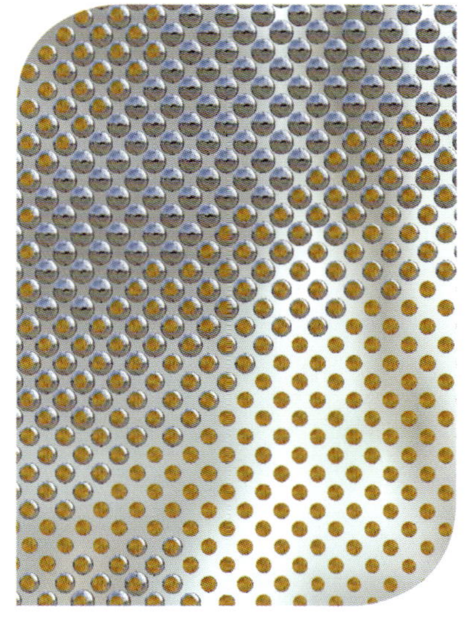

立面表皮 * FACADE ELEVATION

Facade Surface
立面表皮

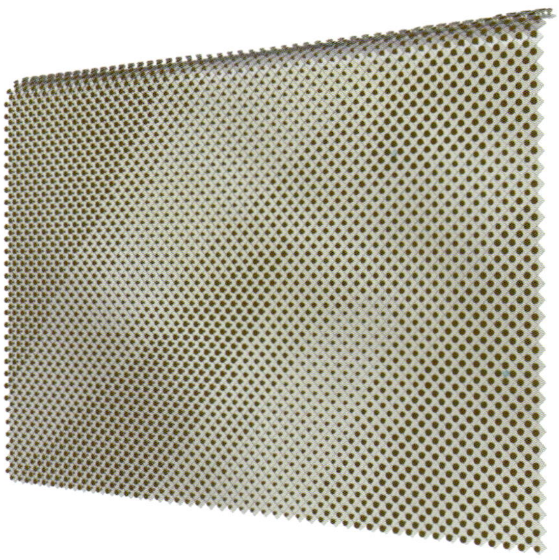

使用模块
USED MODULES

透视图
PERSPECTIVE

facade transition 1
立面过渡 1

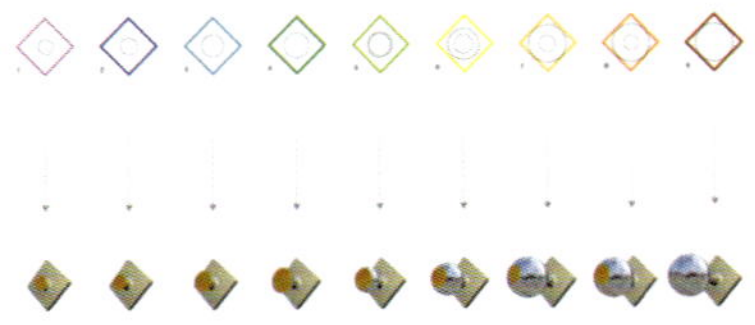

使用模块
USED MODULES

立面
ELEVATION

使用模块
USED MODULES

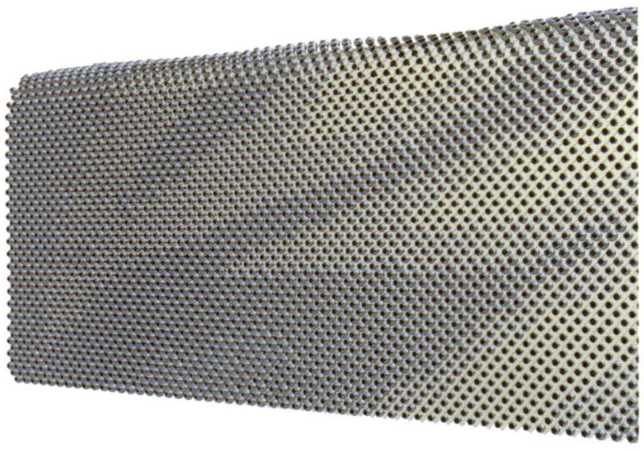

透视图
PERSPECTIVE

facade transition 2
立面过渡 2

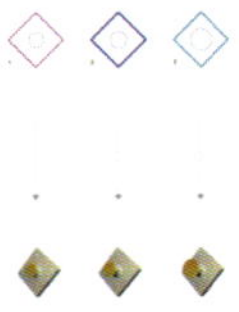

使用模块
USED MODULES

立面
ELEVATION

使用模块
USED MODULES

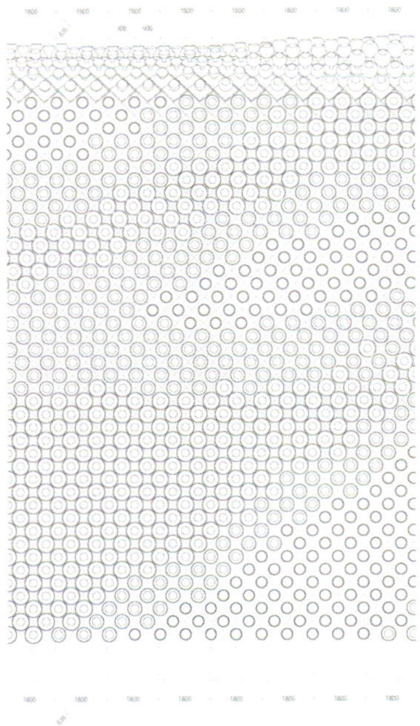

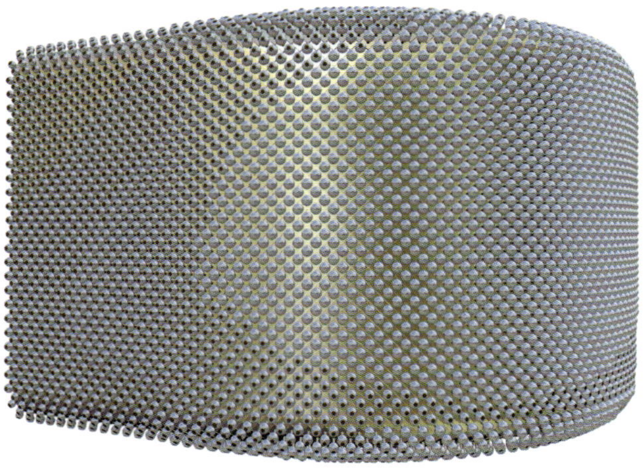

透视图
PERSPECTIVE

facade transition 3
立面过渡 3

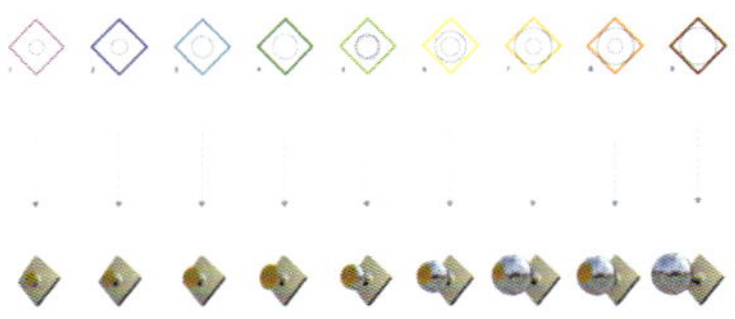

使用模块
USED MODULES

立面
ELEVATION

Facade design

The facade design focuses on achieving a dynamic effect, reflecting the hanccrafted combination of two materials: polished stainless steel and patterned glass. These two materials are crafted into nine differently trimmed, but standardised spheres. Their specific positions in relation to each other recreate the effect of movement and reflection in water, or the sensuous folds of silk fabric.

The geometry ranges from full stainless steel spheres to a sequence of gradually trimmed spheres down to a hemisphere, with an inlay of laminated glass with printed foil. The spheres have a diameter of 600mm and are mounted at various distances on the 900mm x 900mm brushed aluminium panels, which were preassembled and mounted on site.

Synergy of flows

As water was utilised as a main organisational principle in the design for the Wuhan Central Cultural Centre the theme "synergy of flows" is used as a starting point for the organisation of the buildings.For the design of the Hanjie Wanda Square this entails guiding attention and visitor flows from the main routes towards the facades and entrances of the building. From the three main entrances visitor flows are guided to two interior atria.

立面设计

立面设计侧重于实现动态效果，表达了两种材料的手工组合：抛光不锈钢与压花玻璃。这两种材料被制成 9 种不同的标准球体。它们之间特定的位置能创造出运动的效果和水中的反射，或如真丝面料般的褶皱。

立面几何形状成线性变化，从由纯不锈钢制成的球体形状逐步演变成半球体形状。立面为镶嵌式夹层玻璃，表面呈现铝箔色泽。球体直径为 600mm，安装在 900mm x 900mm 的磨砂铝板上，各自之间的间距各不相同。这些磨砂铝板都是在现场组装并安装完成的。

协同和流动

水是设计武汉中央文化中心的主要布局原理。为了与其交相呼应，广场采用了协同和流动的主题，将协同和流动作为布局各建筑的出发点。汉街万达广场的设计旨在引导人们的注意力与人流从主道转向外立面与建筑入口。将人流从 3 个主要入口引向两个正厅。

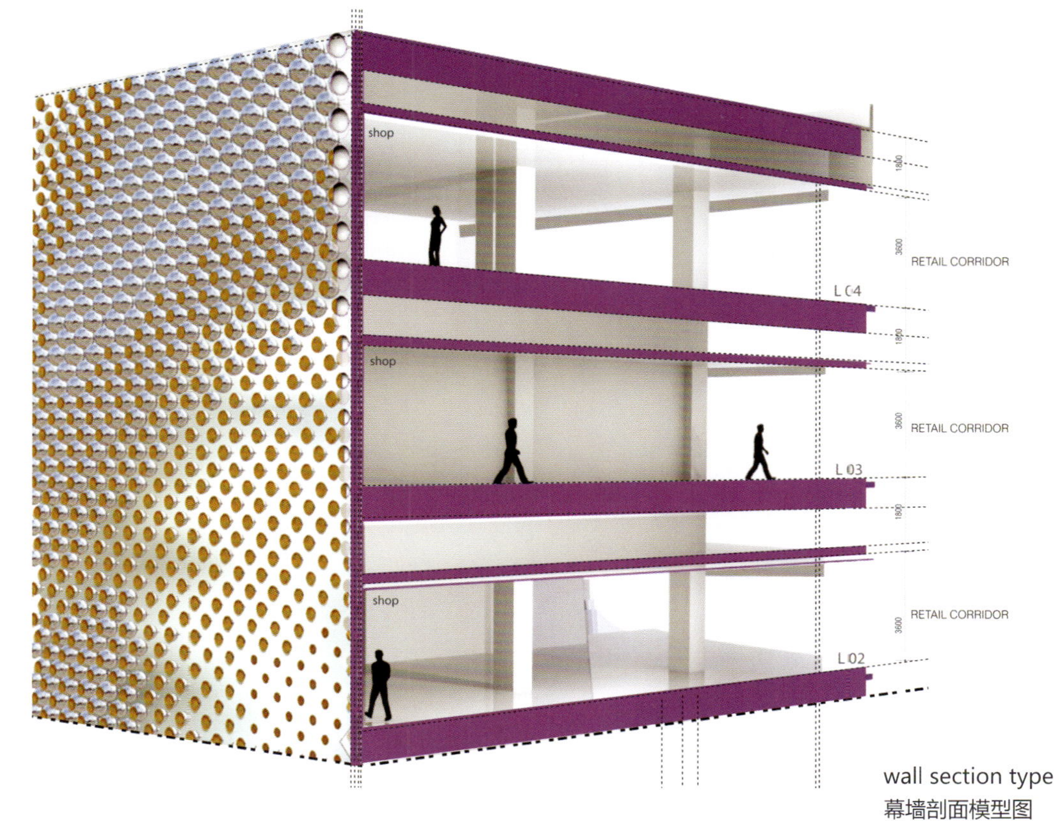

wall section type
幕墙剖面模型图

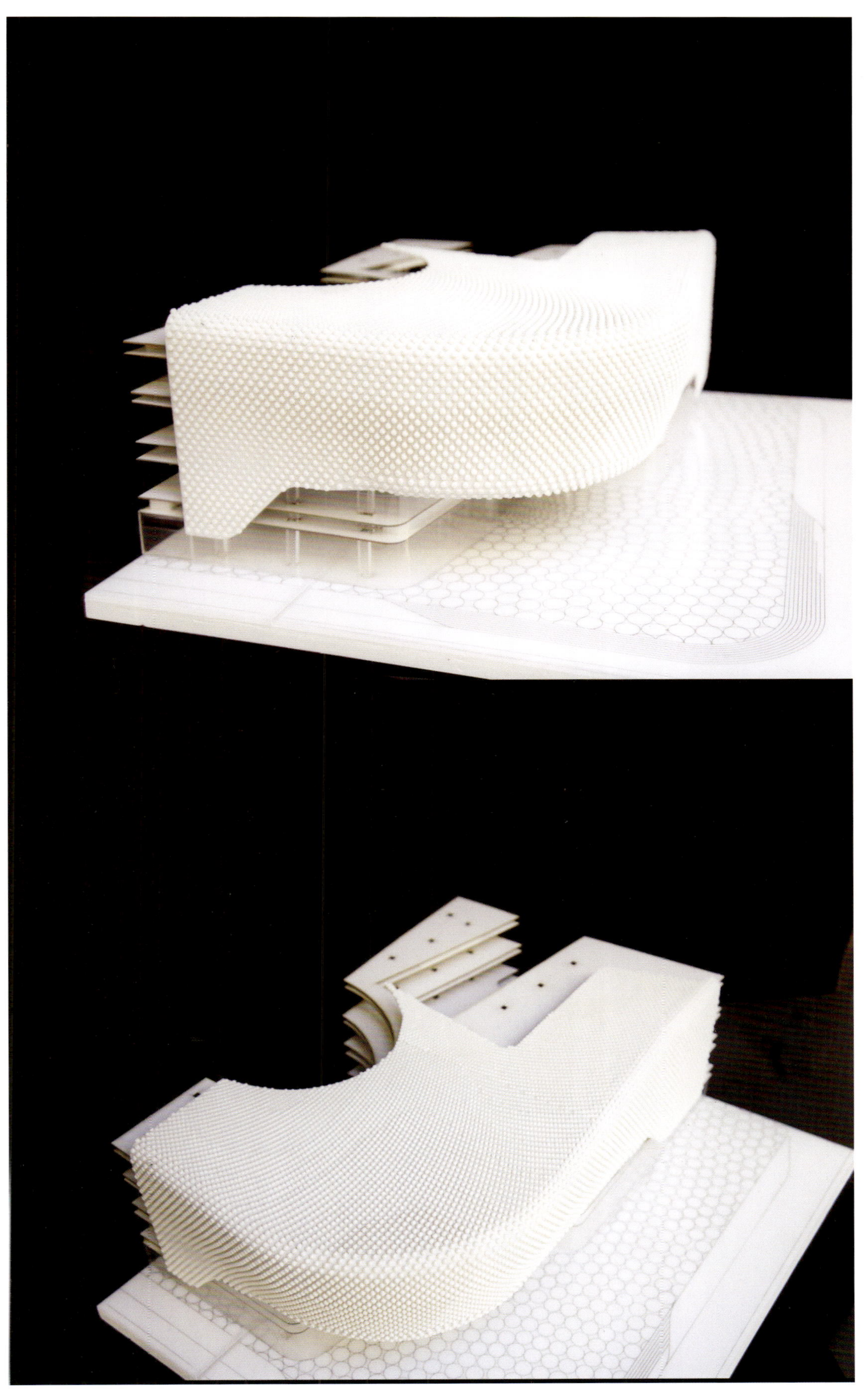

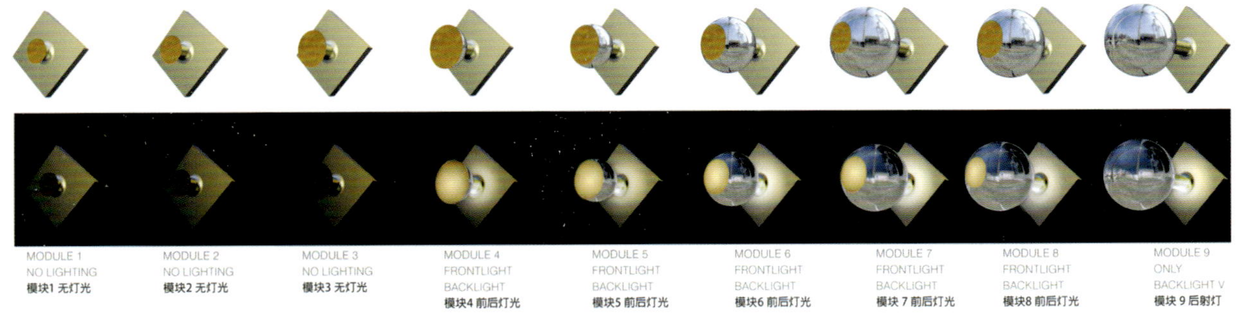

立面模块被分类為"特色性格"的光 每个大模块成為特殊的灯光体,是一个表皮的組成元件同時也是時尚的產品。

FACADE MODULES ARE CATEGORIZED AS 'CHARACTERS' OF LIGHT. EACH OF THE LARGER MODULES BECOMES A UNIQUE LIGHT OBJECT. A FACADE ELEMENT AS WELL AS A SOPHISTICATED AND STYLISH PRODUCT IN ITSELF

渐变研究 * GRADIENT STUDIES

facade lighting
外立面照明

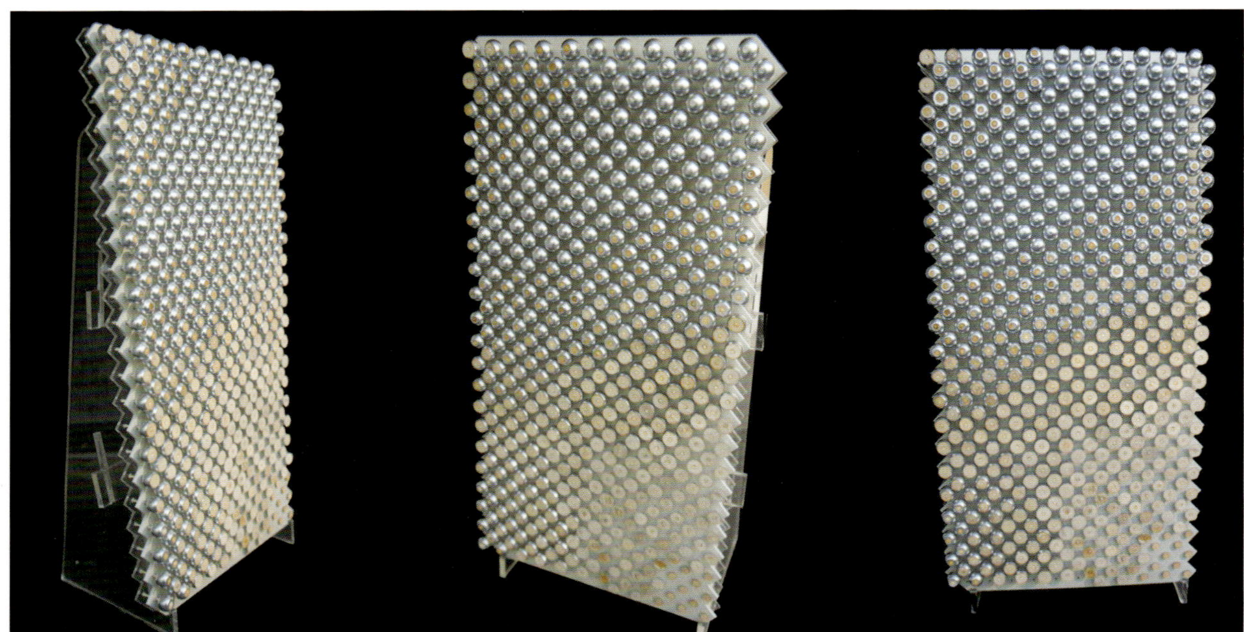

Facade sphere Diagram
外立面球体示意图

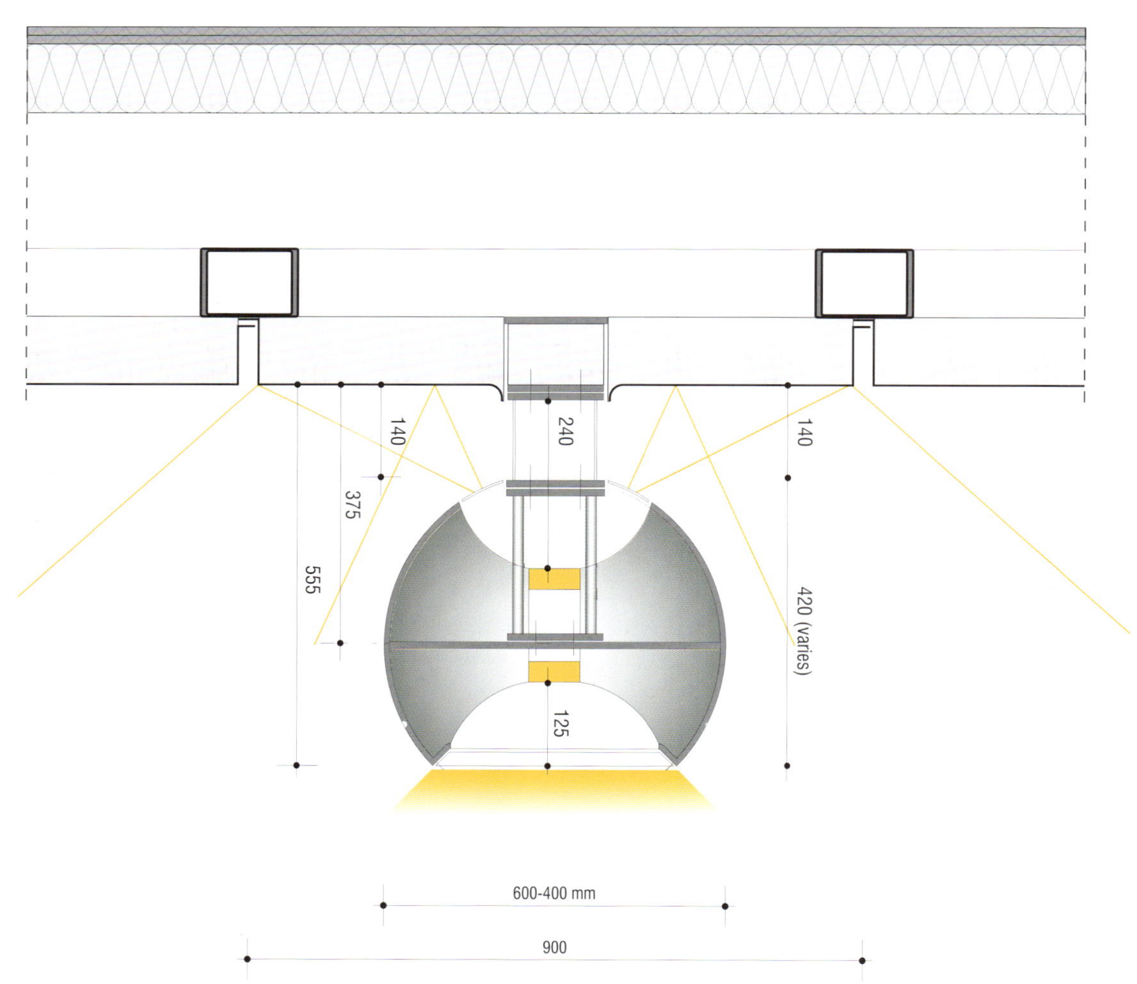

Facade Detail
立面细节图

The concept of synergy of flows is key to all of the design components; the fluid articulation of the building envelope, the programming of the dynamic facade lighting and its content and the interior pattern language which guides customers from the central atria to the upper levels and throughout the building via linking corridors.

The architectural lighting is integrated into the building envelope's 42.333 spheres. Within each sphere LED-fixtures emit light onto the laminated glass to generate glowing circular spots. Simultaneously a second set of LED's at the rear side of the spheres create a diffuse illumination on the back panels. A total of 3,100,000 LED lights where used to cover the 17,894 m². media facade. Various possibilities to combine and control these lights allows diverse media lighting effects and programming of lighting sequences related to the use and activation of the Hanjie Wanda Square.

所有的设计部件：连贯的围护结构，动态立面照明及光影效果的设计，内部从中庭到楼上和所有走廊上的指示标语都体现了协同和流动的理念。

建筑的照明与建筑的围合球体(42.333)融为一体。每个球体中的LED灯将光线投射到夹层玻璃上，产生一种圆形光斑，熠熠生辉，栩栩如生。与此同时，安装在球体背部的另一组LED灯具则负责背板的漫射照明。共3,100,000盏LED灯具覆盖了面积达17,894平米的媒体立面。千百种照明搭配与调控使得缤纷多彩的媒体照明效果与照明布置巧妙地迎合了汉街万达广场的主题，让汉街万达广场充满生机。

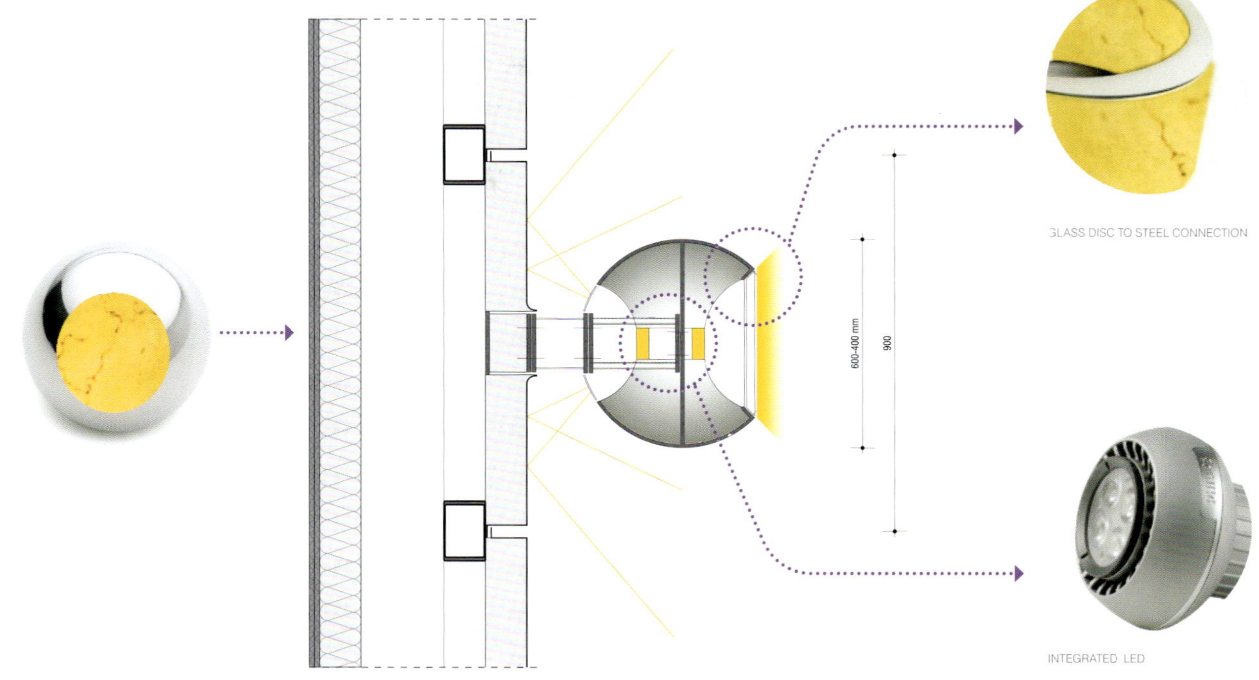

Detail 1
细节图 1

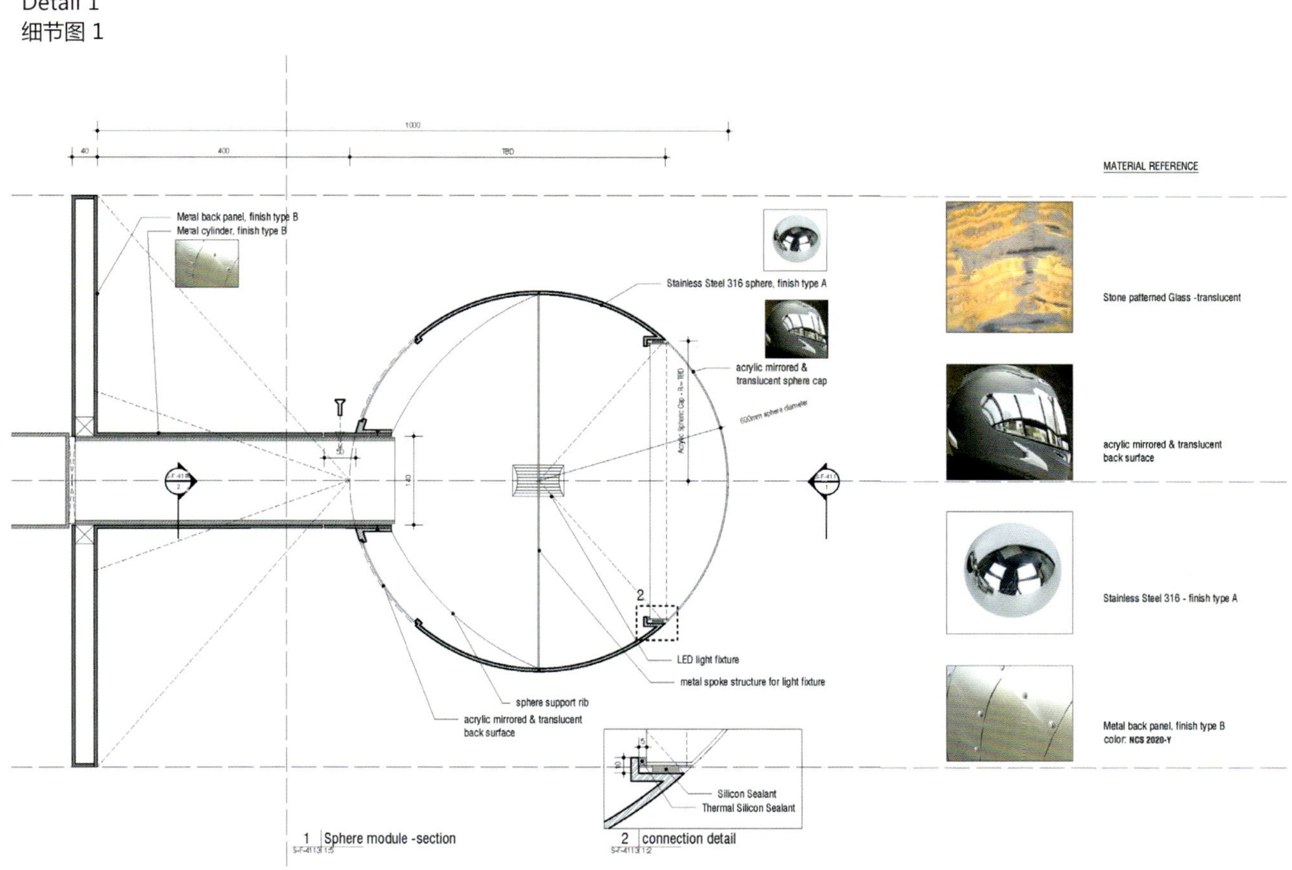

Detail 2
细节图 2

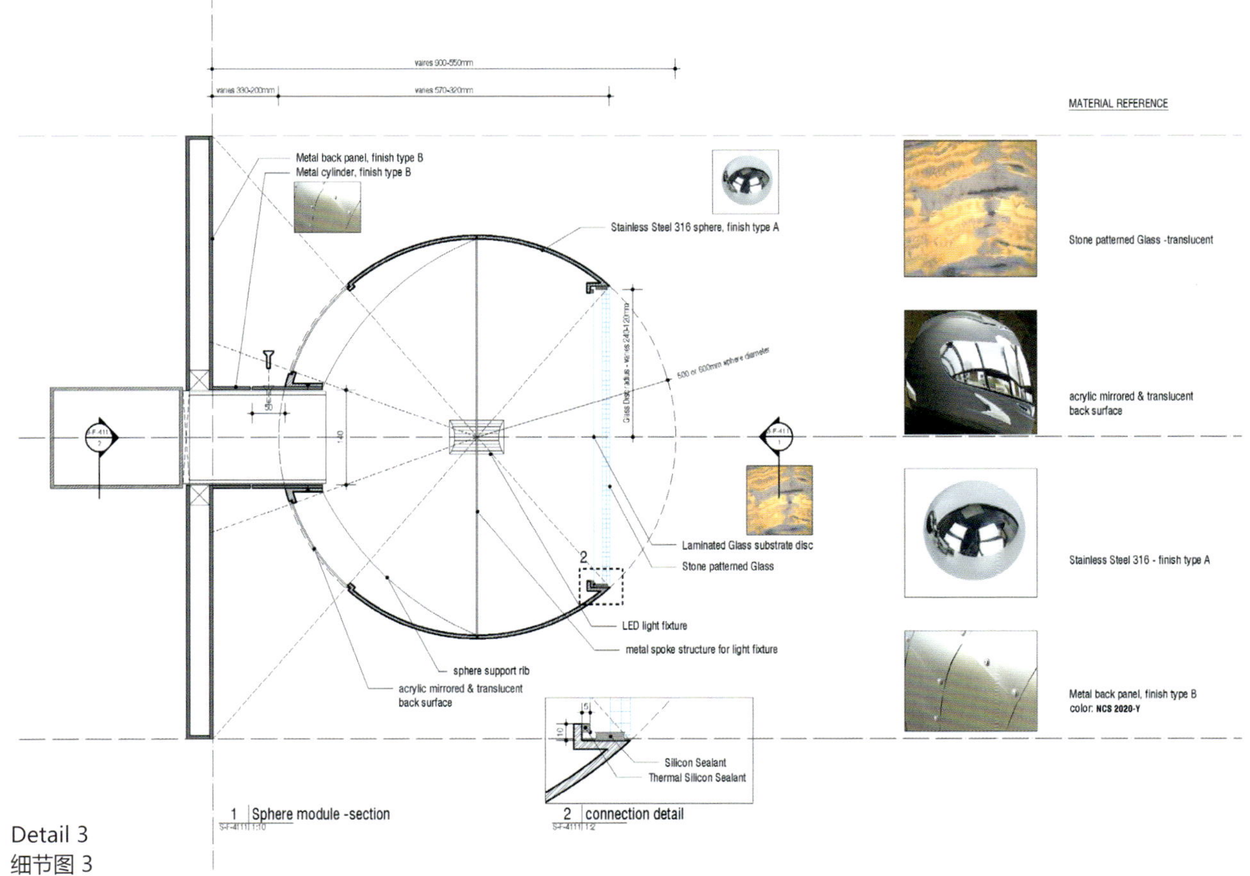

Detail 3
细节图 3

gb
eva ouxiu

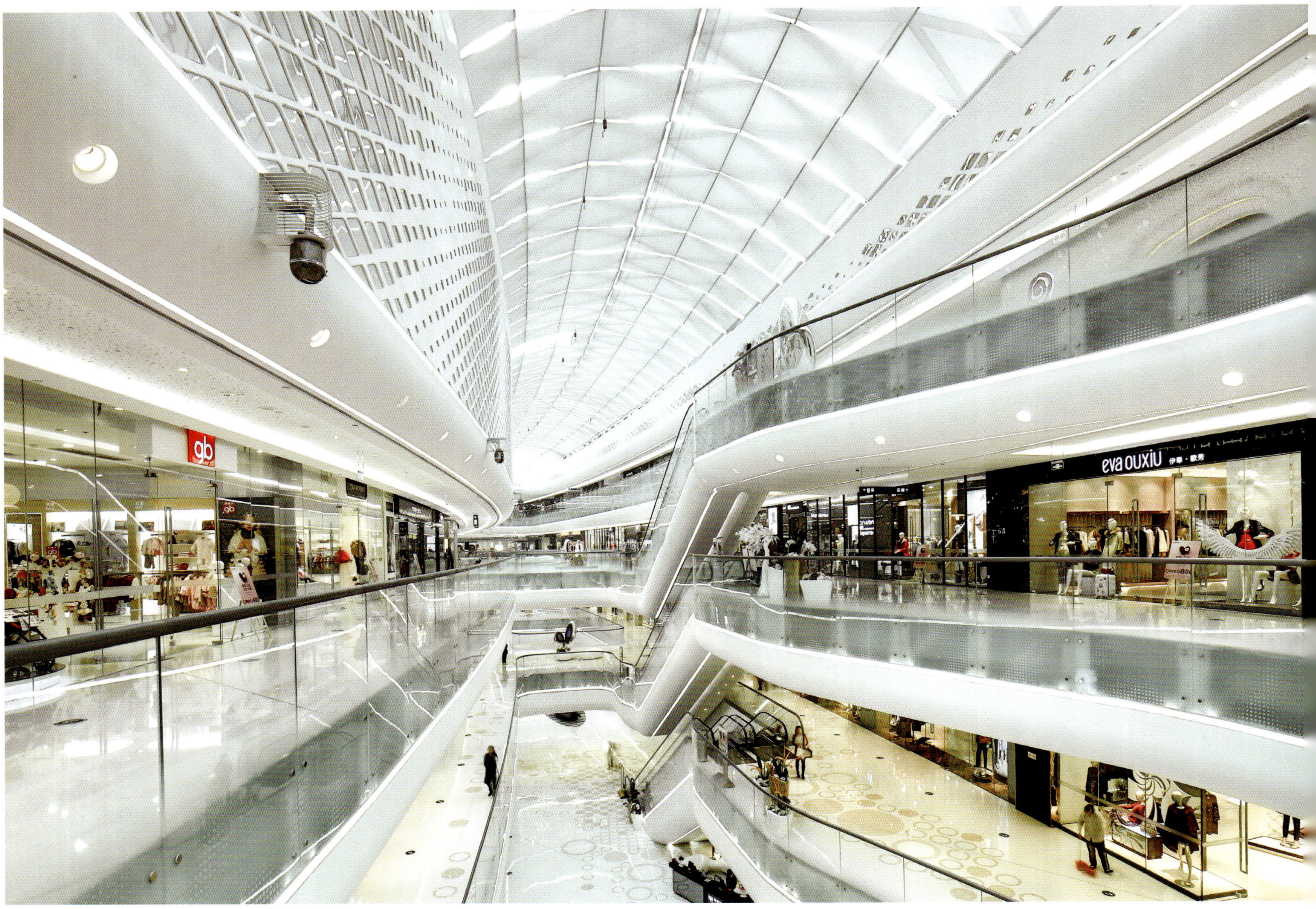

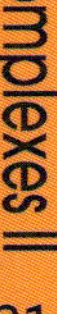

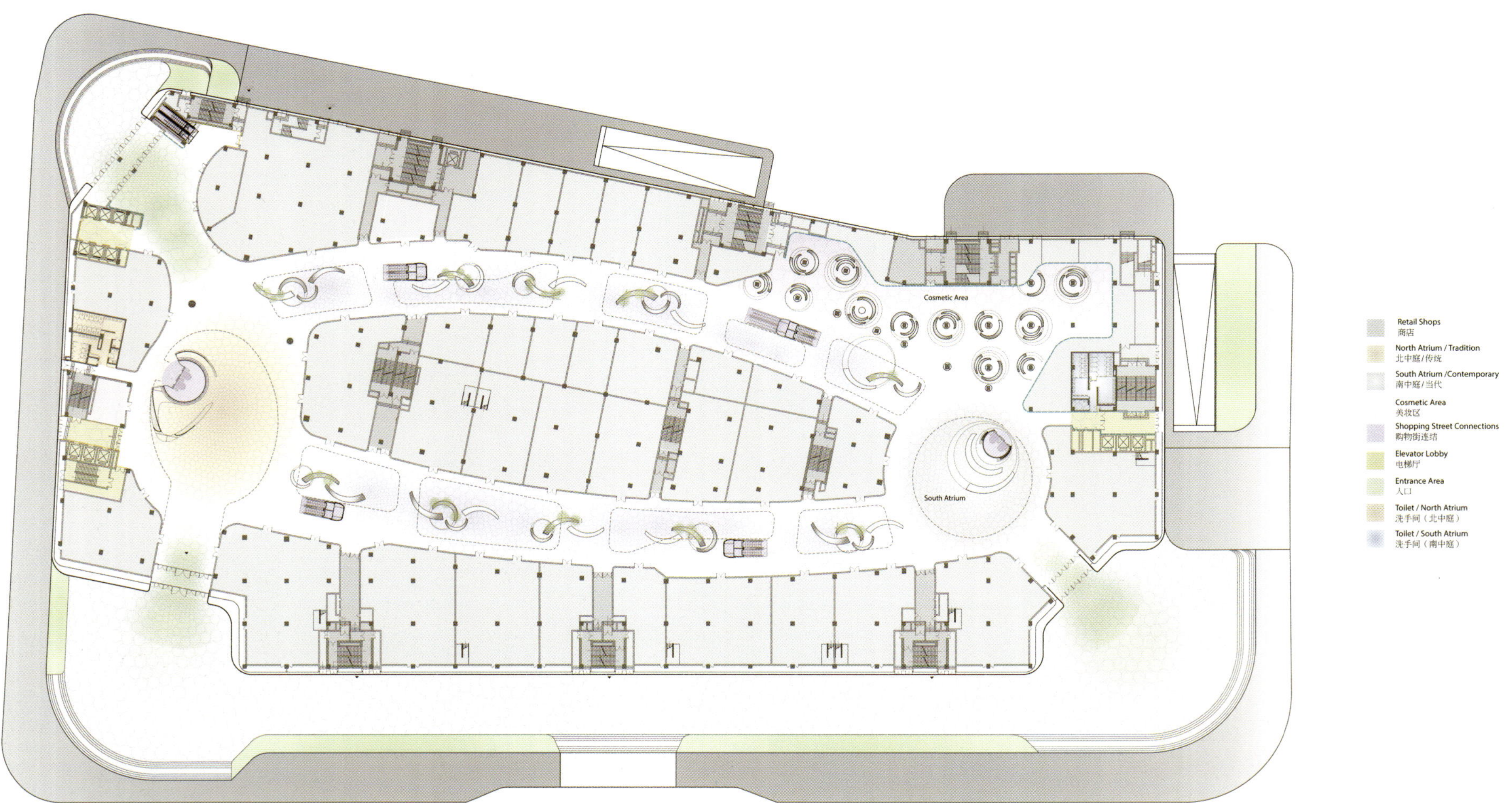

Cosmetic Area
South Atrium
Retail Shops
商店
North Atrium / Tradition
北中庭/传统
South Atrium /Contemporary
南中庭/当代
Cosmetic Area
美妆区
Shopping Street Connections
购物街连结
Elevator Lobby
电梯厅
Entrance Area
入口
Toilet / North Atrium
洗手间（北中庭）
Toilet / South Atrium
洗手间（南中庭）
10
25
50 m

Interior concept

The interior concept is developed around the North and South atria, creating two different, yet integrated atmospheres. The atria become the centre of the dynamic duality of the two Hanjie Wanda Square identities: Contemporary and Traditional. Variations in geometry, materials and details define these differing characters. With two main entrances, the North atrium is recognised as a main venue hall, and the South atrium as a more intimate venue hall. The North atrium is characterised by warm golden and bronze materials reflecting a cultural, traditional identity. In the South atrium Silver and grey nuances with reflective textures reflect the city identity and its urban rhythm. Both atria are crowned by skylights with a funnel structure which connects the roof and the ground floor. The funnel structures are each clad with 2,600 glass panels and are digitally printed with an intricate pattern. In addition, each funnel integrally houses a pair of panorama lifts. While the atria have strong and distinct identities, the corridors act as connectors between the two, whilst maintaining their own character.

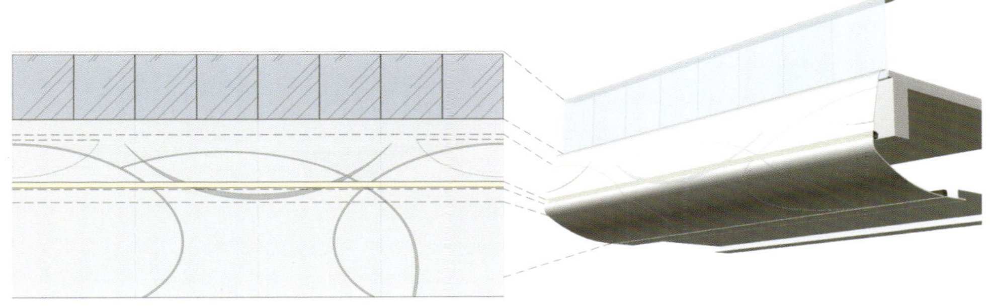

Balustrade Atrium
中庭栏杆

内部设计理念

内部的设计理念是围绕南北正厅，创造两个截然不同，但却浑然一体的氛围。汉街万达广场表达了两种相互矛盾的特点（即现代与传统），而正厅就是这种表达的核心内容。几何形状、材料和细节的变化体现了这些不同的符号。建筑设置了两个主入口，北中庭是主大厅，而南中庭则是更加怡人的大厅。北中庭以温暖的金色和青铜材料为主，体现了文化和传统的气息。南中庭在一些细微之处采用带有反光效果的银色和灰色材料，体现了都市的形象和节奏。南、北中庭的顶部采用了天窗。中庭漏斗形的天窗成为了顶部和地面之间的纽带。漏斗形的天窗共采用了2,600块玻璃墙板，分别通过数字印刷烙上了错综复杂的纹路。此外，漏斗形的天窗还配备了两个全景电梯。尽管两个中庭风格迥异，然而走廊却巧妙地将两者串联，同时也保留了各自的特点。

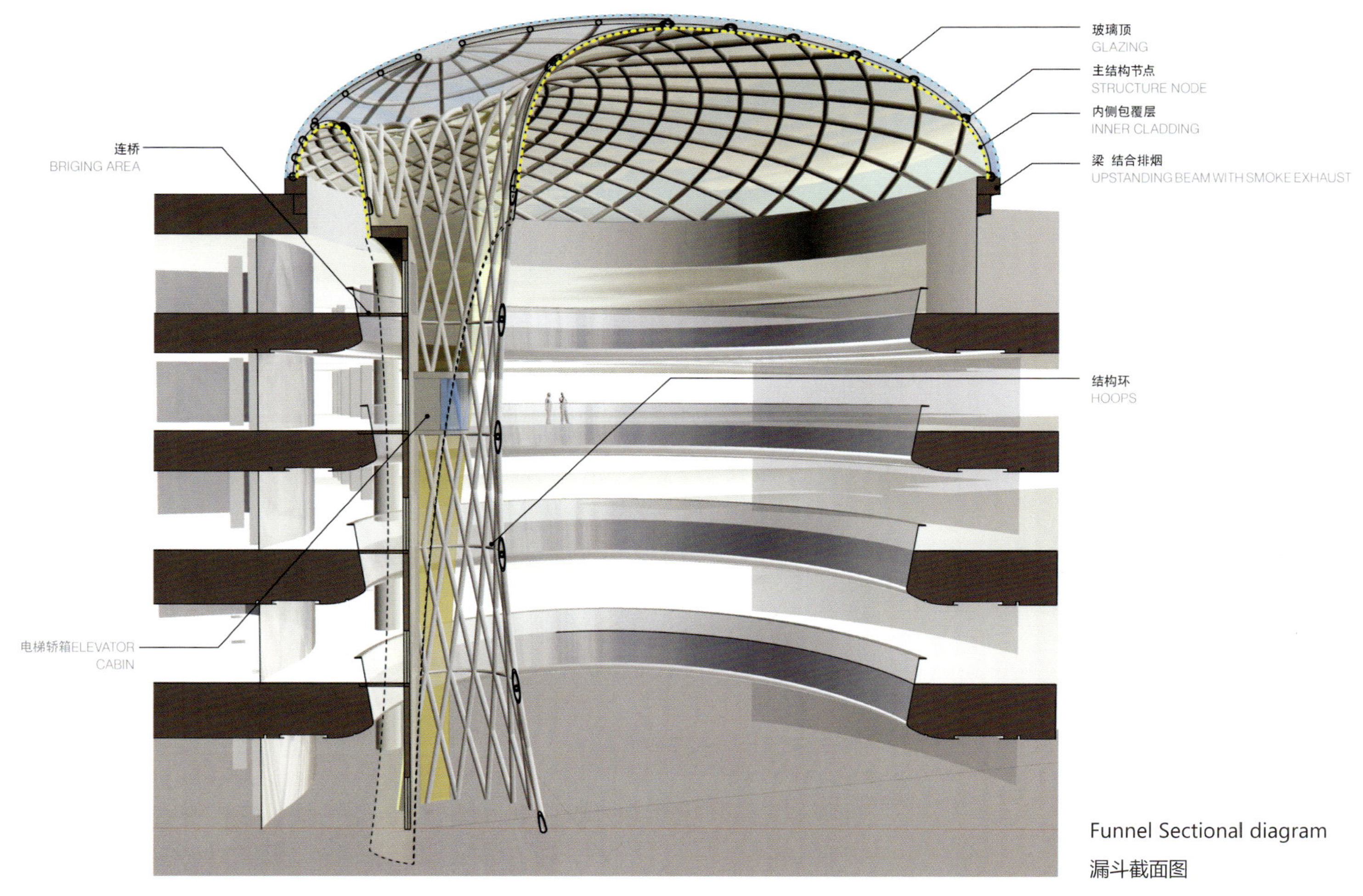

Funnel Sectional diagram

漏斗截面图

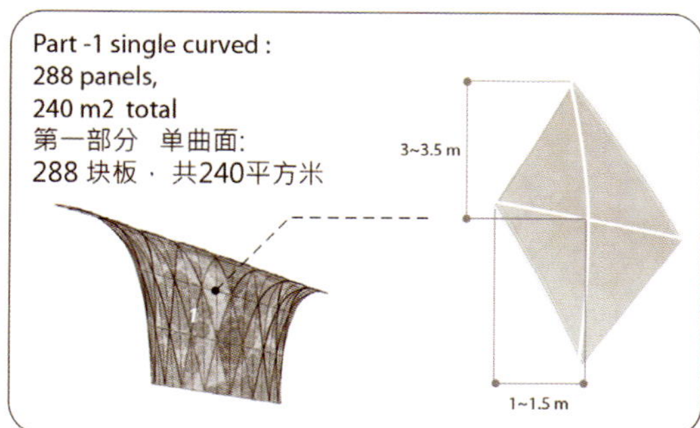

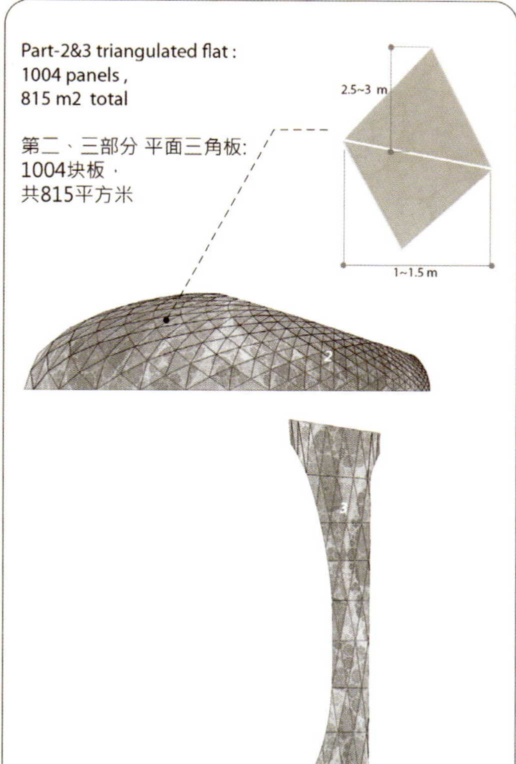

Part -1 single curved :
288 panels,
240 m2 total
第一部分 单曲面:
288 块板 · 共240平方米

3~3.5 m
1~1.5 m

Part -1 single curved panels unfold
第一部分 单曲面板展开

Part-2&3 triangulated flat :
1004 panels ,
815 m2 total

第二、三部分 平面三角板:
1004块板 ·
共815平方米

2.5~3 m
1~1.5 m

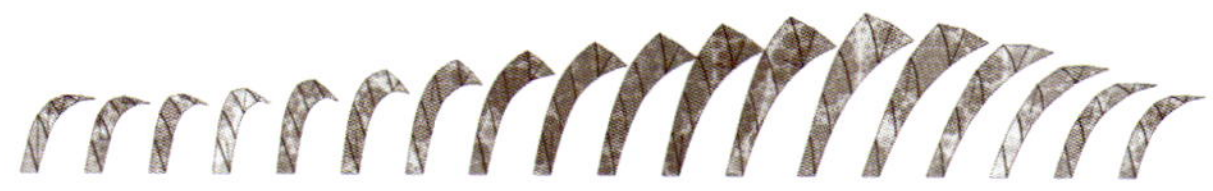

Part -2 triangulated flat panels unfold - skylight
第二部分 平面三角板展开 - 天窗

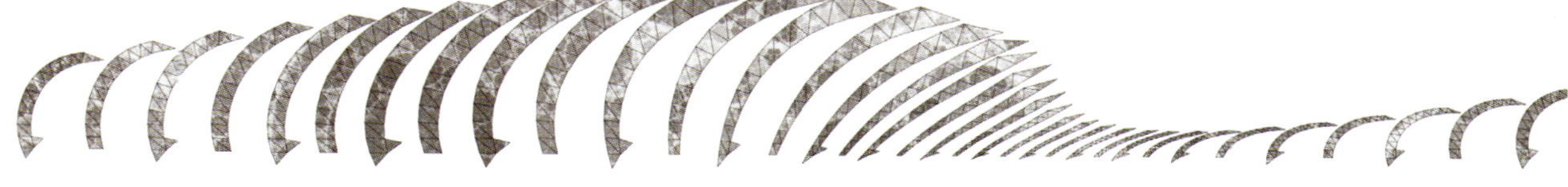

Part -3 triangulated flat panels unfold - funnel stem
第三部分 平面三角板展开 - 漏斗底部

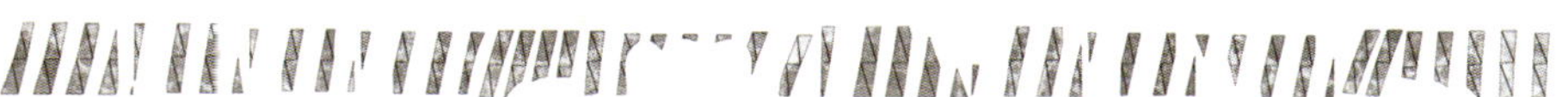

Funnel unfold panels
漏斗展开面板

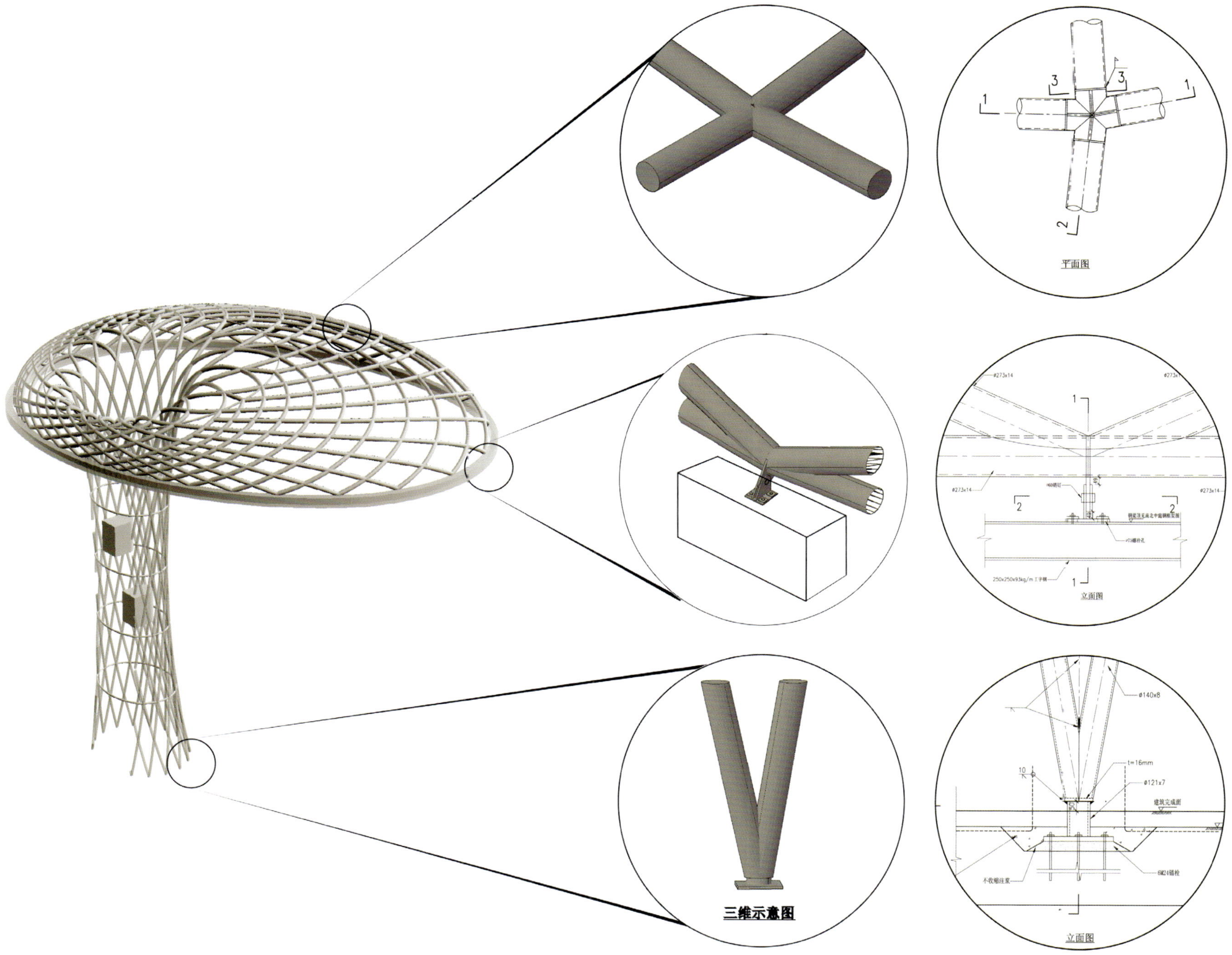

平面图
立面图
三维示意图
立面图

Funnel detail diagram
漏斗的细节图

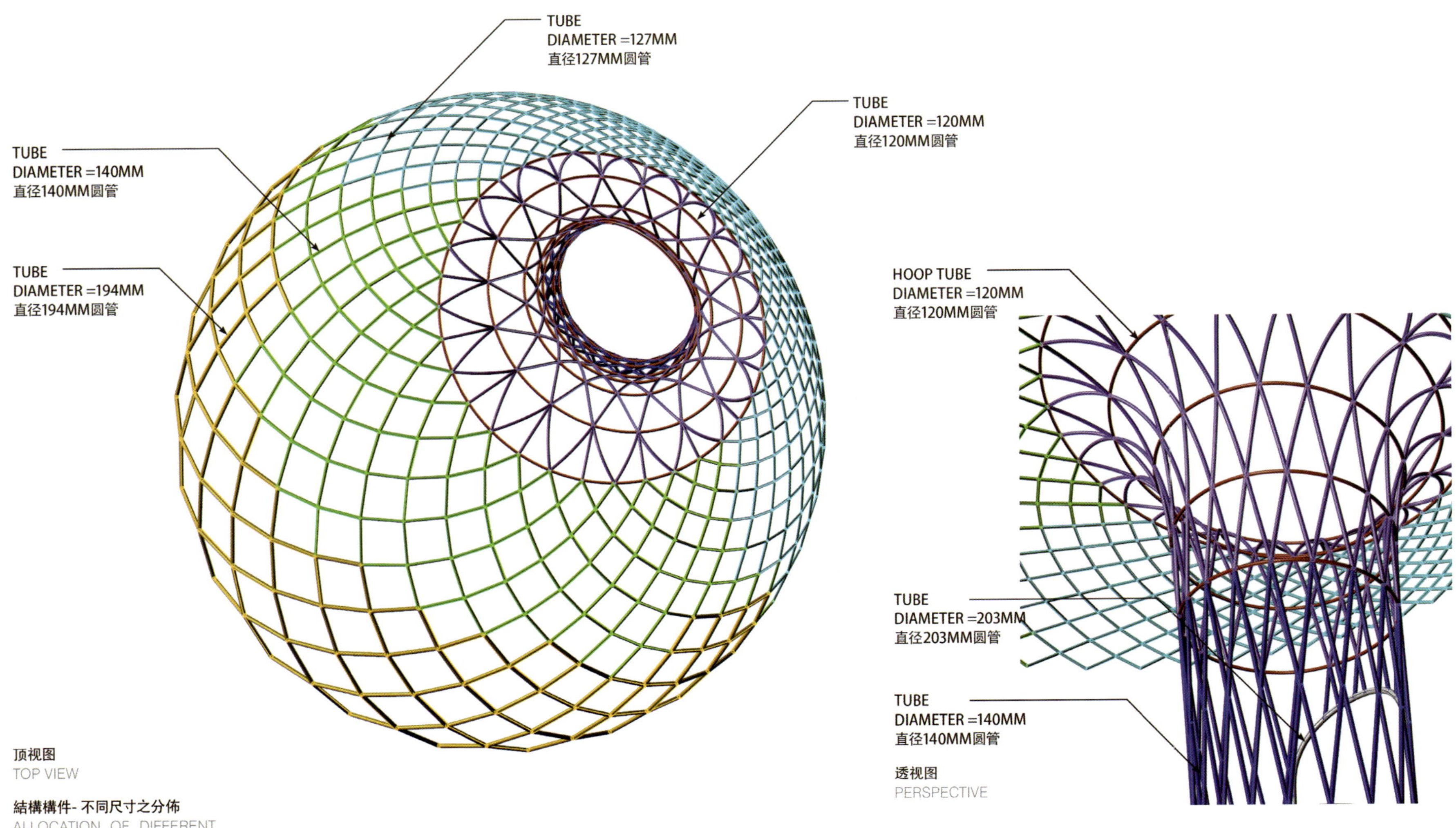

顶视图
TOP VIEW
結構構件- 不同尺寸之分佈
ALLOCATION OF DIFFERENT STRUCTURE MEMBER SIZES

透视图
PERSPECTIVE

Funnel Souh structure
漏斗的南立面结构

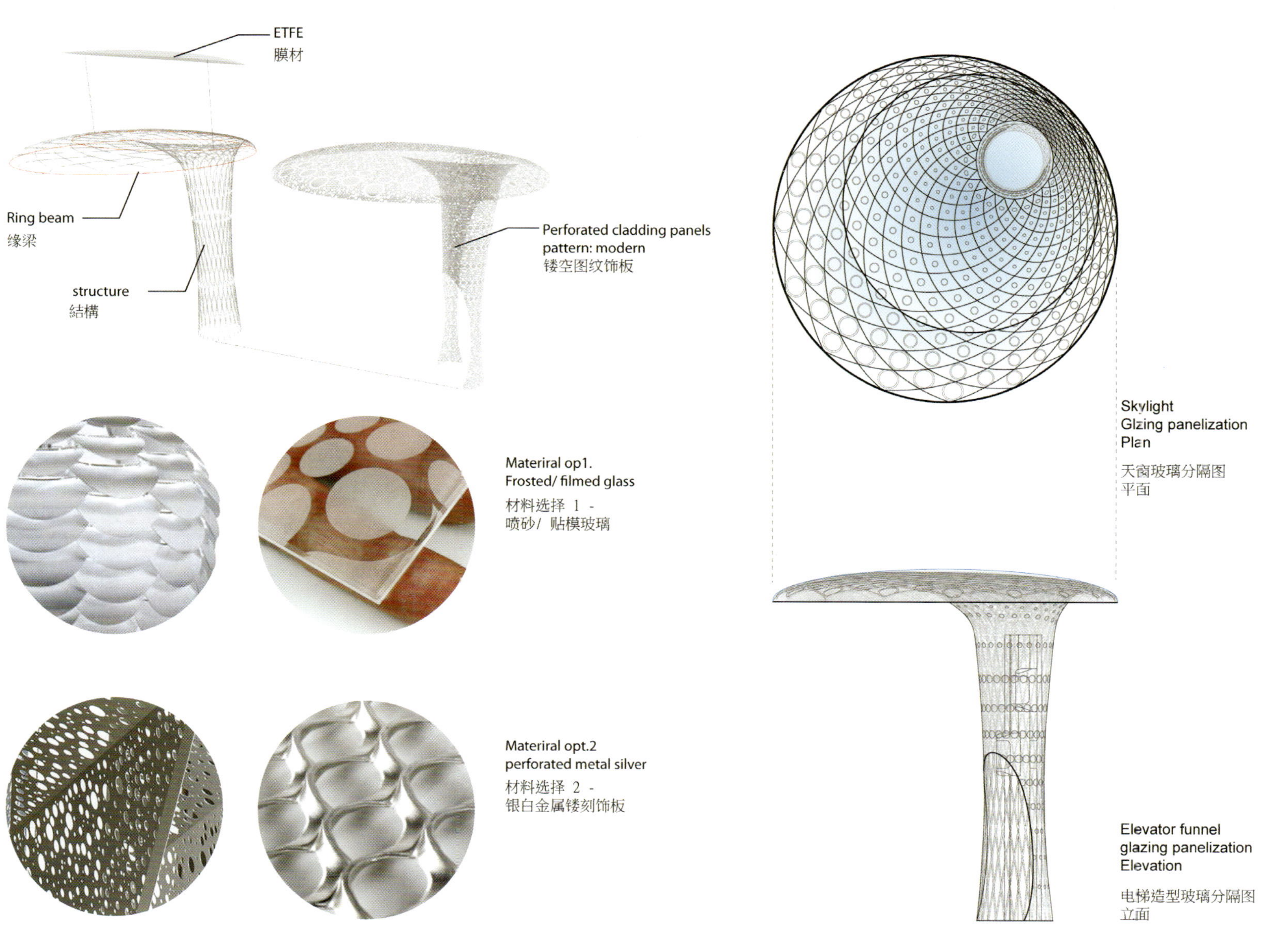

Funnel circle
漏斗圈

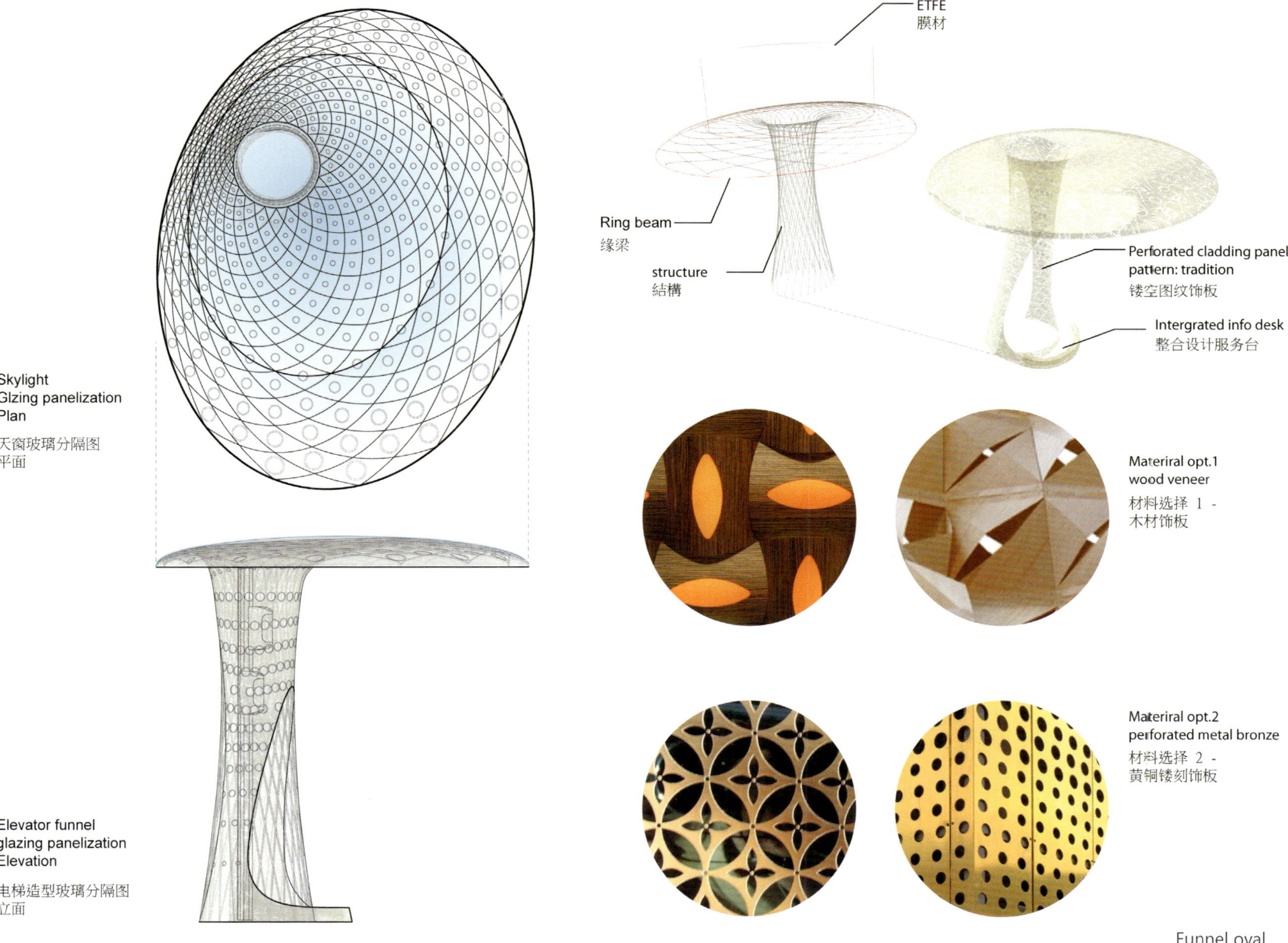

Funnel oval
椭圆形漏斗

PROJECT NAME 项目名称

GLOBAL HARBOR, SHANGHAI
上海环球港

Architect: Chapman Taylor

设计公司：查普门泰勒建筑设计咨询（上海）有限公司

PROJECT INFORMATION 项目信息

Location	Shanghai, China
Area	480,000 m^2
Architecture	Chris,Ben,Hua Lei,Rita
Shopping Mall area	approx. 270,000 m^2
Interior	Rodney,Peter, Gary

地点	中国上海市
面积	480 000 平方米
建筑设计	Chris、Ben、Hua Lei、Rita
购物中心面积	约 270000 平方米
室内设计师	Rodney、Peter、杨广

OVERVIEW 项目概况

Located in a prime location of the centre area,Shanghai Global Harbor is a super large urban complex with a total building area of 480,000m^2. The complex consists of a large shopping centrewith an area of 320,000m^2 and two 80,000m^2 high-rise towers,one of which will become Hyatt Hotel, a five star hotel, and the other isaA-grade office building.The surrounding transport connectionsare complicated with two metro linesintegrated into the buildingand theInner Ring Elevated Road runningbyit; however, on the other hand,it will bring heavy pedestrian flow to the complex. As the lead designer of Shanghai Global Harbor,Chapman Taylor is undertaking the architecturalconcept design, schematic design anddetailed design as well as the interior design.This shopping center opened in 2013,and is so far the largest project which have been designed and completed by Chapman Taylor .

上海环球港是上海市中心的一个超大型城市综合体，总面积达 48 万平方米。该综合体由一个面积达 32 万平方米的大型购物中心和两座 8 万平方米的超高层塔楼组成，其中一座塔楼为五星级凯悦酒店，另一座为甲级写字楼。项目四周交通条件较为复杂，有两条地铁线直接与建筑连为一体，内环高架紧贴在建筑边上，但同时又将给商业带来大量的人流。查普门泰勒公司作为该项目的总建筑设计者，承担了建筑概念、建筑方案、初步设计的工作，以及室内的全部设计工作。该购物中心于 2013 年正式开业，是迄今为止由查普门泰勒公司设计且已竣工的最大项目。

FEATURE ANALYSIS 特色分析

ARCHITECT
Hua Lei

设计师
华镭

This modern commercial building collects and conveys many classical architectural languages. It has the biggest area in Shanghai commercial complex building. It is the epitome for art deco building style in Shanghai. All of these features show that client tries to create a unique classical building shopping experience in China. Complicated decorative elements in patio are very stunning. Nowadays, all modern buildings pursuit the efficient design, it is very difficult to create the classical architectural languages, which require many people and materials. The actual result of this ambitious project cannot get the answer right now.

古典建筑语汇在现代商业建筑的大合体。冠绝上海的商业综合体面积体量。上海地区泛滥的 artdeco 建筑风格的集大成者。种种可供总结的特点都指出这个建筑开发商试图创造一个在全国范围内独一无二的古典式建筑购物体验的野心。建筑内部中庭繁复的装饰元素令人瞠目。因为在讲究高效率的现代建筑设计下要想反其道而行之复刻古典建筑语汇其背后的人力物力可见一斑。这种野心勃勃的项目其实际效果如何，也许需要长期的沉淀后才能知道答案。

环球港
GLOBAL HARBOR
环球港
Global Harbor

采光井
休闲坐凳
太阳伞
服务用房
铺装广场
景观种植
特色水景
木平台休息区
绿篱
小广场
阳光草地

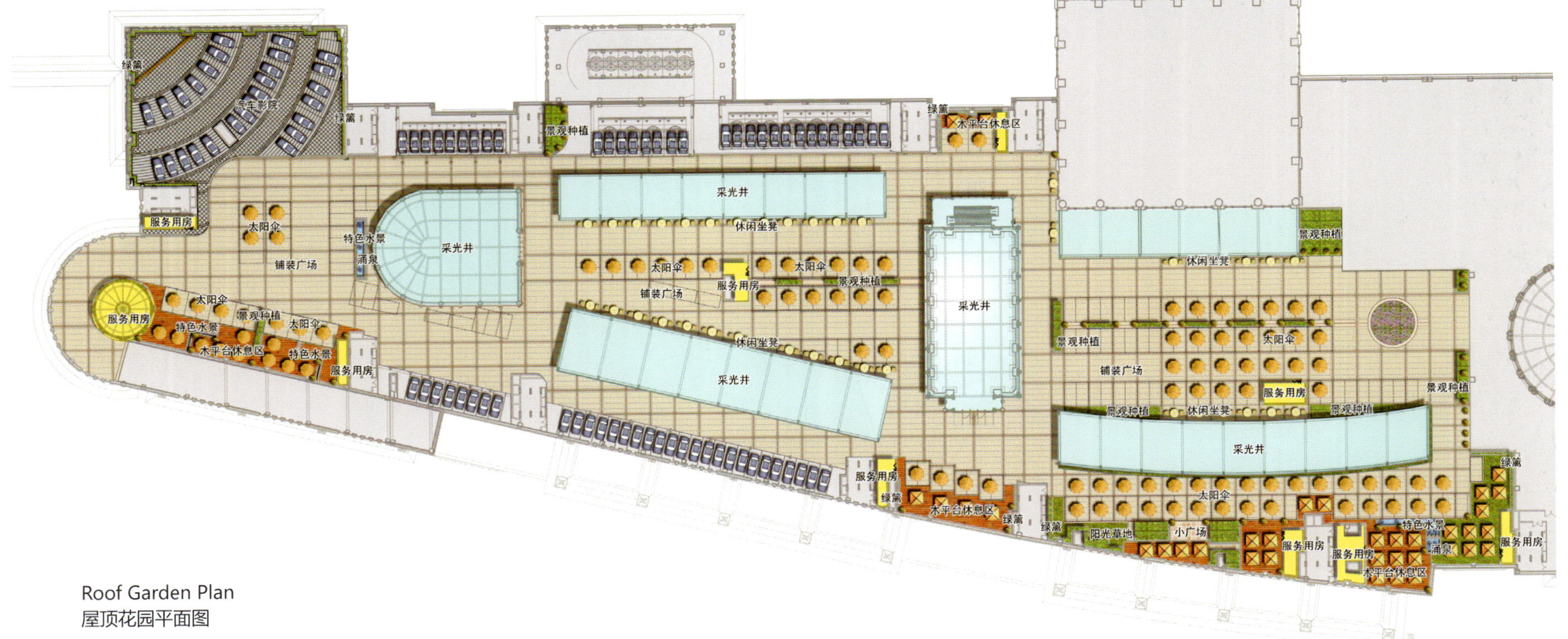

Roof Garden Plan
屋顶花园平面图

The design team of this project, composed of the best and most experienced designers of Chapman Taylor, is led by Chris Lanksbury, an international design master for commercial architectures, and supported by the design team of Chapman Taylor Shanghai office, reviewing the deliverables of every professional field in each stage, and striving to create an international, modern, urban commercial complex.

The retail areaoccupies four abovegroundlevels and two basements.Due to the long narrow shape of the site, the building is a rough rectangle of 250mby 100m, and the internal commercial corridorsarering-shaped. There are three atria in the north, south and central section respectively, with different shapes and styles.The atria,voids and skylights create a strong visibility between retail levels and enable natural daylight to reach B2.

该项目的设计团队集合了查普门泰勒公司各方面最优秀、最有经验的设计师，并由英国总部的国际商业建筑设计大师——克里斯•兰斯伯瑞主笔，上海办公室也组成了一支最强的设计团队全程配合，审核各个工种、各个阶段的设计成果，力争打造一个国际水平的现代化城市商业综合体。

该综合体商业部分地上有四层，地下二层。由于地块狭长，建筑呈一个长250米、宽100米的形状，内部商业走廊为环形结构，设有南北中三个中庭，以不同的形态和风格使空间呈现出丰富的变化。中庭和环线走廊都采用中空的方式上下打通，同时采光屋顶使天光倾泻而下，直通地下二层，上下视觉通透，增加了楼下层面的商业可见性。

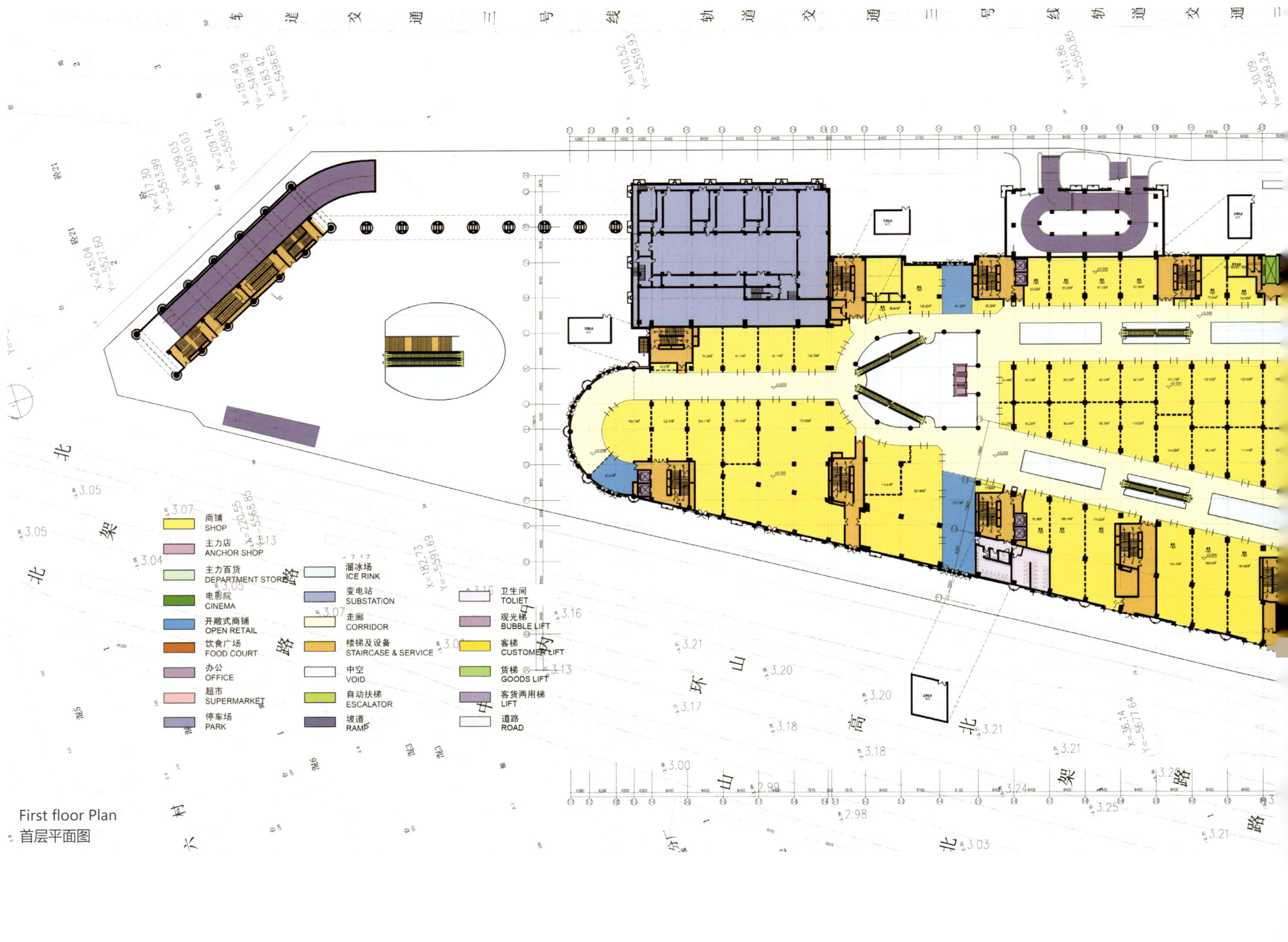

商铺 SHOP
主力店 ANCHOR SHOP
主力百货 DEPARTMENT STORE
电影院 CINEMA
开敞式商铺 OPEN RETAIL
饮食广场 FOOD COURT
办公 OFFICE
超市 SUPERMARKET
停车场 PARK
溜冰场 ICE RINK
变电站 SUBSTATION
走廊 CORRIDOR
楼梯及设备 STAIRCASE & SERVICE
中空 VOID
自动扶梯 ESCALATOR
坡道 RAMP
卫生间 TOLIET
观光梯 BUBBLE LIFT
客梯 CUSTOMER LIFT
货梯 GOODS LIFT
客货两用梯 LIFT
道路 ROAD
轨道交通三号线
北环山路
中山北路

First floor Plan
首层平面图

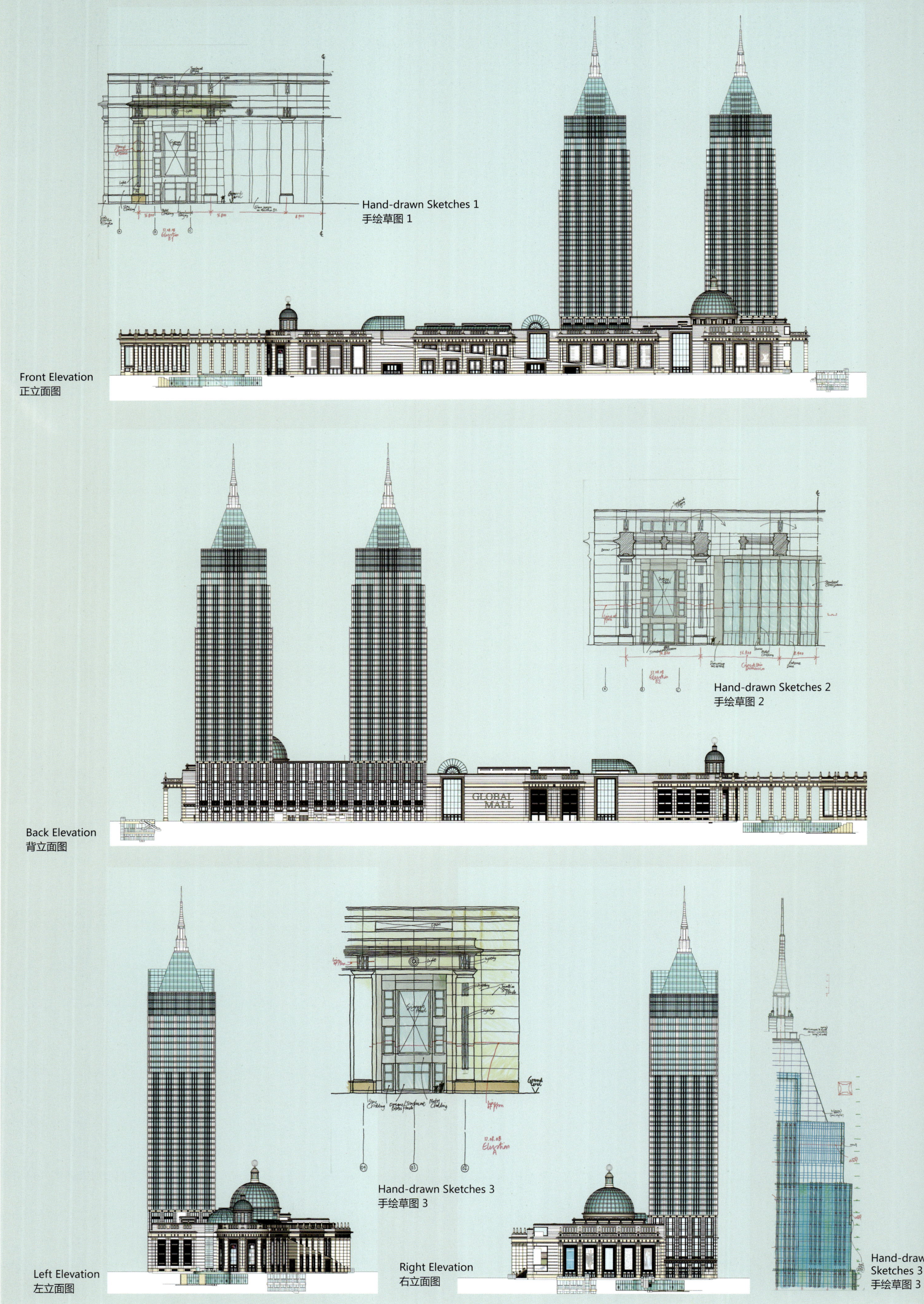

Hand-drawn Sketches 1
手绘草图 1

Front Elevation
正立面图

Hand-drawn Sketches 2
手绘草图 2

Back Elevation
背立面图

Hand-drawn Sketches 3
手绘草图 3

Left Elevation
左立面图

Right Elevation
右立面图

Hand-drawn Sketches 3
手绘草图 3

About the shopping centre, there are two twin towers with a height of 250m due to the height restriction of the building. Vertical lines are used to emphasize their vertical characteristics and height. Compared with other towers, the twin towers are more commercial style.Considering that it is difficult to see the towers in close range and the podium is invisible from far away, the towers are gradually independent from the podiumlower.This kind of design approach can reduce the unnecessary constraints of classical style and makethe towersrelatively simpler.

Stone is the prominent material used for the podiumto reflect the dignity of classicism.The towers use aluminum panels and glazing curtain walls with the same texture and color as the stones to achieve harmony and unificarion.

购物中心上面是一对姐妹双塔，由于建筑高度的限制，塔楼在 250 米处止住。塔楼的设计以竖向线条为主，强调了其纵向特征和高度，风格则更加商业化，与下面的裙房渐渐地脱开独立。由于从近处人们很难看到这两座塔楼，而从远处看又看不到裙房，因此这种分面置之的手法可减少不必要的古典风格对塔楼的制约，使其相对简洁明快。

建筑裙房以石材为主，以体现古典主义的厚重，塔楼则采用了铝板和玻璃幕墙，但在质感和色彩上尽量与裙房保持和谐统一。

As for the tenant layout, standard shops are arranged in the atrium area of each level, and secondary anchor stores are placed at either end. At the south end, there is a department store occupies partial L1-L4; a cinema is placed on the top floor of the north end; a hypermarket occupies the northern area of basements; a food court on B1 and a food street on L4. Anchor stores are evenly distributed to guide and split pedestrian flow to increase the stores' rent rate as a whole. Additionally, the southern end of B2 is seamlessly connected to a Metro station of line 13, and the eastern end of L3 is connected withNo.4 Light rail by a gallery bridge, and there is an entrance on L4 connecting the roof parking, plus the two sunken plazas in the northernand southern squares, as a result of which, more 'direct'pedestrian flow are brought to each retail level with aleasing 'light spot'.

As the client adores traditional European architectures, the building is given a western classical style. The classic design approach is used in the facade design with simplified detailingto make it a commercial architecture rather than a monumental or municipal building. Apart from the precise design approach used in the design,a strong commercial atmosphereis created and advertisement spaces are reasonably arranged.It is worth mentioning that the client's requirement for a roof parking and the subsequent 200m ramp on the west elevation leading up to it,was a big challenge for classical architecture, however, the designer make the ramp be carefully integrated into a colonnade, reducing the adverse visual effect. On the roof, there are three big domes with different shapes, serving as the skylights of the atriums below, and the southern hemispherical shaped dome corresponding with the northern, smaller dome, form the symbol of the Shanghai Global Harbor complex.

业态分布把大小一致的标准店铺放在每层的中庭区域，而将不同的次主力店分布在两端。南端入口上部较大的空间用作主力百货，占据了该端1~4层的空间，北端顶层设有影院，地下室北端是一个大型的超市，地下一层设有美食广场，四层设有美食街。从业态分布上可以看出，设计师平均分布主力店以引导人流流动，从而使整体的店铺租金有了全面的提升。此外，地下二层南端与上海地铁13号线的站台形成全方位的"无缝"连接，三层东侧则通过廊桥与轻轨4号线相连，四楼设有屋面停车场入口，再加上南北广场上的两个大型的下沉式广场，为每层商业带来更多的"直入"人流，使每层都拥有"租赁亮点"。

由于业主对欧洲传统风格的钟爱，建筑采用了西洋古典的风格，外立面设计采用了严格的古典建筑设计手法，但在细部上又进行了适当的简化，使之成为一个商业建筑，而非一个过于严肃的纪念性建筑或政府类建筑。除了严谨的设计手法外，设计还将商业风格充分融入到建筑中，并对广告位进行了合理的安排。值得一提的是由于业主要求在屋顶上设停车场，我们需要在建筑西立面上设计了一条长约200米的坡道直通屋顶，这对于古典建筑的设计来说已经是一个相当艰难的挑战，但是设计师别具匠心地将坡道设置在一排柱廊内，巧妙地削弱了这条斜线带来的负面影响。建筑顶部设有三个大穹顶，用作下面中庭的采光天窗，三个穹顶拥有不同的形态，尤其是南端的半球穹顶与北端的还小圆穹顶南北呼应，成为商业中心的一个象征性标志。

The lighting, landscape and signage design play a key part in the overall effect of the space. We not only providethe same style concept design, but also strictly controlthe detailing, to improve the final effect and enhance the elegance and glory of the classical style used throughout the building.

In terms of architecture technique, wehave applied the most valuable international experience to the commercial architecture design process.Some detailsthat can be easily ignored,such as the window-cleaning machines for the skylights,areconsidered and included in the schematic design stage.

此外，灯光、景观和标识等设计对建筑的空间效果同样有着重要的意义。我们不仅提供了与建筑融为一体的概念设计，而且还严格控制每个环节的设计成果，以期最终效果为整体的建筑效果增添光彩，尤其是强调出古典建筑风格的优雅和恢宏。

在建筑技术上，我们尽量把国际上最有价值的经验应用到该商业建筑的设计过程中，如在采光天窗的设计中，擦窗机的布置等这些容易被人忽视的细节，我们都在方案阶段就将其纳入最初的设计之中了。

Central Plaza Interior Elevation
中央广场室内立面图

We also work hard to create convenient vertical circulation routes that maximize pedestrian flow whilst simultaneously creating an easy shopping experience through the large number of escalators and scenic lifts.

Energy efficient and environment protection has been key to the design of the building. Current mature techniques as well as economical and practical methods have been used to achieve the goal. The biggest energy consumption comes from the heat preservation in winter and thermal insulation in summer, leaving a difficult problem to the design of roof and skylight. In order to solve the problem, we not only apply regular measures like Low-E glasses and reflective glasses, but also add 20% colored glaze dots to the glasses to block direct sunlight. Those dots also reflects the interior light at night, killing two birds with one stone.

我们对室内垂直交通流线进行了反复的研究，以期设计出最便捷的线路和最大的商业流线，布置充裕但不过多的自动扶梯和观光电梯，让人们在购物时感到方便自如。

建筑设计同时把节能环保作为了一个重要的环节，尽可能利用现有成熟的技术和经济实用的手段来达到这一目的。裙房中最大能耗反映在屋顶天窗冬日的保温和夏季的日照方面。在材料的选用中，不仅采用了LOW-E、反光等措施，同时在玻璃上增加了20%的彩釉以阻挡直射的阳光。这些不明显的釉点在夜晚又能向内反映室内的照明，一举两得。

The corridor has a generous width and few visual barriers, with clear vertical lines of site. The atria are either cool or intimate, creating a different spatial effect, breaking the 'lengthy' feeling of the corridor, and reducing the fatigue factor of shopping by creating varied and changing spaces. Those large spaces, designed with different themes and decoration styles, can be also used as platforms for business promotion activities and bring huge rental revenue for the client.

购物中心走廊宽度适中，上下视线通畅，中庭或给人以较大尺度的震撼感，或给人以较为适中的亲切感，形成不同的空间效果，同时还打破了过长的走廊带给顾客的冗长感，赋予空间变化和新奇感，减少视觉疲劳。空间设计赋予这些空间不同的主题和装饰风格，可用作商业促销活动场所，为业主带来巨大的租金收益。

Sun Plaza Interior Elevation
太阳广场室内立面图

即将开业
敬请期待
OPENING SOON
M&S

DESIGNED FOR FREEDOM
为自由而设计
salomon
6月19日 盛大开业

Garden Courtyard Indoor Elevation
花园庭院室内立面图

TISSOT

SHANGHANG

ABC Cooking Studio
MOOCHI

Lily

SUNPLAZA
太阳大厅
GLOBAL HARBOR

PROJECT NAME 项目名称

JOCKEY PLAZA BOULEVARD

赛马广场林荫大道

Architect:Metropolis

设计公司：Metropolis

PROJECT INFORMATION 项目信息

Location	Av. Javier Prado Este Nº 4200	地点	秘鲁
Site Are	3,625.56m²	占地面积	3，625.56 平方米

OVERVIEW 项目概况

Jockey Plaza has always been one of the biggest and most recognized shopping malls in the country; it has always had innovative designs and experiences, which makes it a reference for new standards in shopping malls.

In this new expansion we seek to give a different experience than the rest, making it an avant-garde space, achieved by the new incorporated elements. They consist mainly of more organic elements, these great trees that welcome the visitor, with leaves that have distinct light effects, which resembles a forest, with the tree tops high up.

赛马广场一直是秘鲁规模最大且最具影响力的购物中心之一， 其创新设计和购物体验使其成为其他购物中心的新标杆。

在此次扩建中，设计师力图另辟息路，打造别具一格的购物体验。通过新元素的融合，让其成为所有购物中心的潮流引领者。 新元素以有机植物为主，例如迎接顾客的参天大树，大树叶子能产生独特的光效应，让游客犹如置身于高树参天的森林里。

BRIEF INTERVIEW 访谈录

ARCHITECT
Jose Orrego

设计师
约瑟·奥雷戈

HKASP: What are the highlights and features of the project?

Metropolis: This project was designed to create a memorable experience, the retail business seeks the participation of the visitors in the commercial experience and make it as pleasant as may be unforgettable. When one does this, enters into the collective imagination and create an emotional bond with the place.

The Jockey Plaza has achieved this with costumers, through the creation of semi-urban areas with architectural elements that serve as references and encourage the visitors to explore a worth remembering experience.

HKASP: would you please Introduce the shape, the skin and the layout of the project for us ?

Metropolis: This project has been designed based on a village, where one can cross it and find dystopian elements. This type of expression creates a tension in the visitor, having different experiences in the day than at night. The surfaces become like a skin with a vocabulary that speaks of a reality that does not belong to time, the floors can be marble frames, the ceilings can be heaven or a parametric design suspended with synthetic trees that glows at night and the walls can belong to a past that never existed in Lima city. All of this vocabulary forms a speech that speaks to visitors and invites it to discover every corner of this world.

香港建筑科学出版社：立面宛如被剪过的纸。该项目的设计理念是什么？

Metropolis：该项目旨在打造一种难以忘怀的体验， 让顾客在购物体验中找到参与感，让顾客感受到无微不至的呵护，从而终身难忘。当你进入其营造的集体想象时，你的心已然与此地连为一体。

服装商，城乡结合区的打造，建筑元素的借鉴都促就了赛马广场的成功。建筑元素无时无刻不吸引游客们去探索一种值得回忆的体验。

香港建筑科学出版社：请你简单介绍一下该项目的造型，立面以及布局？

Metropolis：该项目以一个村庄为原型。若你穿过村庄，你便会发现许多乌托邦的反面元素。这种表达是为了在游客心中营造一种紧迫感，让游客在白天而非晚上感受另一番风味。墙体表面酷似一种蕴含着语汇的表皮，向人们述说着一种不会随时间而演变的事实。地面采用大理石构件，天花板采用参数化设计，近乎完美。天花板上悬挂的人造树在夜幕中熠熠生辉，内墙表达出一段利马的历史。所有这些语汇与游客形成精神上的共鸣，激发他们去探索整个世界。

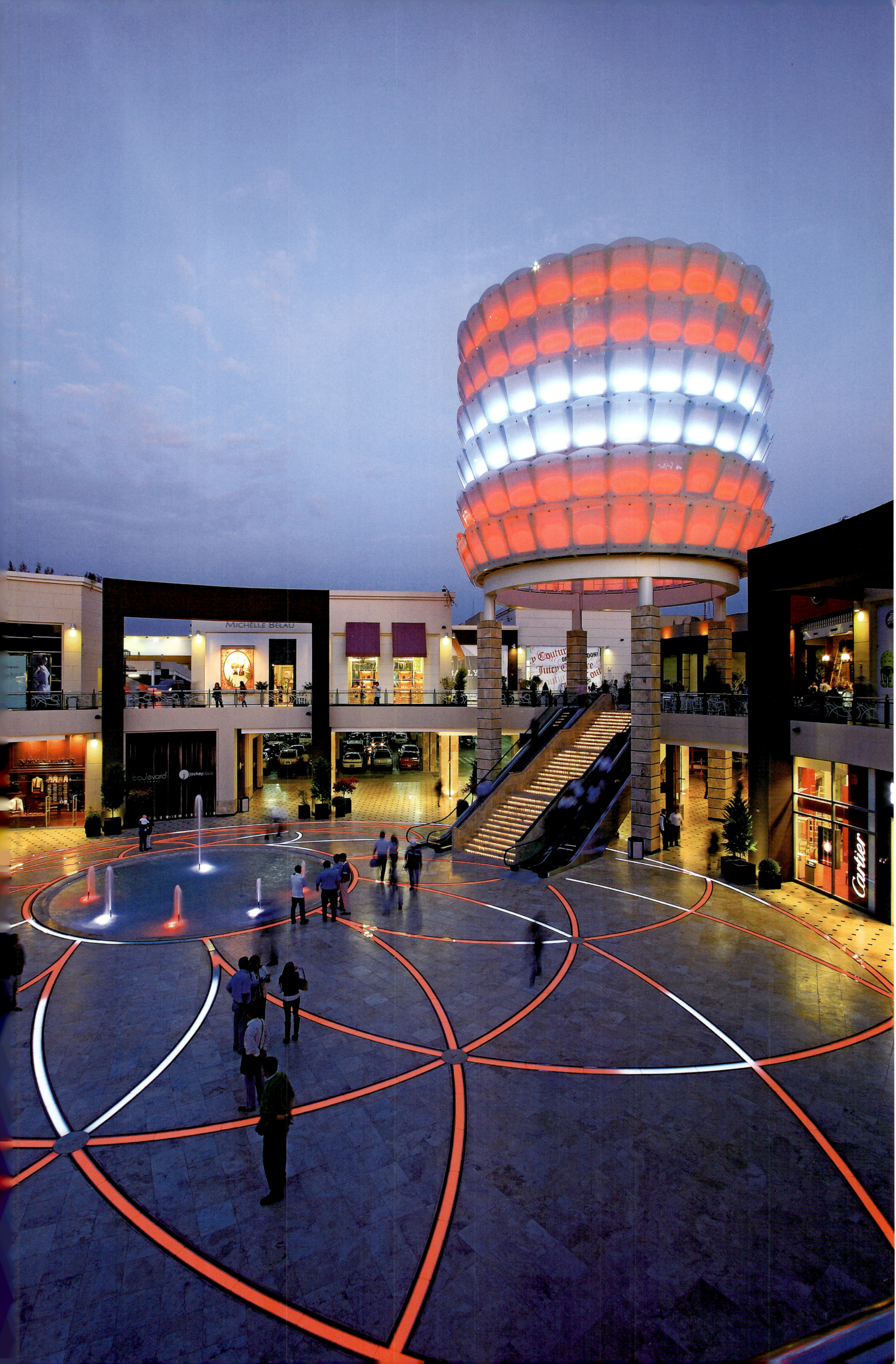
MICHELLE BELAU
Cartier

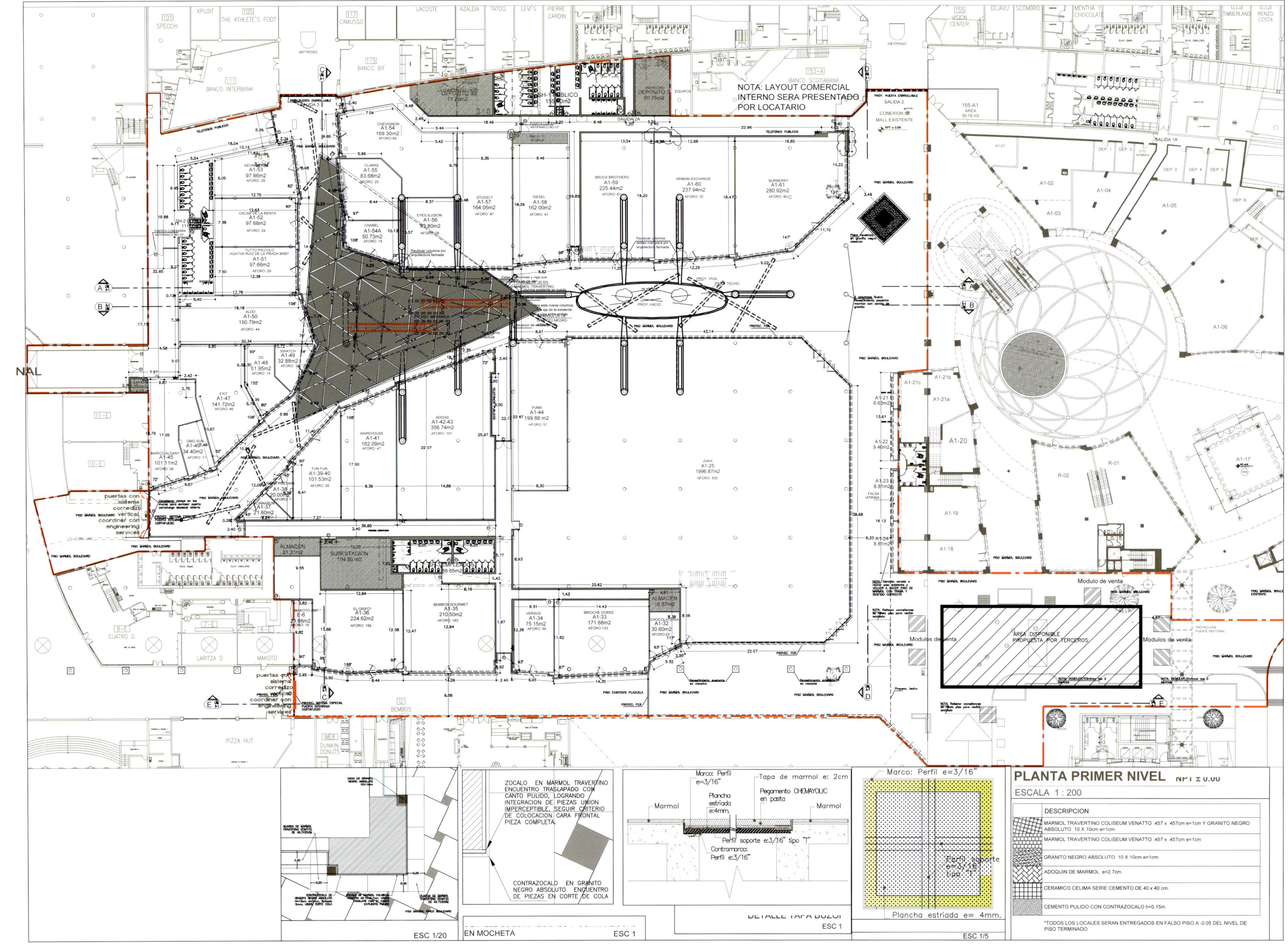

1st Floor Plan
一层平面图

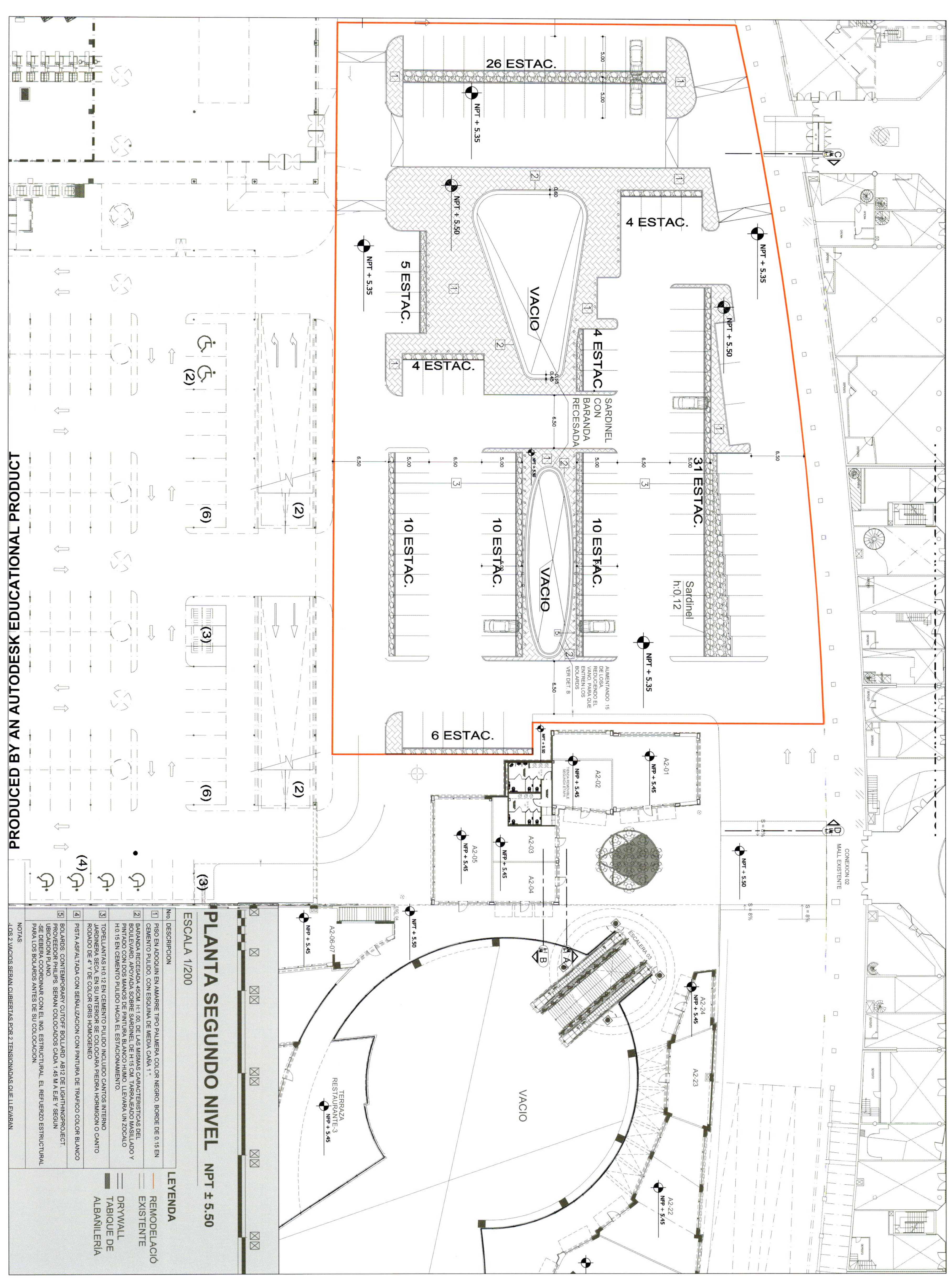

2nd Floor Plan
二层平面图

The lighting in this project plays one of the key roles due to it being what stands out, along with the three-dimensional design that helped us develop this aesthetic. The light complements the luminous tower and they are both part of the synchronization of this almost theatrical scene. In this way the visitors or passer-by not only obtain entertainment in the activities they can achieve in the locales but also the ambient itself.

The walk also has another element, a locale in the shape of a red geode, which adds to the avant-garde affect that we are looking to give and at the same time it gives the walk a different and impactful appearance.

鉴于照明旨在吸引顾客眼球，所以该项目中的照明将扮演重要的角色。此外，在三维设计的衬托下将更显建筑美感。照明让璀璨夺目的大厦更添光彩。它们都是呈现如此魔幻般的剧场舞台效果的一份子。照明灯补充了发光塔的光线，它们都是这个犹如同步戏剧性场景的组成部分。 无论是在购物中，还是在驻足欣赏，顾客或路人们都能感受到无尽的乐趣。

大道还设有另一大元素，即一个红色的形如空心石核的场所。它的存在让我们试图营造的前卫氛围锦上添花。与此同时，也让大道拥有一种与众不同、震撼人心的风格。

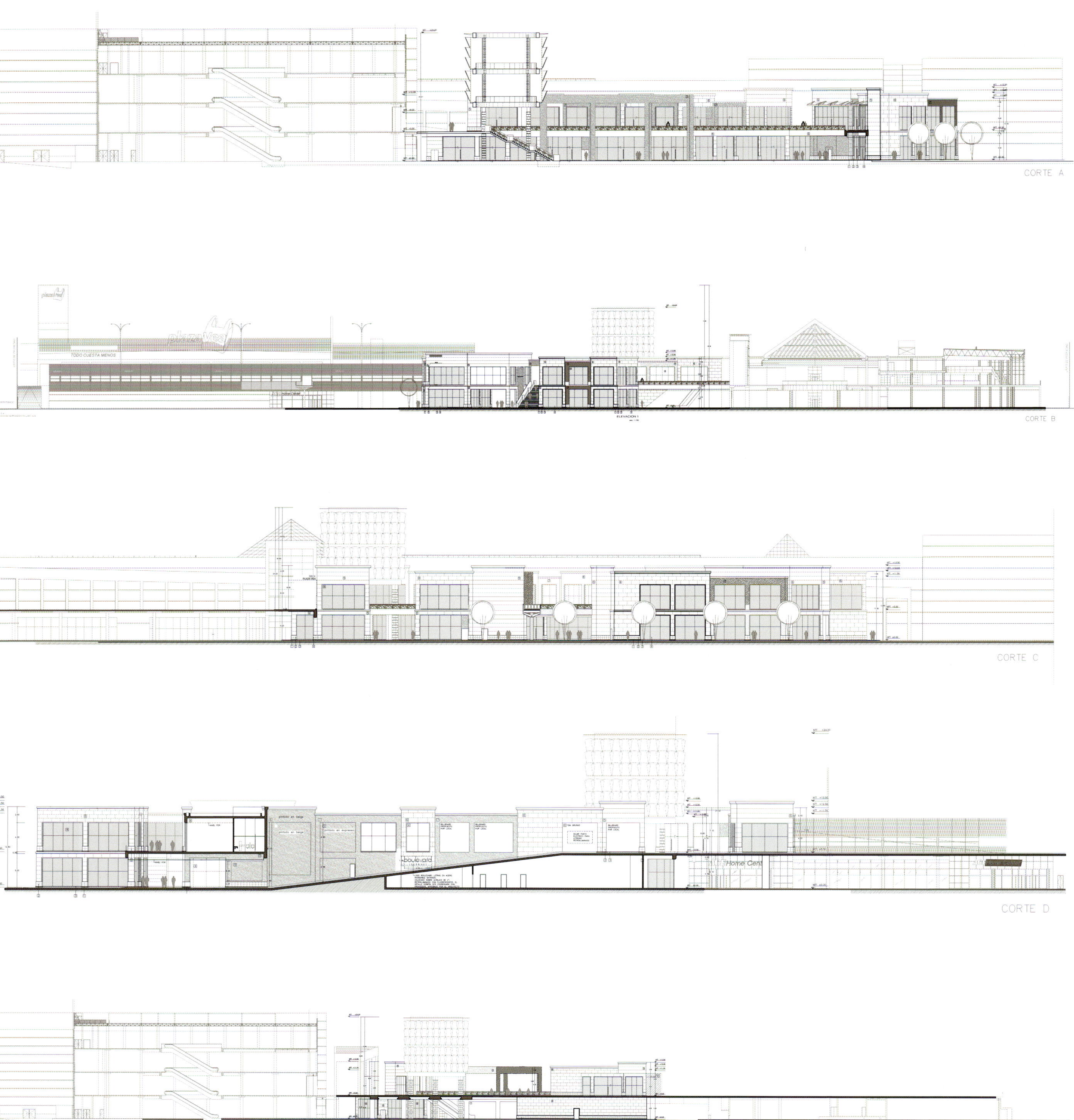

Section
剖面图

This locale is an experience comparable to the greatest shopping malls, for example in Hon Kong, Las Vegas, Dubai or London, that seek that their experience be enriched by the walk about of the place.

The "Jockey Plaza Shopping Center" mall is an edifice constructed by a complex of shopping locales and/or department shops and/or offices, organized inside an integral plan, destined to the buy-sell of goods and/or services, recreation and/or relaxation.

The Jockey Plaza Shopping Center is strategically located; in the intersection of the two most important highway axes in the city. The remodelation project encompasses approximately 3,625.56m² in area.

该场所能与诸如香港、拉斯维加斯、迪拜或伦敦最好的购物中心相媲美。步行于这些购物中心，你的购物体验将丰富多彩。

赛马广场购物中心是由一系列购物场所、百货商店或办公室组成的大厦。内部采用整体规划，集商品买卖、服务、娱乐和休闲为一体。

赛马广场购物中心地理位置优越，地处该市两条最重要的高速公路交叉路口。该项目占地面积约 3,625.56 平方米。

The project labeled as "BOULEVARD THIRD STAGE" is a commercial construct developed in a single floor, destined to activities whose end purposed is the commercialization of goods and services, composed by commercial locales. These locales are places along pedestrian axis that connect the existing mall with the Boulevard on the second floor. The proposal's main idea is the continuation of the creation of the urban space created in the boulevard, generating continuity; a safe and equipped meeting point where neighborhood life can be recreated.

该项目名为"林荫大道第三期工程"，为独栋式商业建筑。内设一系列商场，是商品和服务交易的终端市场。人行轴线两侧商场无数，鳞次栉比。若顺着人行轴线走去，顾客可从现有的商业街通往第二层楼的林荫大道。这样的串联旨在将城市空间延续至林荫大道，创造商场的连续。让这里成为一个安全有序、设施完善、娱乐身心的都市集合场所。

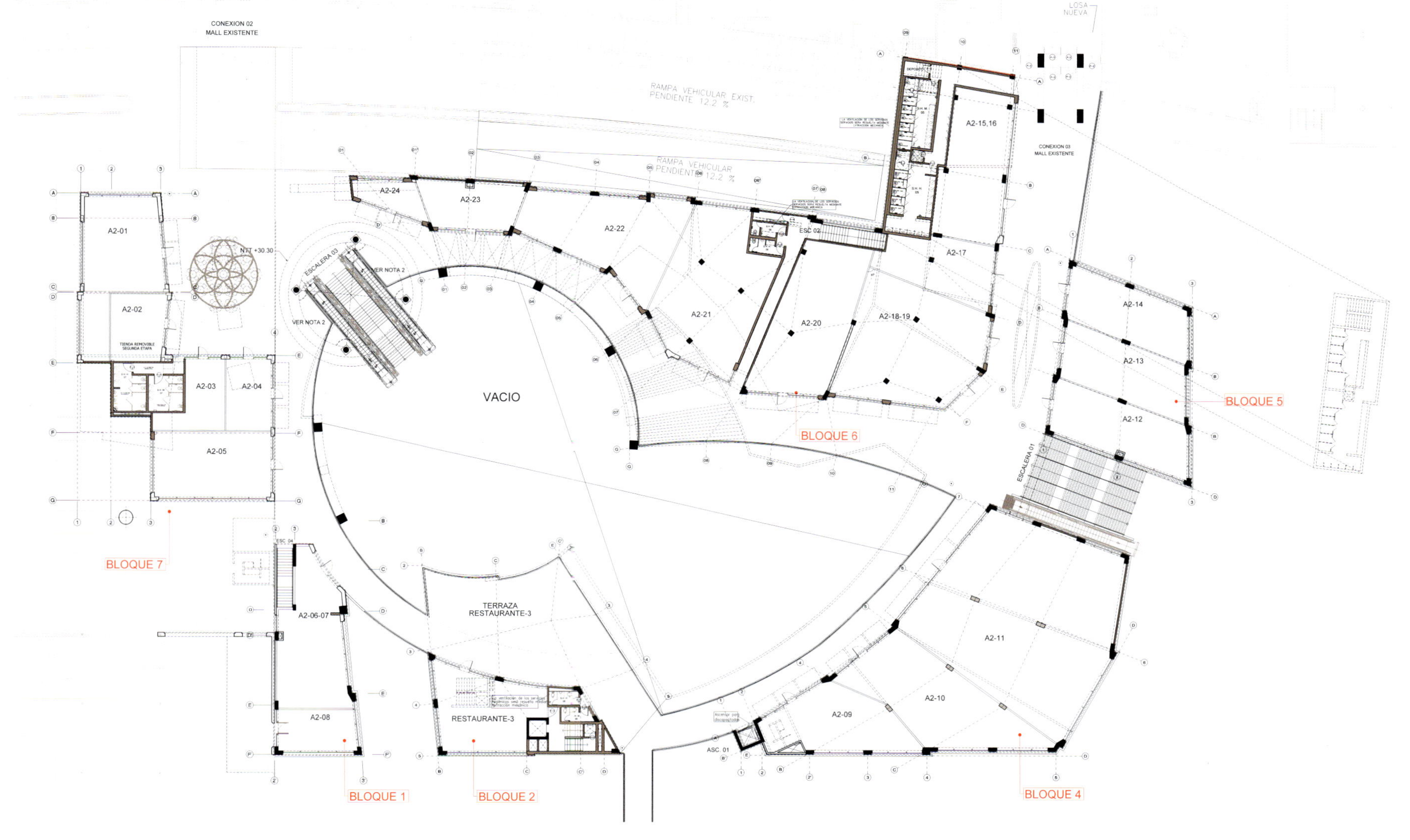

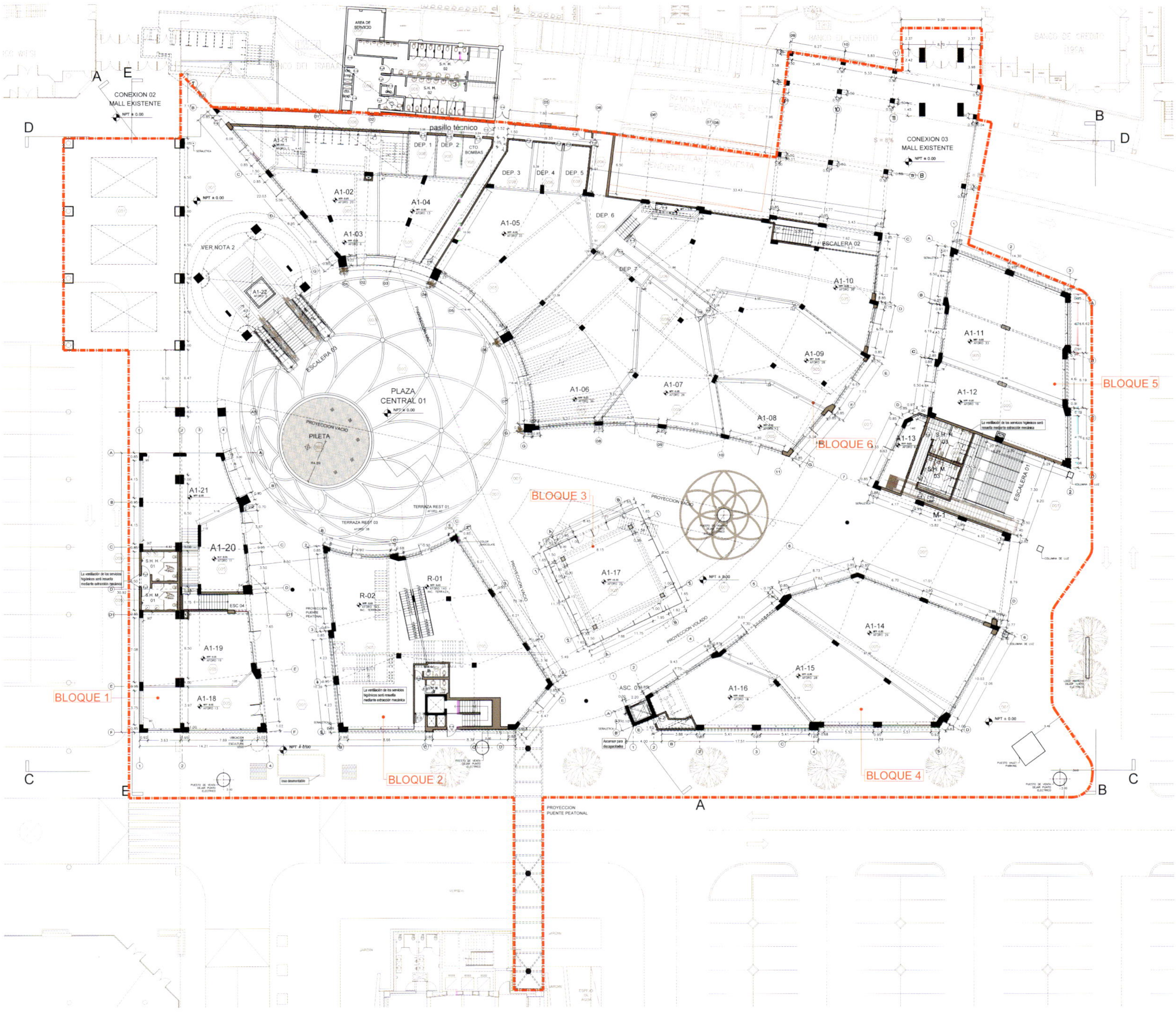

CONEXION 02
MALL EXISTENTE
CONEXION 03
MALL EXISTENTE
pasillo técnico
DEP. 1
DEP. 2
DEP. 3
DEP. 4
DEP. 5
DEP. 6
A1-02
A1-03
A1-04
A1-05
A1-06
A1-07
A1-08
A1-09
A1-10
A1-11
A1-12
A1-13
A1-14
A1-15
A1-16
A1-17
A1-18
A1-19
A1-20
A1-21
R-01
R-02
PLAZA
CENTRAL 01
PILETA
ESCALERA 02
VER NOTA 2
BLOQUE 1
BLOQUE 2
BLOQUE 3
BLOQUE 4
BLOQUE 5
BLOQUE 6
A
B
C
D
E

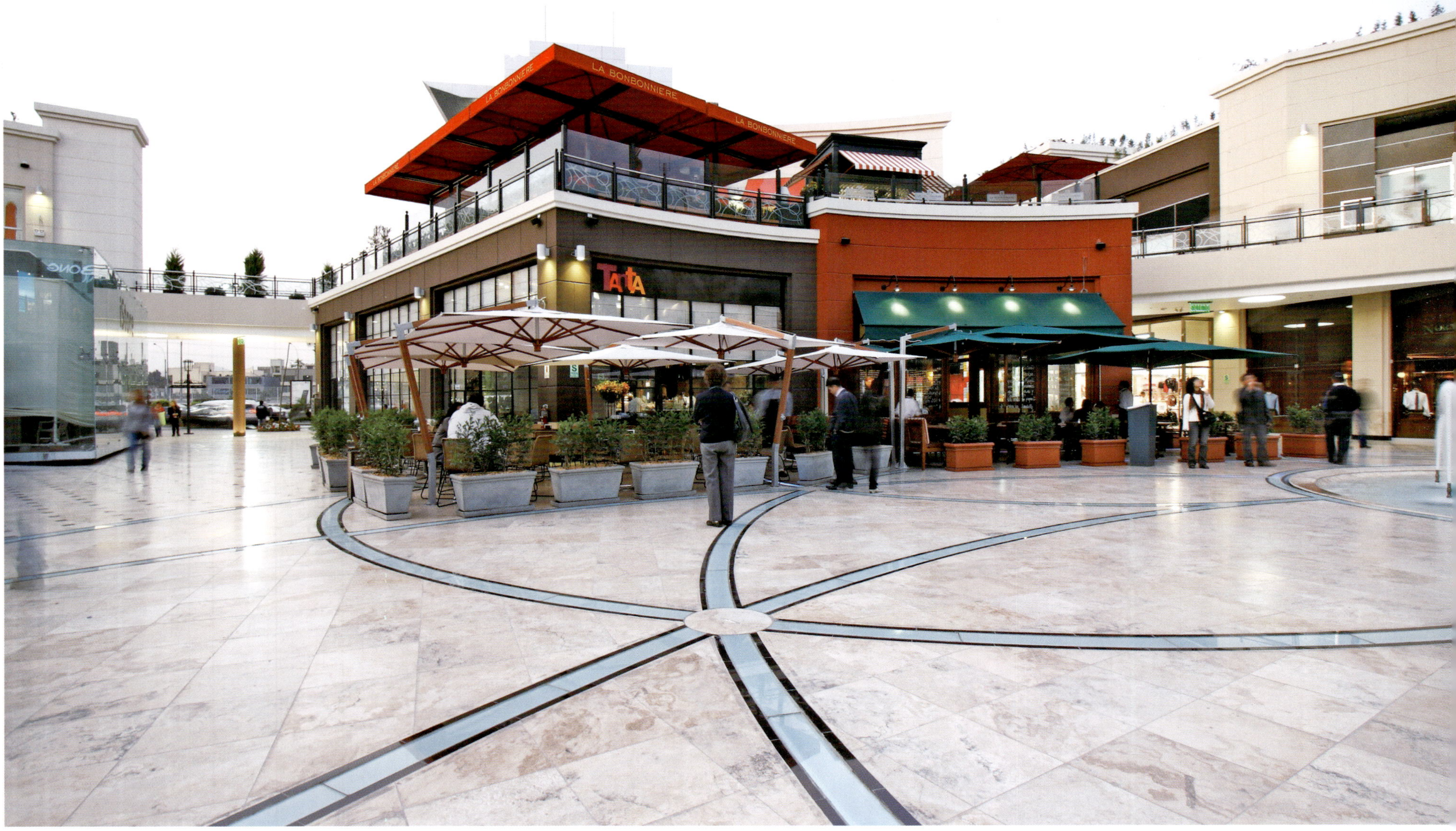
LA BONBONNIERE

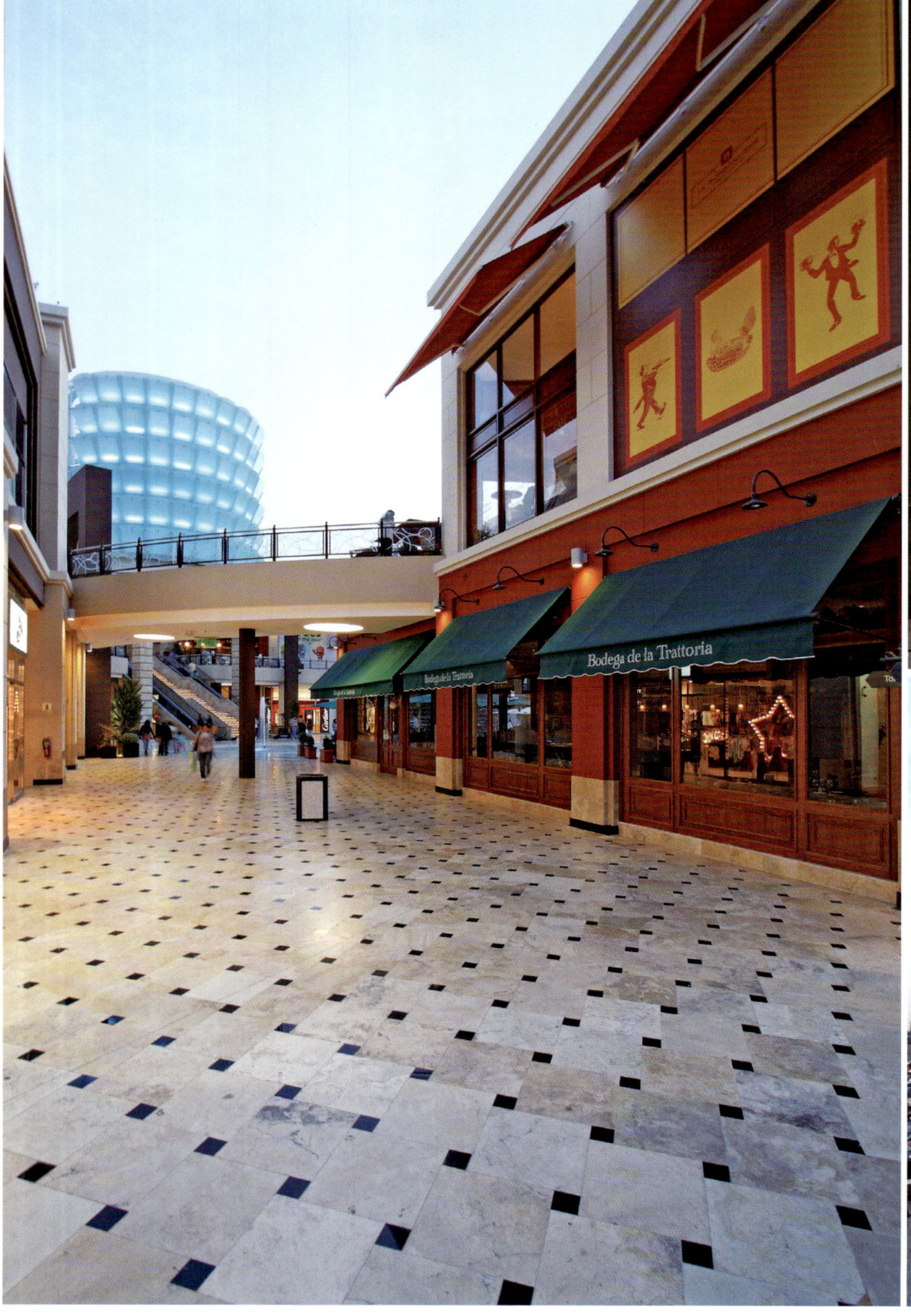

Bodega de la Trattoria

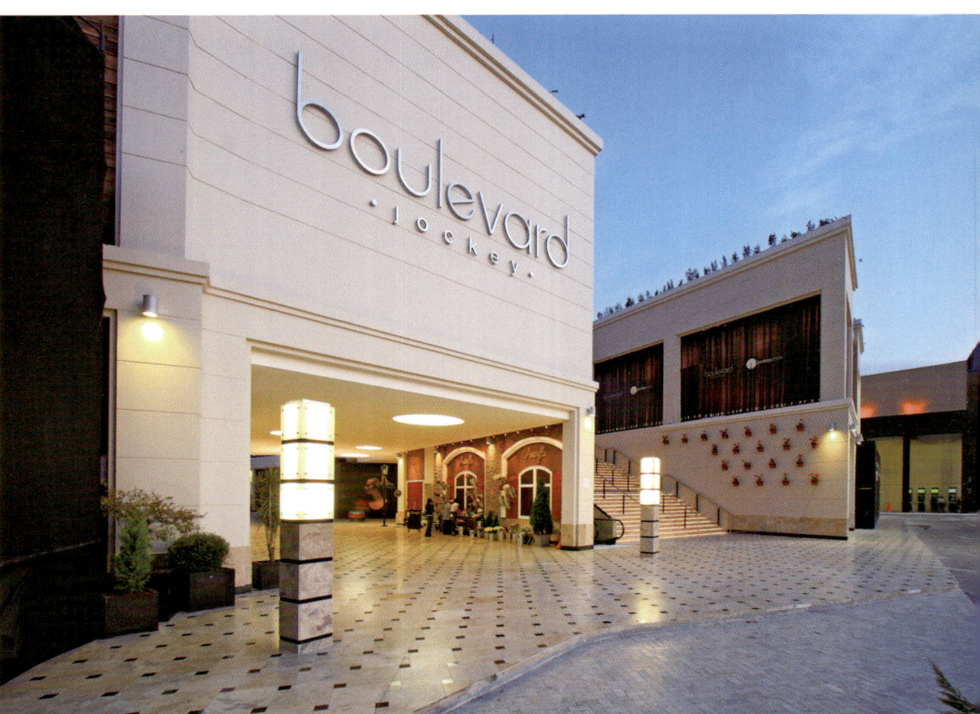

boulevard
jockey

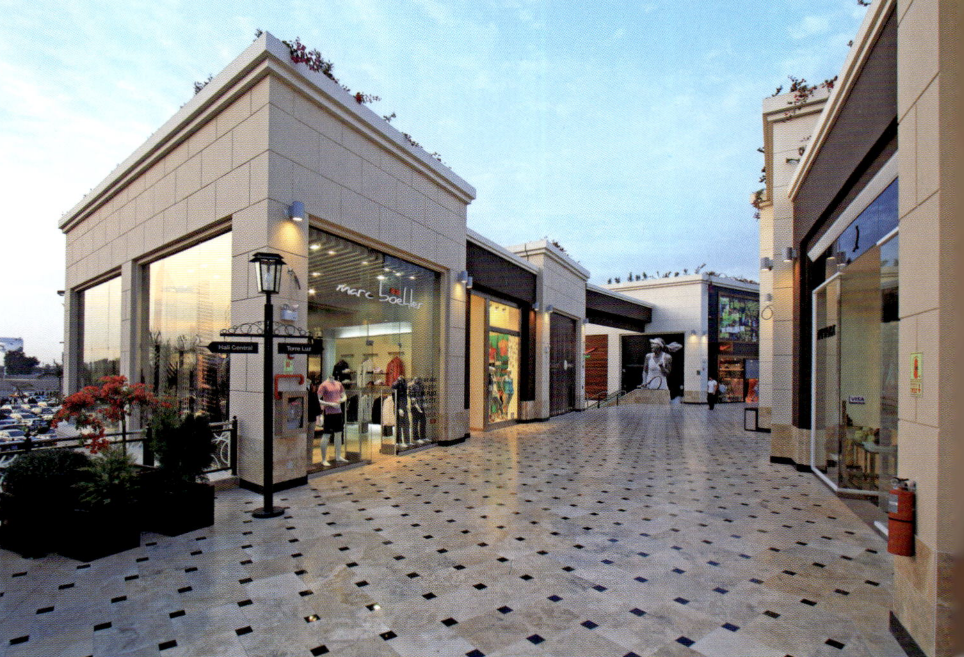

LA BONBONNIERE

BONBONNIERE

The draft for this remodelation started with two articulating elements:

1.Pedestrian circulation axis, serve as connection to the Plaza Vea zone, anchor store market, and the Jockey Plaza Boulevard. These circulations are designed so as to create a continuous, natural pedestrian flow through the project and mall, creating the sufficient tension to generate permanent interior transit that guaranteed the success of all operations

2.Plaza: Exhibition and sale area, this plaza serves as an articulating element for the pedestrian flows that come together in the third stage and as connection with the flows of the second stage. It's a focal point to generate the necessary tension and attraction for the user to navigate the pedestrian axis in a natural way and to ensure commercial success of the locales that are located in the project.

该项目草案以两大承前启下的特征为出发点：

1、人行道串联 Plaza Vea 区、主力店市场和赛马广场大道。人行道旨在引领川流不息的人流来到项目所在地，来到商场。通过提供足够的购买力来创造永恒的内部交通运输系统，从而保障所有商店的成功运营。

2、广场：展览区和卖场区。此广场作为第三期工程中聚集人流量的典型场所，使其承接与第二期工程中的人流量。 这是产生必要人流量的关键措施，并且能够引导行人自发的使用人行通道，以确保该项目中的商业场所的成功运营。

new balance
Columbia

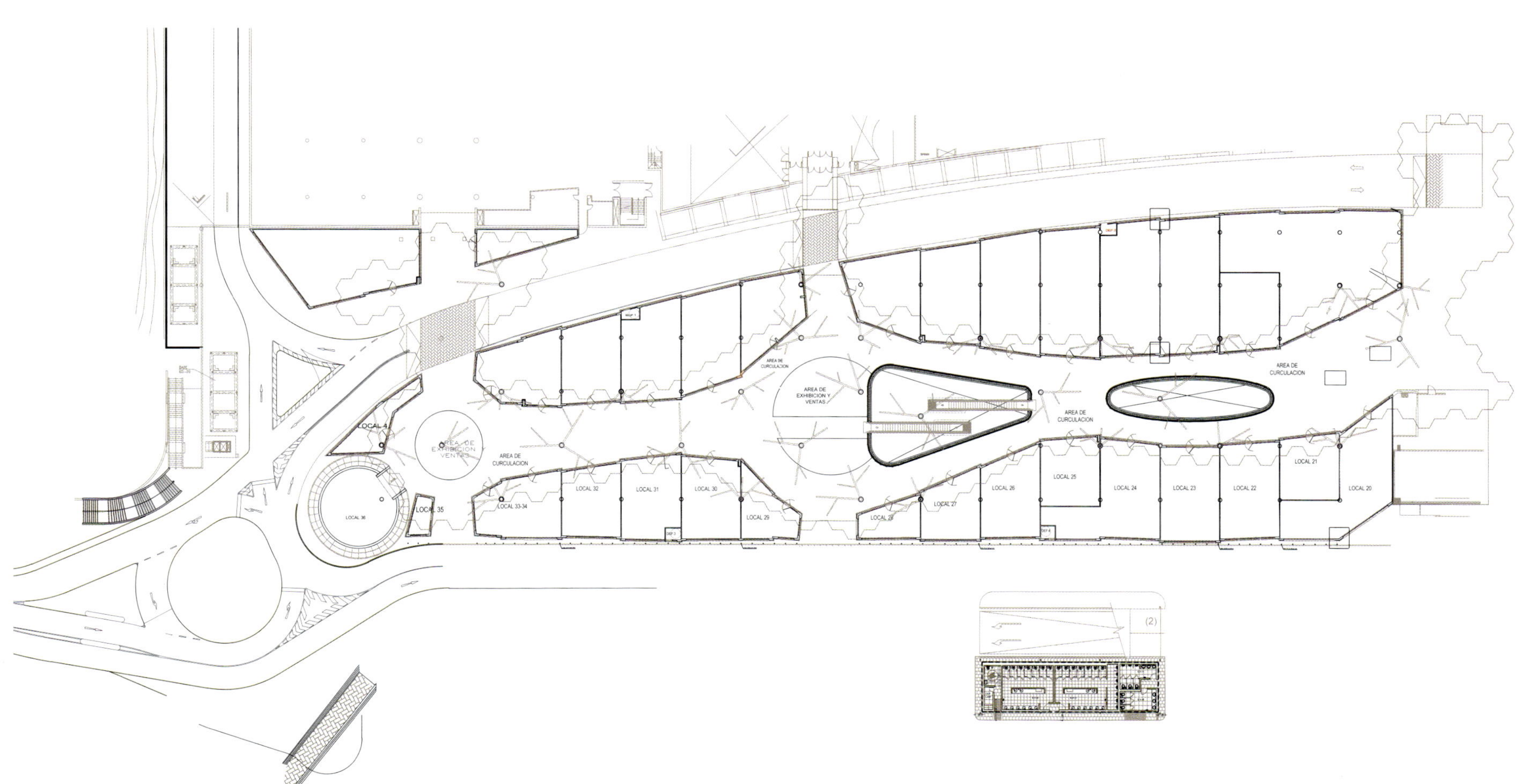

The great contribution of this proposal consists of the creation of successive small plazas in the different stages of the project, in the intersection of the articulating paths that allows having different meeting points and creates value in the interior commercial areas making all stores attractive.

Commercial locales have been planed as distributed around the circulation axis in such a way that a continuous volumetry is generated from the plaza, from the boulevard, to the cinema plaza. important circulation axis and 1 transversal axis that allow the connection and evacuation of the user in case of any contingency have been additionally planed and placed strategically in the project.

The group of facades has been designed to have impact and to show the offer of the shopping mall during day and night with a unique lighting proposal, continuing the boulevard´s. The whole of the Project is planned so as to have a landscape solution that enriches it´s spaces as well as a commercial illumination treatment that values commercial spaces.

随着工期的推移，各小型广场相继登场，这成为了该方案的点睛之笔。另外，各条小路穿插其间，通往四面八方，它们相互形成的叉路口给顾客提供了不同的汇集点。随之而来的是在内部商业区的价值创造，让所有商店颇具吸引力。

我们计划将商场分布在人行环道周围，这样从广场、大道到电影广场便会产生持续的人流量。该项目计划额外建造一条重要的人流轴线和一条横向轴线，位置优越，使得行人易于通行，并且在任何意外事故发生的情况下，能够疏散行人。

该建筑的外立面效果以及独特的照明方案用于凸显购物中心白天与黑夜的不同体验。项目整体规划旨在设计一个丰富空间感的景观方案，以及一个带来商业空间价值的商业照明方案。

FLORSHEIM
ESTABLISHED 1892
CRECEMOS

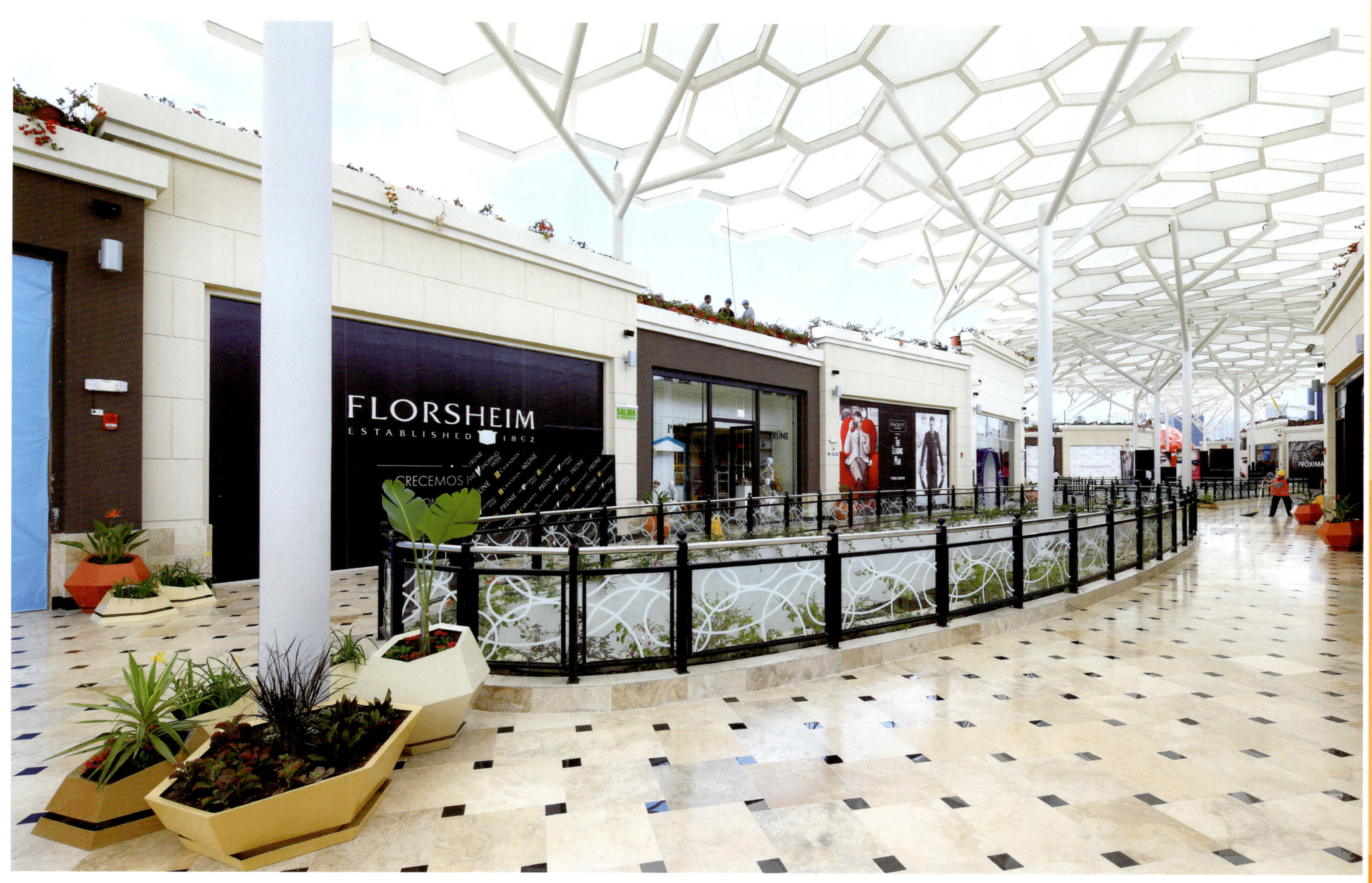

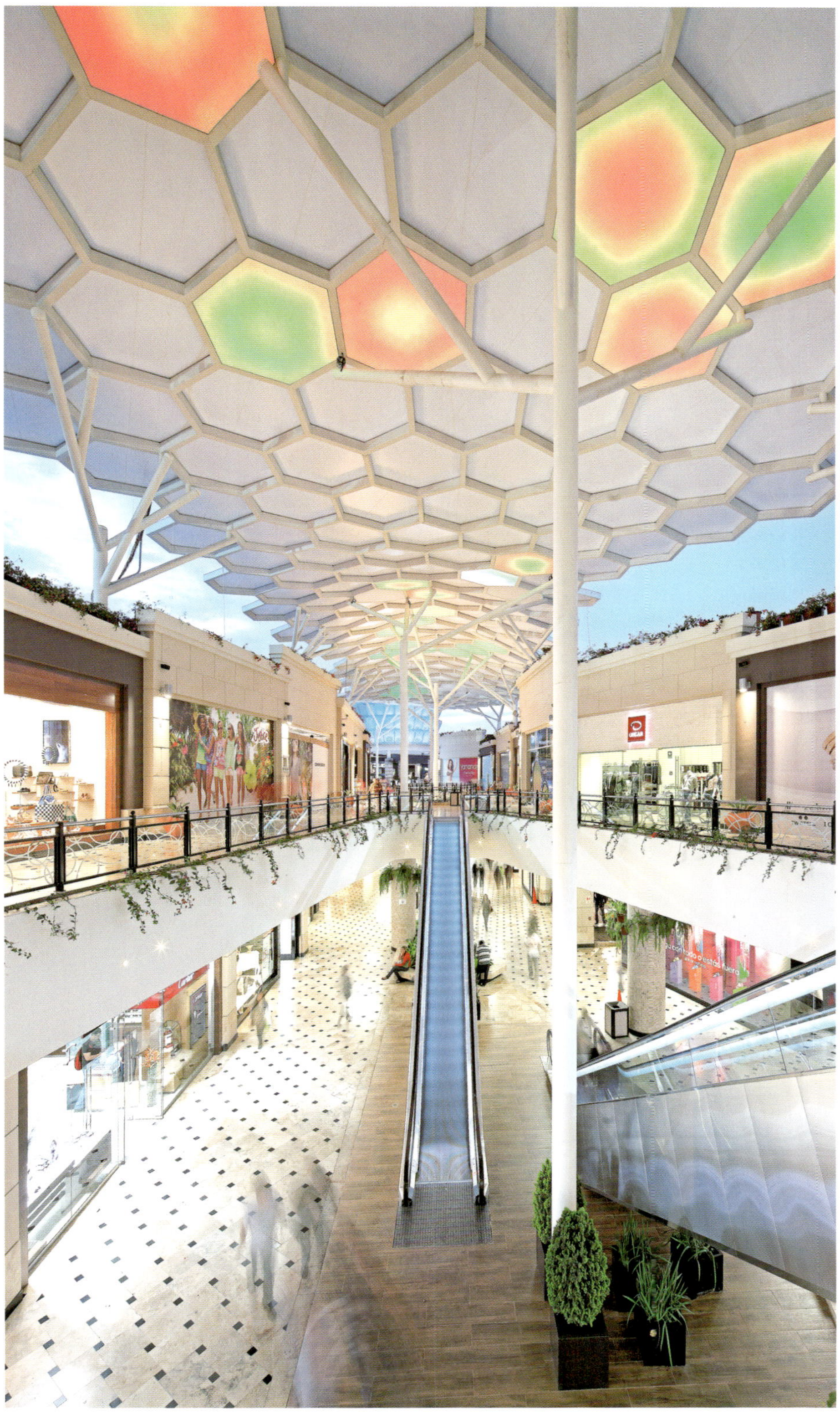

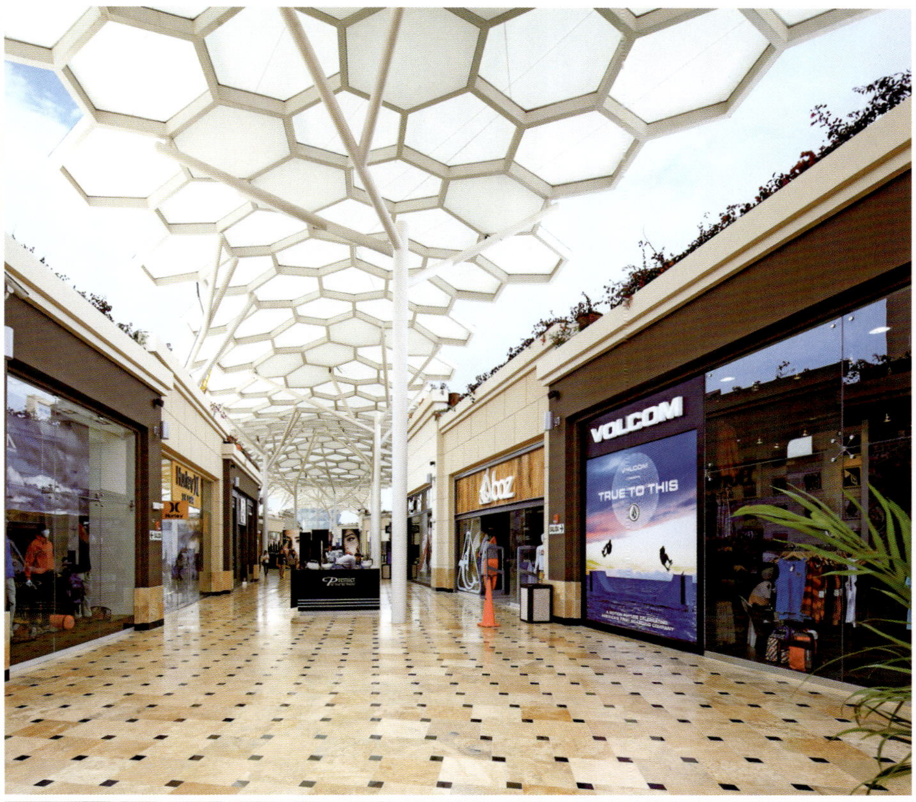
VOLCOM
TRUE TO THIS

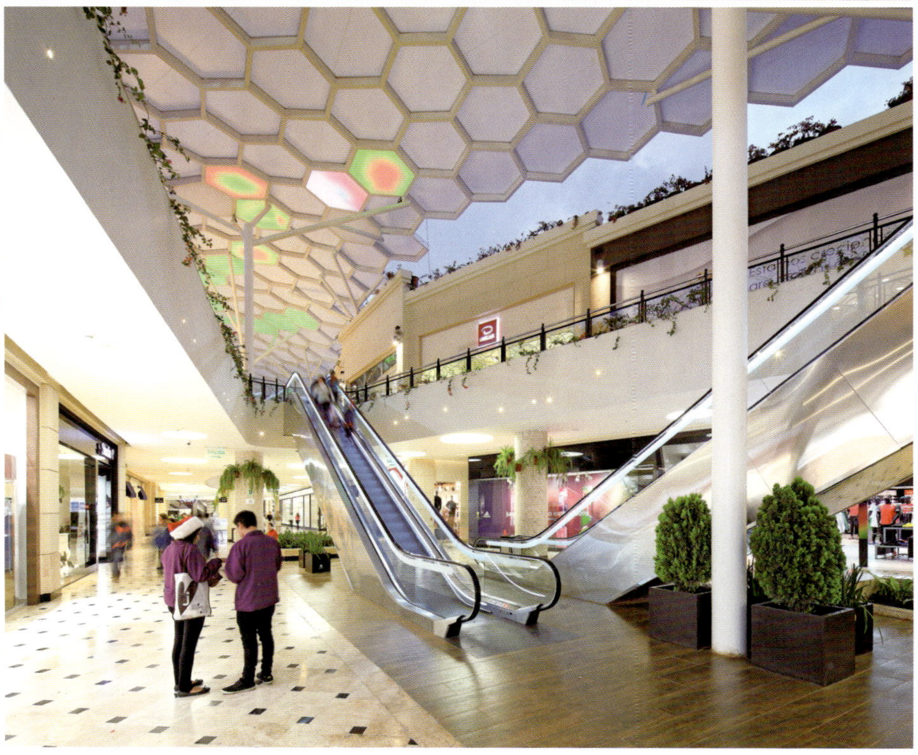

PROJECT NAME 项目名称

SHANGHAI WANDA COMMERCIAL PLAZA

上海万达松江商业广场

Architect:HMD

设计公司：HMD

PROJECT INFORMATION 项目信息

Location	Songjiang, Shanghai	**地点**	上海市松江
Gross Building Area	231,700 m²	**总建筑面积**	231,700 平方米
SiteAre	50,930 m²	**占地面积**	50,930 平方米
Heigh	140 m	**建筑高度**	100 米
Design Type	Shopping Mall, Office Building, Hotel	**设计类型**	购物中心、写字楼、酒店

OVERVIEW 项目概况

Located at Zhongshan street or 9 International Ecological Business Zone, Songjiang district, Shanghai, Songjiang Wanda Commercial Plaza enjoys a planned site area of about 92,700 m^2 and a planned covered area of about 32,2900 m^2. It is designed to have a total covered area of 316,700 m^2 of which 231,700 m^2 is the covered area based on plot ratio and 85,000 m^2 is the underground covered area. The project covers business center, Wanda department store, Wanda international cinema, game center, KTV, electrical appliance store, indoor pedestrian street, outdoor pedestrian street and other facilities. It is a large-sized urban complex that incorporates shopping, catering, culture, entertainment, recreation and other functions. It is the 3rd generation of urban complex that absolutely goes ahead of others in China. It will become a high-end large-size recreation and consumption site locating at Songjiang new town.

松江万达广场项目位于上海市松江区中山街道（国际生态商务区 9 号），总规划用地面积约 92,700 平方米，规划总建筑面积约 32,2900 平方米。设计总建筑面积 316,700 平方米，其中计容建筑面积 231,700 平方米，地下建筑面积 85,000 平方米。项目涵盖了商业中心、万达百货、万达国际影城、电玩城、KTV、电器商场、室内步行街、室外步行街等设施，是融购物、餐饮、文化、娱乐、及休闲等多功能为一体的大型城市综合体，是目前在国内属于绝对领先地位的第三代城市综合体，它将成为松江新城高端的大型休闲消费场所。

BRIEF INTERVIEW 访谈录

HKASP: The tower delivers an elegant and original form. The sense of form as a whole and structural detailing both are impressive. Would you like to talk about design process and the source of concept?

HMD: Two towers sit upon Yixing WANDA square. One is a 5-star prime office tower as high as 153m. The other is a 5-star hotel as high as 110m. The architectural design of towers is part of Yixing WANDA square commercial complex. The cluster of buildings takes a form that is based on the overall planning for Dongjiu new town. Overall space is shaped by vertical linear volume in a strong dynamic movement. The lines, both visible and invisible, run diagonally across the glazing facade and cut the glazing facade into triangle volumes, implying sail and delivering a symbol that Yixing square sails out for success and takes a leadership in the planned Dongjiu new town. On the other hand, the square speaks to the overall waterfront open space in Dongjiu new town. It is an insertion of vertical linear volume in the rational urban fabric. The architectural orientation and exterior layout are integrated into the waterfront space, with a purpose to attract flows of people into WANDA square. The integration of the square into graceful natural landscape forms a beneficial relationship between nature and the town. The Jockey Plaza has achieved this with costumers, through the creation of semi-urban areas with architectural elements that serve as references and encourage the visitors to explore a worth remembering experience.

HKASP: When designing, is there something in particular that you focus on? Like Material and form?

HMD: We were actively engaged through all stages through bidding, finalizing design plan, working with construction drawing, inspection of model and post-construction services when designing the facade. We also conducted effective study and analysis with much care, allowing the plan to be realized fully and taking an efficient cost control right from the scratch which became our focus. Much attention has been paid to creating urban scale, human-friendly scale, scale of stand-alone and local parts as well as creating a rich commercial climate and others. In addition, how to improve the overall image of building by working on all aspects of design was also on the list of our considerations.

It is very important to make a correct selection of materials and their pattern. We paid special attention to material during inspection of model house.

香港建筑科学出版社：塔楼的形式是非常优雅而具有原创性的，整体的形体感和结构的处理都让人印象深刻。能谈一下你们的设计过程以及概念的来源吗？

HMD：宜兴万达广场塔楼一共两座，分别为一座 153 米高的五星级甲级写字楼和一座 110 米高的五星级酒店，塔楼建筑设计作为宜兴万达广场商业综合体的一部分，建筑群的形态立足于东氿新城整体规划带中，建筑以动感强烈的竖向线型体量营造整体的空间，幕墙明、隐框“折线”切分幕墙的三角形体量寓意风帆，象征宜兴万达广场的起航，并将成为东氿新城规划的领航建筑，; 另一方面，该项目与东氿新城整体滨水开放空间取得对话，在理性的城市肌理当中穿插具有强烈竖向线型体量，建筑走势与外部布局顺应东氿整体滨水空间的大关系，将氿新城中的人流引入万达广场，契入东氿新城优美的自然景观当中，形成自然与城市相互渗透的良性关系。

香港建筑科学出版社：在设计的过程中什么是你们特别注重的吗？比如材料和形式方面？

HMD：宜兴万达广场外立面项目设计过程中 ,从投标阶段、方案深化阶段到施工图配合、样板检查阶段及后期服务 ,各个阶段我们都积极投入 ,进行细致有效的研究，分析，使方案从概念到落地，从城市尺度，近人尺度，从单体到局部的尺度，以及商业氛围的强化等等方面，如何从设计的各方面完善建筑的整体形象，真实有效的将方案效果落实到建筑上，有效的控制立面成本，成了我们的设计重点。在整个项目中材料的确定及式样的选择，是很重要的一个环节，我们在项目中样板检查阶段就是专门针对材料这一块的。

HKASP: What do you think is the key to the success of a complex project?

HMD:The success of a complex project lies in many things. That of a commercial complex lies in more than those. Talking about architectural design alone, we have to read the plan first and have a full understanding of art of architectural expression and of how to intensify the features of structural forms and to give the building a layered and dimensional look. What is more, integrating local characterization in microcosmic sense into general composition in macroscopical sense comes along with careful study, prudent and professional drawing, picky selection of materials and an exploration into craftsmanship. In addition, we shall have a severe cost control and bond all professionals into one, deliver excellent services through all stages of construction step by step. Effort shall be made to realize the project exactly as the plan requires. All is about human feeling. With such concept, we are able to deliver vibrant and touching work. Only if you are more demanding on yourself, you can keep up with the time and take the lead.

香港建筑科学出版社：你觉得一个综合体项目成功的最重要的方面是什么？

HMD：一个综合体项目的成功，包含了很多方方面，对于一个商业性质的综合体要求更多了。单从建筑设计这一块来说，首先是对建筑的方案进行解读，要充分理解建筑表现艺术，强化建筑结构形式特点，完善建筑的层次感和立体感，将建筑的整体宏观构图与局部微观刻画相结合，细致的研究，严谨专业的深化图纸，对材料的苛求，对工艺做法的探索。严格把控项目成本，无缝衔接各个专业的配合，分步骤的服务好各个阶段的施工。原汁原味地使方案从概念到落地，建筑完美如初地呈现。一切以人为本，以人的感受为首要，我们就可以做出有生命的、感动人的作品。对自己有更高的要求，才能跟紧时代的潮流，才有可能引领这一领域。

North Elevation of Commercial Plaza
商业广场北立面图

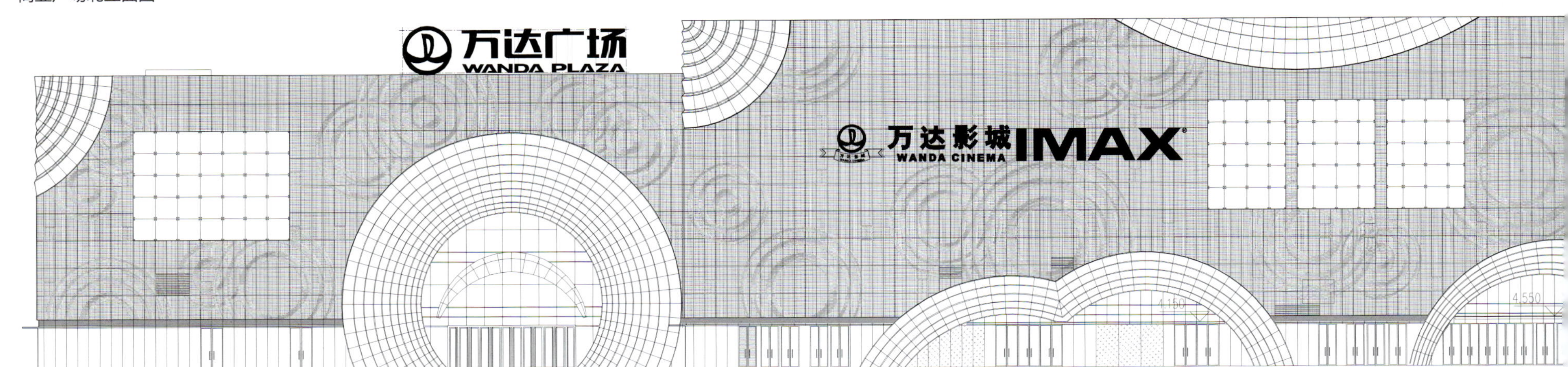

South Elevation of Commercial Plaza
商业广场南立面图

The design concept for Songjiang Wanda

By adopting a different business concept, Wanda made a great success in integrating fast food practice into the operation of large-sized business complex. This made it rank first globally in the creation of complex both in scale and speed. In the mean time, the success comes along with its downside that its projects are in lack of marked regional characters and individual cultural identity. For this project, we try to go deep into the cultural root and make it a unique local landmark.

松江万达的设计构思

万达独特的商业理念，使其成功地将大型商业综合体运作成了快餐模式，这成就了万达世界第一的综合体生产规模和生产速度，但同时也使得万达的项目缺少鲜明的地域性格，缺少独属于每个综合体的文化特性。我们试图为项目寻找一些根源，使其能够成长为独一无二的地域标志。

Apartments Elevation 1
公寓立面图 1

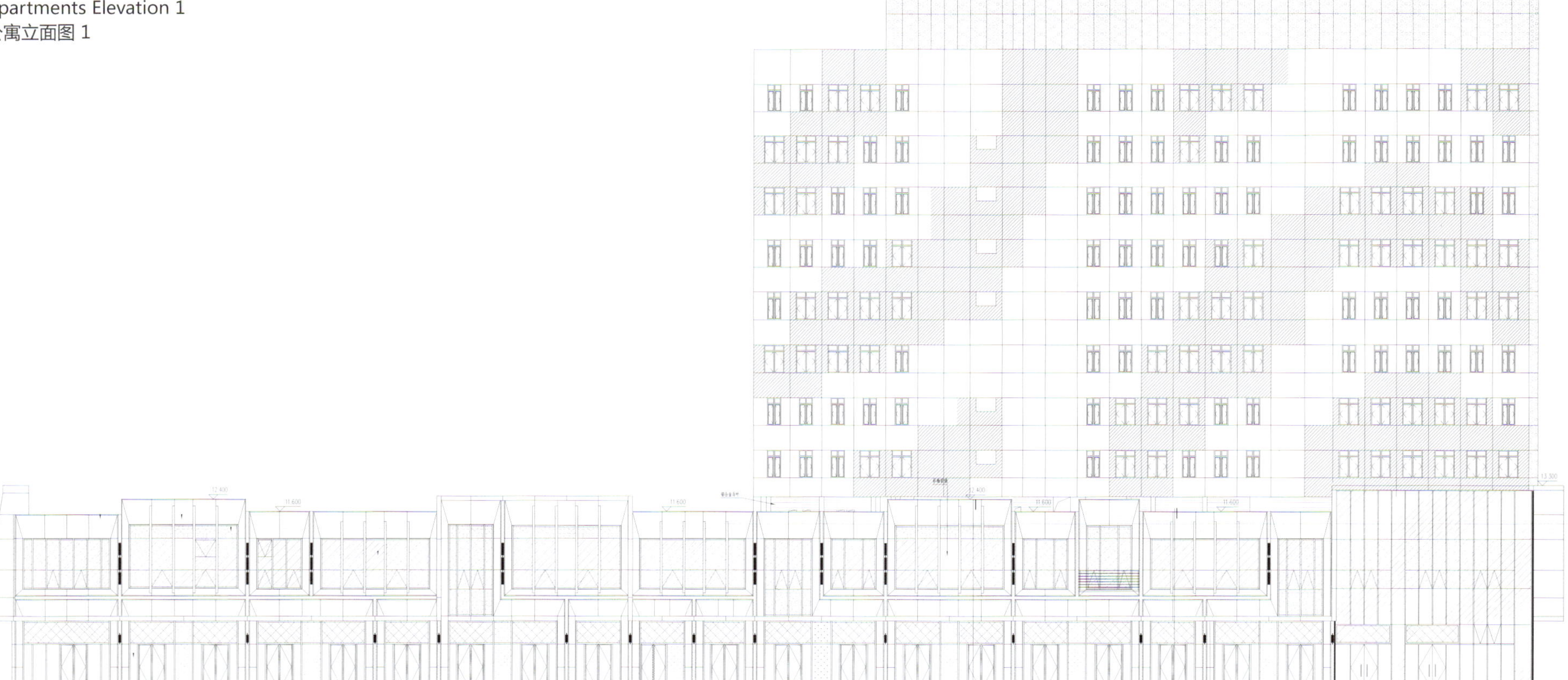

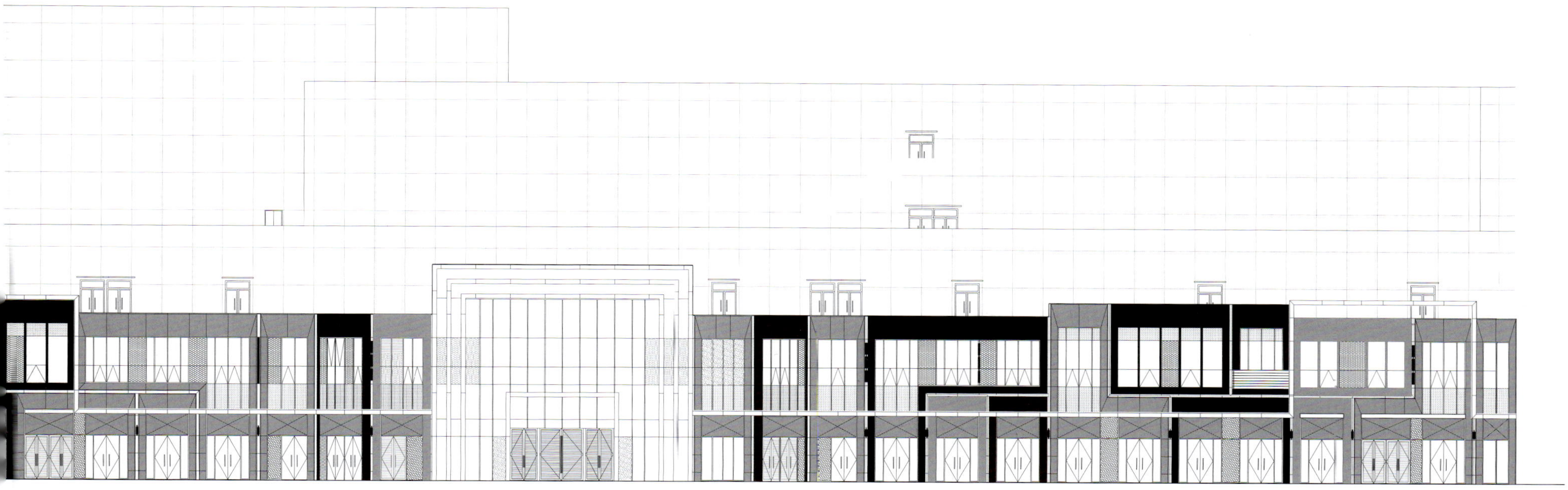

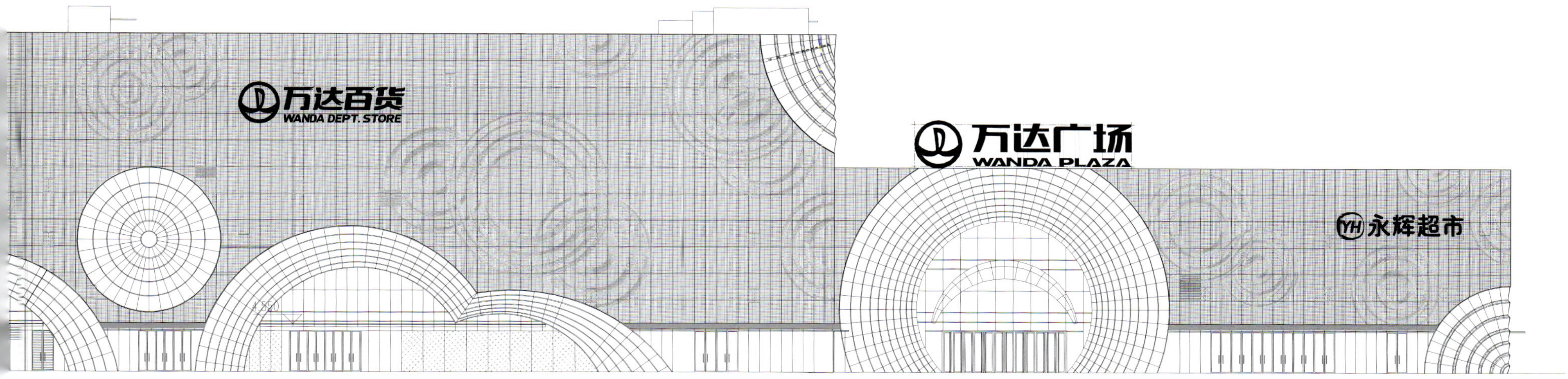

Reputed as Shanghai's cultural root, Songjiang district boasts a long history and a well-developed culture. affluent in architectural cultural heritage. Tangjingzhuang (an ancient stone pillar with Tang dynasty scripture carved on it) from Tang dynasty, Square tower from Song dynasty, Masjid from Yuan dynasty, screen wall from Ming dynasty and Drunken Bai Pond from Qing dynasty and many other cultural relics can all be found here. It is reputed as "a look through history from Tang dynasty to Qing dynasty"

松江历史悠久、文化发达，是上海的文化之根，拥有丰富的建筑文化遗产。有唐代的唐经幢、宋代的方塔、元代的清真寺、明代的照壁和清代的醉白池等众多文物，故有“唐宋元明清，从古看到今”之誉。

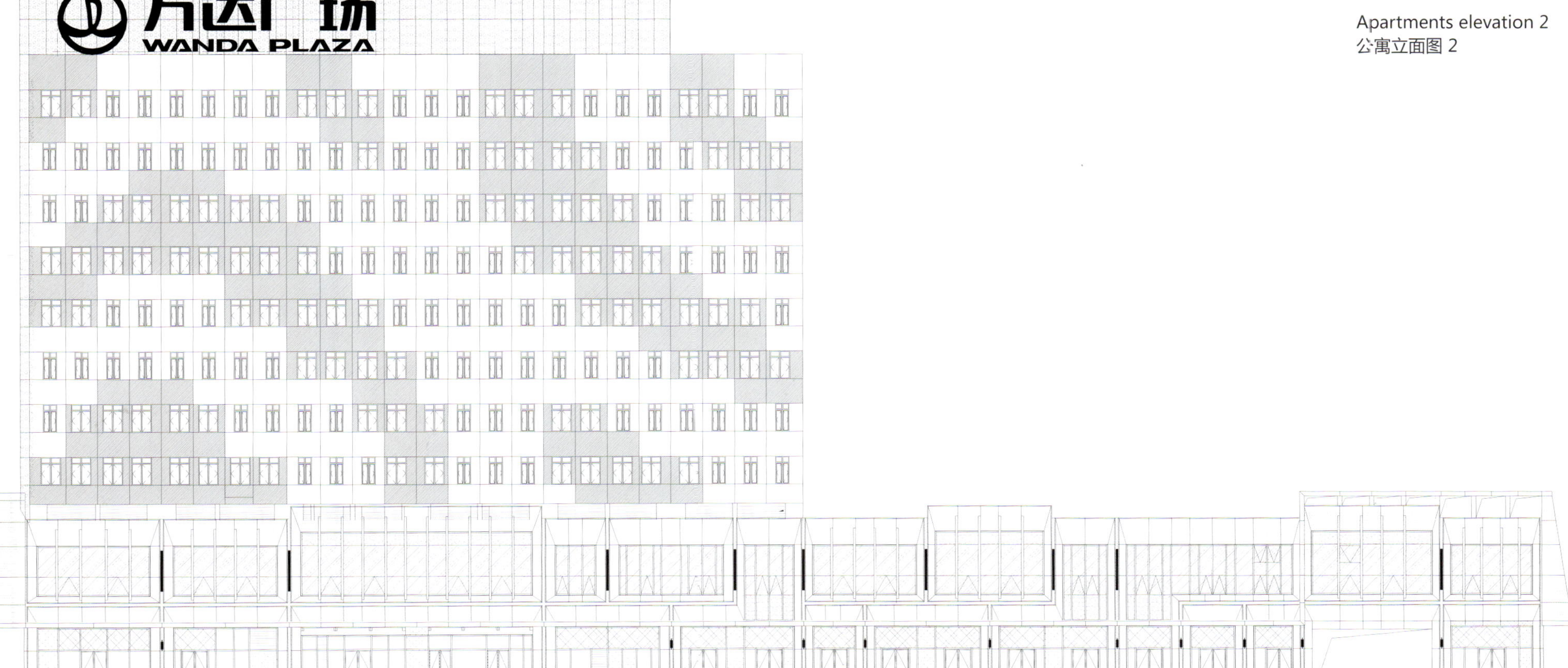

Apartments elevation 2
公寓立面图 2

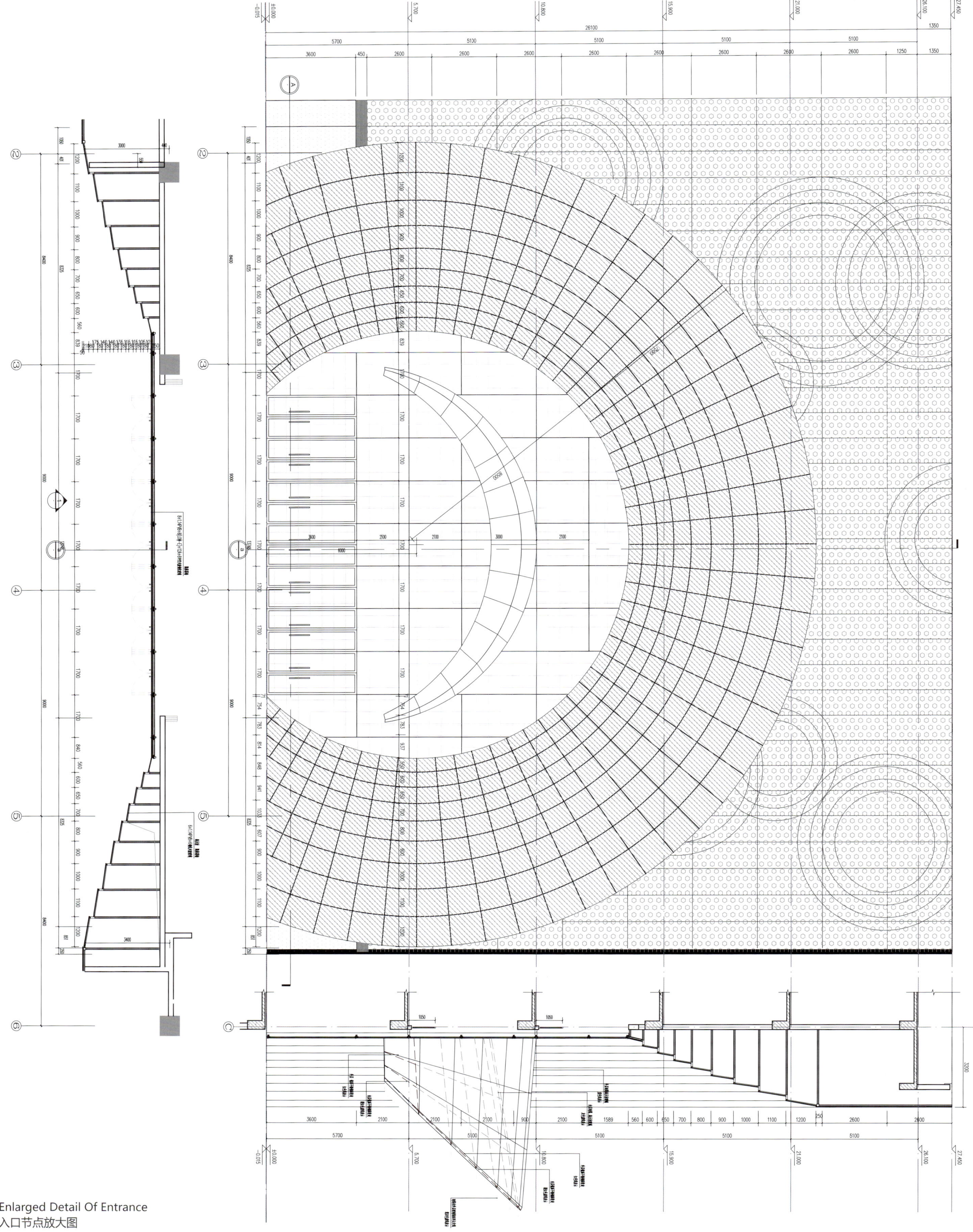

Enlarged Detail Of Entrance
入口节点放大图

Songjiang became famous for its water. As a core part of south Chinese garden, water is closely connected to cultural heritage. Drunken Bai Pond is also one of famous classical south Chinese gardens. A variety of traditional architectural elements are combined to form charming south Chinese architectural clusters, including bridges, water flow and pavilion.

松江因水得名，水也是江南园林的核心特色，这里到处都有与水有关的文化传承，松江的醉白池也是江南著名的古典园林之一。小桥、流水、亭台、楼阁各种各样的传统建筑组成了迷人的江南建筑群落。

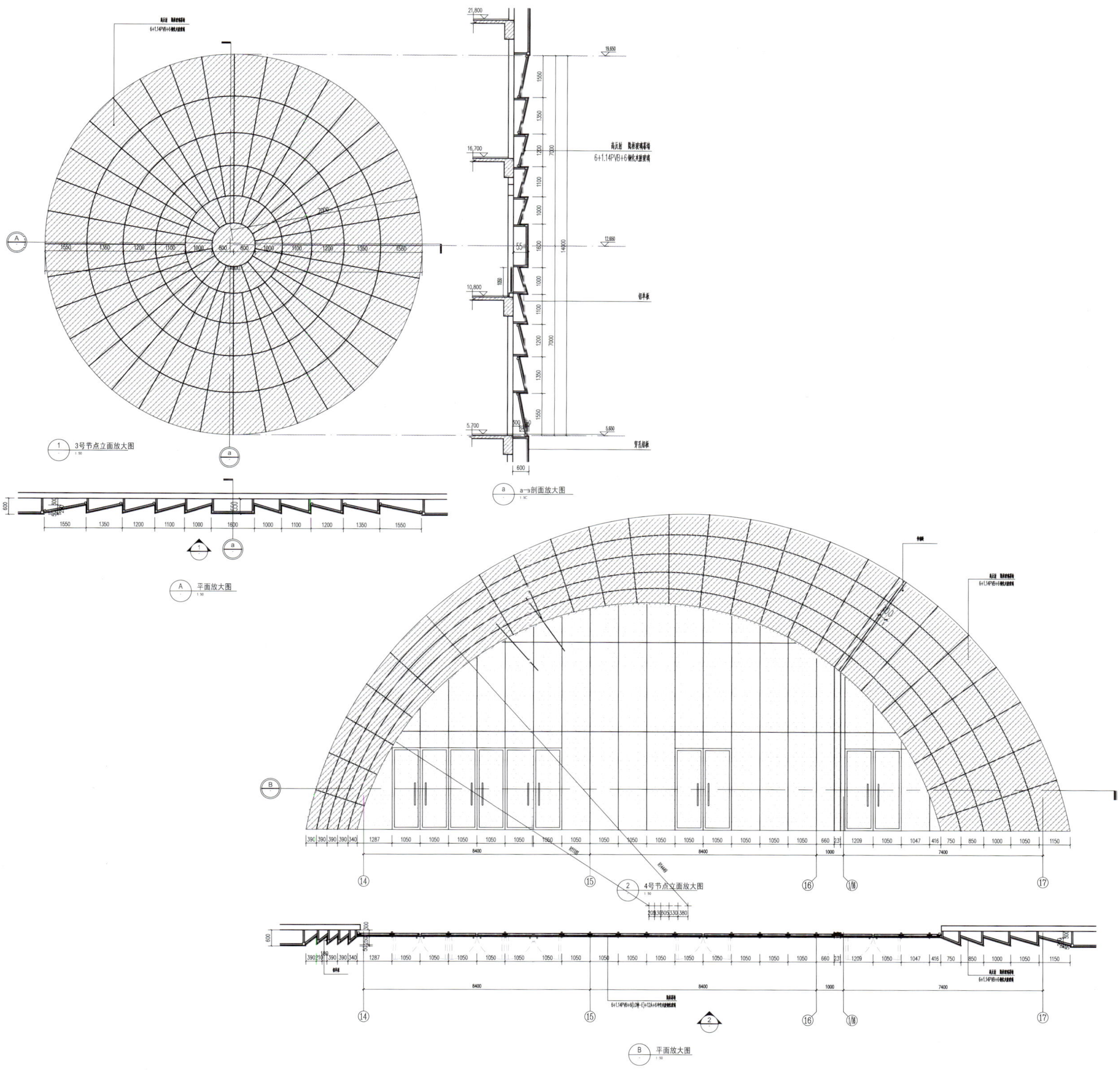

3号节点立面放大图
a—a剖面放大图
平面放大图
4号节点立面放大图
平面放大图

Detail 1
节点图 1

6号节点立面放大图

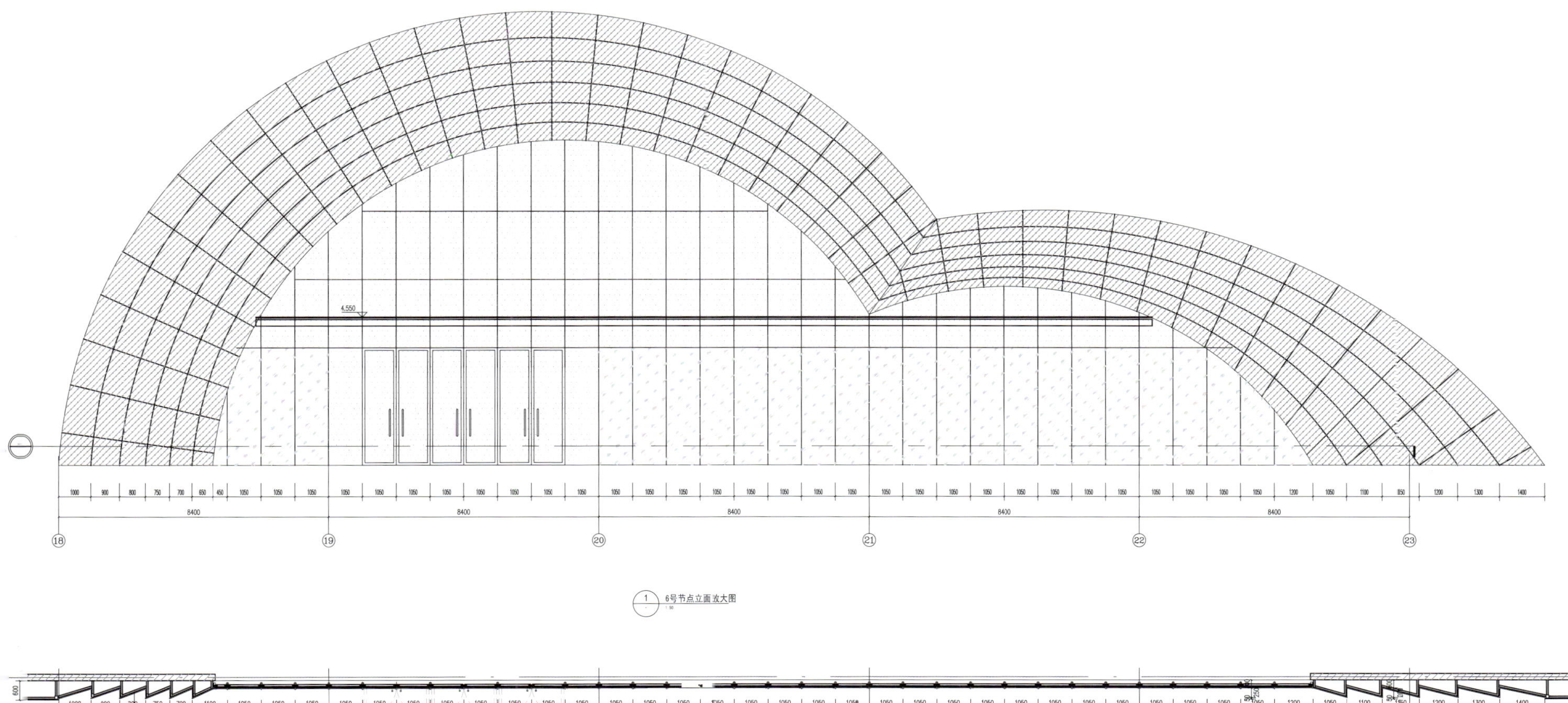

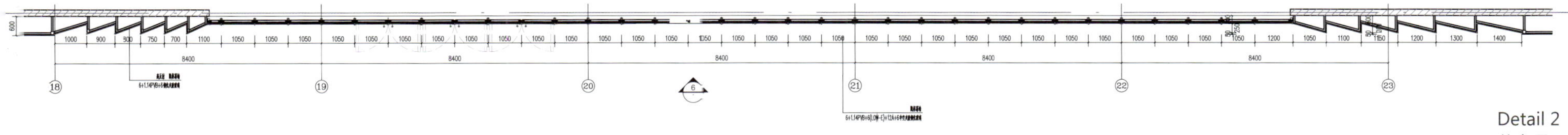

Detail 2
节点图 2

By starting from water drip and by integrating classical architectural culture, design proposal seeks to interact with traditional style with modern material and techniques. Drizzle, lotus pool and garden are epitome of south Chinese scenery. Inspired by them, the design aims at forming an artistic conception of ripple by introducing perforated plate and elaborating unique pattern. By allowing LED to work with perforated plate, water curtain of varied colors is formed at night.

设计方案以水滴为切入点，融合古典建筑文化，试图使用现代的材料和手法与传统的风格相呼应。细雨、荷塘、园林是江南景致的缩影，设计从中汲取灵感，引入穿孔板材料，并精心设计了独特的纹理，形成水晕的意境。穿孔板结合LED灯光，在夜间也能形成色彩变幻的“水幕”。

The main entrance to the indoor business street is designed to integrate the concept of moon gate found at a typical Chinese garden. Terraced glass is used to form a whirlpool-like visual perception, and to attract people to come into the mall, allowing the main entrance to become an intense visual center.

The exquisite woodcarving components found at a classical garden are the essence of architecture, with fine patterns engraved on hanging fascia, lattice window and door leaf. As to outdoor business street, the variation that occurs in repeated classical patterns is used in the design. Based on this, textured facade, rich in variation and uniform in form, is taken into shape by modulization-based facade design and employing varied jigsaw. By doing so, a straight business street is no more monotone in spatial pattern and view changes with each step you make.

Four SOHO high-risings show a visual effect of ripple by allowing windows to change in size, which is the setting for the entire mall. However, the textured pattern presents a dynamic movement as if ripple coming out of water surface spreads far away. We expect the design concept to be consistent throughout the design instead of some standalones only. Hence, we tried a variety of visual effects, trying to establish a link among all buildings.

在室内商业街的主入口设计上，融合中国园林中月亮门的概念，利用玻璃层层叠退的手法使主入口形成漩涡一样的视觉冲击力，吸引人流进入商场，成为强烈的视觉中心。

四栋 SOHO 高层通过窗户大小的变化形成水波纹的效果，成为大商业的背景图案。而整个图案纹理又是变化的，犹如一个平静水面激起的涟漪扩散到远处。我们希望设计概念能够贯穿到整个设计中，而不仅仅是其中的某些单栋建筑。因此我们尝试了不同视觉效果，试图让不同建筑可能够关联起来。

古典园林中精致的木雕构件是建筑的精髓，挂落、花窗、门扇都有着精美图案。在室外商业街的设计中，我们吸收古典图案在重复中变化的特点，通过模数化立面设计，采用变化拼图的方式，形成富于变化又形式统一的立面肌理。妥善解决了平直商业街空间单调的劣势，达到步移景异的效果。

MERICA S
AVORITE
EANS
RAND

WINE
WINE
WINE

The architects attempt to mark the modern commercial architecture with cultural symbol, allowing the architecture to be part of distinct local cultural context. Under the precondition that the architects make greatest effort to inject vogue elements into the commercial architecture, they are able to mark the architecture with tradition and individualize Wanda business complex that employs fast-food practice. Having made a miracle of rapid growth, Wanda believes that it is able to create commercial cultural legend in the future development.

设计者试图为现代商业建筑寻找文化的传承，使其能够融入到独特的地域文脉中。在松江万达的设计过程中，尽可能在满足商业建筑时尚需求之后，能够留下些传统的印记，能够给万达的快餐式商业综合体以个性的沉淀。万达在建立了自己的速度奇迹之后，相信在未来的发展中也能够塑造其商业的文化传奇。

PROJECT NAME 项目名称

TURKEY OPTIMUM IZMIR

土耳其 OPTIMUM IZMIR 综合体

Architect: 5+ design

设计公司：五杰建筑设计

PROJECT INFORMATION 项目信息

Client	Renaissance Development	**客户**	Renaissance Development
Land Area	39,000 m²	**面积**	39，000 平方米
Building Area		**建筑面积**	88，000 平方米
Gross Floor Area	135,575 m²	**总建筑面积**	135，575 平方米

OVERVIEW 项目概况

Optimum Izmir is Renaissance Developments fourth Optimum branded shopping mall in Turkey which opened November 2008 in the country's third largest city, Izmir. Optimum Izmir incorporates a variety of retail and entertainment offers including a large format hypermarket, DIY, electronic market, home wares, and unique boutique retailers. The retail segments are supported with more than 20 fast food units and restaurants and various leisure facilities, including a 10-screen movie theatre, an ice rink, a bowling alley, a 5D cinema and a kids' entertainment centre. Convenient parking is provided below the centre, providing direct access into the projects main retail passages and courts.

Optimum Izmir 综合体项目是文艺复兴开发商在土耳其的第四个品牌商场，于 2008 年 11 月在土耳其第三大城市伊兹密尔市开业。项目包含了多种多样的零售商场和娱乐设施，如大型超市、DIY 手工店、电子市场、家居用品和精品店等。零售商场里还设置了超过 20 个快餐店和餐馆，还有各种各样的休闲设施，如配备了 10 个放映厅的电影院、溜冰场、保龄球场、5D 电影院和儿童娱乐中心等。停车场位于地下，进出便利，能直接连通建筑内的商场通道和庭院。

BRIEF INTERVIEW 访谈录

ARCHITECT
Tim Thurik

设计师
Tim Thurik

HKASP: The facade looks like paper has been cut. What is the concept behind this operation?

5+ design : The facade concept for Optimum Izmir is derived from the topographic context of the site. The project is located in the gentle rolling hills of Izmir. The hills are a combination of cliffs, stones, plateaus and foothills and we wanted the building to mirror the surrounding landscape.

Both the materials and forms of the massing are organic or natural with gentle curves and arcs overlapping to make the building reflect the topography. The result is a harmonious facade, both in color and form, symbolic and unique within its context.

HKASP: How did you make the final decision between different design options? How many choices did you make during the design process?

5+ design : There were many design options but it is ultimately a process of design; the decision is typically made for you thru the drawing process. Typically there are two types of designers; process designers and concept designers. Concept designers have a particular objective (i.e. the building will look like a "Diamond" ring). So they work and work until the building looks like a Diamond Ring. Process designers are different; they let the design process dictate the design of the building. Sketching, 3D technologies, programming, etc. decide the final character of the building. Optimum Izmir's design is really a process driven approach.

HKASP: When designing, is there something in particular that you focus on? (Material, form, use etc.)

5+ design : As it's been said many times by others, we let form follow function (and experience). We believe buildings are as much vessels of experience as they are material objects. In other words, in our office designing unique experiences is as important as designing buildings. Often, the focus is on the space between the walls; the interstitial spaces of streets, plazas, arcades....movement spaces that require careful design consideration to achieve the desired experience. Likewise, materials are chosen for the feelings they convey to people who come into contact with them (warmth, comfort, solidity and strength) as much as for their appearance.

香港建筑科学出版社：立面宛如被剪过的纸。该项目的设计理念是什么？

五杰建筑设计：我们根据场地的地貌环境得出了建筑的立面设计理念。项目坐落于坡度平缓的伊兹密尔群山之中。群山实则是许多悬崖、乱石、高原、山麓小丘汇集而成。于是，我们希望能从建筑的立面来呼应周遭景观的特点。

通过对柔和曲线与弧线的堆叠，采用天然材料，塑造自然形体，让建筑与周遭地貌融为一体。从而，无论是颜色还是形体，都打造出与环境相交融的立面，不仅别具一格，而且相映成趣。

香港建筑科学出版社：你是如何从多个设计方案中做出决定的？设计过程中，你做出了多少选择？

五杰建筑设计：有许多设计方案，但这毕竟只是设计过程。我们通常都是在制图过程中做出决定。通常有两种设计师：过程设计师与概念设计师。概念设计师专注于目标（比如，他们希望建筑看起来像钻戒），然后他们就专注于将建筑设计成宛如钻戒一样。然而，过程设计师则不一样。他们让设计过程主宰建筑的设计，包括诸如制图，3D 技术，程序设计等因素都会决定建筑的最终特点。而对最好的伊兹密尔的设计则是以过程为引导的。

香港建筑科学出版社：设计时，你有什么特别关注的地方吗？（材料、形体、用途等等）

五杰建筑设计：一些人常说，我们让建筑的形体跟着建筑的功能与体验走。我们认为建筑就如同它们是实体一样，是能装下体验的容器。换言之，设计出别具一格的办公感受跟设计建筑同样重要。我们通常关注墙体之间的空间与街道、广场、拱廊之间的空隙，乃至流动的空间。它们都需要我们精心的考量才能实现所希望的体验。同样，所选用的材料也能向人们传达出一种感受，使之与人产生互动，让人感到温馨、舒适、踏实以及力量。同样，材料的外观也能散发出同样的特质。

GREYDER
GREYDER

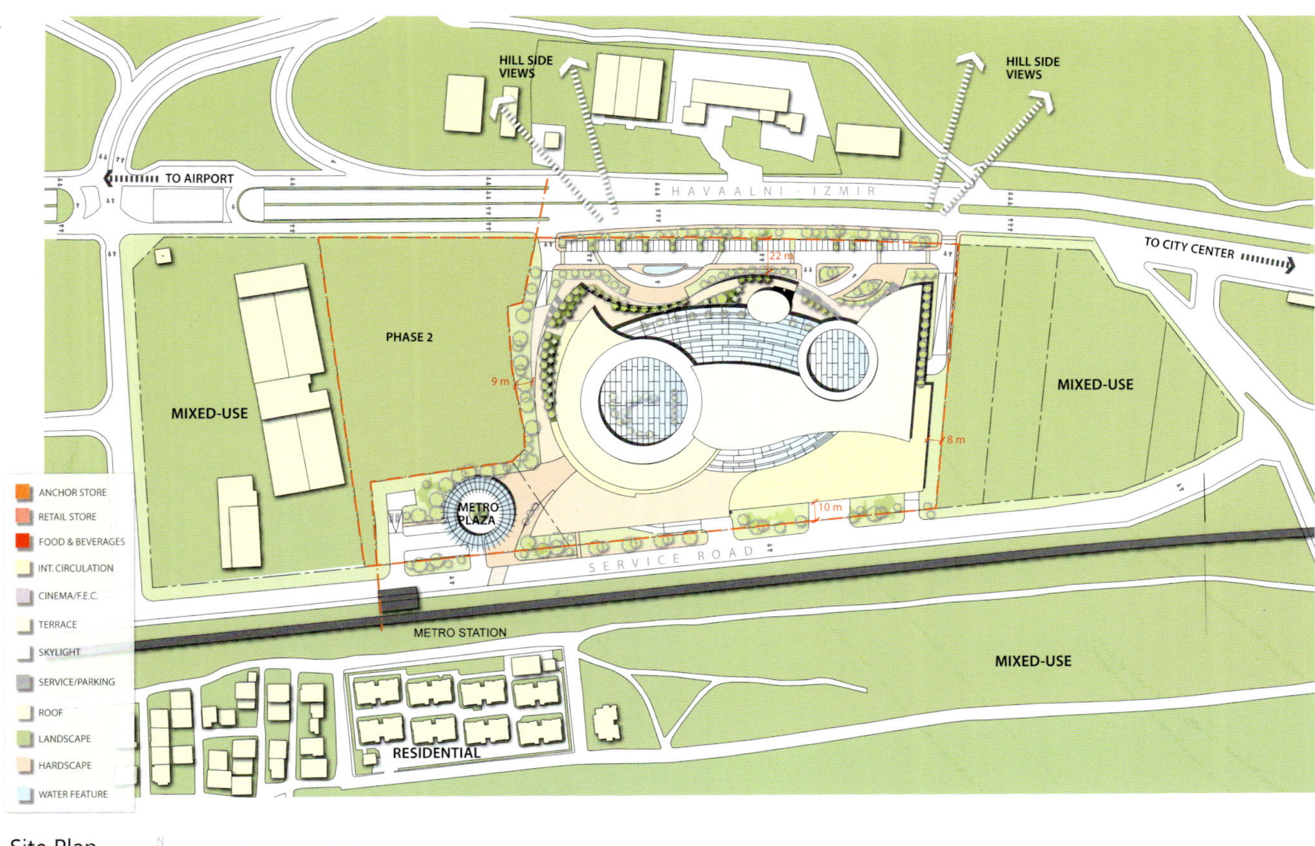

Site Plan
总平面图

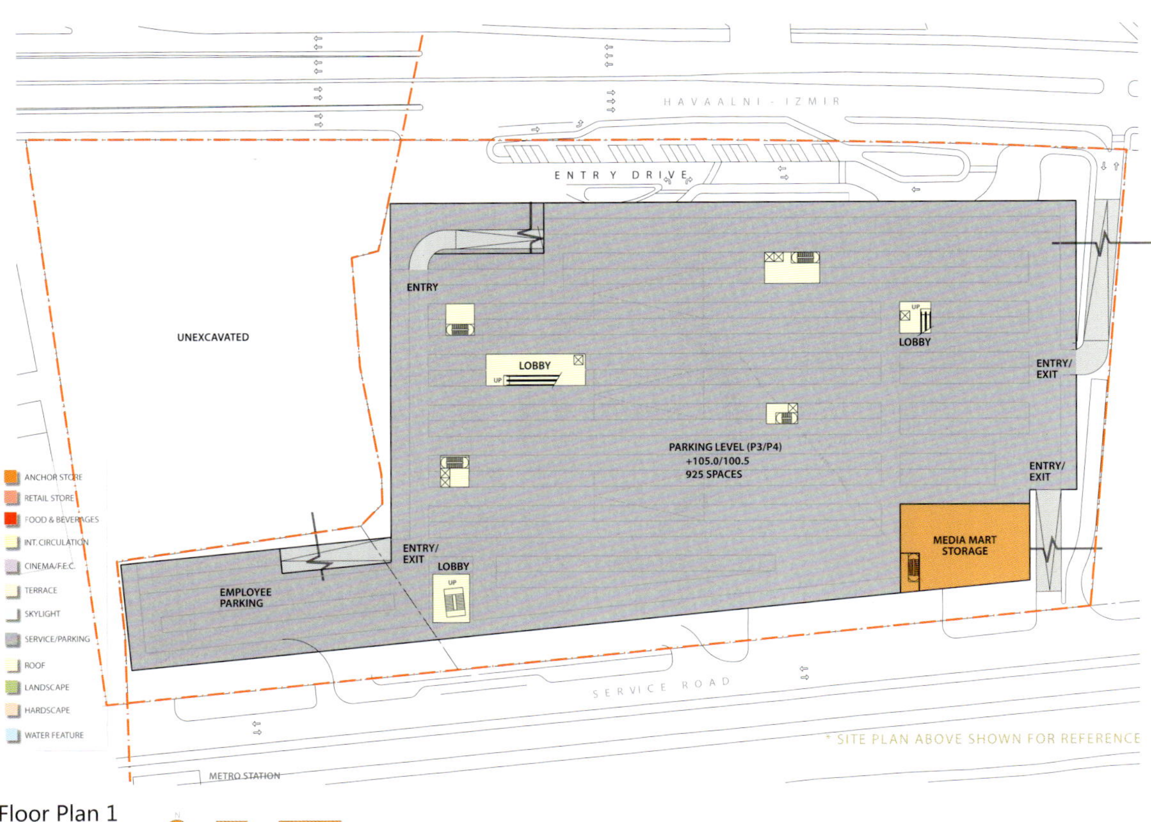

Floor Plan 1
楼层平面图 1

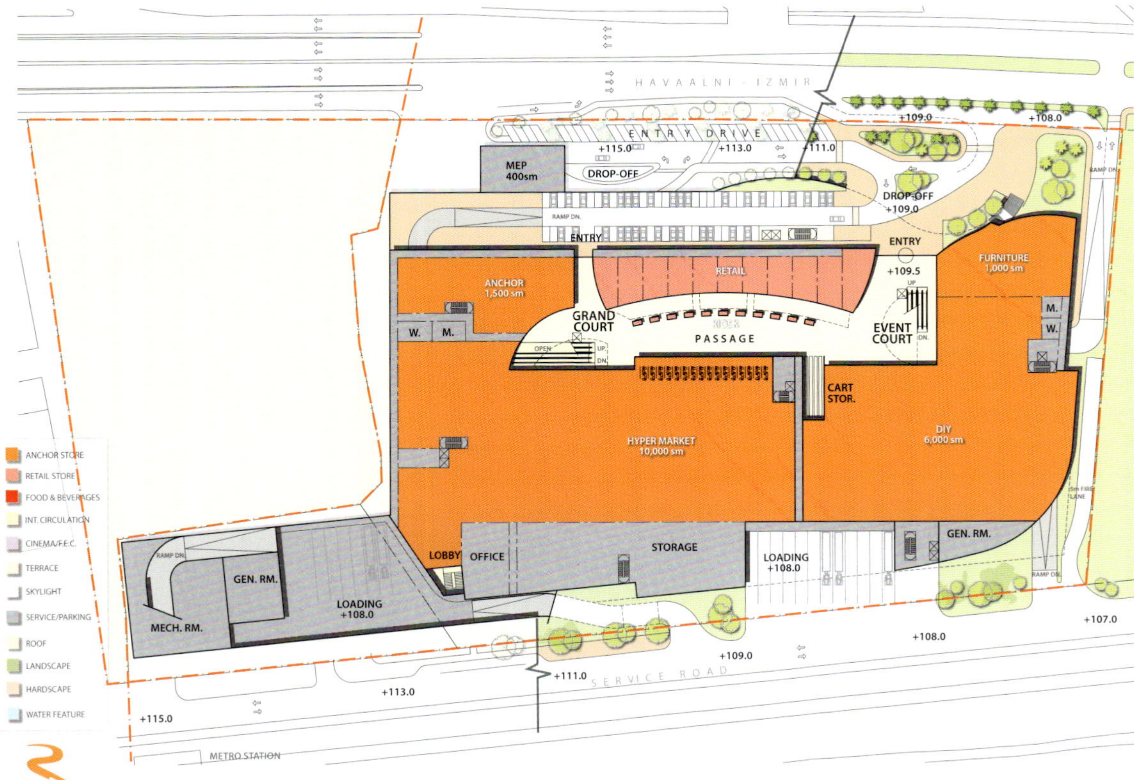

Floor Plan 2
楼层平面图 2

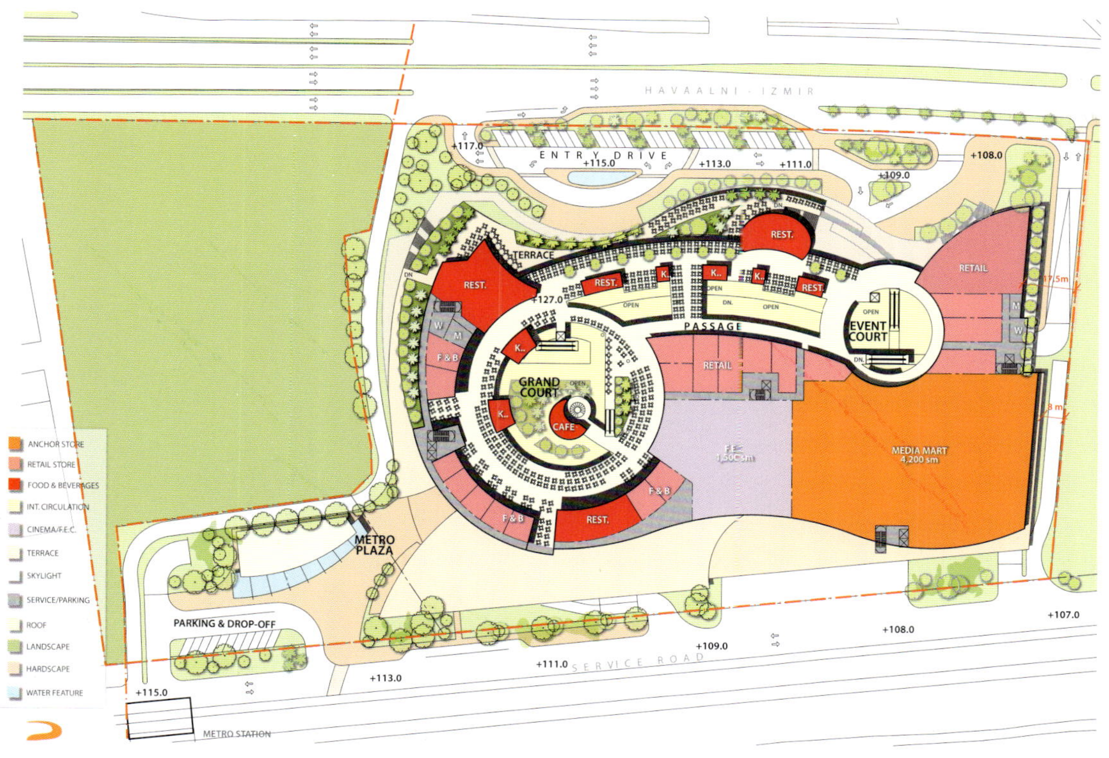

Floor Plan 5
楼层平面图 5

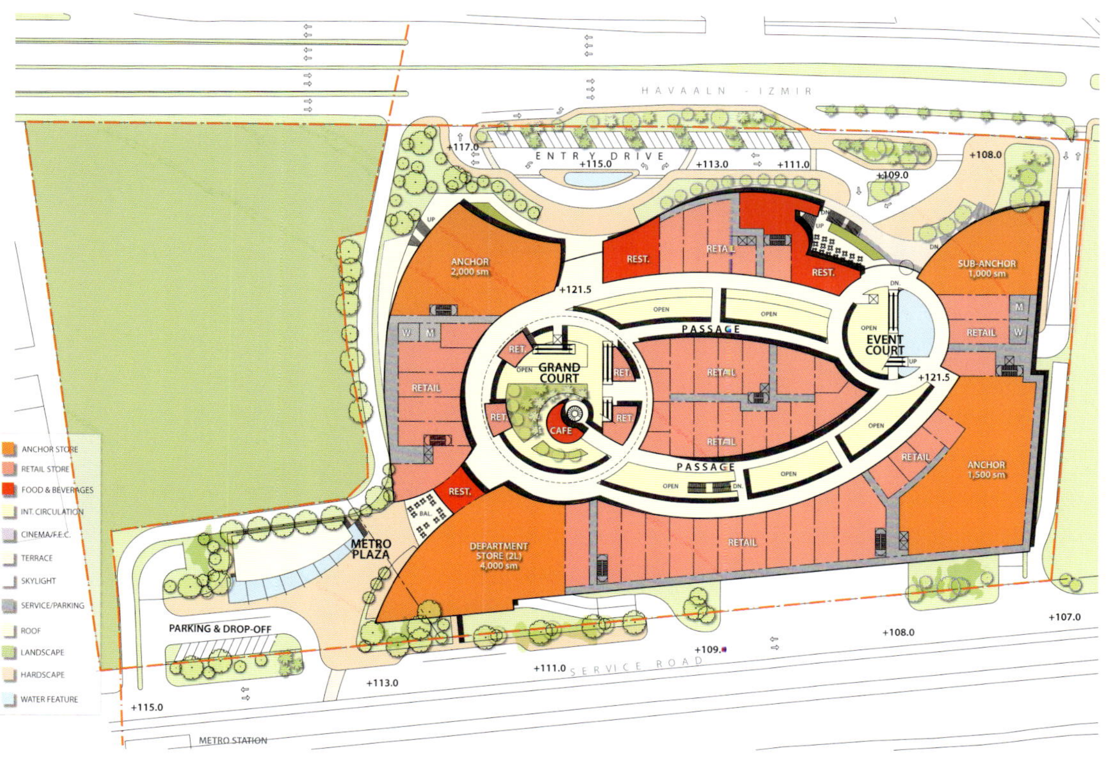

Floor Plan 4
楼层平面图 4

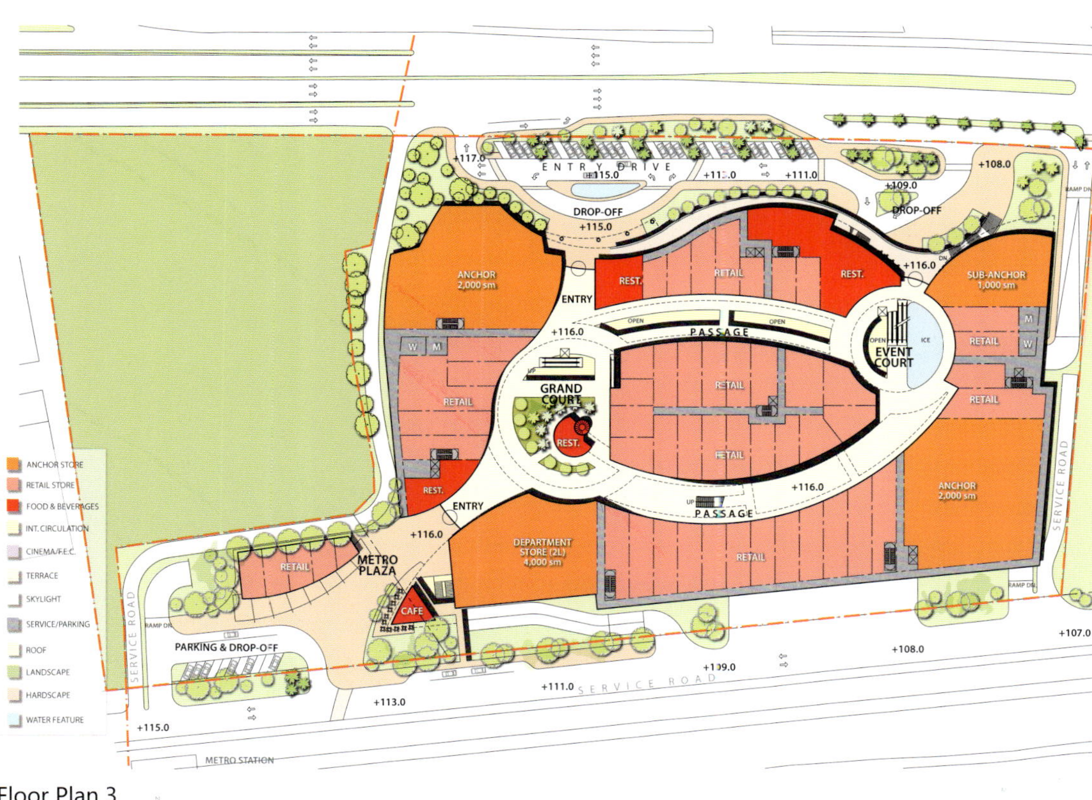

Floor Plan 3
楼层平面图 3

Location & Vicinity

Optimum Izmir is located in the Gaziemir district of Izmir, which lies between the city centre and the Izmir Adnan Menderes Airport. The transit oriented development is easily accessed via public metro and from the Izmir Highway. Optimum Izmir is favorably positioned across the Aegean Free Trade Zone, which has enhanced the development of Gaziemir district and overall commercial strategy for cities developing western communities. Optimum Izmir provides the community with a new landmark retail and entertainment destination.

Project Design

The architectural design of the project is inspired by the terracing landscapes and foothills surroundings of Izmir. True inspiration comes from nature; the building facades and interior pathways reflect the stepping hillsides and organic forms found in the region. The use of natural stone on the facade mirrors the adjacent topography; stepping and carving to create outdoor terraces and feature towers. To enhance the shopping experience on the interior, the outside is brought in with natural light, green landscapes and warm materials. The meandering retail passages provide a unique retail experience for the shopper, giving each tenant a strong identity. The interior is anchored by the grand "ice" court; a three level light filled atrium, activated with cafes, skating performances and fashion boutiques.

区域与周边

Optimum Izmir综合体项目位于伊兹密尔市的Gaziemir区，坐落在市中心和德列斯机场之间。项目注重交通便利性，人们可以通过地铁和伊兹密尔市高速公路快速到达。项目的地理位置也很优越，横跨爱琴海自由贸易区，不仅能增强Gaziemir区的发展和整体商业战略，促进城市西部区域的发展。项目将成为该区域一个新地标和娱乐场所。

项目设计

该项目的建筑设计是得到梯田景观和伊兹密尔市山麓环境的启发。设计师真正的灵感来自于大自然，建筑的立面和室内通道就是取自于该地区特有的梯田式山坡和有机形态。外立面采用天然石材来反映了相邻地区的地形；台阶和雕刻被运用到户外露台上，这也是建筑的特征之一。为提升内部的购物环境，外界的自然光被引入其中，并配上绿色景观和保暖材料。商店里蜿蜒的通道为购物者带来独特的购物体验，也给每个卖家一个独特的身份特征。建筑内部有一座三层高、光线充足的大型“冰”场，周边的咖啡店、滑冰表演和时尚精品店也使其活力四射。

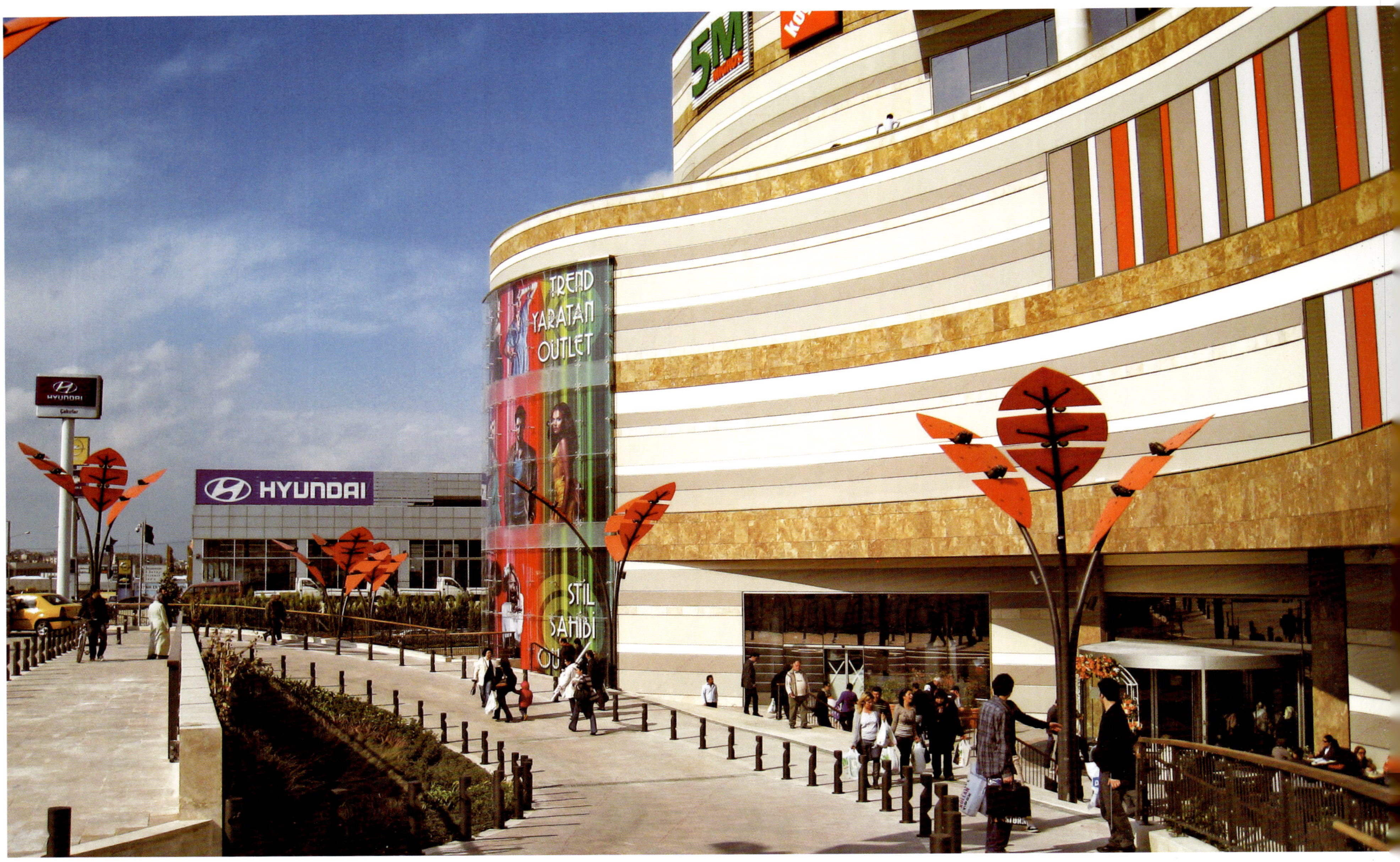
5M
HYUNDAI
TREND
YARATAN
OUTLET
STIL
SAHİBİ

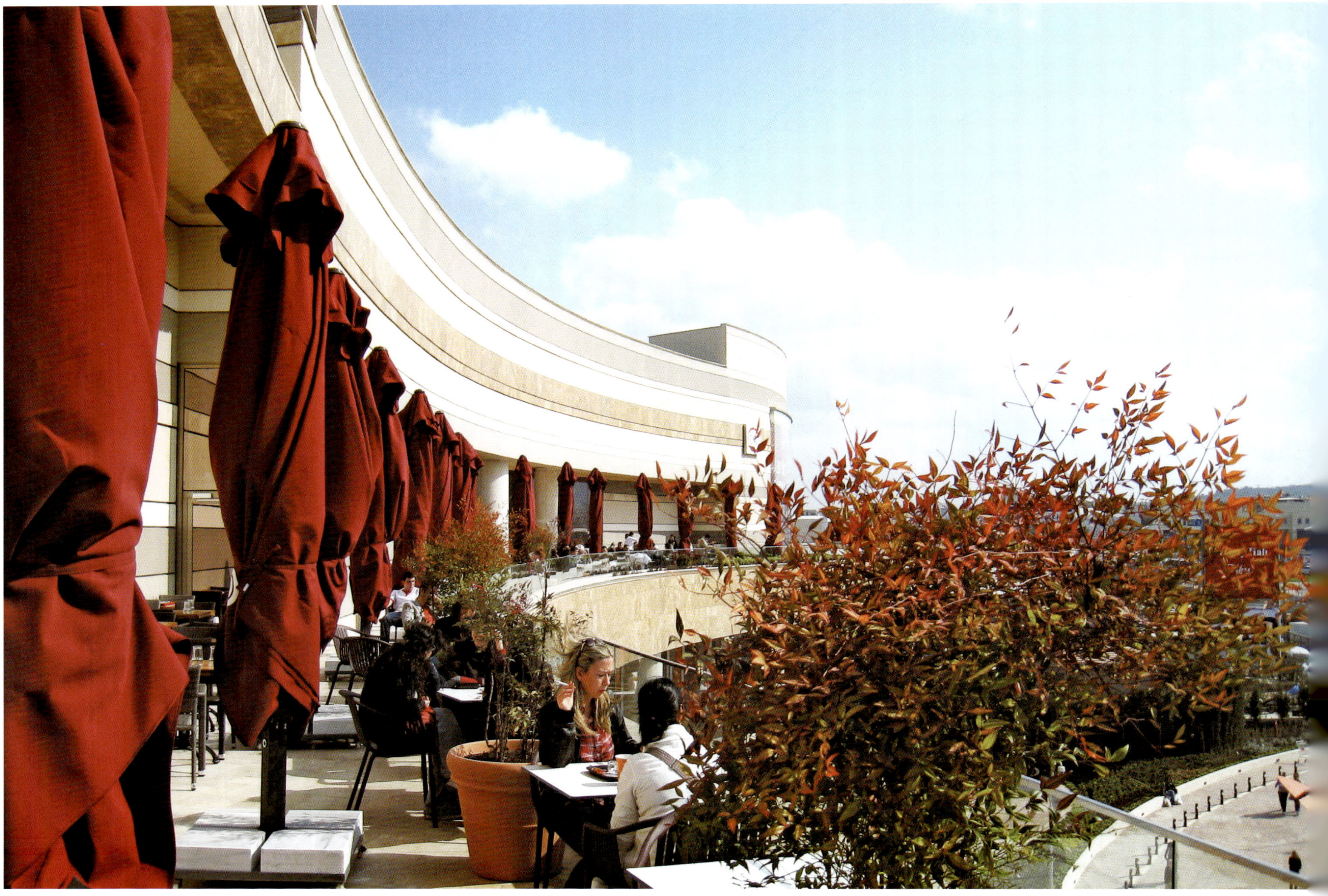

OUTLET STORE

LTB

Polen Tantuni

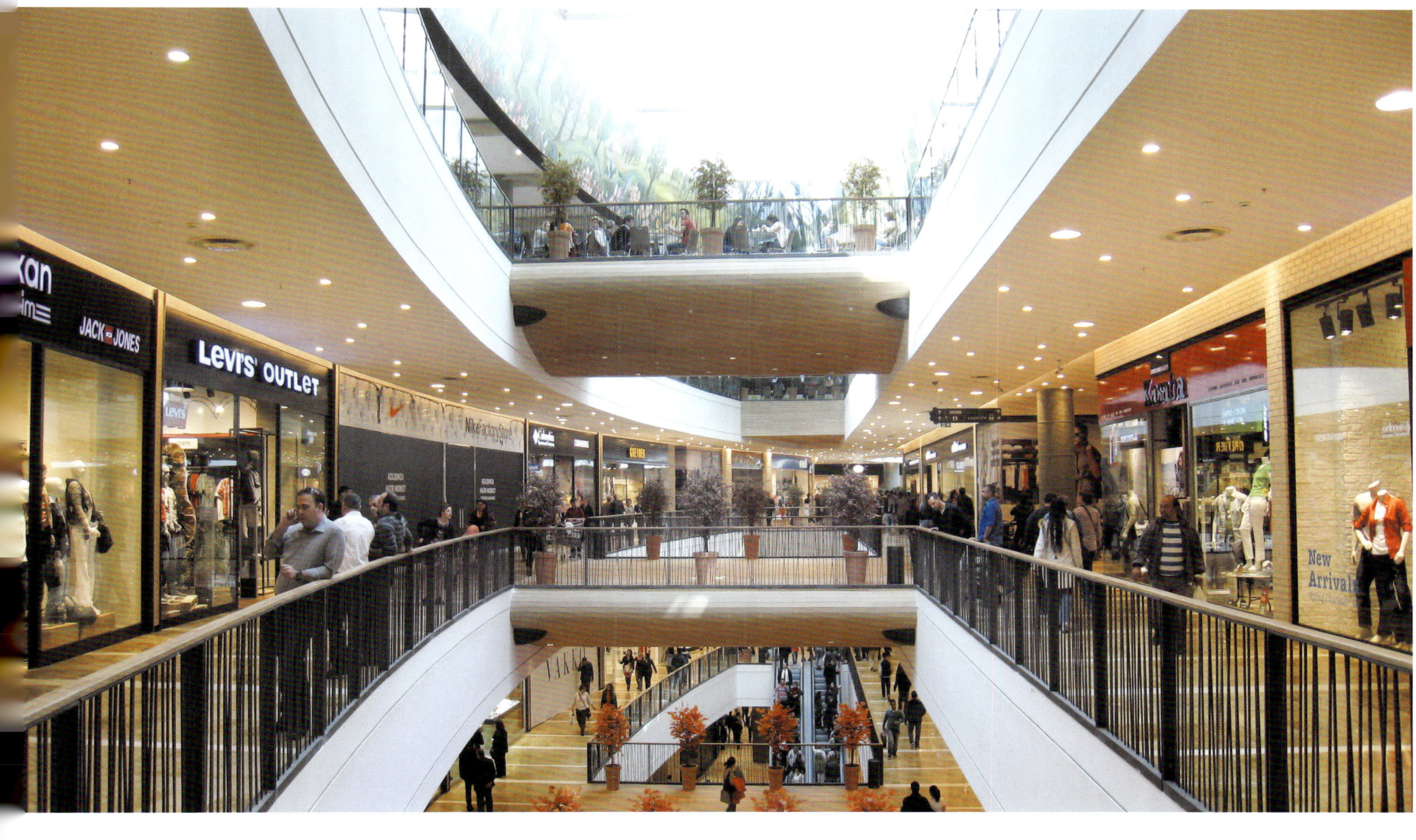

PROJECT NAME 项目名称

TURKEY PIAZZA MARAS

土耳其马拉什广场

Architect: 5+ design

设计公司：五杰建筑设计

PROJECT INFORMATION 项目信息

Client	Renaissance Development	**客户**	Renaissance Development
Site Area	36,000 m²	**占地面积**	36，000 平方米
Building Area	GBA-78,000 m²	**建筑面积**	GBA-78，000 平方米
Site Area	36,029 m²	**占地面积**	36，029 平方米
Gross Floor Area	105,772 m²	**总建筑面积**	105，772 平方米

OVERVIEW 项目概况

One of the most vital commercial and economic centers of Southeastern Turkey, Kahramanmaras has a deep cultural and historical background. Situated at the foothills of the Dibec Mountains, the region is known for its agriculture and spices; most famous for its creation of distinctive ice cream and rich architectural heritage and villages. Naturally, the commercial retail center of Maras Park is a landmark destination for the city and surrounding region. The site is located conveniently near the major ring road of Maras as well as the historic high street corridor of the city center.

作为土耳其东南部最为重要的商业和经济中心之一，卡赫拉曼马拉什拥有深厚的文化底蕴和历史背景。它位于迪北克山脉的丘陵地带，因农产品和香料而闻名于世；最为著名的还是本地制作的特色冰激凌、以及丰富多样的建筑遗产和村落。位于马拉什公园的这个商业中心自然而然地成为这所城市和周边地区的地标性目的地。它位置便利，毗邻马拉什的主环路和市中心的主干道。

BRIEF INTERVIEW 访谈录

ARCHITECT
Tim Thurik

设计师
Tim Thurik

HKASP: What was the main concept behind the whole project?

5+ design : Conceptually, the project required a sensitive and thoughtful design; one that fit within the overall fabric of the historic city but also reflected the contemporary "marketplace" atmosphere of the people of Kahramanmaras. The region is well known not only in Turkey but worldwide for its textiles and agriculture. The city has grown greatly so we wanted a project that reflected that market growth with a nod to the rich material history of the city.

HKASP: When designing, is there something in particular that you focus on? (Material, form, use etc.)

5+ design : The main objective was to create a warm and inviting shopping experience. The historic city center has a regional architectural style; timber balconies, stone arcades, and bay windows. The project references these local building forms and materials but assembles them in a more contemporary way. In many ways, the building is an informal yet contemporary collage of the warm materials and history of Maras. It was important to acknowledge the civic history and give the region a contemporary design. Integral to the design was to bring the outside inside for a holistic concept. Materials, patterns and elements from the facades are introduced to the interior atriums and passages. Filtered daylight, timber colonnades , and natural stone paving create an approachable and inviting experience; a new landmark for a historic city.

香港建筑科学出版社：整个项目的主要设计理念是什么？

五杰建筑设计：概念上，该项目要求设计能迎合周遭环境，能面面俱到。一则要求设计能与历史名城的肌理相匹配，二则要求设计能体现卡赫拉曼马拉什人民的时代意识与当代“商场”特质。该地区以其纺织业与农业不仅在土耳其乃至全世界都闻名遐迩。城市经历了巨大发展，所以我们希望该项目能体现市场的发展，肯定该座城市悠久的物质文明史。

香港建筑科学出版社：设计时，你有什么特别关注的地方吗？（比如，材料、形体、用途等等）

五杰建筑设计：该项目的主要目标就是打造一种温馨且充满吸引力的购物体验。历史名城中心具有显著的当地建筑风格，体现在木阳台、石拱廊以及飘窗。项目借鉴当地建筑形体与材料，再同时以一种当代的方式将这些元素揉捏于一体。通过许多方式，该建筑师表达了温馨感材料与马拉什历史的融合，散发出一种随性的当代气息。设计中，对城市历史给予敬意，注入当代气息非常重要。将建筑里外形成一个统一的整体是设计中不可分割的内容。将立面上呈现的材料、格局与元素沿用至建筑内部的大厅与各个走廊。柔和的日光、木质柱廊、自然石材铺装，这一切都营造出一种温馨、亲民的体验。已然一座历史名城的新地标。

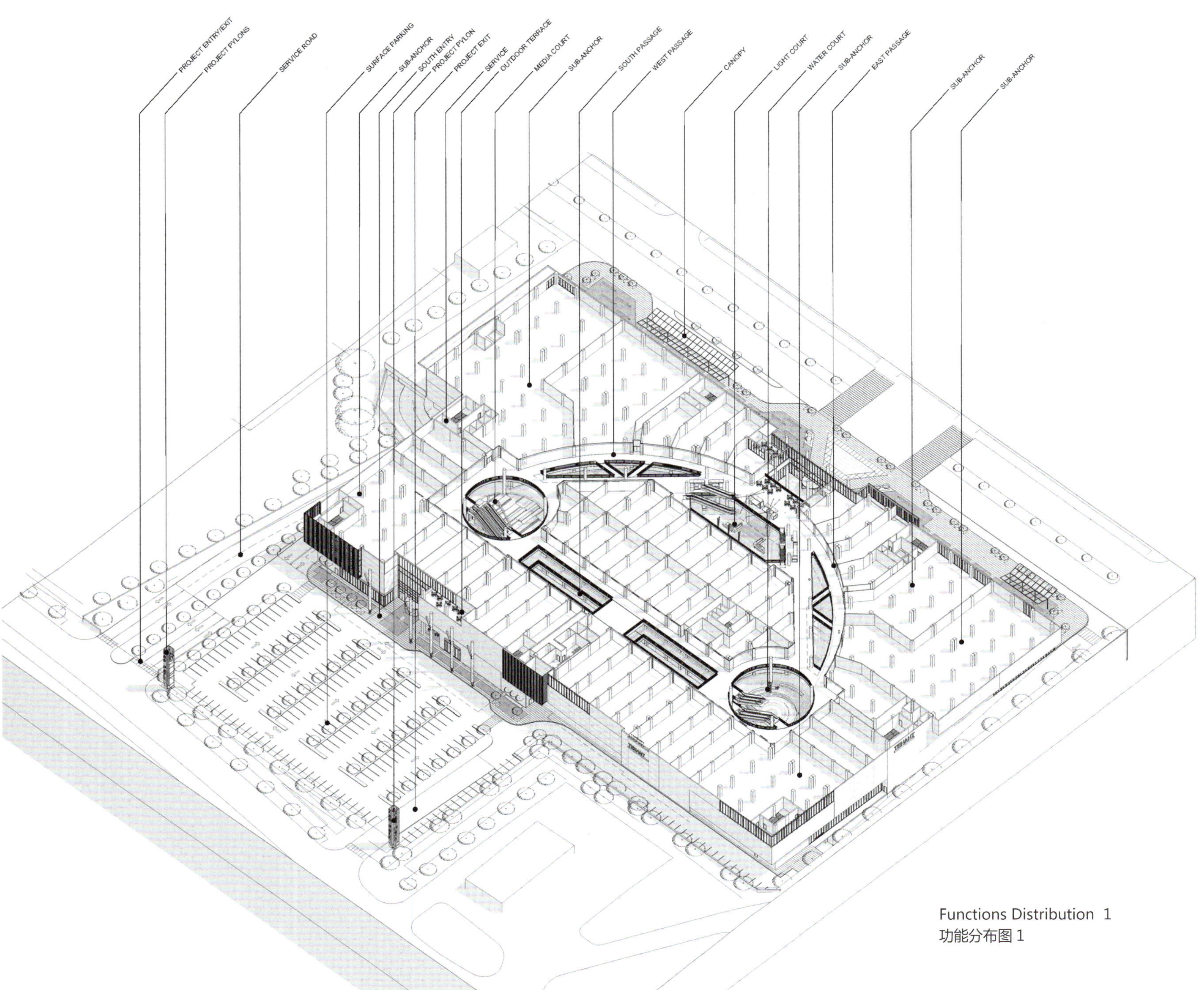

Functions Distribution 1
功能分布图 1

The overall design of the master plan is organized into a sequence of simple unique districts all connected via covered day lit passages. Combining a variety of shops, restaurants and entertainment offerings, the 4-level retail center provides a distinct shopping district for visitors currently not found in Maras. Lifestyle, fashion and homewares anchor each level of the project while the upper level is reserved for the restaurant and entertainment district. The top floor district, a primary destination for the center, is designed in grand scale with outdoor cafes, open kitchen concepts and dining terraces all under an expansive wood and glass skylight. A key element of the design, the undulating skylight opens to the sky above and captures multiple views to the North historic city center and to the Southern Dibec Mountains.

A unique feature of the project is the influence derived from local materials and ancient architecture. Incorporating local materials and textures, the design of building utilizes the vocabulary of the historical city but transforms it into a modern vocabulary. A combination of columned arcades, covered markets and bay windows are all combined in new ways. Timber columns, stone floors and modeled plaster walls create the texture of each space and surface. Each element referenced the historical Maras landscape but transforms the spaces and finishes into a new language. The project recognizes the long history and growth of Kahramnamaras, capturing the unique elements found throughout and incorporating them into a new destination for the city.

总体规划设计由一系列简洁独特的分区通过带顶棚的日光走廊相互连接而成。4 层商业中心由各种各样的店铺、餐厅和娱乐设施组成，为游客们提供马拉什独一无二的特色购物区。该项目各层分为生活用品、时尚用品和家居用品，而上层则留作餐厅和娱乐区。顶楼区是该中心的主要旅游目的地，巨大的木质玻璃天窗下设有大型室外咖啡馆、开放厨房概念区以及就餐露台。该设计的一大关键元素当属波浪形天窗，在此不仅可以抬头仰望辽阔的蓝天，还可捕捉到北部古老的市中心和南部迪贝克山脉的各色迷人风光。

该项目的一大特色就是吸取了当地的材料和古建筑风格。该建筑设计结合了当地材料与结构，吸取当地精华的同时更具现代气息。圆柱拱廊、棚内市场、凸窗都以现代方式结合在一起。木柱、石门和典型的灰泥墙构成了每个空间和装饰。每种元素都参照了马拉什的古老风格，同时通过改变空间和装饰，传递着一种新的语言。该项目颂扬了卡赫拉曼马拉什的悠久历史和长远发展，四处发现并捕捉独特的元素，将它们整合到一起从而形成了这所城市崭新的旅游胜地。

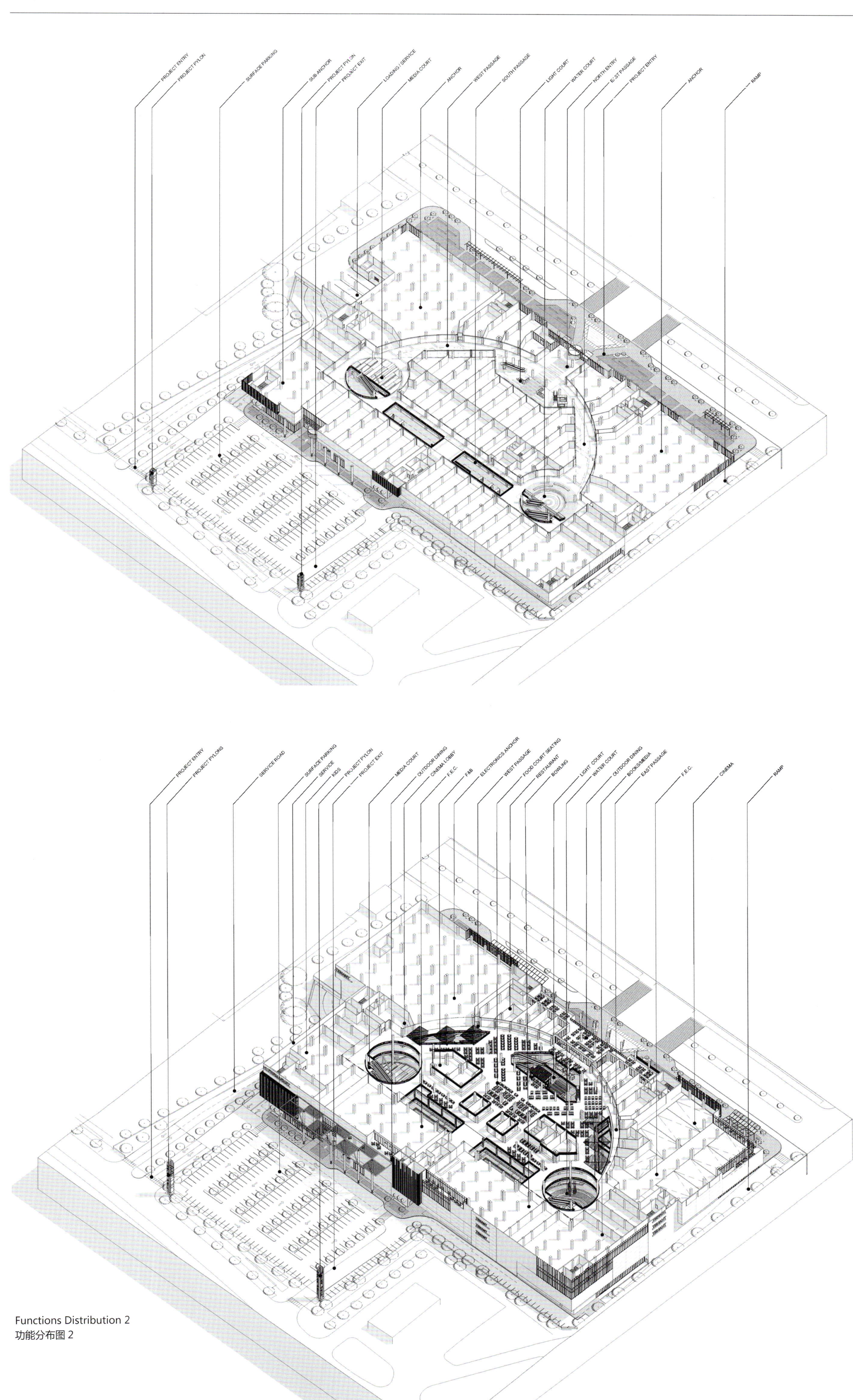

Functions Distribution 2
功能分布图 2

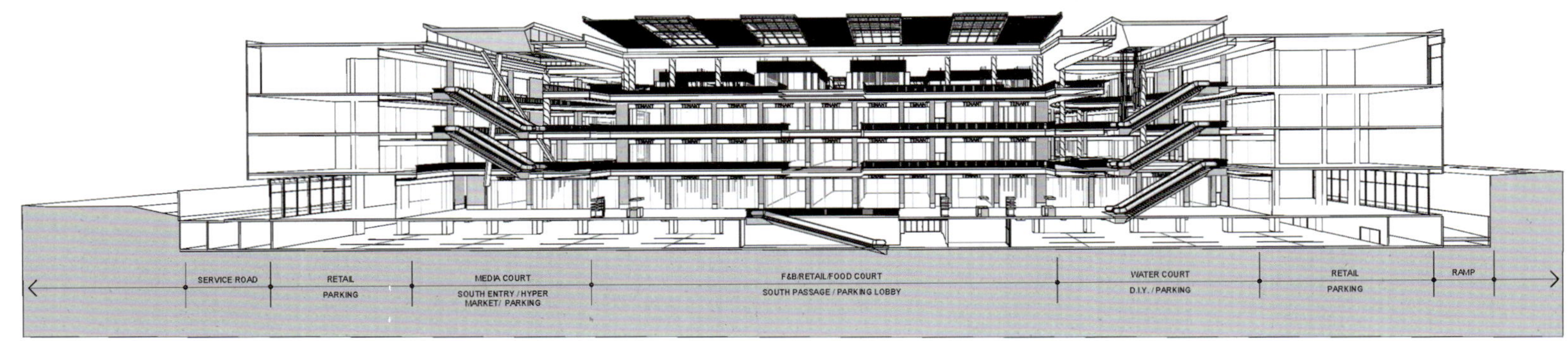

1 LONGITUDINAL SECTION @ SOUTH PASSAGE

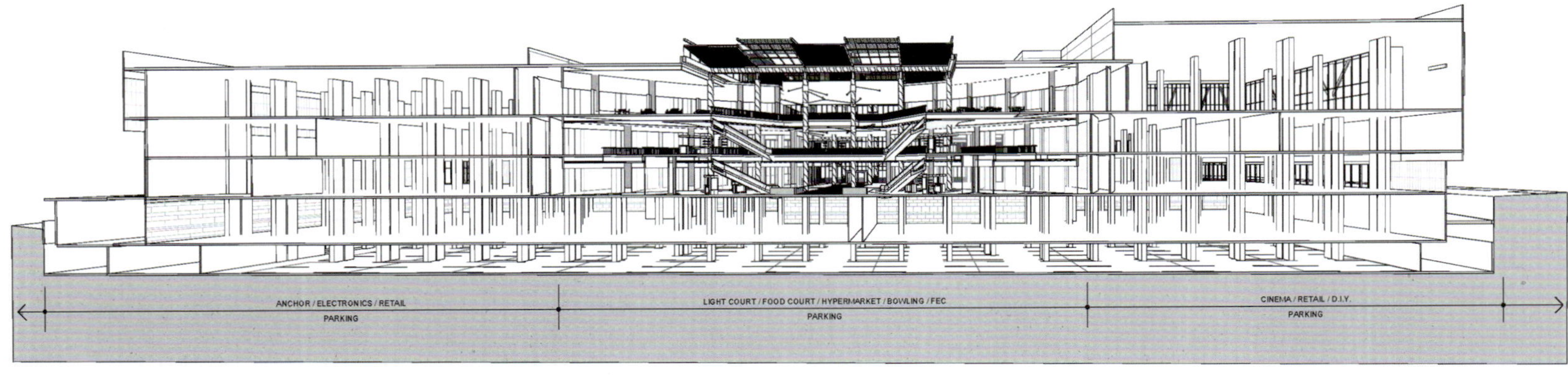

2 LONGITUDINAL SECTION @ GRAND COURT

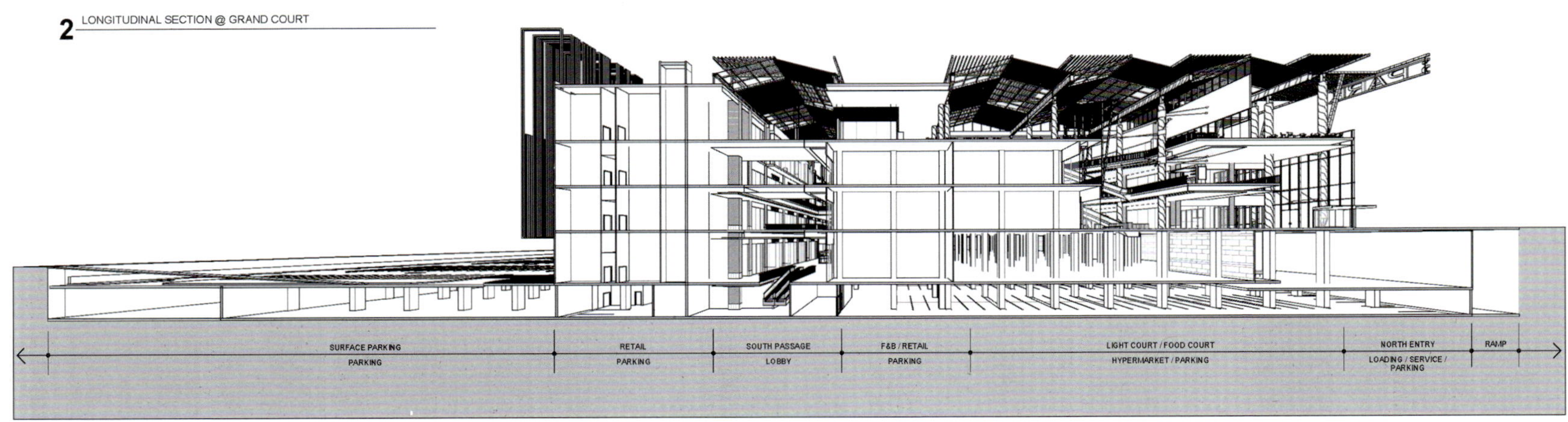

Elevation
立面图

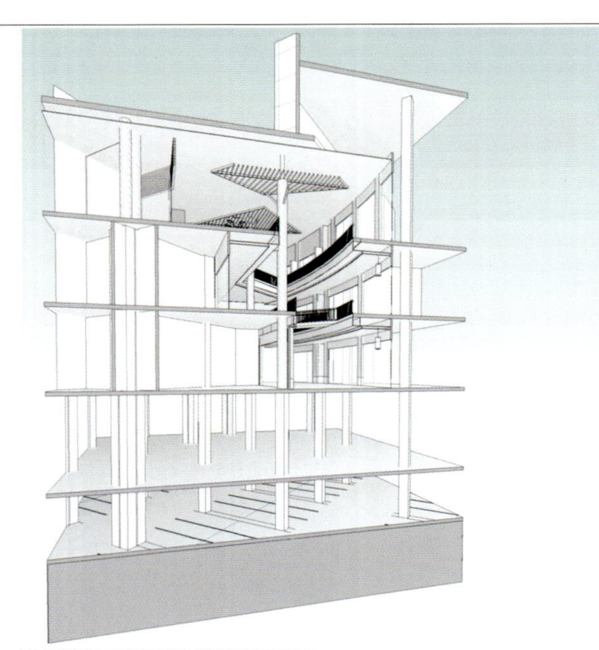

4 ENLARGED SECTION PERSPECTIVE @ EAST PASSAGE

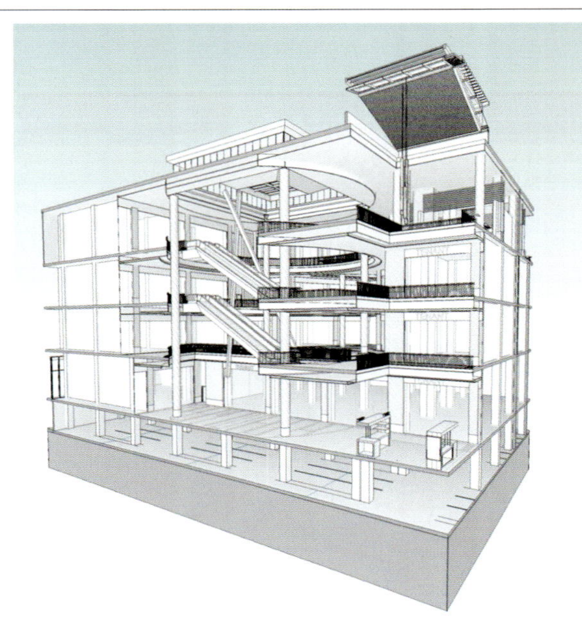

2 ENLARGED SECTION PERSPECTIVE @ MEDIA COURT

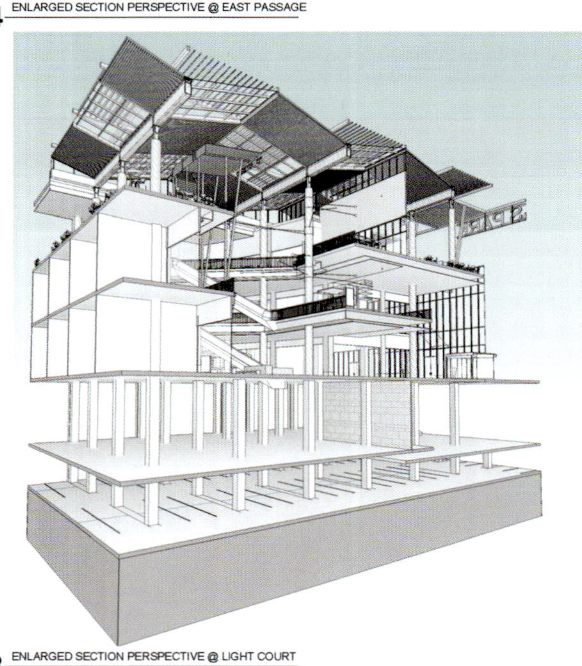

3 ENLARGED SECTION PERSPECTIVE @ LIGHT COURT

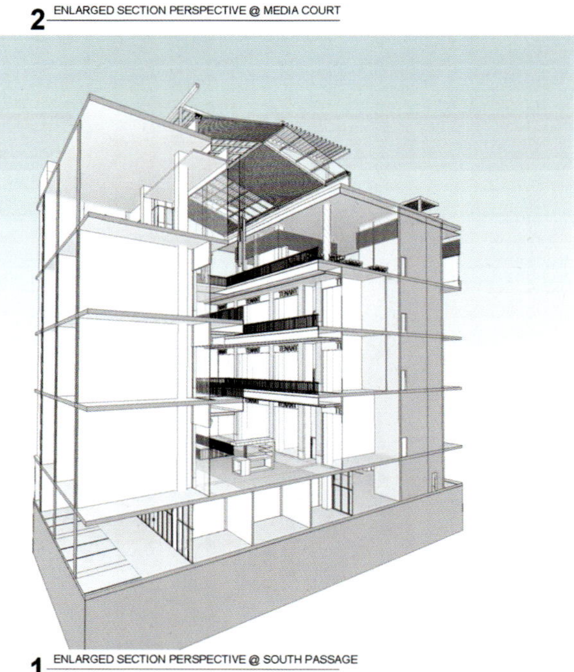

1 ENLARGED SECTION PERSPECTIVE @ SOUTH PASSAGE

Enlarged Section Perspective
放大的剖面透视图

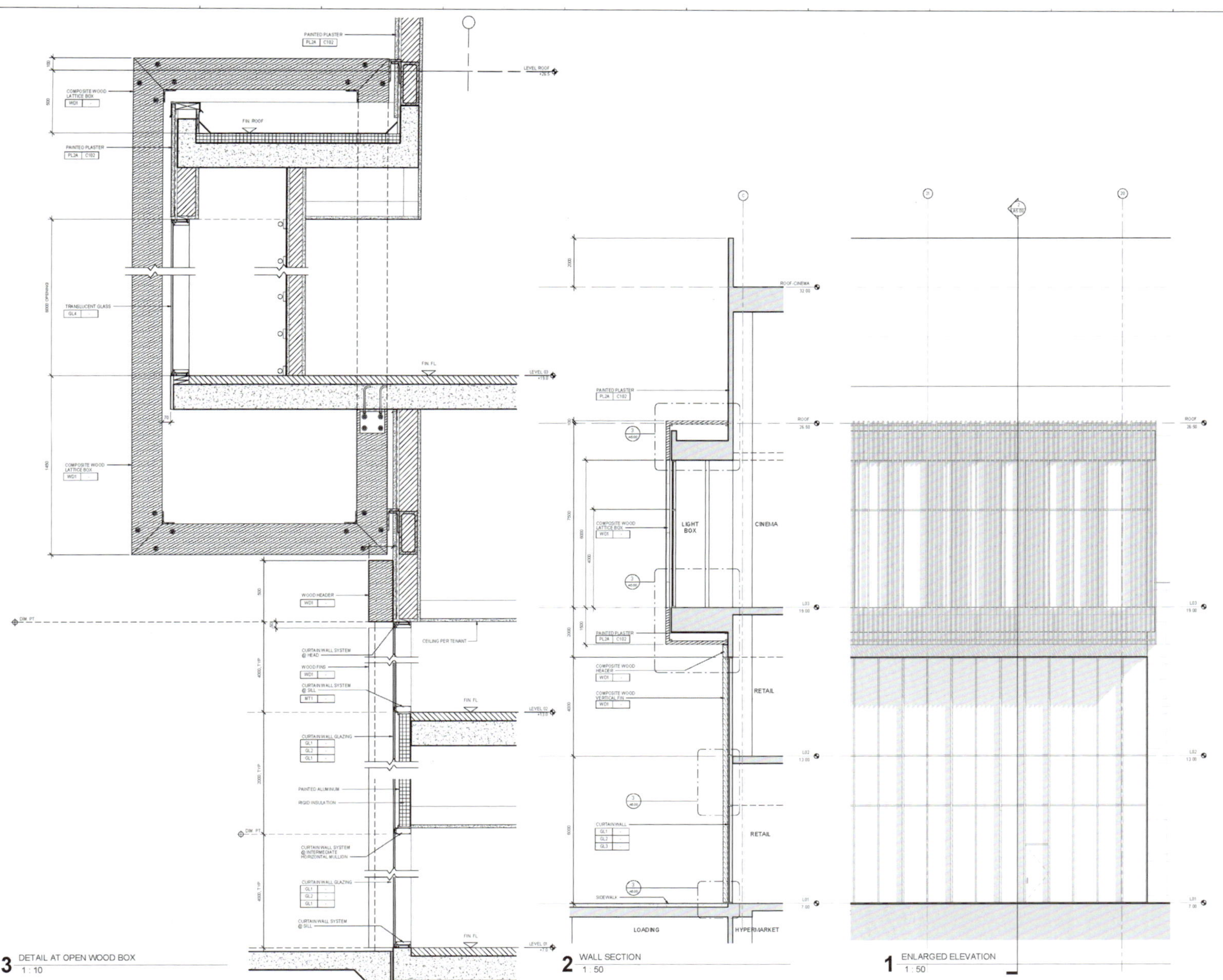

Partial Analysis 1
局部分析图 1

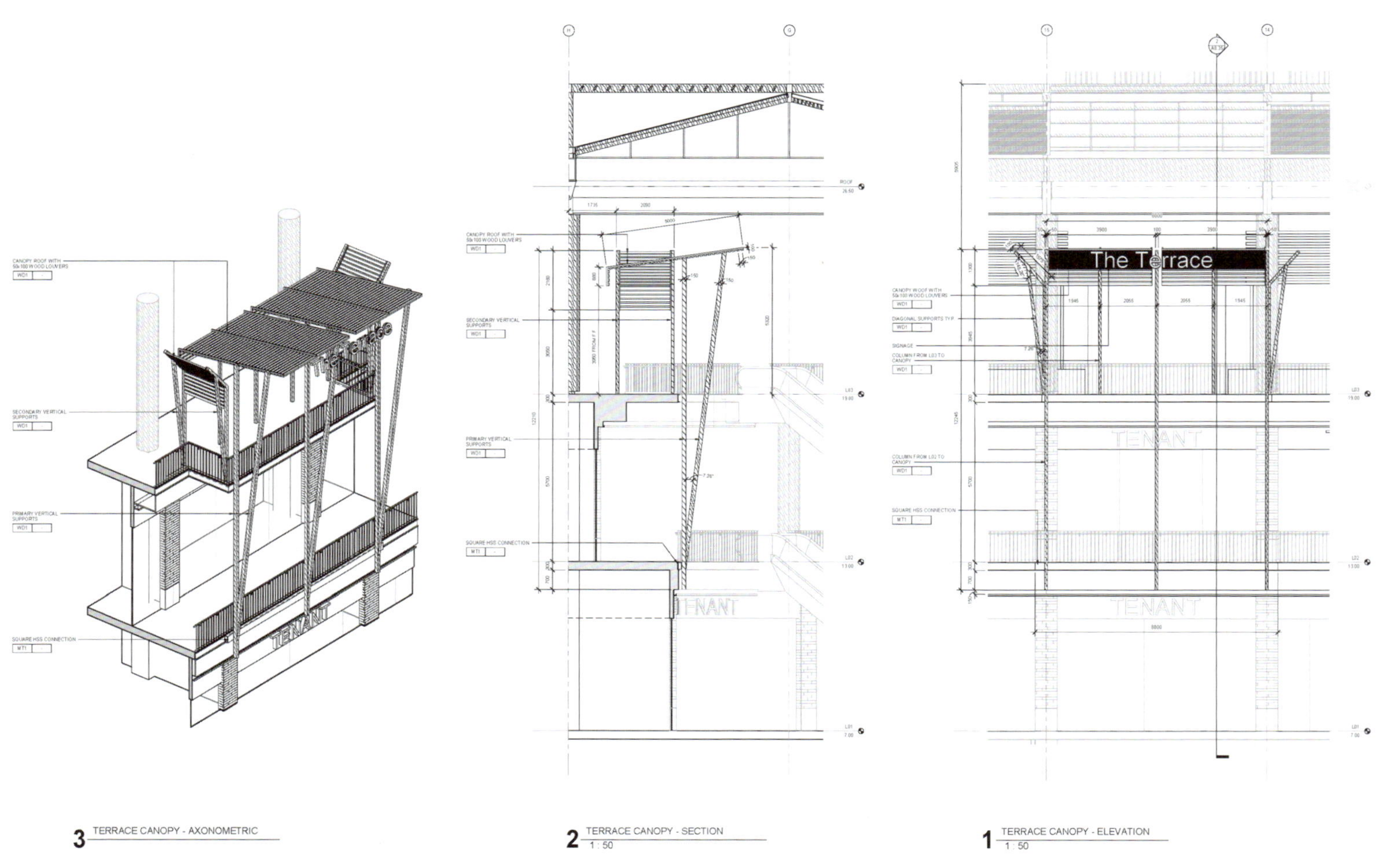

Partial Analysis 2
局部分析图 2

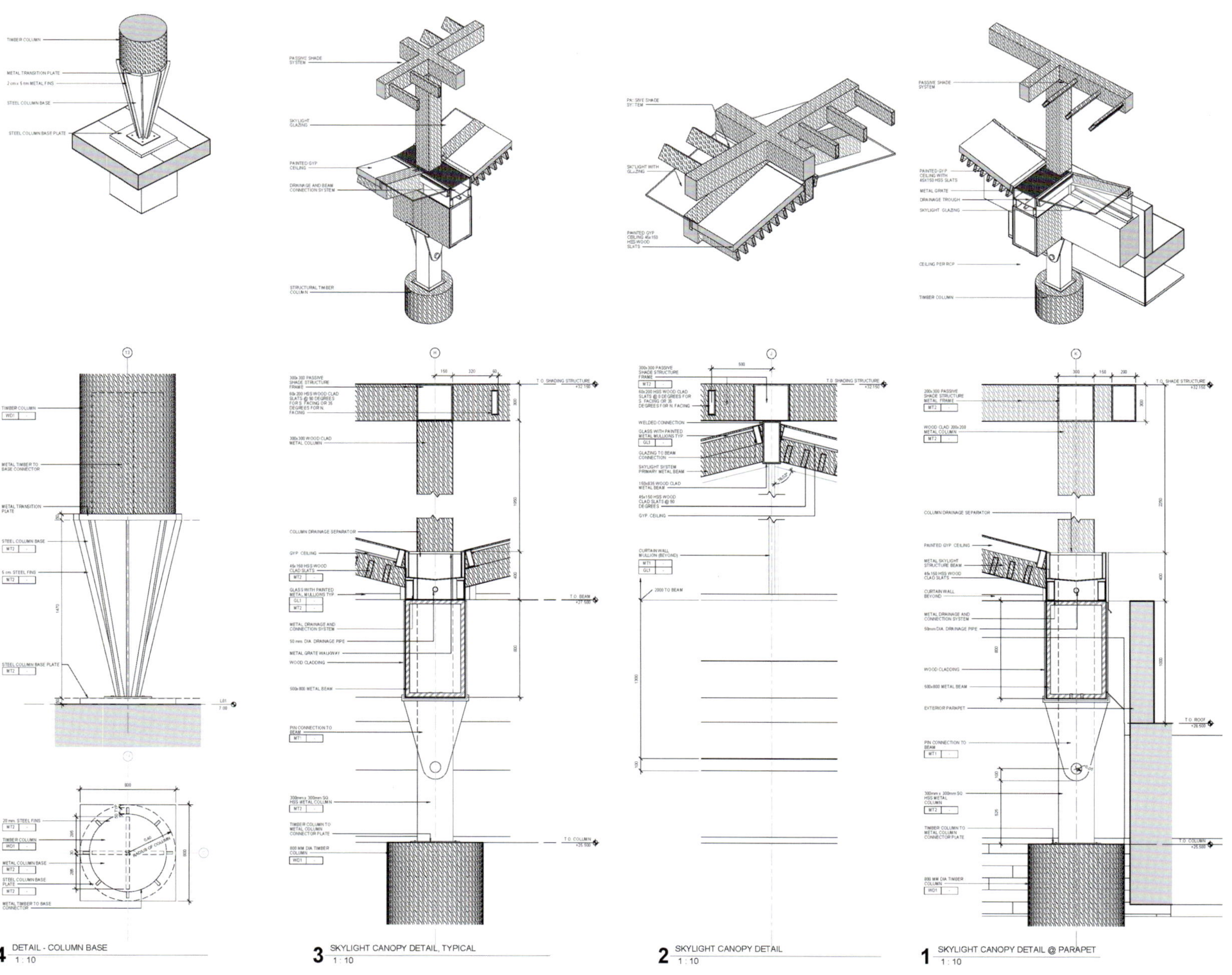

Partial Analysis 3
局部分析图 3

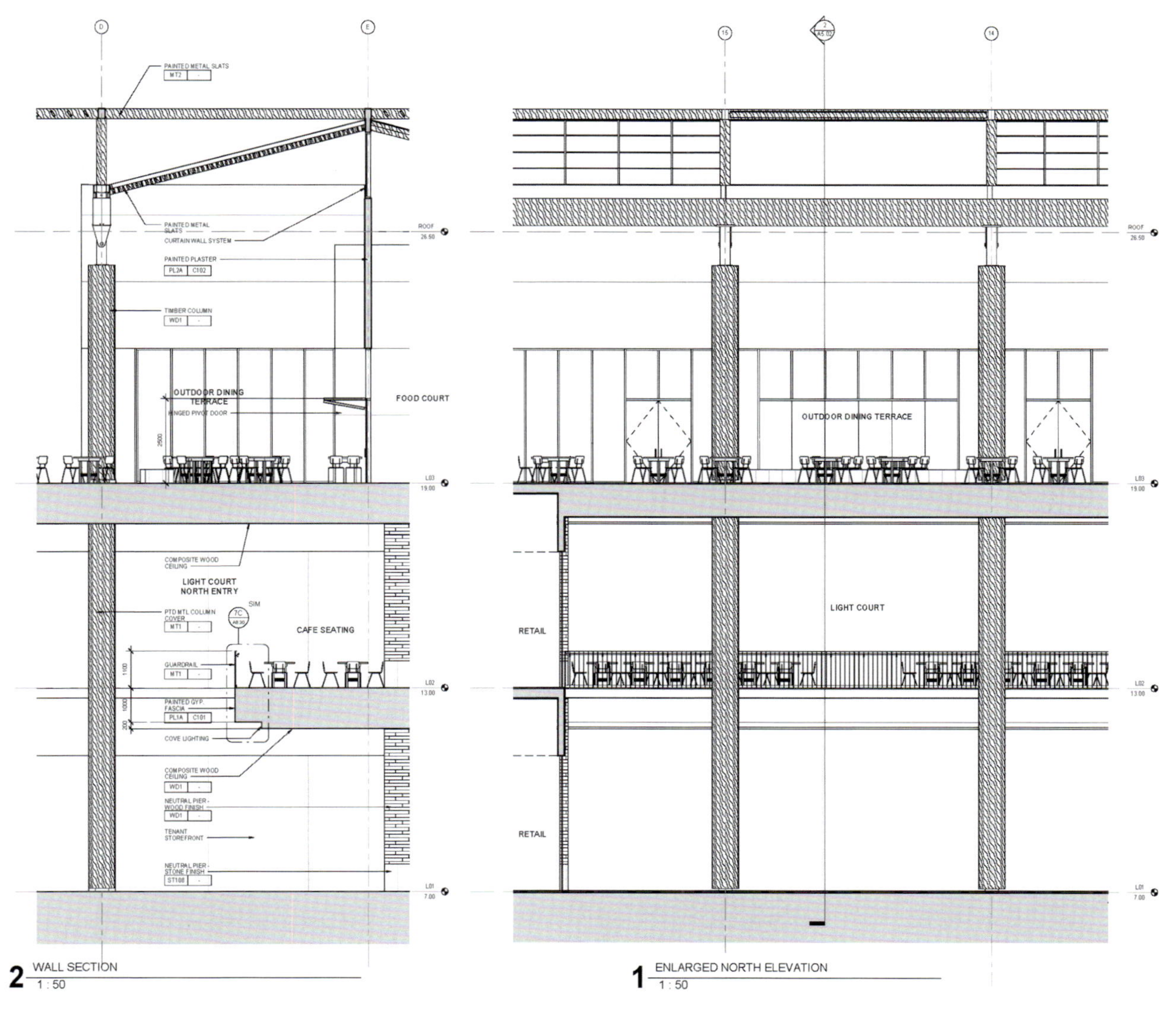

Partial Analysis 4
局部分析图 4

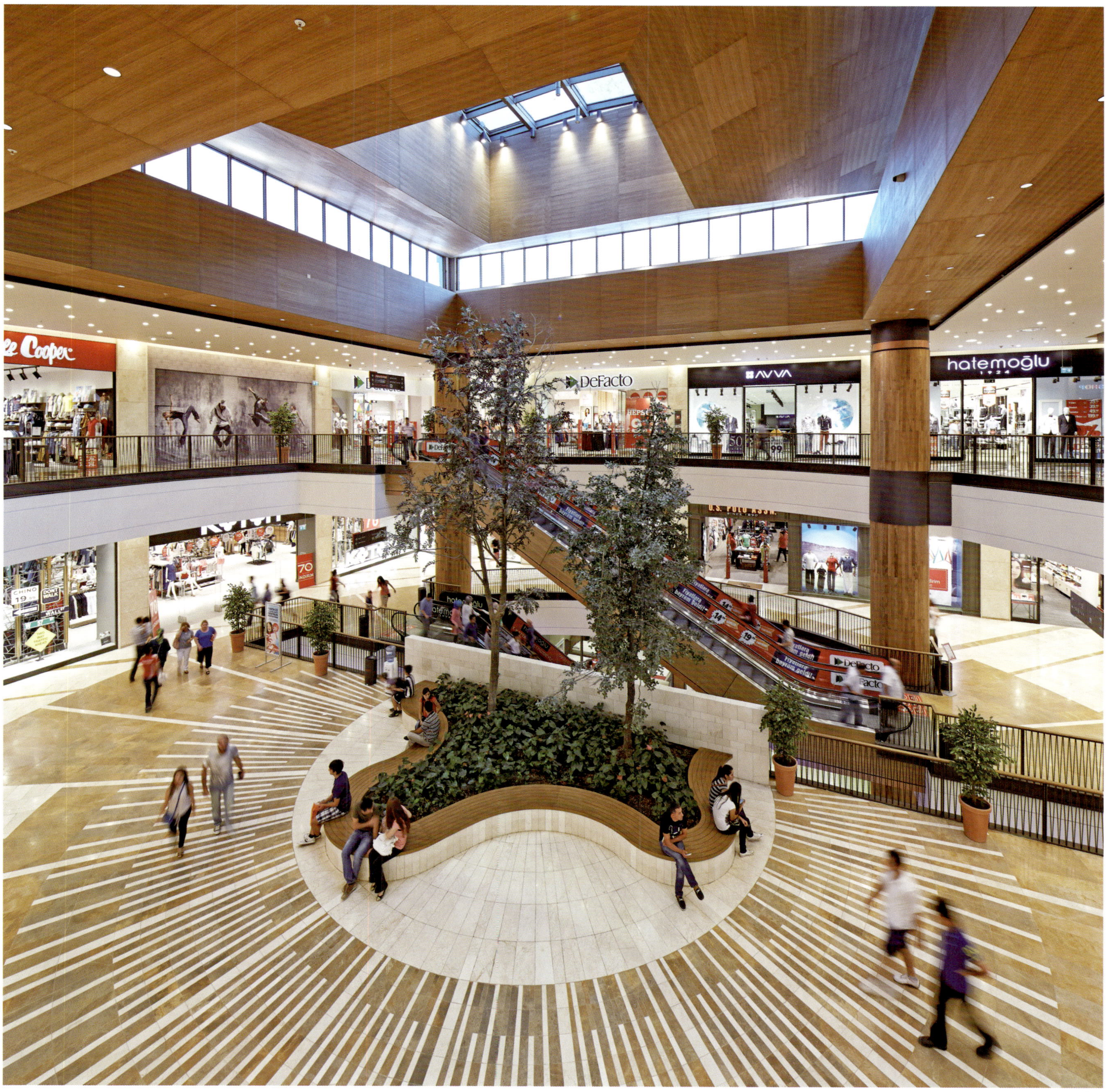
DeFacto
AVVA
hatemoğlu

PUMA
KIĞILI
SARAR

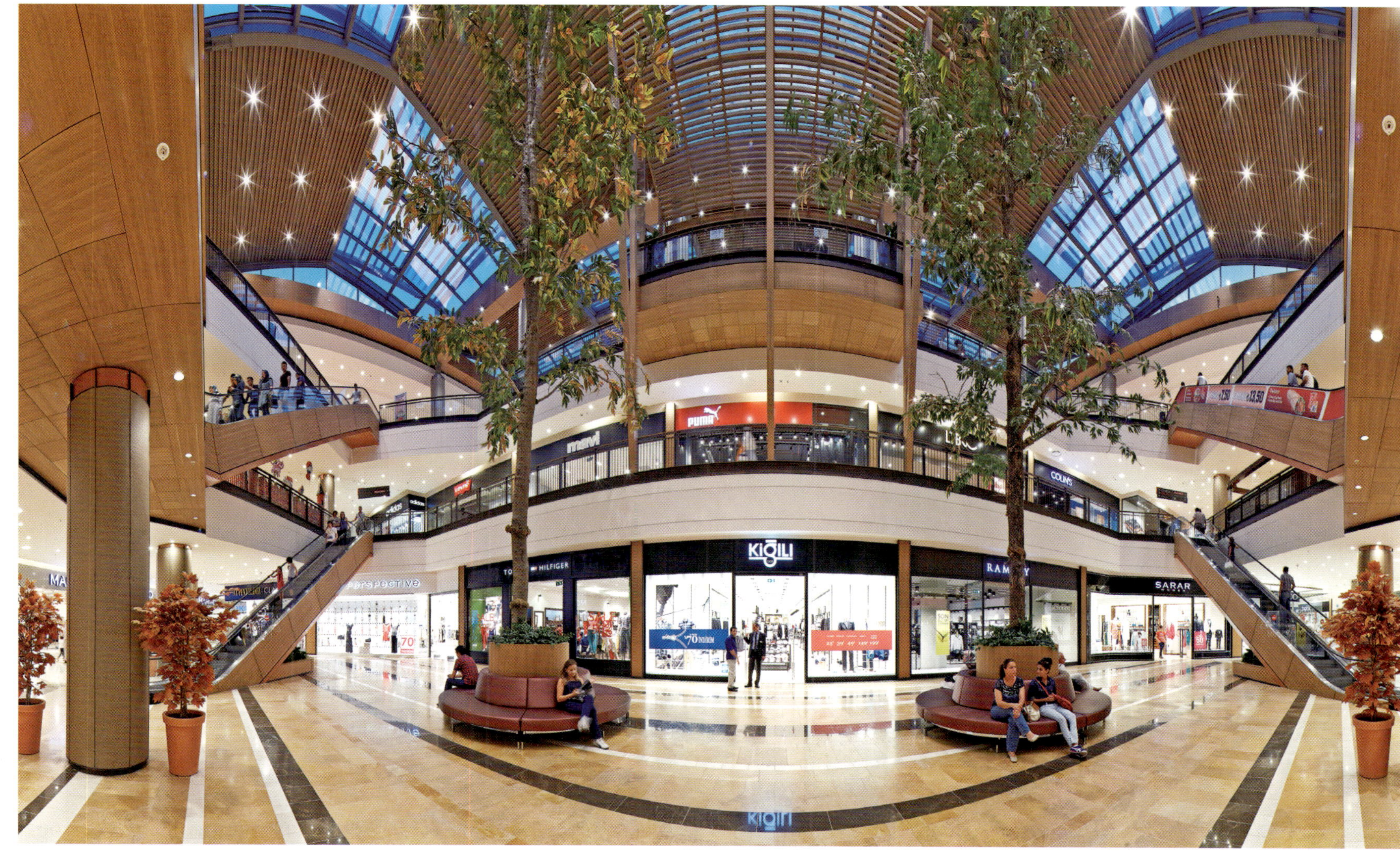

PROJECT NAME 项目名称

CRYSTAL DESIGN CENTRE, BANGKOK, THAILAND

泰国水晶设计中心

Architect: DWP

设计公司：DWP

PROJECT INFORMATION 项目信息

Location	Bangkok, Thailand	**地点**	Bangkok, Thailand
Area	4,830 m²	**面积**	4,830 平方米

OVERVIEW 项目概况

The Crystal Design Centre is a new lifestyle concept and creative hub that combines entertainment with the latest design trends from around the world. This creative centre, designed by world-class architecture and interior design firm dwp (design worldwide partnership) sets the benchmark for Asia's creative industry. dwp tackled, head on, the unique challenge of creating a facility that lastingly enhances design products and services housed within the centre, yet not overtly compete with them.

水晶设计中心是一个新的生活概念和创意中心，结合了娱乐与来自世界各地的最新的设计趋势。这个创意中心，由世界一流的建筑和室内设计公司 dwp 担纲设计，为亚洲创意产业奠定了基准。dwp 正面应对创建一个持久提高产品设计和服务设施独有的挑战，但不与他们公开竞争。

BRIEF INTERVIEW 访谈录

ARCHITECTS
dwp / design
worldwide partnership

设计公司
dwp / design
worldwide partnership

HKASP: How does the concept of "Design Center" come? Is there any interaction between architects and the client about the project vision?

dwp: dwp created the architecture and interior design for the Phase 1 Building E only, and created the masterplanning and architecture for whole of Phase 2, for the Crystal Design Centre. The idea was to carry through the architecture in a similar language for the whole complex, created by the main architect for the original Phase 1 structures, to ensure consistency, but with a high degree of functionality and aesthetics, as a striking focus point.

The client vision for a project is always very important to dwp, as well as the function and flow, circulating through the facility. Dwp's approach to every project is a collaborative one. The spaces needed to reflect a creative hub environment for the city's creative and aspiring minds to meet, research, collaborate, shop and share.

HKASP: How did you manipulate the architecture form with the concept of "Design Center"? Anything in particular you focus on?

dwp: In phase two, the shape of the layout represents a bird's wings. This form is clearly visible from the third floor of building E. This phase of the project also needed a high degree of functionality and good circulation, to ensure maximum accessibility.

HKASP: What are the important things that this project does for the city?

dwp: The Crystal Design Centre (or CDC) is for Bangkok the ultimate design lifestyle district, and the first of its kind in Thailand. It is a complete creative hub and resource for design, retail, education and entertainment. It is currently is the most comprehensive and integrated design centre in Asia, showcasing architectural, interior, decorating and construction products. CDC facilities include product showrooms, an Architecture & Decorative Resource Centre, exhibition and conference facilities, a business lounge, design library, office.

香港建筑科学出版社："设计中心"理念如何得来？建筑事务所和客户就项目愿景进行过相关交流吗？

DWP：Dwp 建筑事务所主要致力于水晶设计中心 Building E 一期的建筑与室内设计，二期工程的总体规划及设计。其理念延续着一期工程骨干建筑师的思路，贯彻在整个建筑群中，不失偏颇。这不仅确保了建筑群之间的相容性，保证了其高功能性，连同美感也未失却，确实引人注目。Dwp 既关注客户的项目愿景，也会考虑到设施功能及便利性，每个细节都至关重要。它每个项目的成功都是合作的成果，也希望同各方携手合作，满足大家共同的需求。那些极富创意的有志者可以来到这里举办会谈，进行研究，协商合作，购物及分享彼此的想法，这里会给他们提供创意性的环境，是他们可以停留的港湾。

香港建筑科学出版社：你们如何通过"设计中心"理念对建筑形式进行巧妙处理？

DWP：在二期工程中，布局规划整体呈现鸟翼状。这在 Building E 三楼显而易见。该项目也需要实现高度功能化及高效流通量以保证流通的最大化。（欲知详情，请参见工程表二期工程）

香港建筑科学出版社：该项目为城市带来何益处？

DWP：水晶设计中心坐落在曼谷，堪称终极生活区设计。该建筑第一次亮相泰国，锋芒毕露。它是一座完备的创意中心，不仅是创作的源泉，也提供零售，教育，休闲服务。在亚洲，目前它算是最全面的设计中心，展示着独特的建筑理念，精美的装饰及建筑产品。水晶设计中心包括产品展厅、建筑及装饰资源中心、展览及会议设施、休息室、设计库及办公区等。

CDC

Site Plan
总平面图

Roof Plan
屋顶平面图

dwp achieved this balance via true design excellence with spaces transformed through the use of organic shapes, specialist lighting, and the use of recognized signature design products. The resulting organic structure extrudes from first floor through three levels to plateau at the centre's apex, where luxurious lounges, ballrooms, meeting rooms and a library are all located. The continuous and amorphous nature of the centre's core is carried through to the intricately designed library and each of the eight meeting rooms, where walls and ceilings curve and flow in one fluid form.

Building on the success of the first phase of this landmark design centre, in Thailand's capital, world-class architecture and interior firm dwp further developed the master plan for a 32,000m² extension.

dwp 通过真正的卓越设计将有机形态的空间，专业的照明设计以及个性化的标识设计相平衡得出一个从一楼到三层顶点通告的有机构筑物。其中设有豪华的休息室，宴会厅，会议室和一个图书馆。连续和无定形自然中心的核心是通过精心设计的图书馆和每八个会议室中的任何一个表现出来，它们的墙壁和天花板弯曲下来，如同流入到一个流体形式。

第一阶段的成功使得业主希望二期发展为一个 32,000 平方米的扩建总体规划。

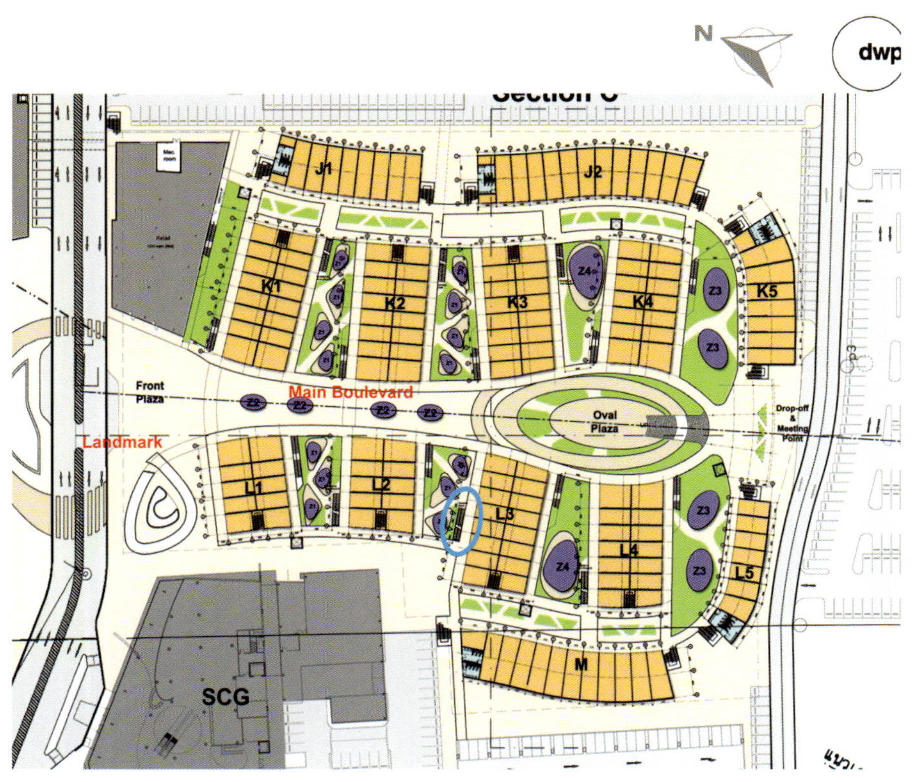

Ground Floor Plan
一层平面图

Floor Plan
楼层平面图

Floor Pattern For Construction
楼层施工结构图

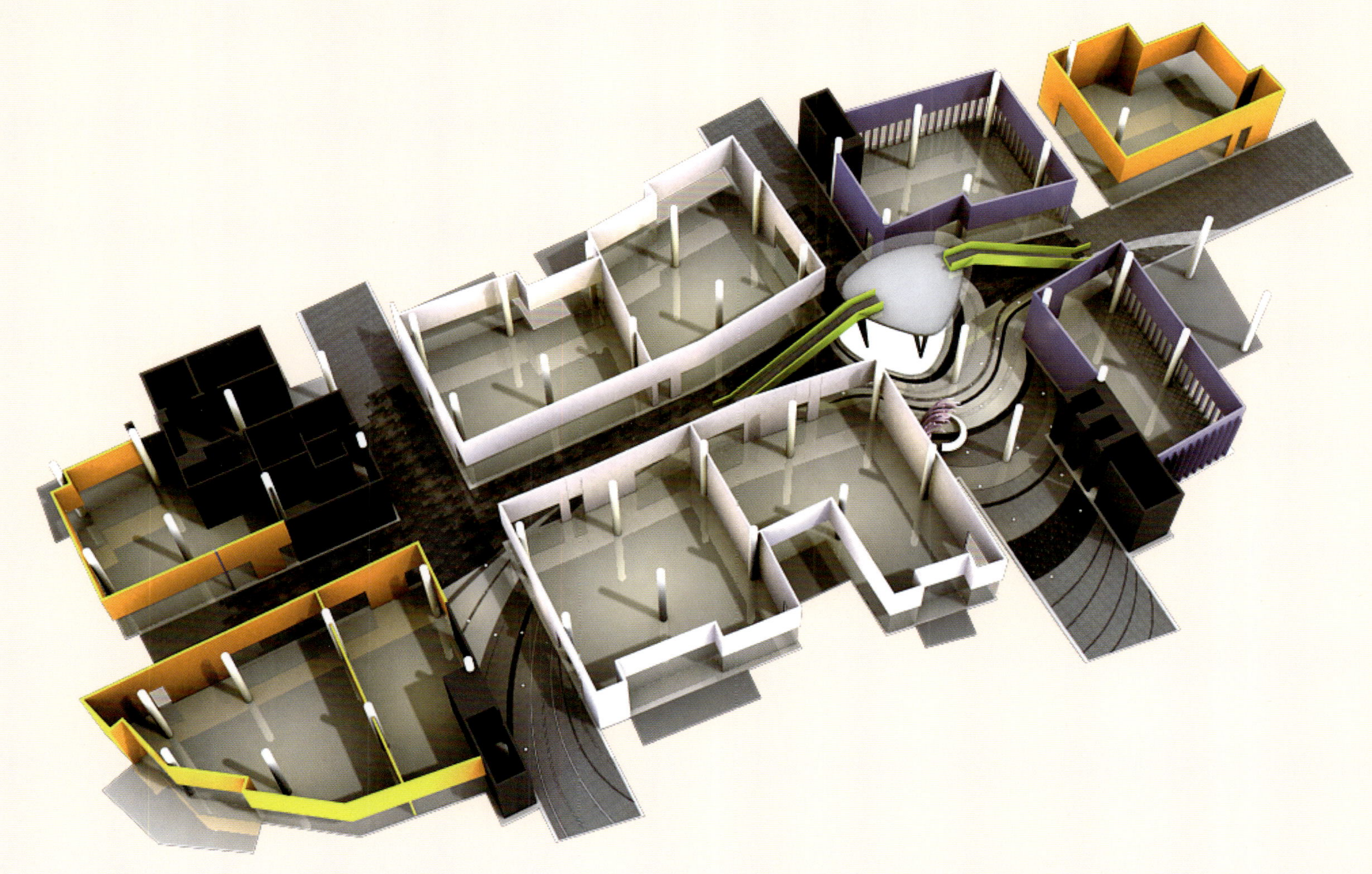

Comprising multiple two-storey units that house small- and medium-sized retail outlets, the design ties together 14 buildings through a series of walkways, bridges and integrated graphics. A central elliptical plaza offers a prime location for events and special activities, as well as an extraordinary view over the Crystal Design Centre Phase 1, also designed by dwp.

通过一系列的人行道，桥梁联系起来一系列小型和中型零售点和 14 幢楼宇。中央椭圆形广场提供了一个优越的地理位置来举行各种公共活动，从中也可以看到 dwp 设计的水晶设计中心一期的美景。

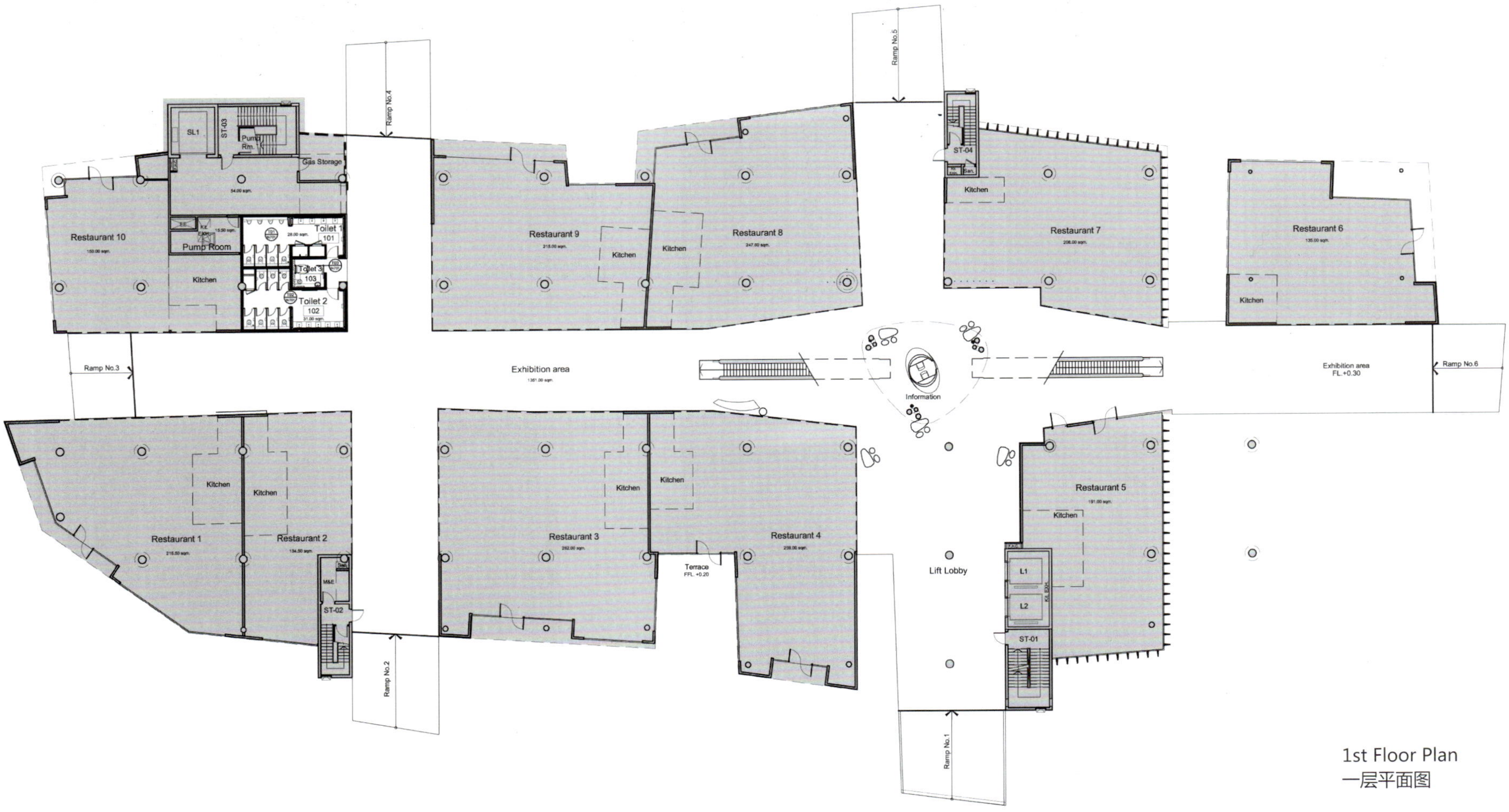

1st Floor Plan
一层平面图

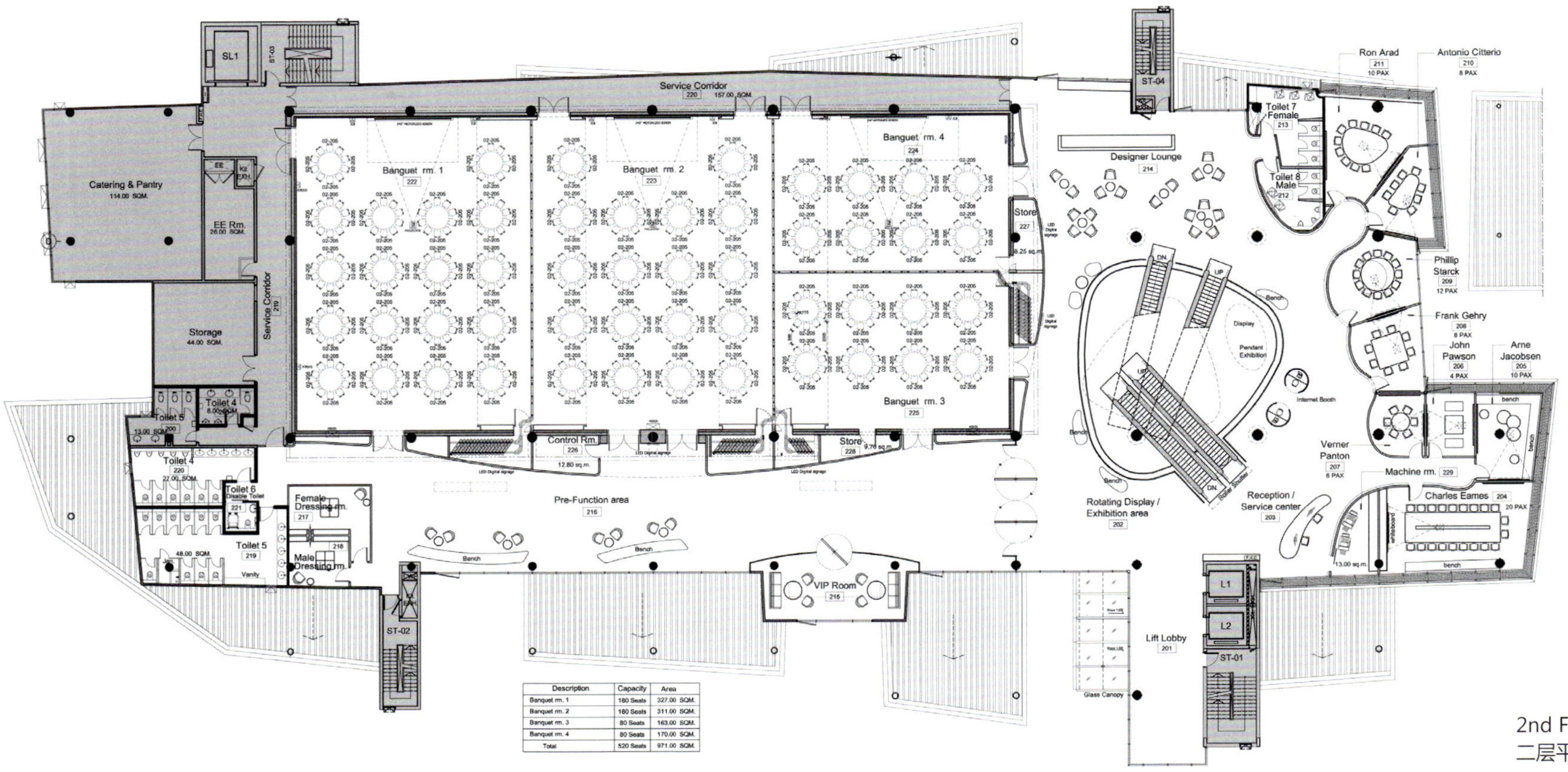

Description	Capacity	Area
Banquet rm. 1	180 Seats	327.00 SQM.
Banquet rm. 2	180 Seats	311.00 SQM.
Banquet rm. 3	80 Seats	163.00 SQM.
Banquet rm. 4	80 Seats	170.00 SQM.
Total	520 Seats	971.00 SQM.

2nd Floor Plan
二层平面图

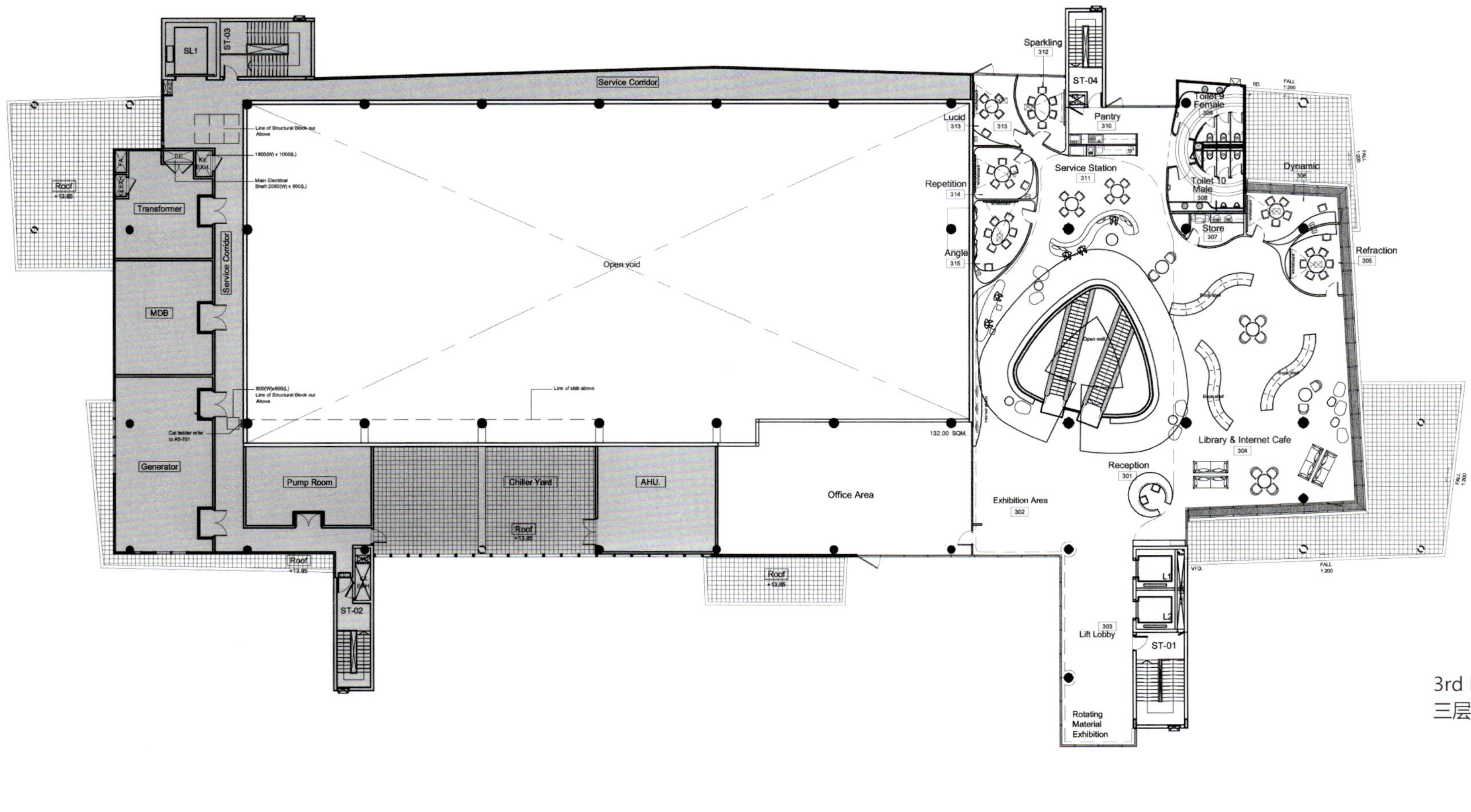

3rd Floor Plan
三层平面图

IWISH

กาแฟ
สด

PP
BY STUDIO 128

Sketch
草图

Between the buildings, a courtyard cleverly clusters a group of small kiosks. The central boulevard of the Phase 2 master plan intentionally continues the main axis from Phase 1, creating a spatial connection between the two. The contemporary design of this educational precinct ensures the Crystal Design Centre's position, as a benchmark for learning and creative facilities, throughout Asia.

Key design leaders have also been acknowledged, within the design, with iconic furniture and styling defining different areas. This permits CDC users to choose their preferred location to work or congregate in, so as to feel the direct impact design can have on any space.

建筑物之间庭院布置了一系列的售货亭。二期总体规划的中央大道有意延续了第一阶段的主轴线，形成两者之间的空间联系。现代化的设计保证了水晶设计中心的地位，使其成为整个亚洲的一个设计创造的核心。

设计的领导者也已经认为，在设计中家具和风格界定不同的区域。这允许 CDC 用户选择自己喜欢的位置工作或者交流。这体现着设计可以在任意地方进行的原则。

PROJECT NAME 项目名称

FOSHAN POLY CANAL CITY

佛山南海保利水城

Architect: GLC

设计公司：杰奥斯建筑设计

PROJECT INFORMATION 项目信息

Client	Poly Group	**客户**	保利集团
Location	Nanhai,Foshan	**地点**	佛山南海
Project Type	Large-Scale Commercial	**项目性质**	大型商业综合体
Building Area	180,000m²	**总建筑面积**	约 180,000 平方米

OVERVIEW 项目概况

The total construction area are 265,000 m², of which the shopping center on the ground are about 100,000 m², in which the retail, leisure, entertainment, life experience are integrated in one commercial complex in east bank; the commercial street of customs and habits on the ground are about 58,000 square meters in west bank, that would be on sale overall.

项目总建筑面积 26.5 万平方米，其中东岸大型购物中心地上约 10 万平方米，集零售、休闲、娱乐、生活体验一体的综合性商业综合体；西岸为风情商业街区，地上约 5.8 万平方米，整体销售。

BRIEF INTERVIEW 访谈录

ARCHITECT

设计师
曾捷

HKASP: Why the project scheme focuses on the element of water?

GLC: Poly Water City takes full account of its own advantage to use the "water" element in a scientific and reasonable way. As this project has the wonderful nature landscape resource - Qiandeng Lake, GLS takes "water" as the project theme, the design concept combines the business needs and "Lingnan Water Village" culture, striving to keep the nature feature of water system of Qiandeng Lake. The planning design adopts the modern commercial architecture design technique to dig out the business feature and brand character of Qiandeng Lake water system, the nature landscape and commercial operation are combined organically here to create the core competitiveness of Water City.

HKASP: What kind of characteristic makes this commercial project different from other projects?

GLC: It should be the commercial layout of "one river and two banks". Poly Water City is divided into eastern square and west street by the Qiandeng Lake canal, two sections are linked by two bridges crossing on the canal, forming a sense of wholeness. The west bank adopts the model of full sales as it is far away from the east bank, but two sections have flexible relationship, so the bad management of west street will not affect the business of eastern square largely.

Meanwhile, eastern square and west street choose complementary commercial types.The eastern square is a full-stop shopping center features shopping, dining, leisure and entertainment while the west street takes priority of characteristic businesses and promotes the night life leisure culture to create the best organized night street with dining, entertainment and leisure functions in Foshan.

HKASP: What is the most crucial point for the successful commercial project?

GLC: The appropriate commercial orientation is the most important factor in the development process of successful project. It could say that the project will lack the congenital advantages without correct commercial orientation. After the research and analysis in the phase of orientation, selling the property in a reasonable way could balance the development fund investment, but the most important one should be the forward-looking orientation. The scientific and proper adjustment and innovation in the post phase continuously meet the needs of business development for commercial project and dig out the self advantages to meet needs of investors, operators and consumers, which improves the project's business value as well as to acquire the biggest benefit.

Professional company that familiar with the business could help to guide the development process. After the deep understanding of market and combination of development trend for while business, the planning takes full account of existing and future commercial needs, providing the accurate market orientation, layout planning for this project after full analysis, helping owners to avoid investment risks by offering the investment basis.

香港建筑科学出版社：方案为什么强调＂水＂这个元素？

杰奥斯建筑设计："水"元素是保利水城项目对于自身的优势最为科学合理的应用。保利水城拥有千灯湖这份先天的自然景观资源，GLC 将"水"作为主题，结合商业需求与佛山"岭南水乡"文化为概念，在规划设计上力求保留千灯湖水系的自然特色，通过现代商业建筑设计手法，充分挖掘千灯湖水系的商业特质与品牌个性，将自然景观与商业经营有机结合，形成水城的核心竞争力。

香港建筑科学出版社：这个商业项目有别于其他一般商业项目的特点是什么？

杰奥斯建筑设计："一河两岸"的商业布局。千灯湖运河将保利水城分割成了东广场与西街两个部分，通过两条横跨运河河面的小桥相连，使两部分维持着一种"整体"关系，由于东西岸从地块条件上相隔一定距离，西街采取了全销售的模式，在经营和运作上东广场和西街是一种可分可合的状态，所以能最大程度地降低"一旦西街经营不善"对东广场商业经营的伤害。

同时，东广场和西街两部分在业态的选择上形成了互补的作用。东广场是一个融合了购物、餐饮、休闲、娱乐为一体的一站式购物中心；西街则以特色经营为主，倡导夜生活休闲文化，打造为佛山最具规模的餐饮、娱乐、休闲购物夜街。

香港建筑科学出版社：如果只说一点，一个商业项目成功的最关键点是什么？

杰奥斯建筑设计：根据成功项目开发运作的流程，一个正确的商业定位是首要的。可以说没有正确的商业定位，项目将失去先天的优势。在定位阶段，通过研究分析，合理销售物业能够平衡一定的开发资金投入，重要的是定位应该具备前瞻性，通过后期科学、适当的调整与创新，不断地满足商业项目经营发展的需求，挖掘自身的优势，满足投资商、经营者、消费者三方所需，极大地激发项目的商业物业价值的提升，获得最大化的收益。

在整个商业的开发运作过程中，需要熟悉商业的专业化公司做指导工作，通过对市场的深入了解，结合整体商业的发展趋势，充分考虑现时和未来的商业需求，进行全面分析，为项目确立精准的市场定位、布局规划，提供投资依据，帮助业主规避投资风险。

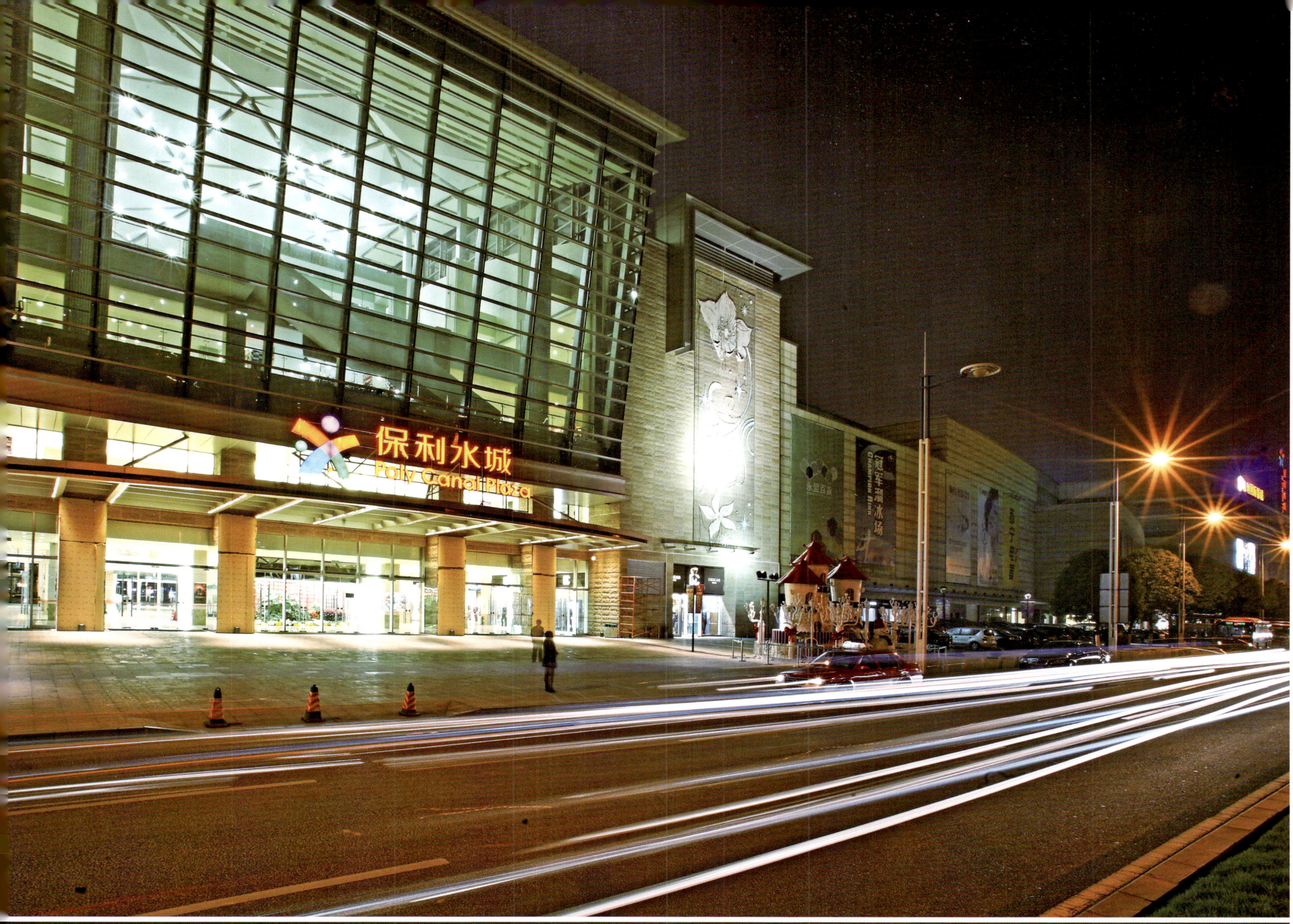
保利水城
Poly Canal Plaza

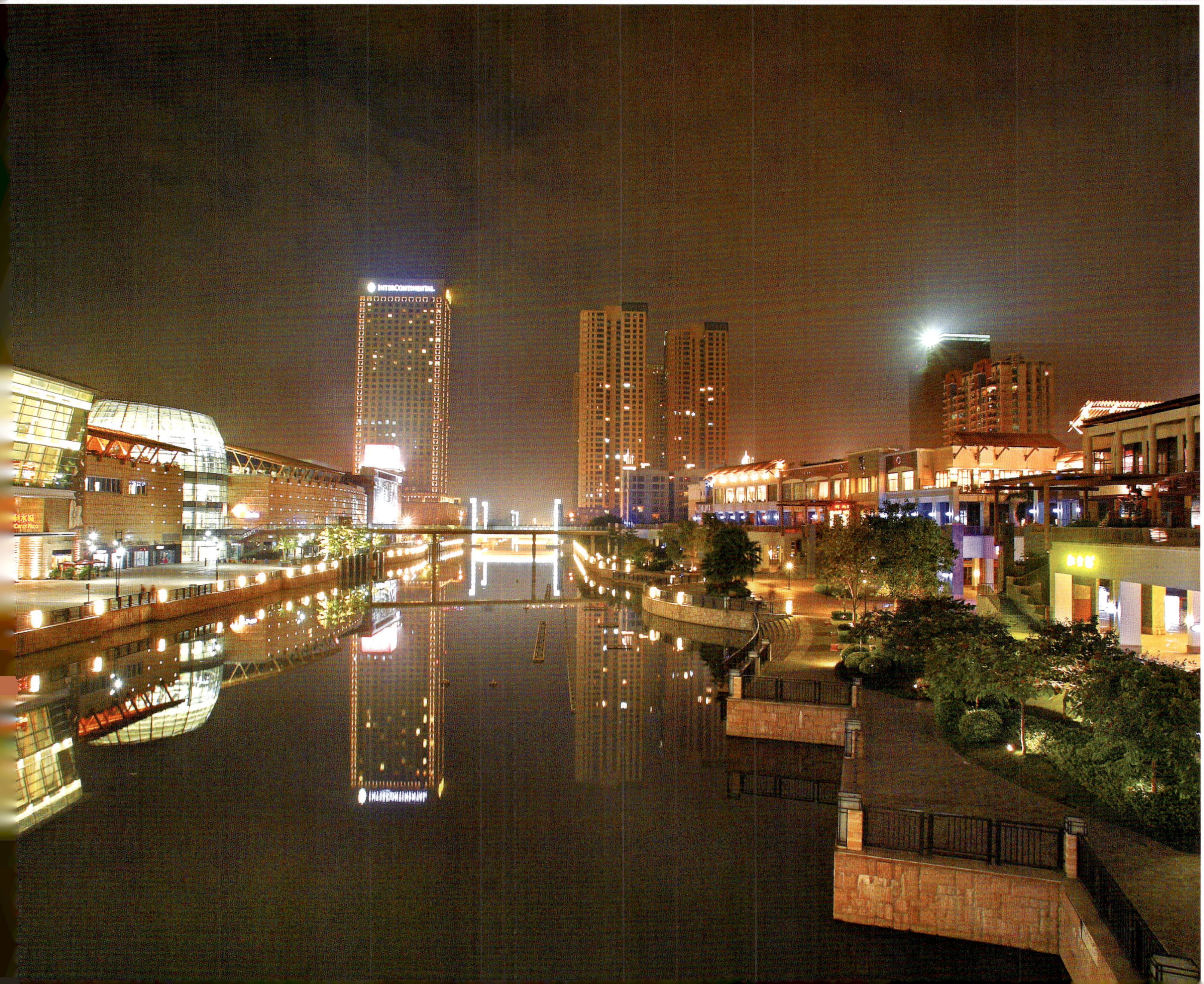
INTERCONTINENTAL

The Poly City of south China Sea is the project of commercial complex cooperated to build by Poly Real Estate and GLE architecture Co., Ltd. with joint hands in strength. The project is located in a land in Foshan City that enclosed by the west and east Den Hu Roads, Fifth and Seventh Sea Roads. The site is separated from east bank and west bank by a river. A bridge on the second floor of both sides forms a loop traffic.

The modern style is given priority to the buildings in east bank, and it integrates with natural elements to create the leisure atmosphere of street in west bank. The whole project officially opened in 2009.

There are rich formats in east bank, such as a Jusco supermarket, Poly theater, ice rink, large restaurants, specialty catering, Suning Appliance, Winman department store, Uniqlo and retail brands of fast fashion , shoe etc; While the leisure entertainment are the main formats , including large Chinese food, specialty catering, KTV, bar street, night clubs, children's education etc..

The design takes "barbell" type on the line layout in east bank. The Winman department store and the cinema at the north side of area and Jusco super market at the south side of area are the main role in pulling people. Because of the deep thickness of

site, it takes pressure in depth control for the self-sustaining shops, and considering to sell part of the property, the sales outlets are set up in the riparian edge of the first layer, thus formed the generatrixof layout. Taking into account of all good business, the reasonable atrium are considered on the two lines in order to separate line area later and to facilitate the updating and business model, thus the second line could effectively eliminate gradually.

The planning of the west bank considered the plenty of parking spaces and the vertical transport to each layer that bring convenience for the future operation. At the same time, commercial blocks in the west bank designed receding platform with an elevator on the second floor to form double deck of commercial shops along the river so as to enhance the price of upward layers greatly.

南海保利水城，由GLC建筑设计有限公司与保利地产强强联手打造的商业综合体，项目位于佛山市灯湖东路与灯湖西路、海五路、海七路围合板块用地，分为东岸及西岸，其间一河之隔，两岸在二层有户外连桥相接，形成环路交通。

东岸建筑以现代风格为主，西岸以现代结合休闲自然元素打造街区氛围。项目整体于2009年正式开业营运。东岸业态丰富，有吉之岛超市、保利院线、真冰溜冰场、大型餐饮、特色餐饮、苏宁电器、永盟百货、优衣库等快时尚零售品牌、鞋城等；西岸业态以休闲娱乐为主，包括大型中餐、特色餐饮、KTV、酒吧街、夜总会、儿童教育等。

在动线布局上，东岸采取“哑铃式”动线设计。北侧以永盟百货及电影院、南侧吉之岛超市作为主力店拉动人流，但由于地块厚度较深，对自持商铺的进深控制有压力，并且当时开发商需要考虑对部分物业进行销售，因此在河岸边缘的首层，设置了销售商铺，从而形成了前后动线。考虑到商业的均好性，GLC在主动线上合理地设置了中庭，以便日后对次动线区域进行板块切割处理，以利于业态的更新与招商，使次动线有效地逐渐消除。

西岸在规划时考虑了充足的停车位，以及足够的垂直交通直达各层，为日后运营带来便利之处，同时西岸商业街区采用了二层退台设计，结合扶手电梯的设置，形成双首层的沿河商铺，大大提升二层以上的售价。

EDISA

BAGANA
BAGANA
MARC

PPGIRL

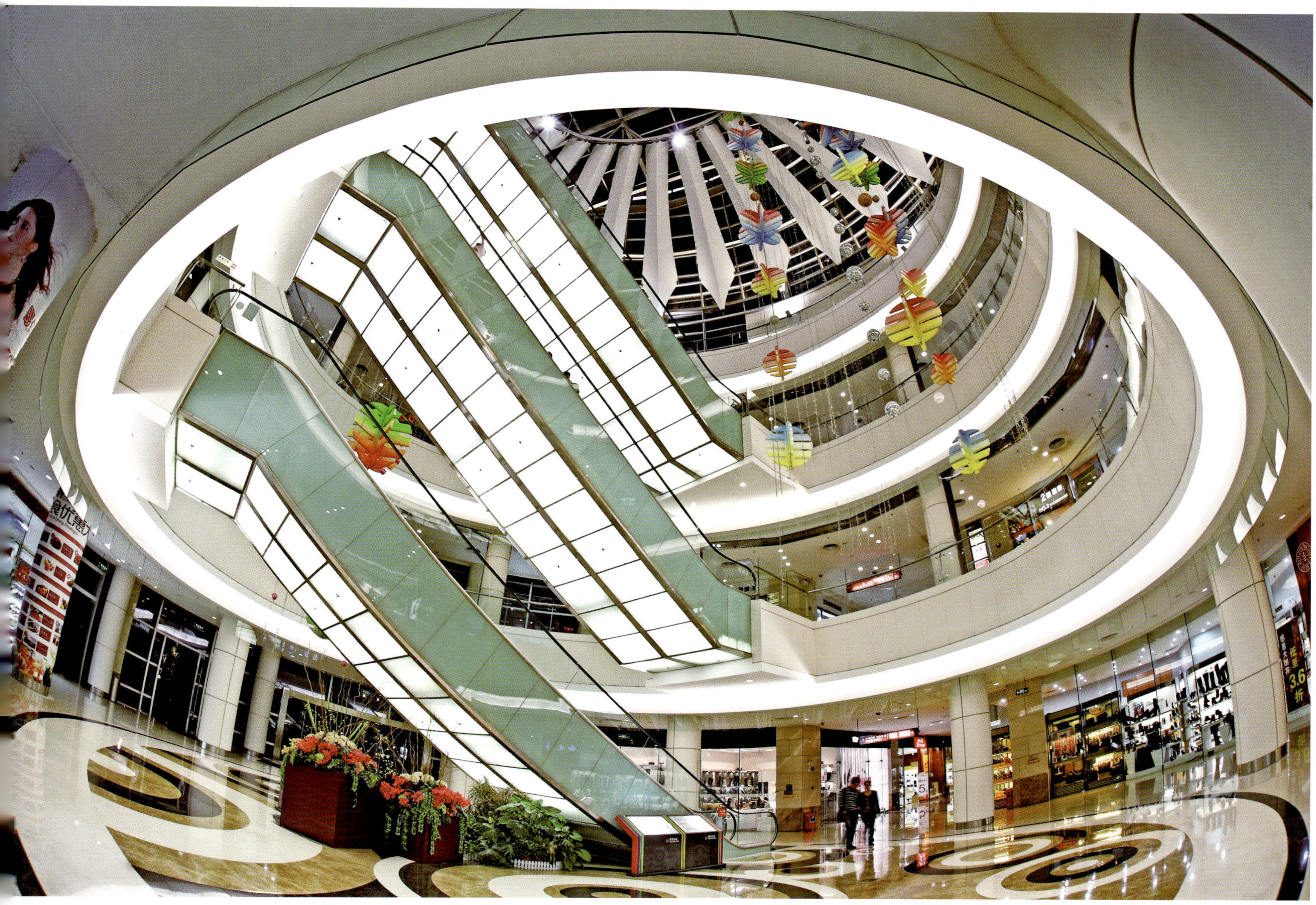

CAV

阿兰达
无国界餐饮
香港星级大厨主理
集世界各国美食
Tel:0757-86318168
Http://www.arlanda.hk

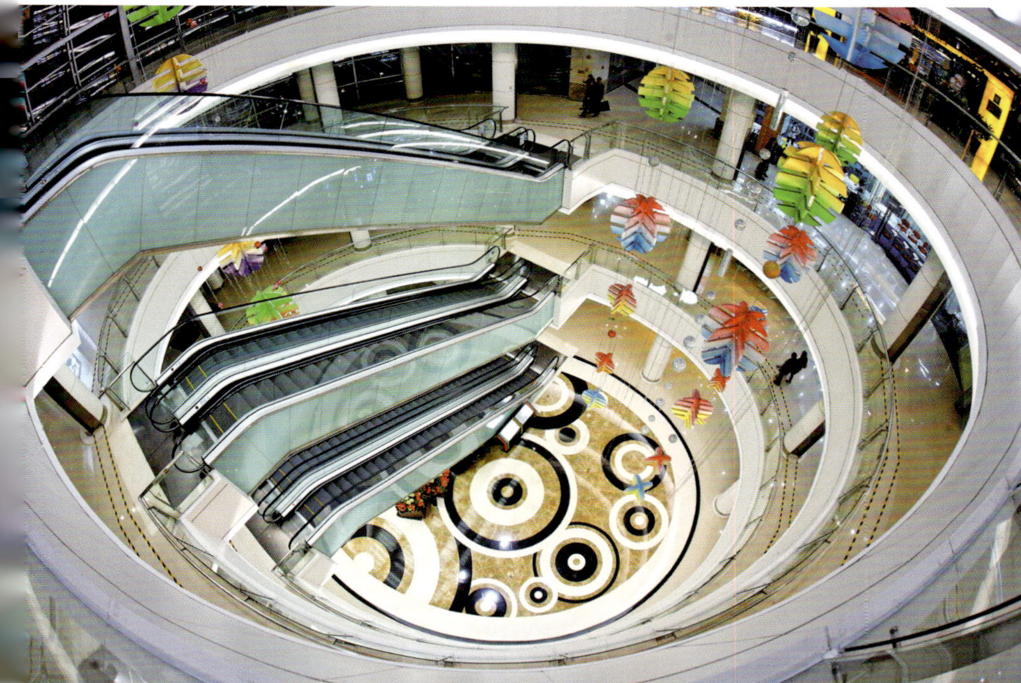

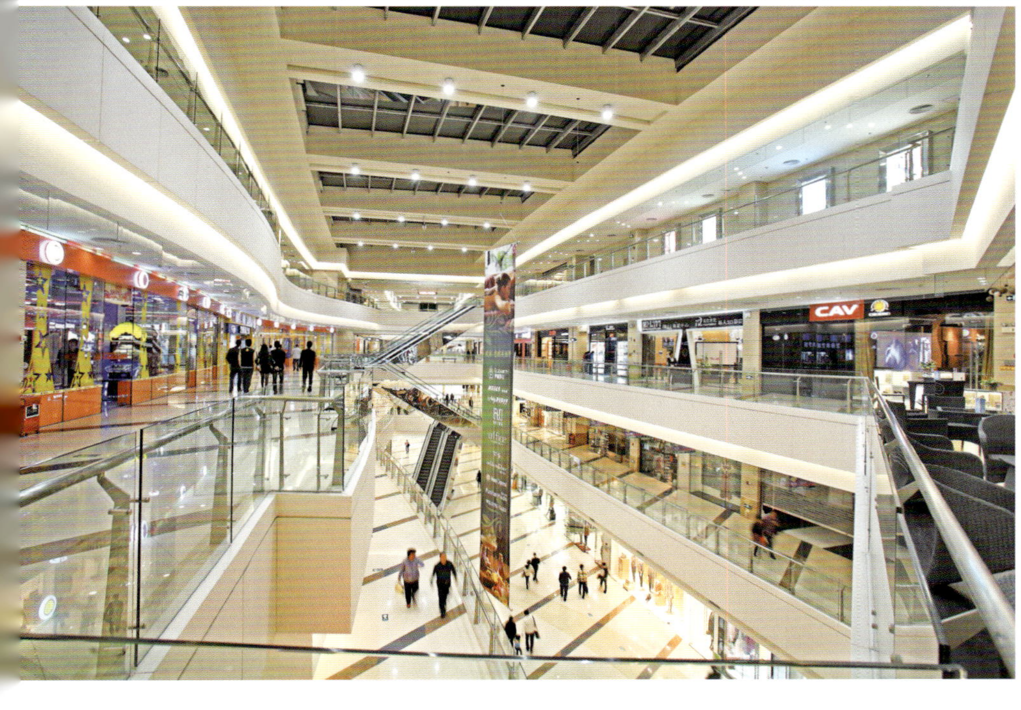

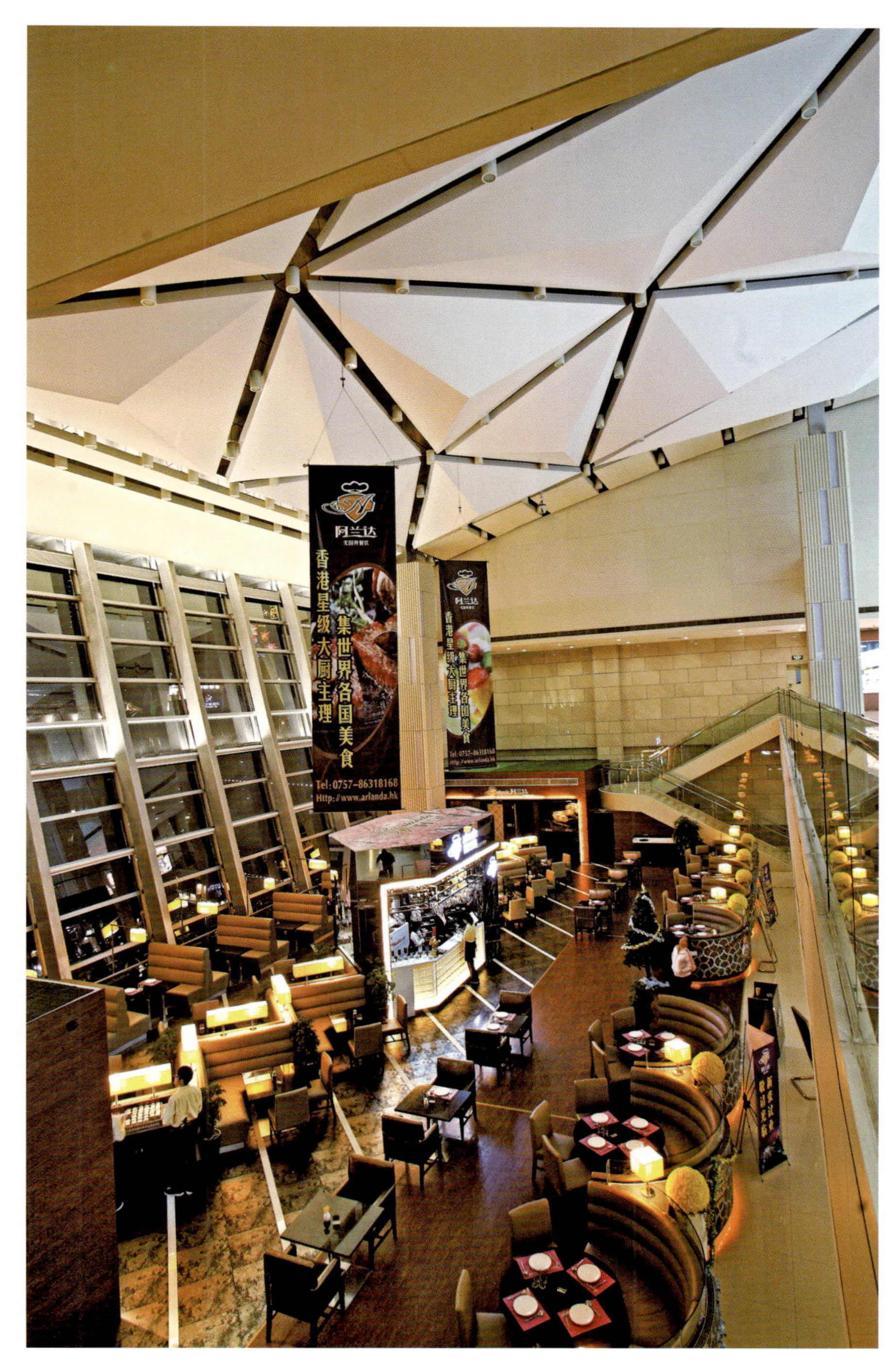

PROJECT NAME 项目名称

CHENGDU SUNING PLAZA
成都苏宁广场

Architect: Nanjing Yangtze River Urban Architectural Design Co.,Ltd.
设计公司：南京长江都市建筑设计股份有限公司

PROJECT INFORMATION 项目信息

Client	Suning Appliance Company	**客户**	苏宁电器公司
Location	chengdu,sichuan,china	**地点**	四川成都
Gross Floor Area	125,335 m²	**建筑总面积**	125，335 平方米
Site Area	26,736 m²	**占地面积**	26，736 平方米

OVERVIEW 项目概况

This project occupies 26,736 m² totally, the base area of construction is 1,604 m² while the plot ratio is 3.5. The gross building area is 125,335 m², comprised by two levels of 31,769 m² underground and six levels of 93,566 m² above the ground. The building height should be 39.15 m.

本项目用地面积 26,736 平方米，建筑基底面积 16,041 平方米，容积率为 3.5。总建筑面积 125,335 平方米，其中地下建筑面积 31,769 平方米，地上建筑面积 93,566 平方米。项目地下二层，地上六层，建筑高度 39.15 米。

FEATURE ANALYSIS 特色分析

The project emphasizes the integration of urban function and form, the building rich more porosity and gives space back to citizens.The project implements in Chengdu architecture and regional emotion, architecture and human interaction and integration, and achieves the concept of modern environmental protection technology to build a super green building. The project hopes to give residents here an exciting experience.Sichuan people like the sunshine, the glass facade and glass atrium roof which can provide a good natural lighting. The project of public space in line with Chengdu citizens' leisure habits. This also deeply reflects the architect concept of "Micro-urban life ".

项目强调整体化都市功能与形式，建筑体富多孔隙性，还空间于市民。该项目实现了成都建筑与地域情感、建筑与人的互动与融合，实现了现代环保技术打造超级绿色建筑的概念，项目希望带给成都市民一种兴奋的体验。四川人喜欢晒太阳，玻璃立面和玻璃中庭屋顶可以提供很好的自然采光，此项目营造的公共空间非常亲近成都市民的休闲习惯，这也是建筑师“微型都市生活体”理念的深刻体现。

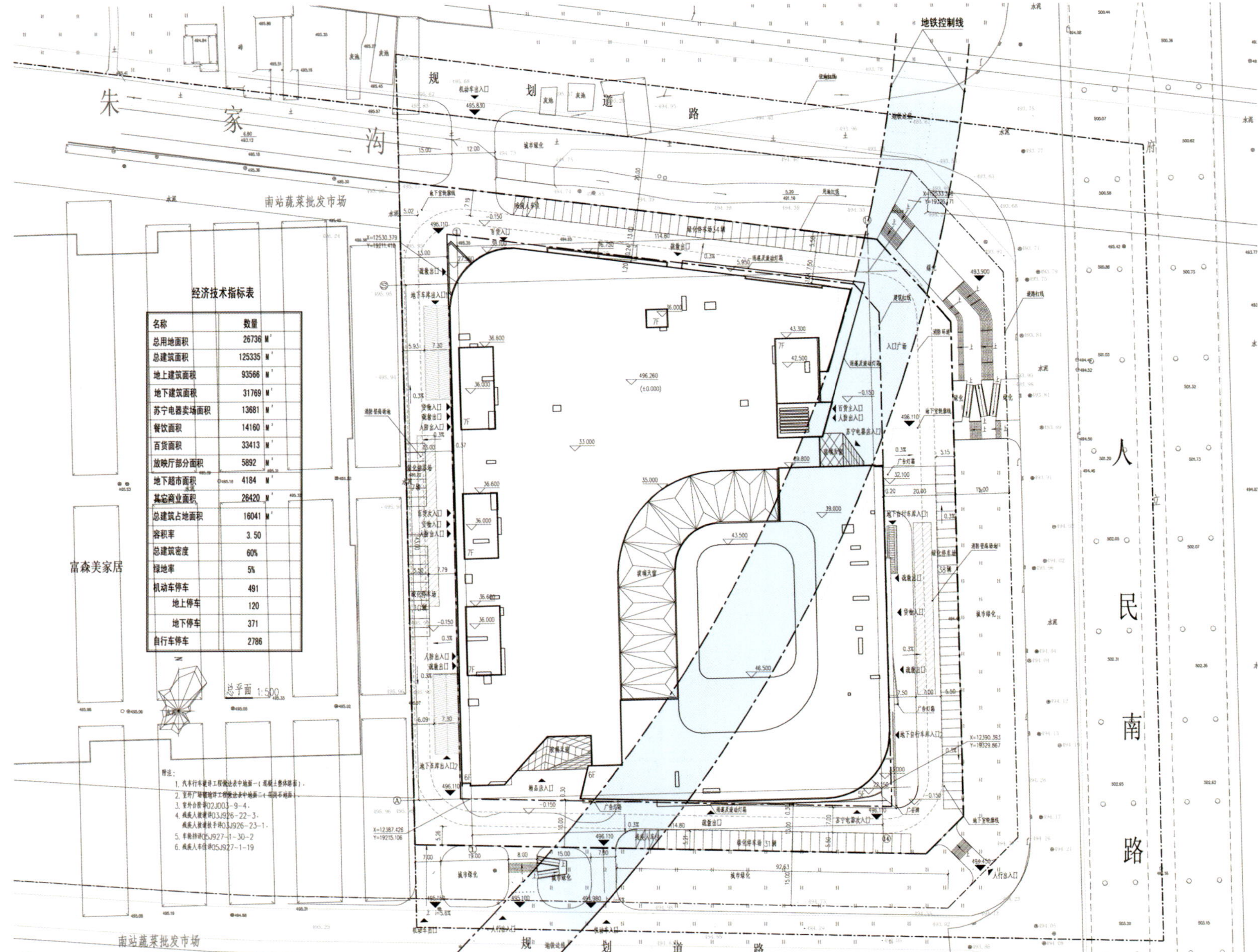

Site Plan
总平面图

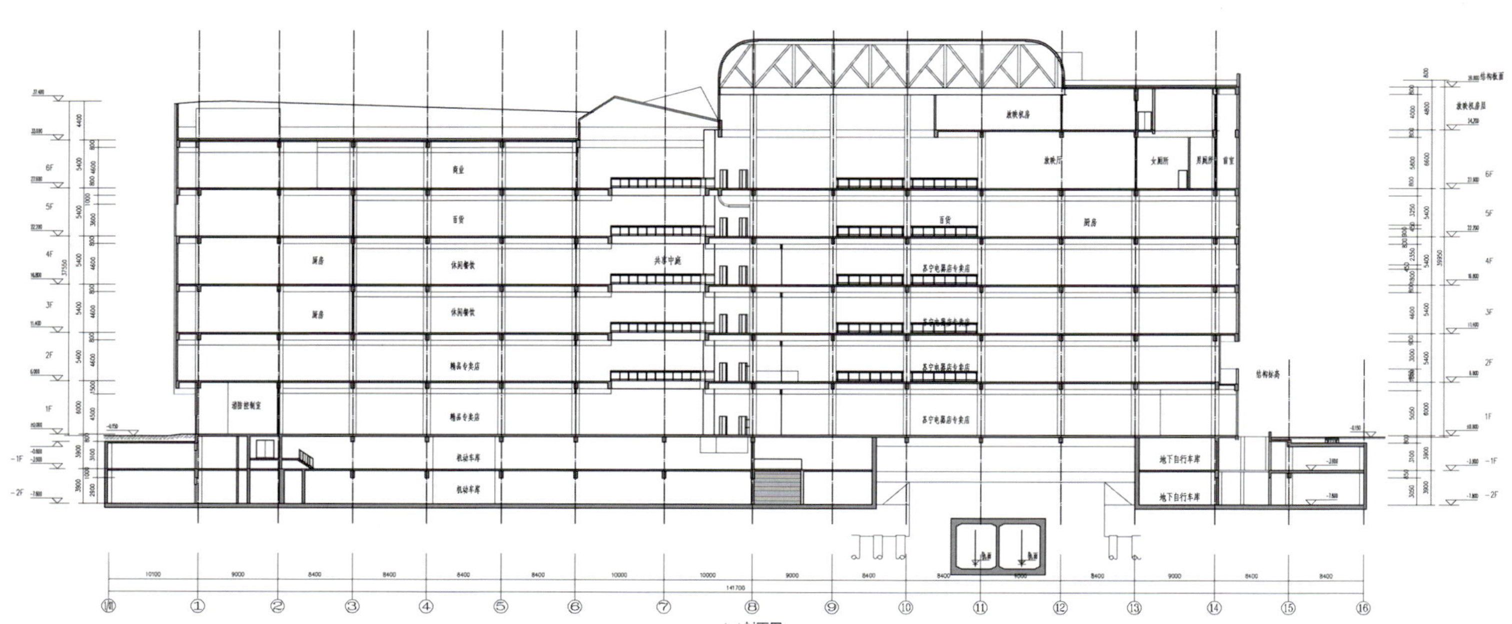

Section A-A
剖面图 A-A

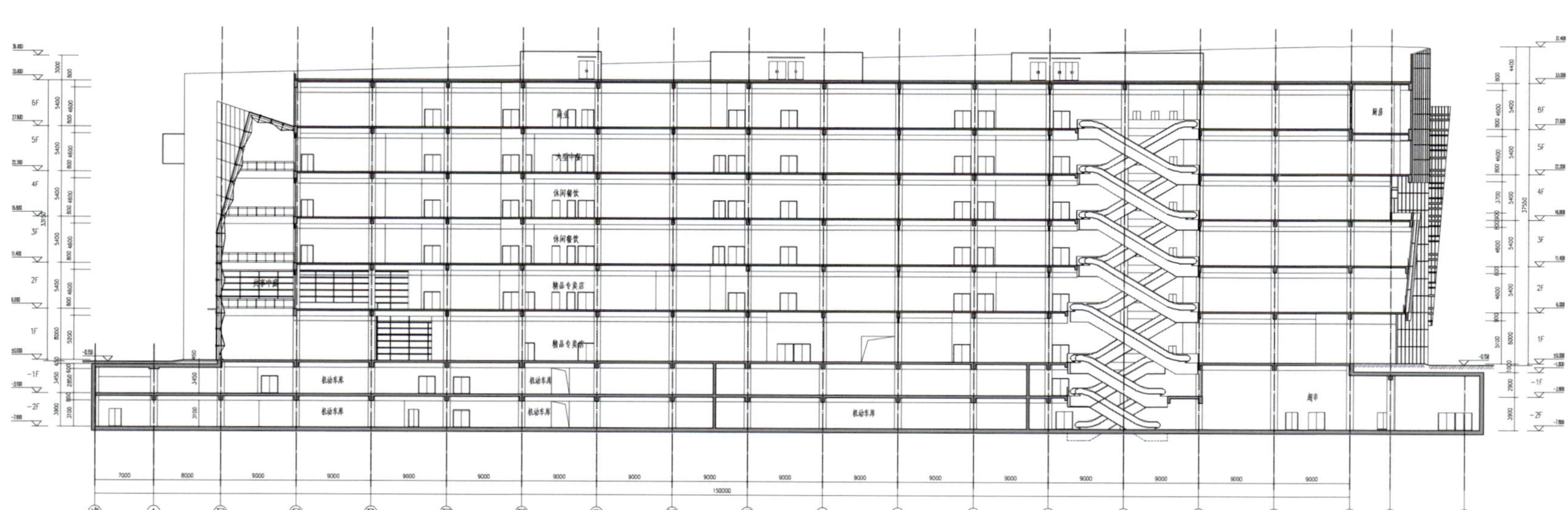

Section B-B
剖面图 B-B

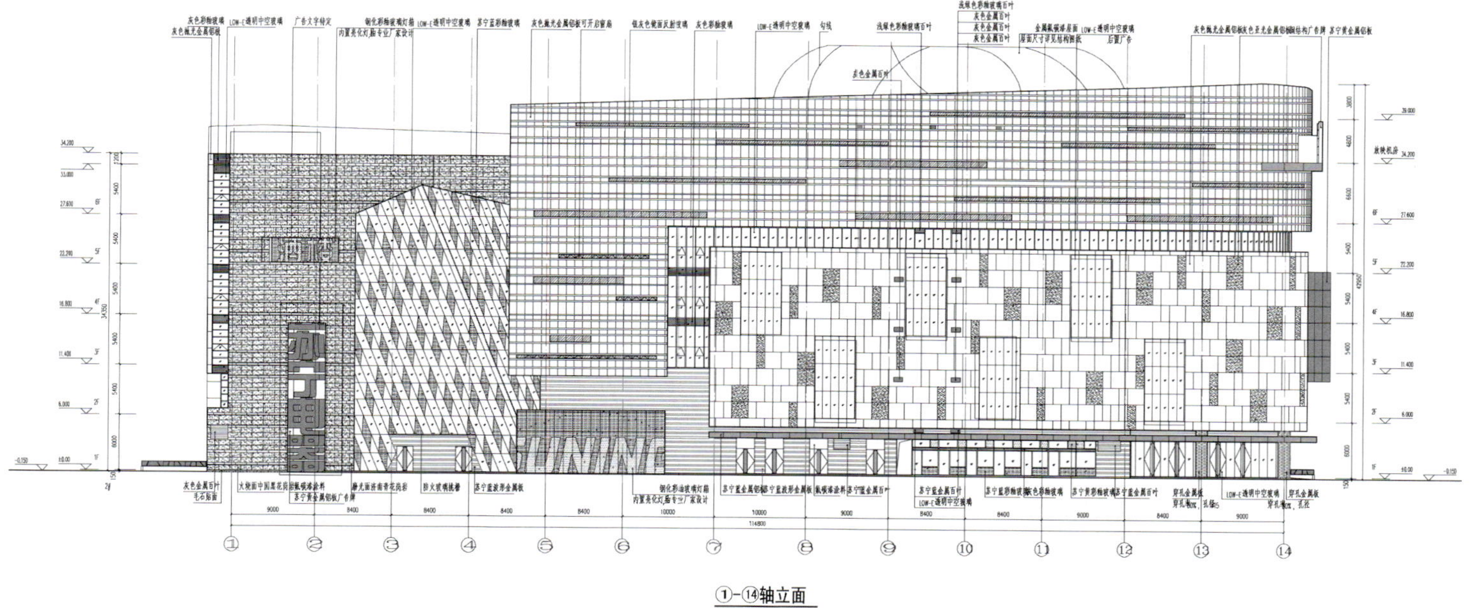

①-⑭轴立面

Elevation
立面图

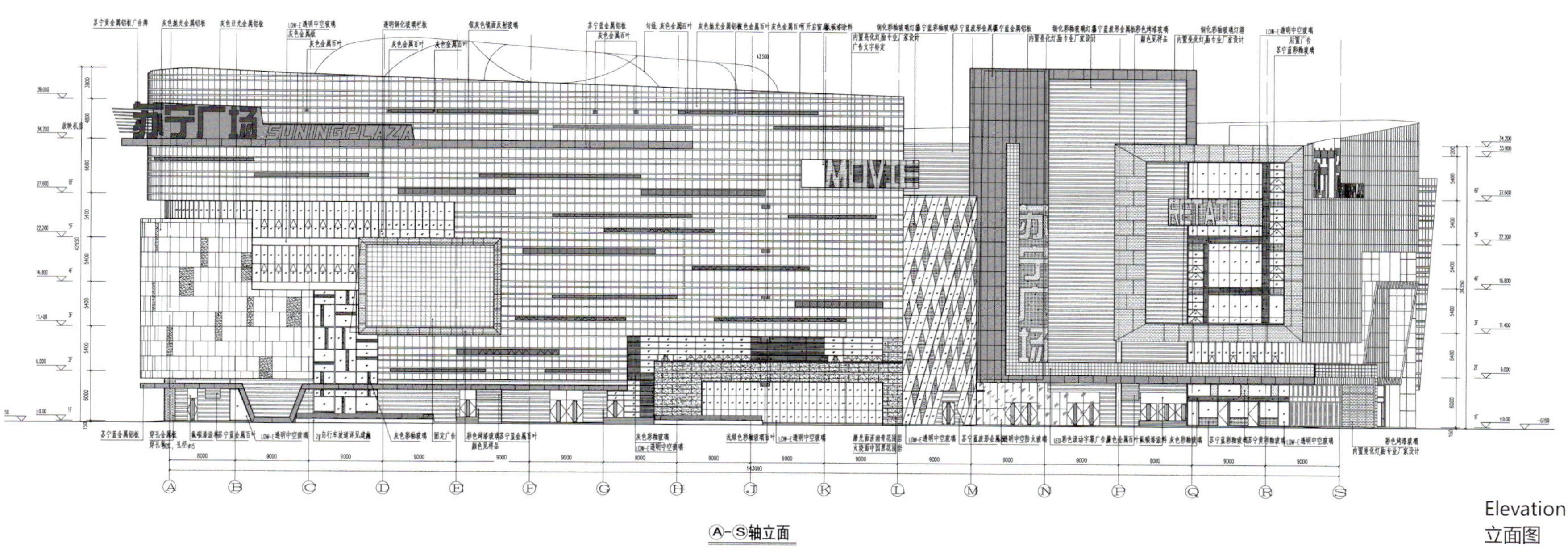

Ⓐ-Ⓢ轴立面

Elevation
立面图

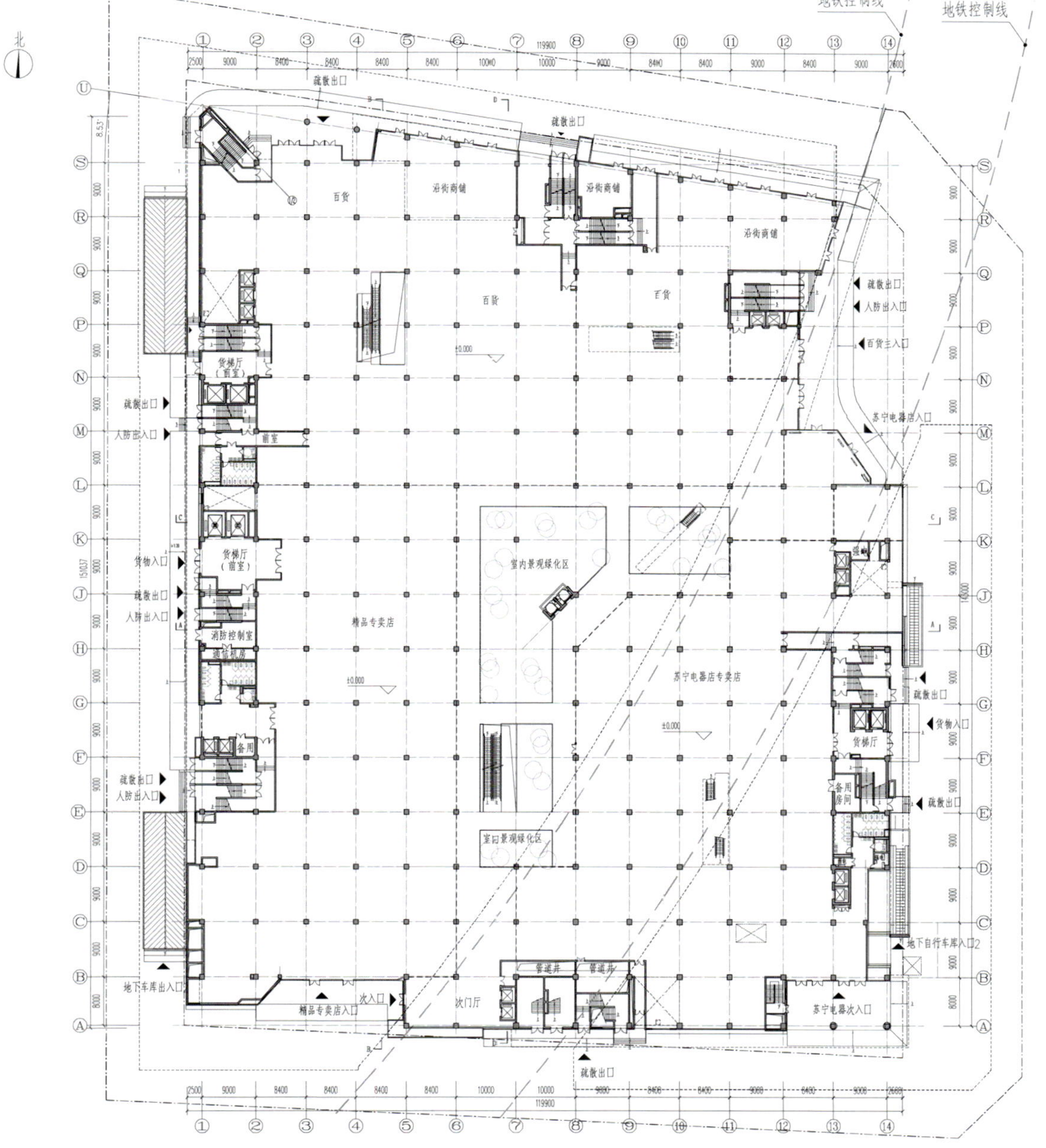

Floor Plan
楼层平面图

By considering the full use of square and flat block, the building centrally rooted on the center of block with circular passages around, which could be used as the fire lane as well as to meet the need of outside parking. The entrance squares on the main entrances are good for personnel evacuating and business events. The overall elevation of roads surrounding the block creates the high west and low east layout, bringing two meters' altitude difference between base and eastern road. Vehicle access was arranged in the south and north direction in the east side of base, 15 meters of green belt lies between the roads and building in the east and south. The outdoor step ramp on the main entrance links the base and roads directly.

项目基地地块方正平整，在充分利用基地覆盖率的基础上，将建筑集中布置在基地中央，四周留有环形通道，既是消防车道，又能满足室外场地停车的需要。建筑的主要入口附近均设计有入口广场，可以满足人员疏散及商业活动的要求。基地周边道路整体标高西高东低，基地和东侧道路约有 2 米高差。在规划设计上，将机动车出入口布置在基地西侧的南北两个方向，建筑东侧、南侧和城市道路之间，有 15 米宽的城市绿化带，在建筑主要入口的方向，通过室外台阶坡道等将基地和城市道路连接起来。

SUNING PLAZA

PROJECT NAME 项目名称

GERMANY HOFGARTEN SOLINGEN SHOPPING CENTRE

德国索林根花园购物中心

Architect: HPP

设计公司：HPP

PROJECT INFORMATION 项目信息

Client	Solingen Shopping Center GmbH	客户	索林根购物中心有限公司
Location	Solingen,Germany	地点	德国索林根
Gross Floor Area	48,412 m²	总建筑面积	48,412 平方米
Retail Surface	29,000 m²	商铺面积	29,000 平方米
Parking Spaces	600	停车位	600 个

OVERVIEW 项目概况

This three-storey HOFGARTEN SOLINGEN shopping centre will be built on the site of the former Karstadt department store on the Neumarkt in Solingen. The main aim of the concept is the creation of a new city centre. There is an integrated car park linking 70 shops with an attractive range of products, many service providers and 16 restaurants. Located directly on Graf-Wilhelm-Platz in the south of the city centre, the shopping centre is directly adjacent to the bus station on Koelner Straße, where up to 30,000 passengers arrive daily.

这栋三层的花园购物中心坐落在德国索林根市新市场，Karstadt 百货公司原址上。设计的理念是要打造一个新的城市中心。购物中心内有 70 家商品丰富的店铺，16 家餐饮和多种服务设施，同时设有停车场。商场建在城市中心南部的格拉夫－威廉－广场上，临近科隆大街的公交车站，每天至少有 30,000 人路径此地。

BRIEF INTERVIEW 访谈录

ARCHITECT
Werner Sübai

设计师
维纳 苏柏

HKASP: What are the important things that this project does for the city?

HPP: The urban scheme of the Hofgarten Solingen was conducted to repair the city center. With the new building, the inner city square is now comprised again on all of its four sides. Furthermore, the pedestrian walk ways have been restored and connect again all of the city's retail locations.

HKASP: If any, what makes this project different from other commercial retail projects?

HPP: The design and programmatic focus are based primarily on the location in Solingen, known as the German City of Blades. The mall has been designed with the themes of nature, industry and fashion. The first two subjects strongly relate to the City of Solingen and its surrounding regions. Within and outside the mall, the topics accentuate the various areas and lead the customers on their way through the building. Thereby creating a local landmark and an important destination for the entire region.

香港建筑科学出版社：你觉得这个项目给这个城市带来了什么重要的东西呢？

HPP: 这个项目的规划设计就是为了修复城市中心。新的建筑使城市广场的四个边界再次完整。另外，步行街也得到了修复，并与其他商业步行街连为一体。

香港建筑科学出版社：这个商业项目有别于其他一般商业项目的特点是什么？

HPP: 设计最初就针对了索林根市作为德国刀片城市出名这一特点。商场以自然、工业、时尚作为设计主题。前两个主题与索林根市及其周边区域息息相关。整个主题围绕着商场的室内室外，并通过强调不同区域的设计来对顾客起引导作用。因此设计成为整个地区的重要场所和地方标志。

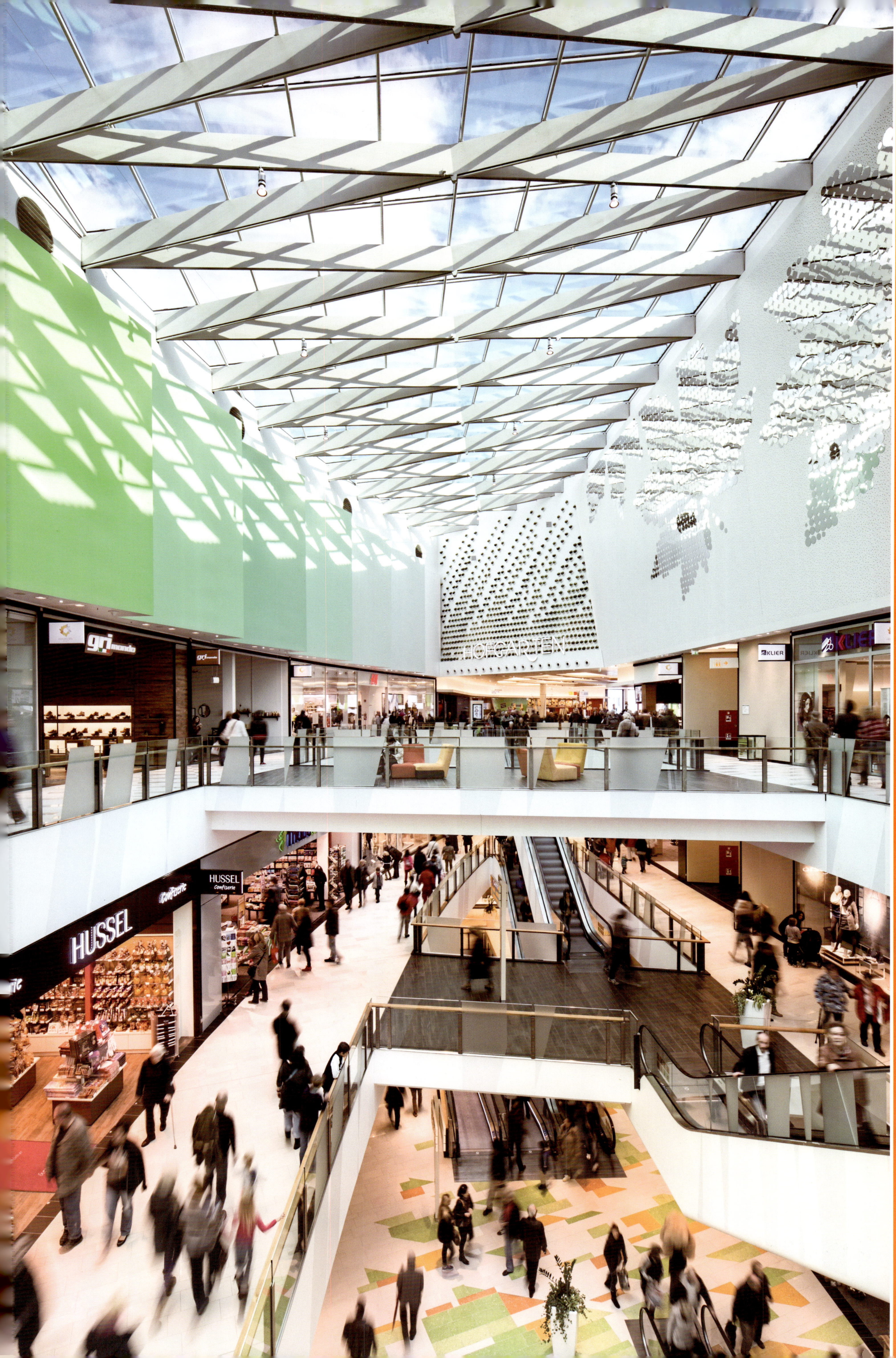
HOFGARTEN
HUSSEL
HUSSEL
Confiserie
KLIER

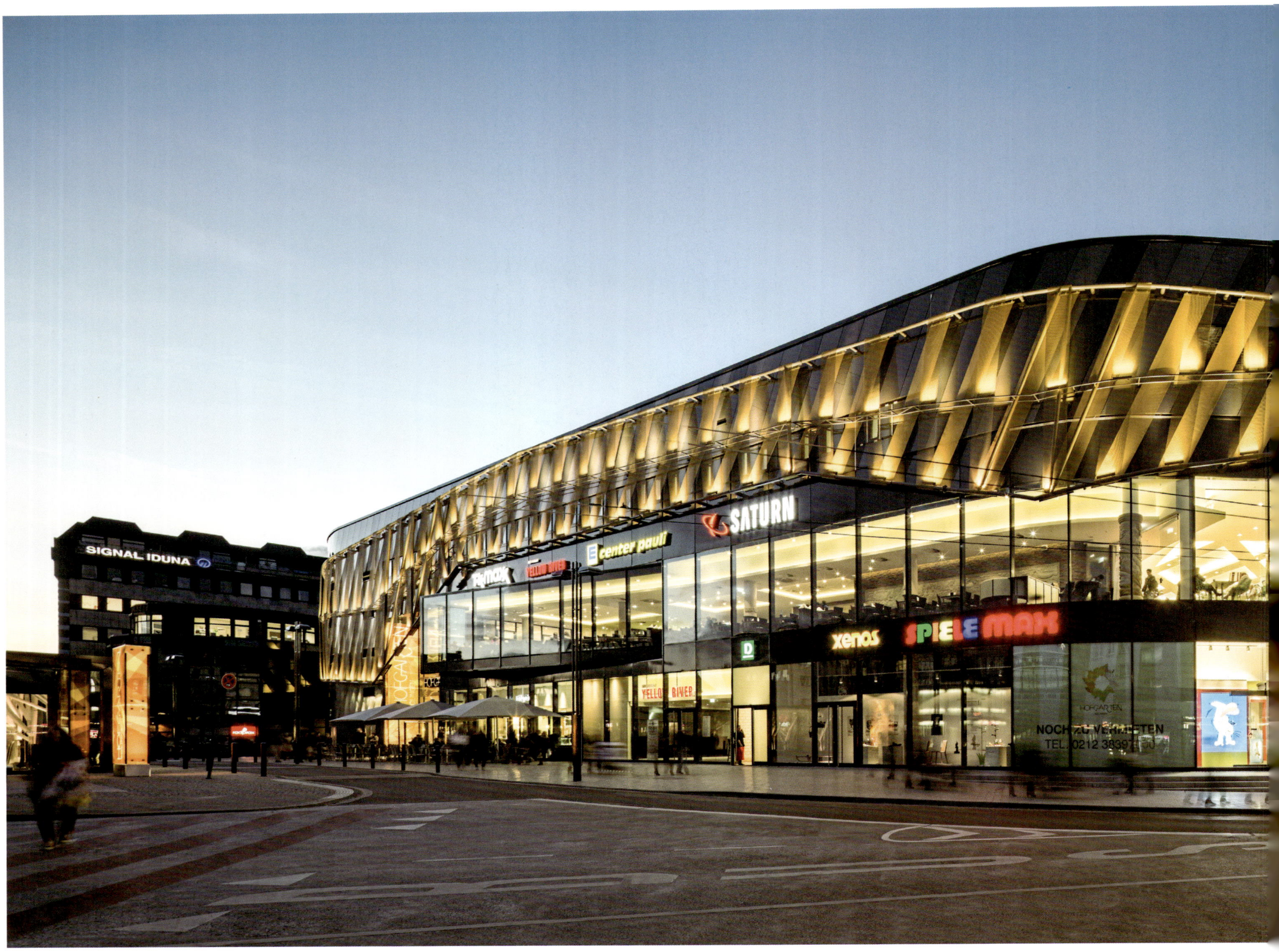
SIGNAL IDUNA
SATURN
center pauli
xenos
SPIELE MAX

T·K·maxx
YELLOW RIVER
center pauli

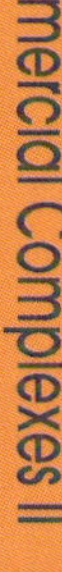

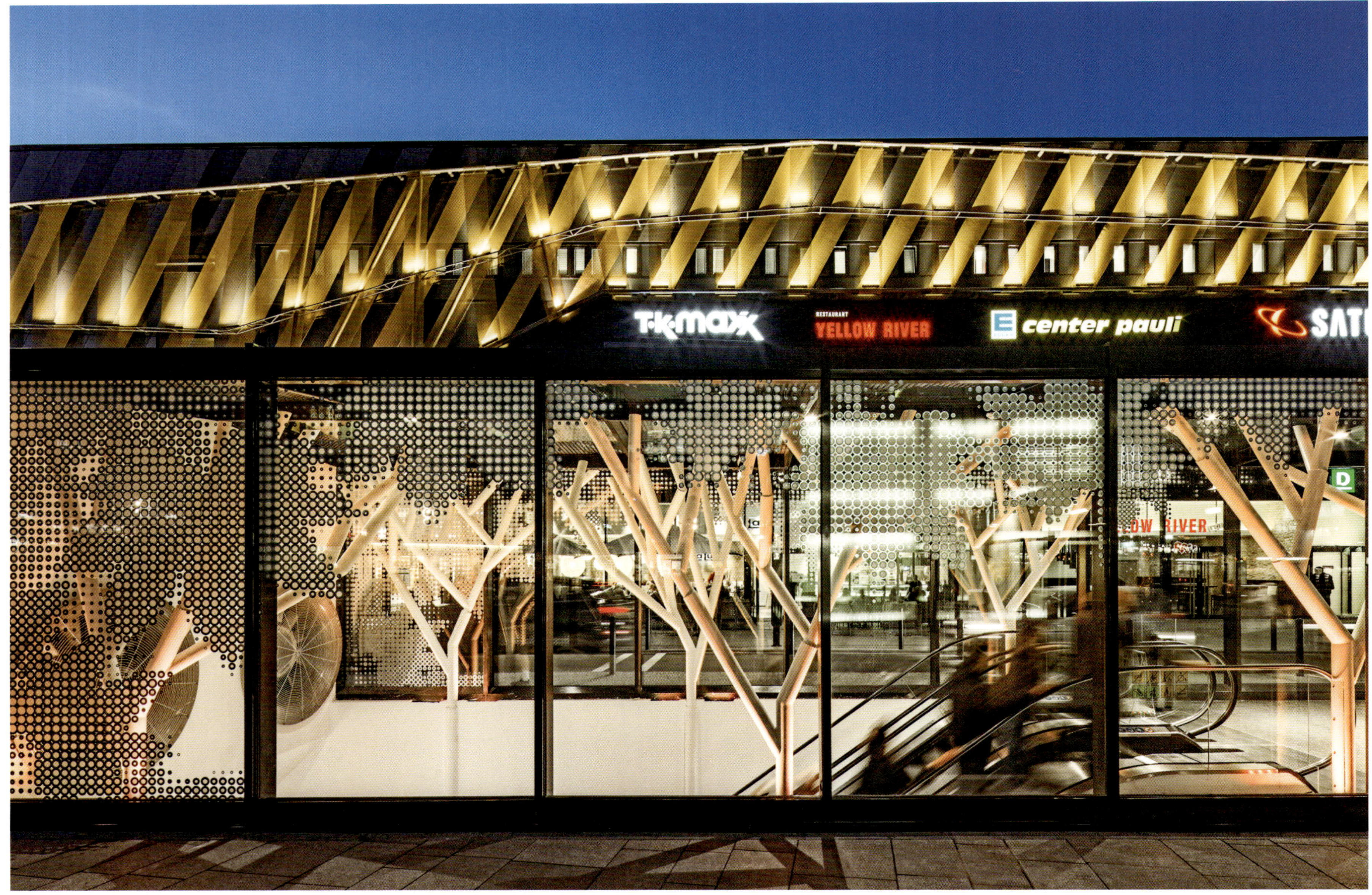

The city of Solingen's main shopping area is concentrated around the northern end of Graf-Wilhelm-Platz: this building will form the fourth side of Graf-Wilhelm-Platz, completing the square. The floor plan is a complex polygon but the shell of the building is clad with a transparent facade that has a second skin of perforated metal, running diagonally over the building and accentuating the main entrance on the Koelner Strasse. Internally, the project comprises three linked sections: the retail floors, the car park and the existing underground passage.

索林根的主要商业区都集中在格拉夫－威廉－广场上，该建筑定义了广场的第四条边。建筑的平面是多变的，外壳则由一层半透明的外皮包裹，即由金属编织网以平行对角线的方式缠绕的装饰立面，使购物中心在科隆大街上的主入口显得特别起眼。建筑内部由三大部分组成：商铺、停车场和原有的地下人行道。

HOFGARTEN
EBENE
-3

HOFGARTEN

Architectural Design

The design and programmatic focus are based primarily on the location in Solingen, known as the City of Blades in the Bergisches Land; the mall has been designed with the themes of nature, industry and fashion. Nature is reflected through the facade; the greened roof crowning the 3rd storey; the open, planted cable net facade of the car park or through the vertical garden above the fountain at the main entrance on Koelner Straße.

The golden metal mesh, woven in a zig-zag pattern, wrapped around the building like a loose scarf expresses the themes of industry and fashion through material and construction.

This light, suspended "wrap" stands for the youthful, dynamic image of the centre. Behind the wrap, the facade is mainly comprised of a three-layered metal facade, each layer a different shade of grey, over an anthracite grey brick base. The dark grey thermal insulation is also partially visible. These dark shades provide a clear contrast to the shiny wrap and are inspired by the local slate facades. The design focuses on the food court, the customer toilets in the first upper storey and the central area of the mall with the large skylight. The food court has been given a structured ceiling with lozenge-shaped light vaults, opened up by means of 6 small skylight domes. The result is a bright space with direct views towards Solingen's pedestrian area.

建筑设计

设计的灵感主要来源于索林根城市的工业历史，由于锋利金属器具的生产，该市以“刀片城市”的称号闻名，因此商场的整体设计便以“自然－工业－时尚”作为主题。自然－反映在立面上：绿色屋顶铺满了整个第三层；开放式的，缠满植被的停车场立面和科隆大街主入口前喷泉上的垂直花园。金黄色的金属编织网，以锯齿的形状缠绕在立面上，体现了工业的意味。时尚则由建筑的材料和结构来体现。轻盈的，吊挂式的金属编织网包裹的立面展现了购物中心的年轻跟活力。

编织网背后的立面则由三层灰度不同的金属板拼接而成，金属板背后的深灰色的隔热层也部分可见。各种灰度意喻了具有地方特色的板岩立面，同时把金黄色的金属网衬托得更加耀眼。

室内设计重点考虑了美食广场，二层的顾客卫生间和中心区域的巨型天窗。美食广场的天花由多个发光的菱形凹槽组成，其中6个为天窗，接受自然采光，形成一个直视索林根步行区域的敞亮空间。

Kö-Bogen
P Tiefgarage
SAN MARCO

EAA

EAA

TURKEY ZORLU CENTER
土耳其佐鲁中心

312

The excellent project should be designed according to the terrain. Row houses under the building shell are configured with a large garden on its first floor,while the residents could enjoy the view of the Bosphorus Bay from the large terrace of second floor. Both the garden and the terrace can be entranced through the open atrium. This atrium is a space that is rich, bright and pleasant.

根据地形来设计的优秀项目。建筑外壳下的联排住宅在一层配置了大型的花园，二层的大露台使住户可以在此欣赏博斯普鲁斯湾的景色。花园和露台都可以经由露天的中庭进入。这座中庭是一处内容丰富、色调明亮、令人愉悦的空间。

The Zorlu Center Site is just at the junction of the Bosphorus Bridge European connection and the glamorous Büyükdere axis that connects the city center with the great business district Maslak. It is reached from various important centers of Istanbul and moreover,topographically is one of the few plain sites that face south, with the old city view. With all these significant qualities, it has been a "subject of desire" and was owned by the Zorlu Property through a tender, being watched by all levels of the public. In this sense, the mixed use project being developed on this area deals with contradictions such as grandeur and modesty, public and private, international and domestic, social and distinguished, together with structural and topographical considerations.

佐鲁中心位于土耳其伊斯坦布尔博斯普鲁斯大桥和迷人的布伊克德尔轴线的交汇处，布伊克德尔轴线连接了市中心和马斯拉克商业区。佐鲁中心不仅连接了城市几个重要的中心地带，同时它也处在城市少有的几处平坦地形之上，靠近南部的旧城区。因其综合这些重要的品质，它被称为"欲望的主体"，佐鲁中心归佐鲁地产所有，是在公众的目光下投标所得。这个多功能项目将多个对立的元素融合在一起：宏伟和谦逊、公开和私密、国际性和本土化、社会化和独特性等都在结构和地形的设计上有所体现。

The commercial building is of neighborhood.

Module design comes along with energy saving. The Middle East economic crisis happened during the creation. But the final design brought value to the investment.

The key to the commercial project lies in the success of sustainability. It will last forever instead of an one-off opening ceremony.

商业属于街区社区类型、小而美；模块化设计结合节能、营造过程经历了中东经济危机、但最终设计为投资带来了价值；业项目最关键的是可持续的成功、而非昙花一现的开幕式、要永不落幕。

OFFICE COMPLEX REAL ESTATE

办公型复合地产

Studio Daniel Libeskind (SDL) +Architect Daniel Libe

Studio Daniel Libeskind (SDL) +Architect Daniel Libe

Kö-Bogen completes the Königsallee boulevard at Hofgarten park and shapes the new Hofgarten promenade and terraces, places that have already become popular with the people of Düsseldorf. The building also gives shape to Schadowplatz square and forms a passage towards Hofgarten, busy with boutiques, restaurants and cafes with outdoor seating.

LAB

LAB_ 尚墨

GERMANY KÖ-BOGEN DÜSSELDORF

德国杜塞尔多夫库伯根项目

332

Kö-Bogen 的存在填补了宫廷公园国王大道的空缺，形成了已受杜塞尔多夫人民热捧的宫廷新散步道、露台与聚集地。此外，建筑的存在不仅塑造了沙多广场，而且还是通往宫廷公园的通道。建筑内设有众多精品店，餐馆，咖啡，并在室外安置了座椅。

On the sides towards Schadowplatz and Gustaf-Gründgens Platz, using components of various heights within the same sized facade elements a horizontal pattern is created. The staggered horizontal bands amplify the dynamic character of the building along the newly shaped pedestrian spaces.

在朝沙多广场与格林德根斯・古斯塔法广场一侧的立面上采用水平格局，在同样宽度的立面元素内采用不同高度的构件。以新形成的步行空间为背景，纵横交错的横条纹更加凸显建筑的动态感。

Kö-Bogen is a six-storey 40,162㎡office and retail complex in downtown Düsseldorf and marking an important transition between urban space and landscape.

建筑高 6 层，建筑面积为 40 162 平方米，兼有办公和零售功能。它位于杜塞尔多夫的市中心，在城市空间和景观空间之间发挥承前启下的作用。

ABU DHABI GUARDIAN TOWER
阿布扎比 GUARDIAN 大厦

344

Permeated cuts into the facades towards Königsallee and Hofgarten allow for the landscape to naturally blend and flow into the building.

人们的视线可穿过立面上的切口，直达国王大道与宫廷公园，让建筑与远处的景观形成自然的交融，成为建筑物一幅美丽的背景画。

PROJECT NAME 项目名称

TURKEY ZORLU CENTER

土耳其佐鲁中心

Architect: EAA

设计公司：EAA

PROJECT INFORMATION 项目信息

Location	Istanbul, Turkey	**地点**	土耳其伊斯坦布尔
Site Area	720,000m²	**面积**	720，000 平方米

OVERVIEW 项目概况

The Zorlu Center Site is just at the junction of the Bosphorus Bridge European connection and the glamorous Büyükdere axis that connects the city center with the great business district Maslak. It is reached from various important centers of Istanbul and moreover,topographically is one of the few plain sites that face south, with the old city view. With all these significant qualities, it has been a "subject of desire" and was owned by the Zorlu Property through a tender, being watched by all levels of the public. In this sense, the mixed use project being developed on this area deals with contradictions such as grandeur and modesty, public and private, international and domestic, social and distinguished, together with structural and topographical considerations.

佐鲁中心位于土耳其伊斯坦布尔博斯普鲁斯大桥和迷人的布伊克德尔轴线的交汇处，布伊克德尔轴线连接了市中心和马斯拉克商业区。佐鲁中心不仅连接了城市几个重要的中心地带，同时它也处在城市少有的几处平坦地形之上，靠近南部的旧城区。因其综合这些重要的品质，它被称为“欲望的主体”，佐鲁中心归佐鲁地产所有，是在公众的目光下投标所得。这个多功能项目将多个对立的元素融合在一起：宏伟和谦逊、公开和私密、国际性和本土化、社会化和独特性等都在结构和地形的设计上有所体现。

FEATURE ANALYSIS 特色分析

The excellent project should be designed according to the terrain. Row houses under the building shell are configured with a large garden on its first floor,while the residents could enjoy the view of the Bosphorus Bay from the large terrace of second floor. Both the garden and the terrace can be entranced through the open atrium. This atrium is a space that is rich, bright and pleasant. Other residential units constitute the three unique towers.The three unique towers is set on the underlying aerial column, by separating with the building shell. Like the row houses, a tower on the structure takes horizontal stretch, rather than build a whole building complex with iconic elements.

根据地形来设计的优秀项目。建筑外壳下的联排住宅在一层配置了大型的花园，二层的大露台使住户可以在此欣赏博斯普鲁斯湾的景色。花园和露台都可以经由露天的中庭进入。这座中庭是一处内容丰富、色调明亮、令人愉悦的空间。其他的住宅单元构成了三座独特的塔楼。这三座塔楼设置在底层架空柱上，以此与外壳相分离。同联排住宅一样，塔楼在结构构成上也采用水平方向伸展的方式，而没有选择成为整个建筑综合体的标志性元素。

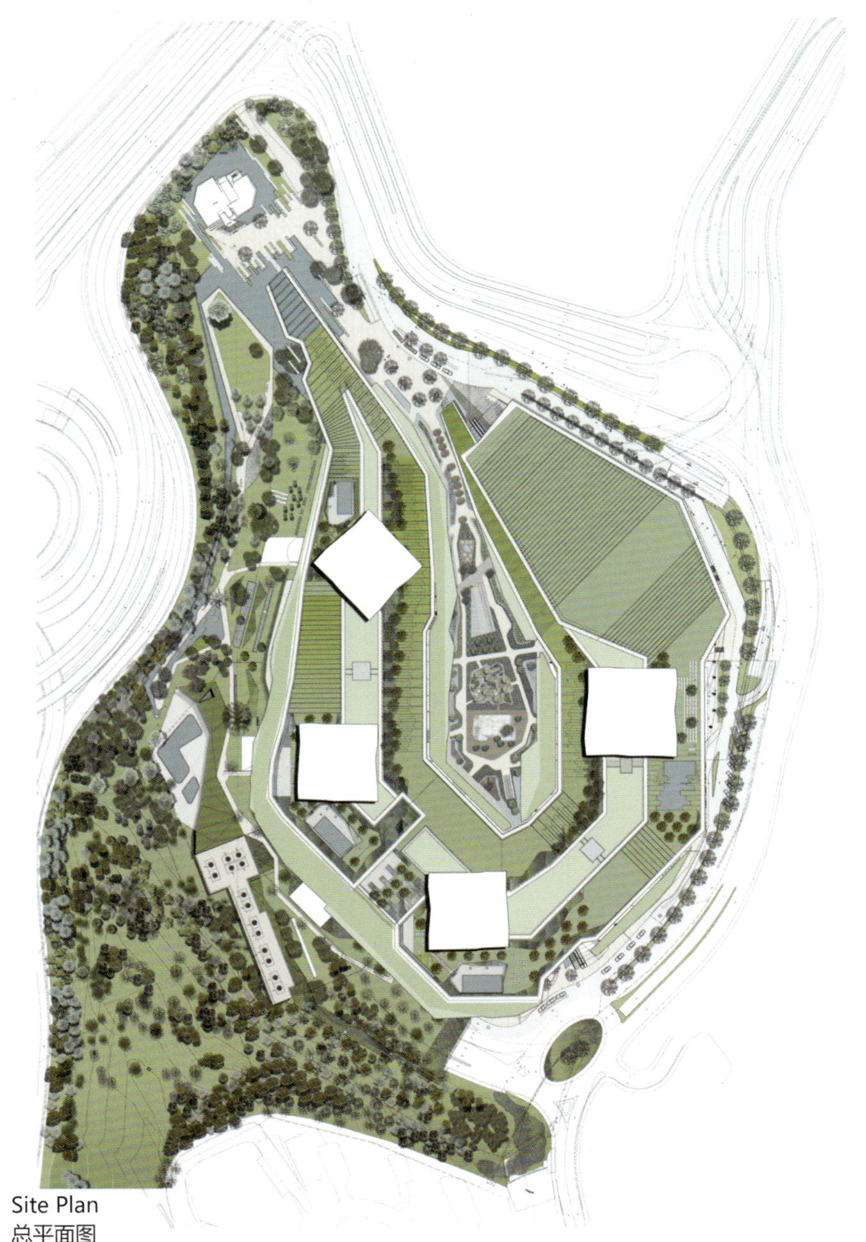

Site Plan
总平面图

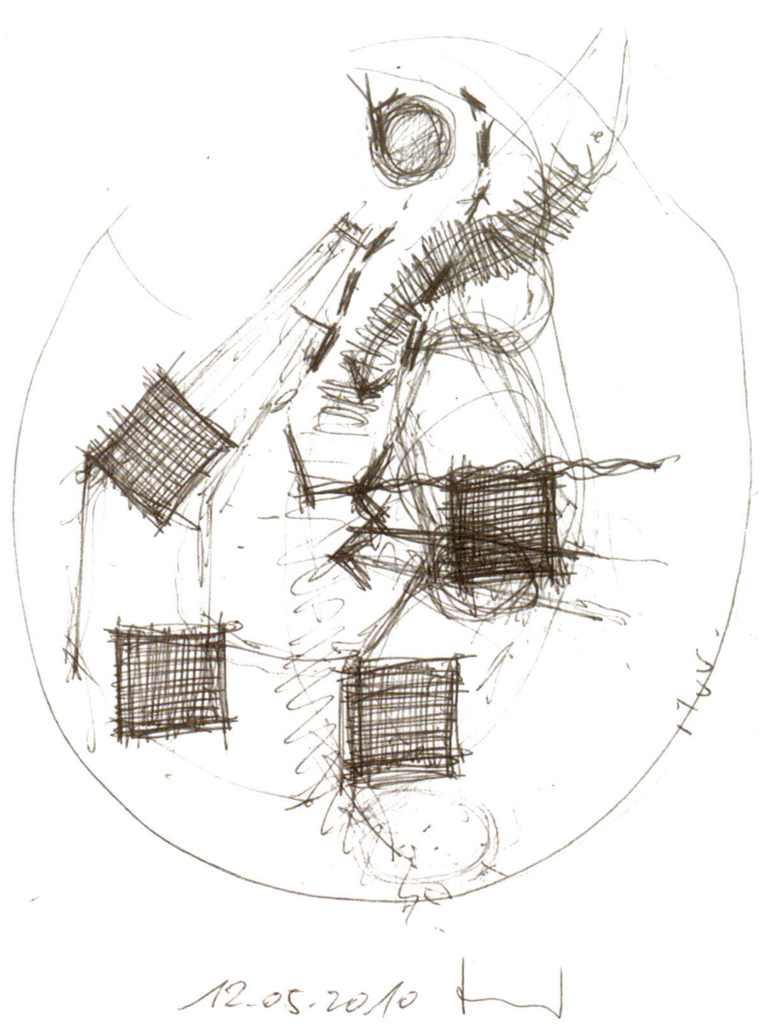

Sketch
草图

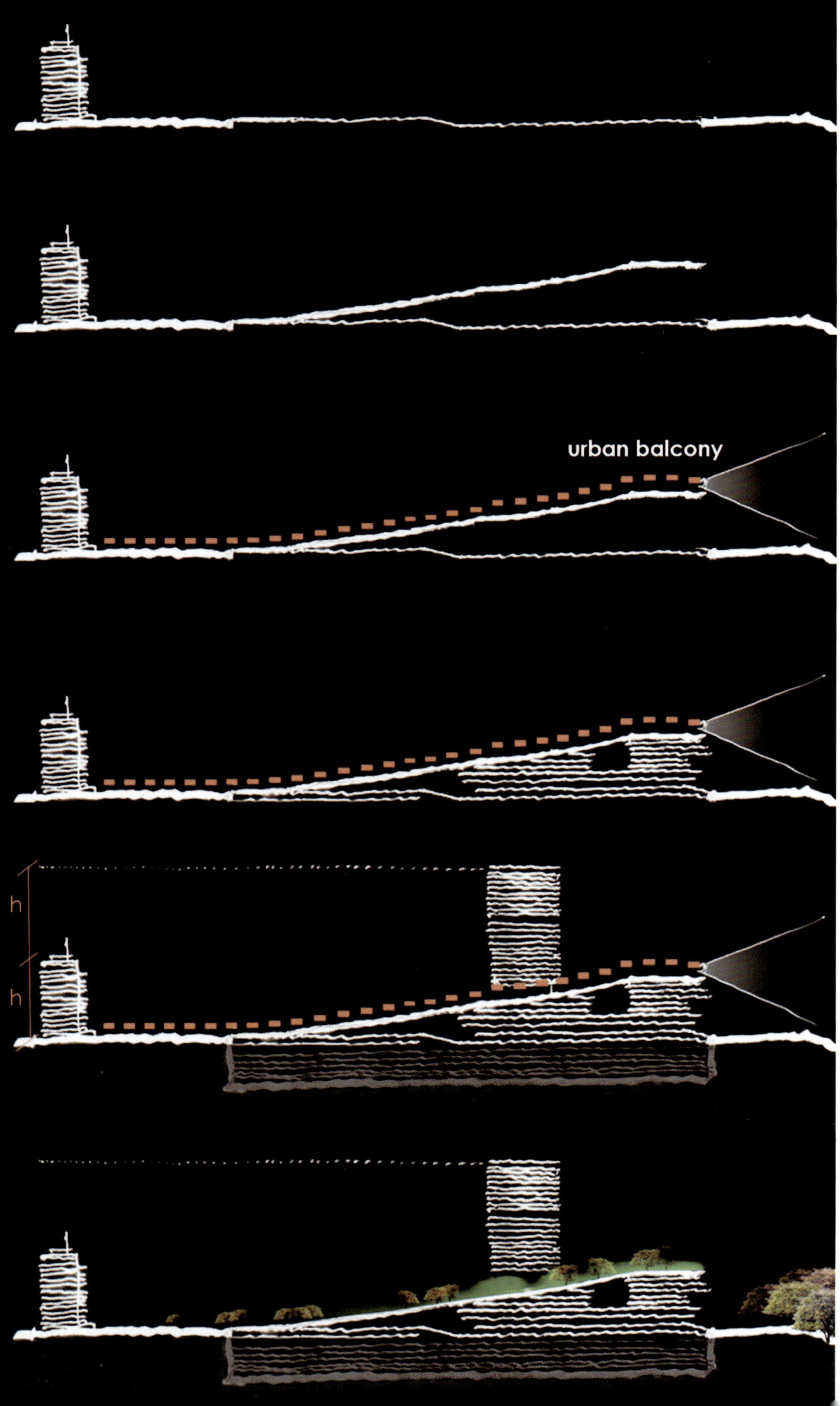

The ground is reconstructed by a topographical interpretation, with a kind of shell that is transformed into an in-between layer for the different functions combined in the complex. The shell starts from the Boulevard Level, with a Public Square at the meeting point with the city, and rises towards south and east. It is split into two arms seperated by level differences, in order to overcome the dichotomy between the private and the public. The inner route, the Public Topography reaches to the 28m. higher Urban Balcony with the marvellous Bosphorus view. The outer ring ends up with a height of 32m creating the Private Topography of the residential units.

项目场址根据地形判断进行了重建，建筑表面有一个作为连接层的外壳，在综合体中起着多种作用。外壳从街道层开始，在城市的交汇点形成了一个公共广场，并朝东南两个方向逐渐攀升，根据水平差不同，形成两条“手臂”，这种设计可以区分公共场所和私人场所。内部的公共空间可达到 28 米高，视野开阔，可以一览博斯普鲁斯的壮丽风景。外环的建筑高 32 米，是私人空间的住宅部分。

büyükdere st via maslak
büyükdere st via taksim
barbaros blvd via beşiktaş
1st bridge (eurasia connectio

Just in the center, at the Boulevard Level is the Piazza surrounded by the retail units, that strives for creating an alternative public space. The Activity Stairs direct the public down to the interior retail units, the Bosphorus Level, that also has another direct entrance on south. The retail level below has the Metro connection and houses cinemas, kids entertainment center, big gourmet market and leisure platforms. The retail center offers both exterior and interior shopping in relation to a Piazza that feeds the whole complex. The Concet Hall of 2,500 people capacity has an entrance amphi as a continuation of the Public Square and the Piazza, that offers a semi-closed space for alternative performances.

在街道层的中心是一个广场，广场周围坐落着很多零售商店，这个地区是公共场所。“活动楼梯”从公共空间一直向下通往室内零售区，在街道层南边还有一个直接入口进入零售区。零售层有地铁、影院、儿童娱乐中心、美食超市和休闲平台。零售中心提供内外部购物体验，连通露天市场一起满足整个综合体的购物需求。音乐厅可容纳 2,500 人，入口与公共广场和露天市场相连，是一个半封闭的建筑，里面可举办各类表演。

Performing Art Center Entrance Sketch
表演艺术中心入口草图

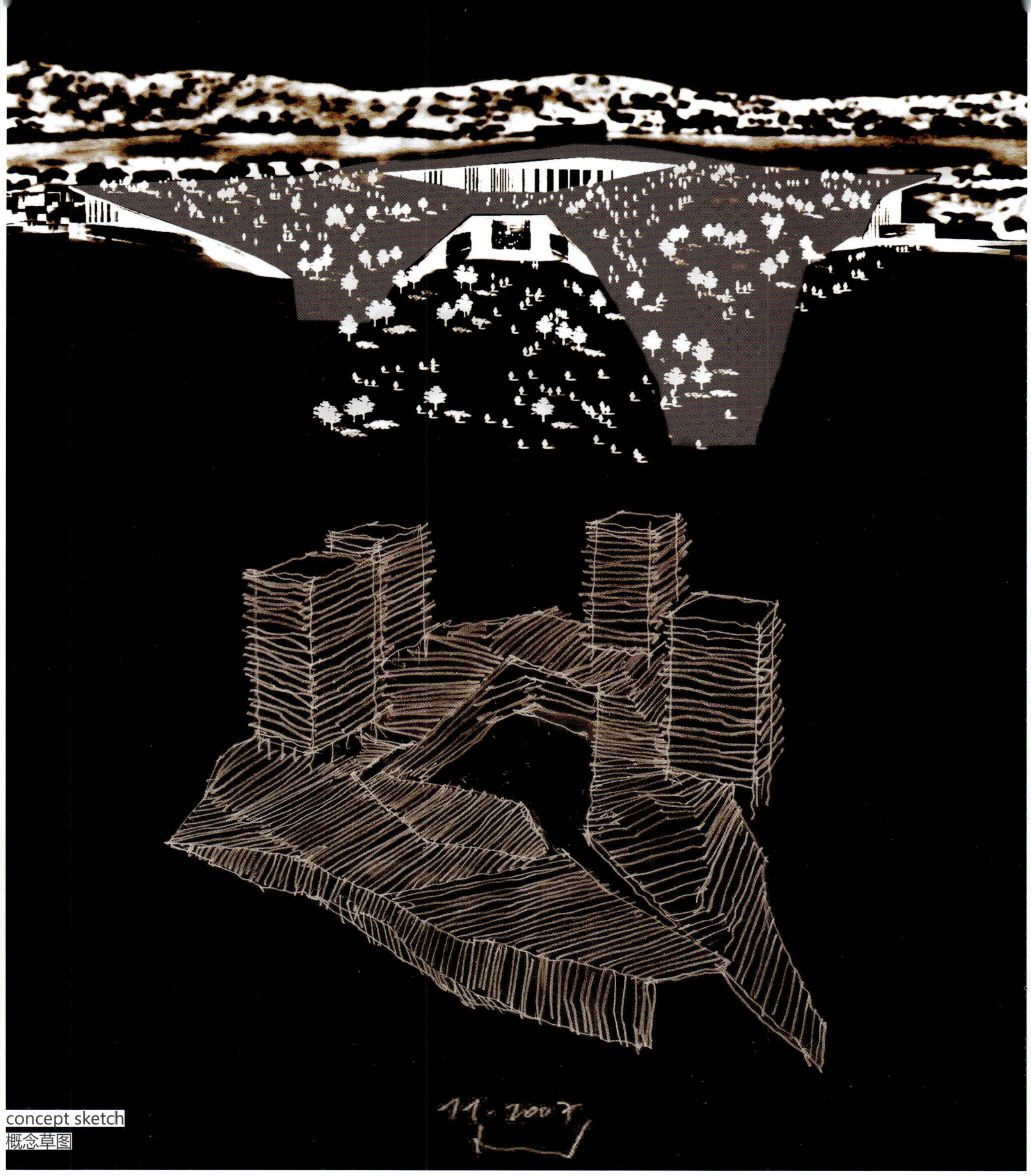

concept sketch
概念草图

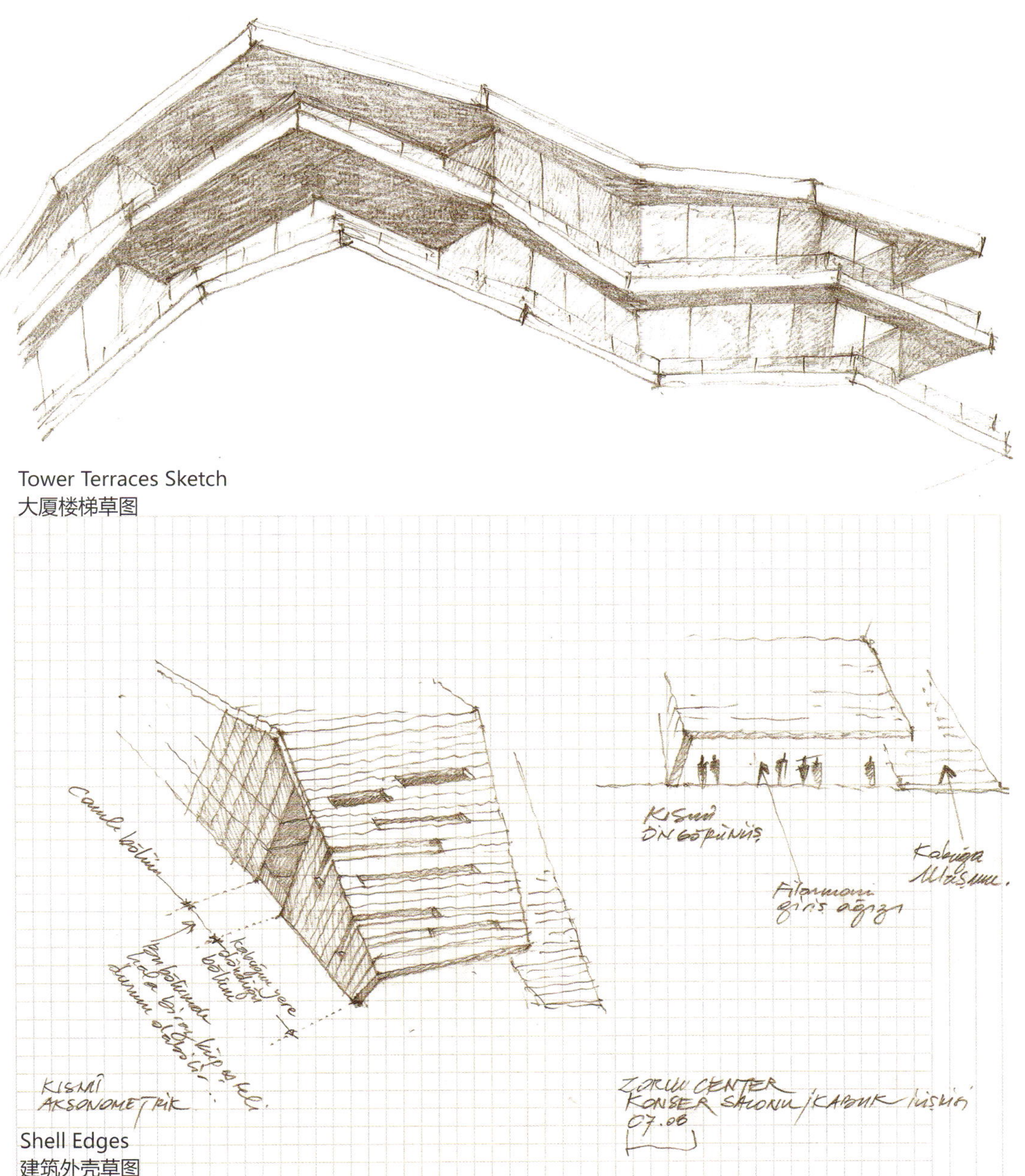

Tower Terraces Sketch
大厦楼梯草图

Shell Edges
建筑外壳草图

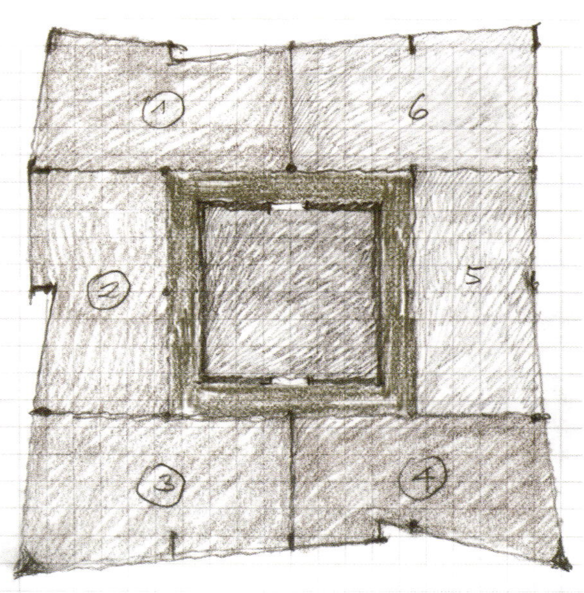

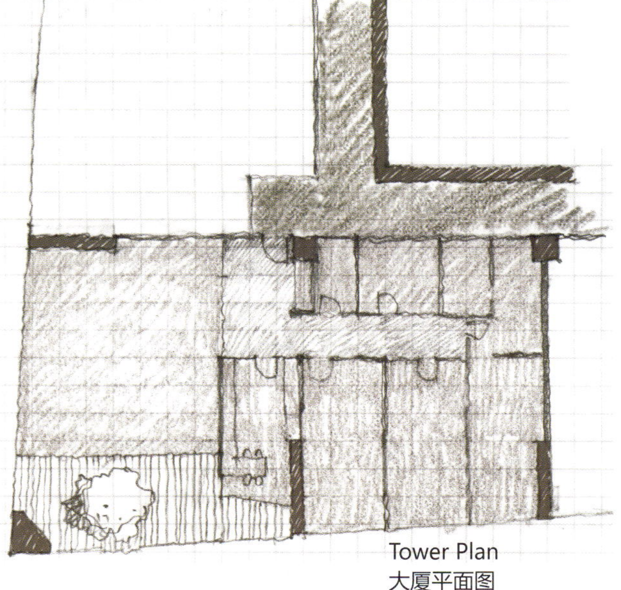

Tower Plan
大厦平面图

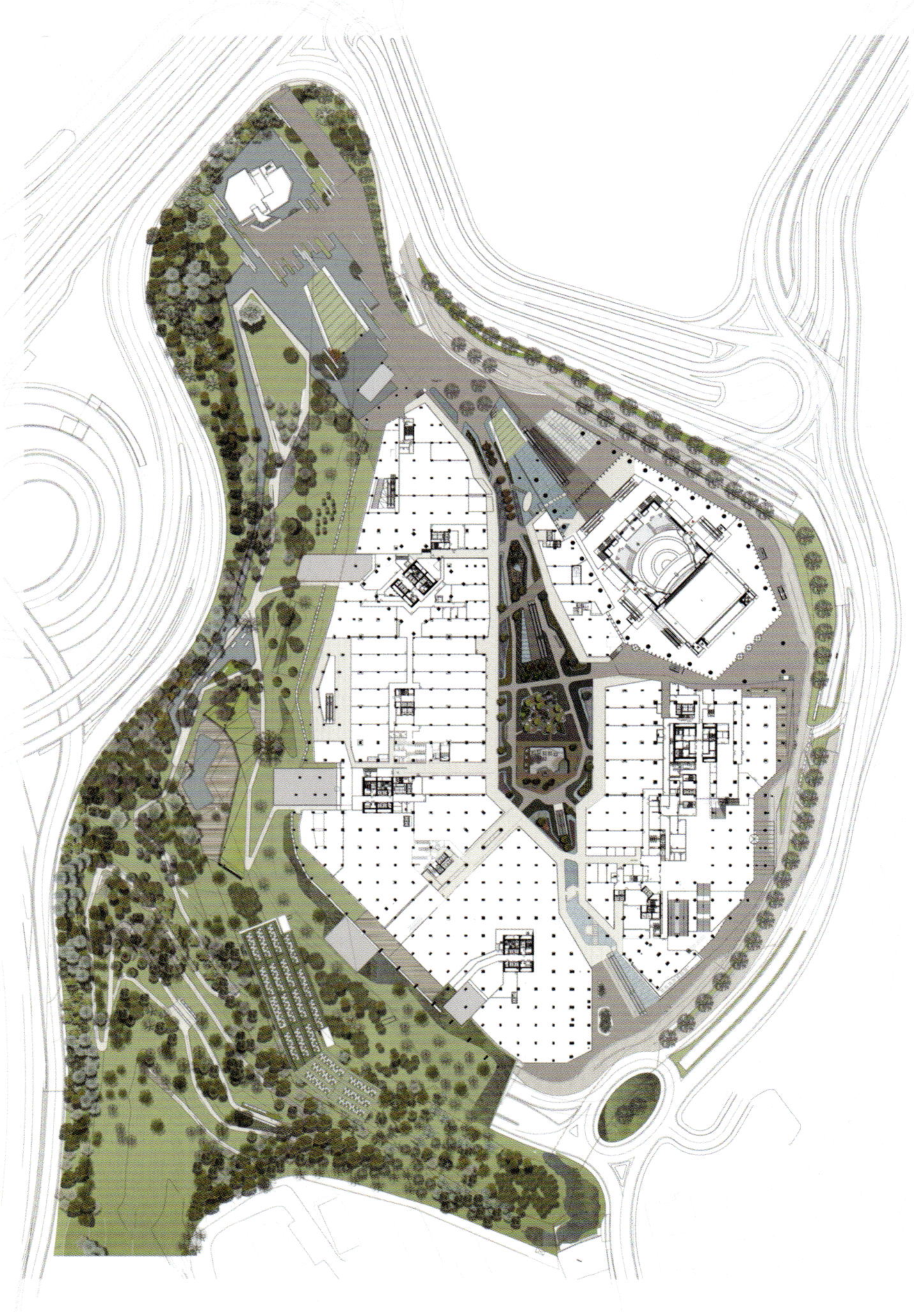

1st Floor Plan
一层平面图

Second (Terrace Residences) Floor Plan
第二个露台住宅平面图

The terrace flats under the shell, are equipped with large gardens on the first level, and with large terraces on the upper levels enjoying the Bosphorus view. They are reached through the linear open air atrium, quite rich, lighted and cheery space. The rest of the residential units form three identical towers, detached from the shell with "piloti" and their structural formation continues the horizontal projections of the terrace flats, without turning into symbollic elements of the complex. The fourth tower is the luxury Bosphorus Hotel.

In the general formation of the complex, instead of using the recent grandiose and gleeming architectural tendency that has been dominant over such big investments of the modern world, an approach that derives its power from public motivations and keeps itself away from the habit of "society of spectacle" has been embraced. mplex. The fourth tower is the luxury Bosphorus Hotel.

外壳下方露台平层的第一层建有大型花园，上面的楼层则设有大型露台，可以欣赏博斯普鲁斯的景色。通过直线型露天中庭可以轻松抵达这些露台，而中庭则是一个光线充足的愉悦空间。住宅区由三栋相同的塔楼组成，与外壳完全分离，设有底层架空柱，其构造形式延续了露台平层的水平结构，与综合体的象征元素风格迥异。第四栋塔楼是奢华的博斯普鲁斯酒店。

综合体的总体构造并没有使用在现代社会的建筑潮流中占据主导地位的宏伟而闪亮的建筑风格，而是从公众动机中汲取能量，从“奇观社会”的习惯中解放出来，形成自己独特的风格。

BURBERRY

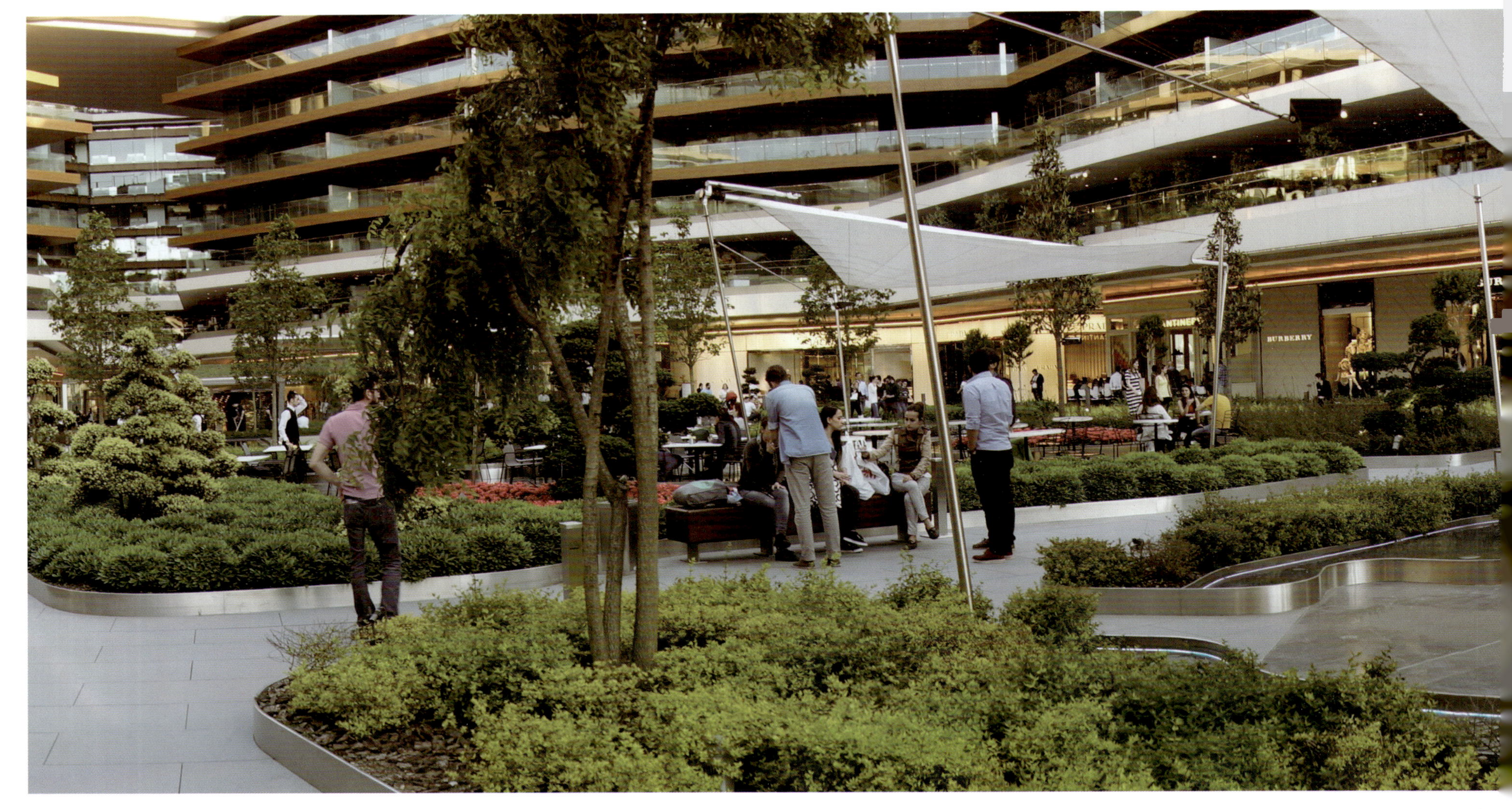

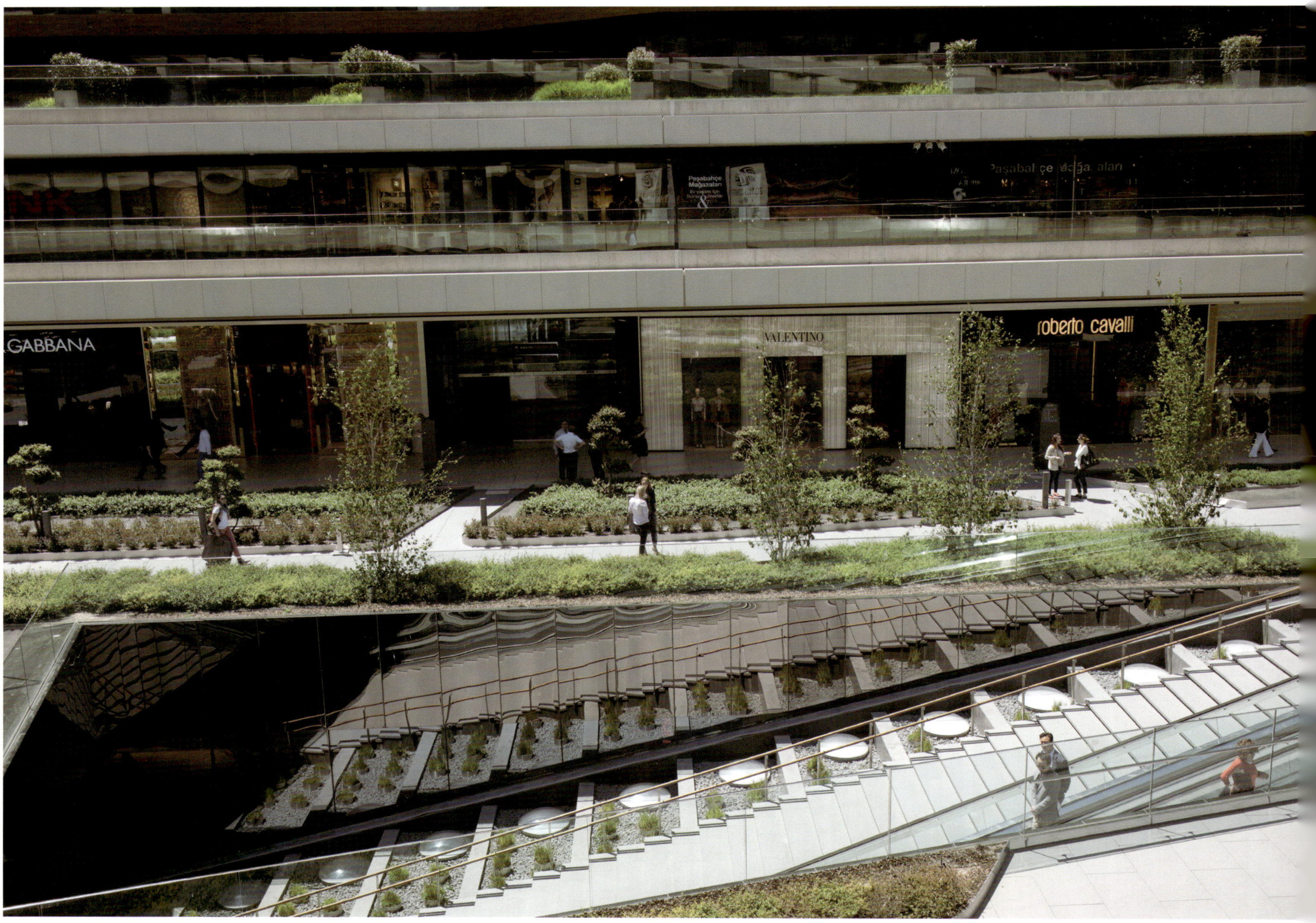
GABBANA
VALENTINO
roberto cavalli

DOLCE & GABBANA
DOLCE & GABBANA
DOLCE & GABBANA

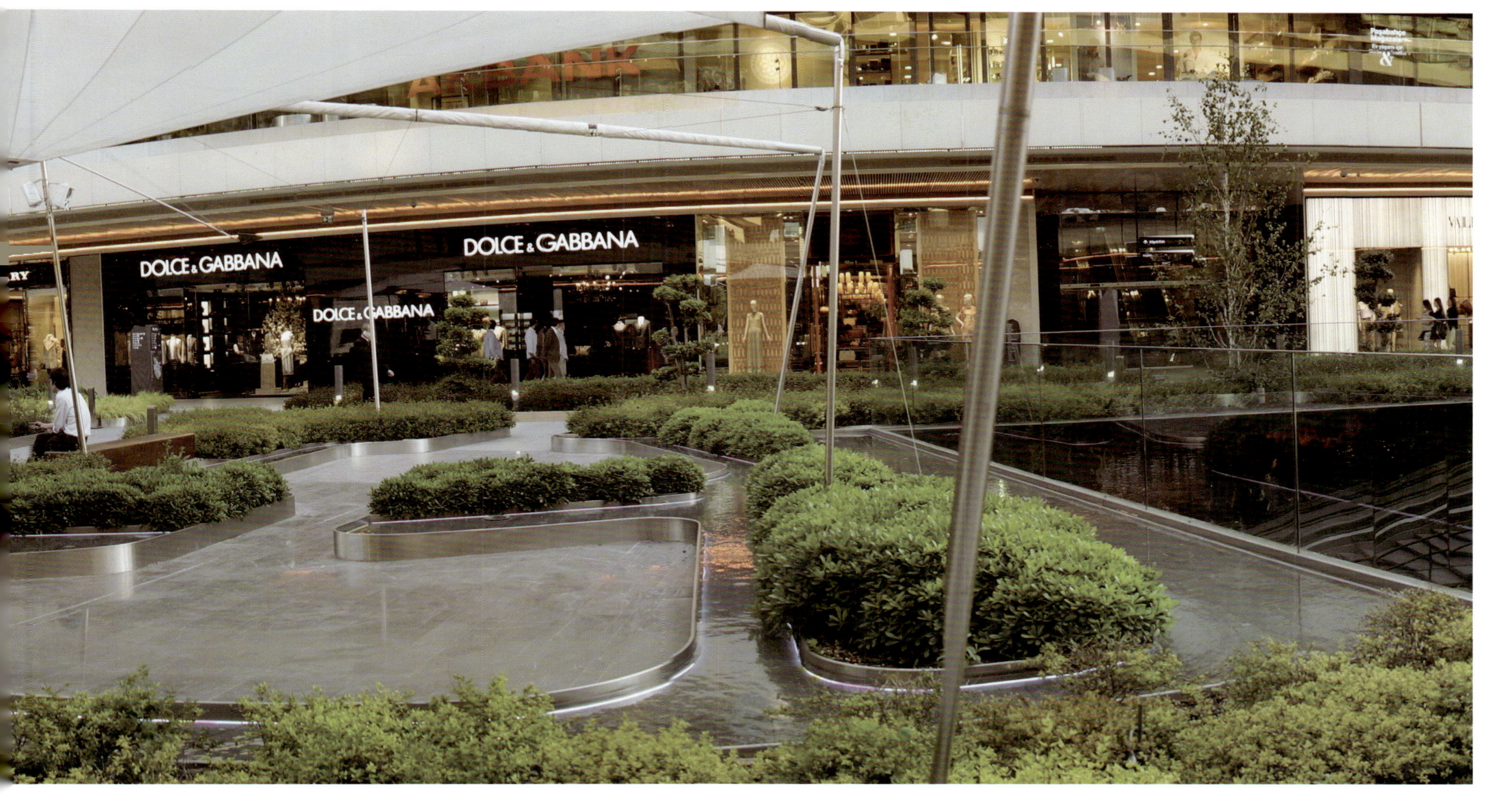

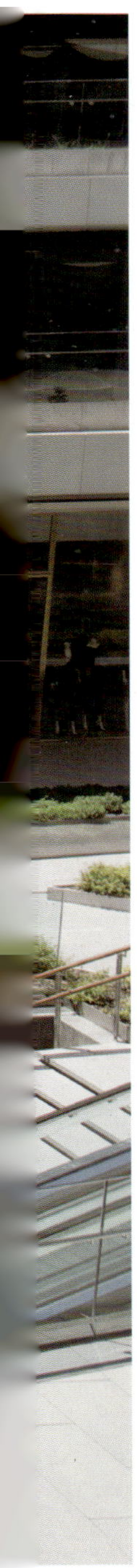

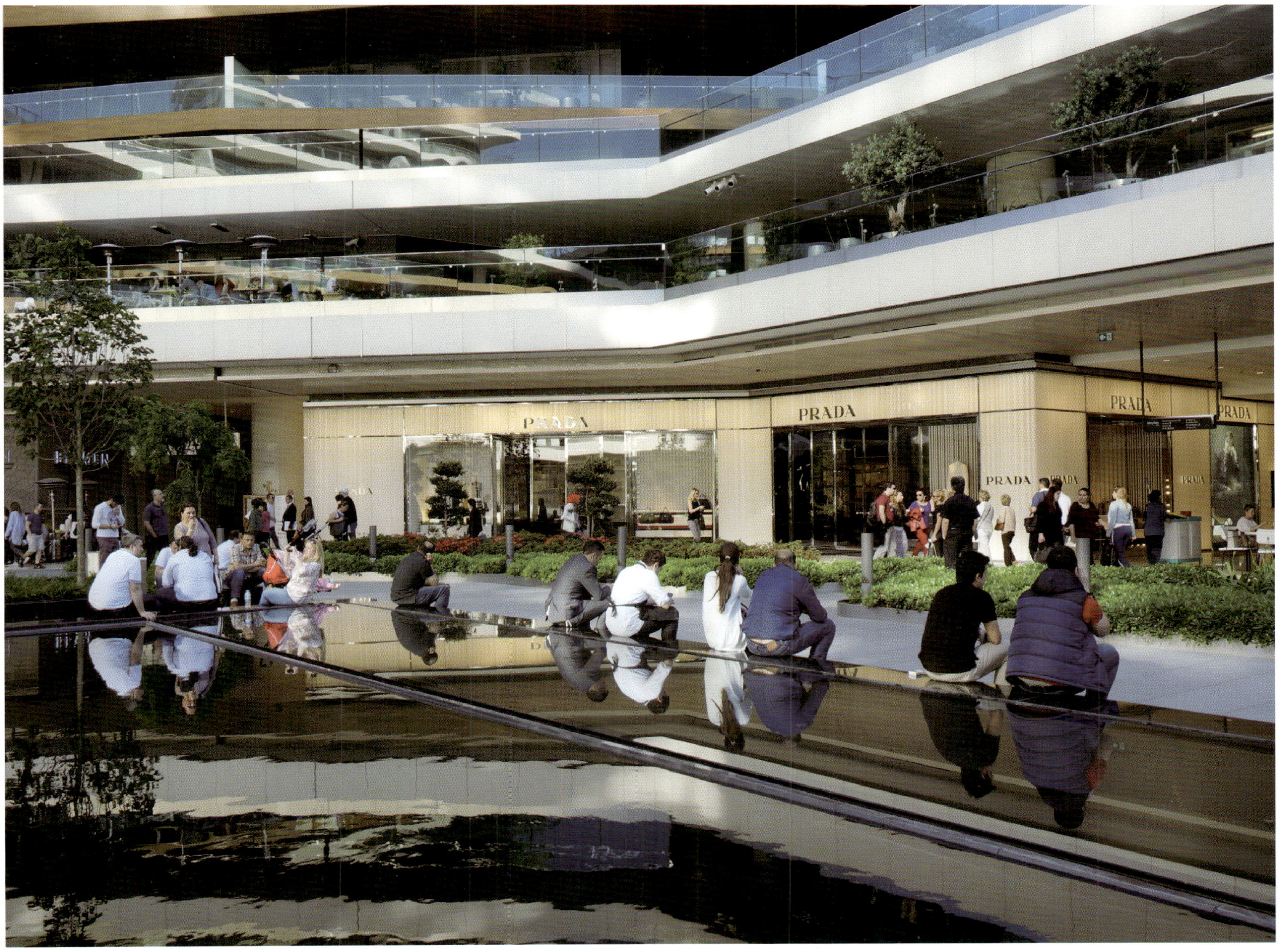
PRADA
PRADA
PRADA
PRADA
PRADA

Patchi

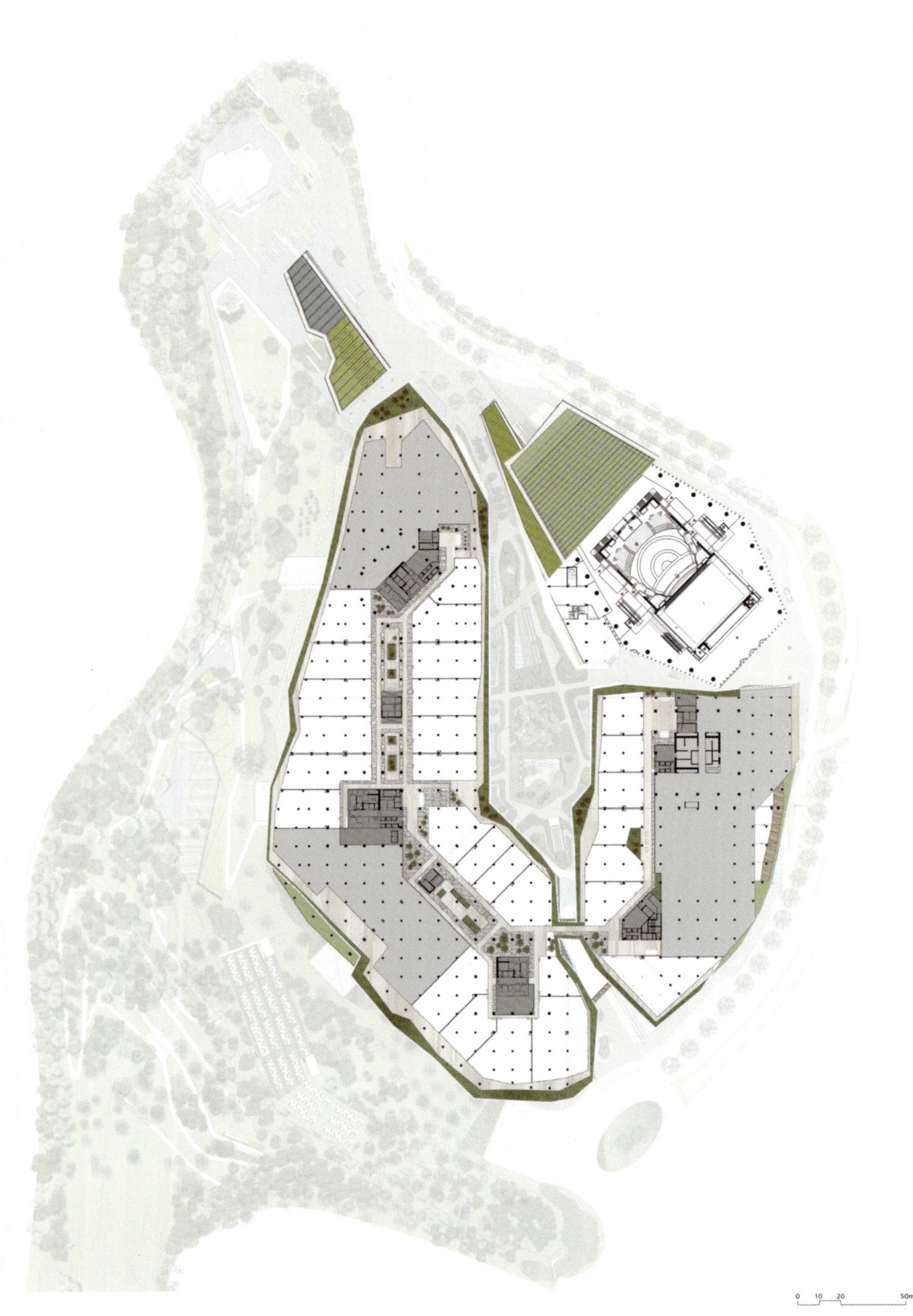

1st Floor Plan
一层（办公室）平面图

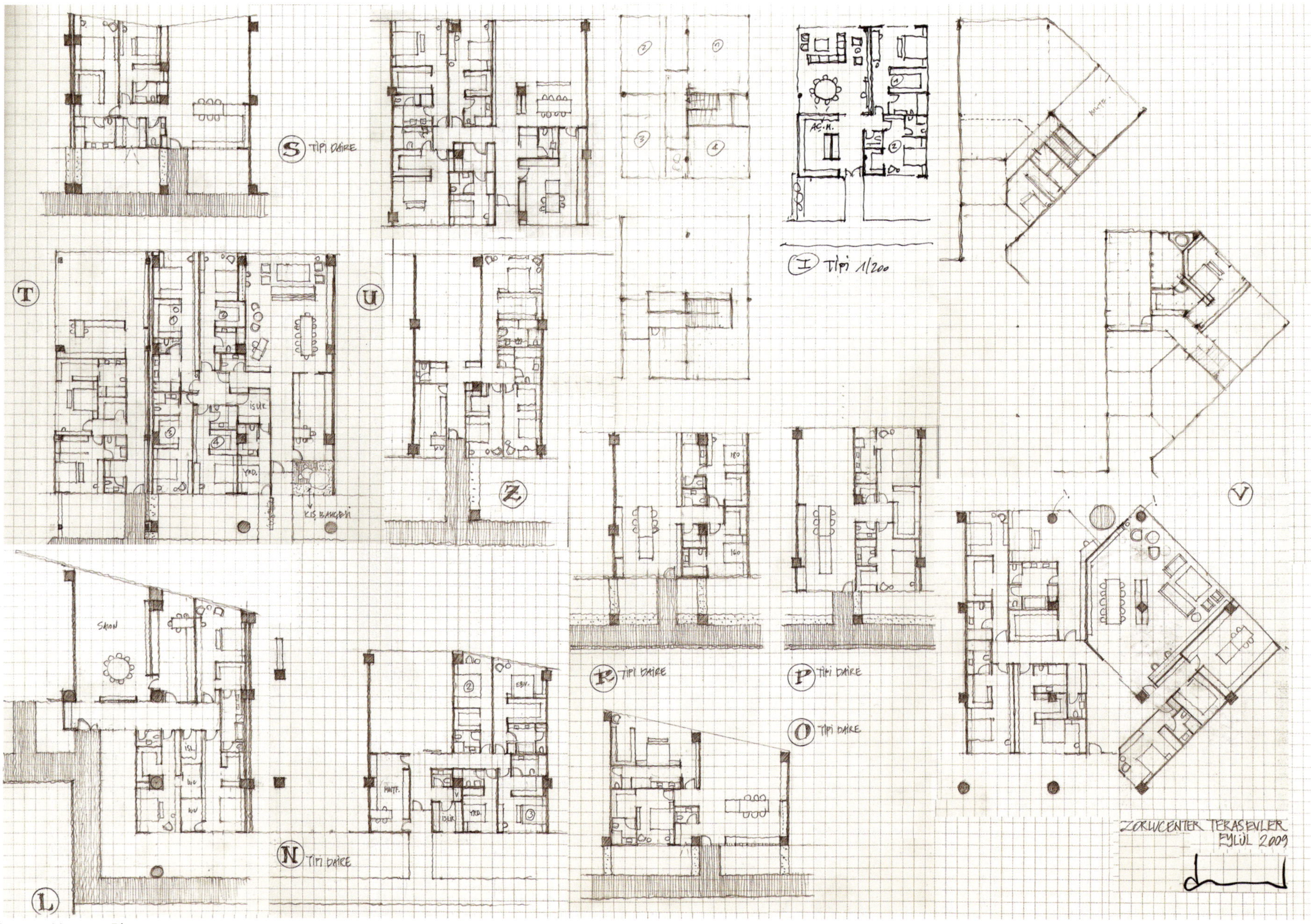

Terrace Houses Plan
露台房屋平面图平面图

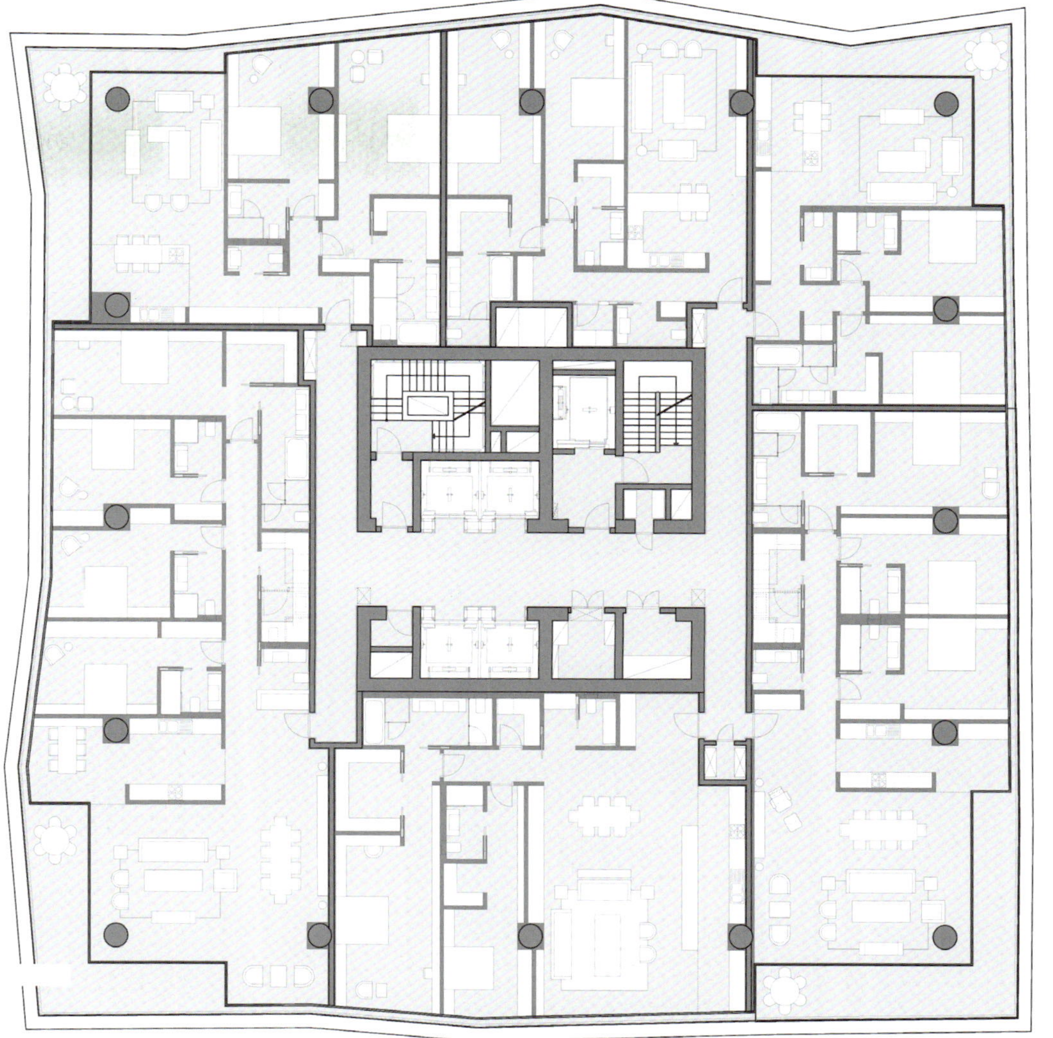

Residential Tower Plan
住宅楼平面图

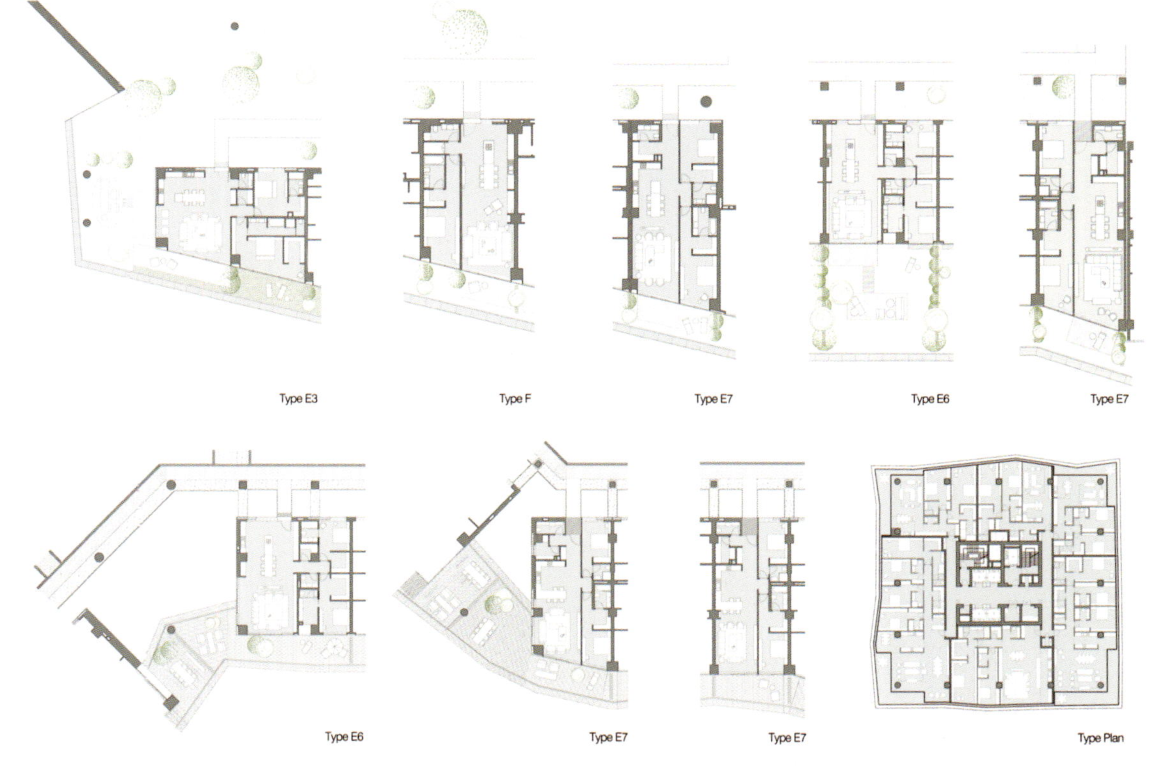

ZC Plans Types 1
佐鲁中心标准平面图 1

ZC Plans Types 2
佐鲁中心标准平面图 2

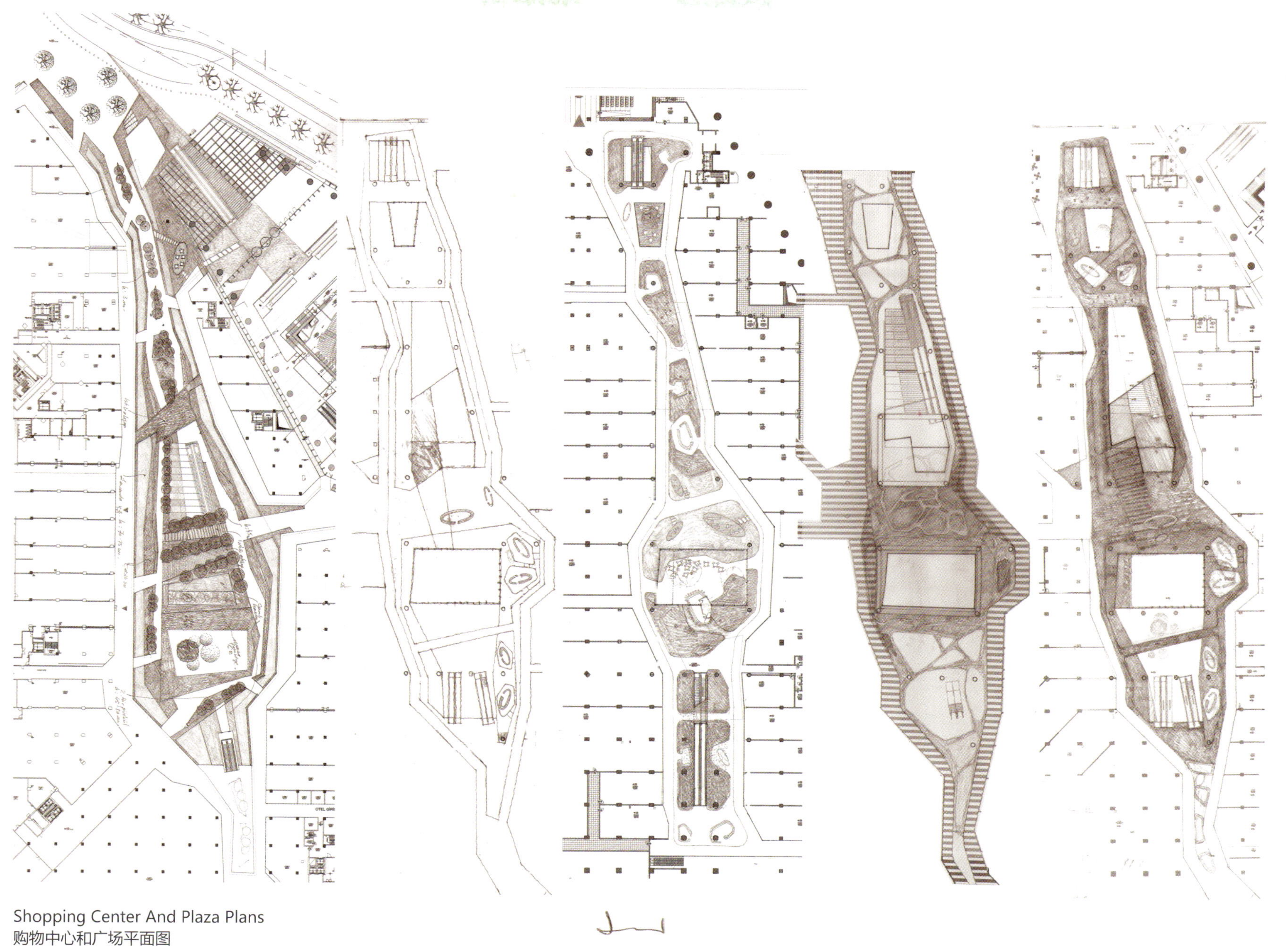

Shopping Center And Plaza Plans
购物中心和广场平面图

Performing Art Center Plans
表演艺术中心平面图

PROJECT NAME 项目名称

GERMANY KÖ-BOGEN DÜSSELDORF

德国杜塞尔多夫库伯根项目

Architect: Studio Daniel Libeskind (SDL) + Architect Daniel Libeskind AG (ADL)

设计公司：Studio Daniel Libeskind (SDL) + Architect Daniel Libeskind AG (ADL)

PROJECT INFORMATION 项目信息

Joint venture partner	Studio Daniel Libeskind with Architekt Daniel Libeskind AG, Zurich		
Location	Dusseldorf , Germany	**地点**	德国杜塞尔多夫
Area	40,000m²	**面积**	40,000 平方米
Building Area	Base Design: 40,165 m²,Underground Parking: 13,547 m², Alternative Design :38,097 m²	**建筑面积**	基础设计：40,165 平方米；地下停车场；13,547 平方米；替代设计：38,097 平方米

OVERVIEW 项目概况

Kö-Bogen, currently under construction, is a six-story 432,300-square-foot office and retail complex in downtown Düsseldorf and marks an important transition between urban space and landscape. Two city blocks will be joined with one continuous roof line, forming a unified space for walking, shopping and working. The building will also create a connected space between the Schadowplatz, a pedestrian street, and the Hofgarten, the central park in Düsseldorf.

目前在建的库伯根项目，位于杜塞尔多夫市中心，是一栋六层 40，000 平方米的办公及零售综合大楼。它标志着城市空间和景观之间的重要过渡。从此，城市的两个街区就会被一个连续的屋顶连接起来，形成连续的行走，购物和工作空间。该建筑也将创建出一个连续空间把 Schadowplatz ，步行街与位于杜塞尔多夫中央公园的宫廷花园联系起来。

BRIEF INTERVIEW 访谈录

ARCHITECT
Stefan Blach

设计师
斯蒂芬 • 布拉克

HKASP: What are the important things that this project does for the city?
Studio Daniel Libeskind (SDL) + Architect Daniel Libeskind AG (ADL): Kö-Bogen is a six-storey 40,162m² office and retail complex in downtown Düsseldorf and marking an important transition between urban space and landscape. Two city blocks, joined by a two-storey bridge with a roof terrace create new urban spaces for shopping and leisure: Kö-Bogen completes the Königsallee boulevard at Hofgarten park and shapes the new Hofgarten promenade and terraces, places that have already become popular with the people of Düsseldorf. The building also gives shape to Schadowplatz square and forms a passage towards Hofgarten, busy with boutiques, restaurants and cafes with outdoor seating. Permeated cuts into the facades towards Königsallee and Hofgarten allow for the landscape to naturally blend and flow into the building.

HKASP: 2.When designing, is there something in particular that you focus on? (Material, form, use etc)
Studio Daniel Libeskind (SDL) + Architect Daniel Libeskind AG (ADL):A particular focus was on the building volume and how it shapes the urban space at this prominent location. Towards Königsallee and Hofgarten, Kö-Bogen is retracing historical buildings lines, while towards Schadowplatz and Gustaf-Gründgens Platz the building's curved outline form new fluid urban public spaces, which are carried into the passage towards Hofgarten. The two individual blocks are joined by a bridge that springs from one building and is received by the other.
Another focus was on how the facades enhance the character of the building and communicate with its urban context. The main facades are made of light-colored Travertine stone and opaque and transparent glass in a flush arrangement. Various sizes of glass and natural stone components form complex patterns that conceal their modular order at first glance. The same system is used in two different configurations: on the sides oriented towards Königsallee and Hofgarten, a vertical pattern is generated, using different widths components within the approximately 1.35 m wide facade elements. On the sides towards Schadowplatz and Gustaf-Gründgens Platz, using components of various heights within the same sized facade elements a horizontal pattern is created. The staggered horizontal bands amplify the dynamic character of the building along the newly shaped pedestrian spaces.

香港建筑科学出版社：你觉得这个项目给这个城市带来了什么重要的东西呢？
Studio Daniel Libeskind (SDL) + Architect Daniel Libeskind AG (ADL):Kö-Bogen 建筑高 6 层，建筑面积为 40，162 平方米，兼有办公和零售功能。它位于杜塞尔多夫的市中心，在城市空间和景观空间之间发挥承前启下的作用。两栋大楼之间通过一座双层天桥连接，天桥最上面一层为观景露台。天桥的连接形成了一个集购物与休闲于一体的新城市空间。Kö-Bogen 的存在填补了宫廷公园国王大道的空缺，形成了已受杜塞尔多夫人民热捧的宫廷新散步道、露台与聚集地。此外，建筑的存在不仅塑造了沙多广场，而且还是通往宫廷公园的通道。建筑内设有众多精品店、餐馆、咖啡，并在室外安置了座椅。人们的视线可穿过立面上的切口，直达国王大道与宫廷公园，让建筑与远处的景观形成自然的交融，成为建筑物一幅美丽的背景画。

香港建筑科学出版社：在设计的过程中，有什么是你们特别关注的吗？（比如材料或者形式）
Studio Daniel Libeskind (SDL) + Architect Daniel Libeskind AG (ADL): 我们特别关注建筑体量。如何通过建筑体量来塑造黄金地段的城市空间。在朝国王大道与宫廷公园一侧，Kö-Bogen 的建筑线条表达出一种对历史建筑的追忆。然而，在朝沙多广场与格林德根斯 • 古斯塔法广场的一侧，建筑的曲线造型勾画出一系列行如流水般的新空间，这样的空间风格一直延续至通往宫廷公园的大道。两栋大楼由一座天桥连接。天桥从一栋大楼起身跳跃，降落到另一栋大楼上。
另外一个关注点就是如何通过立面凸显建筑特色，从而迎合周边环境。主立面采用淡色的石灰华天然洞石，同时在同一平面上配合透明与不透明的玻璃。各种大小的玻璃与天然石材构件形成了复杂的立面肌理，从而轻而易举地隐藏了采板的次序。同样的构件组合通过两种不同的格局展现：在朝国王大道与宫廷公园一侧的立面上采用垂直格局，在大约 1.35 米宽的立面元素中采用不同宽度的构件。然而，在朝沙多广场与格林德根斯 • 古斯塔法广场一侧的立面上采用水平格局，在同样宽度的立面元素内采用不同高度的构件。以新形成的步行空间为背景，纵横交错的横条纹更加凸显建筑的动态感。

HKASP: 3.What was the biggest challenge in this project? Any story you can share with us?

Studio Daniel Libeskind (SDL) + Architect Daniel Libeskind AG (ADL):A particular challenge was that the building was designed before any leases were signed. The ambition was to create a very articulated and varied facade. Once the leases were signed, of course, each tenant had particular requirements regarding the facade and its openings. When Apple got onboard, they asked for all glass facades on both sides of their shop, which would completely break the continuity of the glass and stone patterns we had created. We reviewed, however, the facades along Schadowplatz and increased the glass percentage overall, an improvement even recognized by the city officials who closely watched over the design. Meanwhile on the Hofgarten side we could convince the tenant of the importance of the continuous facade pattern. The juxtaposition of the two facade types gives the space a unique character, finally much appreciated by the tenant and his patrons.

香港建筑科学出版社：此项目中所面临的最大挑战是什么？有什么值得跟我们分享的吗？

Studio Daniel Libeskind (SDL) + Architect Daniel Libeskind AG (ADL): 我们在签订租约之前就开始着手设计了，这是一大挑战。我们目标是创造出过渡自然，变幻莫测的立面效果。一旦签订了租约，当然，每个租户都有权利对建筑立面与各出入口的设计提出自己的要求。在事已成定局的时候，租户们反而要求在店面四周都采用玻璃立面，这样的要求会完全破外我们所创作的玻璃与石材格局的连续性。我们对此进行了评审，最后在沿沙多广场一侧的立面上增加了玻璃立面的面积。虽然在设计调整过程中，当地市政官员们密切关注我们的设计，但最终这样的调整还是得到了他们的认可。在朝宫廷公园一侧的立面，我们会让租户相信保持立面格局连续性的重要性。同时采用两种立面的确赋予空间独一无二的特点。最后，无论是租户还是店主，都非常欣喜这样的立面设计。

Site Plan
总平面图

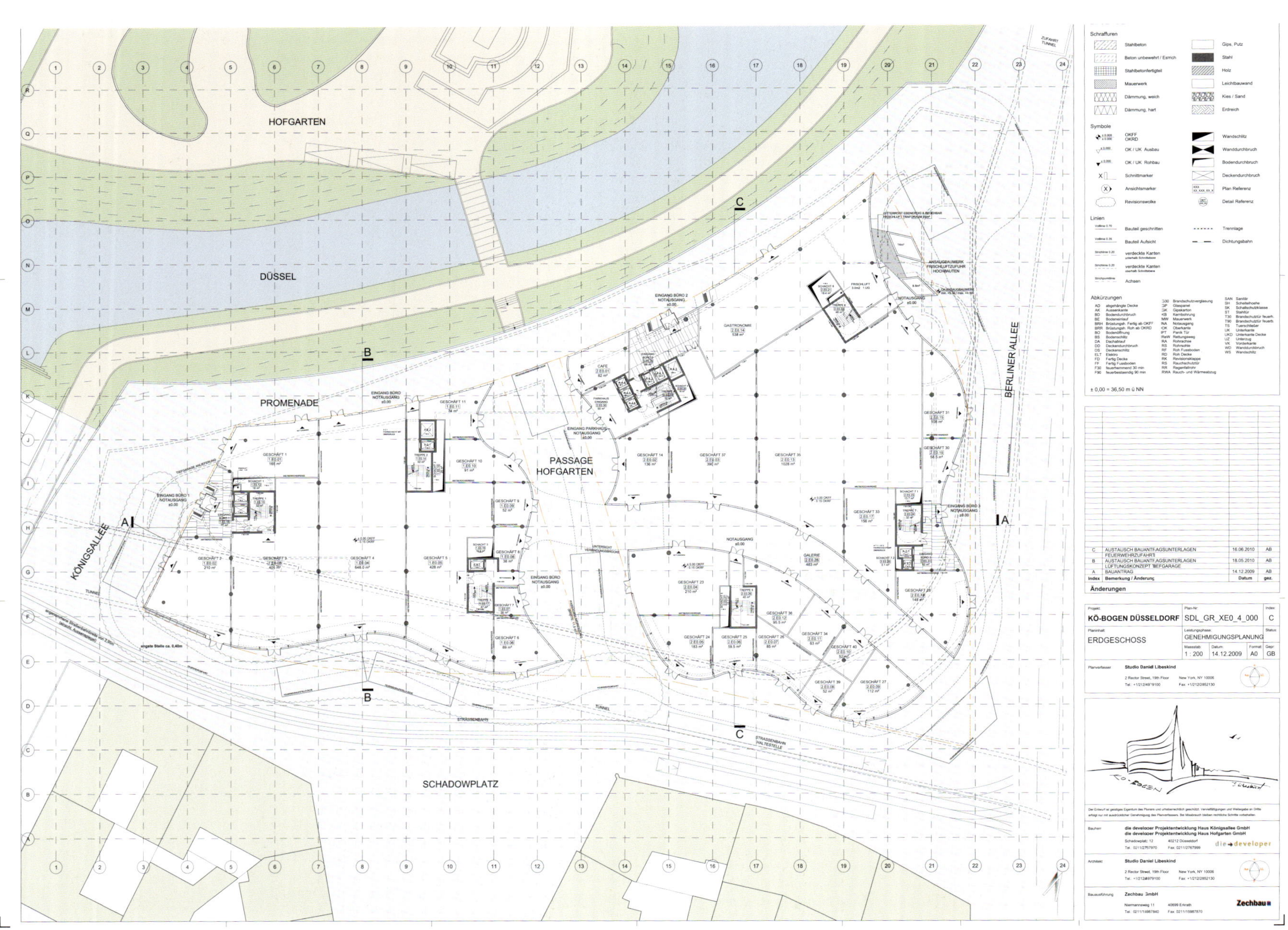

A two-story connecting bridge with roof terrace will connect the east and west blocks of Kö-Bogen and between the two blocks will be green courtyards, which will also provide generous daylight to the interior spaces. Permeated cuts into Kö-Bogen itself will allow for the landscape to naturally blend and flow into the building space. The green courtyards and green roof become part of a new environment that bridges urban space with park space, a fitting entryway to and from the Hofgarten.

带屋顶露台的二层连接桥将连接库伯根的东部和西部两个块。块与块之间将是绿色的庭院，这将把充足的日光引入到室内空间。库伯根建筑本身将可以使得风景自然协调地流入建筑空间。绿色的庭院和屋顶绿化成为横跨在城市空间与公园的空间，使之成为一个合适的入口，并成为新环境的一部分。

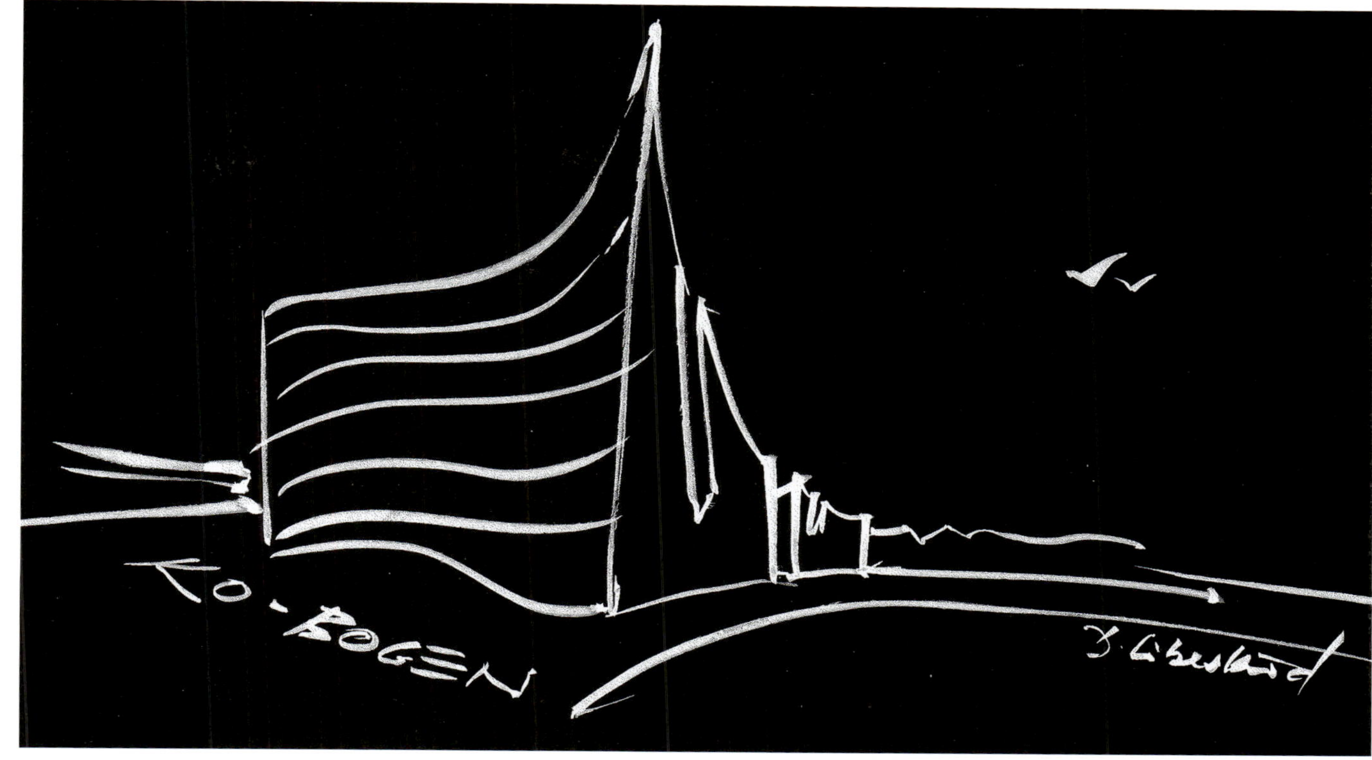

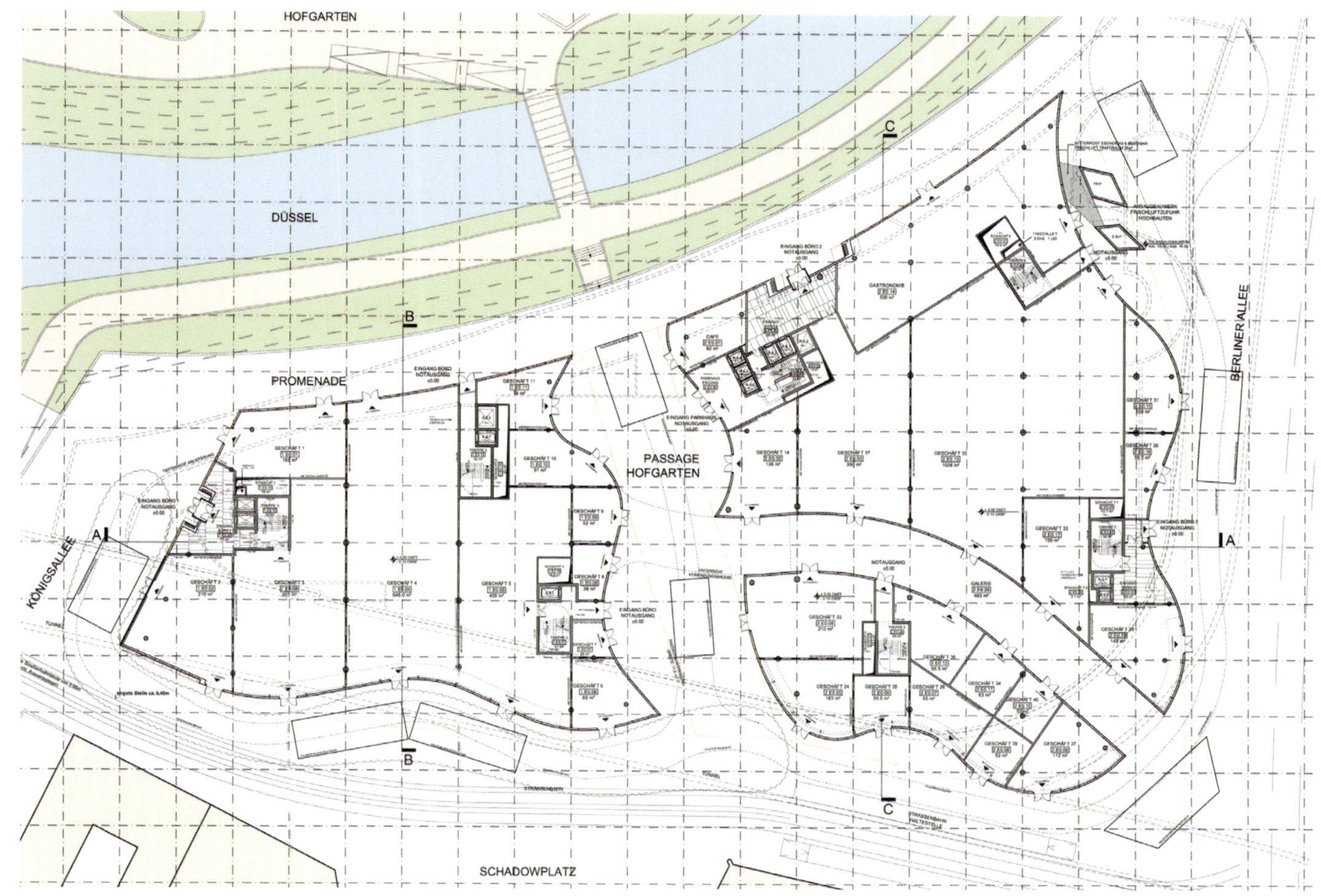

Ground Floor Retail
一楼零售店面图

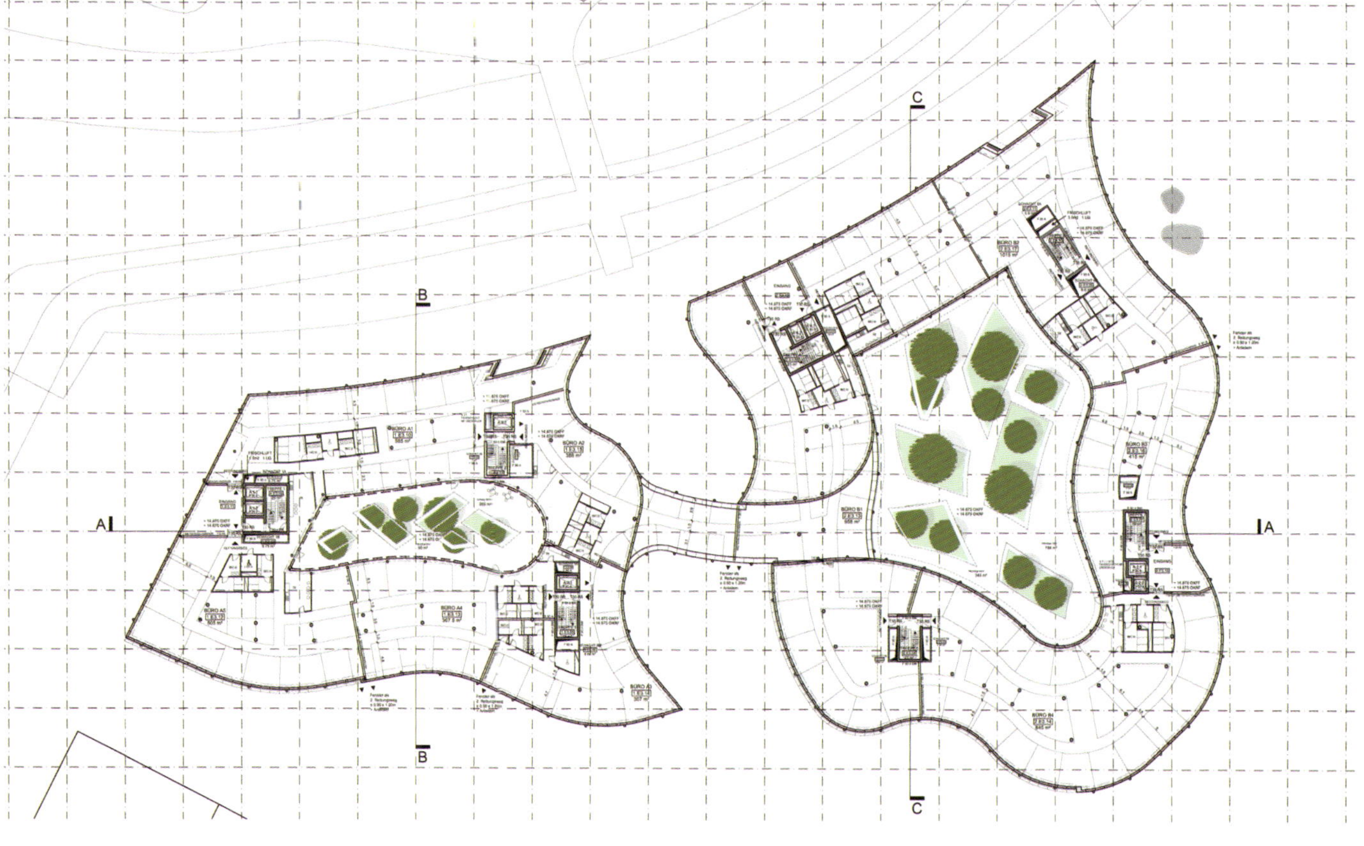

Third Floor Office`
三楼办公室平面图

Elevation 1
立面图 1

Elevation 2
立面图 2

Elevation 3
立面图 3

Elevation 3
立面图 3

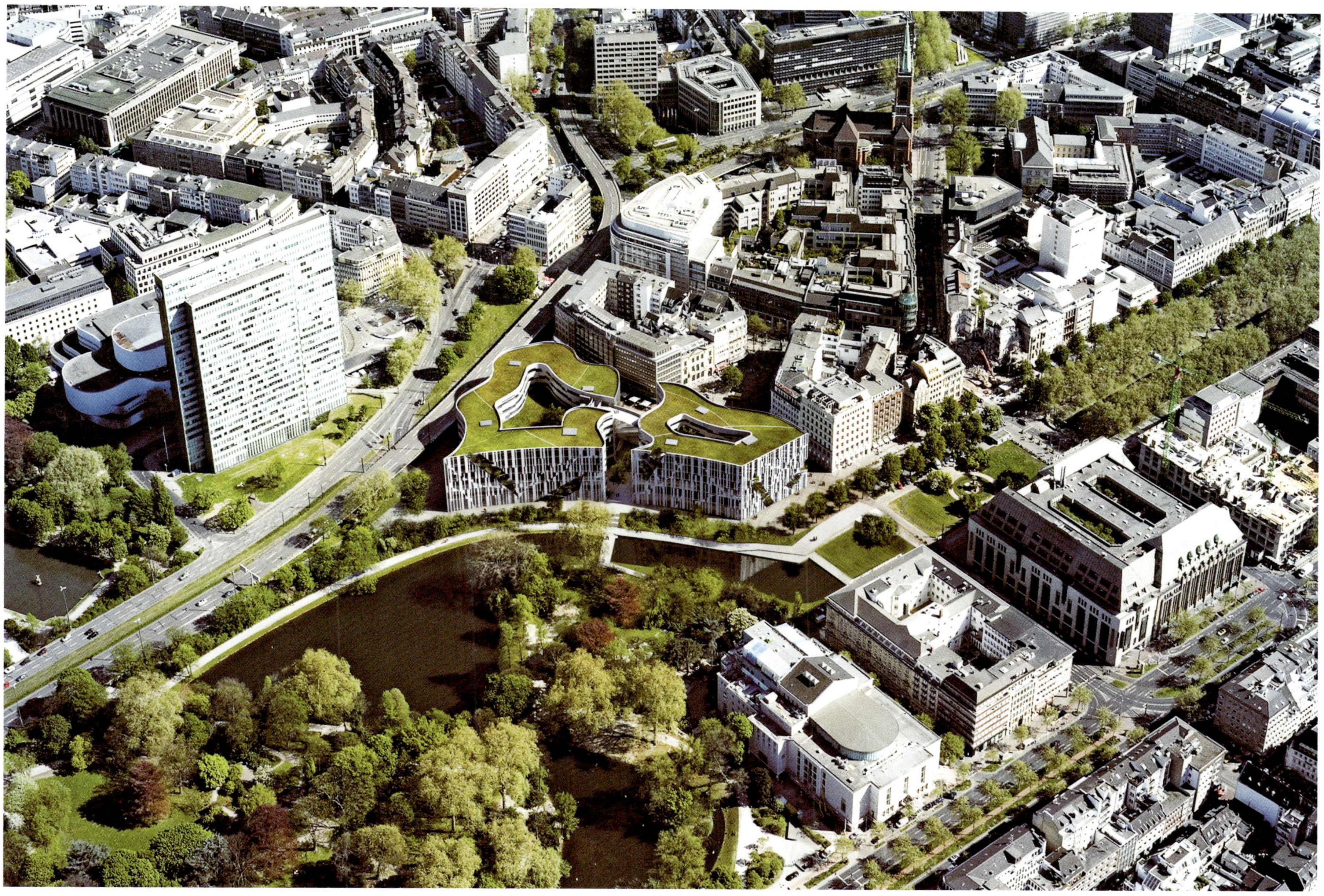

The project is being realized by Studio Daniel Libeskind (SDL) with Architect Daniel Libeskind AG (ADL).

该项目正由丹尼尔·里伯斯金工作室与丹尼尔·里伯斯金 AG 共同设计并实施的。

Kö-Bogen
SAN MARCO

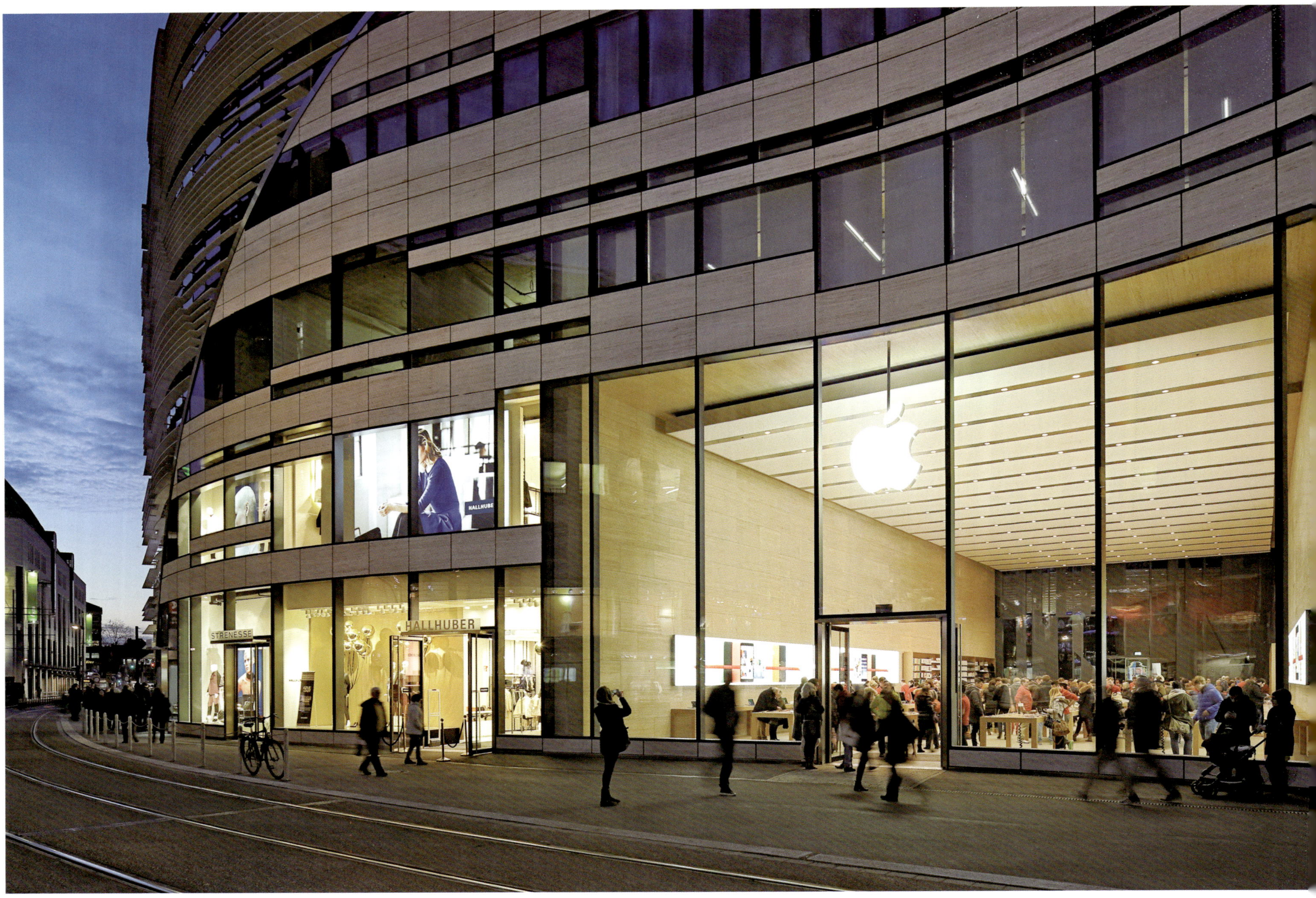
STRENESSE
HALLHUBER

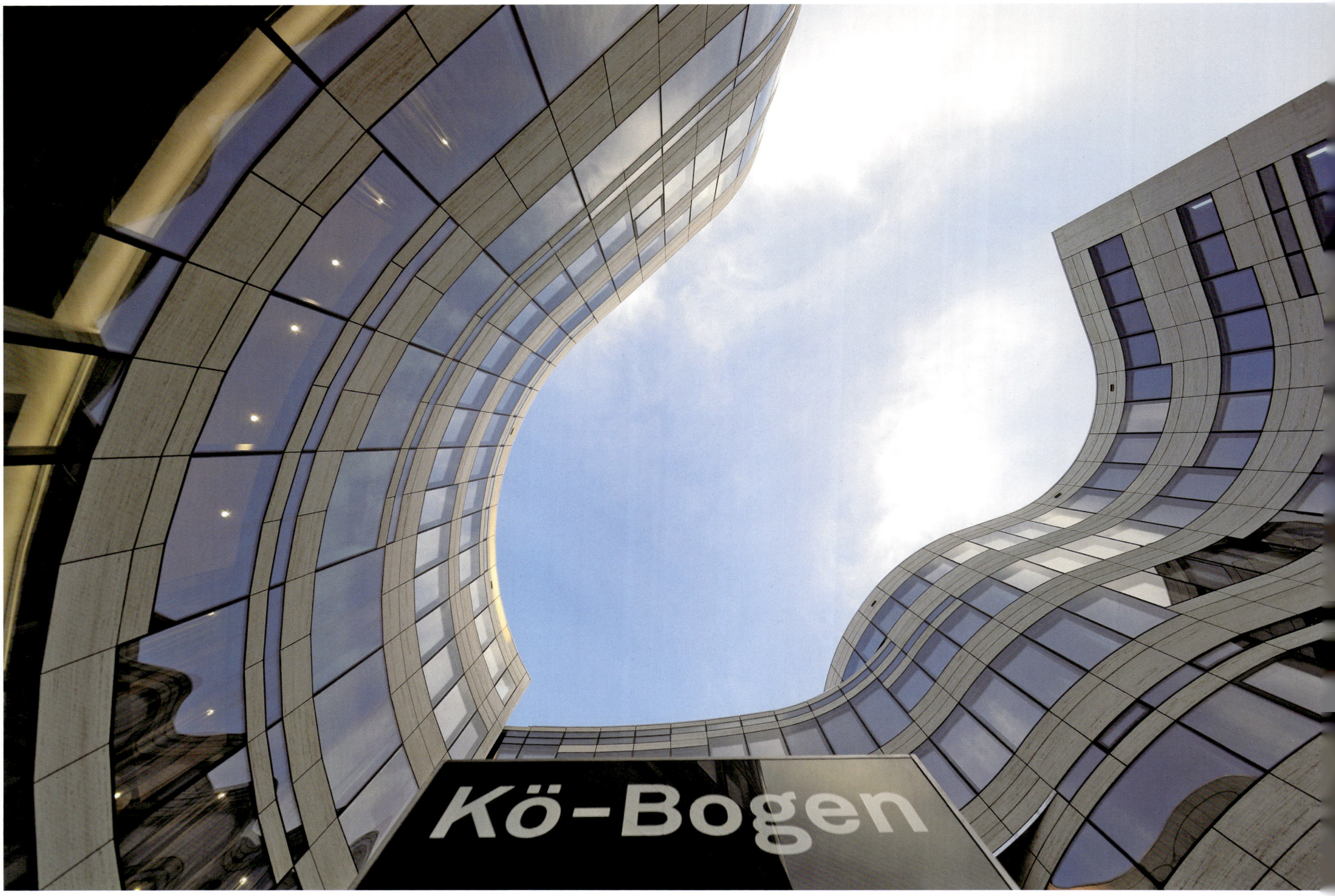
Kö-Bogen

PROJECT NAME 项目名称

ABU DHABI GUARDIAN TOWER

阿布扎比 GUARDIAN 大厦

Architect: LAB

设计公司：LAB_ 尚墨

PROJECT INFORMATION 项目信息

Location	Abu Dhabi, UAE	**地点**	阿联酋阿布扎比
Site area	50,000 m²	**建筑面积**	50，000 平方米
Area	7,000 m²	**用地面积**	7，000 平方米
Type of project:	Residential development, office, business w	**项目类型**	住宅、商务办公、商业

OVERVIEW 项目概况

Guardian tower consists of two parts: high-rise residence and office tower which are linked by retail and services.

Guardian 大厦由两部分组成：高层住宅和高层办公楼，通过零售商业和服务平台相连接。同时，该综合体有三层地下停车场，提供停车服务。

BRIEF INTERVIEW 访谈录

ARCHITECT
Donald L. Bates

设计师
唐纳德 • 贝茨

HKASP: If any, what makes this project different from other commercial retail projects?
LAB: The commercial building is of neighborhood.

HKASP: What was the biggest challenge in this project? Any story you can share with us?
LAB: Module design comes along with energy saving. The Middle East economic crisis happened during the creation. But the final design brought value to the investment.

HKASP:If say one, what is the most important key to be success in a mall?
LAB: The key to the commercial project lies in the success of sustainability. It will last forever instead of an one-off opening ceremony.

香港建筑科学出版社：你觉得这个项目和其他的商业零售项目比起来有什么与众不同的地方？
LAB_ 尚墨：商业属于街区社区类型、小而美。

香港建筑科学出版社：你觉得项目进行过程中最大的挑战是什么？有什么可以和我们分享的吗？
LAB_ 尚墨：模块化设计结合节能、营造过程经历了中东经济危机、但最终设计为投资带来了价值。

香港建筑科学出版社：如果只说一点，你觉得做商业项目要成功最关键的点是什么？
LAB_ 尚墨：商业项目最关键的是可持续的成功、而非昙花一现的开幕式、要永不落幕。

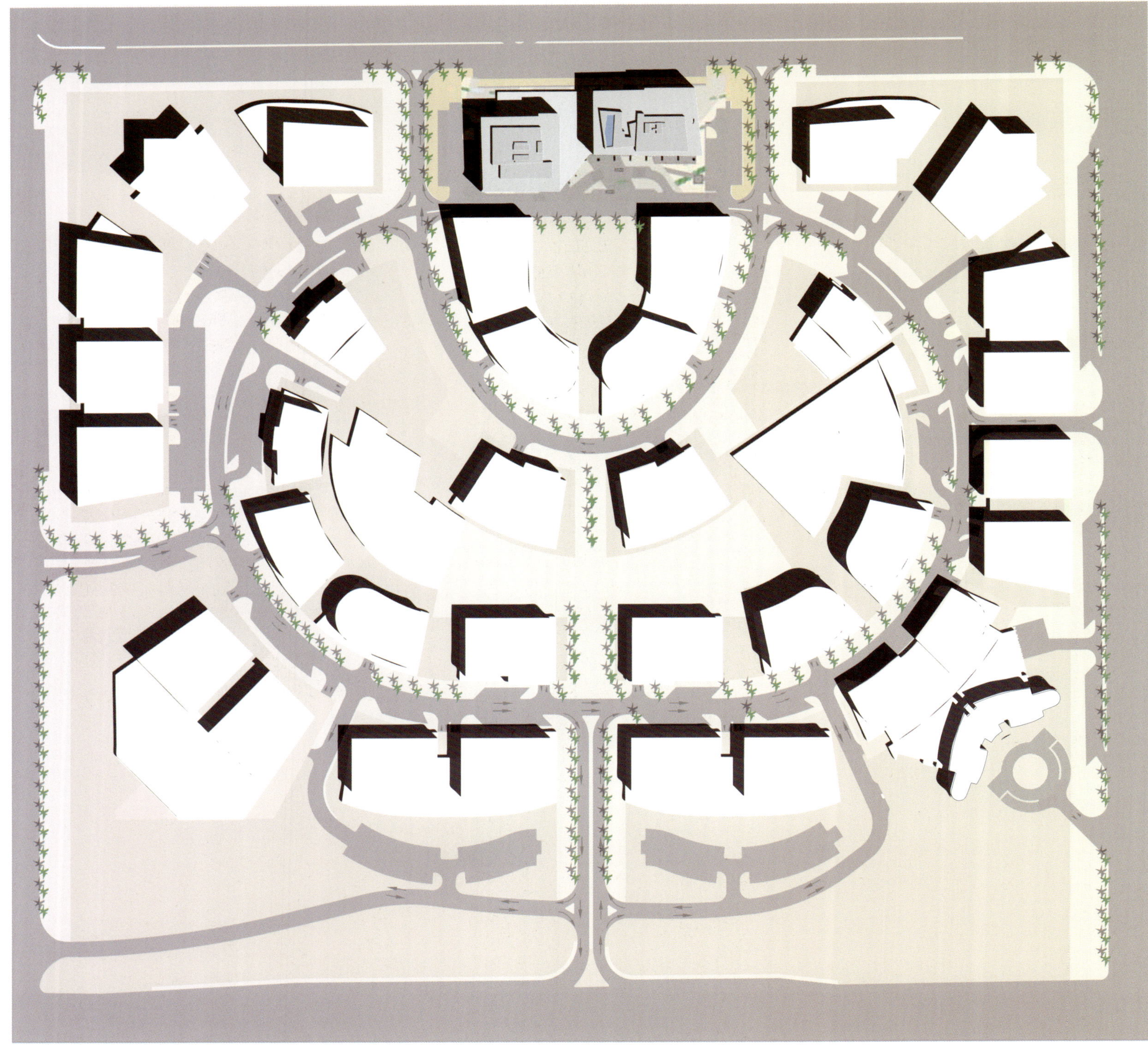

Site Plan
总平面图

The complex enjoys a three-level underground parking lot. Located at the center of the northern base, Guardian tower is designed to be a cellular building, an indication of Abu Dhabi's convention. Within the base, the two towers are linked in a variety of ways, giving opportunities for architectural profile and skyline to have a vibrant interaction in between. The variation also provides information on the thoughts given to the existing buildings in northern base and symmetric layout, the tradition of Abu Dhabi. What is more, it fully conveys the idea of context. Besides the position of the base, the two towers break from the conventional rectangle volume of medium-height architecture with a strong sense of split and deviation. A design delivering a sense of deviation plays a role in defining space and enriching vision, allowing medium-height architecture to be endowed with a new definition.

Guardian大厦位于基地北侧的中心位置，大厦的设计有明显的阿布扎比传统的箱式建筑特色。在基地范围内，两座塔楼之间的关系不断变化，为建筑轮廓和天际线提供了富有活力的互动。这种变化同时表达了对北侧现有建筑以及阿布扎比传统对称布局的思考，更充分地表现了文脉关联。除了基地位置，这两栋更具断裂和偏离感的塔楼打破了传统的中等建筑矩形体量。偏离感的设计使建筑得以作用于空间的限定和视觉的丰富，使得中等高度建筑有了新的定义。

WEST ELEVATION
1:500 @ A3

SOUTH ELEVATION
1:500 @ A3

Elevation
立面图

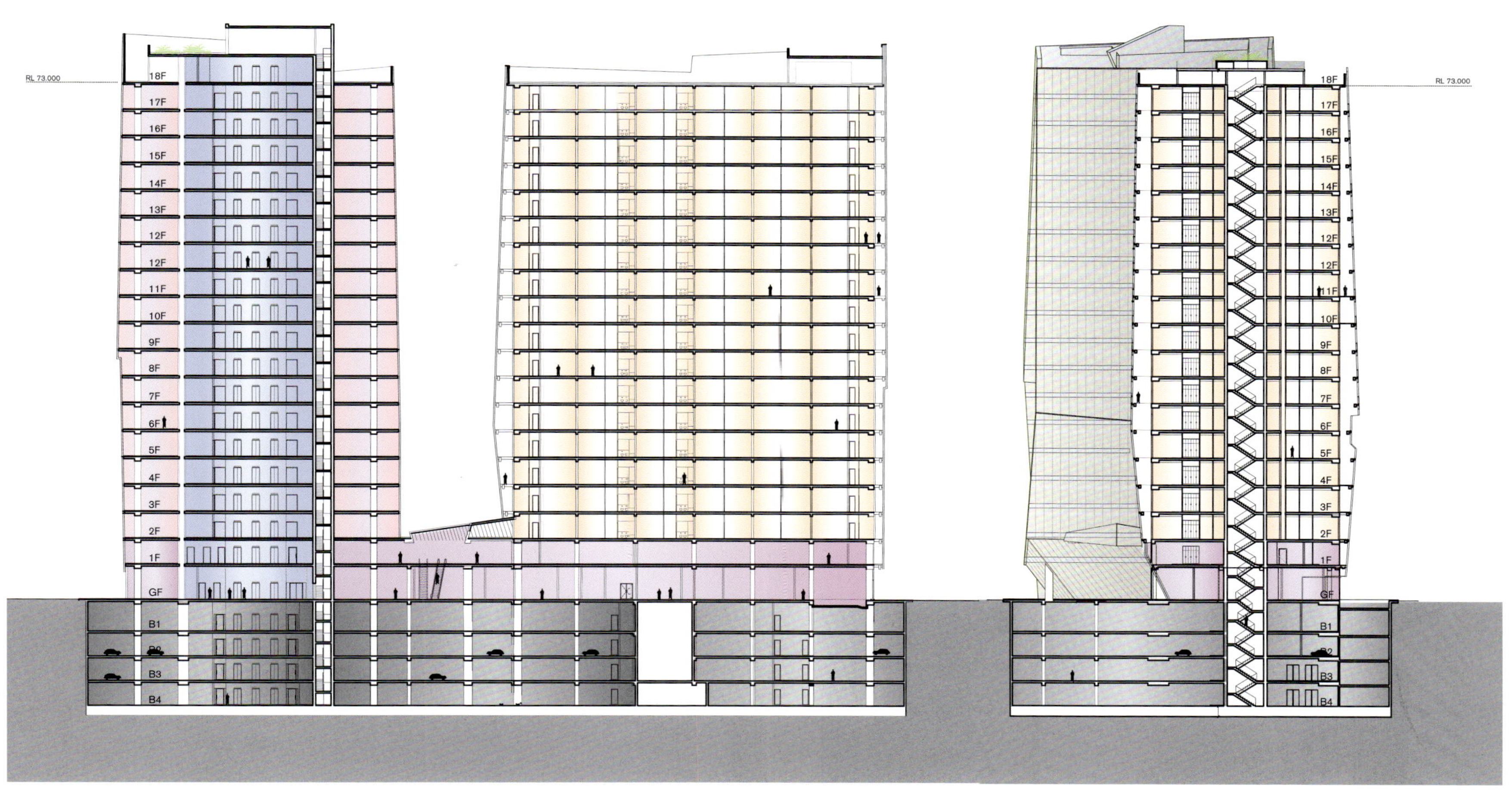

WEST EAST SECTION
1:500 @ A3

SOUTH NORTH SECTION
1:500 @ A3

Section
剖面图

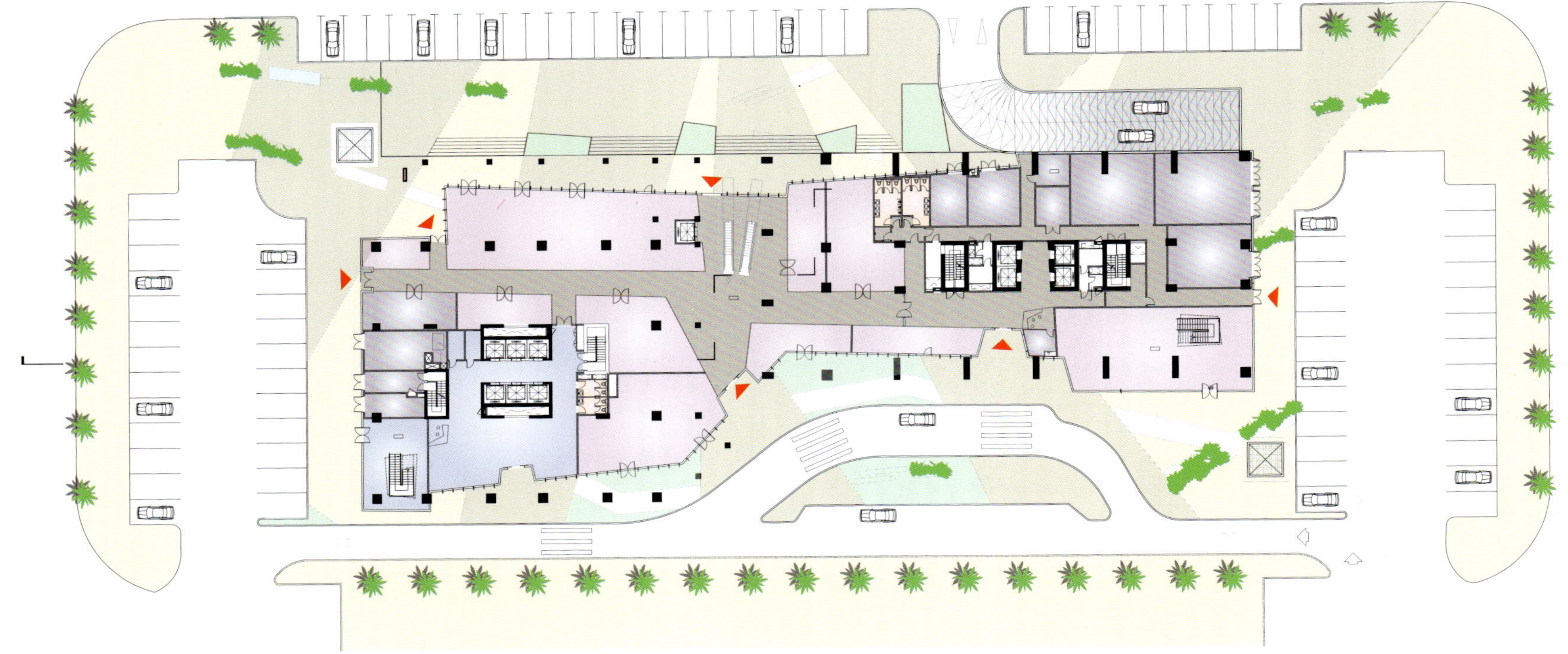

Ground Floor Plan
首层平面图

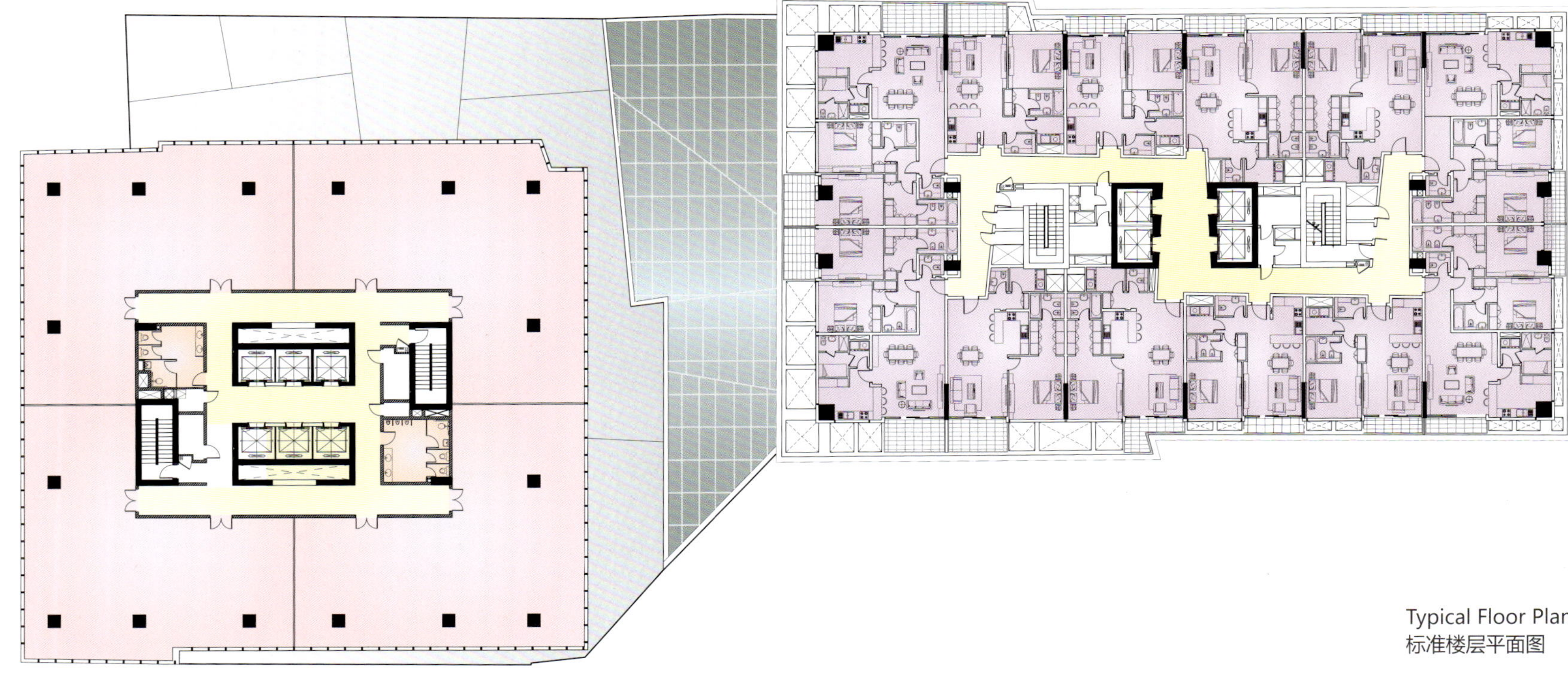

Typical Floor Plan
标准楼层平面图

THE
CLEMENTI
金文泰广场

spatial practice

spatial practice

We truly believed that a the right working environment is generating money! Today we are obligate to create a comfortable wcrking space even though the cost is more expensive in construction but when its get to rent the rent is higher.

我们从骨子里认为，只要能营造出舒适的工作环境，大家就能开心工作、赚钱！尽管建设成本高昂，但从当今社会角度考虑，我们有义务营造出舒适的工作场所，而且还可抬高楼面租金。

Promoting human interaction is an important guideline for spatial practice, we truly believe that its the essence of design today.

促进人际互动是如何布局空间的主要纲领。我们的确认为促进人际互动就是当今设计的核心内容。

The main concept of the Harbin towers was Sharing the same DNA - but positioned differently - the Twin Towers form a new icon for the Haxi Business Development Zone. The Towers creates a balanced relationship between empty and full, mass and void, private and public. Each tower creates a program specific dialogue with the site, with the north SOHO and Service Apartment tower atrium opening toward the Plaza, and the south Office Tower atrium oriented toward the Business District.

哈尔滨大厦的主要设计理念：同样的血统，不同的定位。作为哈西商务开发区的新地标，双子塔在虚与实、私密与公共之间找到了一种平衡关系。大厦的功能定位与场地布局紧密相连。北侧是SOHO与酒店式公寓大厦，其大厅入口正对广场。南侧则是写字楼，其入门大厅正对商务区。

Surbana International Consultants Pte Ltd

Surbana International Consultants Pte Ltd

Clementi Mall stands out because it is part of the first mixed-use development in Singapore that has seamlessly integrated a retail mall with public housing units, an air-conditioned bus interchange as well as a Mass Rapid Transit (MRT) station. The project is a true reflection of what it means to build spaces that are socially-conscious and yet, commercially viable.

由于克莱门蒂商场是新加坡首个综合型商业项目，所以她的存在自然就与众不同。该项目在商场，公共住房单位，空调巴士换乘站以及新加坡地铁站之间形成了无缝连接。项目真实地反应了什么才是既服务大众又适合经商的空间打造。

A mall should not be just another high density development standing in isolation. It should be designed for the community in mind, with features such as interactivity and connectivity incorporated into not only the mall but every aspect of the entire development living, commuting and retail experience.

商场不应是一个独立的且高密集型建筑。设计应该以人为本，考虑到与人的互动，与周边环境的互通。不仅是商场本身，还是整个建筑的各方面，包括住户生活体验、路人感受、购物体验等等，都应体现出一种互动与连通。

ACCESSIBLE COMPLEX REAL ESTATE

交通型复合地产

Benthem Crouwel Architects

Benthem Crouwel Architects

By creating spaces that are amiable to be in and offer the user a pleasant ambience. In addition, it needs the great spaciousness, clear orientation and sightlines, and can lead people's sightline, providing a lot of daylight and pleasant lighting.

创造出和蔼可亲的空间，让人们能感到愉悦。此外，还需要广阔的空间、明确的朝向，能引导人们的视线，充足的自然采光，让人心情舒畅的照明设计。

Uses are changing with new ways of life, and technology affecting our relationship to space and time. New uses will be the most interesting sources of innovations in the future. Form has to follow and serve new uses.

建筑用途正随着新的生活方式发生变化。技术影响着我们跟空间与时间的关系。在未来，首当其冲的是建筑用途的创新，随后才是形式创新，这是因为形式创新是随用途创新而来。

The task was to make a design for a facade which gave the building a "shell" with a unique character, to hide the parked cars on the top floors, while offering enough openings for ventilation. We approached that challenge with the "Wine Leave Facade".

我们的一个目标就是设计出一种具有特色，类似于"壳"的立面，遮住停在顶层的汽车。与此同时，立面还具备保证充分通风的孔洞。最后，我们的解决方法就是"葡萄叶立面"。

Philippe Chiambaretta/PCA

Philippe Chiambaretta/PCA

The essential qualities were the strong incorporating in the urban microstructure of the routes and ways and the easy accessibility of the projects. We wanted an introverted mall but also a building that could function independently and invites the user to stroll throught.

本项目内涵就是从微观层面上看，如何将城市空间中的人流、物流、交通便利性有效地整合在一起。我们既希望打造一个含蓄的商场，也希望打造一个具有独立功能的建筑，可以吸引人们到此畅游。

建筑理所当然应该成为促进社会联系的纽带。

Buildings must contribute to create social links.

SAA Architects Pte Ltd 8 Lead Agency, Benoy Ltd,·AECOM Singapore Pte Ltd,· Beca Carter Hollings & Ferner (SEA) Pte Ltd

SAA 建筑设计 贝诺设计，新加坡 AECOM， Beca Carter Hollings & Ferner (SEA) Pte Ltd

PROJECT NAME 项目名称

HARBIN TWIN TOWERS
哈尔滨双子大楼

Architect: spatial practice
设计公司： spatial practice

PROJECT INFORMATION 项目信息

Client	Kaishengyuan Group	**客户**	凯盛源集团
Location	Harbin, Haxi District, China	**地点**	中国哈尔滨
Function	Office, Residential, Retail, Parking and Landscape	**功能**	办公室、住宅、零售、停车和景观
Partners in charge	Erik Amir, Dora Chi	**合作伙伴**	Erik Amir, Dora Chi
Project Architect	Max Gerthel	**项目设计师**	Max Gerthel
Local Architect	Harbin Institute of Technology	**当地设计单位**	哈尔滨工业大学

OVERVIEW 项目概况

China has the world longest High Speed Rail (HSR) network that connects the entire country from north to south and from east to west. In the city of Harbin, the new West Train Station will become the northern China gateway connecting to China's major cities with daily high-speed links to Beijing, Tianjin, Shanghai and Guangzhou.

中国拥有世界最长的高铁交通网，从北到南、从东到西将整个国家连接了在一起。在哈尔滨，新建成的火车西站将成为中国北部的门户，每日都将有高铁列车将哈尔滨与北京、天津、上海和广州等连成一体。

BRIEF INTERVIEW 访谈录

ARCHITECT
Spatial Practice
Dora Chi
设计师
Spatial Practice
Dora Chi

ARCHITECT
Spatial Practice
Erik Amir
设计师
Spatial Practice Erik Amir

HKASP: What was the main concept behind the whole project?

spatial practice: The main concept of the Harbin towers was : Sharing the same DNA - but positioned differently - the Twin Towers form a new icon for the Haxi Business Development Zone. The Towers creates a balanced relationship between empty and full, mass and void, private and public. Each tower creates a program specific dialogue with the site, with the north SoHo and Service Apartment tower atrium opening toward the Plaza, and the south Office Tower atrium oriented toward the Business District.

HKASP: There are many public space in tower. Regarding the economy issue, how did you convince the client to accept such a design idea?

spatial practice: We truly believed that a the right working environment is generating money! meaning today we are obligate to create a comfortable working space even though the cost is more expensive in construction but when its get to rent the rent is higher.

HKASP: How is this project, representative of your attitude toward design, both public and private?

Architect:spatial practice: Promoting human interaction is an important guideline for spatial practice, we truly believe that its the essence of design today

香港建筑科学出版社：整个项目的主要设计理念是什么？

spatial practice: 哈尔滨大厦的主要设计理念：同样的血统，不同的定位。作为哈西商务开发区的新地标，双子塔在虚与实、私密与公共之间找到了一种平衡关系。大厦的功能定位与场地布局紧密相连。北侧是 SOHO 与酒店式公寓大厦，其大厅入口正对广场。南侧则是写字楼，其入门大厅正对商务区。

香港建筑科学出版社：大厦内部设有许多公共空间。从成本角度考虑，你们是如何说服客户接受这样的设计思路的？

spatial practice: 我们从骨子里认为，只要能营造出舒适的工作环境，大家就能开心工作、赚钱！尽管建设成本高昂，但从当今社会角度考虑，我们有义务营造出舒适的工作场所，而且还可抬高楼面租金。

港建筑科学出版社：这个项目代表了你对设计的观点，你是如何做到公私并存的？

spatial practice: 促进人际互动是如何布局空间的主要纲领。我们的确认为促进人际互动就是当今设计的核心内容。

PREMIUM
OUTLETS
CRH
MaxMara
VERSACE
ORLANDO

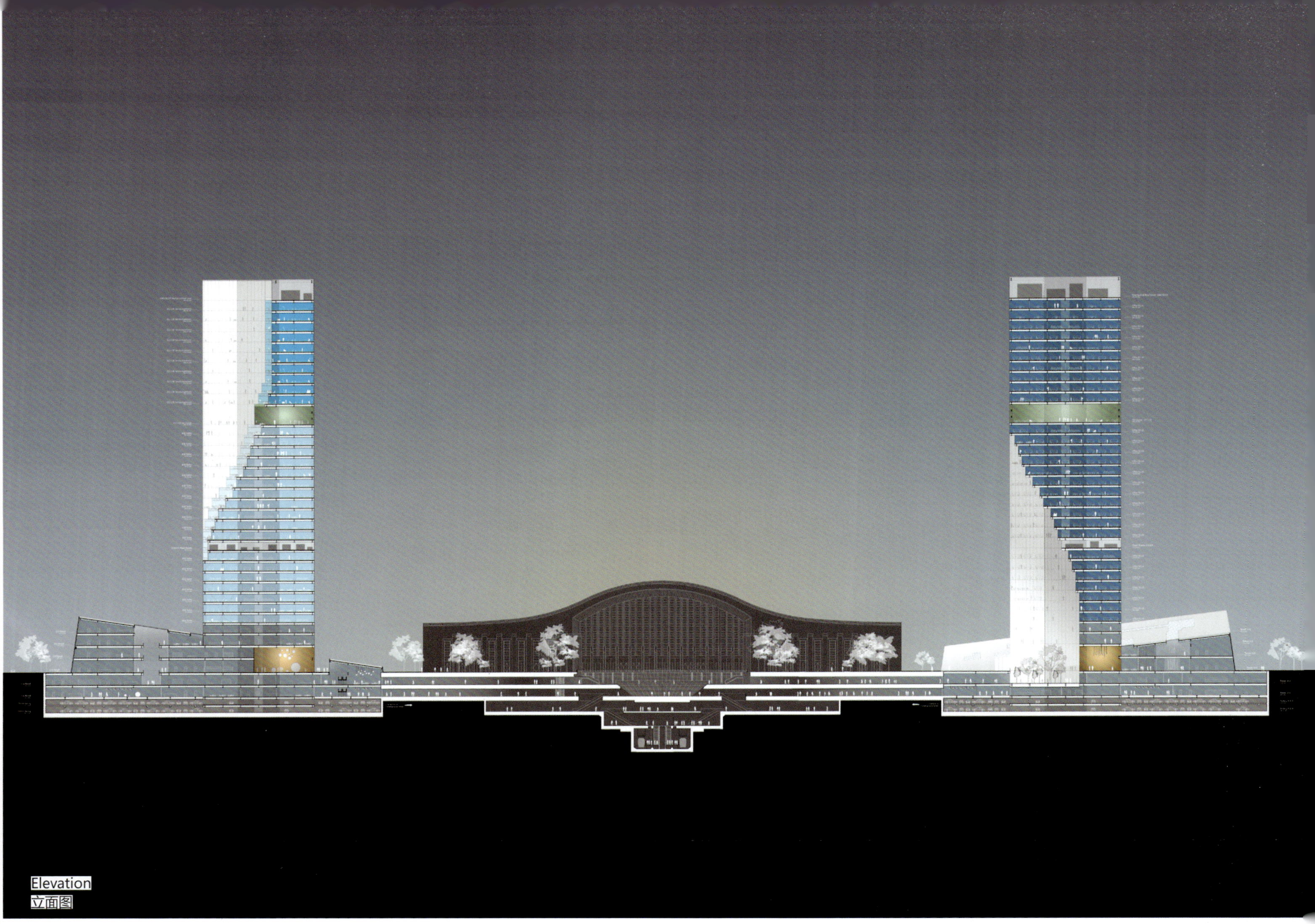

Elevation
立面图

Integration

Harbin West Station is a transportation hub linked with the high-speed train station, Subway and Bus Station.The Kaishengyuan Towers take full advantage of sitting on a transportation hub not only connected to main cities in China but hyper-connected to Harbin City main infrastructure. Distances are shortening, fostering faster business transactions and promoting communication.

整合

哈尔滨火车西站将成为一个交通枢纽，连接起高铁站、地铁和巴士站。凯胜元大楼坐拥临近交通枢纽的优势，不仅连接了中国的大城市，也连接了哈尔滨的主要城市设施。距离的大幅度缩短将有助于未来商业发展和便利交流。

Identity

Sharing the same DNA - but positioned differently - the Twin Towers form a new icon for the Haxi Business Development Zone. The Towers creates a balanced relationship between empty and full, mass and void, private and public. Each tower creates a program specific dialogue with the site, with the north SoHo and Service Apartment tower atrium opening toward the Plaza, and the south Office Tower atrium oriented toward the Business District.

身份象征

双子大楼共享了一样的DNA，只是坐落位置不一样，它们将成为哈西商业发展区的新地标。双子大楼在盈实和空虚、聚合和分散、私人和公共之间创造了一种微妙的平衡关系。每栋大楼都与场地结合凸显出自己的特色，北边的商务公寓设置有对着广场开放的中庭，南边的写字楼则面向商业区。

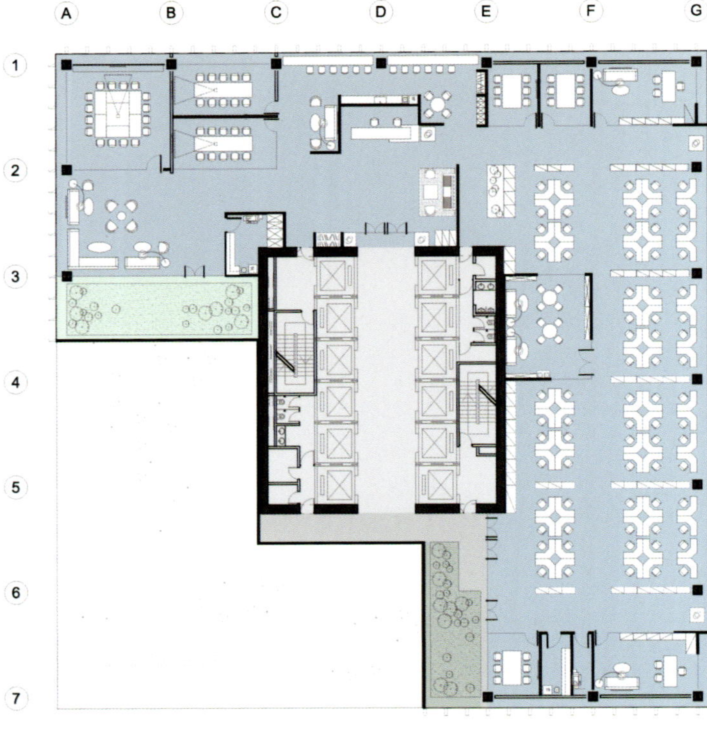

Floor Plan 1
楼层平面图 1

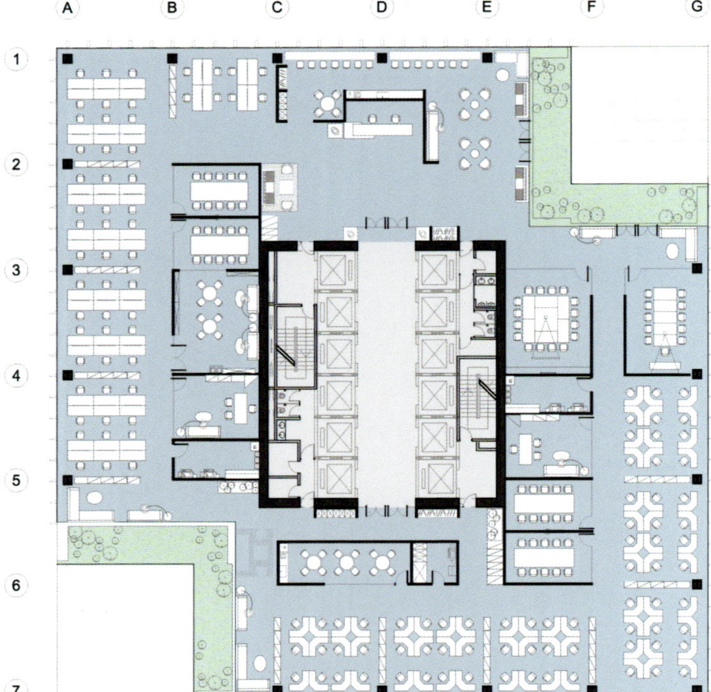

Floor Plan 2
楼层平面图 2

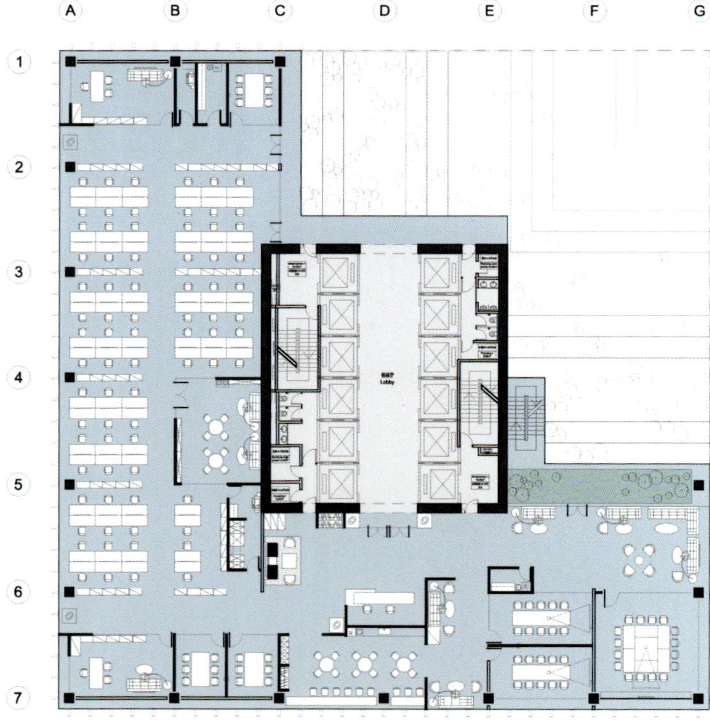

Floor Plan 3
楼层平面图 3

Working & Living

In response to Harbin's extreme climate conditions, interior multi functional green terraces are injected into the upper atrium spaces promoting a high quality and healthy working environment for the office tower, and creating comfortable and climate controlled recreational terraces for the luxury residences.

工作与生活

为了缓解哈尔滨的极端气候条件，室内多功能绿色露台被引入到上层中庭空间，为写字楼提供高品质和健康的工作环境，也为高级住宅楼提供舒适和气候控制系统平台。

Synergy

The towers perform as the Digital Gate framing the city and station. The integrated media facades frame and activate the adjacent plaza promoting communication and social interaction between travellers, commuters and residents. The suspended microclimate atriums create a new typology of indoor spaces that promotes human interactions.

协同效应

双子大楼同时也成为了城市和车站数码门户。多媒体立面为相邻的广场带来了活力，促进旅客、乘客和居民之间的交流和社会交往。微气候空中中庭也为人际交往提供一个新型的室内空间。

PROJECT NAME 项目名称

SINGAPORE CLEMENTI MIXED DEVELOPMENT

新加坡金文泰综合体

Architect: Surbana International Consultants Pte Ltd

设计公司：Surbana International Consultants Pte Ltd

PROJECT INFORMATION 项目信息

Location	Singapore	地点	新加坡

OVERVIEW 项目概况

Clementi's new mixed development embodies the concept of a vertical city, integrating all the basic necessities for living, within a layered stratum of transportation, shops, eateries, residential units and recreational facilities.

This project was devised as a government initiated project to revitalise a mature estate. Devised in three parts, it consists of an air-conditioned bus interchange; a lower level commercial podium and an upper portion of two residential towers.

This project is a landmark development with a renewed vibrancy that enhances the image, value and quality of living for the Clementi community.

本项目旨在表现出垂直城市的概念，集合了生活设施、完整的地面交通系统、商场、餐馆、住宅公寓和娱乐设施等必要的基础设施。

本案是按照政府要求进行设计，目的是要让本地以成熟的房地产业再现活力。设计分为三部分，其中包括空调巴士枢纽、低层商业裙楼和两座高层住宅楼。

本项目作为地标性项目，为金泰文社区提升了其形象、价值和生活质量，并带来了新气象和新活力。

BRIEF INTERVIEW 访谈录

ARCHITECT
Jasmine Teo

设计师
Jasmine Teo

ARCHITECT
Patrick Lee

设计师
Patrick Lee

HKASP: If any, what makes this project different from other commercial retail projects?
Surbana International Consultants Pte Ltd: Clementi Mall stands out because it is part of the first mixed-use development in Singapore that has seamlessly integrated a retail mall with public housing units, an air-conditioned bus interchange as well as a Mass Rapid Transit (MRT) station. The project is a true reflection of what it means to build spaces that are socially-conscious and yet, commercially viable.

HKASP: If say one, what is the most important key to be success in a mall design?
Surbana International Consultants Pte Ltd: A mall should not be just another high density development standing in isolation. It should be designed for the community in mind, with features such as interactivity and connectivity incorporated into not only the mall but every aspect of the entire development living, commuting and retail experience.

香港建筑科学出版社：此项目与其他商业项目有什么不同之处？
Surbana International Consultants Pte Ltd: 由于克莱门蒂商场是新加坡首个综合型商业项目，所以她的存在自然就与众不同。该项目在商场、公共住房单位、空调巴士换乘站以及新加坡地铁站之间形成了无缝连接。项目真实地反应了什么才是既服务大众又适合经商的空间打造。

香港建筑科学出版社：你可以浅谈一下商场设计的成功秘诀是什么吗？
Surbana International Consultants Pte Ltd: 商场不应是一个独立的且高密集型建筑。设计应该以人为本，考虑到与人的互动，与周边环境的互通。不仅是商场本身，还是整个建筑的各方面，包括住户生活体验、路人感受、购物体验等等，都应体现出一种互动与连通。

CLEMENTI
mall
金文泰广场

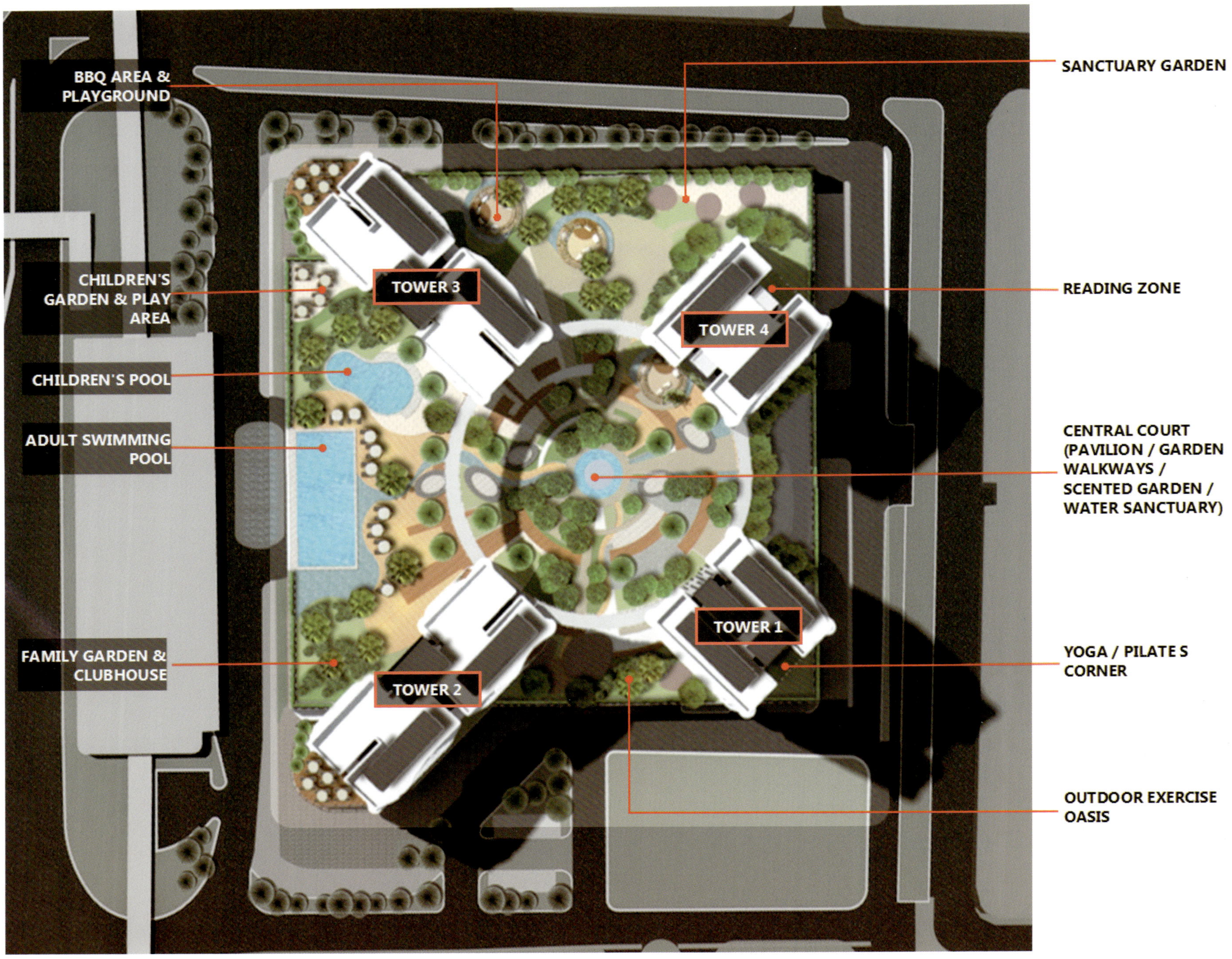

BBQ AREA & PLAYGROUND
CHILDREN'S GARDEN & PLAY AREA
CHILDREN'S POOL
ADULT SWIMMING POOL
FAMILY GARDEN & CLUBHOUSE
TOWER 3
TOWER 4
TOWER 1
TOWER 2
SANCTUARY GARDEN
READING ZONE
CENTRAL COURT (PAVILION / GARDEN WALKWAYS / SCENTED GARDEN / WATER SANCTUARY)
YOGA / PILATE S CORNER
OUTDOOR EXERCISE OASIS

The complexity of interlocking functions appears deceivingly simple. Tucked in beneath the shops and accessible by a network of internal route-ways sits the Clementi Bus Station, wrapped by air-conditioned passenger concourse. Via elevators and lifts, pedestrians can move down to the basement supermarket and public carpark below, or up to the commercial areas, office spaces, Clementi Public Library and a bridge connection to Clementi MRT station. A 24-hour accessible mall offers visual and physical porosity for orientation and accessibility. A new water cum sculpture feature, which replaced the beloved old water feature, provides a sense of memory and place.

项目各个部分都紧密相连，看似复杂其实简单明了。金文泰巴士站设置在商场层的下方，周围的内部道路四通八达，中央候车大厅也配置了空调系统。乘客可以利用扶梯和电梯自由前往地下超市和停车场，或上层的商业和办公空间、金文泰公共图书馆等。另外还有一座小桥连接到金泰文地铁站。24 小时营业的超市布局在实际上还是视觉上也设计得四通八达，方便进出。新设计的水景取代了熟悉的老水景，带来一份怀念感和空间感。

4km
3km
2km
1km
Jalan Jelatek
SITE
MRR2
ated Highway
LRT
Jalan Ampang
Jalan Tun Razak
Commercial-Corp. Offices
Commercial-Shop Lots/Offices
Gov. Institutions
Hospitals
Education
Resi-Low rise
Resi-Med. rise
Resi-High rise
Recreational
Nature Reserve
Industrial

KL CITY CENTRE

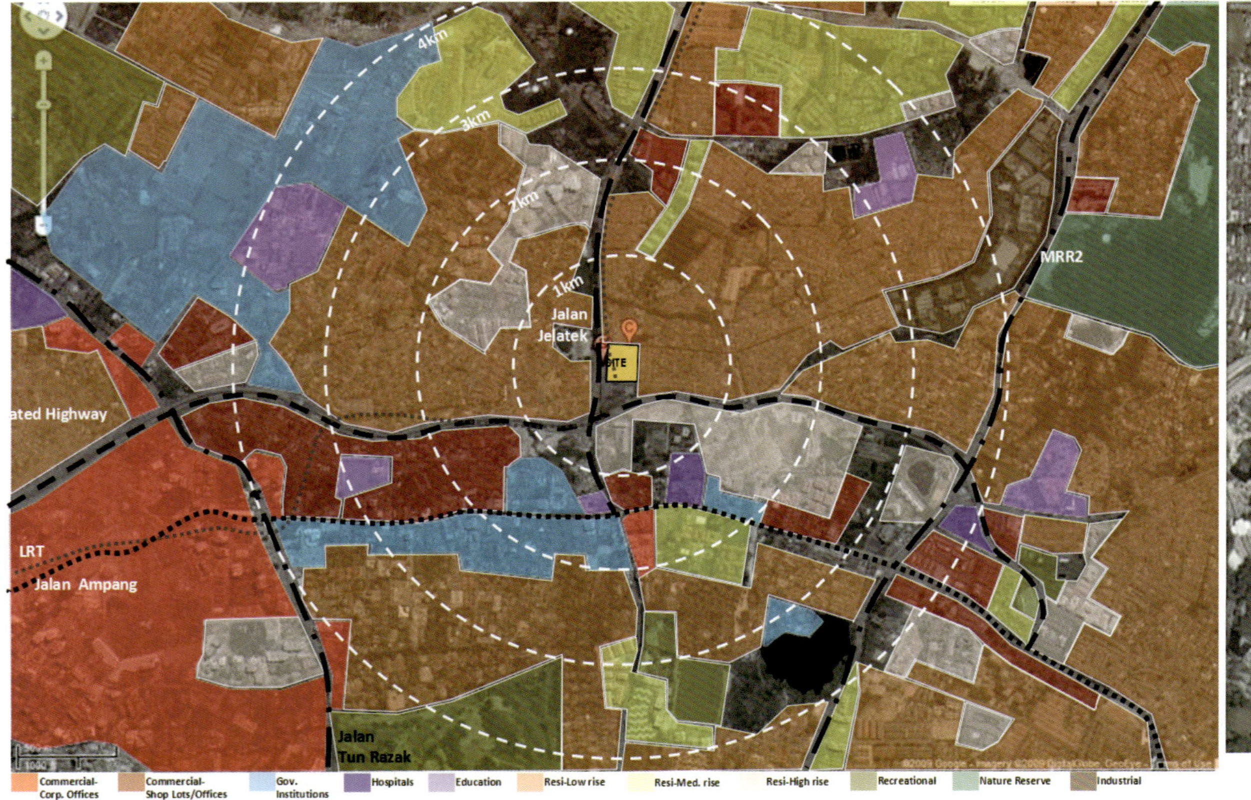

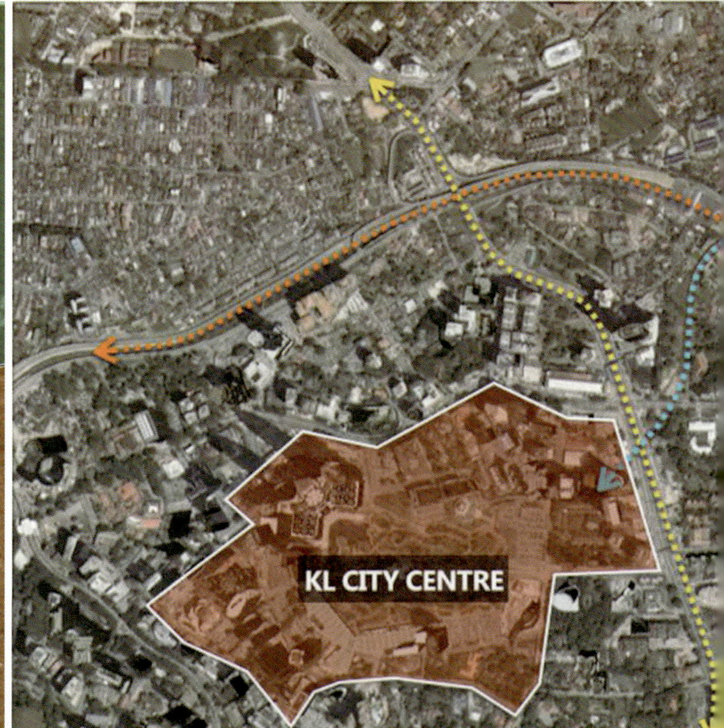

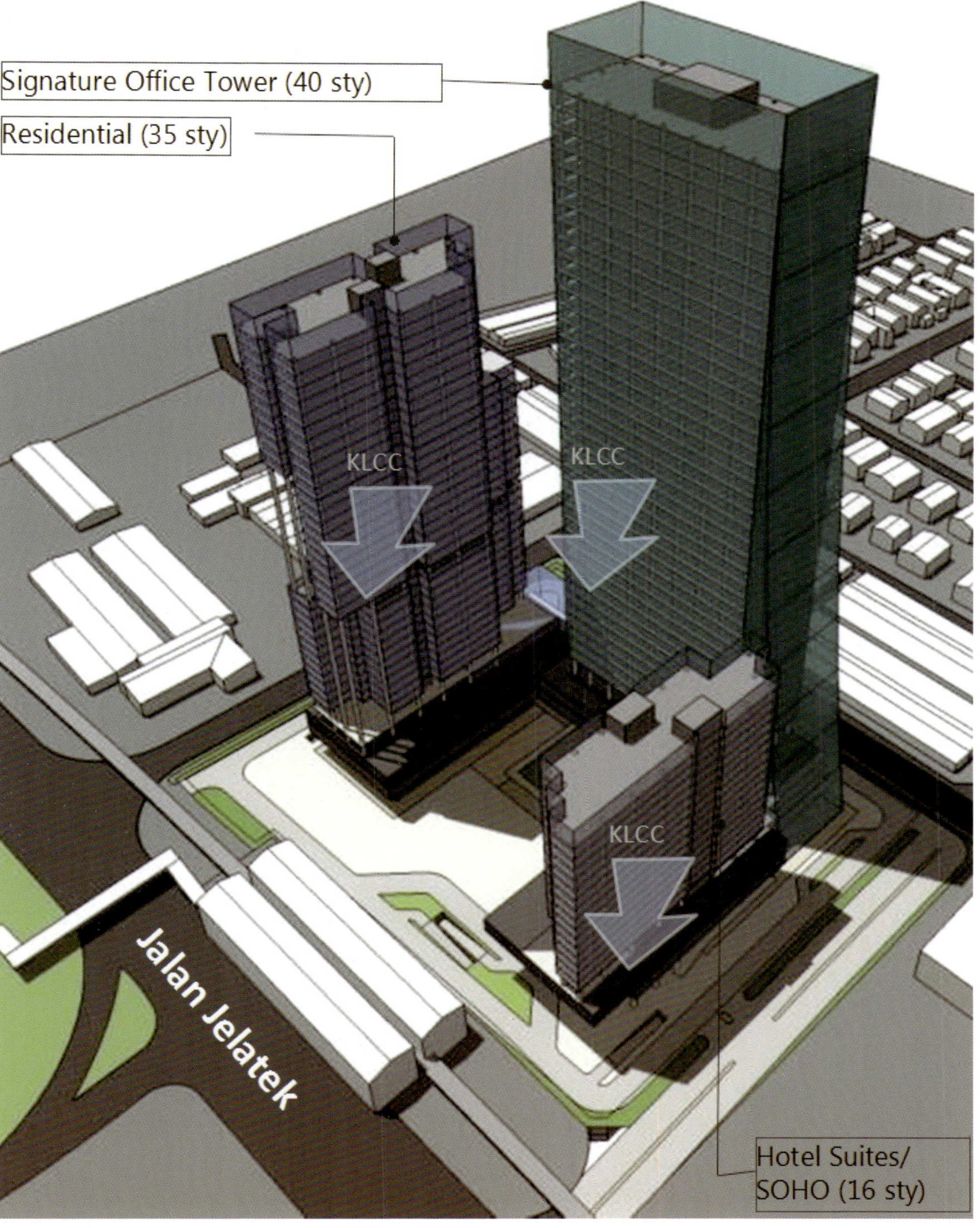

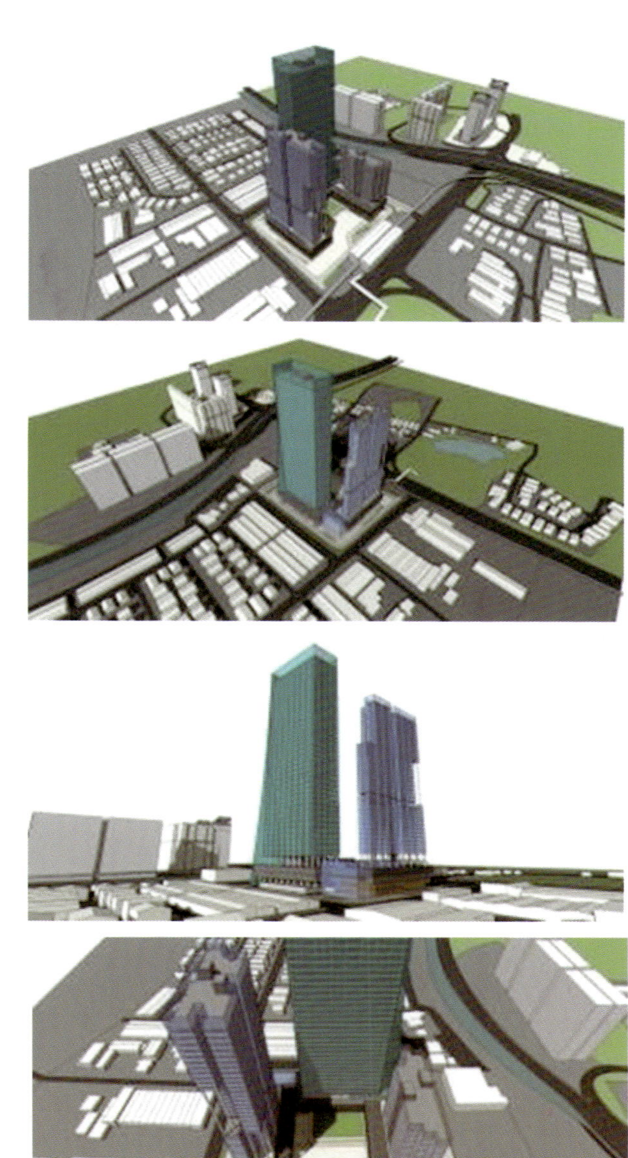

Facade & Roof Design

This development boasts of contemporary architecture which adds a unique charm to Clementi's skyline. There was consideration to break the project's massive scale to create interest to the form and facade. The staggering roof form, the interplay of bay windows and canopies, the rhythm and texture created by the weather shield along the corridor create impressive shadow play to the facade, draping the building form with distinctive character.

立面及屋顶设计

本案展示了现代建筑的独特魅力，为金泰文的天际线增添了新景。设计师为打破建筑的大规模沉重感，在建筑形态和立面上下了功夫。令人咋舌的屋顶形式、凸窗和天蓬的相互作用、走廊上顶棚的纹理和韵律感等，都为立面带来了强烈的阴影效果，让整个建筑具有鲜明的个性。

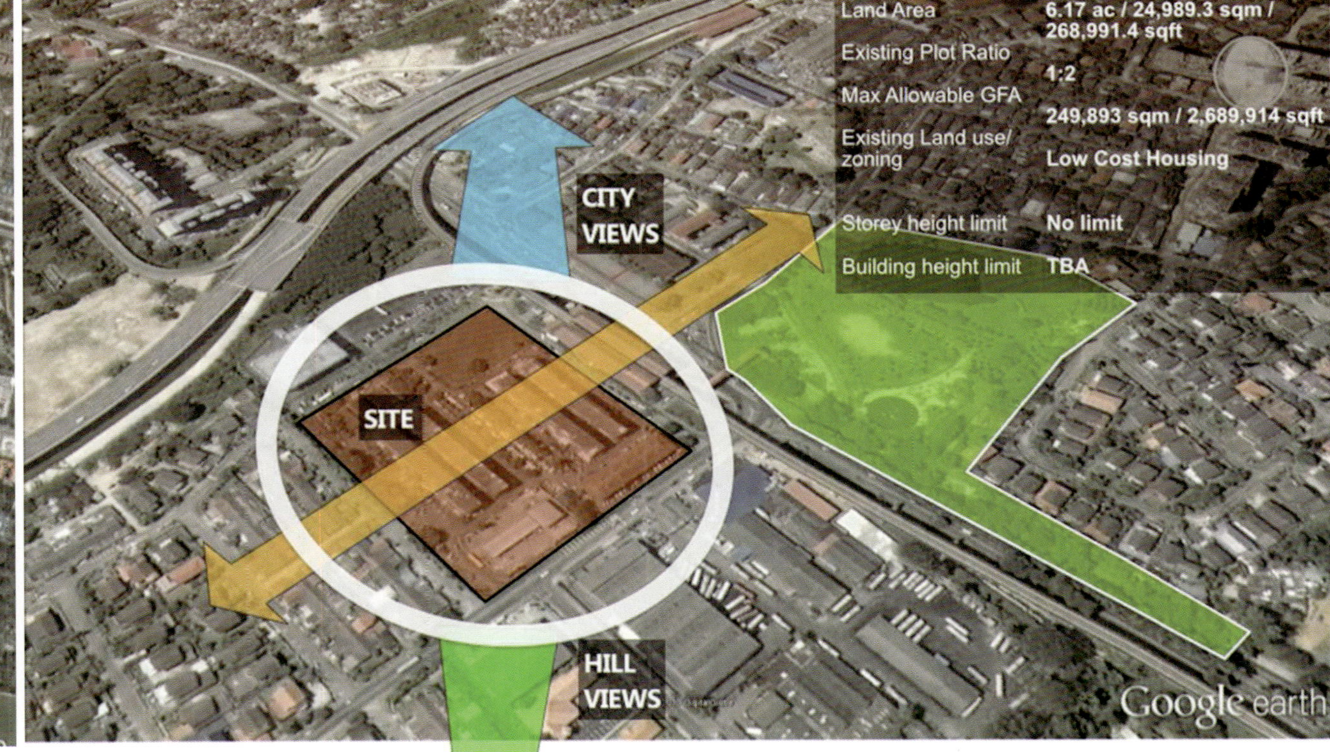

CLEMENTI

Above this commercial dais, two forty storey residential towers, one a linear block, the other a point block, are accessed by high-speed elevators from two main residential lobbies on the ground floor, each with their own external entrance, offering privacy from the surrounding business zones. Car parks take up two floors above the commercial dais, and there is a sky garden on the eighth floor. This landscaped horizontal green not only connects both towers together but offers 3-Generation play facilities and sitting areas, all of which are complemented by an impressive view of the city.

商业楼层的上方是两座 40 层高的住宅楼，一座为长型，另一座为塔式。各自的首层大厅都有配置高速电梯和独立的出入口，以从周围商业区中保护起住户的隐私。停车场共两层，位于商业层上方。第八层设置了一座空中花园。水平延伸的绿色景观不仅连接起两座住宅楼，其中还配置了 3 处游乐设施和休息区，在此可以欣赏整个城市的迷人景色。

PROJECT NAME 项目名称

MALL FORUM MITTELRHEIN, KOBLENZ

科布伦茨中部莱恩的 Mall Forum Mittelrhein

Architect:Benthem Crouwel Architects

设计公司：Benthem Crouwel Architects

PROJECT INFORMATION 项目信息

Client	ECE Projekt management GmbH	**客户**	ECE Projekt management GmbH
Gross floor area Mal	42.500 m²	**商场总面积**	42，500 平方米
Kulturbau	18.600 m²	**Kulturbau 广场**	18，600 平方米
Parkingspace	25.000 m²	**停车空间**	25，000 平方米
Photographer	Jens Kirchner	**摄影师**	Jens Kirchner

OVERVIEW 项目概况

The shopping mall 'Forum Mittelrhein' and the Kulturbau Koblenz, together form the design for the redevelopment of the central plaza, the central square of Koblenz. The central plaza not only connects the various districts of Koblenz with each other but also has an important function as a public transport interchange and place where various pedestrian flows come together.

Forum Mittelrhein 和 Kulturbau Koblenz 购物商场，作为整个中心广场再开发的一部分，不仅仅把 Koblenz 的各个街区有机地联系起来，也起到作为一个交通换乘中心，汇聚步行人流的作用。

BRIEF INTERVIEW 访谈录

ARCHITECT
Markus Sporer

设计师
Markus Sporer

HKASP: The facade looks quite impressive. Can you mention something about your design process of the facade?

Benthem Crouwel Architects:The task was to make a design for a facade which gave the building a shell with a unique character, to hide the parked cars on the top floors, while offering enough openings for ventilation. We approached that challenge with the "Wine Leave Facade".

By using production techniques from car body manufacturing in the architectural process we could stay within the scope of technical requirements, design issues and building costs. By designing one "Wine Leave" element and using it 2.900 times in the facade it was possible to achieve the benchmark of the budget while getting a high end quality of the product. The chosen material aluminium had great advantages and made it feasible to make a lightweight element which saved a lot of primary construction while introduce the deep draw technique in the building sector.

The elements are about 1.25m x 1.25m of size and are deepdrawn to about 0.30 m in total. Laser cut out edges and wholes in combination with the curved and modelled surface gives a lively and expressive emanation. The fixing points are on the same spot at every object – they can be rotated 90°, 180° and 270° in order to achieve a non□repetitive pattern. The surface got a finishing coat of lacquer in three different green colours.

The introduction of industrial methods of production in the building sector offered complete new opportunities for making a relative complicated facade technically possible within the very limited budget while achieving high end quality.

HKASP: How did you convince the client to do a mall with such a radical form strategy? Anything you can share with us?

Benthem Crouwel Architects:The project was preceded by a competition for the mall, the cultural building and the new central square, which we won as we had designed an urban ensemble, which was developed from one design strategy. The essential qualities were the strong incorporating in the urban microstructure of the routes and ways and the easy accessibility of the projects. We wanted an introverted mall but also a building that could function independently and invites the user to stroll throught. Moreover we strongly anchored the mall to the city and gave it its own identity by creating the 'wine leaf' facade (Koblenz is located in the largest wine-growing region of Germany). These conceptual approaches eventually convinced the client, the municipality was already on our side becasue of this concept.

HKASP: If say one, what is the most important key to be success in a mall design?

Benthem Crouwel Architects:By creating spaces that are amiable to be in and offer the user a pleasant ambience. This, in combination with the great spaciousness, clear orientation and sightlines, a lot of daylight and pleasant lighting. t.

香港建筑科学出版社：立面看起来很了不起，你可以谈谈关于立面设计的过程？

Benthem Crouwel Architects: 我们的一个目标就是设计出一种具有特色，类似于“壳”的立面，遮住停在顶层的汽车。与此同时，立面还具备保证充分通风的孔洞。最后，我们的解决方法就是“葡萄叶立面”。

在建筑设计过程中，我们借助了取自于汽车车身的生产工艺，从而帮助我们解决在技术要求，设计以及建造成本方面的困难。我们设计了以“葡萄叶”为单位的立面构件，安装了 2 900 个“Wine Leave”，最终可以在不超出预算的情况下打造出如此高品质的产品。我们选用铝作为材料，铝具有很大的优势，可以制造出轻量的立面构件。这样不仅可以大幅度节约建设成本，而且还可借用汽车制造行业采用的深冲成形工艺。

每个构件尺寸为 1.25 米 x 1.25 米。通过深冲成形工艺，总尺寸变成大约 0.30 米。经过激光切割与修整后的构件再配以弯曲成型的表面呈现出生动且富有表达的散发物。每个构件的固定点都一样。为了营造出多样化的格局，安装时，可将构件旋转 90°、180°以及 270°。构件表面采用 3 种颜色的面漆。

虽然在预算有限的条件下要求实现高品质产品，于是工业工艺的借用，使打造出比较复杂的立面成为现实。

香港建筑科学出版社：你是如何劝说客户接受如此另类的商场建筑形体？有什么可以同我们分享吗？

Benthem Crouwel Architects: 在启动项目之前，我们参加了商场、文化楼、新中央广场的设计竞标。最后，我们凭借出色的城市总体布局方案胜出，这个胜出的方案其实是基于一个设计策略而来。本项目内涵就是从微观层面上看，如何将城市空间中的人流、物流、交通便利性有效地整合在一起。我们既希望打造一个含蓄的商场，也希望打造一个具有独立功能的建筑，可以吸引人们到此畅游。此外，在这座城市中我们赋予该商场以举足轻重的地位，给予她自身的特点，于是我们打造了“葡萄叶”立面主题。（因为科布伦茨坐落于德国最大的葡萄种植和葡萄酒酿造业地区）。这样的设计理念最终赢得了客户的信任。凭借此设计理念，市政府也站在了我们一边。

香港建筑科学出版社：能否浅谈一下什么是商场设计的制胜法宝？

Benthem Crouwel Architects: 创造出和蔼可亲的空间，让人们能感到愉悦。此外，还需要广阔的空间，明确的朝向，能引导人们的视线，充足的自然采光，让人心情舒畅的照明设计。

Lageplan
A. Forum Mittelrhein
B. Kulturbau
C. Zentralplatz
D. Trichterplatz

1. Eingang 01 Center, Altlöhrtor
2. Eingang 02 Center, Trichterplatz
3. Eingang 03 Center, Casinostraße
4. Eingang Center Parkhaus
5. Eingang Center Personal
6. Eingang Center Anlieferung
7. Eingang Kulturbau Zentralplatz
8. Eingang Kulturbau Clemensstraße
9. Eingang Kulturbau Trichterplatz

I. Casinostraße
II. Clemensstraße
III. Görgensstraße
IV. Viktoriastraße
V. Luisenstraße

Site Plan
总平面图

The facade design takes the users into account. The lower two floors with the shops have a glass facade as a strip around the building. The standing glass formats and the expressive shaped click frames of the facade profiles, give a strong vertical orientation. The top three floors of the building are dominated by an artificial "Weinlaub facade" (wine leaf facade). The initial idea of the competition to make a natural over grown facade was developed further artistically and abstractly. The basis of the structure is an abstract image of a vine leaf, which is interpreted freely as a 3D-shape. The entire facade is composed out of only one type of element, which is produced in large quantities and high quality in an industrial thermoforming process. Approximately 2,900 identical, three-dimensional shaped aluminum elements, painted in three different shades of green, form this distinctive facade.

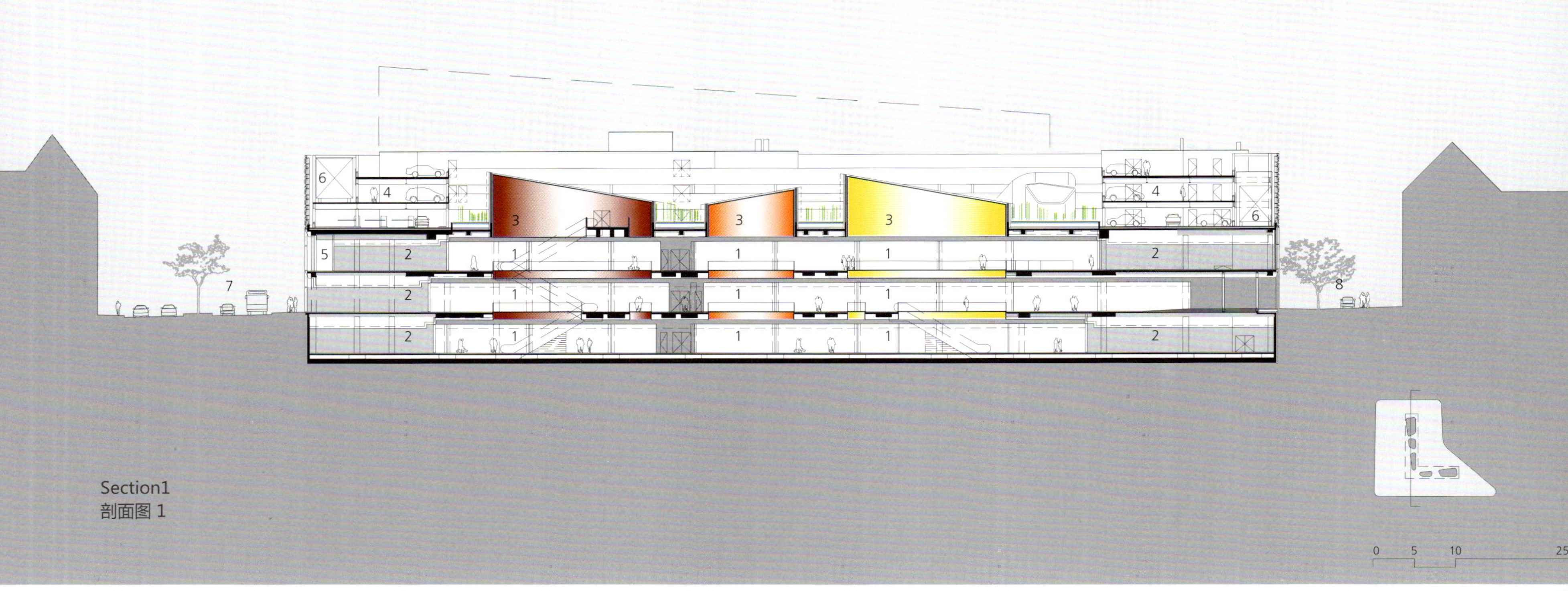

Section1
剖面图 1

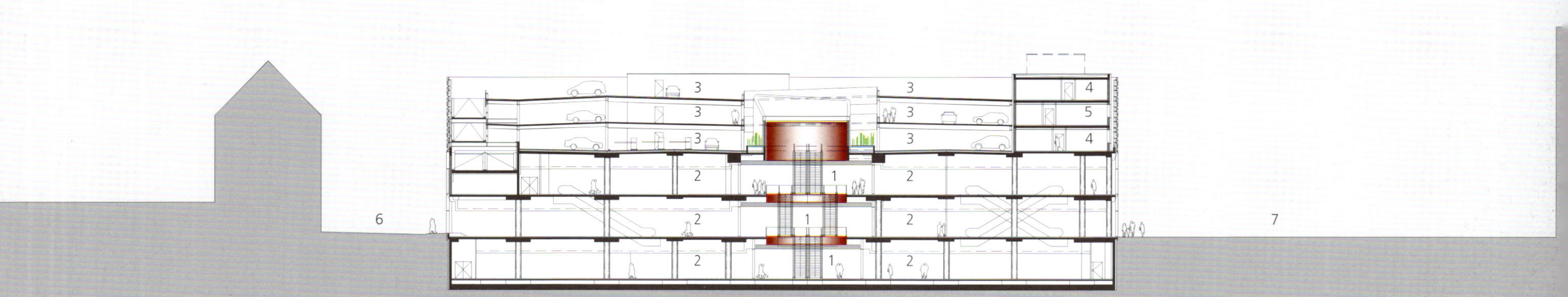

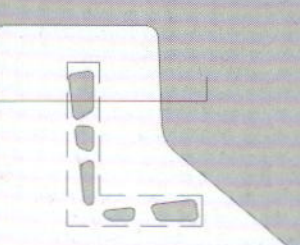

Section2
剖面图 2

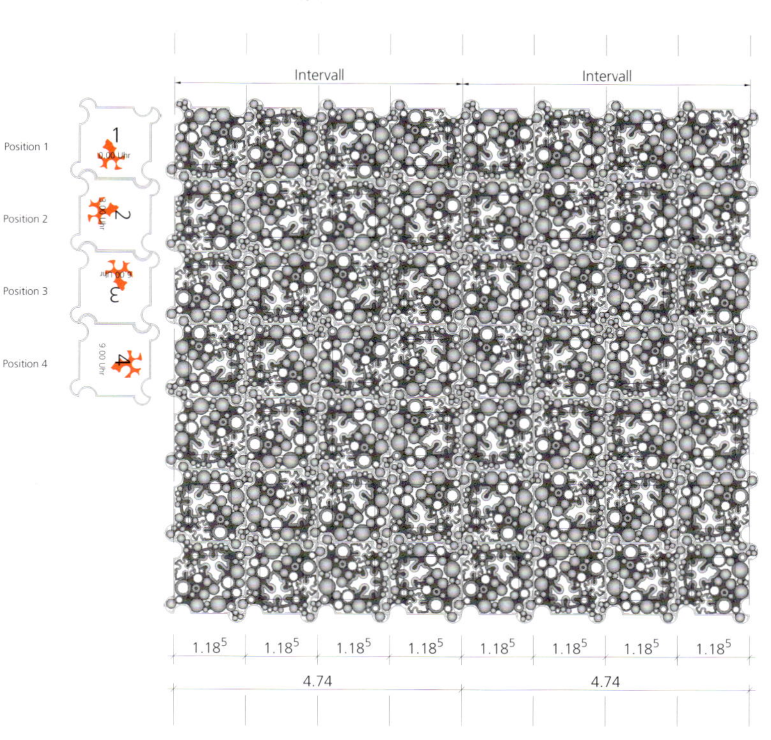

Partial Analysis 1
局部分析图 1

建筑的立面设计考虑了用户的感受。底部两层售货区运用了玻璃和条纹结合的立面。该区域在立面形式给人以强烈的垂直感。此外，大楼的顶部三层是由一个人为的“Weinlaub 立面”为主。由自然杂草丛生的最初的画面经过进一步艺术和抽象发展。该设计的基础是一个藤叶的抽象图像，由先进的工业加工手段创造而来，约 2，900 相同的三维形状的铝制元素，涂上 3 种不同色调的绿色，形成这种独特的外观。

Partial Analysis 2
局部分析图 2

Elevation
立面图

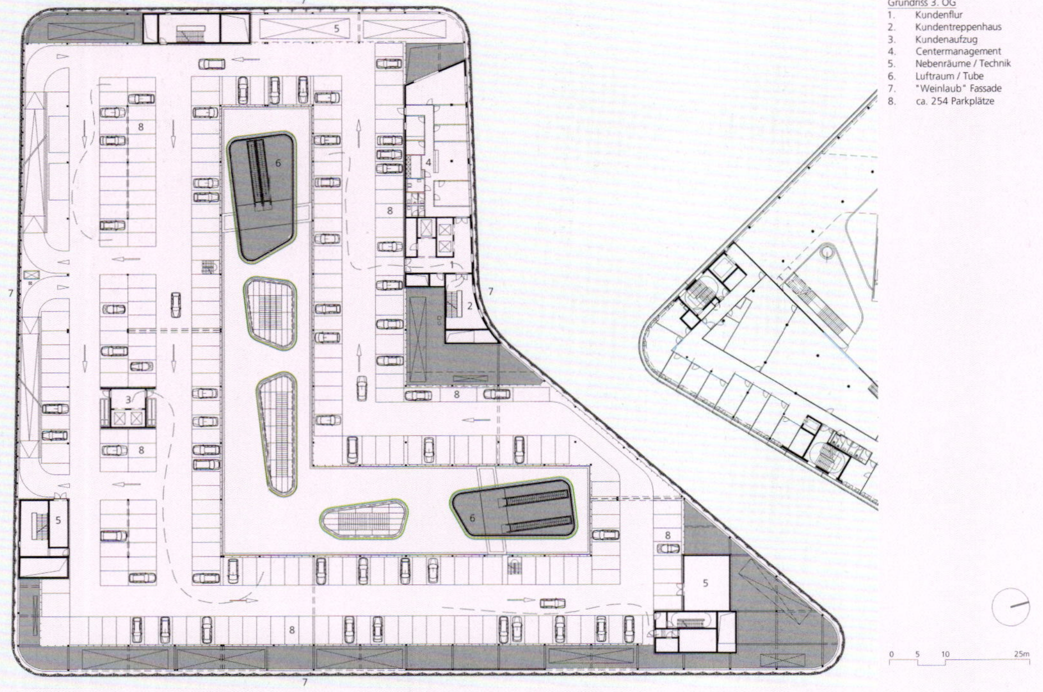

Floor Plan 1
楼层平面图 1

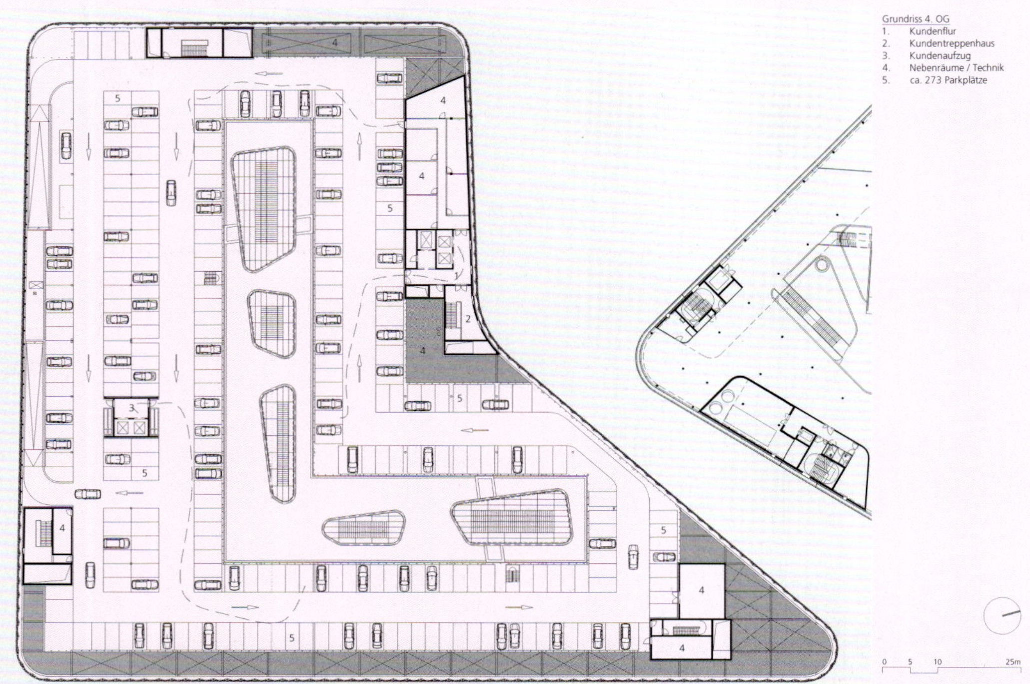

Floor Plan 2
楼层平面图 2

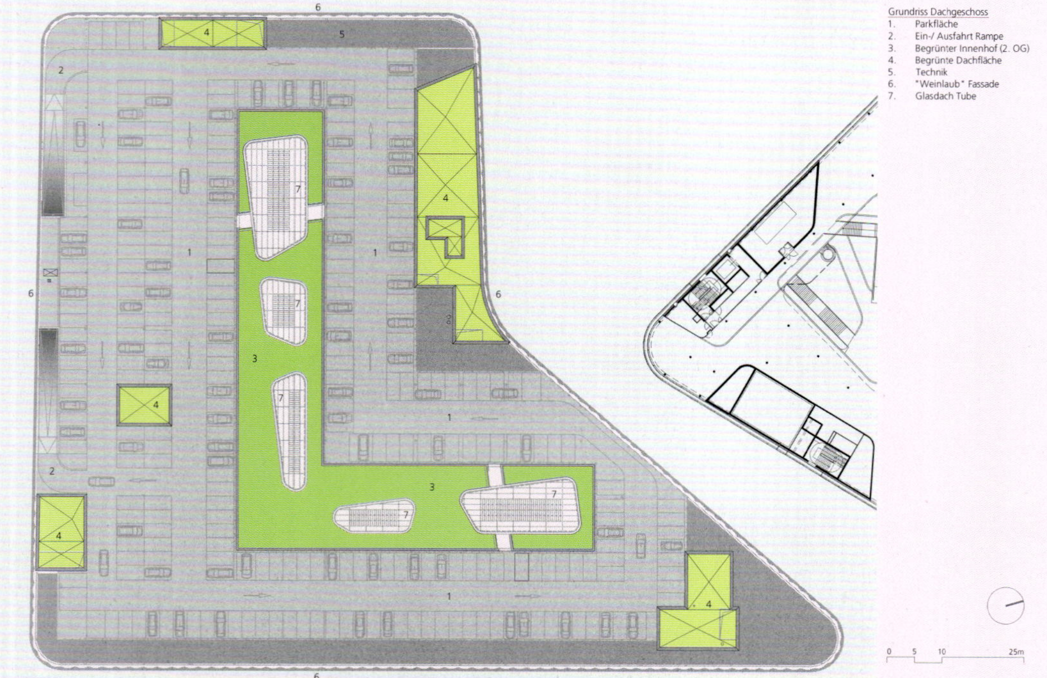

Floor Plan 3
楼层平面图 3

The mall Forum Mittelrhein presents itself as a flat, horizontal layered structure. Due to this powerful format, the buildings volume is reduced efficiently and a pleasant sense of scale is established. On relevant junctions within the urban fabric, the mall offers spacious entrances and invites to follow the pedestrian flows and to 'glide' through the building. The shopping center is characterized by its trapezoidal layout and smooth outlines. The areas intertwined with escalators provide orientation points, divide the building and provide the interior with natural light. This, in combination with the great spaciousness gives a high level of amenity and a pleasant ambience for the user. Across the intense colors of the void edges, powerful accentuations are applied, that create a vivid image.

Forum Mittelrhein商场作为一个水平层状结构。由于这种强有力的形式，建筑体量得以降低到一个宜人的尺度。在其所占据城市街区的各个节点，商场提供宽敞的入口，并通过建筑物布局跟随人流的行径。购物中心的特征在于其梯形布局和光滑轮廓。交织着扶梯的地区提供定位点并划分建筑，同时引入自然光到。由此建筑提供给人们大气的空间和愉快的购物体验。同时鲜艳的色彩的应用也创造出了一副生动的建筑图景。

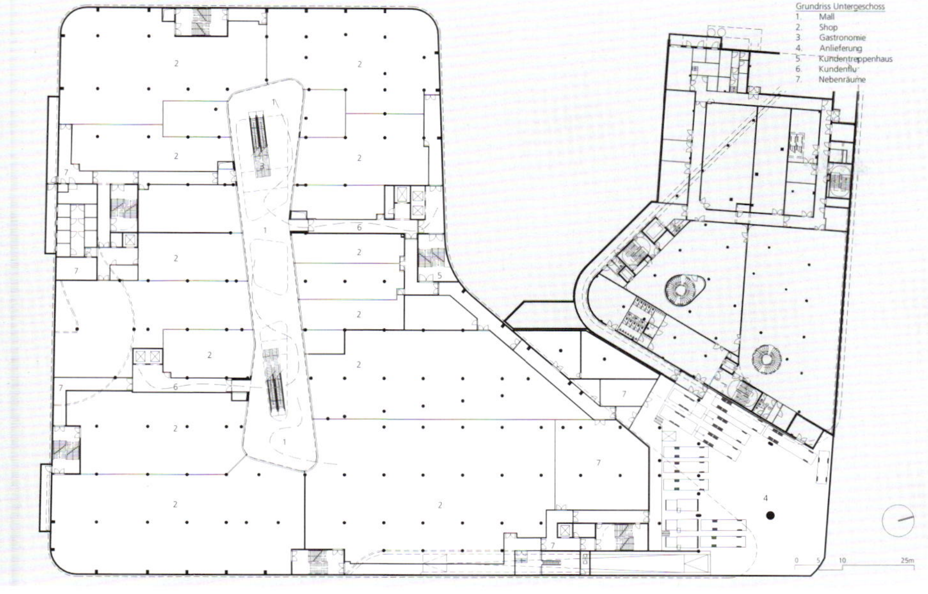

Floor Plan 4
楼层平面图 4

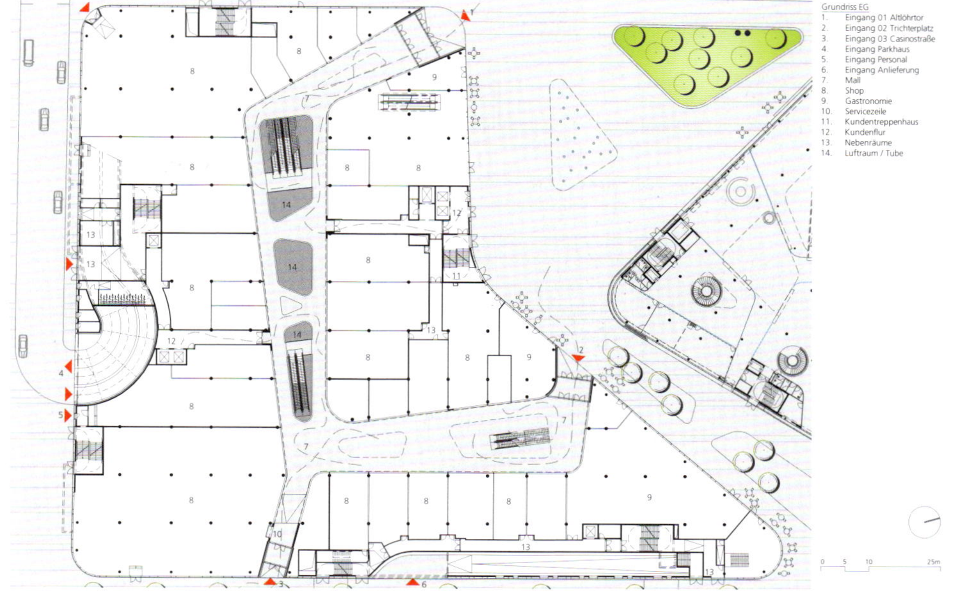

Floor Plan 5
楼层平面图 5

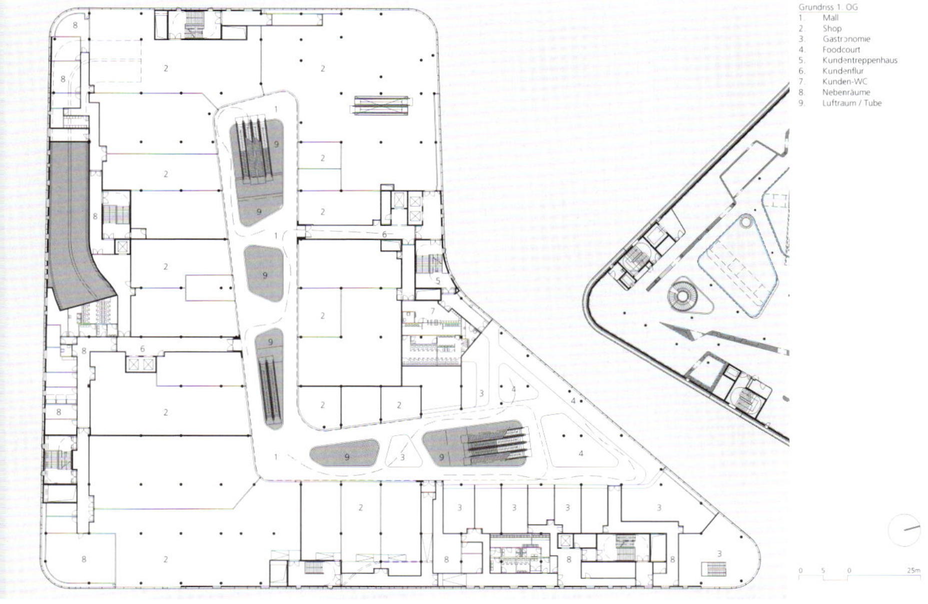

Floor Plan 6
楼层平面图 6

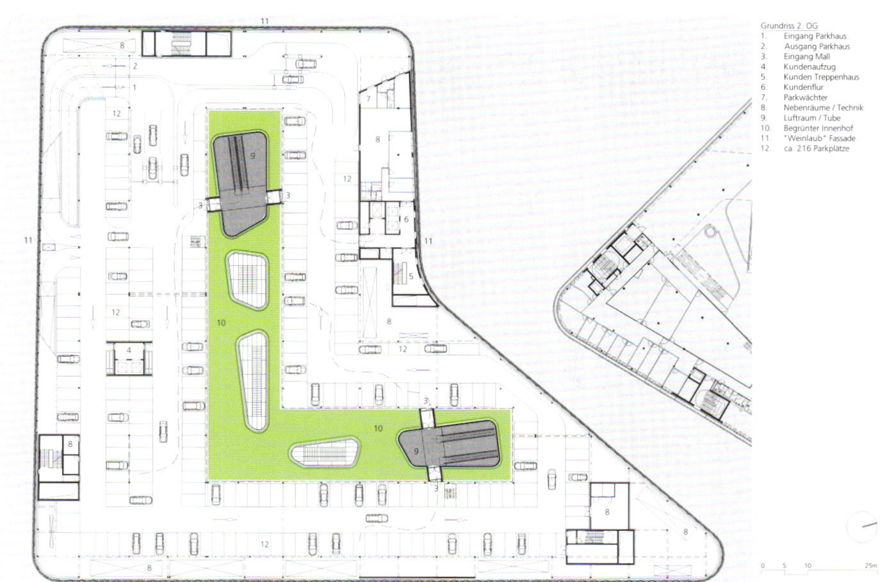

Floor Plan 7
楼层平面图 7

The sales floors are located on level -1, 0 and +1. In the basement the loading and unloading area is organized in such a way that supplying both buildings can be easily coordinated and done collectively. On the second to the fourth floor there are technical facilities and a parking lot for about 740 cars that are organized around a central landscaped courtyard.

销售区位于地下一层，地面层和二层。在地下室的装卸区域的组织方式使得建筑可以很容易地协调货物的装卸。在第二到第四层设有技术设备区和一个容量为 740 的停车场，围绕一个中央景观庭院布置。

SCHUHWERK
SATURN
Aufzug
Center-
Management

PROJECT NAME 项目名称

AEROVILLE

爱萝维莉购物娱乐中心

Architect: Philippe Chiambaretta / PCA

设计公司：Philippe Chiambaretta / PCA

PROJECT INFORMATION 项目信息

Client	Unibail-Rodamco	**客户**	尤尼百 - 洛当科集团
Location	Paris, France	**地点**	法国巴黎
Area	110,000 m²	**面积**	110，000 平方米
Retail Area	84,000 m²	**零售店面积**	84，000 平方米
parking spaces	4,600 m²	**停车场**	4，600 平方米
Interior Design	Saguez & Partners	**室内设计**	Saguez & Partners

OVERVIEW 项目概况

The Paris area airport - Charles de Gaulle – has become the first airport hub in continental Europe because of its advanced technology, its flux of freight and travelers, and its inestimable potential for growth.

This airport zone – consisting of 10 business parks, multiple commercial zones, and professional fairgrounds - is the first employment center in the Ile-de-France region, after La Défense, with over 120,000 employees. The Grand Paris projects (CDG Express or double loop) will soon reinforce the power of the "hub", a node of global interconnection, and a threshold for the capital and the country.

巴黎地区机场——戴高乐机场因其领先的技术，客货运流量和难以估量的增长潜力成了欧洲大陆最大的航空中心。

机场地区是继拉德芳斯之后在巴黎都会区内最大的就业中心，它有 12 万多雇工，有十个商业园，多功能商务区和专业游乐场，大巴黎建设项目（CDB 快速列车或双环路列车）将会很快增强中心作为交互连接的地理节点以及都市与乡村门槛的活力。

BRIEF INTERVIEW 访谈录

ARCHITECT
Philippe Chiambaretta

设计师
Philippe Chiambaretta

PHOTOGRAPHY
Henry Roy

摄影师
Henry Roy

HKASP: When designing, is there something in particular that you focus on?(Material, form, use etc)

Philippe Chiambaretta / PCA : believe use is the first thing to focus on. Uses are changing with new ways of life, and technology affecting our relationship to space and time. New uses will be the most interesting sources of innovations in the future. Form has to follow and serve new uses.

HKASP: What important thing does this project can bring to the city?

Philippe Chiambaretta / PCA : Buildings must contribute to create social links.

香港建筑科学出版社：在设计的过程中，有什么是你们特别关注的吗，比如材料、形式、用途等等？

Philippe Chiambaretta / PCA：我认为用途是首先需要关注的。建筑用途正随着新的生活方式发生变化。技术影响着我们跟空间与时间的关系。在未来，首当其冲的是建筑用途的创新，随后才是形式创新，这是因为形式创新是随用途创新而来。

香港建筑科学出版社：你觉得该项目给这座城市带来了什么重要的东西呢？

Philippe Chiambaretta / PCA：建筑理所当然应该成为促进社会联系的纽带。

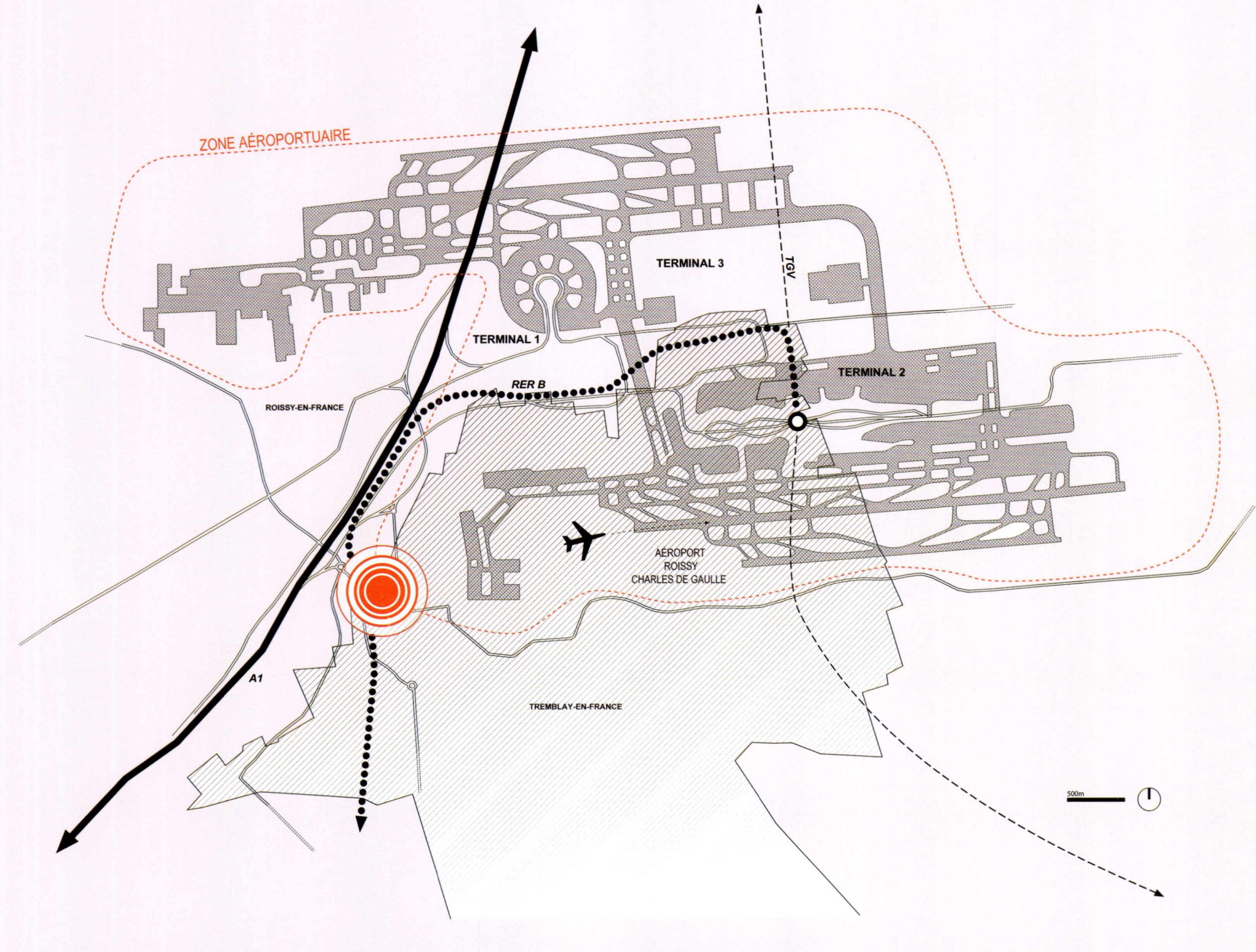
ZONE AÉROPORTUAIRE
TERMINAL 3
TGV
TERMINAL 1
TERMINAL 2
RER B
ROISSY-EN-FRANCE
AÉROPORT
ROISSY
CHARLES DE GAULLE
A1
TREMBLAY-EN-FRANCE
500m

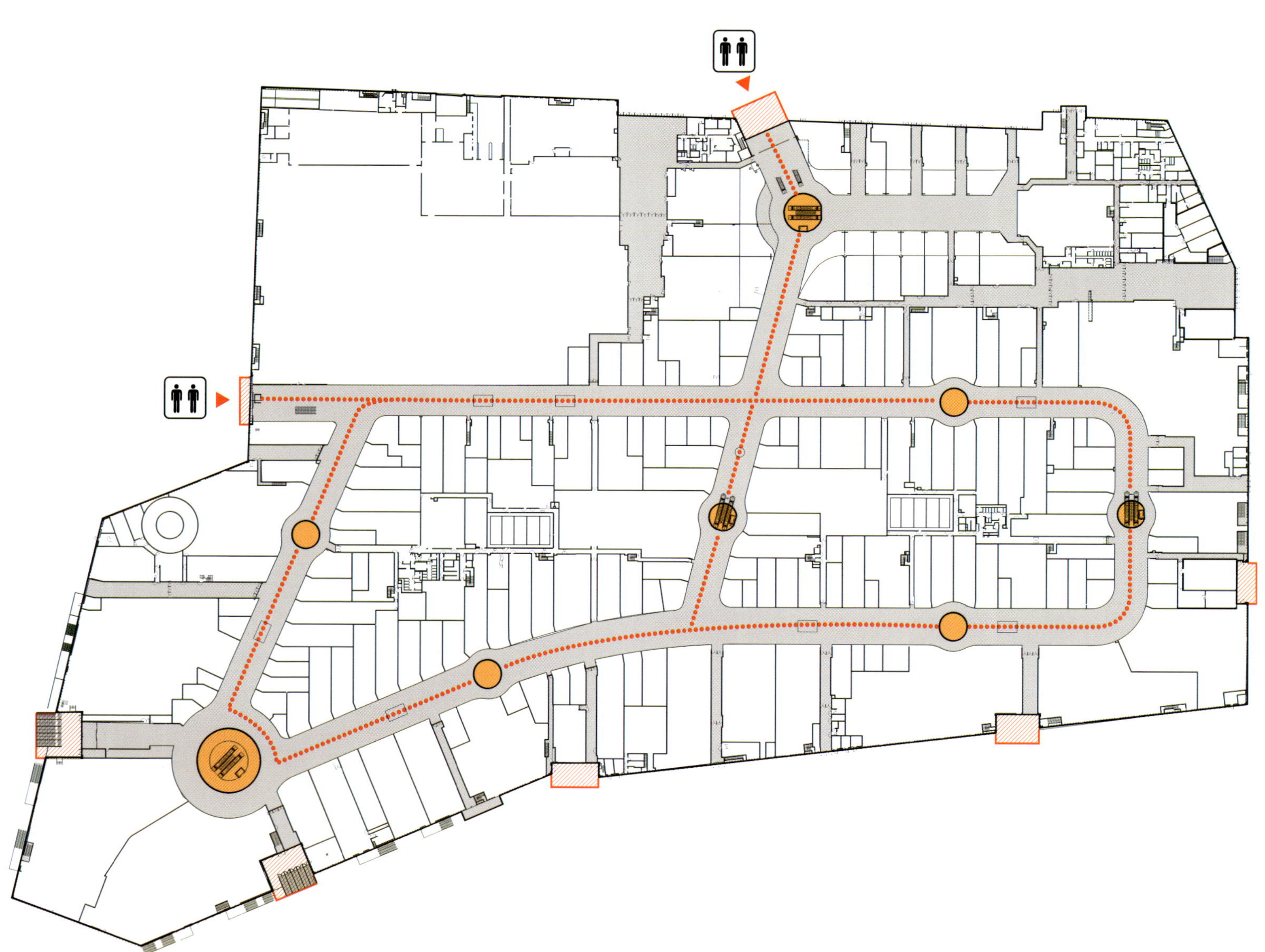

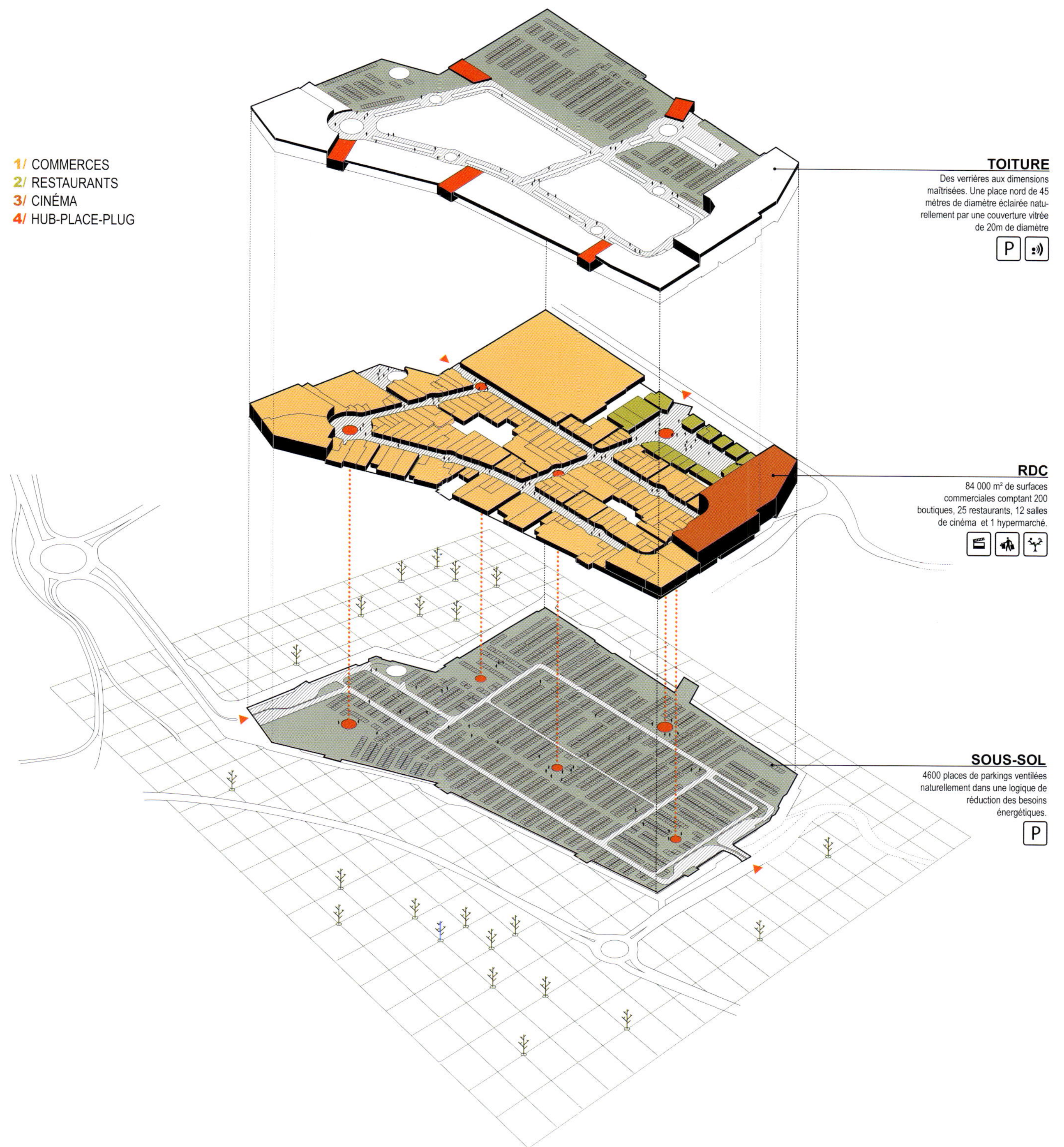

Mixed-use retail and entertainment hub at Roissy-Charles de Gaulle Airport, France.

This area has suffered from a lack of identity of space and centrality which could offer its users the facilities of a city center: services, shopping, entertainment, and culture. To overcome this absence, Aéroports de Paris, in partnership with the Unibail-Rodamco group have for a decade envisioned a long awaited mixed-use and entertainment complex at the fringes of the airport zone, less than 10 minutes by car or bus for employees of the area, and for travelers and residents of Roissy and Tremblay. Less than 30 minutes by car, there is a population of 1.8 million people that is affected by the project, between the highly dense zones towards Paris and the more scattered zones to the north.

In 2010, Unibail-Rodamco appointed Philippe Chiambarettc/PCA with the design and development of this complex called Aeroville. After less than four years of studies and construction, the project is open today.

法国戴高乐机场综合购物和娱乐中心

这一地区长期苦于因不能为其住户提供城市中心功能而造成的空间及中心特性的缺失，诸如服务、购物、娱乐、文化等。为了找回这些方面的缺失，巴黎戴高乐机场与尤利百一洛当科集团实行一项十年合作计划，在机场区的外围兴建一座人们期待已久的集休闲娱乐于一体的综合建筑体。这样一来，机场的职员、罗茜及特郎布莱的居民和游客乘车抵达的时间都用不了十分钟。处于巴黎方向的人口稠密区和北部地带人口分散区之间的 180 万人口直接受益于该项目，他们抵达的车程也不足三十分钟。

2010 年，尤利伯一洛当科指定由 Philippe Chiambaretta 建筑事务所（PCA）设计开发这个叫做爱萝维莉的综合体，随后经过不到四年的设计建设，项目于今年落成启用。

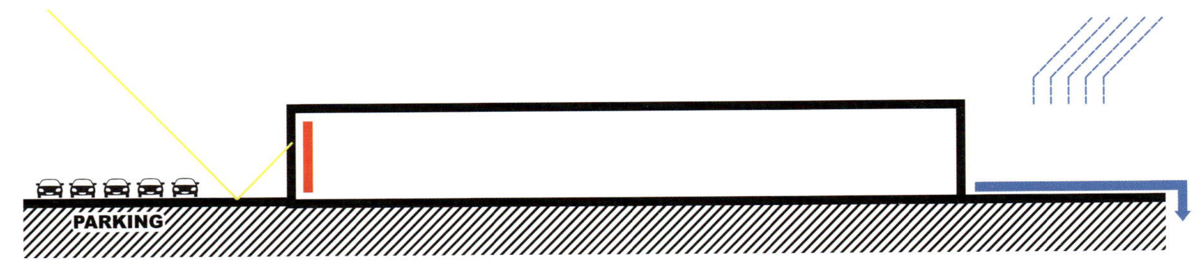

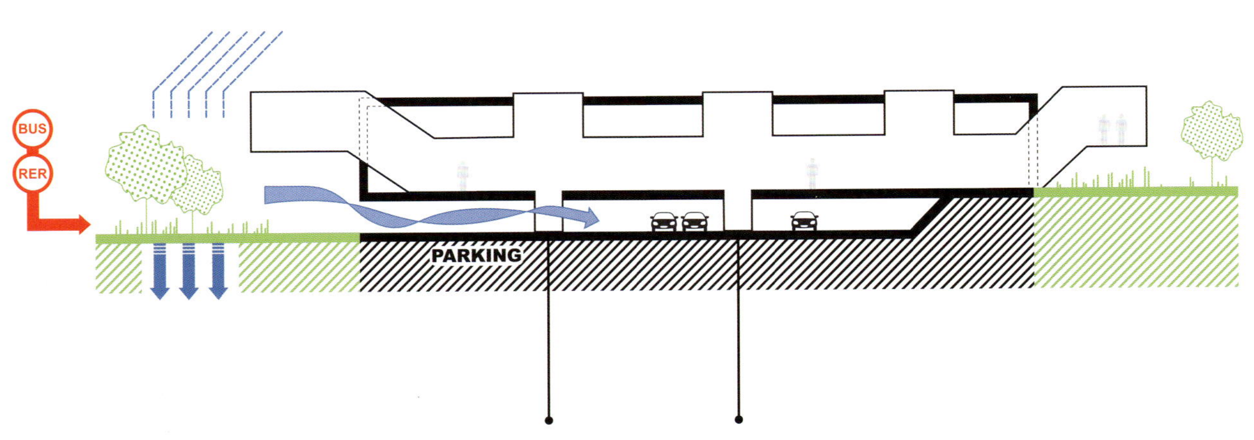

AN ARCHITECTURAL CONCEPT THAT BRIDGES THE GAP FROM THE AIRPORT TO THE CITY CENTER

The Aeroville mall is designed in the manner of a city rail system, making a clear distinction between the public space and the built environment. The commercial program around the interior streets is fragmented into blocks of varying heights and dimensions referring to the islands of the city. The project is in contrast with the usual proportions of this type of program, flat and uniform, and consistent with its function as a participant to travel and escape. The opening of the building and its character, non-generic and non-repetitive, form a space devoted to commerce, a public form that promotes exchanges and strolls.

桥接从机场到城市中心之间的边缘区的建筑理念

爱萝维莉被设计成城铁系统样式，其公共空间和建成环境有着明确的区分，其内街的商业项目散布在不同高低和大小的像各种岛屿一样的城市街区中。建筑规模与商业项目配套恰当、均匀一致，符合人群集散要求。建筑的开放性、特异性和不可复制性，使其成为吸引人们闲逛购物的公共商业空间。

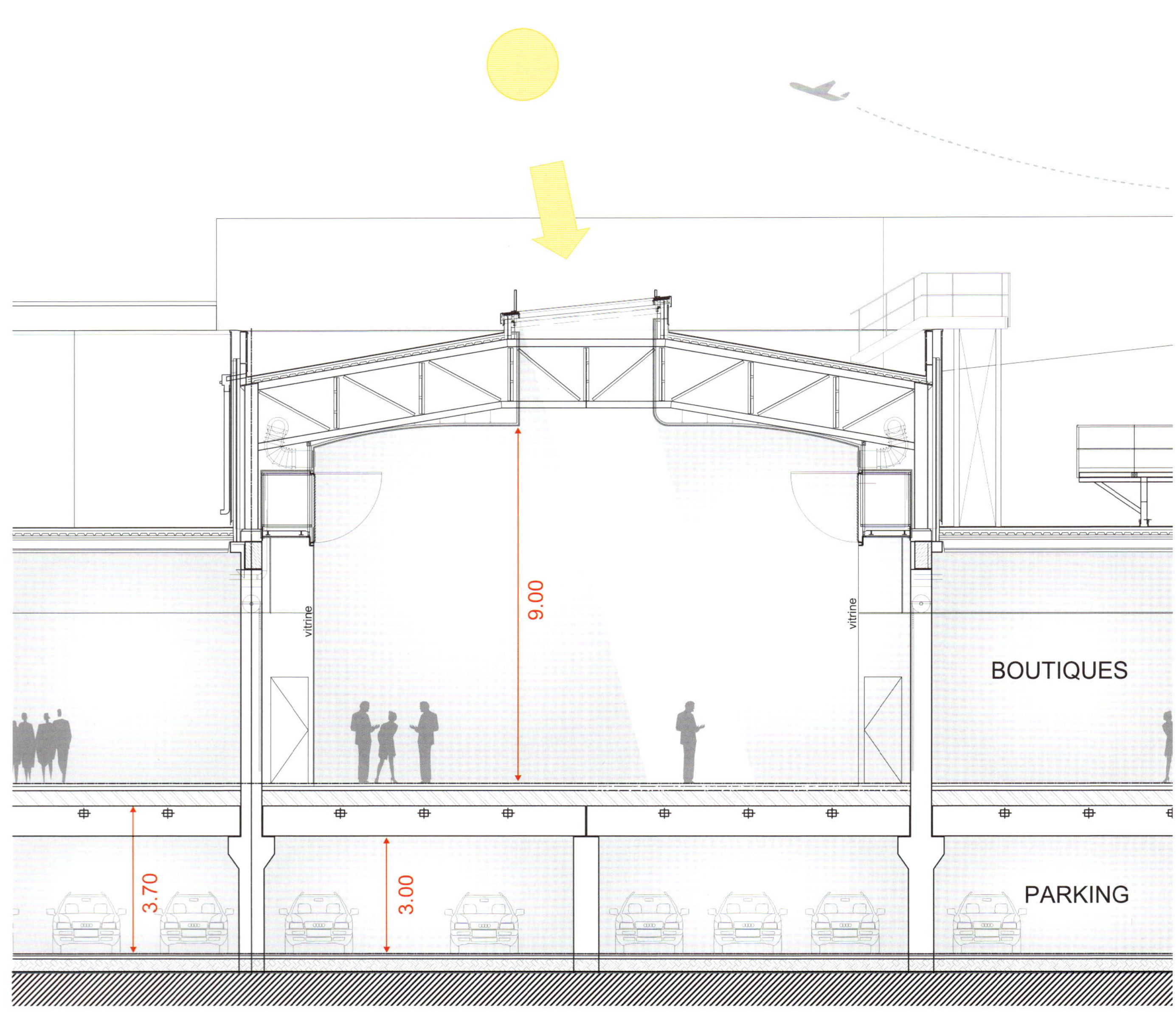

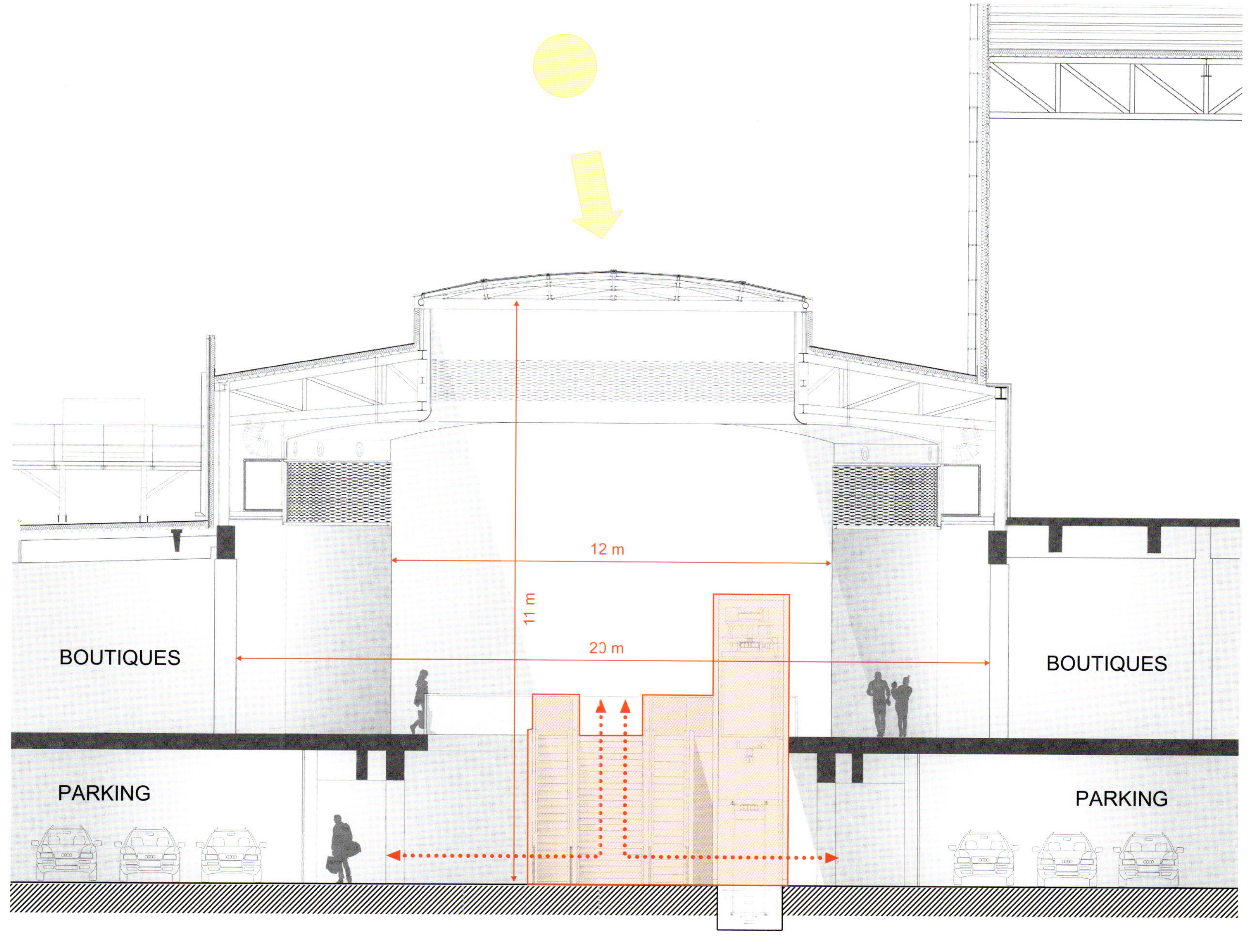

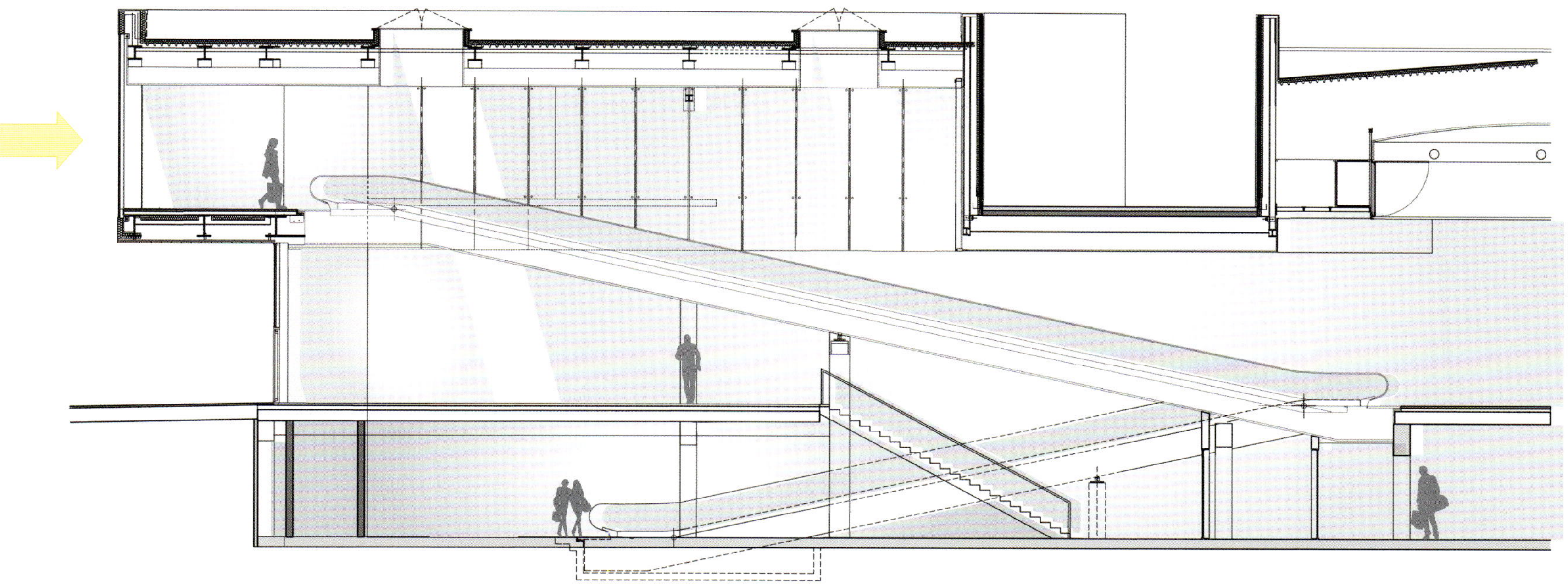

AN ORGANIZATION IN THREE STRATUMS PLAYING WITH NATURAL TOPOGRAPHY

The architectural design presents the originality of this type of development solely on a single level of retail around a covered street in the form of the number eight, along which are arranged the program components. This inner street level is accessed from rue des Buissons, facing the bus stop and offices of the freight area.

与自然地貌共生的三层结构里的组织系统

建筑设计的创意在于用八种形式在一个闭合的街道内创造单一零售的独特发展模式，沿着这条街分布着零售项目的各个要素。内街的标高接近外面的灌木丛，朝向货运区的汽车站和办公室。

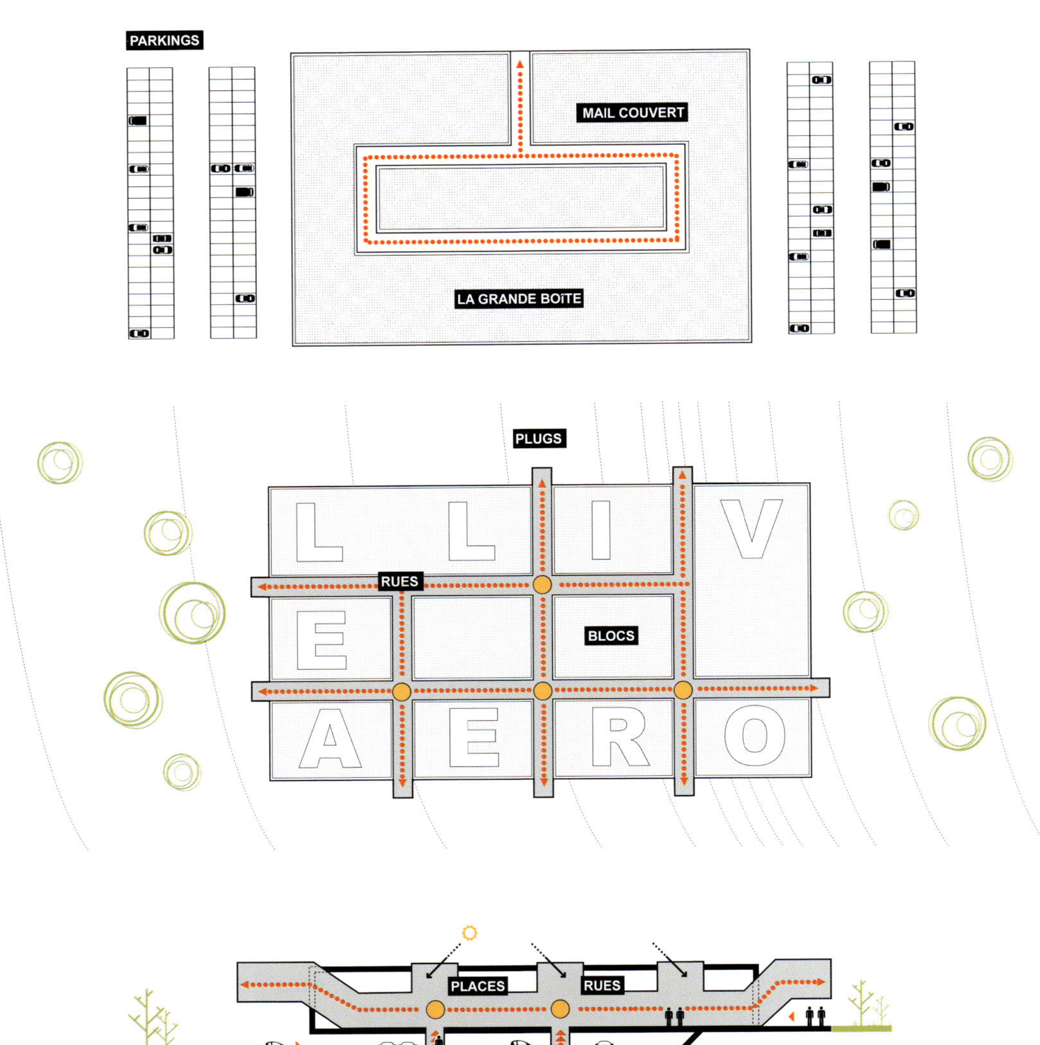

Parking is hidden under and on street level. The project has taken part of the sloping site, and the north entrance to the parking is on the natural terrain, providing natural light and ventilation to the parking lot. The parking for staff and the cinema are located in the center. The surroundings are freed from vehicles and are vegetated allowing the reconstitution of an ecosystem.

停车场隐藏在街道标高以下，利用部分斜坡地块，其北部入口依靠天然地势为车库提供自然照明和通风。职员和影院的停车区处于中央，四周是免费停车区。这样布置有利于植被生态系统的重建。

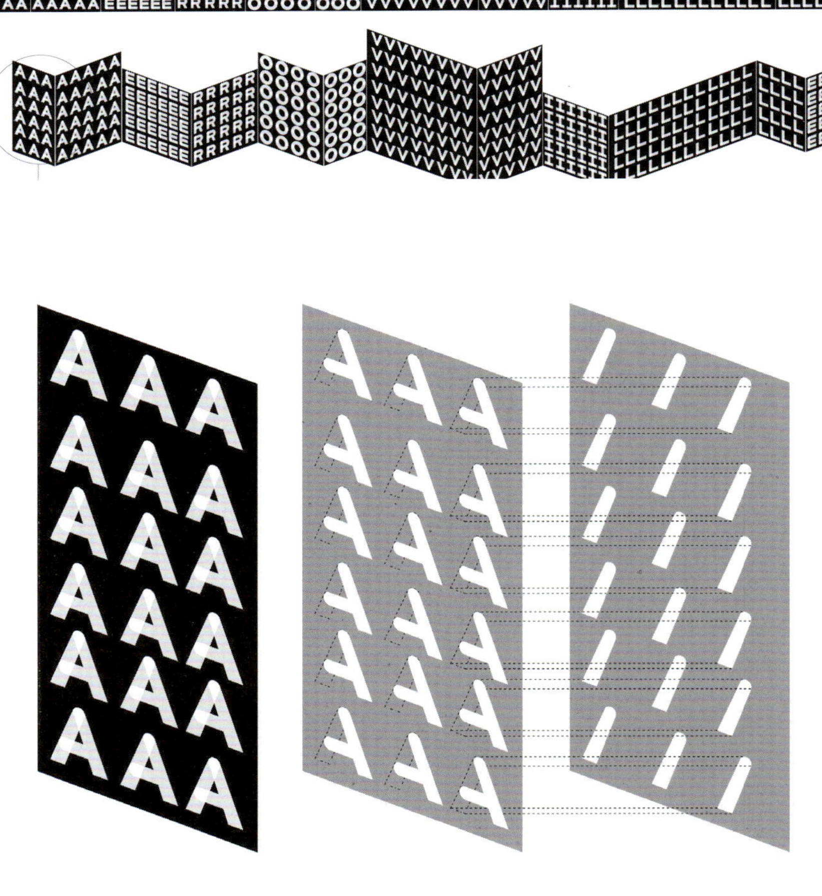

THE ENVELOPE

The envelope of the blocks, inspired by the codes of the city center, was thought out with the image of the periphery. International brands have become a major component of the global imagery. A, E, R, O, V, I, L, L, E or the original monogram of the imaginary brand. In "tattooing" graphically the skin of the shopping center, these letters refer to this fictitious brand that would be Aeroville, transforming the object of international consumption into collective creation.

表层

灵感来自城市中心符号的各建筑单元的表皮通体充满着想象，国际品牌已成为其全球形象的重要组成部分，A，E，R，O，V，I，L，L，E 这些虚构品牌的字母醒目地镶嵌进购物中心的表皮，字母所构成的虚拟品牌就是爱萝维莉，如今它已将这座国际消费综合体变换成集体创作的结晶。

A STRUCTURAL PRINCIPLE DICTATED BY THE SPECIFICTY OF THE CONSTRUCTION SITE

The structural specificity of the project was driven by its sprawl and the limited duration of construction. The use of prefabrication helped respect the quick deadline. The very large size of the building, not allowing the construction level by level, imposed a device capable of providing a definitive stability with limited phases without the need for ulterior interventions on the work. The structural core of the building has been built for every level in advance.

由场地特点所决定的建筑结构

项目结构的特性受其建筑的蔓延性和有限的施工工期所决定，预制件的使用有效地加快了工期，巨大的建筑体量已没时间逐层去建造，加强设备阶段性稳定工作能力，减少干扰非常重要，每一层结构的核心都提前建好。

The principle developed to allow for this feat consists of implementing the prefabricated posts at full height (10m and 16m), whose stability and bracing is done directly by the embankment into its foundation (almost all the bracings of this buildings is provided by these embankments). Since their installation, the posts are stable and well braced and can support two or three floor levels. No temporary bracing and shoring is required. Only the structure crossing the mall and parking is an exception to this rule. Large spans and continuity in volumes naturally leads to a realization in the metal frame, which are also prefabricated.

The North node is an exception to this rule; the 45m diameter required a reconstituted/welded metal frame on site with a glass canopy of 20m in diameter is the centerpiece.

这一庞大的工程使用了全长度预制桩（10 米和 12 米），它由基于地基的堤防提供稳定和支撑（这座大厦的几乎所有的支撑都是由这些堤防提供）。这样的安装使预制桩能同时稳定支撑两至三层楼层而无须临时支护。结构交叉于购物中心和车库时，则采用大型连续钢梁，钢梁也是预制的。

北部的节点处则不用上述方法，这里使用了直径 45 米的现场拼装曲型钢梁，梁上是一个直径 20 米的装饰玻璃顶盖。

A PROJECT OF HIGH ENVRIONMENTAL QUALITY (BREEAM Excellent certification)

• Mastering the sealing
- Use of serviced land and non-agricultural land
- Overlay the building and parking to free outdoor spaces
- Controlling water discharges through a retention basin of 4500 m^3

• Respecting and valuing natural resources
- Limit earthworks
- Making a compensatory landscape promoting biodiversity
- Reducing the impact on the water cycle
- Use of geothermal energy

• Reduced energy needs
- Refresh the external environment and create masks with a landscaped space
- Protect against solar radiation by controlling the size of the windows
- Naturally ventilate parking

优秀环境品质的项目（获英国环评组织优秀证书）

主动环境控制
利用即有土地和非农业用地
有效控制建筑和停车场的室外免费空间
一个容量 4、500 立方米的蓄水池用来控制排水

尊重和重视自然资源
限定土方规模
形成补偿景观，促进生态多样化
减低对水文循环的影响
利用地热能

降低能耗
恢复外部环境提高景观空间的遮蔽性
控制窗子的尺寸防护太阳辐射
停车场采用自然通风

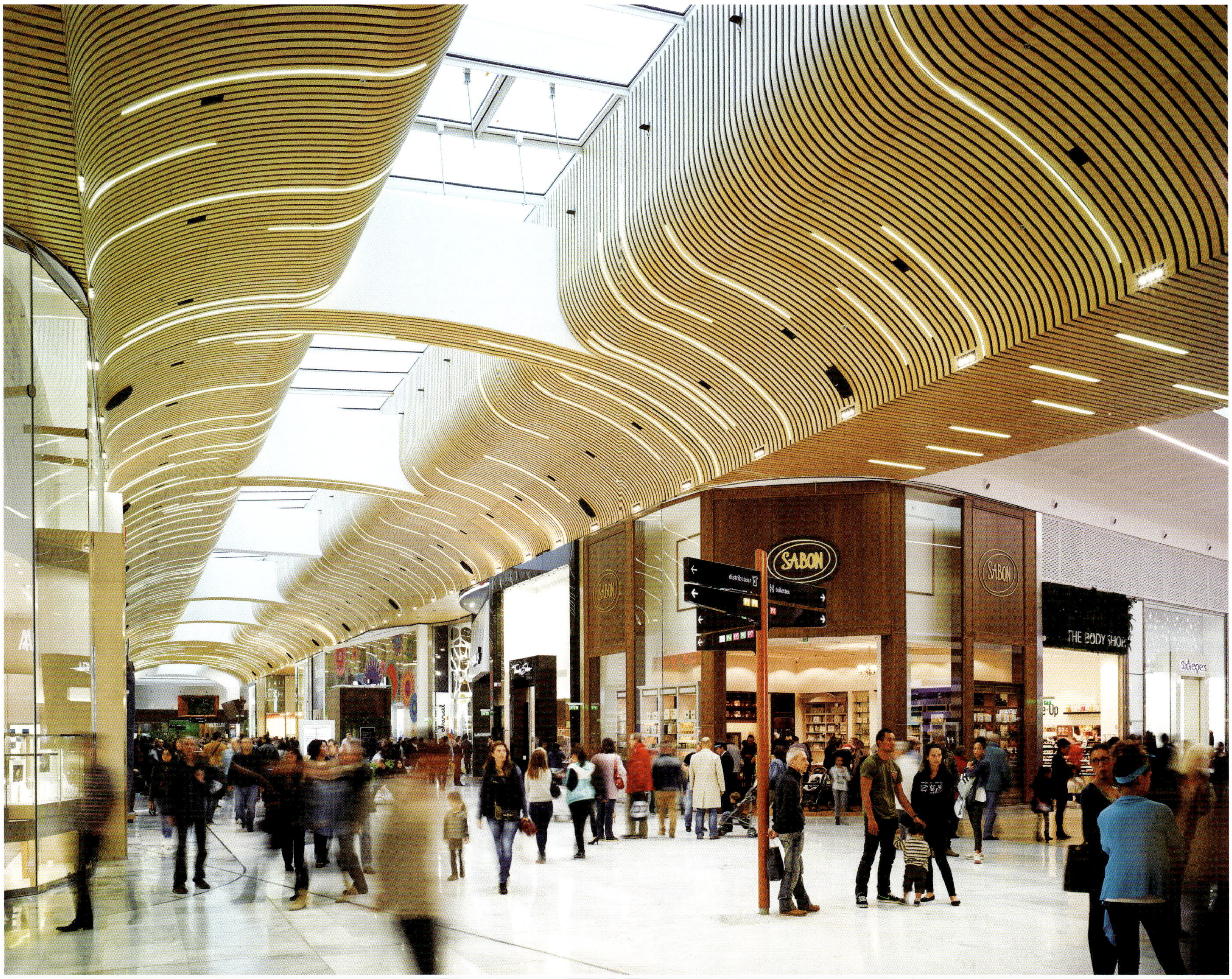
SABON
THE BODY SHOP

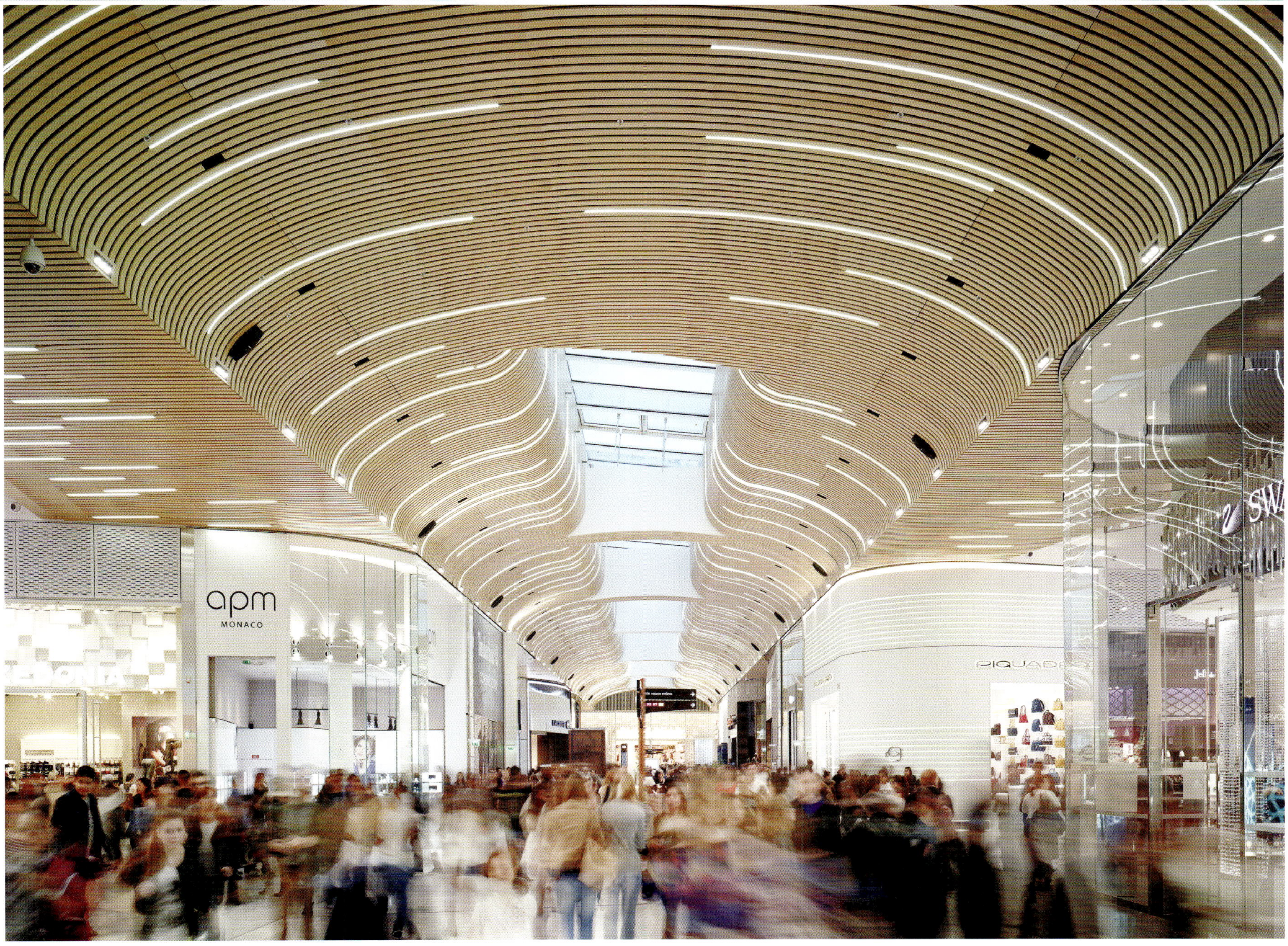
apm
MONACO

PROJECT NAME 项目名称

SINGAPORE CHANGI AIRPORT TERMINAL 4

新加坡樟宜机场 4 号航站楼

Architect: SAA Architects Pte Ltd – Lead Agency, Benoy Ltd,· AECOM Singapore Pte Ltd,· Beca Carter Hollings & Ferner (SEA) Pte Ltd

设计公司：SAA 建筑设计 贝诺设计， 新加坡 AECOM， Beca Carter Hollings & Ferner (SEA) Pte Ltd

PROJECT INFORMATION 项目信息

Client	Changi Airport Group (CAG)	**客户**	樟宜机场集团 (CAG)
Location	Singapore	**地点**	新加坡
Gross floor area	195,000m²	**总建筑面积**	195，000 平方米

OVERVIEW 项目概况

Set to redefine the travel experience, Changi Airport's new terminal will be located along Airport Boulevard, and will accommodate up to 16 million passengers a year. The 195,000m² building has been designed to celebrate both physical and visual transparency. The arrival experience will be surrounded by lush vertical landscaping and an impressive double-storey glazed facade. Inside, the concept is dynamic, vibrant and colourful with feature skylight lanterns illuminating the terminal. Gardens have been incorporated to enliven the airport interiors with green walls and an abundance of elegant tall trees growing beneath the natural light.

樟宜机场的新航站楼位于机场大道，年旅客流量将达到 1600 万，赋予了旅行体验新的定义。面积为 195，000 平方米的建筑设计体现了物理和视觉上的透明感。旅客抵达大厅，即被郁郁葱葱的垂直绿植景观和令人难忘的双层高光墙面包围。航站楼内部采用动感设计理念，整个空间充满活力、色彩斑斓，特色天窗灯笼设计照亮了整栋大楼。花园的绿墙和众多优雅的高大树木在自然光的沐浴下生机勃勃，使机场内部空间变得活跃起来。

FEATURE ANALYSIS 特色分析

The large areas of vertical greening and interior green garden, are exactly consist with the title of "garden city" of Singapore, creating the comfortable interior green life. In addition, two layers of glaze appearance, colorful light lanterns hanging in the entrance hall and unique old Nyonya-style buildings, show people the brand-new feelings.

项目大面积的垂直绿化、室内的绿色花园，与新加坡的“城市花园”的称号非常相符，营造非常舒适的室内林荫生活。另外，两层内釉面外观、色彩斑斓的天窗灯笼挂在入口大厅，以及设计独特的娘惹风格建筑，给人耳目一新的感觉。

The new concept for the highly anticipated Terminal 4 (T4) at Singapore Changi Airport has been unveiled at the T4 groundbreaking ceremony on 5 November 2013. Appointed by Changi Airport Group (CAG), Singapore's award-winning SAA Architects, the lead consultant and executive architect of the Architect & Design Consortium (Consortium), collaborated with UK-founded design firm Benoy Limited on the concept and interior design of the new terminal.

万众瞩目的新加坡樟宜机场 4 号航站楼的新概念在 2013 年 11 月 5 日的开工奠基仪式上正式揭开帷幕。接受樟宜机场集团（CAG）的委任后，新加坡备受赞誉的 SAA 建筑设计有限公司（建筑和设计团队的首席顾问和总建筑师）和联合英国贝诺建筑设计有限公司完成了新航站楼的概念和内部设计。

Yeo Siew Haip, Managing Director of SAA Architects, explained the complexity of the large-scale project, "Since winning the project in mid February 2013, the SAA-led Consortium worked hand in hand with CAG and Benoy to bring the design of T4 from concept to commencement of piling works on-site. SAA provided the Consortium leadership in managing concept refinement, stakeholder engagement, fast-track scheduling and value engineering.Finalising the overall design of T4 for the Main Contract Tender within the time frame we had is a feat in itself for the industry, especially with over ten consultants and specialists collaborating intimately in the intricate work scope, keeping the project on schedule."

SAA 建筑设计公司的总经理 Yeo Siew Haip 对大型项目的复杂性进行了解释，他说："自 2013 年 2 月中旬中标以后，以 SAA 为首的团队携手 CAG 和贝诺为 T4 提供设计方案，从概念设计到现场开工打桩，我们尽量做到精益求精。SAA 主要负责管理概念深化、利益相关方、快速调度和工程估价方面的工作。在规定的时间内完成主合同招标中 T4 的整体设计是行业内一次难得的壮举，超过 10 名顾问和专业人士亲密合作，同心协力完成复杂的工作，确保项目工作进度更是难能可贵。

"The planning agenda has centred on introducing efficiency and comfort to the travel experience", explained Meeta Patel, Director at Benoy. "State-of-the-art facilities including self check-in kiosks and self bag-drops will provide travellers with a quick and easy airport journey. To shape the boutique atmosphere of T4, Benoy has created walk-through retail zones, Peranakan-inspired shop fronts and mezzanine dining hubs which will offer views over the central interior gardens".

The main focal point of the building is the "Central Galleria"; a glazed, open space that visually connects the departure, check-in, arrival and transit areas across the terminal.

David Buffonge, Director at Benoy said, "We are extremely excited about Terminal 4 at Changi Airport. We believe in the concept that has embraced energy and motion; creating a dynamic yet timeless design in a welcoming environment. The terminal has been designed to provide visitors access to a new level of travel comfort outside their traditional airport experiences."

"SAA's role as lead consultant and architect is not unlike a music conductor in orchestrating all processes to bring the design of Terminal 4 at Changi to reality. With CAG and Benoy, we strive to create a unique T4 experience that pushes the boundaries and inspires the traveller like never before", said Yeo Siew Haip.

The Consortium comprises a number of members responsible for various aspects of T4 including: architecture, design, civil & structural engineering, mechanical & electrical engineering, landscaping, acoustics and safety.

贝诺的主管Meeta Patel解释道："我们的规划议程主要集中在提供高效而舒适的旅行体验，许多先进的设施包括自助登机终端和自助行李托运设备让旅客可享受快捷而简单的机场服务。为了营造机场的精品氛围，贝诺设计了通道式零售区，土生华人式店面和可欣赏到中央内部花园景观的夹层餐饮空间。"

建筑的主要焦点是"中心长廊"，这是一个饰有玻璃的开放式空间，可连接航站楼内的离港区、办理登机手续区、抵达区和中转区。

贝诺的主管David Buffonge说："我们对樟宜机场4号航站楼的设计非常兴奋。我们的设计理念集合了活力和动态，打造了一个动感而永恒的设计，营造出温馨的迎客氛围。这个航站楼的设计旨在为旅客提供有别于传统机场体验的全新舒适旅行感受。"

Yeo Siew Haip说："SAA 作为首席顾问和总建筑师的作用与音乐指挥家并无不同，将会对所有流程进行调配，努力将樟宜机场4号航站楼的设计变为现实。通过与CAG和贝诺的合作，我们将极力打造一个独一无二的4号航站楼，跨越所有边界，为旅客提供前所未有的旅行体验。"

设计团队囊括了众多专业人士，负责T4的各个方面，其中包括：建筑、设计、土木和结构工程、机械和电气工程、景观、建筑声学和安全系统。

TOURISM COMPLEX REAL ESTATE

旅游型复合地产

GDS Architects

GDS 建筑事物所

Careful consideration is paid to zoning and building arrangement within the site to maximize views and ventilation to all buildings, while at the same time maintaining the existing important sight lines and breeze corridors. Leisure facilities are designed on podium rooftops raised from the undulating landscape, while spaces are carved into the high-rise towers to form sky gardens for residents.

设计师细心考虑了基地分区和基地内建筑物的布局，以获得最佳的景观效果及自然通风，但同时也保留了现有的景观和通风回廊。在高低起伏的景观的烘托下，裙楼屋顶设计了休闲设施，同时高层塔楼上挖出空间，为住户打造空中花园。

BEIJING TONGZHOU RESORT CITY 392

北京通州度假城

The main concept for the project was to create a unique year-round mixed-use resort destination in the heart of Tongzhou while providing a dramatic silhouette along the Wenyu River.

该项目的主要设计理念就是在通州的核心地段打造一个四季开放的综合型度假胜地，给人们带来另一番风味的体验。建筑在文宇河边画出美丽的轮廓，生机快然。

While the curving nature of the design concept references the historical narrative of a traditional Sampan boat sailing along the river it also serves the functional purpose of providing a larger footprint area to be designated for public plaza and gathering spaces.

中国自古以来就有小船荡漾在河上的美景。以此为灵感，我们在设计理念中引入了曲线的元素。从功能上说，度假胜地给游客带来更宽阔的散步空间，引领游客通往公共广场与聚集空间。

10 DESIGN

10 DESIGN（拾稼设计）

The question is a challenge to an architect. Many architects would hold a rejection attitude toward it. I believe a project's features would generate more factors that influence the design during the stage of design. For an architect, more opportunities to show value of design emerge during designing. As for a commercial building, the architects tend to give a full study to the business operation and investment return. The fact is that digging deep into an issue can give birth to a solution during designing.

这个问题对建筑师是挑战，很多建筑师持排斥态度，我想在建筑设计进程中因项目的特点，产生了更多影响设计的因素，对建筑师而言，其设计的过程会更显设计的价值。对商业建筑，建筑师充分研究商业运营与投资回报也是从不可少的课题，只有了解了问题的实质，才能在设计中合理的解决。

GALAXY MOONBAY RENAISSANCE HOTEL AND MIXED USE DEVELOPMENT 400

星河澜月湾万丽酒店及综合发展

The masterplan design was inspired by the local craft of bamboo carving and the aerodynamic shapes of naval design. The landscape design forms the foundation of the overall planning and design of the masterplan. A mixture of public spaces including parks, plazas, an amphitheatre and playgrounds are designed to support a variety of uses. The nature of public usage of landscape areas allows the site to integrate seamlessly with the existing lake-side promenade to the east of the site.

此总体规划设计的灵感来自当地竹雕工艺以及具有流线外形的现代船舶设计。景观设计构建了总平面规划和设计的基础。一系列的公共空间如公园、广场、圆形剧场和操场为多种用途提供支持。景观区域的公共用途性质使基地与东面现有的湖滨人行道无缝对接。

The buildings are curved to reflect the fluidity of the lake. A section of each tower is carved to house a large floating garden to give the masterplan a softer, resort like feel.

建筑物呈弧形设计，以呼应湖泊的流动性。每座塔楼的一部分都被挖开，镶嵌大型的漂浮花园，使总体规划看起来更柔软、更具度假地的美感。

STARH Architects

STARH Architects

412 INTERNATIONAL BUSINESS CENTER AND INTERCONTINENTAL HOTEL

国际商务中心与洲际酒店

A certain dualism has been sought in the project- a reference and connection between Mount Ararat and the twin peaks together with the dynamic equilibrium of the two parts as a whole. The hotel building has been designed as an accent both in the architectural composition of the complex and in the general layout of the city.

该项目力图寻找某种两重性，寻找阿勒山双子峰之间的关联；同时当两者作为一个整体时，两者之间形成的一种动态平衡。无论在综合体建筑布局方面，还是在城市总体布局方面，酒店大楼都是焦点。

Combining three functions- hotel, office and residential building in one complex is always challenging. Following the design concept of the two integral elements, considering them not as separate units, but as a part of the whole, point our idea. The volumes appear as a united complex of ovals by plan, but each expresses its individual purpose.

功能上，该综合体集酒店、办公以及家居为一体。如何实现功能的集合，总是颇具挑战。遵循合二为一的设计理念，我们既要将各建筑视为一个整体，同时又传递出他们的不同之处。从平面图上看，各建筑好似融合在一起的综合体，但同时也表达出各自不同的用途。

The first job is to integrate and plan commercial functions to cater to business practice and deliver an excellent organization of flows when a commercial project is not influenced by any specific external factor.

对于商业项目，在无特定的外部条件影响下，首要的是将商业功能整合规划成符合商业运营的模式，组织好各种流线。

Zhongshen Architectural Design Co., Ltd. Shenzhen

深圳中深建筑设计有限公司

CHENGDU'S NEW CENTURY GLOBAL CENTER 420

成都新世纪环球中心

The project was small in scale in the early phase. The design proposal is quite based on concept. With change of external factors, we saw an increasingly improved core of this project which became a signature project in Chengdu. And the project saw an enhancement both in scale and functions.

项目的前期规模不大，设计方案也是在设计理念基础上进行，但是随着外部因素的变化，项目主体不断提升，成为成都市的名片项目，其规模和功能也不断的放大。

The energy of the space is very important. We really focused on the spatial flow of the spaces as this is important to connect back to the streets of Kuta so the people can flow and walk in naturally at the surrounding areas,beachwalk became an extension of the street in a natural way. It is the first semi open lifestyle commercial hub in Indonesia with a great focus on nature and landscape design.

赋予空间以活力是非常重要的要素。保持与库塔街风格的连贯至关重要，于是我们的确把重心放在了如何营造出一种过渡自然的空间。这样，人们很自然地穿行于周边各个区域，而且海滩步道也自然地成为库塔街的延伸。这是有史以来在印度尼西亚第一次采用半开放式生活体验购物中心，如此关注自然，如此关注景观设计。

SAHID KUTA LIFESTYLE RESORT 432

萨希迪库塔生活方式度假村

Envirotec Indonesia

镜艺

PROJECT NAME 项目名称

BEIJING TONGZHOU RESORT CITY
北京通州度假城

Architect: GDS Architects
设计公司：GDS 建筑事务所

PROJECT INFORMATION 项目信息

Client	Shin Kong Real Estate Management Co., Ltd.	客户	新光房地产有限公司
Location	TongZhou,Beijing,China	地点	中国北京通州
Gross Floor Area	463,941 m²	建筑总面积	463，941 平方米
Drawings and Plans	46,704 m²	占地面积	46，704 平方米

OVERVIEW 项目概况

Located in the heart of the City of Tongzhou, Beijing and along the Wenryu River, the Tongzhou Resort City will become a mixed-use urban resort destination that provide a striking visual silhouette. The design concept provides an iconographic silhouette referencing the traditional sails along the waterfront with an all season dome and podium structure featuring an Urban Entertainment Center, Specialty Retail, Shin Kong Department Store, indoor Waterpark and arboretum, and pedestrian bridge linkages to surrounding sites and Yuan Toudaolsland.

通州度假城位于北京通州的中心地带，靠近温榆河边，其拥有引人注目的视觉轮廓并将成为多功能城市度假目的地。该项目的设计理念是沿着水滨建立极具象征意义的传统风帆架构以及四季穹顶和中庭结构，打造都市娱乐中心、专营零售空间、新光百货商店、室内水上乐园和植物园，一座人行天桥将周围的空间和源头岛连接起来。

BRIEF INTERVIEW 访谈录

ARCHITECT
Michael Collins

设计师
Michael Collins

HKASP: What was the main concept behind the whole project?

GDS Architects: The main concept for the project was to create a unique year-round mixed-use resort destination in the heart of Tongzhou while providing a dramatic silhouette along the Wenyu River. While the curving nature of the design concept references the historical narrative of a traditional Sampan boat sailing along the river it also serves the functional purpose of providing a larger footprint area to be designated for public plaza and gathering spaces. The design intent was to energize the commercial street frontage, activate the adjacent waterfront while also engaging the nearby Yuan Toudao island.

In order to allow for a true live, work, play environment, the design provides several key programs that achieve this synergy and critical mass. These include an 80-story Landmark Commercial Tower with a 6-star Atrium hotel and Observation deck located on the upper levels, 53-story Office Tower, 41-story Residential Tower, two All-Season enclosed Resort Domes with indoor waterpark, Department Store, Arboretum, Discovery Museum and Urban Entertainment Center.

HKASP: The tower facade looks quite impressive. Can you share with us of your research process?

GDS Architects: Our initial research allowed us to better understand the local history and cultural significance of the site and importance to the region. This area is known to be of historical significance with respect to having been a location where traders and visitors sailing along the river in Sampans would wait for the opportunity to meet with the Emperor. The curving silhouette of the towers acknowledges the significance of this cultural identity while providing a dramatic skyline for today. For sake of economy and ease of construction, the towers are intended to be reinforced concrete with a conventional curtainwall system with Low-E flat glazing, both in plan and section. The final "curved aesthetic" of the facade will be achieved by using a non-structural curved sunshade.

The project will incorporate many leading examples of Green Technology including Low-E glass, Natural daylighting, BIPV for all domes and canopies, Pre-fabricated ETFE panels and Bio-tops roofing and gray water cistern and recycling. The two main enclosed domes will utilize ETFE panels capable of spanning great distances while weighing 1% of the weight of glass.

香港建筑科学出版社：整个项目的主要设计理念是什么？

GDS 建筑事务所：该项目的主要设计理念就是在通州的核心地段打造一个四季开放的综合型度假胜地，给人们带来别一番风味的体验。建筑在文宇河边画出美丽的轮廓，生机快然。中国自古以来就有小船荡漾在河上的美景。以此为灵感，我们在设计理念中引入了曲线的元素。从功能上说，度假胜地给游客带来更宽阔的散步空间，引领游客通往公共广场与聚集空间。设计旨在点燃正街的商业氛围，让毗邻的滨河地区充满生机，同时还唤醒附近的源头岛。

为了满足真实生活、工作以及娱乐的要求，还设立了若干重要的服务设施，以实现多种业态优势互补，成熟的商业模式。其中包括一栋 80 层高的地标性商业楼（商业楼内设有一家六星级天庭酒店与位于高层的观景台），一栋 53 层高的写字楼，一栋 41 层高的公寓，两栋四季封闭式度假圆顶建筑（内设水上公园、百货商店、植物园、探索博物馆以及娱乐城）。

香港建筑科学出版社：大厦立面让人印象深刻。你可以跟我们分享你的探索历程吗？

GDS 建筑事务所：探索历程之初，我们需要加深对当地历史人文的了解，什么对这个地区重要。当地以悠久历史而闻名，这里曾经是商人、游客坐船等待一窥皇帝的宝地。大厦的曲线外形正好贴合了这一历史文化特点。如今，曲线外形还增添了一道栩栩如生的天际线。鉴于对节约建设成本与降低建设难度的考虑，大厦采用钢筋混凝土结构与传统的低辐射平板玻璃幕墙。呈曲线的遮阳帘为非结构材料。它的存在将最终实现立面的“曲线美感”。

该项目应用了多项先进的环保技术，比如低辐射玻璃、自然采光技术、光伏建筑一体化（用于圆顶与顶篷）、预制四氟乙烯板、生态房顶、污水池以及污水循环利用技术。两个主要的封闭圆顶采用可以横跨大空间四氟乙烯板。四氟乙烯板的重量只有玻璃的 1%。

HKASP: What are the important things that this project does for the city?

GDS Architects: Tongzhou Resort City (TRC) provides a truly unique, year-round mixed-use resort destination in the heart of Tongzhou. The development provides much needed program opportunities to Tongzhou and the surrounding area. TRC will serve as an icon for the city while providing a much needed civic amenity as it becomes an urban oasis and cultural entertainment destination for all.

香港建筑科学出版社：该项目对这座城市具有怎样的重要意义？

GDS 建筑事务所：通州度假城（简称 TRC）坐落在通州核心地段，为一处全年开放式综合型度假胜地，这里游客可享受名副其实且别具一格的度假体验。此项目给通州及周边地区打造了人们渴望的服务设施。通州度假城将成为这座城市的一张名片，给人们提供所渴望的民心服务。此外，她还将成为城市里的一片绿洲，众人渴望的文化娱乐圣地。

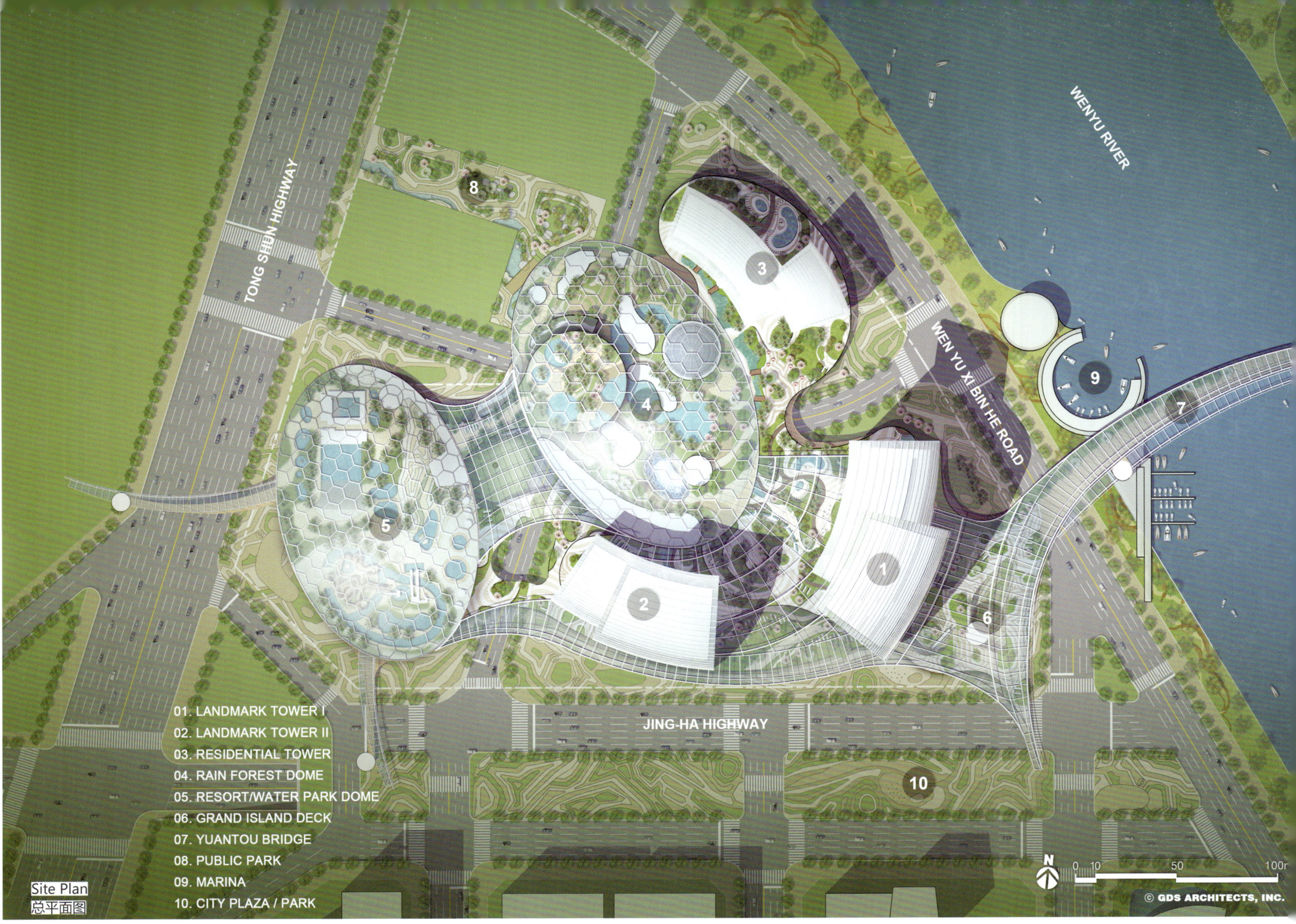

TONG SHUN HIGHWAY
WENYU RIVER
WEN YU XI BIN HE ROAD
JING-HA HIGHWAY
01. LANDMARK TOWER I
02. LANDMARK TOWER II
03. RESIDENTIAL TOWER
04. RAIN FOREST DOME
05. RESORT/WATER PARK DOME
06. GRAND ISLAND DECK
07. YUANTOU BRIDGE
08. PUBLIC PARK
09. MARINA
10. CITY PLAZA / PARK
N
0 10 50 100m
© GDS ARCHITECTS, INC.

Site Plan
总平面图

CONCEPT

DOME + TOWERS

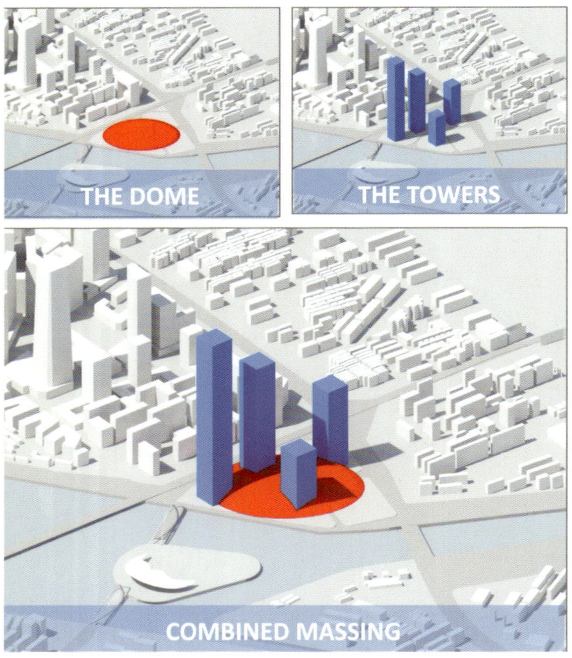

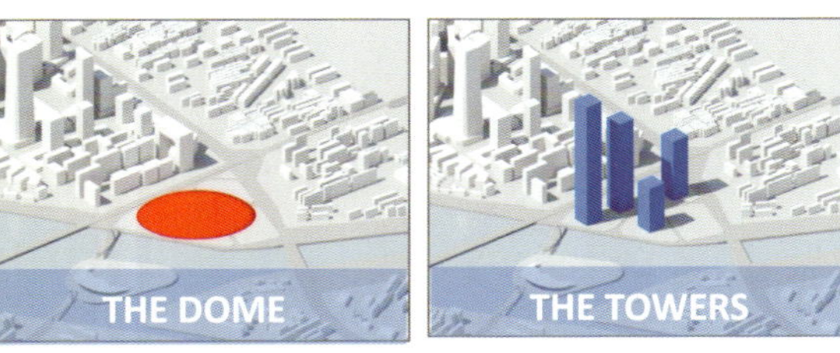

THE DOME
THE TOWERS
COMBINED MASSING

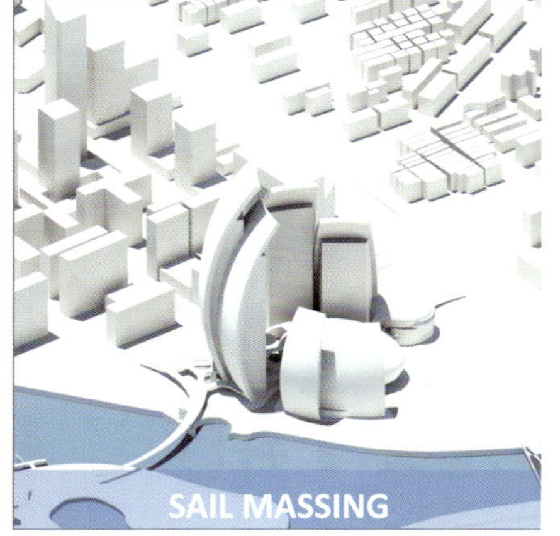

KEY DESIGN STRATEGY

1. STRATEGICALLY POSITIONED TOWERS FOR MAXIMUM WATERFRONT EXPOSURE AND VIEW POTENTIALS
2. DOME TO COMBINE ALL PODIUM PROGRAM ELEMENTS TO BECOME THE "HAMMER" FOR THE PROJECT, CREATING THE DIFFERENTIATING BRAND
3. UNIQUE AND POWERFUL ARCHITECTURAL CHARACTER COMBINED WITH THE "FOUR SEASONS" BRAND CONCEPT WILL PROVIDE THE NECESSARY BUSINESS MODEL FOR SUCCESSFUL DEVELOPMENT PROJECT FOR SHIN KONG

SAIL MASSING

PROGRAM SUMMARY- SAIL

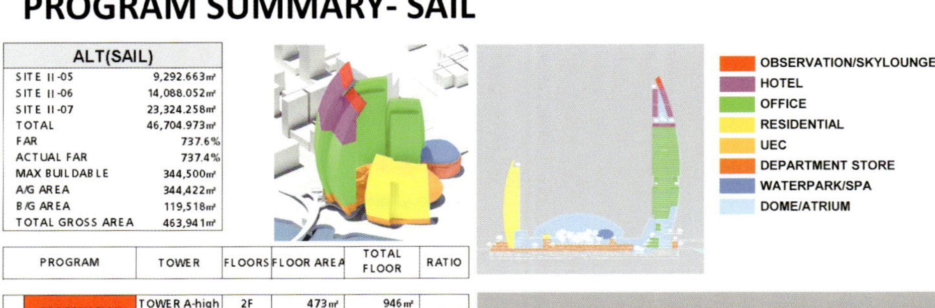

ALT(SAIL)	
SITE II-05	9,292.663㎡
SITE II-06	14,088.052㎡
SITE II-07	23,324.258㎡
TOTAL	46,704.973㎡
FAR	737.6%
ACTUAL FAR	737.4%
MAX BUILDABLE	344,500㎡
A/G AREA	344,422㎡
B/G AREA	119,518㎡
TOTAL GROSS AREA	463,941㎡

- OBSERVATION/SKYLOUNGE
- HOTEL
- OFFICE
- RESIDENTIAL
- UEC
- DEPARTMENT STORE
- WATERPARK/SPA
- DOME/ATRIUM

	PROGRAM	TOWER	FLOORS	FLOOR AREA	TOTAL FLOOR	RATIO
TOWER	OBSERVATION /SKYLOUNGE	TOWER A-high	2F	473㎡	946㎡	
		TOWER A-low	2F	481㎡	962㎡	
				SUBTOTAL	1,908㎡	0.6%
	HOTEL	TOWER A	17F	1,908㎡	32,434㎡	
		TOWER B	17F	1,655㎡	28,128㎡	
				SUBTOTAL	60,562㎡	17.6%
	RESIDENTIAL (OFFICETEL)	TOWER C	41F	2,080㎡	85,262㎡	
				SUBTOTAL	85,262㎡	24.8%
	OFFICE	TOWER A	56F,37F	1,908㎡	88,566㎡	
		TOWER B	35F,26F	1,655㎡	52,133㎡	
				SUBTOTAL	140,699㎡	40.9%
DOME	WATER PARK		2F		6,008㎡	
				SUBTOTAL	6,008㎡	1.7%
	UEC	2 STORY MALL	2F		21,832㎡	
				SUBTOTAL	21,832㎡	6.3%
	DEPARTMENT STORE		4F		28,152㎡	
				SUBTOTAL	28,152㎡	8.2%
		TOTAL ABOVE GRADE AREA			344,422㎡	100.0%

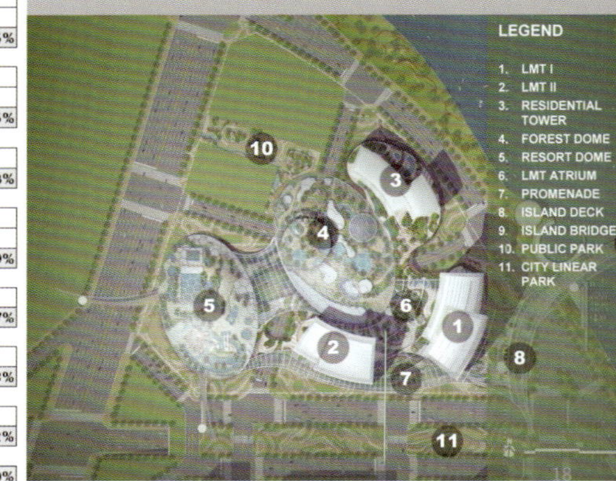

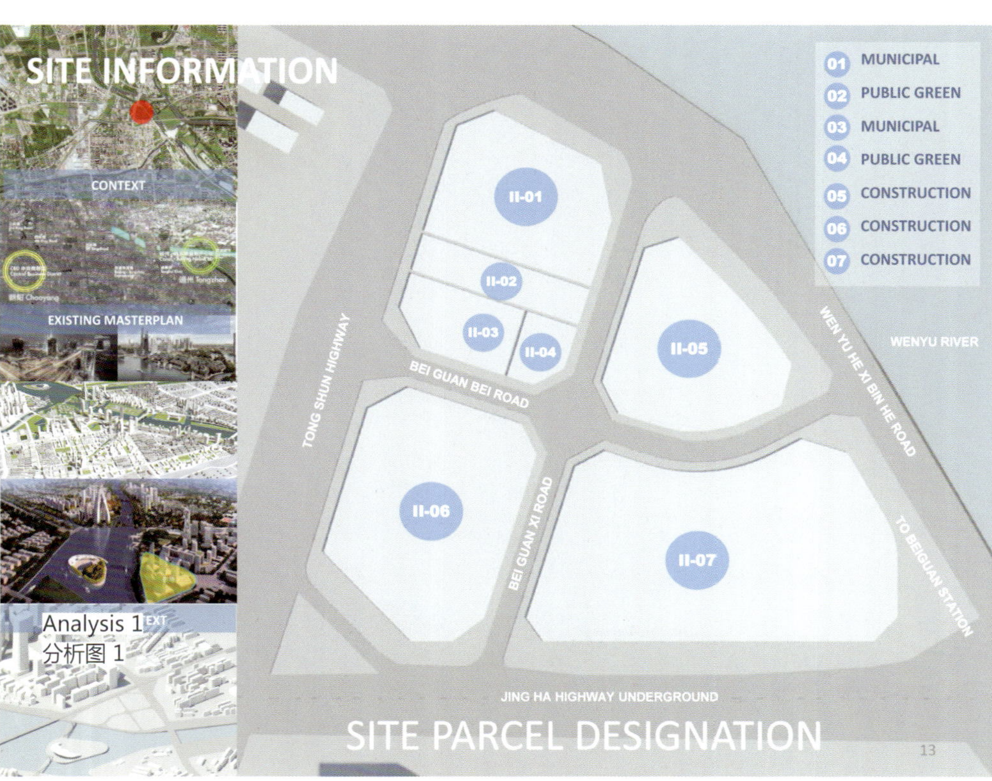

LEGEND
1. LMT I
2. LMT II
3. RESIDENTIAL TOWER
4. FOREST DOME
5. RESORT DOME
6. LMT ATRIUM
7. PROMENADE
8. ISLAND DECK
9. ISLAND BRIDGE
10. PUBLIC PARK
11. CITY LINEAR PARK

SITE INFORMATION
CONTEXT
EXISTING MASTERPLAN
01 MUNICIPAL
02 PUBLIC GREEN
03 MUNICIPAL
04 PUBLIC GREEN
05 CONSTRUCTION
06 CONSTRUCTION
07 CONSTRUCTION
II-01
II-02
II-03
II-04
II-05
II-06
II-07
TONG SHUN HIGHWAY
BEI GUAN BEI ROAD
BEI GUAN XI ROAD
WEN YU HE XI BIN HE ROAD
WENYU RIVER
TO BEIGUAN STATION
JING HA HIGHWAY UNDERGROUND
SITE PARCEL DESIGNATION
13

Analysis 1
分析图 1

SITE INFORMATION
01
02
03
04
05
06
07
TONG SHUN HIGHWAY
WENYU RIVER
JING HA HIGHWAY
PARCEL INFORMATION

SITE VOLUME DIAGRAM

TOTAL SITE AREA:	74,611 SM
CONSTRUCTION AREA:	46,705 SM
ROAD AREA:	12,753 SM
PUBLIC GREEN AREA:	4,050 SM
MUNICIPAL AREA:	11,102 SM

LANDUSE

- COMMERCIAL
- MUNICIPAL
- PUBLIC GREEN

	LANDUSE	SITE AREA (SM)	BUILDING SIZE
01	MUNICIPAL	8,046	
02	PUBLIC GREEN	2,729	
03	MUNICIPAL	3,055	
04	PUBLIC GREEN	1,321	
05	CONSTRUCTION	9,292	55,800
06	CONSTRUCTION	23,324	198,100
07	CONSTRUCTION	14,088	90,600

14

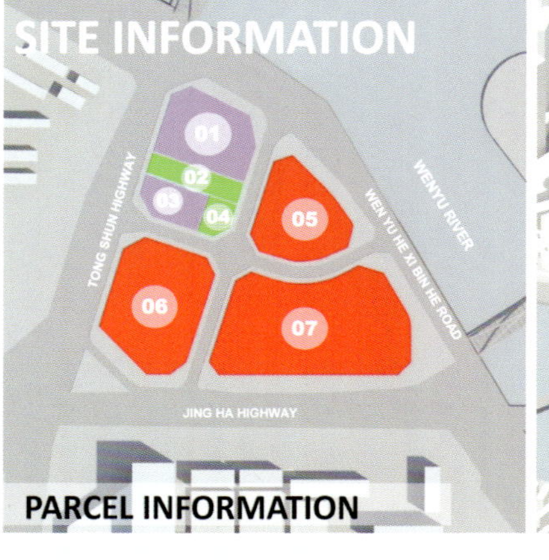

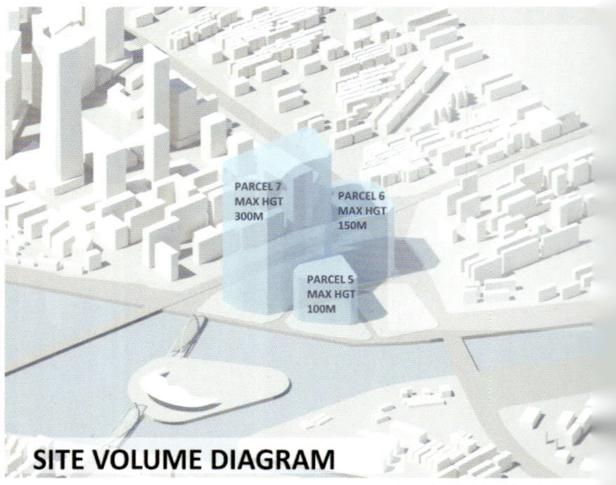

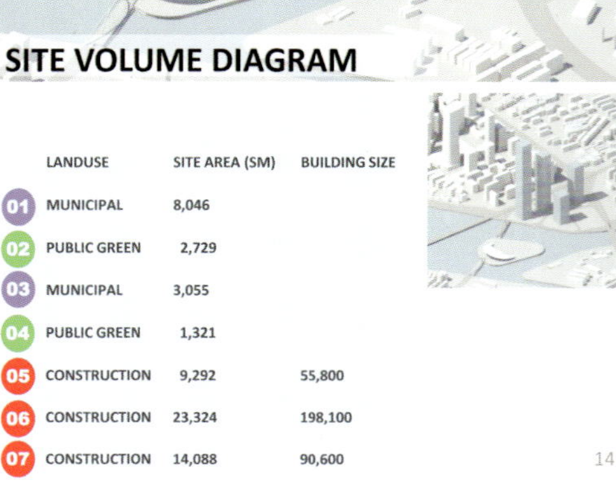

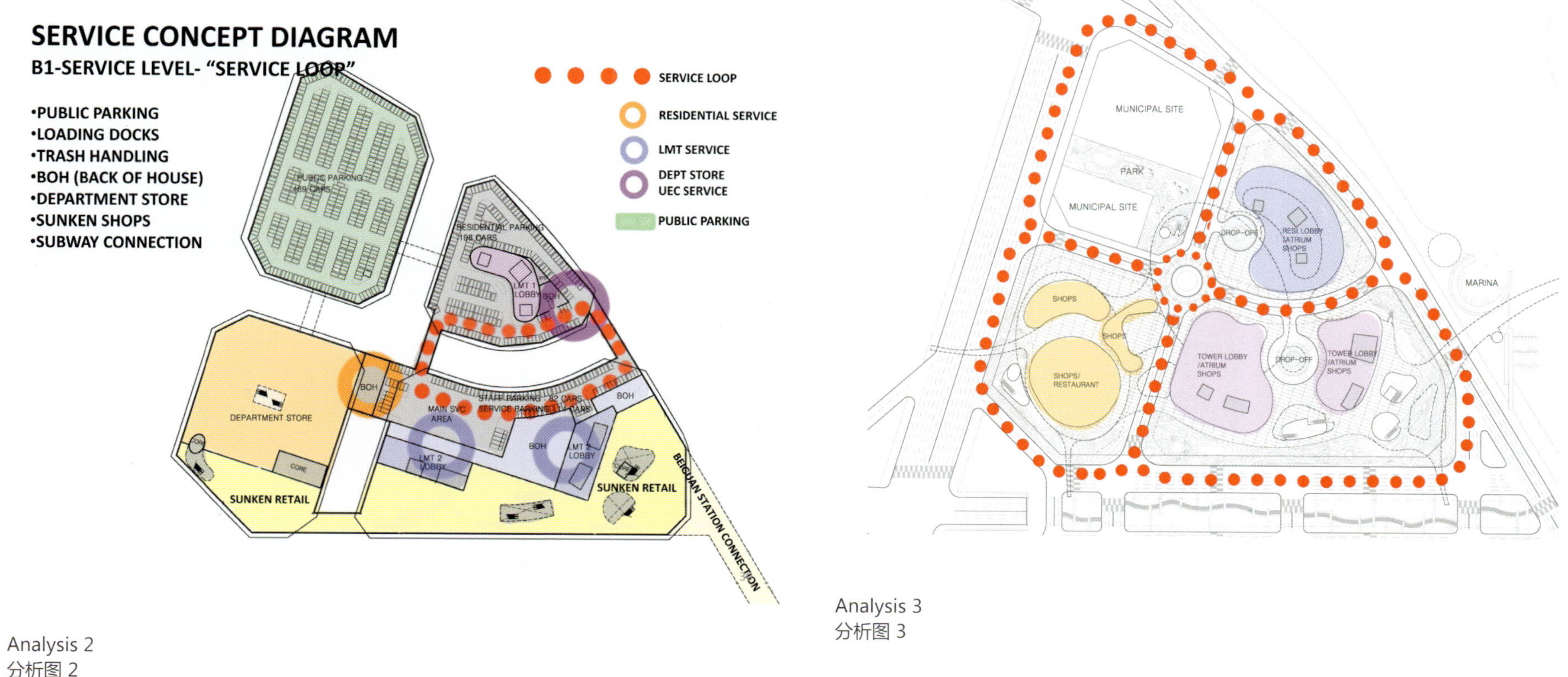

Analysis 2
分析图 2

Analysis 3
分析图 3

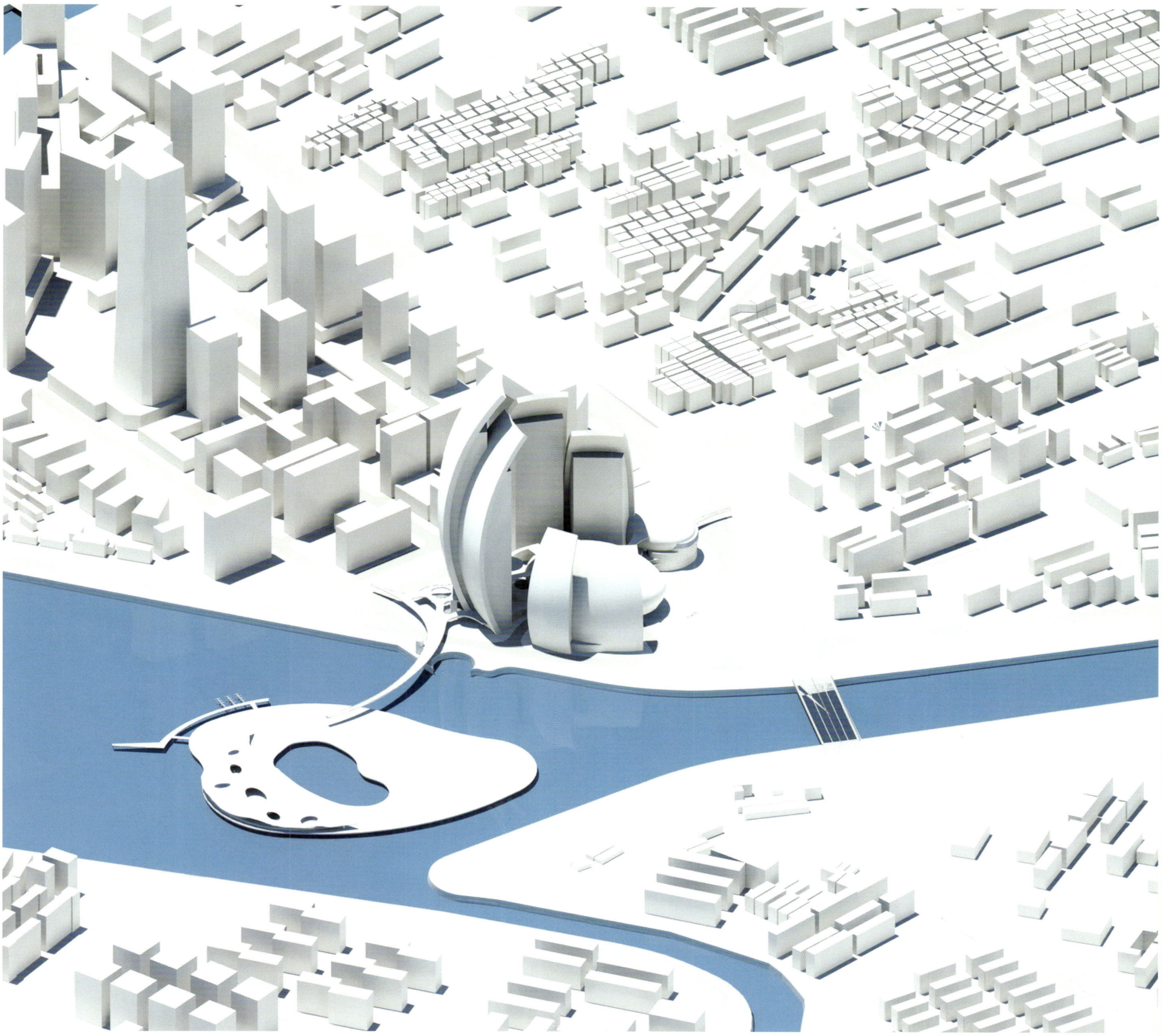

北京通州度假城

旅游型复合地产

大商业 2

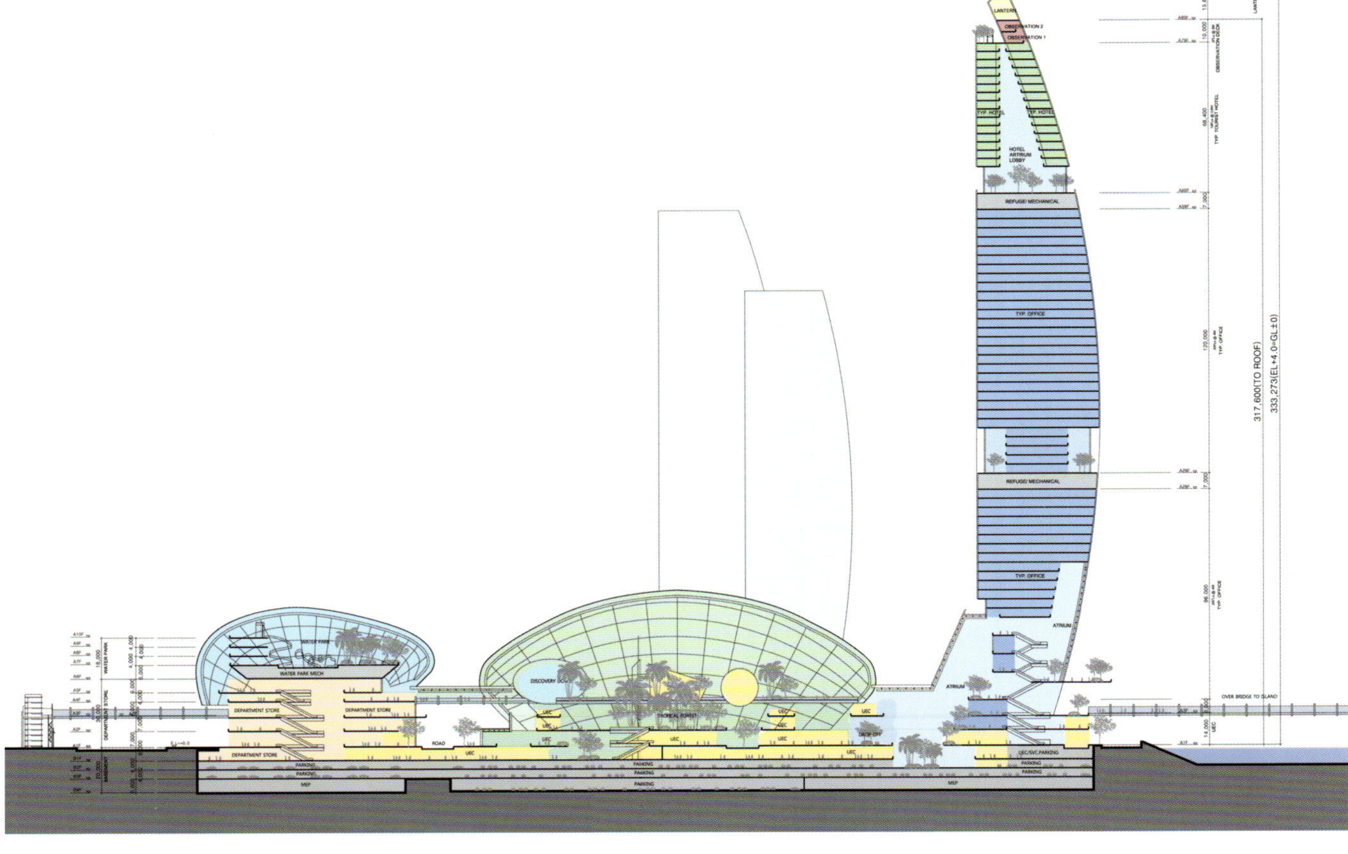

Elevation Analysis
立面分析图

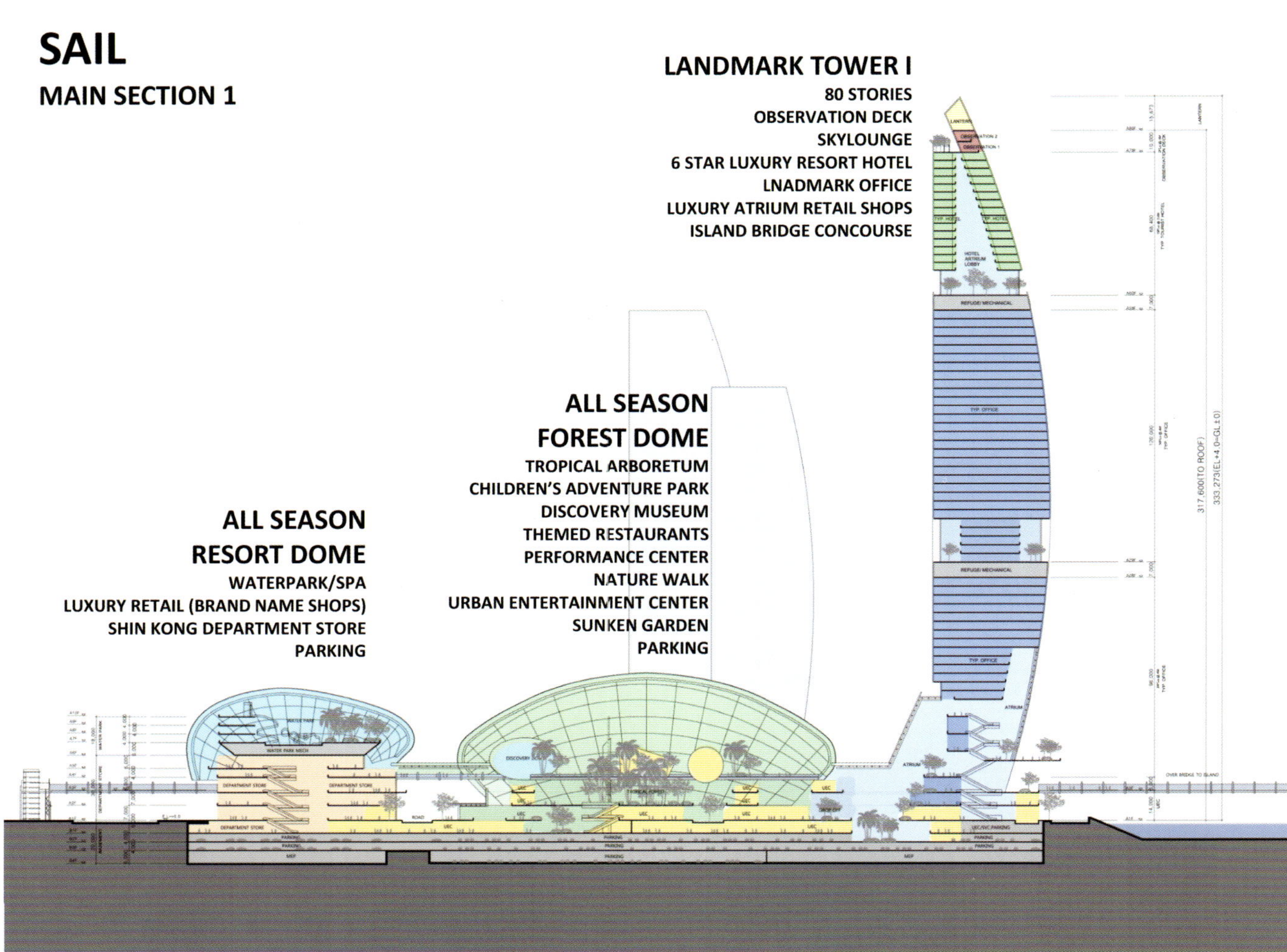

Elevation Analysis
立面分析图

SAIL
MAIN SECTION 2

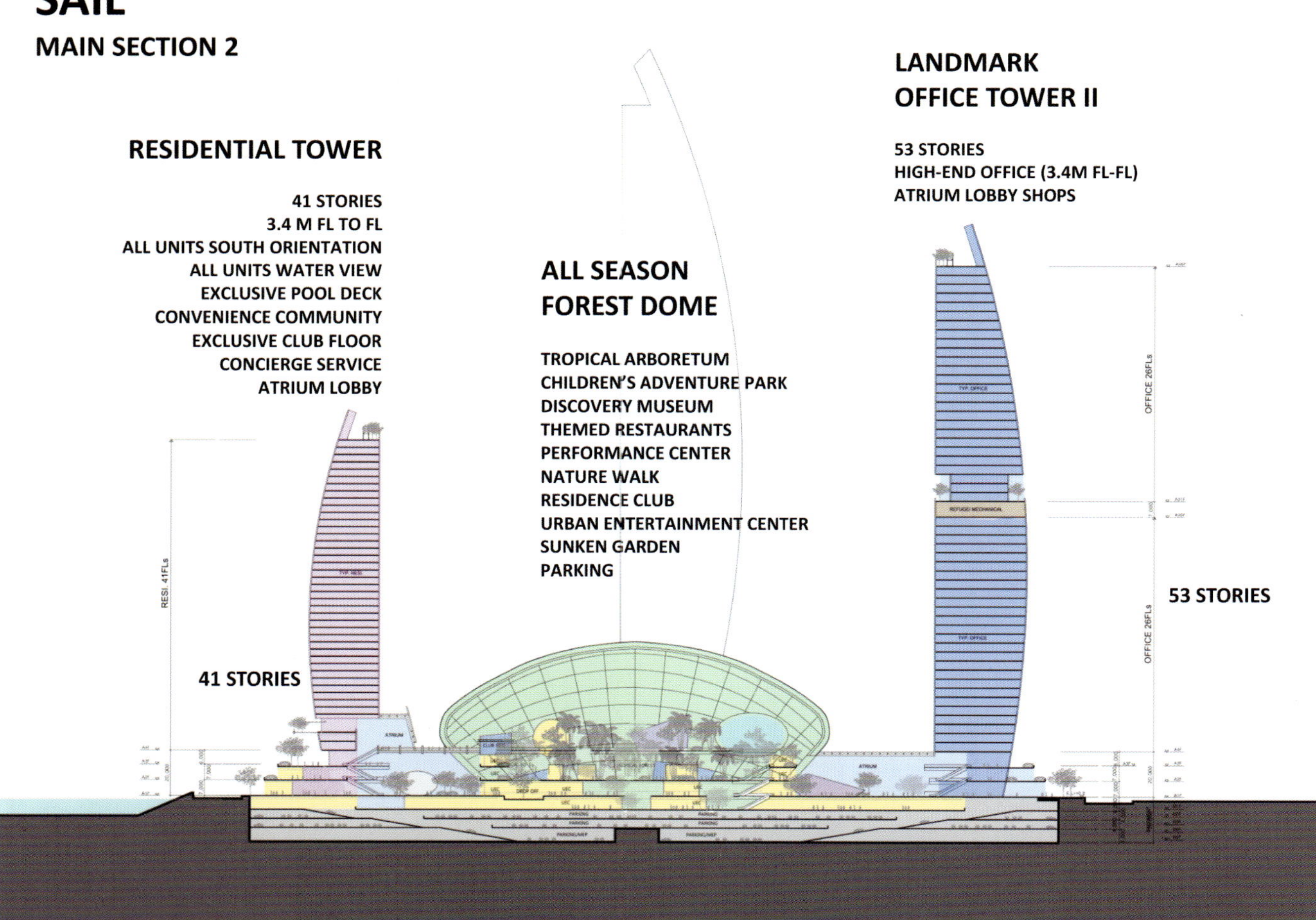

Elevation Analysis
立面分析图

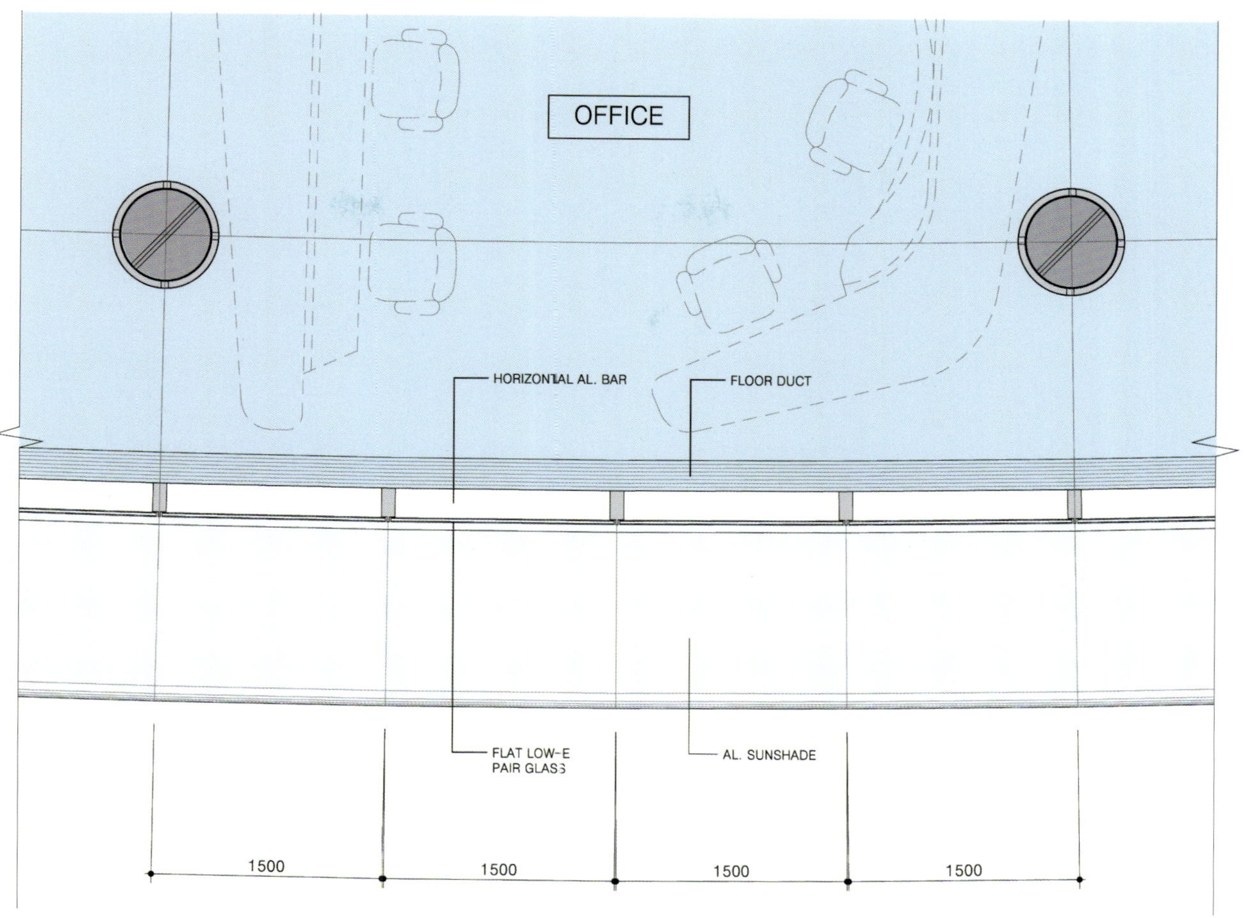

Analysis 1
分析图 1

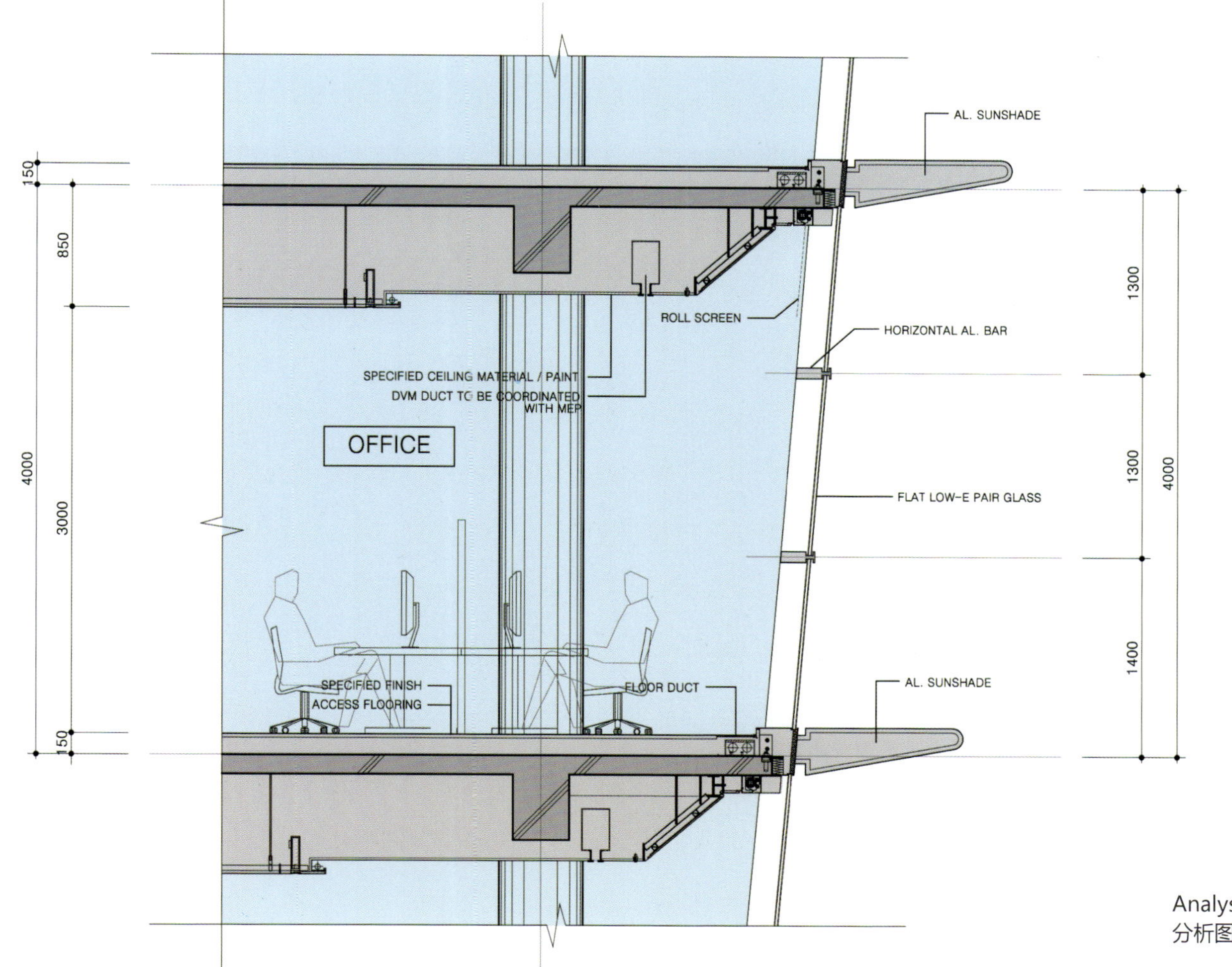

Analysis 2
分析图 2

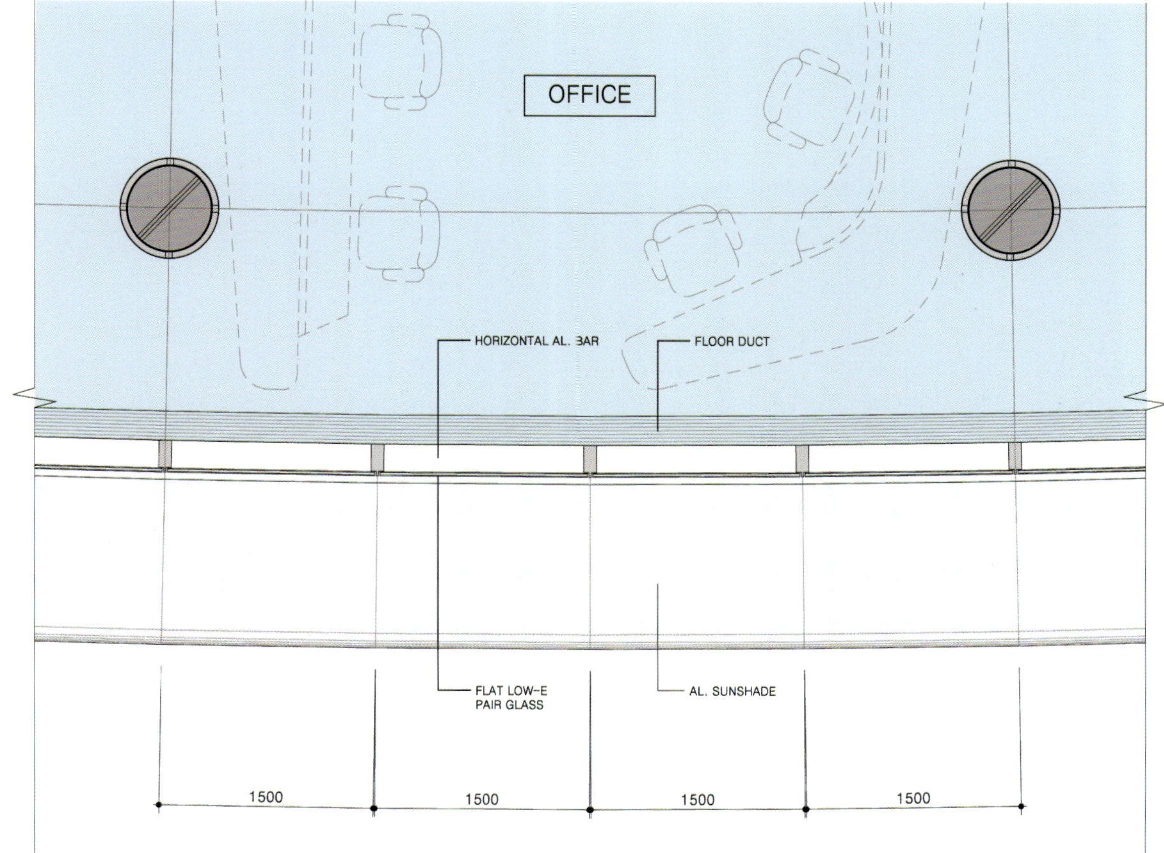

Analysis 3
分析图 3

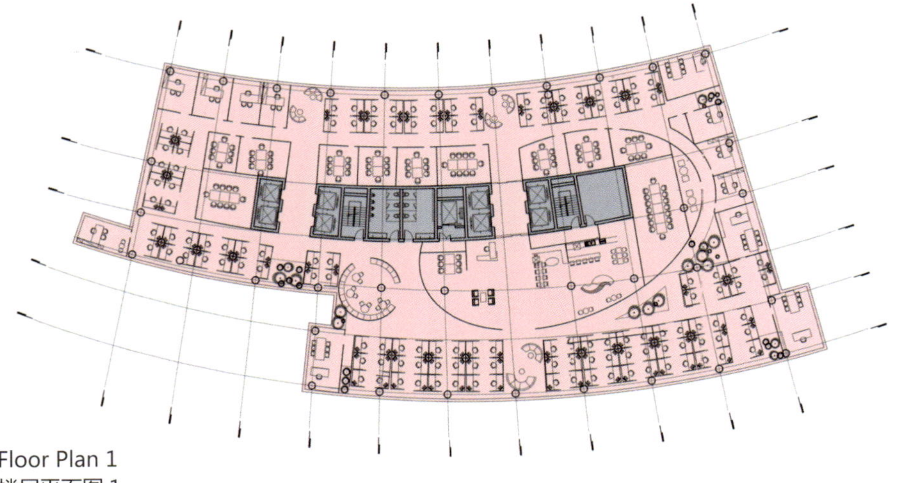

Floor Plan 1
楼层平面图 1

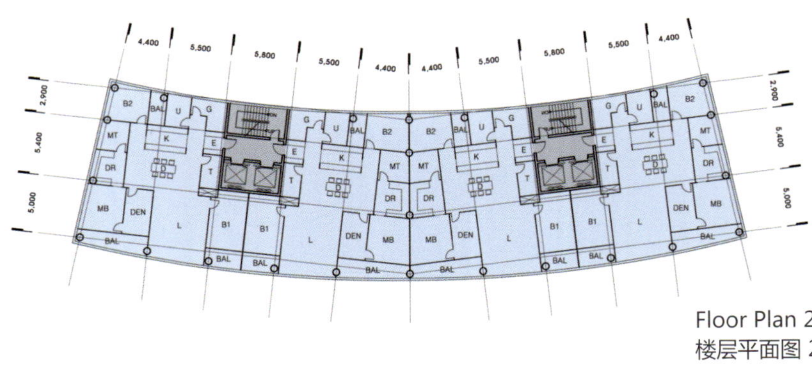

Floor Plan 2
楼层平面图 2

Floor Plan 3
楼层平面图 3

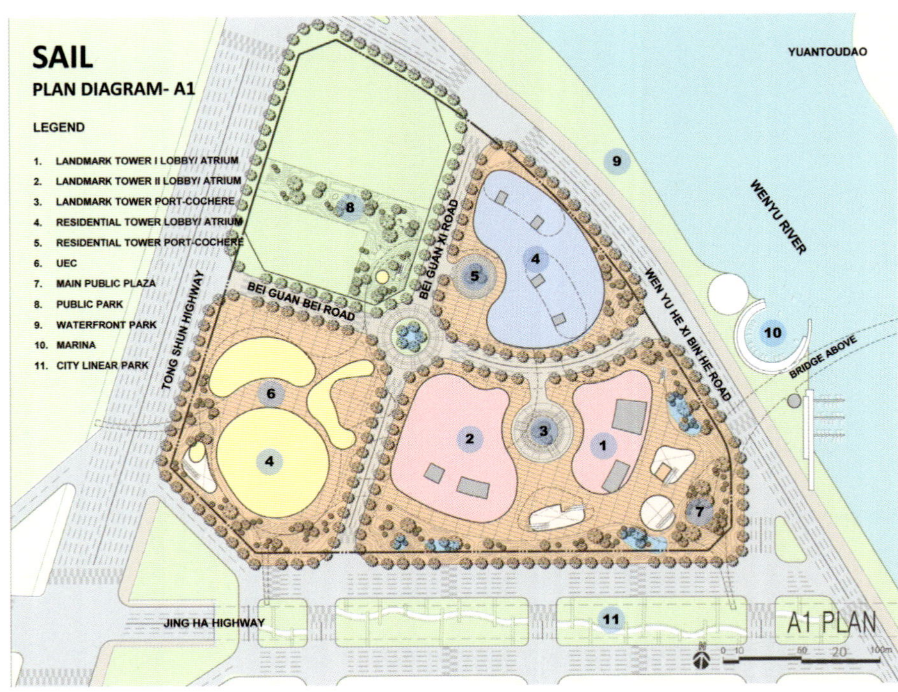

1st Floor Plan
一层平面图

2nd Floor Plan
二层平面图

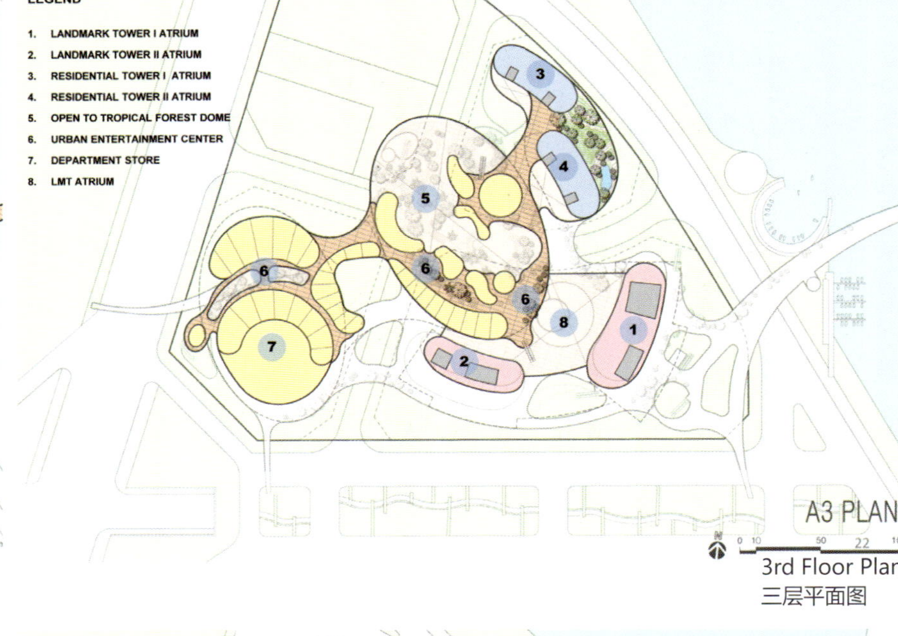

3rd Floor Plan
三层平面图

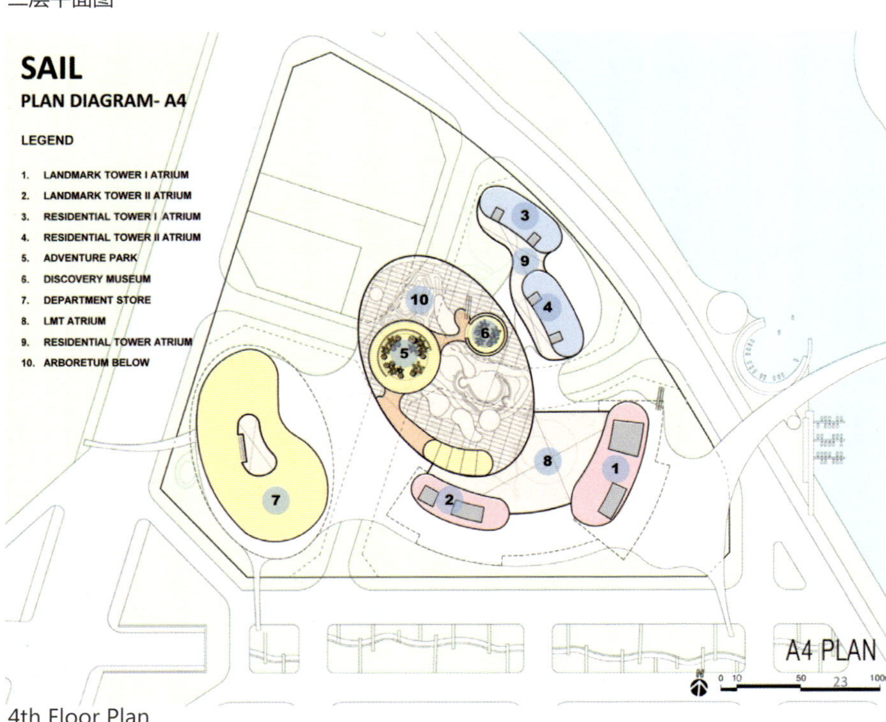

4th Floor Plan
四层平面图

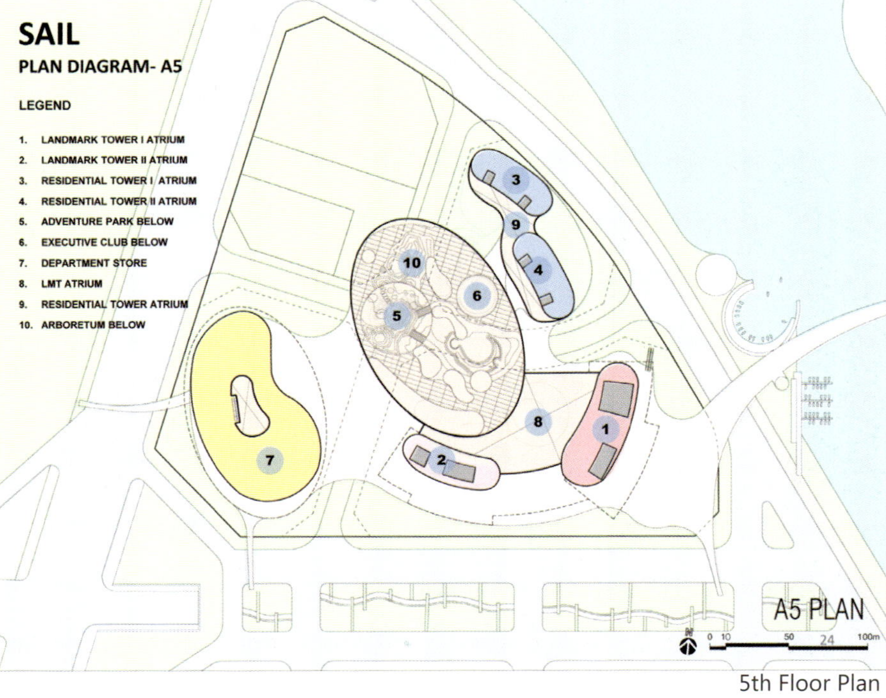

5th Floor Plan
五层平面图

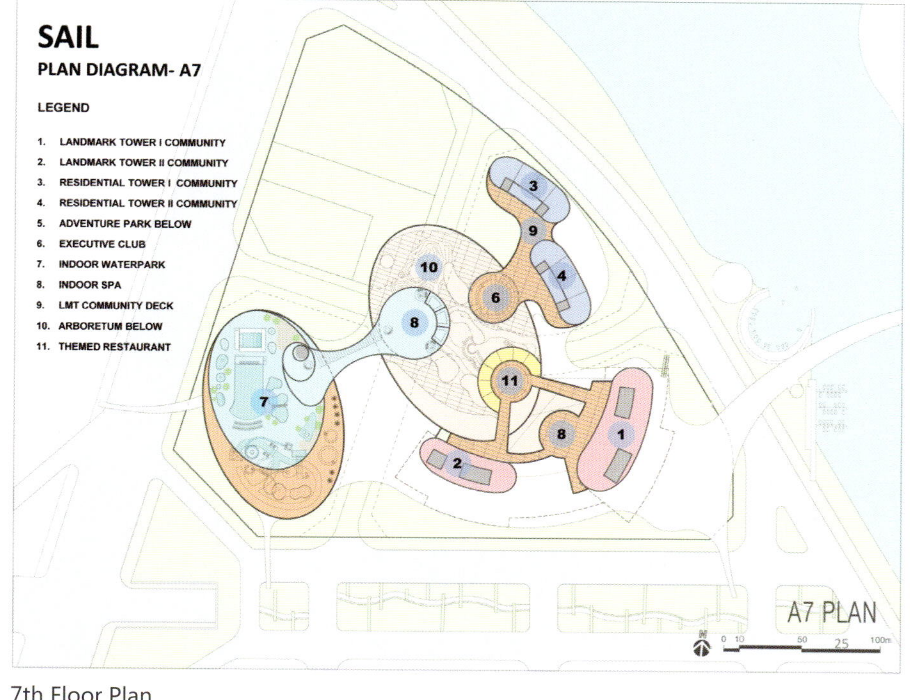

7th Floor Plan
七层平面图

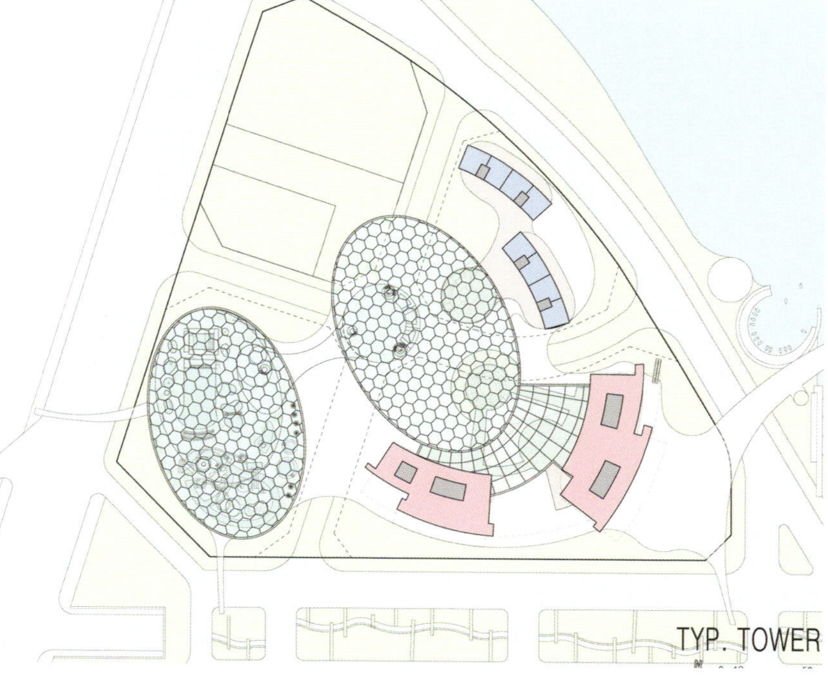

typical Tower Plan
标准塔楼平面图

PROJECT NAME 项目名称

GALAXY MOONBAY RENAISSAN HOTEL AND MIXED USE DEVELOPMENT

星河澜月湾万丽酒店及综合发展

Architect: 10 DESIGN

设计公司：10 DESIGN（拾稼设计）

PROJECT INFORMATION 项目信息

Designer Partner	Ted Givens	**设计合伙人**	其文特
Client	Galaxy Group	**客户**	星河集团
Location	Changzhou, Jiangsu Province, China	**地点**	中国江苏常州
Site Area	132,298 m²	**占地面积**	132，298 平方米
GFA	304,285 m²	**总建筑面积**	304，285 平方米

OVERVIEW 项目概况

10 DESIGN Creating a “Floating Garden” in Changzhou West Tai Lake.The project is located in the West Tai Lake’s ecological and leisure area, positioned to be one of the most important vacation resorts in the Delta Region of Yangtze River. The 31,000,000m² of development will form a modern leisure and commercial community, providing an iconic luxury hotel, serviced apartments, conference centers, offices and public spaces. Site construction started in 2012 and anticipated completion by 2014.

拾稼设计为常州西太湖打造“漂浮花园”。本项目位于常州市武进区滨湖新城的西太湖生态休闲区，将成为长江三角洲一个重要的旅游度假区。项目总面积达 31 万平方米，地块规划将形成一个现代化的休闲及商业社区，发展业态包括一间标志性的豪华酒店、酒店式公寓、会议中心、办公楼及公共空间等。项目 2012 年动工，预计工程 2014 年竣工。

BRIEF INTERVIEW 访谈录

ARCHITECT
Fed Givens

设计师
其文特

HKASP: What is the main concept behind the whole project?

10 DESIGN :The masterplan design was inspired by the local craft of bamboo carving and the aerodynamic shapes of naval design. The landscape design forms the foundation of the overall planning and design of the masterplan. A mixture of public spaces including parks, plazas, an amphitheatre and playgrounds are designed to support a variety of uses. The nature of public usage of landscape areas allows the site to integrate seamlessly with the existing lake-side promenade to the east of the site.

Careful consideration is paid to zoning and building arrangement within the site to maximise views and ventilation to all buildings, while at the same time maintaining the existing important sight lines and breeze corridors. Leisure facilities are designed on podium rooftops raised from the undulating landscape, while spaces are carved into the high-rise towers to form sky gardens for residents. The hotel is located towards the east with maximum panoramic views to the lake. The form of the hotel sweeps down into the garden to create a conference facility within a public park in the centre of the site.

The buildings are curved to reflect the fluidity of the lake. A section of each tower is carved to house a large floating garden to give the masterplan a softer, resort like feel.

香港建筑科学出版社：方案背后的主要概念是什么？

10 DESIGN（拾稼设计）：此总体规划设计的灵感来自当地竹雕工艺以及具有流线外形的现代船舶设计。景观设计构建了总平面规划和设计的基础。一系列的公共空间如公园、广场、圆形剧场和操场为多种用途提供支持。景观区域的公共用途性质使基地与东面现有的湖滨人行道无缝对接。

设计细心考虑了基地分区和基地内建筑物的布局，以获得最佳的景观效果及自然通风，但同时也保留了现有的景观和通风回廊。在高低起伏的景观的烘托下，裙楼屋顶设计了休闲设施，同时高层塔楼上挖出空间，为住户打造空中花园。酒店朝向东面，尽享极致的湖泊全景。其结构延伸至花园内，在位于基地中心的公共公园内创造出一个会议设施空间。

建筑物呈弧形设计，以呼应湖泊的流动性。每座塔楼的一部分都被挖开，镶嵌大型的漂浮花园，使总体规划看起来更柔软、更具度假地的美感。

Site Plan
总平面图

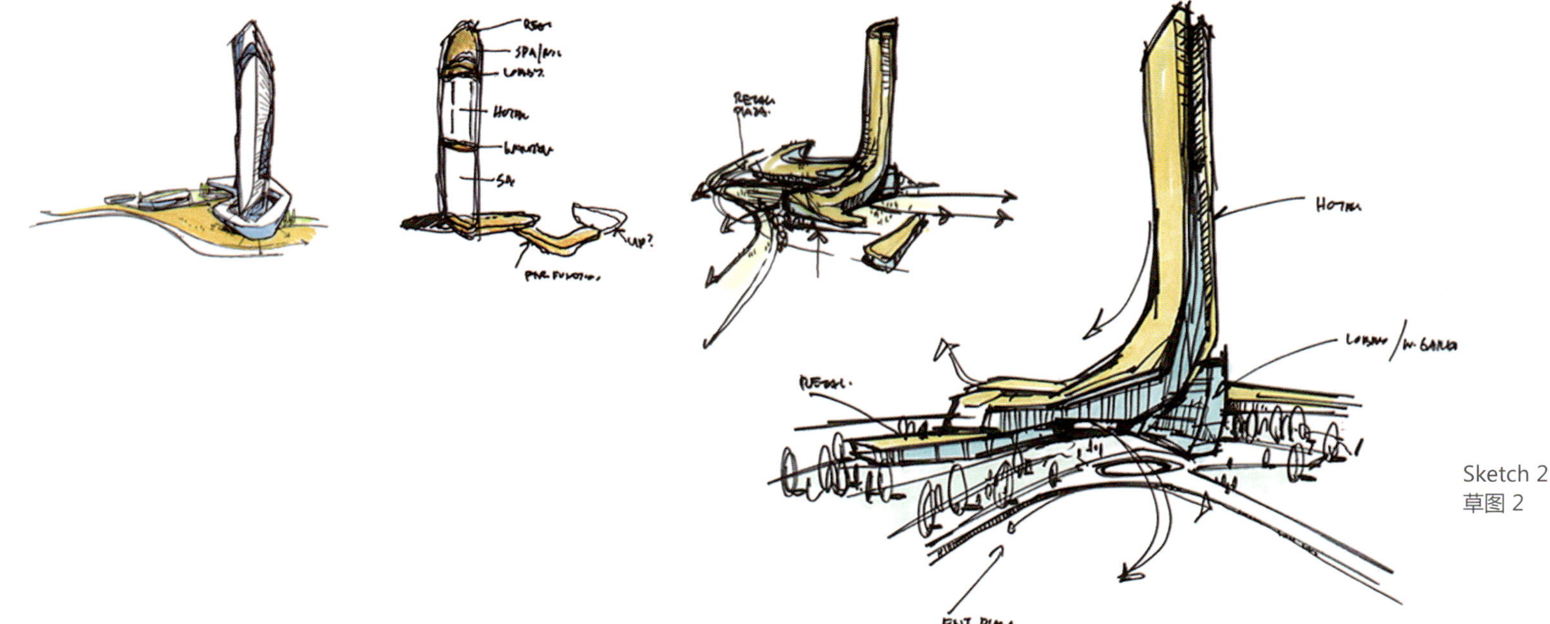

Sketch 2
草图 2

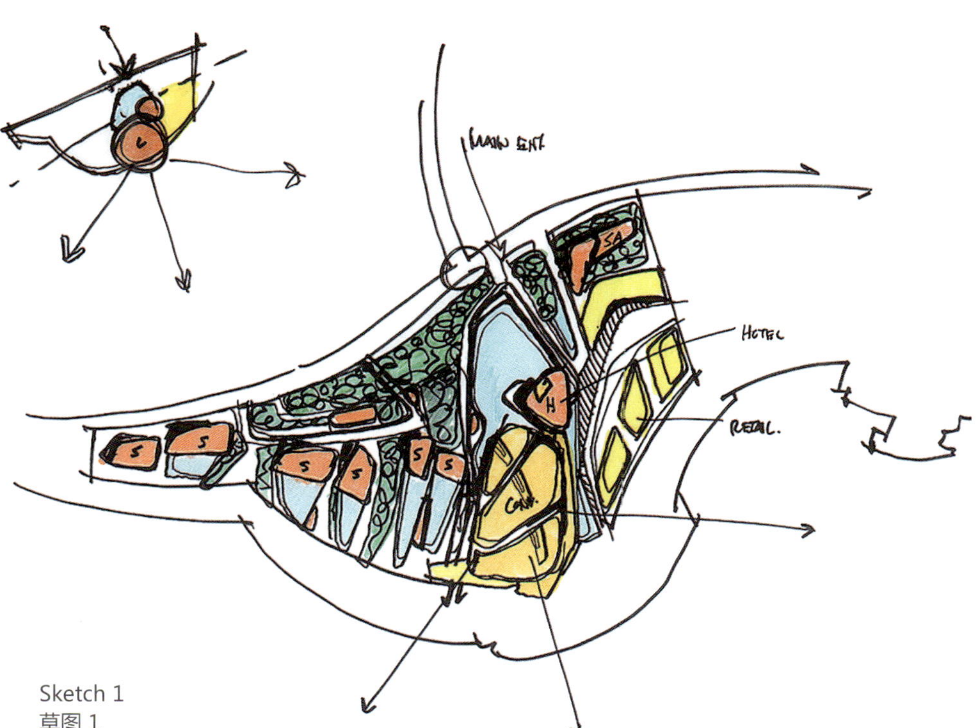

Sketch 1
草图 1

Architectural design and planning arrangement respond both to its surrounding environment and the site itself. Careful consideration was paid to zoning and building arrangement within the site to maximize views and ventilation to all buildings, while at the same time retaining the existing view and breeze corridors. The concept of green design is further implemented via the introduction of green spaces above ground plane.

建筑设计及规划布局与周边环境及基地本身互相呼应，相得益彰。设计细心考虑了基地分区和基地内建筑物的布局，以获得最佳的景观效果及自然通风，但同时亦保留现有景观及通风回廊。通过进一步引入绿地空间彰显绿色设计的概念。

10 DESIGN Creating a "Floating Garden" in Changzhou West Tai Lake. The project is located in the West Tai Lake's ecological and leisure area, positioned to be one of the most important vacation resorts in the Delta Region of Yangtze River. The 31,000,000m^2 of development will form a modern leisure and commercial community, providing an iconic luxury hotel, serviced apartments, conference centers, offices and public spaces.

The master plan design was inspired by the local craft of bamboo carving and the aerodynamic shapes of modern boat design. The buildings are all curved to reflect the fluidity of the lake.

其文特——10 DESIGN 设计合伙人说："由于项目地处独特的地理位置——沿揽月湾 14 千米长的海岸线，客户与我们分享了他们对本项目的愿景，激发了我们以花园环境提升滨湖公共空间品质，来打造本项目的灵感。"

此总体规划设计的灵感来自当地竹雕刻工艺及具有流线外形的现代船舶设计。建筑物呈弧形设计，以反映湖泊的流动性。

Hand-drawn sketches 1
手绘草图 1

An iconic luxury hotel is located towards the east with maximum panoramic views to the lake. The form of the hotel sweeps down into the garden to create a conference facility, housed within a passive public park in the centre of the site. The conference centre will be a sculptural building acting as a focal point in the entry sequence into the site.As an additional sustainable concept the hotel tower can be clad in a titanium dioxide nano-coating. The coating neutralizes air pollution and cleans the air. If this concept is applied; the tower can become an iconic symbol of the clean air of Changzhou.

一栋标志性的豪华酒店位于基地东侧，坐拥最佳的湖景。酒店坐落在基地中心的公共花园，建筑外型从屋顶伸延至花园以形成一个会议中心。会议中心将作为一个雕塑建筑，使其成为入口视觉空间序列的焦点。另一个可持续的绿色设计概念是将二氧化钛纳米涂料用于酒店塔楼外墙。该种涂料可以中和空气中的污染物，清洁空气。如果此概念得以运用，该酒店将会成为常州清洁空气的象征建筑。

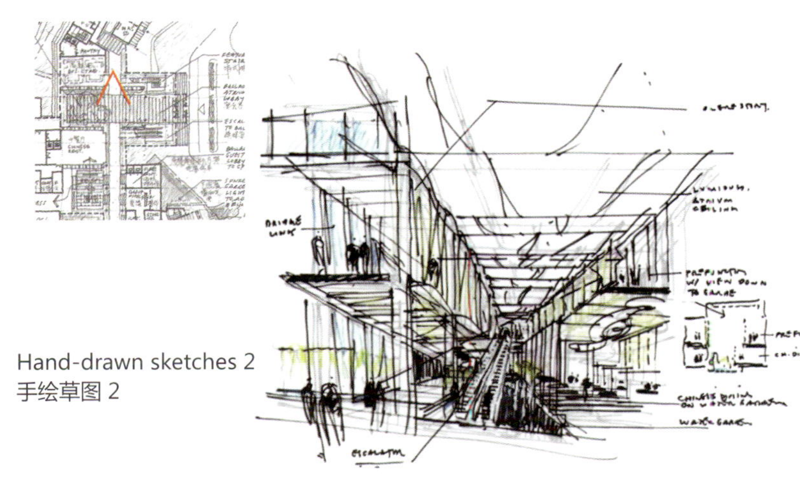

Hand-drawn sketches 2
手绘草图 2

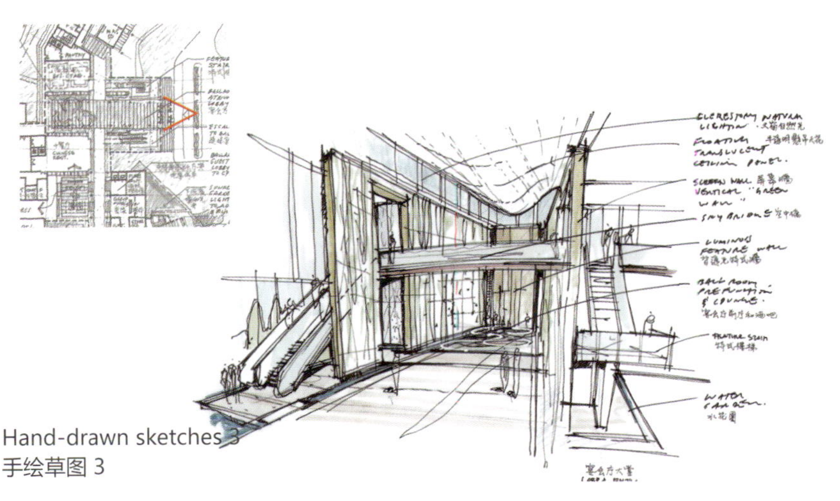

Hand-drawn sketches 3
手绘草图 3

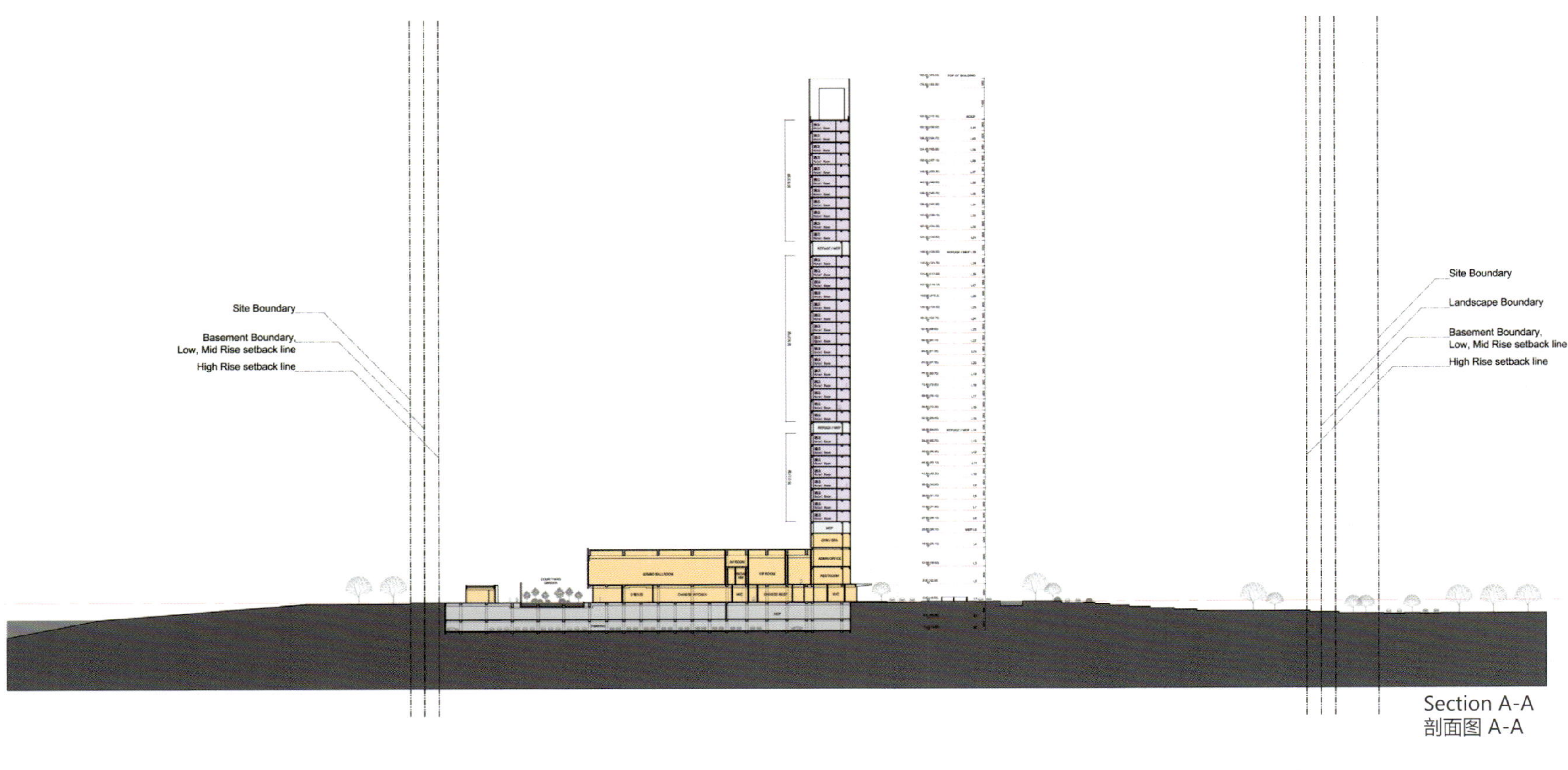

Section A-A
剖面图 A-A

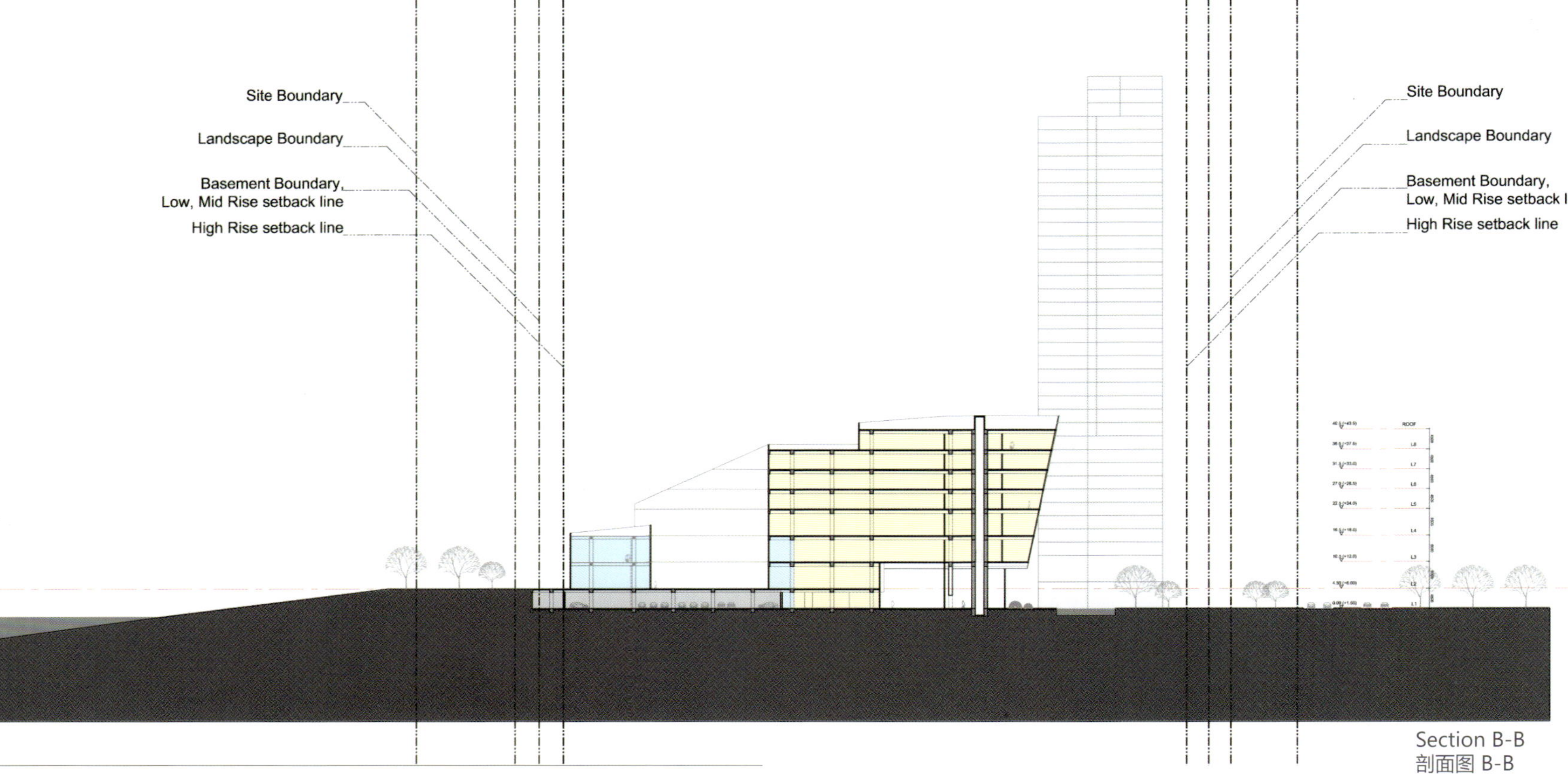

Section B-B
剖面图 B-B

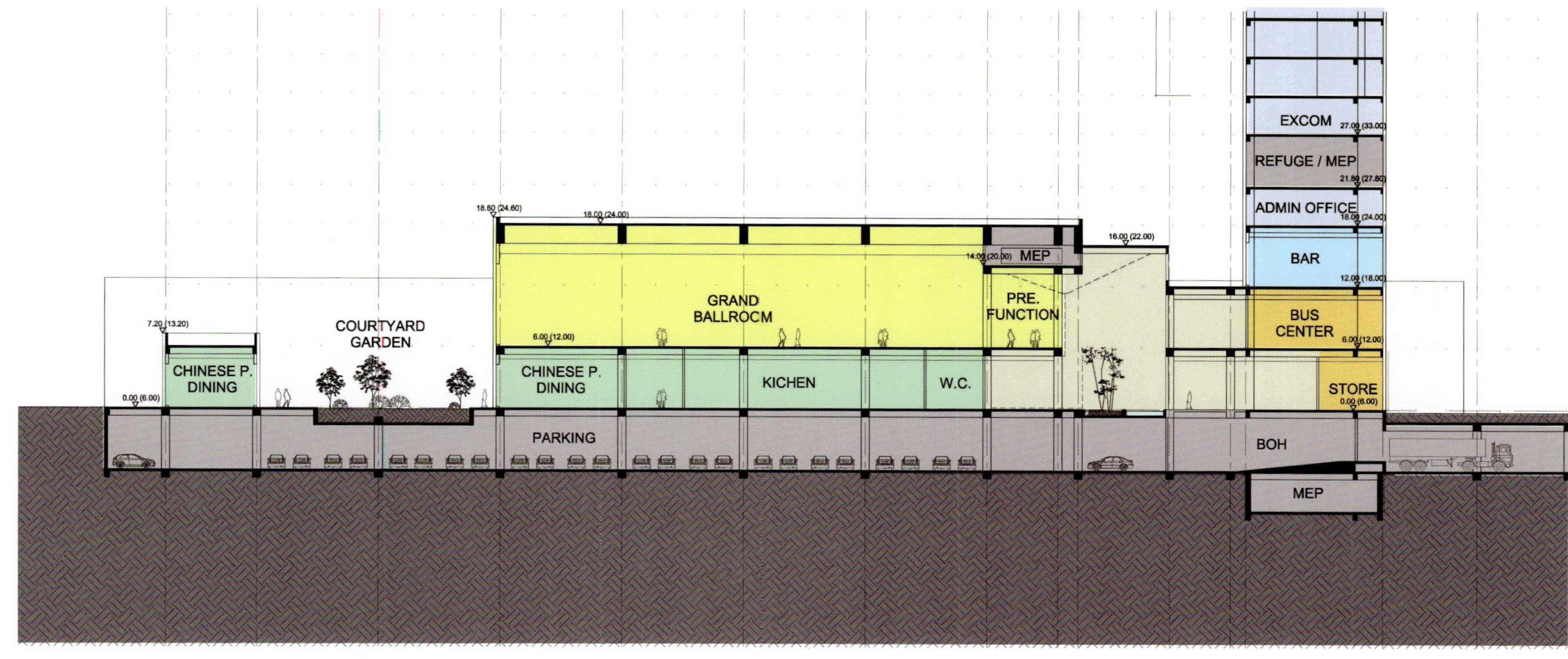

Section C-C
剖面图 C-C

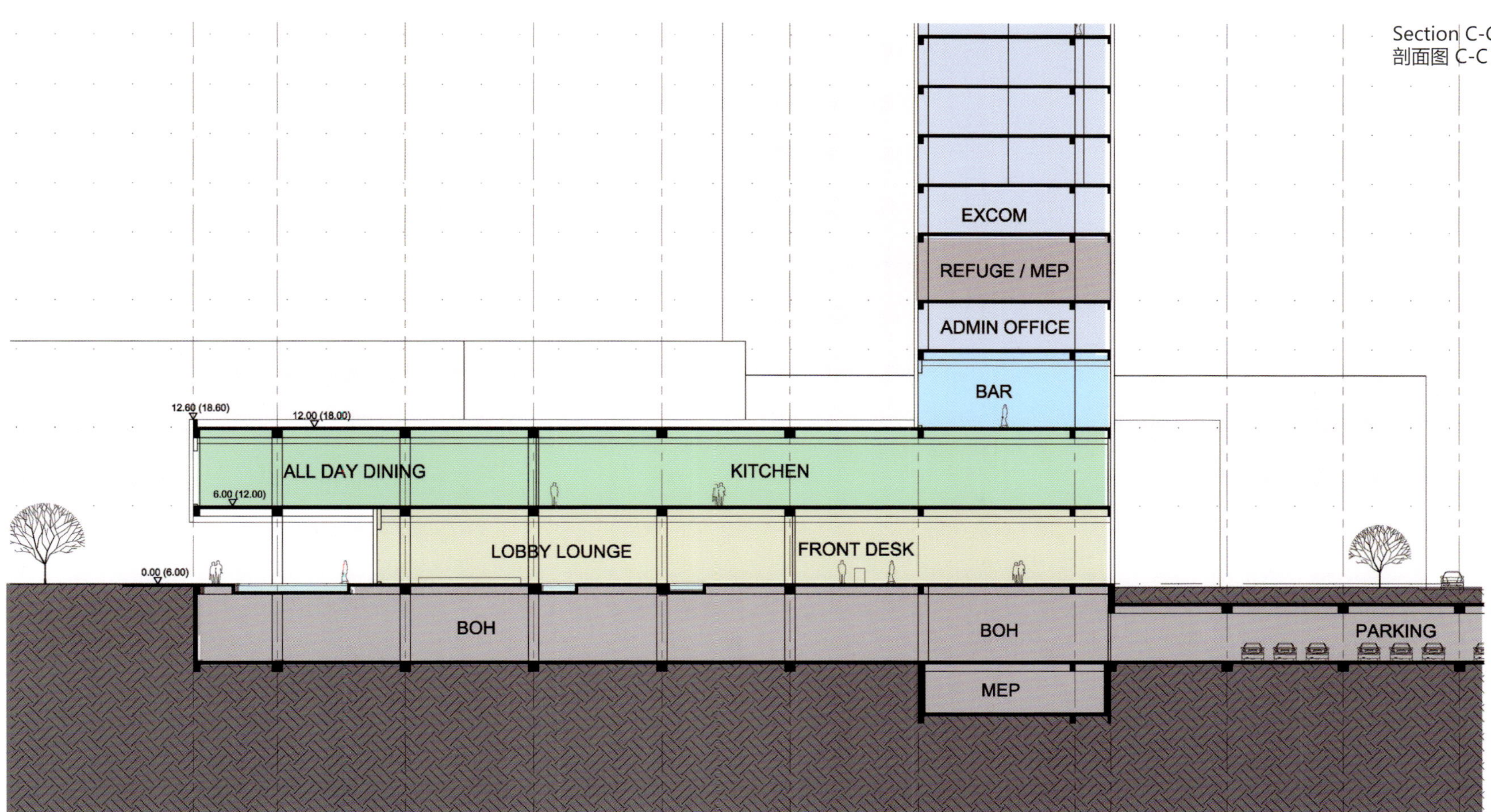

Section D-D
剖面图 D-D

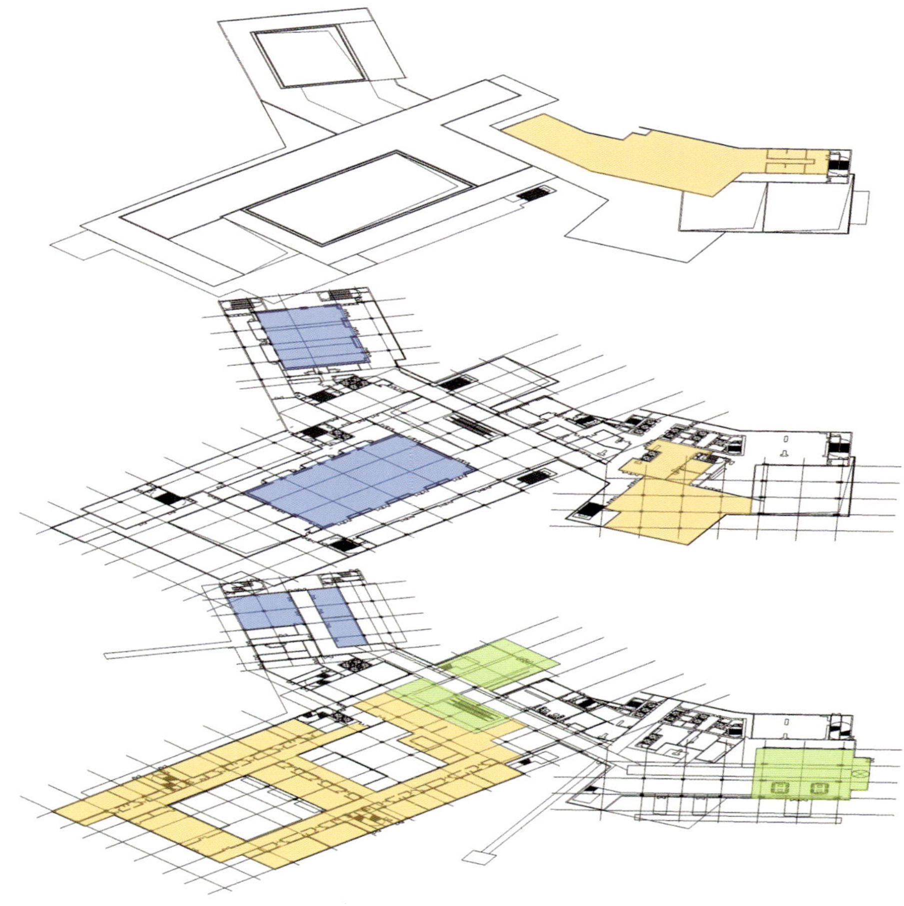

Hotel Podium Plan
酒店裙房平面图

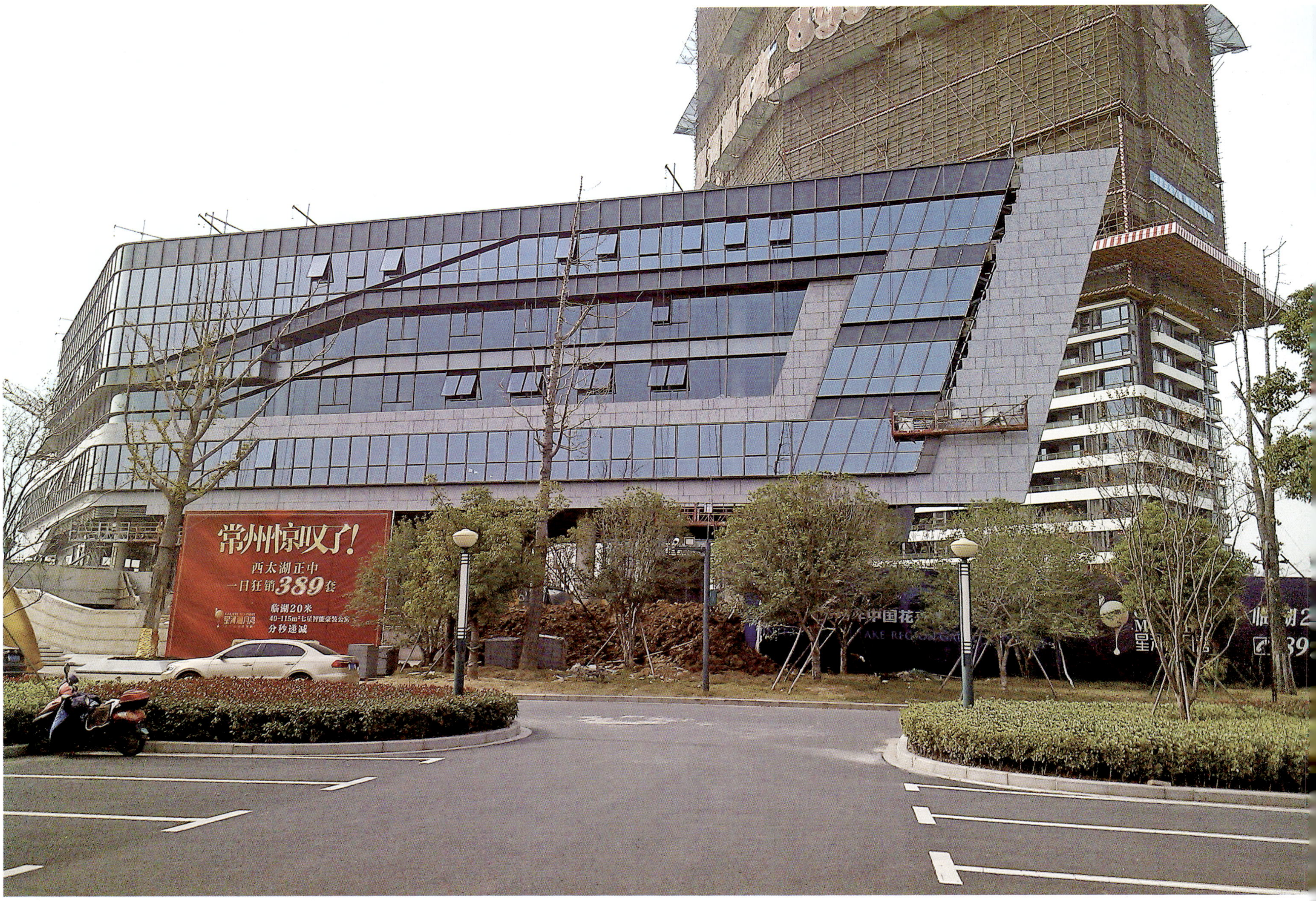
常州惊叹了!
西太湖正中
一日狂销389套
临湖20米
分秒递减

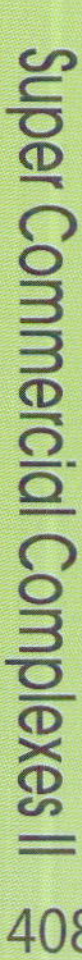

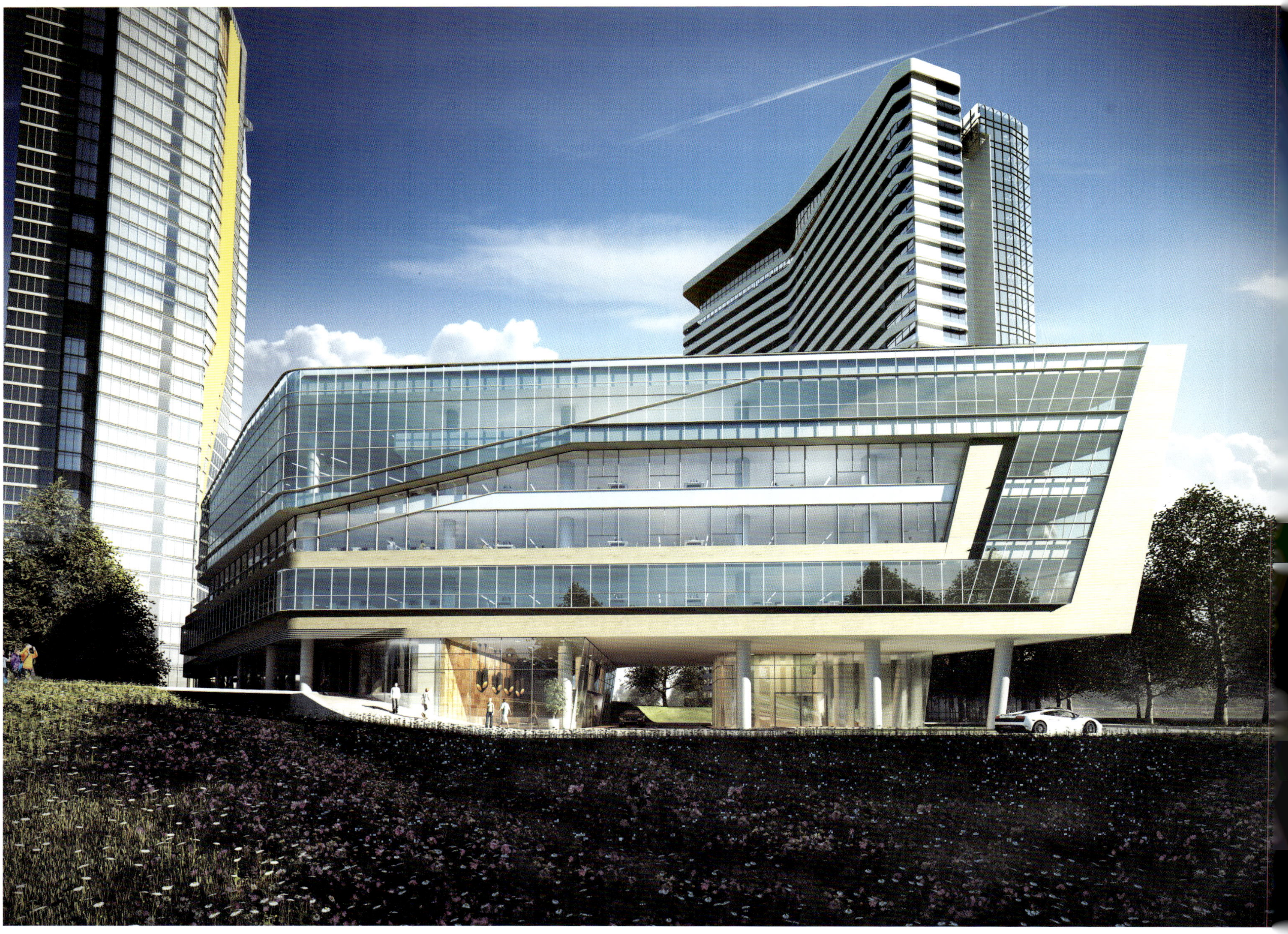

The MLP design is centered around 6 main design objectives:
To create an iconic high rise building facing the lake; Arranging the buildings so they do not to block the view of the lake from properties located behind/north of the site; Minimize impact of shadows cast by towers on sites to the north of the MLP site；To seamlessly integrate the retail and F+B facilities with the existing park to the east to help support the existing park and pull visitors into the MLP site; To provide each of the new residential units with views of the lake; To maximize the possibility of cross ventilation for the buildings and to maintain lake breezes in all the garden areas.

总平面的设计围绕 6 个主要的设计目标：
创建一个临湖的标志性的高层建筑；合理安排楼宇位置，避免其相互遮挡遮挡，以便使处于基地北部的楼宇均能享受到良好的湖景；将建筑物的阴影遮挡减少到最小；将基地内的餐饮购物设施与东侧的公园实现“无缝对接”，既可以补充完善公共空间的服务设施，亦可将游客吸引至基地内；为每一个新建的住宅单位提供优美的湖景；最大限度地保持建筑物的自然通风，使湖面的微风吹进花园的各个角落。

PROJECT NAME 项目名称

INTERNATIONAL BUSINESS CENTER AND INTERCONTINTAL HOTEL
国际商务中心与洲际酒店

Architect: STARH Architects
设计公司：STARH Architects

PROJECT INFORMATION 项目信息

Client	Avant-grade motors	客户	Avant-grade motors
Location	Armenia, Yerevan	地点	美国埃里温
site area	1,253 m²	占地面积	1，253 平方米
build area	133,672 m²	建筑面积	13，3672 平方米

OVERVIEW 项目概况

The architectural concept of the International Business Center and the Intercontinental hotel appears as a prominent solution for the contemporary appearance of the central part of the city of Yerevan. The land on which the concept is developed takes active part in the urbanization resolution, communicating with the Armenian capital's most impressive Republic square, by Teryan Street and Abovyan Street. The square is in the heart of the transportation and communications scheme of the city, and is surrounded by public buildings such as Government House NO. 1, Ministry of Finance, Ministry of Foreign Affairs, Historical Museum, Art Gallery, Comedy Theatre, subway station, etc. The high rising landscape of the multifunctional complex reveals a panoramic view of the city centre and Mount Ararat, as well as a unique visual completion of the street perspectives composed along Teryan and Saralanji St. The direct contact between the architectural complex and the biblical Mountains of Ararat by an axis, passing through the central part of Yerevan, defines the need for dominant vertical shapes. The silhouette of Ararat's twin peaks serves as a natural background of Yerevan, providing infinite dialogue for visitors and inhabitants of the complex.

国际商务中心与洲际酒店的建筑理念成为富有现代气息的埃里温市中心的标志 。亚美尼亚首都共和国广场紧邻Teryan大街与Abovyan大街，是亚美尼亚首都最富盛名之地。此时，将这一建筑理念付诸于实践的这片土地，将以积极的姿态迎接城市化的到来，希望与亚美尼亚首都共和国广场遥相呼应。广场是这座城市交通的中心枢纽，周边公共建筑林立，有1号政府大楼、财政部大楼、外交部大楼、历史博物馆、美术馆、喜剧剧院、地铁站等等。站在多用途综合体高层景观处，你可俯瞰整个市中心与阿勒山。于此同时，可以从独特的视角欣赏Teryan与Saralanji大街。城市中轴线穿过埃里温市中心，串联建筑综合体与阿勒圣经山，引发在此轴线建设标志性大厦的需求。埃里温市以阿勒山的双子峰为其自然背景，让综合体的游客与住户尽享美景。

BRIEF INTERVIEW 访谈录

ARCHITECT
Svetoslav Stanislavov

设计师
Svetoslav Stanislavov

HKASP: What are the important things that this project does for the city?
STARH Architects:The plot of the project is situated in a dominant position in the city scape. The buildings will be visible from wide range and will define the contemporary urban model.

HKASP: When designing, is there something in particular that you focus on? (Material, form, use etc)
STARH Architects: A certain dualism has been sought in the project- a reference and connection between Mount Ararat and the their twin peaks together with the dynamic equilibrium of the two parts as a whole. The hotel building has been designed as an accent both in the architectural composition of the complex and in the general layout of the city.

HKASP: What was the biggest challenge in this project? And how did you solve that?
STARH Architects: Combining three functions- hotel, office and residential building in one complex is always challenging. Following the design concept of the two integral elements, considering them not as separate units, but as a part of the whole, point our idea. The volumes appear as a united complex of ovals by plan, but each expresses its individual purpose.

香港建筑科学出版社：该项目对于这座城市而言，具有怎样的重要意义？
STARH Architects: 从城市景观而言，该项目地块占据了举足轻重的位置。在宽阔的范围内都能看见此建筑，他将树立当代城市建筑典范。

香港建筑科学出版社：在设计过程中，你有什么特别关注的地方吗？（材料、形体、用途等等）
STARH Architects: 该项目力图寻找某种两重性，寻找阿勒山双子峰之间的关联；同时当两者作为一个整体时，两者之间形成的一种动态平衡。无论在综合体建筑布局方面，还是在城市总体布局方面，酒店大楼都是焦点。

香港建筑科学出版社：此项目对你而言最大的挑战是什么？ 你是如何解决的？
STARH Architects: 功能上，该综合体集酒店、办公以及家居为一体。如何实现功能的集合，总是颇具挑战。遵循合二为一的设计理念，我们既要将各建筑视为一个整体，同时又传递出他们的不同之处。从平面图上看，各建筑好似整合在一起的综合体，但同时也表达出各自不同的用途。

INTERCONTINENTAL
YEREVAN

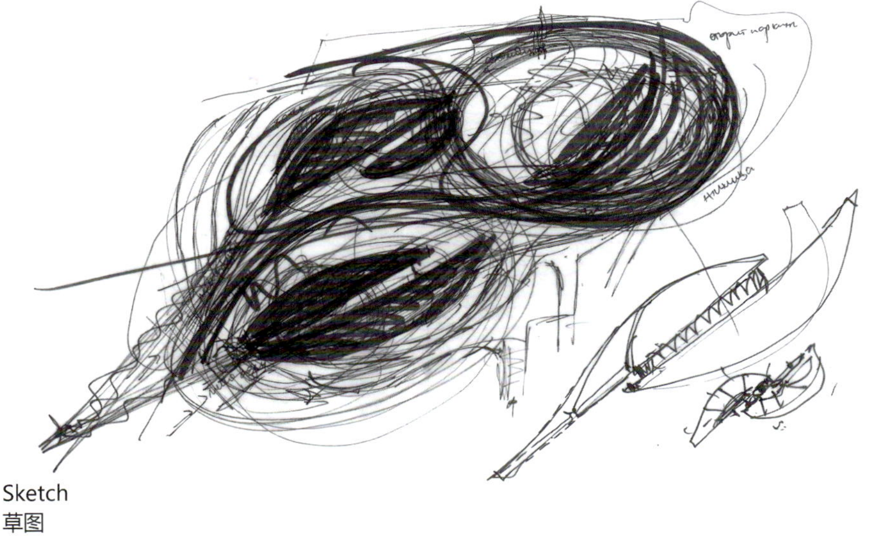

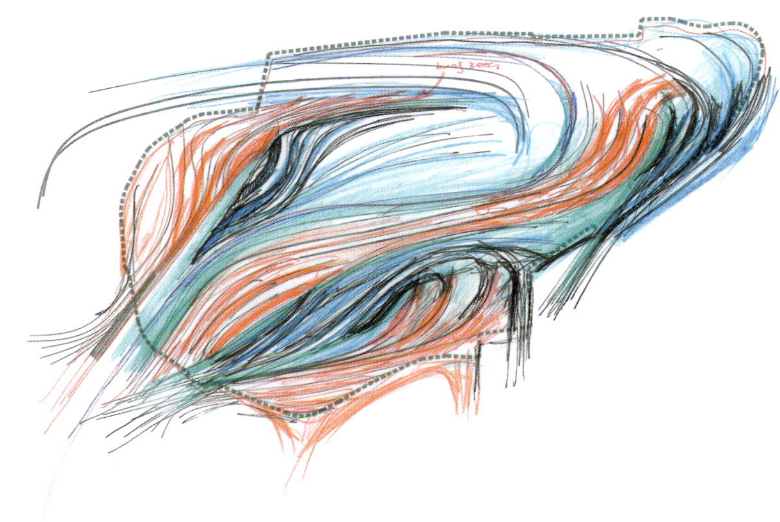

Sketch
草图

According to the general terms announced by the organizer of the competition, Avangard Motors LTD, as well as the materials and data gathered during the preliminary research, we base our architectural concept on the following three main tasks:

Looking for a certain dualism; a connection between Mcunt Ararat its twin peaks Greater and Lesser Ararat; a dynamic balance of both parts as a whole.

1.Accent of the hotel building design and its status as a symbol of the whole complex, and the city as well.

2.The functional zoning of the complex aiming to provide superior functionality, proper communications and harmonic inhabitance.

根据比赛组织方（先锋汽车股份有限公司）公布的比赛总则，再加之在初步研究中所收集的资料与数据，我们将根据以下三项主要任务来找到我们的建筑设计理念：

寻找某种两重性，即在阿勒山的双子峰（大阿勒山于小阿勒山）之间形成关联；整体层面上，在两部分之间构建动态平衡。

1. 重点放在酒店建筑的设计上，将其定位为整个综合体乃至整座城市的象征性建筑。

2. 对综合体按功能分区，旨在形成理想的功能配置，合理的交通分配与和谐的家居环境。

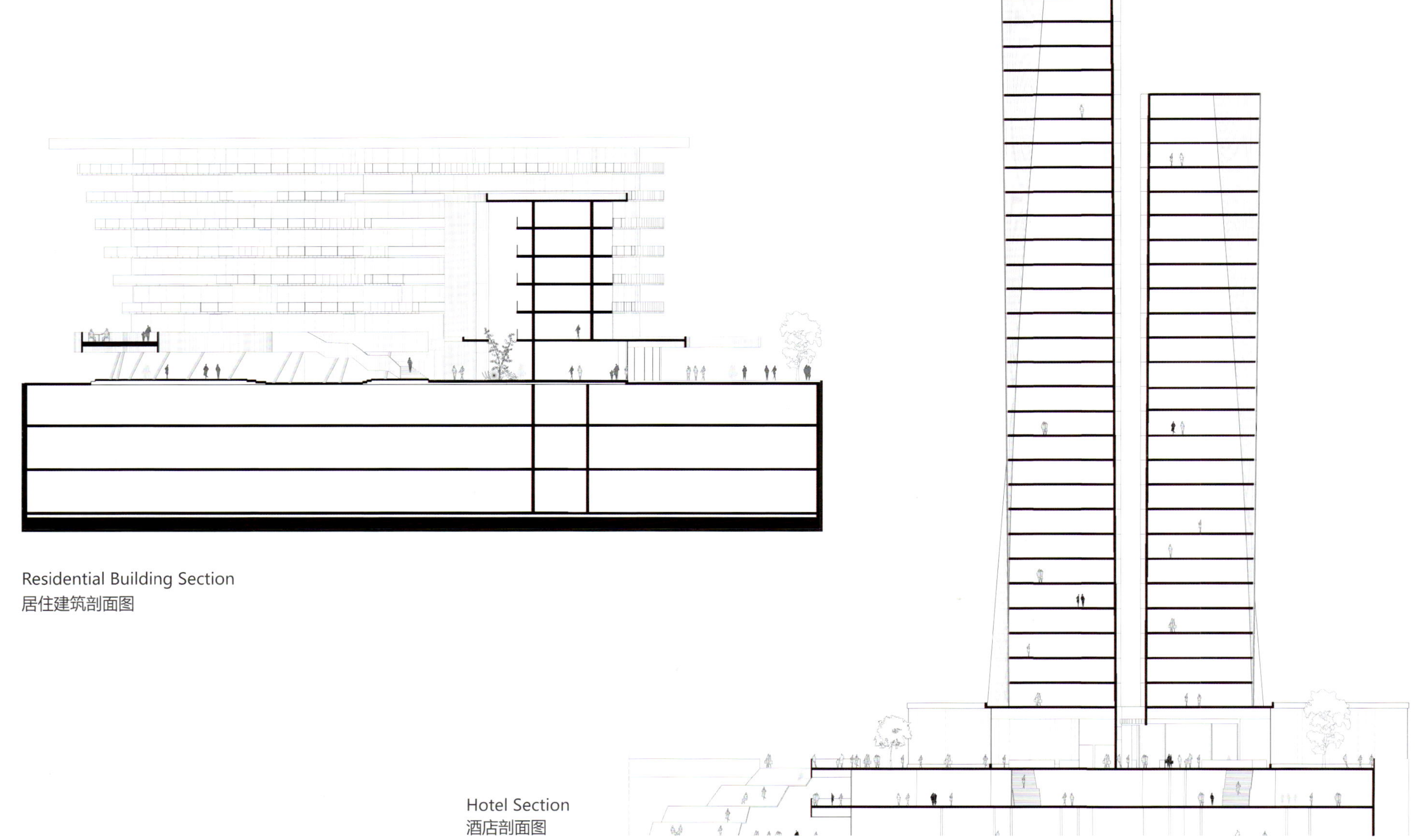

Residential Building Section
居住建筑剖面图

Hotel Section
酒店剖面图

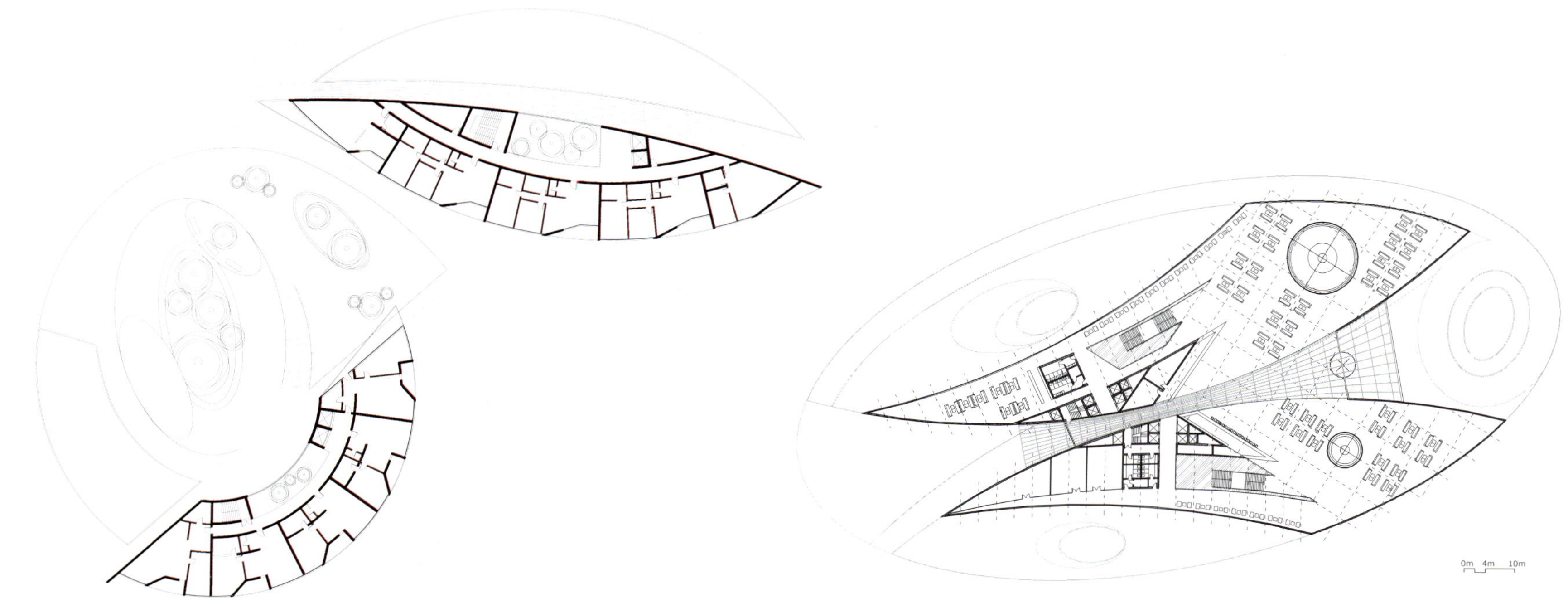

Residential Building Typical Floor
住宅楼层图

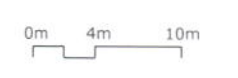

Hoyel Grond Floor
酒店首层平面图

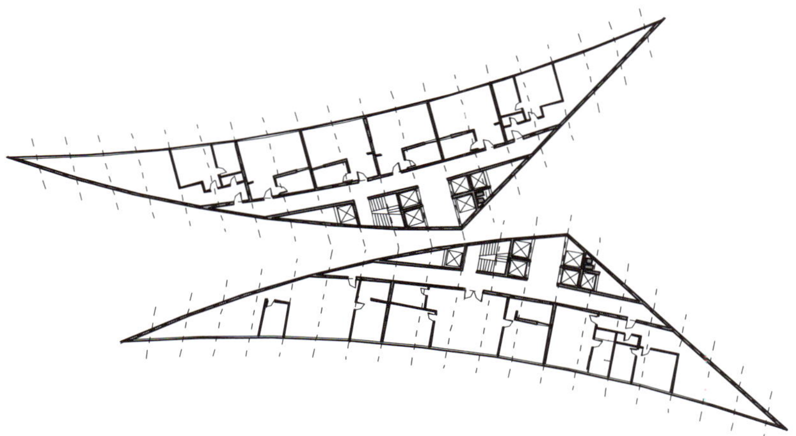

Hotel Typical Floor
酒店楼层图

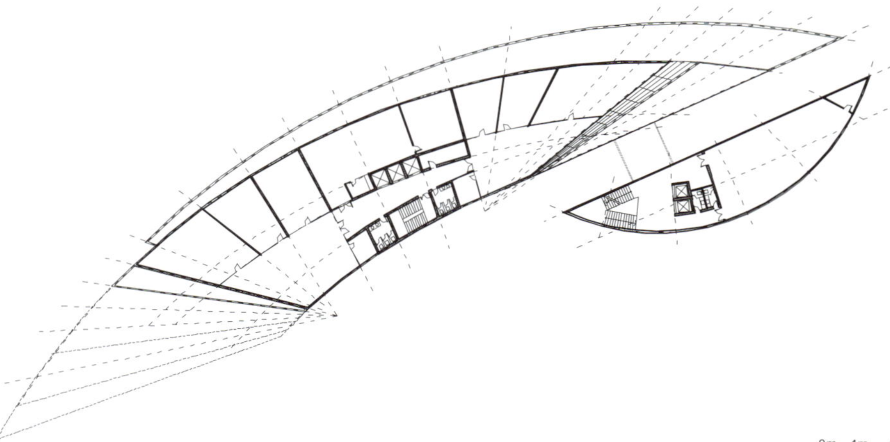

Business Center Typical Floor
商业中心楼层图

The parcel is located 2 km north-east from Republic square and approximately 100 meters above the central square. The link to the central part of the city goes south through Abovyan square, whereas Saralanji st, which rises above the complex, connects east and west Yerevan. The south part of the land rises above Abovyan Square 35 meters on average, and its north part levels with Saralanji Street. The overall vertical displacement is slight with the land sliding 3 to 5 percent south-west. Due to the specific geographical terrain features, we are looking to establish the main transportation connection in the north part, as this provides the possibility to organize the ground and underground traffic into one approach. The main elements of the entire planning solution and functional division of the complex are two ellipses sized 98/160 m and 75/156 m respectively, which tangent at a 7° angle.

The ellipse on the east is a road that goes around the residential part and provides access to the hotel. Driving on this road displays a unique panorama of Yerevan and Mount Ararat. The western ellipse frames the zone of the hotel, which is exclusively pedestrian. The business center is zoned above the ellipses. A very strong component cf the planning solution is the "Sky Way" (stairway, skywalk) – a staircase imaginary extending Teryan St, which divides the hotel zone and the business center, and crosses the parcel to reach the main level of the complex.

An ellipse in the north part represents the main transportation junction connecting ground and underground communications with the outer streets. Another ellipse to the east of the hotel provides guests with access to the welcome lobby and features a lot of green and water areas. The glass opening in the middle lets day light pass to the underground floors of the complex. The fundamental principle of proper organization of basic level communications is solved by directing traffic to underground levels. In that way the vehicles crossing the main level are limited to the maximum. Only vehicles servicing the hotel guests on the west hoop and vehicles using the open parking on the west side of the property will pass through. The main access to underground levels for all vehicles going to the three zones is provided in the northern part right off the main roundabout.

项目地块在共和国广场以东2公里处，其海拔大约比中央广场高100米。通往市中心的道路向南延伸，穿过阿博维扬广场。Saralanji大街的海拔高于综合体，连接市区的东部与西部。地块南部的平均海拔比阿博维扬广场高35米。地块北部的海拔与Saralanji街相同。地块呈现少量垂直位移，微微偏向于西南方向3~5个百分点。鉴于如此多地形特征，我们力求在地块北部设立交通枢纽，因为这样既顾及了地面交通，也兼顾了地下交通。构成整个规划方案与综合体功能分区的主要要素就是两个椭圆地块（尺寸分别为：98/160 m，75/156 m；正切角为：7度）。

东侧的椭圆地块外围实则一条环绕居住区的交通道路，人们可从此到达酒店。当驾车行驶在这条道路上时，一幅通过独特视角的城市全景与阿勒山画尽收眼底。西侧仅供步行的椭圆地块设定了酒店的区域范围。商务中心就将从此椭圆地块拔地而起。“天空路”的构建（即楼梯、天空步道）是规划方案的一大亮点。这是一条通往Teryan大街的虚构阶梯。这条天空步道构成了酒店区域与商务中心的分界线，并且横跨地块，直抵综合体的主楼层。

北侧的椭圆地块是地面与地下交通连接外街区的主交通枢纽。而酒店以东的椭圆地块则是人们通往酒店接待大厅的入口，这里设置了草坪与水景。阳光穿过中间的玻璃窗直入综合体的地下楼层。为了让首层的交通实现合理的布局，基本原理就是将来往车辆引入地下楼层。这样，穿越主楼层的车辆数量将受到限制。而只有在西侧环路上接送酒店宾客的车辆与拥有位于地块西侧的开放式停车场使用权的车辆才能通行。通往地下楼层的主入口位于北侧的椭圆地块（就在主环路的出口处）。所有车辆都可以从此主入口通往这3个区域。

The solution of the underground levels transportation scheme resembles the functional areas of the main level, like parking lots and public service areas, and includes a spiral platform in the middle, reaching to the three underground levels. The main roundabout, distributing all vehicles to the three functional areas, is situated around this platform. Both the platform and the roundabout are ellipse shaped by plan. Each group of buildings has access to the underground levels through the vertical main bodies (cores, facilities).

The business center is also designed as two buildings with no direct link between them. The office spaces are situated in the larger body, which is also higher with seven floors compared to the smaller one with three floors. The first floor includes the entrance lobby with information desk, shops and restaurant for the employees in the building. Each of eighteen offices located on the recurring floors is designed to provide flexibility according to the specific requirements of the future occupants. The other building is a three-floor conference center and offers one conference hall on every floor, each with a capacity of 80 people. This division allows the conference center to serve the business center employees and accommodate independent external events at the same time. The underground levels below the business center are designed for parking, while the zone with access to the "Sky Way" is commercial. The provided 250 parking spaces for the business center are accessible by one core featuring four elevators and stairs.

根据交通设计方案，地下楼层也设有停车场与公共服务区域，与主楼层的功能划分如出一辙。此外，地下楼层的中间将设一个螺旋平台。通过此螺旋平台，人们可直抵地下3个楼层。主环路环绕整个平台，发挥将车辆分流至3个功能区域的功能。根据规划，把平台与环路都设计成椭圆形。在每个建筑群里的人们可通过垂直主体（核心体，各项设施）通往地下楼层。

根据设计，商务中心为两栋完全隔离的大厦。体量较大的大厦拥有7层楼的办公空间，而相对较低的另一座大厦拥有3层楼的办公空间。第一层楼设有入口大厅。大厅中设有咨询台以及供在本大厦的工作人员享用的商店与餐馆。根据未来户主的指定要求，每个若干层楼设有18间办公室，以保障灵活多变的需求。另外一栋大厦则为一个3层高的会议中心，每层楼都设有一间会议大厅，每间会议大厅能容纳80人。这样的配置即可顾及商务中心工作员工的需求，也可顾及外包会议的需求。商务中心大厦的地下楼层用于停车。设置了通往“天空路”的区域为商业服务区。商务中心提供了250个停车位，人们分别可以从4个电梯与楼梯进入车库。

The residential area is situated in the east part of the property in order to provide sunlight all day long. The facades positioning allows not only sunlight, but also a visual contact with Yerevan and Mount Ararat. There are two residential complexes with two buildings each. They are also oval shaped by plan, rising eight floors maximum. The residential area provides space for living and for development of activities, which will ensure better life and correct functioning as well. There are areas for sports and recreation, shopping areas, restaurants and bars. The buildings in the eastern part are higher – one with eight floors and one with two floors. The other couple is five floors and two floors high respectively.

All facades of the business building are finished in glass and two of them have a very steep slope coming from the rotation of the floors in the plan. The volume is aggressive featuring two sharp edges and the areas covered with metal shutters complete the modern look of the building. The architectural concept of the residential buildings is more relaxed, the ovals by plan rise vertically into facade plains, separated by glass and white flash. The sharp ends of the balconies and their growing size as floors increase refer to the vision of the hotel and the business center. The north facades are composed of more flesh and less glass, while the lower bodies for public services are light and fretwork. Around the whole residential area the division and the human scale are more notable in the open areas and the buildings. Richer landscaping in the common areas and the open spaces exalt the feeling for different functionality. The architectural idea for the whole international complex achieves nature purity with fewer materials used, whereas the vertical rising of sharp edges creates quite expressive and spectacular visual perspectives.

为了满足全天的采光，故将居住区设在地块的东侧。立面的布置不仅考虑到自然采光，而且还考虑到如何提供观赏埃里温市区与阿勒山的最佳视角。该项目共设两个家居综合体，每个综合体分别由两栋家居建筑组成。根据设计方案，家居建筑也呈椭圆形，最多8层楼。家居区域提供了生活空间与活动空间，不仅保障了高品质生活，而且还发挥合理的作用。此外，家居区域还设置了运动场所、休闲娱乐场所、购物场所、餐厅及酒吧。西侧两栋楼分别为5层与2层，相比西侧建筑，东侧的建筑更高，一栋楼为8层，另一栋为2层。

商务建筑的所有立面均采用玻璃幕墙。从设计图中可见，由于楼层的扭转变形，致使其中两栋楼呈现非常明显的坡度。该体量传达出气势恢宏的讯息，主要体现在锋利的边缘与金属制的百叶窗上，最终给建筑营造出富有现代气息的风貌。家居建筑的设计理念则倾向于一种轻松；惬意的表达。根据设计，椭圆的建筑拔地而起形成一个立面，立面穿插着玻璃窗与打底白色。阳台采用了大幅收缩造型。此外，随着楼层的升高，阳台的面积也随之增大。这一切都是出于保证酒店与商务中心拥有宽阔视野的考虑。北面立面则更多地采用不透视墙体，而更少的采用玻璃幕墙。然而，公共服务场所（位于底下几层）的楼体采用轻量构造与浮雕细工。整个家居区域的开放区域与建筑都更突显功能划分与人性尺度。共用区域与露天场所被赋予了更加丰富的景观元素，从而更加突出区域的功能符号。虽然整个国际综合体的设计思路力求少用材料，传达出对纯真自然的追求，但挺拔的锋利边缘则营造了一种富有深意且壮观的视觉效应。

PROJECT NAME 项目名称

CHENGDU'S NEW CENTURY GLOBAL CENTER

成都新世纪环球中心

Architect: Zhongshen Architectural Design Co., Ltd. Shenzhen

设计公司：深圳中深建筑设计有限公司

PROJECT INFORMATION 项目信息

Client	Chengdu Century City New International Exhibition Center Co., Ltd.	**客户**	成都世纪城新国际会展中心有限公司
Location	Chengdu,Sichuan,China	**地点**	中国四川成都
Gross Floor Area	1,700,000 m^2	**总建筑面积**	1,700,000 平方米
Site Area	467,000 m^2	**占地面积**	467,000 平方米
Plot ratio	2.52	**容积率**	2.52
Building density	42.0%	**建筑密度**	42.0%

OVERVIEW 项目概况

This project is located on the west of Tianfu Avenue, the south extension line of Chengdu Sichuan. It adjoins Chengdu high-speed beltway in the south, incubation park of the high-tech zone in the north and a municipal sports and greening park in the west. With the core of an 8,000 m² "Recreational Island•Ocean Wonderland", it will be a centralized urban complex with hotel, meeting, multi-shopping and business rolled into one.

项目位于四川省成都市南延长线——天府大道的西侧。南邻成都市绕城高速；北为高新区孵化园；西为市级体育绿化公园。项目是以 8,000 平方米“游乐风情岛·海洋乐园”为核心，集酒店、会议、多重购物、办公为一体的集中式城市综合体。

BRIEF INTERVIEW 访谈录

ARCHITECT
Hu Ran

设计师
忽然

HKASP: How do you rationalize the planning of site when designing the project?

Zhongshen Architectural Design Co., Ltd. Shenzhen:The first job is to integrate and plan commercial functions to cater to business practice and deliver an excellent organization of flows when a commercial project is not influenced by any specific external factor.

HKASP: Considering such a project of gigantic scale, how does the design progress? What is the greatest challenge you face?

Zhongshen Architectural Design Co., Ltd. Shenzhen:The project was small in scale in the early phase. The design proposal is quite based on concept. With change of external factors, we saw an increasingly improved core of this project which became a signature project in Chengdu. And the project saw an enhancement both in scale and functions.

The greatest challenge comes from the huge scale and high-density concentrated functional complex themselves. On one hand, there is no reference to consider. We had to take a blind approach all the way through the 6-year-long design process. It was quite difficult. On the other hand, the crossing among all flows posed as a noticeable issue along with the conflict between functional rationalization and normalized fire fighting.

HKASP: From the view of architectural design, how to better help the developers achieve their investment plan?

Zhongshen Architectural Design Co., Ltd. Shenzhen:The question is a challenge to an architect. Many architects would hold a rejection attitude toward it. I believe a project's features would generate more factors that influence the design during the stage of design. For an architect, more opportunities to show value of design emerge during designing. As for a commercial building, the architects tend to give a full study to the business operation and investment return. The fact is that digging deep into an issue can give birth to a solution during designing.

香港建筑科学出版社：在项目设计中如何合理的规划场地？

深圳中深建筑设计有限公司：对于商业项目，在无特定的外部条件影响下，首要的是将商业功能整合规划成符合商业运营的模式，组织好各种流线。

香港建筑科学出版社：本项目巨大的规模，其设计进程是怎样？最大的难点是什么？

深圳中深建筑设计有限公司：项目的前期规模不大，设计方案也以较为理念的方式进行，但是随着外部因素的变化，项目主体不断提升，成为成都市的名片项目，其规模和功能也不断的放大。

项目最大的难点是由其巨大的规模和高度集中的复合性功能体所产生的。一方面没有可借鉴的项目为依据，摸着石头过河，设计进程长达 6 年，非常艰辛；另一方面项目产生巨大的各种流线的交叉问题，以及与功能合理性与消防规范的矛盾。

香港建筑科学出版社：从建筑设计角度，如何更好地协助开发商实现投资计划？

深圳中深建筑设计有限公司：这个问题对建筑师是挑战，很多建筑师持排斥态度，我想在建筑设计进程中因项目的特点，产生了更多影响设计的因素，对建筑师而言，其设计的过程会更显设计的价值。对商业建筑，建筑师充分研究商业运营与投资回报也是从不可少的课题，只有了解了问题的实质，才能在设计中合理的解决。

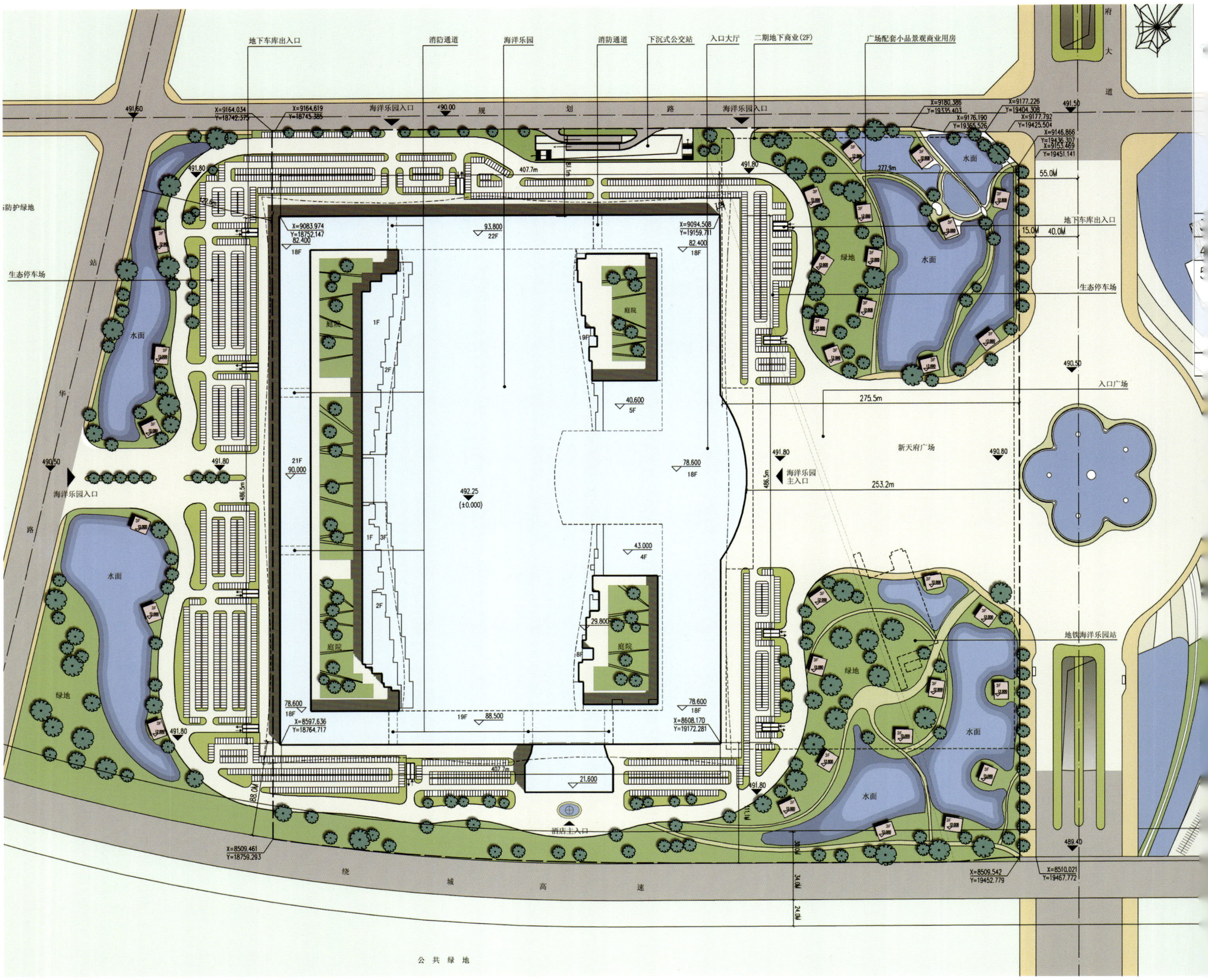

Site Plan
总平面图

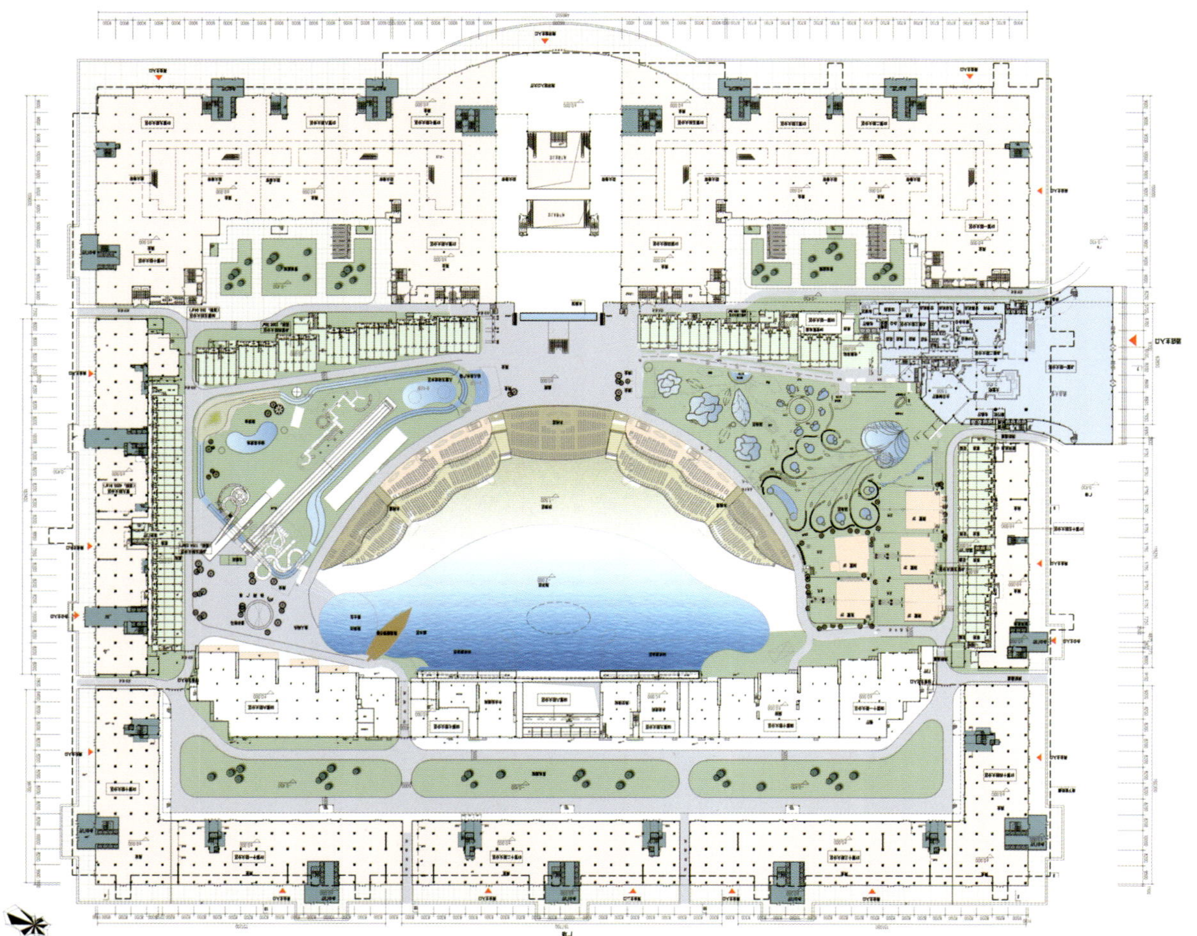

1st Plan
一层平面图

The first scheme
第一方案图

The second scheme
第二方案图

Design Concept

Focusing on ocean park right from the beginning to construction phase, the project delivers a form that revolves around ocean. The floor area was initially only 60 000m². The concept of design features a "flying sea gull" which implies the project flies to Chengdu like a sea gull along with see breeze.

The scale of this project has been increasingly enlarged to 450,000m², with architectural plane dimension reaching 500m x 450m. With a concept of "give Chengdu sea waves", the building is designed to be like sea waves floating atop Chengdu, giving Chengdu a dynamic rhythm.

设计理念

由于项目从前期到实施都以海洋乐园为核心，造型始终围绕海洋主题为依据，最初项目建筑面积只有60,000 平方米，设计是以“飞行的海鸥”为理念，寓意项目像海鸥飞临成都大地，带来海洋的气息。

在项目规模不断扩大至 450,000 平方米后，建筑的平面尺度达 500mx450m，设计以“给成都一片海浪”为理念将建筑设计成漂浮在成都大地上的海浪，让这片土地律动起来。

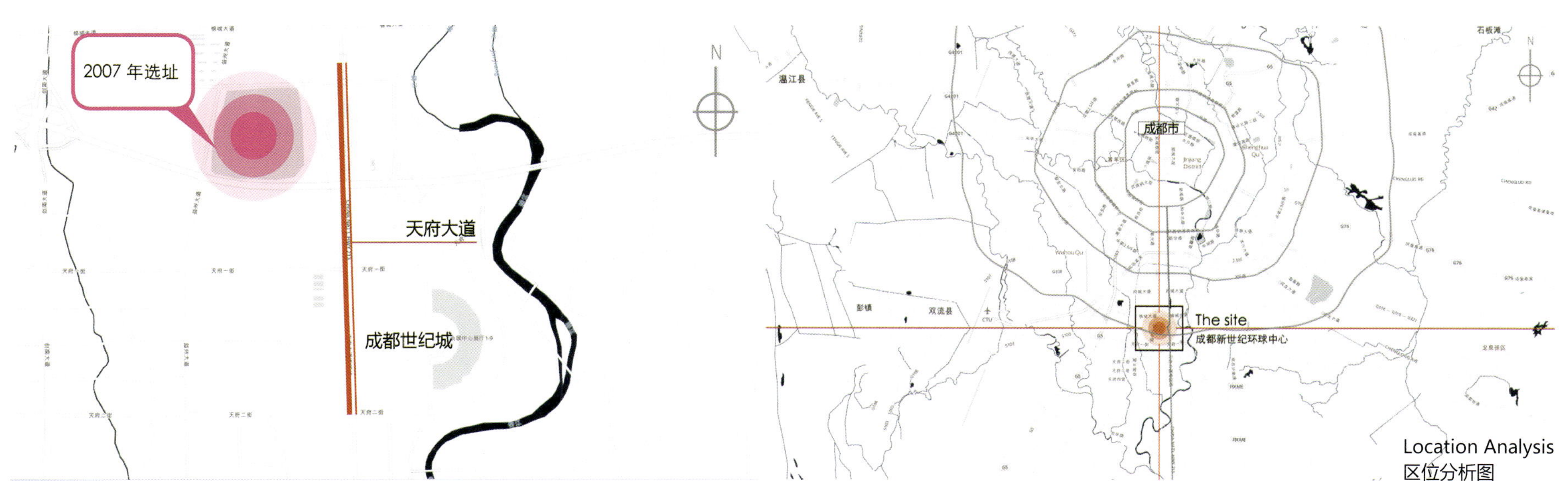

Location Analysis
区位分析图

ODA
ICBC 中国工商银行

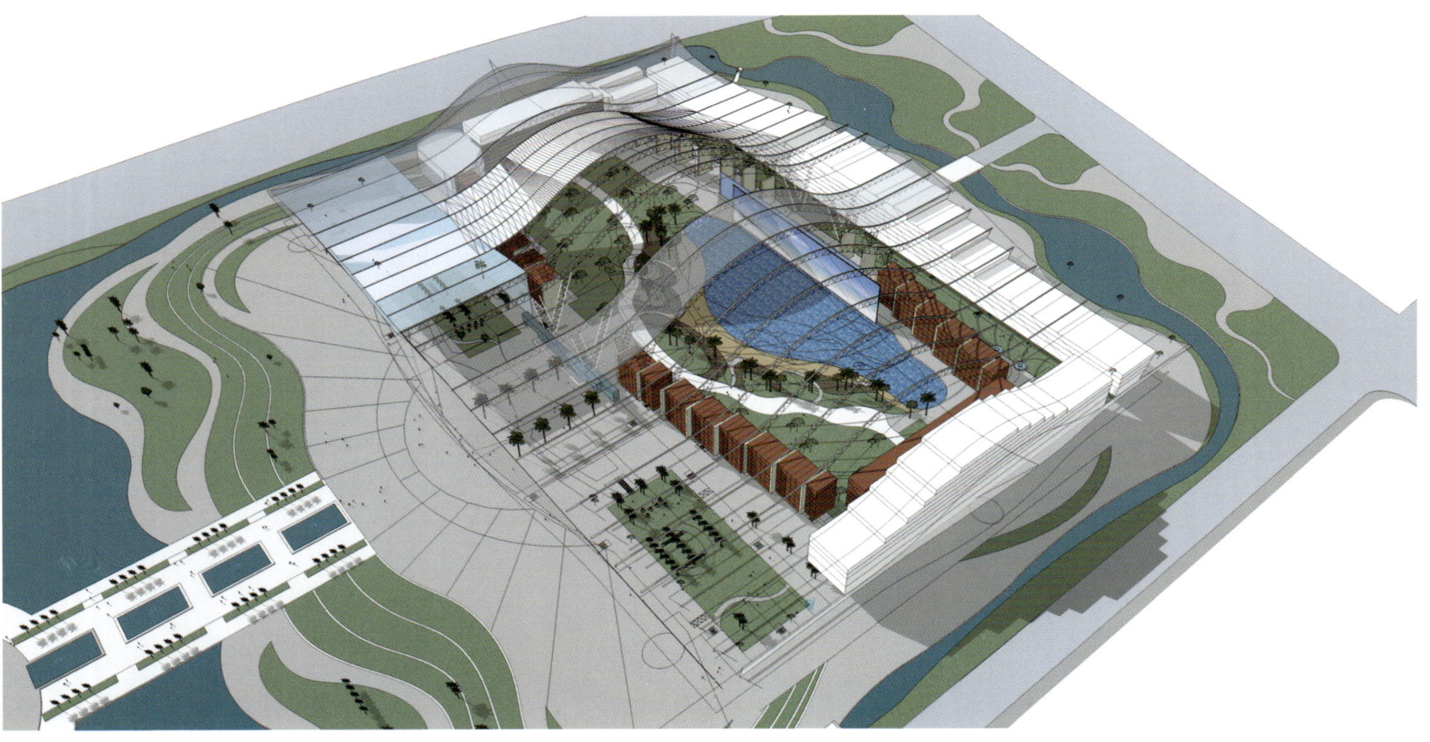

The main building body of Paradise Island Ocean Wonderland is a rectangle in plane view with a length of 486.5 m and a width of 407.7 m. To the east is the main entrance and there are subsidiary exits and entrances to the south, west and north.

The project is characterized by meeting people's demands for entertainment, shopping, recreational life experience, business, hotel and other programs within a huge space in a most effective way. The project serves as an integral complex of urban life.

The project features a core area for entertainment and hotel where an astylar glazed structure covering an area of 80, 000 m^2 locates. It is as high as 100 m which also serves as the most powerful appeal for this project.

Shaped as a flying and floating shell, the major construction space meets all building demands and presents as column-free space with a long span.

天堂岛海洋乐园的建筑主体平面呈长方形，长向:486.5 米，短向:407.7 米；东侧为主要入口，其南、西、北面均设有附属出入口。

项目的特点是在一个大空间内，最有效解决了人们的游乐、购物、休闲生活、商务、酒店等多种需要，是一个城市生活的完整综合体。

项目的特色是核心区（游乐、酒店区）布置在一个 80,000 平方米的无柱玻璃体大空间，其高度达 100 米这也是项目最吸引人的地方。

建筑主功能空间形态以飞翔、漂浮的壳体，将建筑功能全部复盖；且为无柱的大跨度空间。

Functional organization in Paradise Island Ocean Wonderland vary inside-out, with the ocean, recreational island and water park in the center, hotel area in the second circle and commercial and office area in the third circle. Each function is relatively independent and correlated, making it a large comprehensive project with recreation, shopping, relaxation and business rolled into one.

天堂岛海洋乐园的功能由里向外按不同功能布置，核心部分为：海洋、风情岛、水上乐园等；第二圈为酒店区；第三圈为商业和办公区。各功能相对独立，又互为联系，使其成为一个集游乐、购物、休闲、办公为一体的大型综合项目。

How do you consider sustainability when designing?

Sustainable operation is a major issue for this project of such a huge scale. When designing, we tried to realize the project's ecological balance and sustainability in the following ways:

1.An energy center is used throughout the project to maximize mutual use of energy and minimize consumption of energy.

2.The energy center employs geothermal heat pump technology which enhances project's dependence on municipal supply of energy.

3.A special energy saving assessment is conducted for the core area, a huge space with a floor area of 80,000 m^2. The predominant use of free ventilation along with use of openable glass roof exerts an effective control of consumption of energy in such a huge space.

4.For environment: besides planning a large area of greenbelt at the perimeter of site, there will be three atria of large scale within the functional area inside the building. Meanwhile, there will be a 7,000 m^2 water surface and a dense woodland within the core area, allowing for improved physical environment.

Constrained by investment and concept, this project saw an incomplete realization in sustainability although unremitting efforts have been made in design.

对于这样一个大项目，可持续性的运营是一个重要的问题，在项目设计过程中，对项目的生态、可持续性从几个方面入手：

①整个项目共享一个的能源中心，使能源能最大程度的相互利用，将能耗尽量减少。

②能源中心采用地源热泵技术，增强项目能耗对市政供给的依赖。

③对核心区大空间（80,000平方米空间）进行专项节能评估，以利用自由通风为主导，采用开启式玻璃屋盖，使大空间的能耗得到有效控制。

④环境方面：除利用项目周边场地规划出大片绿化外，在建筑的内部功能区规划了3个较大尺度的绿化中庭；同时在核心区大空间内，布置了约7,000平方米的水面以及大量的树林，使项目的物理环境得到改善。

由于投资和理念方面的限制，设计虽做了多种努力，但本项目在可持续性方面的尝试不尽完善。

LOTTE
1000
元
4

PROJECT NAME　项目名称

SAHID KUTA LIFESTYLE RESORT
萨希迪库塔生活方式度假村

Architect: Envirotec Indonesia
设计公司：镜艺

PROJECT INFORMATION　项目信息

Client	PT.IPI	**客户**	PTI.PI
Location	KUTA,BALIINDONESIA	**地点**	印度尼西亚巴厘岛萨希迪库塔
Site Are	52,462 m²	**占地面积**	52，462 平方米

OVERVIEW　项目概况

Sweeping 250m along a bustling beachside street, the Sahid Kuta Lifestyle Resort offers a new lifestyle hub typology. The project covers 32,000m² and contains two zones: the "Beachwalk" retail lifestyle hub and the five-star Sheraton Bali Kuta Resort. The design concept was inspired by the terraced paddy fields that dot the Balinese landscape.

海滨小街呈现一片热闹景象。与海滨小街并行 250 米的萨希迪库塔生活方式度假村同样给人们带来了一种全新的生活体验中心。此项目共占地 32,000 平方米，总体分为两个部分："海滩长廊"零售店生活体验中心；巴厘岛库塔五星级喜来登度假酒店。其建筑风格设计灵感来自散布于巴里岛景区各处的水稻梯田。

BRIEF INTERVIEW　访谈录

ARCHITECT
Chew TaiEng,
Ming Zhou,
Ardianto Rushy

设计师
Chew TaiEng,
Ming Zhou,
Ardianto Rushy

HKASP: How did you arrange people experience in this project?

Envirotec Indonesia: The experience came naturally for everyone in the project. From conceptualising right from the start, to revisions in the middle till the end for construction. The client, the appointed contractor, the suppliers, the designers and us also the interior consultants, landscape, lighting consultants all experienced the true essence of building a fantastic big scaled project in Bali. As everyone will know that Indonesia is probably one of the hardest places to construct a building, of this scale but also of such complexity which intertwines, a lot of spatial effects, landscape elements to remain true to the Balinese roots. The experience became different for different people because everyone was involved in different way but in depth, right up to installing the actual terrazzo or terracotta materials on site.

We also have to experience to deal with the Balinese government to get the approval for building permit which took us a year and wasnt easy because of many strict rules and also the controlled 3 storey height of the buildings. For us we experienced that there is a must to be flexible, to achieve something with a low budget yet creating something the Balinese community at heart can use. Hence the experience goes down to the common people living in Bali, for the tourist to enjoy an escapade from the hot Bali sun to the gardens and for the workers and staff working at Beachwalk a place to enjoy the scenery. All layers of activities, interaction, human connection are interlaced with a natural flow of positive energy just like the Oasis pond flow to the sea. It was truly a blessed project right from the start.

HKASP: .When designing, is there something in particular that you focus on? (Material, form, use etc)

Envirotec Indonesia: The energy of the space is very important. We really focused on the spatial flow of the spaces as this is important to connect back to the streets of Kuta so the people can flow and walk in naturally at the surrounding areas. Beachwalk became an extension of the street in a natural way. It is the first semi open lifestyle commercial hub in Indonesia with a great focus on nature and landscape design. The concepts of "elliptical" glass shops with interwinding shopping corridors or alfresco space is a very new concept in Indonesia. No other developer has done this and it was an encouraging step to create something fresh and for the people. THe gardens became the important space and feature and the building no longer looked like a building but rather big padi fields. The materials was integral in creating the entire ambience. We sourced for local materials and raw ones so it became part of the street fabric that Balinese people were familiar to. It was important to reach out and connect the familiarity.

香港建筑科学出版社：你是如何调配此项目的人力资源的？

镜艺：此项目的人力资源调配遵循顺其自然的原则。从最初的构思开始，到中途的概念调整，一直到最后的竣工，我们都遵循顺其自然的原则。从客户，到指定承建商，再到材料供应商，设计事务所，我们自己，以及室内设计咨询公司，景观设计事务所，照明设计咨询公司，都体会到了在巴厘建设如此大规模，如此神奇建筑的真正含义。众所周知，印度尼西亚是世界上最难修建建筑的地方之一，特别是这种规模，这种复杂程度的建筑更是如此。建筑的复杂是为了保持最真实一面的巴厘风情，而营造出一种盘根错节的空间与景观效果。每个人参与项目的方式不同，程度也不同（比如参与水磨石或陶瓦材料铺装的工人就有不同的体验），所以每个人都有属于自己的体验。

巴厘政府出台了多项严格的规定，将楼层限制在 3 层。于是为了获得建设许可，我们不得不与政府折腾了一年之久。这可谓一段充满艰辛的历程。对于我们而言，我们务必要找到一个切入点，以低预算在巴厘社区核心地段创造出宜人的建筑。因此，该建筑将更贴近在巴厘生活的平民百姓，给游客带来一片躲避巴厘烈日的花园，让这里的工人与工作人员也可饱览美景。如同绿洲池汇入大海，一股自然的正能量将各类活动、人流、人景互动都相互交融，汇聚一体。

香港建筑科学出版社：在设计过程中，你有什么特别关注的地方吗？（材料、形体、用途等等）

镜艺：赋予空间以活力是非常重要的要素。保持与库塔街风格的连贯至关重要，于是我们的确把重心放在了如何营造出一种过度自然的空间。这样，人们很自然的穿行于周边各个区域，而且海滩步道也自然地成为库塔街的延伸。这是有史以来在印度尼西亚第一次采用半开放式生活体验购物中心，如此关注自然，如此关注景观设计。采用椭圆形玻璃橱窗概念的商店与购物走廊的结合或与户外空间的结合是印度尼西亚的首创概念。没有哪个开发商有过这样的尝试。这代表了创新，服务于人们的创新迈出了鼓舞人心的一步。花园成为了空间与特色的焦点，建筑也不再像建筑，反而酷似广阔的稻田。材料成为了打造整个环境不可分割的一部分。我们寻求本地材料，原生态的材料，让材料与巴厘人民所熟悉的街道肌理融为一体。当然，努力去寻找当地人所熟悉的是非常重要的。

Sheraton
Bali
KUTA
RESORT
Hotel Lobby
Parking
Sunset Gathering
ENTRY

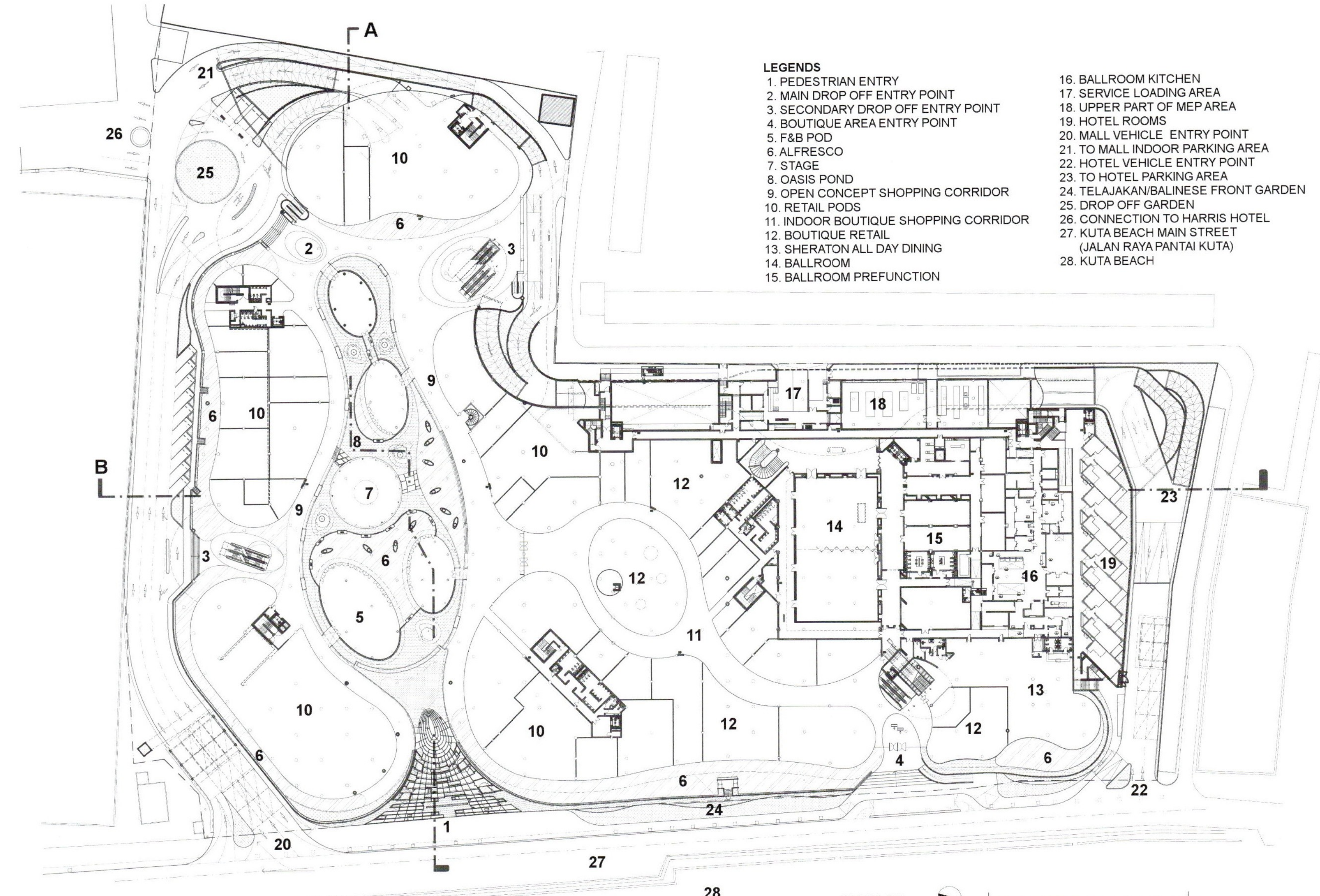

Site Plan
总平面图

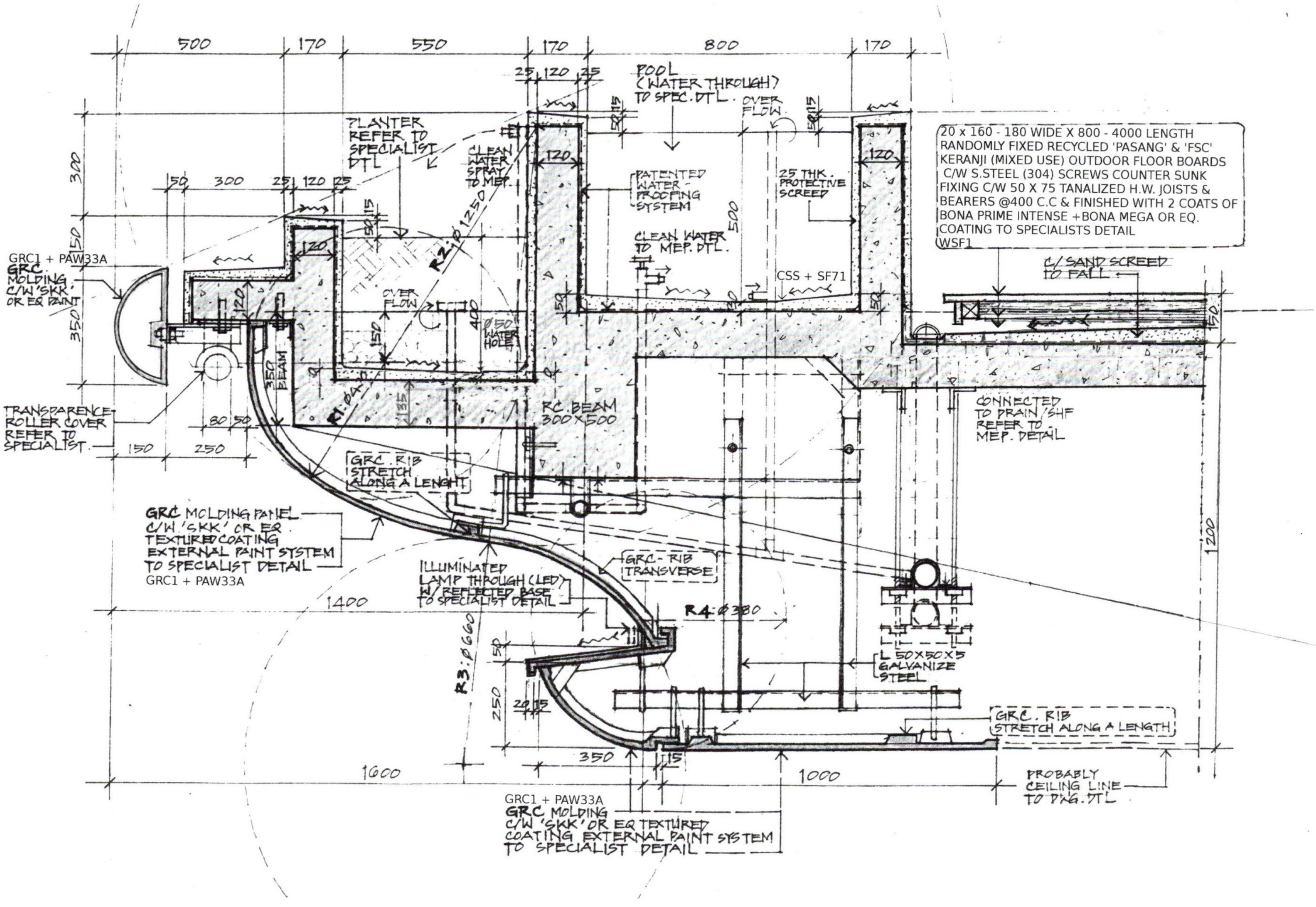

20 x 160 - 180 WIDE X 800 - 4000 LENGTH RANDOMLY FIXED RECYCLED 'PASANG' & 'FSC' KERANJI (MIXED USE) OUTDOOR FLOOR BOARDS C/W S.STEEL (304) SCREWS COUNTER SUNK FIXING C/W 50 X 75 TANALIZED H.W. JOISTS & BEARERS @400 C.C & FINISHED WITH 2 COATS OF BONA PRIME INTENSE +BONA MEGA OR EQ. COATING TO SPECIALISTS DETAIL
WSF1

GRC1 + PAW33A

CSS + SF71

GRC1 + PAW33A

GRC1 + PAW33A

permeterer planter edge detail section
周边植被区域边缘细节剖面图

PERIMETER PLANTER EDGE DETAIL SECTION

0 1M

LEGENDS
1. KUTA BEACH MAIN STREET (JALAN RAYA PANTAI KUTA)
2. MAIN PEDESTRIAN ENTRY STEP
3. PEDESTRIAN ENTRY PLATFORM
4. F & B PODS
5. ROOF GARDEN PODS
6. ALFRESCO
7. OASIS POND
8. RETAIL PODS
9. KIDS PLAYGROUND AREA
10. OPEN CONCEPT SHOPPING CORRIDOR
11. CAR PARK
12. MEP DECK
SECTION A
0
50 M

LEGENDS
1. DRIVEWAY TO MALL DROP OFF
2. ALFRESCO
3. RETAIL PODS
4. ART & CRAFT AREA
5. OPEN CONCEPT SHOPPING CORRIDOR
6. OASIS STAGE
7. OASIS ALFRESCO
8. ENTRY TO BOUTIQUE SHOPPING AREA
9. BOUTIQUE SHOPPING AREA
10. BALLROOM
11. BALLROOM PREFUNCTION
12. BALLROOM KITCHEN
13. SHERATON HOTEL TRANSIT LOBBY
14. SHERATON HOTEL RECEPTION
15. SHERATON HOTEL ROOMS BLOCK
16. HOTEL ROOF GARDEN (WITH SUN DECK AND JOGGING TRACK)
SECTION B
0
50 M

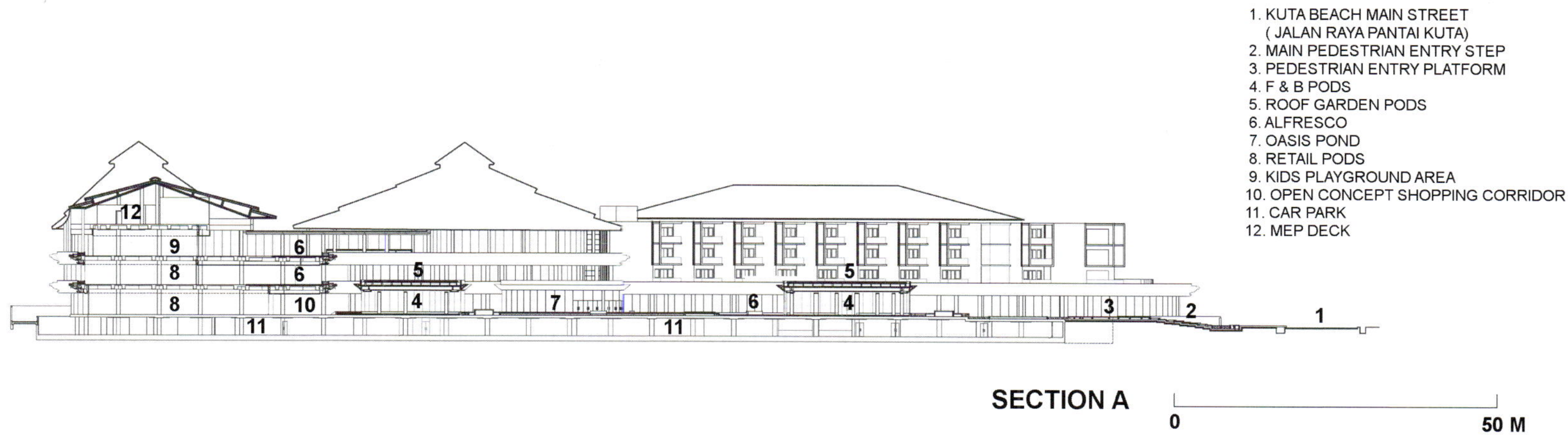

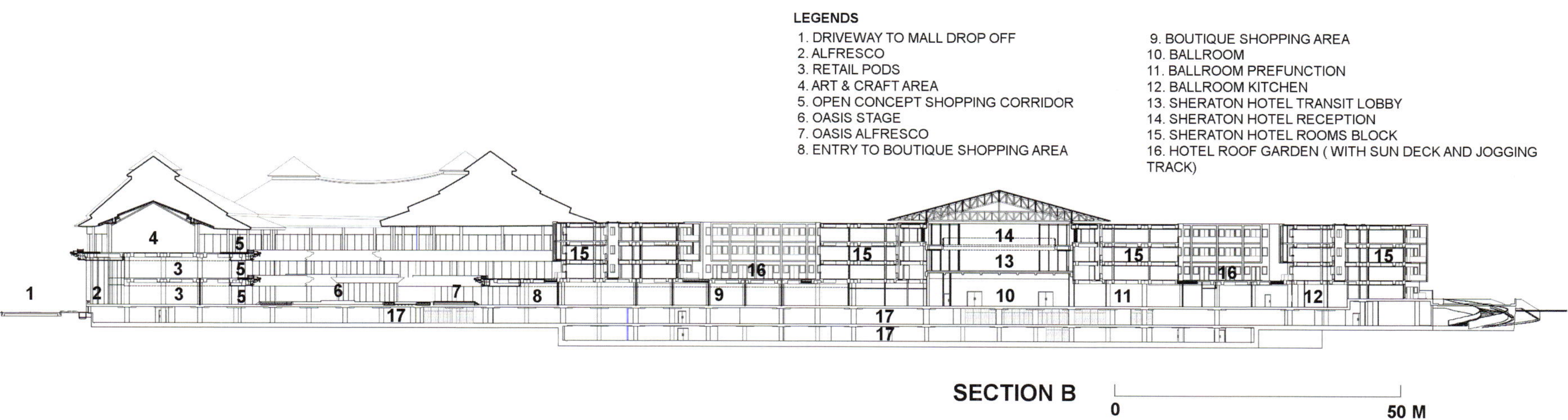

Section
剖面图

The name "Beachwalk" is suggestive of a sensory dimension. Semi-open and naturally ventilated, Beachwalk consists of a series of terraced landscaped plates that create a "soft" environment and serve as viewing decks. The looping circulation eliminates dead-end spaces. Roofs take the shape of a local farmer's hat. Hanging vines and water channels contribute to the resort atmosphere. The material for this project mostly from local material & environmental friendly. Like the retail floor at Beachwalk which using teracotta, produced locally in Bali, also local high-grade paras stones.

之所以取名为“海滩长廊”是对一种感官维度的暗示。半开放式的海滩长廊采用自然通风。各层楼依次叠加，形如阶梯，再加之植被景观的点缀就构成了海滩长廊。海滩长廊不仅是一种供游客欣赏的“软”景观，更是一个供游客欣赏美景的地方。环形步行路消除了“死胡同”的存在。屋顶形如当地农民戴的帽子。吊蔓与水渠让度假村的惬意氛围锦上添花。该项目基本上采用本地材料，达到环保效果。就拿海边散步走廊的零售店楼层举例，该层楼采用当地产的陶瓦与高级灵石构筑。

A soft veil of hanging vines and shallow water channels around the periphery of every building plate contribute to the lifestyle resort's atmosphere of layered poetic idiosyncrasy. The development is perched on a landscaped deck that is elevated above street level. The earth-coloured base wall is lined with deep terracotta colour tiles in "Majapahit"proportioned sizes which depict the islands of Indonesia – including Bali. It seems to be floating on a strip of water. The water flows down from the oasis (the"heart" of Beachwalk) to the stone-terraced entry where the base walls are flanged on both sides.

吊蔓如轻柔的面纱，浅浅的水渠环绕建筑四周，这一切赋予生活方式度假村诗意特质，层层流露，回味无穷。建筑坐落在一个经景观设计的露天平台之上。而露天平台高于邻近街道。土色的底层墙镶有采用符合“满者伯夷”传统尺寸的深色陶瓦。这样的设计体现了印尼群岛（包括巴厘岛）的传统。整个建筑犹如漂浮于一条水带之上。水从绿洲流下（绿洲是海滩长廊的中心），流入梯形石砌入口，入口两边则是底层墙。

The hotel also takes an 'open" design concept. The arrival sequence involves vehicular access through a small patterned lane before a double-volume lobby space, delivering a spectacular and unhindered sea view. Two sets of U-shaped hotel wings gesture toward the sea, with gardens at the centre of each wing. The double-loaded hotel rooms are diagonally oriented to allow all guests to enjoy the sunset from their private balconies.

酒店同样采用“开放式”的设计理念。有一条采用图案装饰的小路位于空间翻番的大厅前方，游客可经由此路驾车驶入酒店。站在大厅内，游客可将壮观的海景尽收眼底。酒店的两组U形侧楼摆出一副投向于大海的姿态，公园分别位于侧楼中心位置。为了让游客从私人阳台尽情欣赏到日落的美景，两排客房成对交错而立。

The Sahid Kuta Lifestyle Resort breathes new life into the old Kuta that we know and love. Through its creation of semi-outdoor garden spaces, the necessity for air conditioning is minimised. By using locally available and recycled materials, local industries are promoted and consumption of resources during transport is reduced. In addition, the architects applied a rainwater collection and water recycling system for maintaining the water features and gardens to reduce the stress on Bali's already overburdened water supplies.

The project represents the architects' push toward environmental and social sustainability in the built environment.

萨希迪库塔生活方式度假村给我们所熟知且热爱的传统库塔生活注入了新的活力。半开放式的花园空间使得人们对空调的依赖降至最低。对本地再生材料的巧妙运用推动了本地企业的发展。与此同时，这还降低了运输途中对资源的消耗。此外，设计师在水景与花园的维护上采用了水收集与循环系统，这样有效缓解了巴厘岛水供应短缺的压力。

此项目表现了设计师在建筑环境中为推动环境与社会可持续发展所做出的努力。

TOPSHOP

ACKNOWLEDGEMENTS

鸣谢

UNStudio

GP 建筑设计有限公司

Architects 61

MAD 建筑事务所

广东省建筑设计研究院

5+ design

10 DESIGN

查普门泰勒建筑设计咨询（上海）有限公司

SPARK 思邦

Studio Daniel Libeskind

COOP HIMMELB(L)AU Prix, Dreibholz & Partner ZT GmbH

amphibianArc

DWP

HPP

EAA

Perkins Eastman

Metropolis

王及王有限公司

澳大利亚柏涛建筑设计有限公司

UA 国际

Sohne & Partner Architects + BET Architects

HMD

LAB_ 尚墨

阿特拉斯建筑事务所

GDS 建筑事务所

Envirotec Indonesia

杰奥斯建筑设计

Benthem Crouwel Architects

南京长江都市建筑设计股份有限公司

Surbana International Consultants Pte Ltd

Philippe Chiambaretta

SAA Architects

深圳中深建筑设计有限公司

深圳市同济人建筑设计有限公司

STARH Architects

spatial practice

Special thanks to the architects above for their high-quality projects and nice supports.Contributions or s uggestions are welcomed at any time to:
news-eu@hkaspress.com

特别鸣谢以上设计公司的一贯支持，为本书提供优质的作品，如有任何问题或建议请联系：
news-eu@hkaspress.com

图书在版编目（CIP）数据

大商业. 2，多元复合商业地产 / 香港建筑科学出版社编著. -- 北京 : 中国林业出版社，2015.6
ISBN 978-7-5038-7980-7

Ⅰ. ①大… Ⅱ. ①香… Ⅲ. ①城市商业－房地产－案例－世界 Ⅳ. ①F299.1

中国版本图书馆CIP数据核字(2015)第093721号

大商业2—多元复合商业地产

编　　著　香港建筑科学出版社
责任编辑　纪　亮　王思源
策划编辑　高雪梅
流程编辑　黄　姗
特约编辑　徐霆威
文字编辑　王加丽　申婷婷
采　　编　张燕清　尹伊君
装帧设计　廖爱霞

出版发行　中国林业出版社
出版社地址　北京西城区德内大街刘海胡同7号，邮编：100009
出版社网址　http://lycb.forestry.gov.cn/
经　　销　全国新华书店
印　　刷　深圳市汇亿丰印刷科技有限公司

开　　本　280mm×400mm
印　　张　55.5
版　　次　2015年6月第1版
印　　次　2015年6月第1次印刷

标准书号　ISBN 978-7-5038-7980-7
定　　价　880.00元（USD 168.00）（精）

图书如有印装质量问题，可随时向印厂调换（电话：0755-82413509）。